MASTERING

MODERN WORLD HISTORY

MACMILLAN MASTER SERIES

Accounting
Advanced English Language
Arabic
Astronomy
Banking
Basic Management
Biology
British Politics
Business Communication
Business Law
Business Microcomputing
C Programming
Chemistry
COBOL Programming
Commerce
Computer Programming
Computers
Databases
Economic and Social History
Economics
Electrical Engineering
Electronic and Electrical Calculations
Electronics
English as a Foreign Language
English Grammar
English Language
English Literature
English Spelling
French
French 2
German

German 2
Human Biology
Italian
Italian 2
Japanese
Manufacturing
Marketing
Mathematics
Mathematics for Electrical and
    Electronic Engineering
Modern British History
Modern European History
Modern World History
Pascal Programming
Philosophy
Photography
Physics
Psychology
Pure Mathematics
Restaurant Service
Science
Secretarial Procedures
Social Welfare
Sociology
Spanish
Spanish 2
Spreadsheets
Statistics
Study Skills
Word Processing

MASTERING
MODERN WORLD HISTORY

SECOND EDITION

NORMAN LOWE

MACMILLAN

First published 1982 by
THE MACMILLAN PRESS LTD
Houndmills, Basingstoke, Hampshire RG21 2XS
and London
Companies and representatives
throughout the world

ISBN 0–333–46576–8

Printed in Malaysia

First edition reprinted six times
Second edition 1988
10
00   99   98   97   96

CONTENTS

Acknowledgements   xii
Maps   xiii
Preface to the Second Edition   xiv
Foreword by Keith Foreman   xvii

1 The world in 1914:   1.1   Prologue   1
   outbreak of the   1.2   The world in 1914   1
   First World War   1.3   Events leading up to the
                                 outbreak of war   4
                     2.4   What caused the war, and
                                 who was to blame?   7

2 The First World War   2.1   1914   18
   and its aftermath   2.2   1915   19
                     2.3   1916   21
                     2.4   The war at sea   22
                     2.5   1917   24
                     2.6   1918: the Central Powers
                                 defeated   26
                     2.7   The problems of making a
                                 peace settlement   27
                     2.8   The Treaty of Versailles
                                 with Germany   29
                     2.9   The peace Treaties with
                                 Austria–Hungary   33
                     2.10   The settlement with
                                 Turkey: Treaty of
                                 Sèvres (1920) and
                                 Bulgaria: Treaty of
                                 Neuilly (1919)   34

3 Russia: 1905–24   3.1   After 1905: were the 1917
                                 revolutions inevitable?   44
                     3.2   The two revolutions:
                                 March and November
                                 1917   47
                     3.3   Lenin and the Bolsheviks
                                 take power 1917   49
                     3.4   How successful were
                                 Lenin and the Bolsheviks
                               in dealing with these
                               problems (1917–24)?   50

CONTENTS

4 Britain: 1918–39

4.1 The Lloyd George coalition 1918–22   60

4.2 Conservative interlude: October 1922 to January 1924   64

4.3 Why did the Liberal Party continue to decline?   65

4.4 The first Labour government: January to October 1924   66

4.5 Stanley Baldwin's Conservative government 1924–9   69

4.6 The General Strike (4–12 May 1926)   70

4.7 The second Labour government (1929–31) and the Great Depression   73

4.8 The National government: financial problems and recovery   74

4.9 Unemployment in the 1930s   75

5 France in decline 1918–40

5.1 What were the problems facing French governments, and with what success did they attempt to solve them?   84

5.2 Why did France collapse so rapidly in 1940?   87

6 Italy 1918–45: the first appearance of Fascism

6.1 Why was Mussolini able to come to power?   94

6.2 What did the term 'Fascism' stand for?   98

6.3 Mussolini introduces the Fascist state   99

6.4 What benefits did Fascism bring for the Italian people?   101

7 The USA and the world economic crisis

7.1 The great boom of the 1920s   109

7.2 The Great Depression arrives: October 1929   111

7.3 Roosevelt and the New Deal   115

8	**Germany 1918–39: the Weimar Republic and Hitler**	8.1	Why did the Weimar Republic collapse?	127
		8.2	What did National Socialism stand for?	135
		8.3	Hitler consolidates his power	136
		8.4	How was Hitler able to stay in power for the next 12 years?	137
		8.5	Nazism and Fascism	143
		8.6	How successful was Hitler in domestic affairs up to 1939?	144
9	**Stalin and the USSR 1924–39**	9.1	How did Stalin manage to get to supreme power?	153
		9.2	What were the economic problems, and how successful was Stalin in solving them?	155
		9.3	Political and social problems, and Stalin's solutions	159
		9.4	Was the Stalin approach necessary?	161
10	**Turkey, Japan and Spain between the wars**	10.1	Turkey	167
		10.2	Japan	170
		10.3	Spain	171
11	**The Empires between the wars**	11.1	Britain and the Commonwealth	181
		11.2	Britain and Ireland 1916–39	182
		11.3	The Indian struggle for independence	185
		11.4	Britain and her Middle East mandates	187
12	**The League of Nations**	12.1	What were the origins of the League?	197
		12.2	How was the League organised?	198
		12.3	The successes of the League	199
		12.4	Why did the League fail to preserve peace?	200

CONTENTS

13 Foreign affairs and international relations 1919–33

13.1 What attempts were made to improve international relations, and how successful were they? 208

13.2 How did France try to deal with the problem of Germany between 1919 and 1933? 211

13.3 How did relations between the USSR and Britain, Germany and France develop between 1919 and 1933? 214

13.4 United States foreign policy 1919–33 217

13.5 The trouble-makers: Poland, Italy and Japan 218

14 Foreign affairs and international relations 1933–9

14.1 Relations between Japan and China 225

14.2 Mussolini's foreign policy 226

14.3 What were Hitler's aims in foreign policy, and how successful had he been by the end of 1938? 229

14.4 What is meant by the term 'appeasement'? How could such a policy be justified, and what part did it play in international affairs between 1935 and 1939? 232

14.5 Munich to the outbreak of war: September 1938 to September 1939 236

14.6 Why did war break out? Was Hitler or were the appeasers to blame? 238

15 The Second World War 1939–45

15.1 Opening moves: September 1939 to December 1940 250

15.2 The Axis offensive widens: 1941 to the summer of 1942 253

15.3 The offensives held in check: summer 1942 to summer 1943 257

	15.4	What part was played by Allied naval forces in the war?	260
	15.5	What contribution did air power make to the defeat of the Axis?	261
	15.6	The Axis Powers defeated: July 1943 to August 1945	262
	15.7	Why did the Axis Powers lose the war?	265
	15.8	What were the effects of the war?	266
16 The Cold War: problems of international relations after the Second World War	16.1	What caused the Cold War?	278
	16.2	How did the Cold War develop between 1945 and 1953?	279
	16.3	Why was there a 'thaw' in the Cold War after 1953, and what form did it take?	285
17 The spread of Communism outside Europe and its effect on international relations	17.1	Chiang or Mao? Troubled years in China 1918–49	297
	17.2	War in Korea 1950–3	302
	17.3	Cuba: why did Fidel Castro come to power, and how were Cuba's foreign relations affected?	306
	17.4	Castro's problems, measures, successes and failures	308
	17.5	The wars in Vietnam: 1946–54 and 1961–75	310
	17.6	Chile under Salvador Allende 1970–3	314
	17.7	*Détente*: international relations in the 1970s	317
	17.8	*Détente* under strain: the 1980s	318
18 Internal affairs of the Communist states of Eastern Europe	18.1	The USSR	330
	18.2	The USSR and the states of Eastern Europe	336

CONTENTS

19	China under the Communists	19.1	What were the problems facing Mao Tse-tung, and how successful was he in dealing with them?	352
		19.2	Life after Mao	356
20	The United Nations Organisation	20.1	The structure of the United Nations Organisation	367
		20.2	What are the main differences between UNO and the League?	370
		20.3	How successful has UNO been as a peace-keeping body?	371
		20.4	What are the weaknesses of UNO?	375
21	Western Europe since 1945	21.1	The growth of unity in Western Europe	381
		21.2	Britain	386
		21.3	France	398
		21.4	West Germany	403
22	The USA, the Americas and Japan after 1945	22.1	The United States of America	412
		22.2	Latin America	424
		22.3	Japan	430
23	The end of the Empires	23.1	Why, and how, was India partitioned in 1947?	441
		23.2	Malaya and Cyprus	442
		23.3	The British in Africa	443
		23.4	Portugal	446
24	The new Commonwealth states	24.1	What is the Commonwealth, and what use is it?	454
		24.2	India	455
		24.3	Pakistan	460
		24.4	Malaysia	462
		24.5	The African nations	465
25	Problems in Africa	25.1	The Congo	485
		25.2	Rhodesia	486
		25.3	South Africa	491
26	The Middle East	26.1	Arab unity and outside interference	503

26.2   The creation of Israel and
       the Arab–Israeli war of
       1948–9   506
26.3   The Suez war 1956   507
26.4   The Six Day war 1967   509
26.5   The Yom Kippur war
       1973   510
26.6   Camp David and the
       Egyptian – Israeli peace
       1978–9   512
26.7   The Iraqi – Iranian war
       1980   513
26.8   Chaos in the Lebanon   515
Further Reading   524
Index   533

ACKNOWLEDGEMENTS

The author and publishers wish to thank the following who have kindly given permission for the use of copyright material.

Edward Arnold for extracts and tables from *Years of Change* by Robert Wolfson, 1978;

Chatto and Windus Ltd and the Estate of the author for 'Anthem for Doomed Youth' by Wilfred Owen from *Collected Poems of Wilfred Owen* edited by C. D. Lewis;

Collins Publishers for extracts from *Hope Against Hope* by Nadezhda Mandlestam;

The Daily Telegraph plc for extracts adapted from 10 August 1978 issue of the *Daily Telegraph*;

The Guardian for extracts from 'Africa's New Dawn in a Poor Light' by Haroub Othman, 6 February 1987, and from the 11 December 1986, 30 October 1986, 3 February 1987 and 5 March 1987 issues of the *Guardian*;

Heinemann Educational Books Ltd for a figure and a table from *World Powers in the Twentieth Century* by Harriet Ward, Heinemann Educational/BBC;

London and East Anglian Group, Midland Examining Group, Northern Examining Association and Southern Examining Group for questions from specimen examination papers;

Longman Group UK Ltd for material from *A People's History of the United States* by Howard Zinn;

The Observer for an extract by Dennis Bloodworth, Observer Foreign News Service, November 1971, and for extracts from the 9 November 1986, 25 January 1987 and 24 May 1987 issues of the *Observer*;

Simon & Schuster for extracts from a poem by A. O. Audienko from *Stalin*, ed. T. H. Rigby, Prentice-Hall, Inc.;

Society for Anglo-Chinese Understanding for an abbreviated extract from *China Now*, March 1973.

Times Newspapers Ltd for material from an article by Michael Jones, *The Sunday Times*, 28th August 1988.

Every effort has been made to trace all the copyright-holders, but if any have been inadvertently overlooked the publishers will be pleased to make the necessary arrangement at the first opportunity.

MAPS

1.1	The Balkans in 1913 showing changes of territory from the Balkan Wars (1912–13)	3
2.1	The Western Front	18
2.2	The Eastern Front	25
2.3	European frontiers after the First World War and the Peace Treaties	31
2.4	Africa and the Peace Treaties	32
2.5	Turkey, Bulgaria and the Peace Treaties	35
14.1	Hitler's gains before the Second World War	230
15.1	Main German thrusts in 1940	251
15.2	North Africa and the Mediterranean	253
15.3	The war in the Pacific	257
15.4	The Russian Front	259
15.5	The Western Front 1944–5	264
16.1	Europe after 1945	280
17.1	China after the First World War	298
17.2	The war in Korea	303
17.3	The wars in Vietnam	311
22.1	Latin America	424
23.1	Africa becomes independent	449
24.1	The Indian subcontinent after 1947	456
24.2	Malaysia and Indonesia	463
24.3	The Kashmir and Indus River disputes between India and Pakistan	481
26.1	The Middle East	504

PREFACE

TO THE

SECOND EDITION

The second edition of the book brings the story of world affairs right up to 1988 and includes topics such as the Reagan era, the Gorbachev 'reforms' and the crisis in South Africa. The main change is that the question sections have been completely rewritten in order to prepare students to meet the new demands of GCSE.

The GCSE National Criteria for History specify *four* main assessment objectives which the examinations and coursework of all Boards must test. These are the ability to:

1. recall, evaluate and select relevant knowledge and to deploy it in a clear and coherent form;
2. make use of and understand the concepts of cause and consequence, continuity and change, similarity and difference;
3. look at events and issues from the perspectives of people in the past (empathy);
4. show the skills necessary to study a wide variety of historical sources such as primary and secondary written sources, statistical and visual material, artefacts, textbooks and orally transmitted information:

(a) by comprehending and extracting information from it;
(b) by interpreting and evaluating it – distinguishing between fact, opinion and judgement; pointing to deficiencies in the material as evidence; detecting bias;
(c) by comparing various types of historical sources and reaching conclusions based on this comparison.

The first requirement of a history textbook must still be to provide the student with the basic information which he or she will be required to recall about the period, and so I have left the first edition text largely unchanged except for minor corrections and updating. The analytical approach should be suitable for helping students to understand cause and consequence, continuity and change, similarity and difference, so that assessment objectives 1 and 2 are taken care of.

The question sections are much longer in the new edition; I have tried to provide a wide variety of primary and secondary sources, to give students plenty of practice for assessment objective 4; and I have included examples of 'empathy' questions for assessment objective 3. The boards define three possible levels of empathy:

1. Everyday empathy. This is where the candidate understands that people in the past were similar in many ways to those of today in that they were motivated by recognisable human ideas. However, weaker candidates do not get far beyond this, and tend to ascribe modern ideas and motives to people in the past.
2. Stereotype historical empathy. This is where the candidate realises that people in the past did have different ideas about their society from people today. However, these candidates tend to assume that everybody in the society under study thought in the same way.
3. Differentiated historical empathy. The best candidates are those who have the further perception that ideas and motives differed even within a past society. For example, the attitudes of Russians in 1917 towards the events of that year would vary widely depending on whether they were aristocrats, landowners, peasants, kulaks, liberals, social revolutionaries or Bolsheviks.

The Examination Boards have chosen to test these objectives in different ways. The Southern Examining Group (SEG) in *World Powers since 1917* has two papers arranged as follows:

Paper One Section A

A compulsory multi-part question based on a variety of sources to test mainly objective 4.

A multi-part question requiring an answer in 'continuous writing', similar to the traditional essay type question, testing objectives 1 and 2.

Section B

A multi-part question based on one source, testing objectives 1, 2 and 4.

Paper Two Section A

Questions which may or may not be multi-part, requiring 'continuous writing' and testing objectives 1 and 2.

Section B

Questions which require 'continuous writing', testing objective 3.

The coursework consists of two assignments, one mainly concerned with objective 3, the other mainly with objective 4. Some of the questions in the book will provide excellent practice for such coursework assignments.

The Northern Examining Association (NEA), on the other hand, has a Paper One which tests mainly assessment objectives 2 and 4, but which 'may also test 1 and 3'. Paper Two tests mainly assessment objectives 1 and 2 but 'may also test 3 and 4'. A wide variety of historical sources will be used in both papers. There is a minimum of four pieces of coursework 'collectively testing' all four objectives.

I have included as wide a variety of questions as possible, given the limitations of space. Some are taken or adapted from specimen papers, but most are my own. The number(s) after each question indicates which assessment objective(s) is being tested.

Marks to be awarded for parts of questions are not shown. History GCSE papers are marked on a 'levels of response' marking scheme designed to give candidates credit for showing positively what they know, understand and can do; the marking scheme might well be adjusted after the examination, depending on how the majority of candidates interpreted the question.

Once again, I must thank my colleagues Greta Hill and Kevin Bean for their help, and Peter Somerfield and his team who so expertly typed the additional material.

1988   NORMAN LOWE

FOREWORD

I am pleased to write this Foreword to Norman Lowe's *Modern World History*, one of the first of a new series of basic texts. It is a valuable addition to the growing list of books which cover this complex century, and to my mind it has a number of advantages. Mr Lowe's approach has been to cover the major topics of world history in a clear and concise style, following a consistent pattern in each chapter. After a general introduction, themes are developed in more detail with headings, key words and phrases underlined. Students will find the system of cross referencing easy to follow, while the problem-solving approach will be of considerable benefit to those taking examinations. Controversial issues are highlighted and discussed with refreshing clarity and fairness, admitting the fallibility of human judgement.

Mr Lowe's style is economical yet avoids the sterility of note form. It is lively and comprehensible, with major terms and concepts carefully explained. The text is supported by relevant maps and by sample examination questions including those involving stimulus material which are fast becoming a feature of the 'new' history. The bibliography will be of particular benefit to those who wish to develop themes in greater depth.

I believe that *Modern World History* will provide an excellent basic text for examinations at 16+ in schools and colleges, and will also be a first-class introduction for higher level study. Students taking General and Liberal Studies and the general reader will find its approach comprehensive and well signposted. Although it is written with the examination candidate in mind it is not narrowly conceived, dealing as it does with some of the topics of world history frequently omitted in other basic texts. One particular merit is its treatment of the post-1945 period to which ten chapters are devoted. Events of the very recent past, including, for instance, developments in Latin America, the crisis in Poland, the Russian occupation of Afghanistan and the policies of the Carter Administration are included.

As a teacher and examiner of modern world history over many years I can recommend this book. It has long been needed to fill a gap in the available literature.

March 1981

KEITH FOREMAN
Warden
The Village College
Comberton
Cambridge

CHAPTER 1

THE WORLD IN 1914: OUTBREAK OF THE FIRST WORLD WAR

1.1 PROLOGUE

Under cover of darkness late on the night of 5 August 1914, five columns of German assault troops, which had entered Belgium two days earlier, were converging on the town of Liège, expecting little resistance. To their surprise they were halted by determined fire from the town's outlying forts. This was a setback for the Germans: control of Liège was essential before they could proceed with their main operation against the French. They were forced to resort to siege tactics, using heavy howitzers. These fired up shells which plunged from a height of 12,000 feet to shatter the armour-plating of the forts. Strong though they were, these Belgian forts were not equipped to withstand such a battering for long; on 13 August the first one surrendered and three days later Liège was under German control. This was the first major engagement of the First World War, that horrifying conflict of monumental proportions which was to mark the beginning of a new era in European and world history.

1.2 THE WORLD IN 1914

(a) Europe still dominated the rest of the world in 1914 and most of the decisions which moulded the fate of the world were taken in the capitals of Europe. Within Europe, *Germany* was the leading power both militarily and economically. She had overtaken Britain in the production of pig iron and steel, though not quite in coal, while France, Belgium, Italy and Austria–Hungary (the Habsburg empire) were well behind. Russian industry was expanding rapidly, but had been so backward to begin with that she could not seriously challenge Germany and Britain. But it was outside Europe that the most spectacular industrial progress had been made over the previous 40 years. In 1914 the USA produced more coal, pig iron and steel than either Germany or Britain and now ranked as a world power. Japan too had modernised rapidly and was regarded as a power to be reckoned with after her defeat of Russia in 1904–5.

(b) **The political systems of these world powers varied widely.** The USA, Britain and France had democratic forms of government, which means that they each had a parliament containing elected representatives of the people, which had an important say in running the country. Some systems were not as democratic as they seemed: Germany had an elected lower house of parliament (*Reichstag*) but real power lay with the Chancellor (a sort of prime minister) and the *Kaiser* (emperor); Italy was a monarchy with an elected parliament, but the franchise (right to vote) was limited; Japan had an elected lower house, but here too the franchise was restricted and the emperor and the privy council wielded most of the power. Far removed from the democracy of the west were Russia and Austria–Hungary. The tsar (emperor) of Russia and the emperor of Austria (who was also king of Hungary) were *autocratic* rulers: this means that although parliaments existed, the monarchs could largely ignore them and rule according to their own whims.

(c) **The European powers had taken part in a great burst of imperialism,** the building up of empires in the years after 1880, rushing to take hold of territory overseas, mainly to satisfy the desire for new markets and raw materials. The Scramble for Africa, as it became known, was accompanied by intervention in the crumbling Chinese empire; the European powers, as well as the USA and Japan, all at different times forced the helpless Chinese to grant trading concessions. Exasperation at the incompetence of their government led the Chinese to overthrow the ancient Manchu dynasty and to set up a *republic* (1911).

(d) **Europe itself had divided into two alliance systems:** the *Triple Alliance* of Germany, Austria–Hungary and Italy, and the *Triple Entente* of Britain, France and Russia. In addition, Japan and Britain had signed an alliance in 1902. Friction within the two systems – sometimes referred to as 'the armed camps' – had on several occasions since 1908 seemed likely to cause a war.

(e) **Causes of friction.** There were many causes of friction which threatened to upset the peace of Europe: Anglo-German naval rivalry; French resentment at the loss of Alsace and Lorraine to Germany at the end of the Franco-Prussian War (1871); German resentment at Britain, Russia and France for allegedly trying to 'encircle' her; and Russian hostility at Austrian ambitions in the Balkans. Perhaps most dangerous of all was Serbian *nationalism* (the desire to free one's nation from the control of people of another nationality). Serbia had ambitions of uniting all Serbs and Croats, many of whom lived inside the Habsburg Empire, into a South Slav kingdom (Yugoslavia). This would involve acquiring certain areas from Austria–Hungary threatening to cause the disintegration of the ramshackle Habsburg Empire, which contained people of many different nationalities. If the Serbs and Croats left the fold, others such as the Italians, Czechs, Slovaks and Poles would demand their independence too. Consequently many Austrians were keen for a 'preventive' war against Serbia to destroy her before she became strong enough to destroy Austria–Hungary. Springing from these resentments and tensions came a series of events which culminated in the *outbreak of war* in late July 1914.

Fig. 1.1 *the Balkans in 1913 showing changes of territory from the Balkan wars (1912–13)*

1.3 EVENTS LEADING UP TO THE OUTBREAK OF WAR

(a) The Morocco crisis (1905–6) was an attempt by the Germans to test the recently signed Anglo-French agreement (the 1904 *Entente Cordiale*) with its understanding that France would recognise Britain's position in Egypt in return for British approval of a possible French occupation of Morocco, one of the few remaining areas of Africa not controlled by a European power. The Germans announced that they would assist the Sultan of Morocco to maintain his country's independence, and demanded an international conference to discuss its future. A conference was duly held at Algeciras in southern Spain (January 1906). The British believed that if the Germans had their way it would be an acknowledgement of German diplomatic domination. To the amazement of the Germans, Britain, Russia, Italy and Spain supported the French demand to control the Moroccan bank and police. This was a serious diplomatic defeat for Germany, who realised that the new line up of Britain and France was a force to be reckoned with, particularly as the crisis was soon followed by Anglo-French 'military conversations'.

(b) The British agreement with Russia (1907) was seen by the Germans as a hostile move. In fact it was a logical step, since Russia and France, Britain's Entente partners, had signed an alliance in 1894. For years the British had viewed Russia as a major threat to her interests in the Far East and India, but recently the situation had changed. Russia's defeat by *Japan* (1904–5) had weakened her considerably, and she no longer seemed so much of a threat. The Russians were keen to end the long-standing rivalry and anxious to attract British investment. The agreement therefore settled their remaining differences. It was not a military alliance and not necessarily an anti-German move, but the Germans saw it as a confirmation of their fears that Britain, France and Russia were planning to 'encircle' them.

(c) The Bosnia Crisis (1908) heightened the tension. The Austrians, taking advantage of a revolution in Turkey, annexed the Turkish province of *Bosnia*. This was a deliberate blow at the neighbouring state of Serbia which had also been hoping to acquire Bosnia since it contained about 3 million Serbs among its population. The Serbs appealed for help to their fellow Slavs, the Russians, who called for a European conference, expecting French and British support. When it became clear that Germany would support Austria in the event of war, the French drew back, unwilling to become involved in a war in the Balkans. The British, anxious to avoid a breach with Germany, did no more than protest to Austria. The Russians, still smarting from their defeat by Japan, dared not risk a war without the support of their allies. There was to be no help for Serbia, no conference took place, and Austria kept Bosnia. It was a triumph for the Austro-German alliance, *but it had unfortunate results*: Serbia remained bitterly hostile to Austria, and it was this quarrel which led to the outbreak of war. The Russians were determined to avoid any further humiliation and embarked on a massive military build-up. They intended to be prepared in the event of any further Serbian appeals for help.

(d) The Agadir Crisis (1911) was a further development in the Morocco situation. French troops occupied Fez, the Moroccan capital, to put down a rebellion against the Sultan. A French annexation of Morocco seemed imminent; the Germans sent a gunboat, the *Panther*, to the Moroccan port of Agadir, hoping to pressurise the French into giving Germany some compensation, perhaps the French Congo. The British were worried in case the Germans acquired *Agadir*, a possible naval base for threatening Britain's trade routes. In order to strengthen France's resistance, Lloyd George, in his famous *Mansion House Speech*, warned Germany that Britain would not stand by and be taken advantage of 'where her interests were vitally affected'. The French stood firm, making no major concessions, and eventually the German gunboat was removed. The Germans agreed to recognise the French protectorate over Morocco in return for two strips of territory in the French Congo. This was seen as a triumph for the Entente powers but in Germany public opinion became intensely anti-British, particularly as the British were now drawing slowly ahead in the 'naval race': at the end of 1911 they had built eight of the new and more powerful 'Dreadnought' type battleships, compared with Germany's four.

(e) The Balkan Wars (1912 and 1913)
  (i) The *First Balkan War (1912)* broke out when Serbia, Greece, Montenegro and Bulgaria (calling themselves the Balkan League) attacked Turkey, capturing most of her remaining territory in Europe. Together with the Germans, Sir Edward Grey, the British Foreign Secretary, arranged a peace conference in London. He was anxious to avoid the conflict spreading, and also to demonstrate that Britain and Germany could still work together. The resulting settlement apportioned the former Turkish lands among the Balkan States. However, the Serbs were not happy with their gains: they wanted *Albania*, giving them an outlet to the sea, but the Austrians, with German and British support, insisted that Albania should become an independent state. This was a deliberate Austrian move to prevent Serbia becoming too powerful.
  (ii) The Bulgarians were also dissatisfied: they were hoping for Macedonia but most of it was given to Serbia. Bulgaria therefore attacked Serbia, starting the *Second Balkan War (1913)*. The Bulgarian plan misfired badly when Greece, Rumania and Turkey rallied to support Serbia. The Bulgarians were defeated, and by the *Treaty of Bucharest*, forfeited most of their gains from the first war. Anglo-German influence had apparently prevented an escalation of the war by restraining the Austrians, who were itching to attack Serbia.

(iii)   In reality though, the *consequences of the Balkan Wars were serious*: Serbia had been strengthened and was determined to stir up trouble among the Serbs and Croats inside Austria–Hungary; the Austrians were equally determined to put a stop to Serbia's ambitions. The Germans took Grey's willingness to co-operate as a sign that Britain was prepared to be detached from France and Russia.

(f) The assassination of the Austrian Archduke Franz Ferdinand at *Sarajevo (28 June 1914)* was the event which sparked off the war. The Archduke, nephew and heir of the Emperor Franz Josef, was paying an official visit to Sarajevo, the Bosnian capital, when he and his wife were shot dead by a Serb terrorist. The Austrians blamed the Serbian government, and sent a stiff ultimatum. The Serbs accepted most of the points in it, but the Austrians, assured of German support, were determined to use the incident as an *excuse for war*. On 28 July, Austria–Hungary declared war on Serbia. The Russians, anxious not to let the Serbs down again, ordered a general mobilisation (29 July). The German government demanded that this should be cancelled (31 July), and when the Russians failed to comply, Germany declared war on *Russia* (1 August) and on *France* (3 August). When German troops

illus 1.1 *Archduke Franz Ferdinand and his wife, shortly before their assassination in Sarajevo*

entered Belgium on their way to invade France, Britain (who in 1839 had promised to defend Belgian neutrality) demanded their withdrawal. When the Germans ignored this, *Britain* entered the war (*4 August*). The escalation was completed when Austria–Hungary declared war on Russia (6 August).

The war was to have profound effects on the future of the world. *Germany was soon to be displaced*, for a time at least, from her mastery of Europe, and Europe never quite regained its dominant position in the world.

1.4 WHAT CAUSED THE WAR, AND WHO WAS TO BLAME?

It is difficult to analyse why the assassination at Sarajevo developed into a world war, and even now historians cannot agree. Some blame Austria for being the first aggressor by declaring war on Serbia; some blame Russia, the first to order full mobilisation, some Germany for supporting Austria, and others Britain for not making it clear that she would definitely support France – which, it is argued, might have dissuaded Germany from declaring war on France.

(a) The point which is beyond dispute is that **the quarrel between Austria and Serbia**, which had become increasingly more explosive since 1908, sparked off the outbreak of the war when Austria seized on the assassination as the pretext for a preventive war with Serbia. Austria genuinely felt that realisation of Serbian and Slav nationalist ambitions for a Yugoslav state would bring about the collapse of the Habsburg empire: Serbia must be curbed. In fairness, they probably hoped the war would remain *localised* like the Balkan Wars. The Austro-Serb quarrel explains the outbreak of the war, but not why it became a *world war*. Several reasons have been suggested for the escalation of the war.

(b) The alliance system or 'armed camps' made war inevitable. This explanation is *not convincing*: there had been many crises since 1904 (Morocco, Bosnia, Agadir, Balkan Wars), none of which had led to a major war. In fact, there was nothing *binding* about these alliances. France had not supported Russia when she protested against the Austrian annexation of Bosnia, Austria took no interest in Germany's unsuccessful attempts (Morocco and Agadir Crises, 1906 and 1911) to prevent France taking over Morocco, and Germany had restrained Austria from attacking Serbia during the Second Balkan War. Italy had agreements with both camps and though still a member of the Triple Alliance in 1914, entered the war against it in 1915. No power actually declared war because of an *alliance treaty*.

(c) Colonial rivalry in Africa and the Far East. *Again, not convincing*: although there had certainly been disputes, they had always been sorted out *without war*. In early July 1914 Anglo-German relations were good, an agreement extremely favourable to Germany having just been reached over a possible partition of Portuguese colonies in Africa. One by-product of colonial rivalry which did, however, cause dangerous friction was the *naval race*.

(d) The naval race between Britain and Germany. Starting with the Tirpitz Navy Laws (1898), the growth of the German fleet probably didn't worry Britain too much at first because she had an enormous lead; but with the introduction of the powerful British Dreadnought battleship in 1906, which rendered all other ships obsolete, the Germans could begin building Dreadnoughts on equal terms. The ensuing naval building race was the main bone of contention between the two right up to 1914. According to Churchill, however, in the spring and summer of 1914 naval rivalry had ceased to be a cause of friction, because 'it was certain that we [Britain] could not be overtaken as far as capital ships were concerned'.

(e) Economic rivalry. It has been argued that the desire for economic mastery of the world caused German businessmen and capitalists to want war with Britain, who still owned about half the world's tonnage of merchant ships in 1912. There isn't much *evidence* to support this theory: Germany was already well on the way to victory in that area; as one leading German industrialist remarked in 1913: 'Give us three or four more years of peace and Germany will be the unchallenged economic master of Europe.'

None of these reasons (b) to (e) gets to the crux of the matter. *More plausible* are the following:

(f) Russia made war more likely by backing Serbia, probably making her more irresponsibly anti-Austrian than she might have been. Russia was the first to order a *general mobilisation*, which provoked Germany to mobilise. The Russians were worried about the Balkans situation where both Bulgaria and Turkey were under German influence; this would enable Germany and Austria to control the Dardanelles, the main Russian trade route, thereby strangling the Russian economy (this happened during the war). Thus Russia felt herself threatened, and once Austria declared war on Serbia, saw it as a struggle for survival. Also the Russians must have felt that their prestige as *Slav leader* would suffer irreparable damage if they failed to support Serbia. Perhaps the government even saw war as a good idea to divert attention away from domestic problems. Perhaps the blame lies more with Austria: though she must have hoped for Russian neutrality, she ought to have realised how difficult this would be for Russia, and given possible Russian reaction the most careful consideration.

(g) German backing for Austria was crucially important. It is significant that in 1913 Germany *restrained* Austria from declaring war on Serbia, but in 1914 *egged them on*, the *Kaiser* urging them to attack Serbia and

illus 1.2 *Hitler celebrates the outbreak of the First World War. This fascinating picture shows Hitler in the crowd which heard the declaration of war in Munich on 2 August 1914*

promising German help without conditions. The important question is: *why did German policy towards Austria change?* The answer is the subject of much controversy:

(i)   Some historians including the German, Fritz Fischer, claim that Germany deliberately provoked war with Russia, France and Britain in order to achieve *world domination*.

(ii) Others argue that Germany wanted war because she felt encircled and threatened by British naval power and by the massive Russian military expansion. The German generals decided that a 'preventive' war, a *war for survival*, was necessary, and that it must take place before the end of 1914; *after that Russia would be too strong*.

(iii) Some historians reject both (i) and (ii) and suggest that Germany did not want a major war at all; the *Kaiser* and Chancellor Bethmann-Hollweg believed a strong line in support of Austria would *frighten the Russians into remaining neutral* – a sad miscalculation, if true.

(h) The mobilisation plans of the various powers accelerated the tempo of events and reduced almost to nil the time available for negotiation. The German *Schlieffen Plan*, first approved in 1905 and modified by Moltke (German Commander-in-Chief) in 1911, assumed that France would automatically join Russia, so the bulk of German forces were to be sent through Belgium to knock France out in six weeks, after which they were to be switched across to face Russia, whose mobilisation was expected to be slow. Once Moltke knew that Russia had ordered a general mobilisation, he demanded immediate German mobilisation so that the plan could be put into operation as soon as possible. However, Russian mobilisation did not necessarily mean war – their troops could be halted at the frontiers; unfortunately the Schlieffen Plan, depending as it did on the rapid capture of Liège in Belgium, involved the first *aggressive act outside the Balkans* when German troops entered Belgium on 4 August. Almost at the last minute the *Kaiser* and Bethmann tried to avoid war and urged Austria to negotiate with Serbia (30 July), which perhaps supports point (iii) above. Wilhelm also suggested a partial mobilisation against Russia only, instead of the full plan, hoping that Britain would stay neutral if Germany refrained from attacking France. But it was too late: Moltke, scared of being caught on the hop by the Russians and French, insisted on the full Schlieffen Plan; there was no time to modify it. It looks as though the *generals had taken over control of affairs from the politicians*. It also suggests that a British announcement on 31 July of her intention to support France would have made no difference to Germany: it was the Schlieffen Plan or nothing even though Germany at that point had no specific quarrel with France.

The most convincing conclusion to be drawn from all these suggestions is that put forward by L. C. F. Turner. Perhaps the Germans did not deliberately provoke a war; it was caused by 'a tragedy of miscalculation'. Most of the leading rulers and politicians seemed to be incompetent. The Austrians miscalculated by thinking Russia would not support Serbia, Germany did so by promising to support Austria, with *no conditions attached*; therefore the Germans were certainly blameworthy, as were the Austrians, because they *risked a major war*. Politicians in Russia and Germany miscalculated by assuming that mobilisation would not necessarily mean war; generals, especially Moltke, miscalculated by sticking rigidly to their plans in the belief that this would bring a quick decisive victory. No wonder Bethmann, when asked how it all began, raised his arms to heaven and replied: 'Oh – if I only knew!'

QUESTIONS

1. Origins of the First World War
Study the Sources below, and then answer the questions that follow.

Source A
Note to the Cabinet from the Prime Minister, Lord Salisbury, in May 1901:

> The British Government cannot undertake to declare war, for any purpose, unless it is a purpose of which the people of this country would approve . . . I do not see how we could invite nations to rely upon our help in a struggle which must be formidable, where we have no means whatever of knowing what may be the attitude of our people in circumstances which cannot be foreseen.

Source B
An interview with *Kaiser* Wilhelm II, published in the *Daily Telegraph*, 28 October 1908.

> You English are like mad bulls; you see red everywhere! What on earth has come over you, that you should heap on us such suspicion? What can I do more? I have always stood forth as the friend of England.

(Extract.)

Source C
From a speech made in the German Reichstag, November 1911.

> Now we know where our enemy stands. Like a flash of lightning in the night, these events have shown the German people where its enemy is . . . When the hour of decision comes we are prepared for sacrifices, both of blood and of treasure.

Source: M. Balfour, *The Kaiser* (Cresset, 1964).

Source D
Lenin in 1911.

> A war with Austria would be a splendid thing for the revolution. But the chances are small that Franz Josef and Nicholas will give us such a treat.

Source: E. H. Carr, *The Bolshevik Revolution* (Macmillan, 1951, vol. 1).

Source E
The cartoon 'A Chain of Friendship' (Fig. 1.2) published in the *Brooklyn Eagle*, July 1914 (Britain is at the end of the line):

Fig. 1.2

Source F
Telegram from Nicholas II of Russia to George V of England, sent on 2 August 1914:

> Ever since the presentation of the Austrian ultimatum at Belgrade, Russia has devoted all her efforts to some peaceful solution of the questions raised by Austria's action. The effect of this action would have been to upset the balance of power in the Balkans which is of such vital interest to my Empire. Every proposal put forward was rejected by Germany and Austria.

(a) **(i)** Which event had caused the 'Austrian ultimatum at Belgrade' referred to in Source F? **1**

  (ii) Explain briefly how the situation shown in Source E had come about in the twenty years before 1914. **1,2,4**

(b) **(i)** According to Source F, why was the Tsar so worried about 'Austria's action'? **1,4**

  (ii) What caused the outburst of German criticism in Sources B and C? **1,2,4**

(c) Sources A and E show that a considerable change took place in British foreign policy between 1901 and 1914.

  (i) Using Sources A and E, explain what this change was. **4(a)**

  (ii) Using any of these Sources, and your own knowledge, explain why this change in policy took place. **1,2,4**

(d) 'Nobody really wanted war in 1914.'

  (i) What evidence do you think these sources provide to help you decide whether this statement is true or not?

(ii) How reliable do you think each of these sources is to a historian trying to decide who was to blame for the war?

4(a,b,c)

[Reproduced by permission of the Midland Examining Group.]

2. Origins of the First World War
Study the Sources below, and then answer the questions that follow.

Source A
A lecture given in October 1913 by an Englishman, J. A. Cramb. He had lived in Germany and studied at a German university, and had become an admirer of German culture.

In regard to Germany we are faced with certain circumstances that deserve our consideration here in England. There is, for instance, the annual appearance in Germany of very nearly seven hundred books dealing with war; I doubt whether twenty books a year on the art of war appear in this country. The German answer to all our talk about the limitation of armaments is: Germany shall increase to the utmost of her power irrespective of any proposals made to her by England or by Russia or by any other State upon this earth.

I have lived among Germans and I have been impressed by the splendour of that movement which through the centuries has brought Germany to her position today. But with the best will in the world I can see no solution to the present collision of ideals but a tragic one. England desires peace and will never make war on Germany. But how can the youth in Germany, that nation great in war, accept the world-predominance of England? The outcome is certain and speedy. It is war.

Source: J. C. G. Röhl (ed.), *From Bismarck to Hitler* (Longman, 1970, extract).

Source B
The Diary of Admiral von Muller, head of the *Kaiser*'s Naval cabinet, 8 December 1912 (meeting with the *Kaiser* and top military and naval personnel).

General von Moltke [Chief of German General Staff] said: I believe war is unavoidable; war the sooner the better. But we ought to do more through the press to prepare the popularity of a war against Russia. The Kaiser supported this. Tirpitz (Naval Minister) said that the navy would prefer to see the postponement of the great fight for one and a half years. Moltke says the navy would not be ready even then and the army would get into an increasingly unfavourable position, for the enemies were arming more strongly than we. That was the end of the conference; the result amounted to almost nothing.

Source: J. C. G. Röhl (ed.), *From Bismarck to Hitler* (Longman, 1970, adapted extract).

Source C

A report of a conversation held in May or June 1914. It was written from memory by Gottlieb von Jagow, after Germany's defeat in the war. In 1914, Jagow was the German Foreign Secretary:

On 20 May and 3 June 1914 our Majesties gave lunches in honour of the birthdays of the Emperor of Russia and the King of England. On one of these occasions – I cannot remember which – Moltke said he would like to discuss some matters with me. In his opinion there was no alternative to making preventive war in order to defeat the enemy while we still had a chance of victory. I replied that I was not prepared to cause a preventive war and I pointed out that the Kaiser, who wanted to preserve peace, would always try to avoid war and would only agree to fight if our enemies forced war upon us. After my rejection, Moltke did not insist further. When war did break out, unexpectedly and not desired by us, Moltke was very nervous and obviously suffering from strong depression.

Source: J. C. G. Röhl (ed.), *From Bismarck to Hitler* (Longman, 1970, extract).

Source D
Statistics:

Table 1   Relative strengths of Germany and Britain in battleships and Dreadnoughts, 1907–11

| Year | Battleships | | | | Dreadnoughts | | | |
| | Less than 15 yrs | | Under construction | | Completed | | Under construction | |
	GB	G	GB	G	GB	G	GB	G
1907	47	21	5	8	1	0	3	4
1908	40	21	8	9	1	0	6	7
1909	43	22	6	10	2	0	6	10
1910	45	23	9	8	5	2	9	8
1911	43	24	10	9	8	4	10	9

Table 2   Fleet sizes (4 August 1914). Figures in brackets indicate ships under construction

	Germany	*Great Britain*
Battleships	33 (+7)	55 (+11)
Battlecruisers	3 (+3)	7 (+3)
Cruisers	9	51
Light cruisers etc	45 (+4)	77 (+9)
Destroyers	123 (+9)	191 (+38)
Torpedo ships	80	137 (+ 1)
Submarines	23 (+15)	64 (+22)
Dreadnoughts	13	20

Source: R. Wolfson, *Years of Change* (Arnold, 1978).

Source E
A British cartoon (Fig. 1.3) from *Punch*, 12 August 1914.

Fig. 1.3

BRAVO, BELGIUM!

(a) **(i)** What evidence is there in Source A that Cramb was an admirer of Germany?

    (ii) What evidence does Cramb mention in support of his opinion that war was likely soon?   **4(a)**

(b) **(i)** Do you think Source D supports Moltke's statement in Source B that 'the enemies were arming more strongly than we'?

    (ii) What evidence do Sources B and C contain about how the *Kaiser* felt about the prospect of war? Do you think the sources support or contradict each other on this point?   **4(c)**

(c) What weaknesses are there in Source C which might reduce its value to the historian?

(d) **(i)** Using your own knowledge and the cartoon in Fig. 1.3 (Source E), explain what ideas the cartoonist was trying to express?

                                          1 and 4(a)

    (ii) What points in the cartoon tell you that it is biased?

                                           4(b)

(e) What evidence do Sources B, C, D and E provide which help the historian to decide whether or not Germany was to blame for the outbreak of the First World War?   **4(a,b,c)**

3. **(a)** Why was there so much unrest and rivalry among the nations and empires of South-East Europe in the early years of the twentieth century?

    (b) Why did Gavrilo Princip assassinate the Archduke Franz Ferdinand on 28 June 1914?

    (c) Why were the great powers able to contain the Balkan crises of 1908 and 1911–12 but unable to prevent the Balkan crisis of 1914 from developing into a widespread European War?   **1,2**

4. It is August 1914. As a German nationalist/conservative member of the Reichstag, write the draft of a speech to be made in the Reichstag, referring to international relations over the last ten years and explaining why you support the war with Britain, Russia and France.   **1,2,3**

CHAPTER 2

THE FIRST WORLD WAR AND ITS AFTERMATH

SUMMARY OF EVENTS

The two sides in the war were the *Central Powers*: Germany, Austria–Hungary, Turkey (entered November 1914) and Bulgaria (October 1915); and the *Allies*: Russia (left December 1917), France, Britain, Italy (entered May 1915), Rumania (August 1916) and the USA (April 1917).

The war turned out to be quite different from what most people had anticipated. It was widely expected to be a short decisive affair, like other recent European wars; hence Moltke's nervous determination not to be left at the post when it came to mobilisation. However, the Schlieffen Plan failed to achieve the rapid defeat of France. Although the Germans penetrated deeply, Paris did not fall, and *stalemate quickly developed on the western front* – with all hope of a short war gone. Both sides dug themselves in and spent the next four years attacking and defending lines of trenches which were difficult to capture because the increased fire-power provided by magazine rifles and machineguns made frontal attacks suicidal and rendered cavalry useless.

In eastern Europe there was more movement, with Russian successes against the Austrians, who constantly had to be helped out by the Germans, causing friction between the two allies. But by December 1917, the Germans had captured *Poland* (Russian territory) and forced the defeated Russians *out of the war*. Britain, suffering heavy losses of merchant ships through submarine attacks, and France, whose armies were paralysed by mutiny, seemed on the verge of defeat. Gradually the tide turned; the Allies, helped by the entry of the USA in April 1917, wore down the Germans, whose last despairing attempt at a decisive breakthrough in France failed in the spring of 1918. The success of the British navy in quietly blockading German ports and defeating the submarine threat by defending merchant convoys, was also telling on the Germans. By the late summer of 1918 they were nearing exhaustion. An *armistice* was signed on *11 November 1918*, although Germany itself had scarcely been invaded; a controversial *peace settlement* was signed at *Versailles* the following year.

2.1 **1914**

(a) On the western front the Schlieffen Plan was held up by unexpectedly strong Belgian resistance; it took the Germans over two weeks to capture *Brussels*, an important delay because it gave the French time to organise and left the channel ports free so that the British Expeditionary Force was able to land. Instead of sweeping round in a wide arc, capturing the Channel ports and approaching Paris from the west, the Germans found themselves making straight for Paris just east of the city. They penetrated to within twenty miles of Paris and the French government withdrew to Bordeaux; but the nearer they got to Paris, the more the German impetus slowed up; there were problems in keeping the armies supplied with food and ammunition and the troops became exhausted by the long marches in the August heat. In September the faltering Germans were attacked by the French under Joffre in the *Battle of the Marne* and driven back to the River Aisne, where they were able to dig trenches. This battle was *vitally important*; some historians even call it one of the most decisive battles of modern history. It ruined the Schlieffen Plan once and for all: France would not be knocked out in six weeks; hopes of a short war were dashed and the Germans would have to face *full-scale war on two fronts*. The war of movement was over; the trench lines eventually stretched from the Alps to the Channel coast, and

Fig. 2.1 *the Western Front*

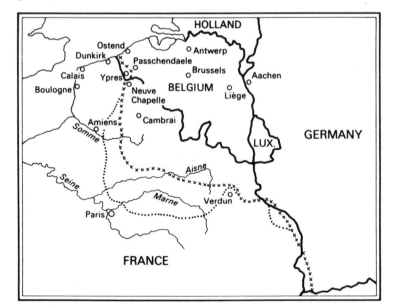

······· Limit of the German advance in 1914

ˣˣˣˣˣ The trench line for most of the war

there was time for the British navy to bring to bear its crippling blockade of German ports. The other important event of 1914 was that though the Germans took Antwerp, the British Expeditionary Force held grimly on to *Ypres*, which probably saved the other Channel ports so that more British troops could be landed and kept supplied.

(b) On the eastern front the Russians, having mobilised more quickly than the Germans expected, made the mistake of invading both *Austria* and *East Prussia* at the same time. Though they were successful against Austria, occupying the province of Galicia, the Germans called Hindenburg out of retirement and twice defeated the Russians at *Tannenberg* (August) and the *Masurian Lakes* (September), driving them out of Germany. *These battles were important*: the Russians lost vast amounts of equipment and ammunition which had taken years to amass. Although they had six and a quarter million men mobilised by the end of 1914, a third of them were without rifles. The Russians never recovered from this setback, whereas German self-confidence was boosted. When *Turkey entered the war*, the outlook for Russia was bleak, since Turkey could cut her main supply line through the *Dardanelles*. One bright spot for the Allies was that the Serbs drove out an Austrian invasion in fine style at the end of 1914, and Austrian morale was at rock bottom.

2.2 **1915**

(a) In the west, the stalemate continued, though several attempts were made to break the trench line. The British tried at Neuve Chapelle and Loos, the French in Champagne while the Germans attacked again at Ypres. These, like all attacks on the western front until 1918, *failed*; always the *difficulties were the same*: there was no chance of a surprise attack because a massive artillery bombardment always preceded the infantry attack to clear the barbed wire from no man's land between the two lots of trenches, and generally to soften up the enemy; reconnaissance aircraft and observation balloons could spot troop concentrations on the roads leading up to the trenches. Even when the trench line was breached, advance was difficult because the ground had been churned up by the artillery barrage and there was deadly machinegun fire to contend with. Any ground won was difficult to defend since it usually formed a *salient or bulge in the trench line*, of which the flanks were vulnerable. At Ypres the Germans used poison gas but when the wind changed direction it was blown back towards their own lines and they suffered more casualties than the Allies, especially when the Allies released some gas of their own.

(b) In the east, Russia's fortunes were mixed: they had further successes against Austria, but met defeat whenever they clashed with the Germans, who captured *Warsaw* and the *whole of Poland*. The Turkish blockade of the Straits was beginning to hamper the Russians, who were

illus 2.1 *Soldiers blinded by poison gas*

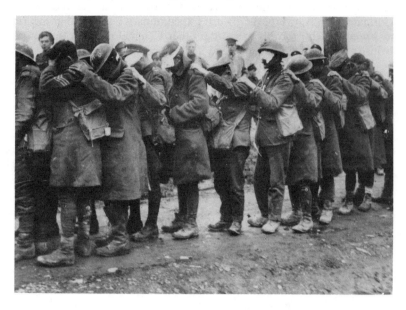

already running short of arms and ammunition. It was partly to clear the Dardanelles and open up the vital supply line to Russia via the Black Sea that the *Gallipoli Campaign* was launched. This was an idea strongly pressed by Winston Churchill (First Lord of the Admiralty) to escape the deadlock in the west by eliminating the Turks, thought to be the *weakest* of the Central Powers because of their unstable government. Success against Turkey would enable help to be sent to Russia and might also bring Bulgaria, Greece and Rumania into the war on the Allied side; it would then be possible to attack Austria from the south. The campaign was a *total failure*; the first attempt in March, an Anglo-French naval attack through the Straits to capture Constantinople, failed because of mines. This ruined the surprise element, so that when the British attempted landings at the tip of the Gallipoli peninsula, the Turks had strengthened their defences and no advance could be made (April). Further landings by Australian and New Zealand troops (Anzacs) in April and British in August were equally useless and positions could be held only with great difficulty. In December the entire force was withdrawn. The *consequences were serious*: besides being a blow to Allied morale, it turned out to be the last chance of relieving Russia via the Black Sea and probably decided Bulgaria to join the Central Powers. A Franco-British force landed at Salonika in neutral Greece to try and relieve Serbia, but it was too late. When Bulgaria entered the war in October, Serbia was quickly overrun by Bulgarians and Germans. The year 1915 therefore was not a good one for the Allies; even a British army sent to protect Anglo-Persian oil interests against a possible

Turkish attack became bogged down in Mesopotamia as it approached Baghdad and was besieged by Turks at *Kut-el-Amara* from December 1915 until March 1916, when it was forced to surrender.

(c) In May, Italy declared war on Austria, hoping to seize Austria's Italian-speaking provinces as well as territory along the eastern shore of the Adriatic. A *secret treaty* was signed in London in which the allies promised Italy Trentino, the south Tyrol, Istria, Trieste, part of Dalmatia, Adalia, some islands in the Aegean and a protectorate over Albania. The Allies hoped that by keeping thousands of Austrian troops occupied, the Italians would relieve pressure on the Russians. But the Italians made little headway and their efforts made no difference to the eventual Russian defeat.

2.3 1916

(a) On the western front, 1916 is remembered for two terrible battles, *Verdun* and the *Somme*.

(i) *Verdun* was an important French fortress against which the Germans under *Falkenhayn* launched a massive attack in February; they hoped to draw all the best French troops to its defence, destroy them and then carry out a final offensive to win the war. But the French under *Pétain* defended stubbornly and the Germans had to abandon the attack in June. The French lost heavily (about 315,000 men) as the Germans intended, but so did the Germans with over 280,000 dead, and nothing to show for it.

(ii) *The Battle of the Somme* was a series of attacks, mainly by the British, beginning on 1 July and lasting through to November. The *aim* was to relieve pressure on the French at Verdun, take over more of the trench line as the French army weakened, and keep the Germans fully committed so that they would be unable to risk sending reinforcements to the eastern front against Russia. At the end of it all the Allies had made only limited advances varying between a few hundred yards and seven miles along a thirty-mile front. The *real importance of the battle* was the *blow to German morale*, as they realised that Britain (where conscription was introduced for the first time in May) was a military power to be reckoned with. Losses on both sides, killed or wounded, were appalling (Germans 650,000; British 418,000; French 194,000) and Haig (British Commander-in-Chief) came under severe criticism for persisting with suicidal frontal attacks: Hindenburg himself admitted in his Memoirs that they could not have survived many more campaigns like Verdun and the Somme. The Somme also contributed to the fall of the British Prime Minister, *Asquith*, who resigned in December 1916, after mounting criticism.

(b) David Lloyd George became Prime Minister, and his *contribution to the Allied war effort and the defeat of the Central Powers was invaluable*. His methods were dynamic and decisive; already as Minister of Munitions since May 1915 he had improved the supply of shells and machine-guns, encouraged the development of new weapons (the Stokes light mortar and the tank) which *Kitchener* (Minister of War) had turned down, and taken control of mines, factories and railways so that the war effort could be properly centralised. As Prime Minister during 1917 he set up a small *war cabinet* so that quick decisions could be taken, brought shipping and agriculture under government control and introduced the Ministry of National Service to organise the mobilisation of men into the army. He also played an important part in the adoption of the convoy system (see Section 2.4(e)).

(c) In the east, the Russians under *Brusilov* attacked the Austrians in June (in response to a plea from Britain and France for some action to divert German attention away from Verdun), managed to break the front and advanced 100 miles, taking 400,000 prisoners and large amounts of equipment. The Austrians were demoralised, but the strain was exhausting the Russians as well. The Rumanians invaded Austria (August) but the Germans swiftly came to the rescue, *occupied the whole of Rumania* and seized her wheat and oil supplies – not a happy end to 1916 for the Allies.

2.4 THE WAR AT SEA

The general public in Germany and Britain expected a series of *naval battles* of the Trafalgar type between the rival Dreadnought fleets. But both sides were cautious and dared not risk any action which might result in the loss of their main fleets. The British *Admiral Jellicoe* was particularly cautious; as Churchill pointed out, he 'was the only man on either side who could have lost the war in an afternoon.' Nor were the Germans anxious for a confrontation because they had only 16 of the latest Dreadnoughts as against 27 British.

(a) The Allies aimed to blockade the Central Powers, preventing goods entering or leaving, and slowly starving them out. At the same time *trade routes* had to be kept open between Britain, her empire and the rest of the world, so that the Allies themselves would not starve. A third function of the navy was to transport British troops to the continent and keep them supplied via the Channel ports. The British were successful in carrying out these aims: they went into action against German units stationed abroad and at the *Battle of the Falkland Islands* destroyed one of the main German squadrons. By the end of 1914 nearly all German armed surface ships had been destroyed, apart from their main fleet (which did not venture out of the Heligoland Bight) and the squadron blockading the Baltic to cut off supplies to Russia. In 1915 the navy was involved in the *Gallipoli Campaign* (see Section 2.2(b)).

(b) The Allied blockade caused problems: Britain was trying to prevent the Germans using the neutral Scandinavian and Dutch ports to break the blockade; this involved *stopping and searching all neutral ships* and confiscating any goods suspected of being intended for enemy hands. The USA objected strongly to this, being anxious to continue trading with both sides.

(c) The Germans retaliated with mines and submarine attacks, which was their only alternative since their surface vessels were either destroyed or blockaded. At first, they respected neutral shipping and passenger liners, but it was soon clear that the German U-boat blockade was not effective, partly because of insufficient U-boats and partly because of problems of identification, as the British tried to fool the Germans by flying neutral flags and using passenger liners to transport arms and ammunition. In April 1915 the British liner *Lusitania* was sunk by a torpedo attack. (It has recently been proved that the *Lusitania* was armed and carrying vast quantities of arms and ammunition, as the Germans well knew; hence their claim that the sinking was not just an act of barbarism against defenceless civilians.) This had *important consequences*: out of the thousand dead, 118 were Americans. President Wilson therefore found that the USA would have to take sides to protect her trade; whereas the British blockade did not interfere with the safety of passengers and crews, German tactics certainly did. For the time being, however, American protests caused Bethmann to tone down the submarine campaign, rendering it even less effective.

(d) The Battle of Jutland (31 May) was the main event of 1916, the only time the main battle-fleets emerged and engaged each other; the result was indecisive. The German Admiral *von Scheer* tried to lure part of the British fleet out from its base so that that section could be destroyed by the numerically superior Germans. However, more British ships came out than he had anticipated, and after the two fleets had shelled each other on and off for several hours, the Germans decided to retire to base firing torpedoes as they went. On balance, the Germans could claim that they had won the battle since they lost only 11 ships to Britain's 14, but the *real importance of the battle* lay in the fact that the Germans had *failed to destroy British sea power*: the German High Seas Fleet stayed in Kiel for the rest of the war leaving Britain's control of the surface complete. In desperation at the food shortages caused by the British blockade, they embarked, with fatal results, on 'unrestricted' submarine warfare.

(e) 'Unrestricted' submarine warfare (January 1917). As they had been concentrating on the production of U-boats since the Battle of Jutland, this campaign was extremely effective. They attempted to sink all enemy and neutral merchant ships in the Atlantic and although they knew that this was bound to bring the USA into the war, they hoped that Britain and France would be *starved into surrender* before the Americans could make any vital contribution. They almost did it: the peak of German

illus 2.2 *Troops crossing the sea of mud at Passchendaele, 1917*

success came in *April 1917*, when 430 ships were lost; Britain was down to about six weeks' corn supply and although the USA came into the war in April, it was bound to be several months before their help became effective. However, the situation was saved by Lloyd George who insisted that the Admiralty adopt the convoy system in which a large number of merchant ships sailed together protected by escorting warships. This drastically reduced losses and the German gamble had failed. The *submarine campaign was extremely important* because it *brought the USA into the war*. The British navy therefore, helped by the Americans, played a vitally important role in the defeat of the Central Powers, and by the middle of 1918 had achieved its three aims.

2.5 **1917**

(a) In the west, 1917 was a year of *Allied failure*. A massive French attack under Nivelle in Champagne achieved nothing except mutiny in the French army, which was successfully sorted out by Pétain. From June to November the British fought the *Third Battle of Ypres*, usually remembered as *Passchendaele*, in appallingly muddy conditions; British casualties were enormous – 324,000 compared with 200,000 Germans for a four-mile advance. *More significant was the Battle of Cambrai*, which demonstrated that tanks, properly used, might break the deadlock of trench warfare. 381 massed British tanks made a great breach in the German line, but lack of reserves prevented the success from being followed up. However, the lesson had been observed and Cambrai became the model for the successful attacks of 1918. Meanwhile the Italians were heavily defeated by Germans and Austrians at *Caporetto* (October) and retreated in disorder. This rather unexpectedly proved to be an important *turning point*. Italian morale revived, perhaps because they were faced with having to defend their homeland against the hated Austrians. The defeat also led to the setting up of an *Allied Supreme War Council*. The new French premier *Clemenceau*, a great war leader in the Lloyd George mould, rallied the wilting French.

(b) On the eastern front, disaster struck the Allies when *Russia withdrew from the war*. Continuous defeat by the Germans, lack of arms and

Fig. 2.2 *the Eastern Front*

≡≡≡ Allied territory (Russia, Serbia, Rumania and Italy)
occupied by forces of the Central Powers
early in 1918

--- New Russian frontier after the Treaty of
Brest-Litovsk

supplies and utterly incompetent leadership caused two revolutions (see Section 3.2) and the Bolsheviks, who took over in November, were willing to make peace. Thus in 1918 the entire weight of German forces could be thrown against the west; without the USA the Allies would have been hard pressed. Encouragement was provided by the British capture of *Baghdad* and *Jerusalem* from the Turks, giving them control of vast *oil supplies.*

(c) **The entry of the USA (April)** was caused partly by the *German U-boat campaign*, and also by the discovery that Germany was trying to persuade *Mexico* to declare war on the USA, promising her Texas, New Mexico and Arizona in return. The Americans had hesitated about siding with the autocratic Russian government, but the overthrow of the tsar in the March revolution removed this obstacle. The USA made an important *contribution to the Allied victory*: they supplied Britain and France with *food, merchant ships and credit*; actual military help came slowly. By the end of 1917 only one American division had been in action, but by mid-1918 over a half a million men were fighting. Most important was the *psychological boost* which the American potential in resources of men and materials gave the Allies and the corresponding blow it gave to German morale.

2.6 1918: THE CENTRAL POWERS DEFEATED

(a) **The German spring offensive** was launched by Ludendorff in a last desperate attempt to win the war before too many US troops arrived and before *discontent in Germany led to revolution*. It almost came off: throwing in all the extra troops released from the east, the Germans broke through on the *Somme* (March) and by the end of May were only *40 miles from Paris*; the Allies seemed to be falling apart. However, under the overall command of the French Marshal *Foch* they managed to hold on as the German advance lost momentum and created an awkward bulge.

(b) **An Allied counter-offensive began (8 August)** near *Amiens*, with hundreds of tanks attacking in short sharp jabs at different points instead of on a narrow front, forcing the Germans to withdraw their entire line. Slowly but surely the Germans were forced back until by the end of September the Allies were through the Hindenburg Line. Though Germany itself had not yet been invaded. Ludendorff was convinced that they would be defeated in the spring of 1919. He insisted that the German government ask President Wilson for an *armistice* (3 October) hoping to get less severe terms based on Wilson's 14 points (see Section 2.7(a)). By asking for peace in 1918 he would save Germany from invasion and preserve the army's reputation. Fighting continued for another five weeks, but eventually an *armistice was signed on 11 November.*

(c) Why did the Central Powers lose the war? The reasons can be briefly summarised:

(i)   Once the Schlieffen Plan had failed, removing all hope of a quick German victory, it was bound to be a strain for them, facing *war on two fronts*.

(ii)   Allied *sea power* was decisive, enforcing the deadly blockade which caused desperate food shortages, while keeping Allied armies fully supplied.

(iii) The German submarine campaign failed in the face of *convoys* protected by British, American and Japanese destroyers; the campaign itself was a mistake because it brought the USA into the war.

(iv) The entry of the USA brought vast *resources* to the Allies.

(v)   Allied political leaders at the critical time – Lloyd George and Clemenceau – were probably more *competent* than those of the Central Powers; the unity of command under Foch in 1918 probably helped, while Haig learned lessons from the 1917 experiences about the effective use of tanks and the avoidance of salients.

(vi) The continuous strain of heavy *losses* was telling on the Germans – they lost their best troops in the 1918 offensive and the new troops were young and inexperienced; an epidemic of deadly Spanish flu did not help the situation, and morale was low as they retreated.

(vii) Germany was badly let down by her *allies* and was constantly having to help out the Austrians and Bulgarians. The defeat of Bulgaria by the British (from Salonika) and Serbs (29 September) was the final straw for many German soldiers, who could see no chance of victory now. When Austria was defeated by Italy at Vittoria-Veneto and Turkey surrendered (both in October), the end was near.

The combination of military defeat and dire food shortages produced a great *war weariness*, leading to mutiny in the navy, destruction of morale in the army and revolution at home.

2.7 THE PROBLEMS OF MAKING A PEACE SETTLEMENT

(a) When the war started none of the participants had any specific ideas about **what they hoped to achieve**, beyond that Germany and Austria wanted to preserve the Habsburg empire, and to this end thought it necessary to *destroy Serbia*. As the war progressed, some of the governments involved, perhaps to encourage their troops by presenting them with some clear objectives to fight for, began to list their *war aims*:

(i)   *Britain*: Lloyd George mentioned (January 1918) the *defence of democracy* and the righting of the injustice done to France in

1871, restoration of Belgium and Serbia, an independent Poland, democratic *self-government* for the nationalities of Austria–Hungary, *self-determination* for the German colonies and an *international organisation to prevent war.*

(ii) *USA*, Woodrow Wilson's famous *14 points* (January 1918) were: (1) abolition of secret diplomacy; (2) free navigation at sea for all nations in war and peace; (3) removal of economic barriers between states; (4) all-round reduction of armaments; (5) impartial adjustment of colonial claims in the interests of populations concerned; (6) evacuation of Russian territory; (7) restoration of Belgium; (8) liberation of France and restoration of Alsace–Lorraine; (9) readjustment of Italian frontiers along lines of nationality; (10) self-government to the peoples of Austria–Hungary; (11) Rumania, Serbia and Montenegro to be evacuated and Serbia given access to the sea; (12) self-government to the non-Turkish peoples of the Turkish empire and permanent opening of the Dardanelles; (13) an independent Poland with secure access to the sea; (14) a general association of nations to preserve peace. These points achieved publicity when the Germans later claimed that they had expected the peace terms to be based on them, and that since this was not the case, they had been *cheated.*

(b) When the peace conference met (January 1919), it was soon obvious that a settlement would be difficult because of the **differing Allied views about how to treat the defeated powers:**

(i) *France* (represented by *Clemenceau*) wanted a harsh peace to ruin Germany economically and militarily so that she could never again *threaten French frontiers.*

(ii) *Britain (Lloyd George)* was in favour of a less severe settlement enabling Germany to recover quickly so that she could resume her role as a *major customer for British goods.* However, Lloyd George had just won an election (November 1918) with such slogans as 'hang the Kaiser' and talk of getting from Germany everything 'that you can squeeze out of a lemon and a bit more'; the British public therefore expected a harsh settlement.

(iii) *USA (Woodrow Wilson)* had earlier been in favour of a lenient peace, but Wilson's attitude changed after the Germans ignored his 14 points and imposed the harsh *Brest-Litovsk treaty* on Russia; he now felt that the Germans needed to be punished, and agreed to the British and French demands for *reparations* (compensation for damages) and German disarmament. Wilson was also in favour of *self-determination*: nations should be freed from foreign rule and given *democratic governments of their own choice.*

By June 1919, the conference had come up with the Treaty of Versailles for Germany, followed by other treaties dealing with Germany's former allies. The Treaty of Versailles in particular was one of the most controversial settlements ever signed and was criticised even in the Allied countries on the grounds that it was too hard on the Germans who were bound to object so violently that *another war was inevitable*, sooner or later; in addition many of the terms (reparations and disarmament) proved *impossible to carry out*.

2.8 THE TREATY OF VERSAILLES WITH GERMANY

(a) The terms were:

(i) *Germany had to lose territory in Europe*: Alsace–Lorraine to France; Eupen, Moresnet and Malmédy to Belgium; North Schleswig to Denmark (after a plebiscite); West Prussia and Posen to Poland, though Danzig (the main port of West Prussia) was to be a *free city* under League of Nations administration, because its population was wholly German, Memel was given to Lithuania; the Saar was to be administered by the League of Nations for 15 years, when a plebiscite would decide whether it should belong to France or Germany. In the meantime France was to have the use of its *coal-mines*. Germany's *African colonies* were taken away and became 'mandates' under League supervision: this meant that various member states of the league 'looked after' them. Union between Germany and Austria was forbidden. Estonia, Latvia and Lithuania, handed over to Germany by Russia at Brest-Litovsk, were taken away from Germany and set up as independent states – examples of *self-determination* in practice.

(ii) *German armaments were strictly limited*: a maximum of 100,000 troops and no conscription (compulsory military service); no tanks, armoured cars, military aircraft or submarines, and only six battleships. The *Rhineland* was to be *permanently demilitarised* (German troops were not allowed in the area).

(iii) *The War Guilt clause* fixed the *blame* for the outbreak of the war *solely on Germany and her allies*.

(iv) *Germany was to pay reparations* for damage done to the Allies; the actual amount was not decided at Versailles, but announced later (1921) after much argument and haggling as *£6,600 million*.

(v) *A League of Nations* was set up, its aims and organisation being set out in the *League Covenant*.

The Germans had little choice but to sign the treaty, though they objected strongly. The ceremony took place in the Hall of Mirrors at Versailles, where the German empire had been proclaimed less than 50 years earlier.

(b) Why did the Germans object, and how far were their objections justified?

(i) *It was a dictated peace*: the Germans were not allowed into the discussions at Versailles; they were simply presented with the terms and told to sign. Although they were allowed to criticise it in writing, all their protests were ignored except one (see point (iii) below). Some historians feel that the Germans were justified in objecting, that it would have been reasonable to allow them to join in the discussions which might have toned down some of the harsher terms, and would certainly have deprived the Germans of the argument much used by Hitler that because the peace was a *diktat* it should *not be morally binding*. On the other hand, one can argue that the Germans could scarcely have expected any better treatment after the scant consideration they had shown the Russians at Brest-Litovsk, also a *diktat* (see Section 3.3b).

(ii) They claimed that they had been promised terms based on Wilson's 14 points, that many of the provisions were *not in accordance with the 14 points*, and were therefore a swindle. This is probably not a valid objection: the 14 points had never been accepted as official by any of the states involved, and the Germans themselves had pointedly ignored them in January 1918, when there still seemed a chance of outright German victory. By November, German tactics (Brest-Litovsk, destruction of mines, factories and public buildings during their retreat through France and Belgium) caused the Allied attitude to harden and Wilson to add *two further points*: Germany should pay for damage to *civilian population and property* and should be reduced to 'virtual impotence' – in other words, Germany should be *disarmed*. The Germans were aware of this when they accepted the armistice and, in fact, most of the terms do comply with the 14 points and the additions. There were also objections on specific points.

(iii) *Loss of territory in Europe* (including *Alsace–Lorraine* and especially *West Prussia* to give Poland access to the sea). However, both were mentioned in the 14 points. Originally, *Upper Silesia*, an industrial region with a mixed population of Poles and Germans, was to be given to Poland, but this was the one concession made to the German written objections: after a plebiscite Germany was allowed to keep about two-thirds of the area. In fact most of the German losses could be justified on grounds of nationality. The Germans probably had more grounds for objection to the loss of their *African colonies* which was hardly an 'impartial adjustment'. The *mandate system* in which Britain took over German East Africa (Tanganyika) and parts of Togoland and the Cameroons, France most of Togoland and the Cameroons, and South Africa acquired German South West Africa (now known as Namibia), was really a device by which the Allies *seized the colonies* without actually admitting that they were being annexed.

Fig. 2.3 *European frontiers after the First World War and the Peace Treaties*

 Territory lost by Germany

||||| Former territory of tsarist Russia

/// Austria–Hungary until 1918

•••• Curzon Line – proposed by Britain (Dec. 1919) as Poland's eastern frontier. Russian territory east of the line was seized by Poland in 1920

32

Fig. 2.4 *Africa and the Peace Treaties*

≡≡≡ German colonies taken away as mandates by the
Versailles Treaty, 1919

(iv) *The disarmament clauses were deeply resented*, the Germans claiming that 100,000 troops were not enough to keep law and order at a time of political disturbance. Perhaps the German objection was justified to some extent, though one can also sympathise with the French desire for a weak Germany. The Germans became more aggrieved later as it became clear that none of the other powers intended to disarm, even though Point 4 mentioned 'all-round reduction of armaments'; however, disarmament was impossible to enforce fully, since the Germans were determined to exploit every loophole.

(v) *The War Guilt clause*: the Germans objected to being saddled with the *entire blame* for the outbreak of war. There are some grounds for objection here, because although later research seemed to indicate Germany's guilt, it was hardly possible to arrive at that conclusion in the space of six weeks during 1919, which is what the Special Commission on War Responsibility did. However, the Allies wanted the Germans to *admit responsibility* so that they would be liable to *pay reparations*.

(vi) *Reparations* were the final humiliation for the Germans, and though there could be little valid objection to the general principle of reparations, it is now agreed that the actual amount decided on was *far too high* at £6,600 million. Many people thought so, including J. M. Keynes, an economic adviser to the British delegation at the conference, who urged the Allies to take £2,000 million, a more reasonable amount which Germany would be able to afford. The figure of £6,600 million enabled the Germans to protest that it was *impossible to pay*, and they soon began to default on their instalments. This caused *resentment among the allies* who were relying on German cash to pay their own war debts to the USA, and there was international tension when France tried to force the Germans to pay (see Section 13.2(c)). Eventually the allies admitted their mistake and reduced the amount to £2,000 million (*Young Plan, 1929*), but not before reparations had proved to be disastrous, economically and politically.

The Germans did have some grounds for complaint, but it is worth pointing out that the treaty could have been *even more harsh*: if Clemenceau had had his way, the *Rhineland* would have become an *independent state*, and *France* would have *annexed the Saar*. However, Germany was still the strongest power in Europe economically, so that the unwise thing about Versailles was that it annoyed the Germans yet did *not render them too weak to retaliate*.

2.9 THE PEACE TREATIES WITH AUSTRIA–HUNGARY

When Austria was on the verge of defeat in the war, the *Habsburg empire disintegrated* as the various nationalities declared themselves independent. Austria and Hungary separated and declared themselves *republics*. Many important decisions therefore had already been taken before the peace conference met; however, the situation was chaotic and the task of the conference was to *formalise and recognise what had taken place*.

(a) The Treaty of St Germain (1919) dealt with Austria, which lost Bohemia and Moravia (wealthy industrial provinces with a population of 10 million) to the new state of *Czechoslovakia*; Dalmatia, Bosnia and Herzegovina to Serbia which, with Montenegro, now became known as

Yugoslavia; Bukovina to Rumania; Galicia to the reconstituted state of Poland; the south Tyrol (as far as the Brenner Pass), Trentino, Istria and Trieste to Italy.

(b) The Treaty of Trianon dealing with Hungary was not signed until *1920* because of political uncertainties in Budapest where the Communists under Bela Kun seized power and were then overthrown. Slovakia and Ruthenia were given to Czechoslovakia; Croatia and Slovenia to Yugoslavia; Transylvania and the Banat of Temesvar to Rumania. Both treaties contained the League of Nations Covenant.

These settlements may seem harsh, but it has to be remembered that much of it had already happened, and on the whole the *spirit of self-determination* was adhered to. More people were placed under governments of *their own nationality* than ever before in Europe, though they were not always as democratic as Wilson would have liked (especially in Hungary and Poland). There were some anomalies, such as the three million Germans placed in Czechoslovakia (in the Sudetenland) and a million in Poland (by the Treaty of Versailles), but these were justified on the grounds that the new states needed them to be *economically viable*. It was unfortunate that both these instances gave Hitler an excuse to begin *territorial demands* on these countries.

The treaties left both Austria and Hungary with *serious economic problems: Austria* was a small republic, its population reduced from 22 million to 6.5 million, and its *industrial wealth* lost to Czechoslovakia and Poland. Vienna, once the capital of the huge Habsburg empire, was left high and dry surrounded by farming land which could hardly support it. Not surprisingly Austria was soon facing a severe economic crisis and was constantly having to be helped out by loans from the League of Nations. *Hungary* was just as badly affected, her population reduced from 21 million to 7.5 million, and some of her richest *corn land* lost to Rumania. Matters were further complicated when all the new states quickly introduced tariffs which hampered the flow of trade through the whole Danube area and made the industrial recovery of Austria particularly difficult. In fact there was an excellent economic case to support a *union* between Austria and Germany.

2.10 THE SETTLEMENT WITH TURKEY; TREATY OF SÈVRES (1920) AND BULGARIA; TREATY OF NEUILLY (1919)

Turkey was to lose Eastern Thrace, many Aegean islands and Smyrna to Greece; Adalia and Rhodes to Italy; the Straits were to be permanently open; Syria became a French mandate and Palestine, Iraq and Transjordan British mandates. However, the loss of so much territory to Greece, especially *Smyrna*, outraged Turkish *national feeling* (self-determination was being ignored to some extent here). Led by *Mustafa Kemal*, they rejected the treaty and chased the Greeks out of Smyrna. The Italians

Fig. 2.5 *Turkey, Bulgaria and the Peace Treaties*

||||| Turkish territory lost to Greece by the Treaty of Sèvres (1920)
but returned by the Treaty of Lausanne (1923)

▓ Turkish territory lost to Italy

≡ Bulgarian territory lost to Greece by the Treaty of Neuilly (1919)

▨ Bulgarian territory lost to Yugoslavia

and French withdrew their occupying forces from the Straits area, leaving only British troops at *Chanak*. Following the Chanak incident (1922) (see Section 4.1(b)(vii)) a compromise was reached and the settlement revised by the *Treaty of Lausanne (1923)* by which Turkey regained Eastern Thrace including Constantinople, and Smyrna. Turkey, therefore, was the first state *successfully to challenge the Paris settlement.* One legacy of the Treaty of Sèvres which was to cause problems was the situation in the mandates which were peopled largely by Arabs who had been hoping for independence after their brave struggle, led by the

English officer, *T. E. Lawrence* (Lawrence of Arabia), against the Turks. Nor were the Arabs happy about the talk of establishing a Jewish 'national home' in Palestine (see Section 11.5).

Bulgaria lost territory to Greece (depriving her of her Aegean coastline), Yugoslavia and Rumania and could complain, with some justification, that at least a million Bulgars were under foreign governments as a result.

In conclusion it has to be said that this collection of peace treaties was *not a conspicuous success*. It had the unfortunate effect of dividing Europe into the states which wanted to *revise the settlement* (Germany being the main one), and those which wanted to *preserve it*. On the whole, the latter turned out to be lukewarm in support. The USA failed to ratify the settlement (see Section 12.4(b)) and never joined the League of Nations; this in turn left France completely disenchanted with the whole thing because the Anglo-American guarantee of her frontiers *could not now apply*. Italy felt cheated because she had not received the *full territory promised her in 1915*, and *Russia was ignored*. All this tended to sabotage the settlement from the beginning, and it became increasingly difficult to apply the terms fully. But it is easy to criticise after the event; Gilbert White, an American delegate at the conference, put it perfectly when he remarked that given the intricacy of the problems involved, 'it is not surprising that they made a bad peace: what is surprising is that they managed to make peace at all.'

QUESTIONS

1. The First World War
Study the Sources below, and then answer the questions that follow.

Source A

Strategically, the battle of the Somme was an unredeemed defeat . . . The Somme set the picture by which future generations saw the First World War: brave helpless soldiers; blundering obstinate generals; nothing achieved. After the Somme men decided that the war would go on forever.

Source: A. J. P. Taylor, *The First World War* (Penguin, 1963).

Source B
British soldiers (Illus. 2.3) manning a captured German trench on the Somme.

illus 2.3

Source C
The first day of the Somme – a German view.

The men in the dugouts . . . waited ready, belts full of hand-grenades around them gripping their rifles . . . It was of vital importance to lose not a second in taking up position in the open to meet the British infantry which would advance immediately behind the artillery barrage . . .

At 7.30 a.m. the hurricane of shells ceased . . . Our men at once clambered up the steep shafts leading from the dugouts to daylight and ran . . . to the nearest craters. The machine-guns were pulled out of the dugouts and hurriedly placed in position . . . As soon as the men were in position, a series of lines were seen moving forward from the British trenches. The first line appeared without end to right and left. It was quickly followed by a second, then a third and fourth . . .

'Get ready' was passed along our front from crater to crater . . . A few minutes later, when the leading British line was within a hundred yards, the rattle of machine-gun and rifle broke out along the whole line of shell holes.

Whole sections seemed to fall . . . The advance rapidly crumbled under the hail of shells and bullets. All along the line men could be seen throwing up their arms and collapsing, never to move again. Badly wounded rolled about in their agony . . .

Source: A. H. Farrar-Hockley, *The Somme* (Pan/Severn House, 1976).

Source D
Two poems written by soldiers serving in the British army.

(i)
        If I should die, think only this of me:
                That there's some corner of a foreign field
        That is for ever England. There shall be
                In that rich earth a richer dust concealed;
        A dust whom England bore, shaped, made aware,
                Gave, once, her flowers to love, her ways to roam,
        A body of England's, breathing English air,
                Washed by the waves, blest by suns of home.

                                                Rupert Brooke

(ii)
        What passing-bells for these who die as cattle?
                Only the monstrous anger of the guns.
                Only the stuttering rifles' rapid rattle
        Can patter out their hasty orisons.
        No mockeries for them from prayers or bells,
                Nor any voice of mourning save the choirs, –
        The shrill, demented choirs of wailing shells;
                And bugles calling for them from sad shires.

                                                Wilfred Owen

(a) How do you know that the soldiers shown in Source B are British?
                                                                    1,4
(b) Explain what is meant in Source C by the following terms:
    (i) artillery barrage
    (ii) dugout
    (iii) crater   **1,4**
(c) Source B shows British soldiers manning a German trench captured during the Battle of the Somme. Does this prove that the author of Source A is wrong in his judgement, or is there some other explanation? Give full reasons for your answer.   **1,4**
(d) Source D(i) and D(ii) were written by soldiers who served in the British army. One of these soldiers died in 1915. Using all the sources to help you decide, which poem would you say was most likely to have been written by the soldier who died in 1915? Explain your answer fully.   **4(a,c)**
(e) How reliable do you think the following sources of evidence would be if you wanted to use them to help you write a report about life in the trenches on the Western Front?
    (i) poems written by soldiers who were there (as in Source D);
    (ii) photographs (as in Source B);

(iii)   accounts given by soldiers on the front line (as in Source C)?

4(b)

[Reproduced by permission of the Midland Examining Group.]

2.   The First World War

Study the Sources below, and then answer the questions that follow.

Source A

Two maps – The Schlieffen Plan, 1905 (Fig. 2.6a); The German invasion, 1914 (Fig. 2.6b).

Fig. 2.6

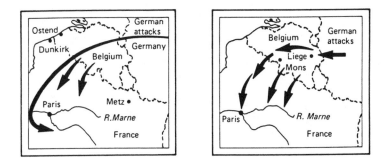

Source B

Tanks were the only way to break the stalemate produced by trenches and machineguns (illus. 2.4).

illus 2.4

Source C

The use of the blockade became an increasingly important issue in the war. The British were able to stop ships before they entered Germany or while they were in the unmined North Sea. They could therefore use surface ships and so search them rather than sink on sight. Consequently they were able to operate an effective blockade. It has been estimated that the Germans were receiving only about 1000 calories a day by the end of the war. German agriculture was hit disastrously by the war. The conscription of agricultural workers hit Germany harder than the other combatant countries.

Source: R. Wolfson, *Years of Change* (Arnold, 1978, adapted).

Source D

(i) German agricultural production (million tons)

	1912–13	1918
Potatoes	52.0	26.4
Rye	11.9	7.2
Oats	9.1	4.3
Wheat	4.9	2.5
Barley	3.6	2.1

(ii) German civilian deaths.

1915 – 88,000
1916 – 120,000
1917 – 260,000
1918 – 294,000

(a) **(i)** Explain the Schlieffen plan shown in Source A (Fig. 2.6a) and how the Germans hoped it would bring them a quick victory.

(ii) Using Fig. 2.6b (Source A) and your own knowledge, explain why the Schlieffen plan did not work out as the Germans hoped, and show what results the German failure had.

1,2,4(a)

(b) **(i)** Suggest a battle in which the scene shown in Source B could have taken place. Give reasons for your answer.   **1,4(a)**

(ii) Describe and explain how tanks played an important part in the First World War.   **1,2**

(c) Show how the evidence in Source D supports the claims made in Source C.   **4(a,c)**

(d) Using all the sources and your own knowledge, write a brief summary of the reasons why Germany lost the First World War.

1,2,4

3. The Versailles Treaties

Study the Sources below, and then answer the questions that follow.

Source A

A speech made by President Woodrow Wilson to the United States Congress on 8 January 1918, in which Wilson outlined his Fourteen Points for the establishment of future peace.

The programme of the world's peace, therefore, is our programme; the only possible programme, as we see it, is this:

Four. Adequate guarantees given and taken that national armaments will be reduced to the lowest point consistent with domestic safety.

Five. A free, open minded, and absolutely impartial adjustment of all colonial claims based upon a strict observance of the principle that in determining all such questions of sovereignty the interests of the populations concerned must have equal weight with the equitable claims of the Government whose title is to be determined.

Thirteen. An independent Polish State should be erected which should include the territories inhabited by indisputably Polish populations, which should be assured a free and secure access to the sea, and whose political and economic independence and territorial integrity should be guaranteed by international covenant.

Source: J. H. Bettey (ed.), *English Historical Documents* (Routledge & Kegan Paul, 1967, extract).

Source B

From the Treaty of Versailles.

Clause 87: Germany recognises the complete independence of Poland, and renounces in her favour all rights and title over the territory.

Clause 119: Germany renounces in favour of the principal Allied and Associated Powers all her rights and titles over her overseas possessions.

Clause 160: The German Army . . . must not exceed one hundred thousand men, including officers . . . The Army shall be devoted exclusively to the maintenance of order within the territory and to the control of the frontiers . . .

Clause 231: Germany accepts the responsibilities of Germany and her allies for causing all the loss and damage to which the Allied governments have been subjected as a consequence of the war imposed upon them by the aggression of Germany and her allies [War Guilt Clause].

Source: J. H. Bettey (ed.), *English Historical Documents* (Routledge & Kegan Paul, 1967, extract).

Source C
From a speech by a German MP in parliament – 1919.

> The criminal madness of this peace [The Versailles Treaty], will drain Germany's national life-blood. It is a shameless blow in the face of common-sense. It is inflicting the deepest wounds on us Germans as our world lies in wreckage about us.

Source: J. W. Hiden, *The Weimar Republic* (Longman, 1974, adapted extracts).

Source D
From a British historian.

> The Treaty of Versailles was not excessively harsh on Germany, either territorially or economically. It deprived her of about $13\frac{1}{2}$ per cent of her territory (including Alsace–Lorraine), about 13 per cent of her economic productivity and about 7 million of her inhabitants – just over 10 per cent of her population – as well as her colonies and large merchant vessels. However, the German people were expecting victory and not defeat. It was the acknowledgement of defeat as much as the treaty terms themselves, which they found so hard to accept.

Source: Ruth Henig, *Versailles and After* (Methuen, 1984).

(a)   (i)   Why did the Germans reject the Fourteen Points (Source A) when they were first offered, yet accepted them in November 1918?   **1,4(a)**

    (ii)   Why were the Germans prepared to accept the Fourteen Points rather than any peace proposal offered by Britain or France?   **1,4(a)**

(b)   (i)   How far were the points (4, 5 and 13) given in Source A kept to by the clauses of the Treaty of Versailles given in Source B?   **4(a,c)**

    (ii)   Which of the clauses of the Treaty of Versailles given in Source B is not referred to in Source A? Explain why there was no mention of this clause in the Fourteen Points.   **4,1,2**

(c)   What evidence in Sources B and D seems to support the views expressed by the speaker in Source C?   **4(a,c)**

(d)   (i)   In what ways does the passage by Ruth Henig (Source D) seem to contradict the statement by the speaker in Source C?   **4(a,c)**

    (ii)   Why do you think these two sources present such different views?   **4(b)**

(e)   Which of the sources A, B, C and D, are primary sources, and which secondary? Give reasons for your answers, and explain the difference between a primary and a secondary source.   **4**

4. **Select** *two* of the following episodes of the First World War:
   (a) The Schlieffen Plan.
   (b) The Dardanelles (Gallipoli) campaign.
   (c) The German submarine campaign.
   For each of your *two* choices, show what was its *main purpose*, and why it *eventually failed*.   **1,2**
   [Southern Examining Group – Specimen Question.]

5. Write *three* short letters to newspapers in 1921, criticising parts of the Versailles Settlement which affected your country:
   (a) As a German ex-soldier.
   (b) As a Frenchman living in Alsace.
   (c) As a Turkish civilian living in Smyrna.   **1,2,3**

CHAPTER 3

RUSSIA: 1905–24

SUMMARY OF EVENTS

In the decade before 1914, Russia was in a troubled state. The tsar *Nicholas II* (1894–1917) insisted on ruling as an *autocrat* (someone who rules a country as he sees fit, ignoring such constraints as parliaments) but had failed to deal adequately with the country's many problems. Unrest and criticism of the government had reached a climax with the Russian *defeats* in the *war with Japan* (1904–5) and in 1905 had burst out in a general strike and an attempted revolution, forcing Nicholas to make concessions (the October Manifesto) including the granting of an elected *parliament (Duma)*. When it became clear that the *duma* was ineffective, unrest increased and culminated, after the disasters of the First World War, in *two revolutions*, both in *1917*. The *first (March) overthrew the tsar* and set up a *moderate provisional government*; but when this fared no better than the tsar, it was itself overthrown by the *Bolshevik revolution (November)*. The new Bolshevik government was shaky at first and its opponents' (Whites) attempts to destroy it caused a *civil war* (1918–20). Thanks to the leadership of *Lenin* and *Trotsky*, the Bolsheviks (now calling themselves *communists*) survived and Lenin was able to begin the task of leading Russia to recovery (until his death in 1924).

3.1 AFTER 1905: WERE THE 1917 REVOLUTIONS INEVITABLE?

Nicholas had survived 1905 because his *opponents were not united*, because there was *no central leadership* (the whole thing having flared up spontaneously) and because he had been willing to compromise at the critical moment. Tsarism now had a breathing space in which Nicholas had a chance to make a constitutional monarchy work, and to throw himself in with the people demanding moderate reforms: improvements in industrial working conditions and pay, cancellation of redemption payments (annual payments to the government by peasants in return for their freedom, following the abolition of serfdom in 1861), which had reduced over half the rural population to abject poverty, more freedom for the press, and genuine democracy in which the *Duma* would play an important part in running the country. Unfortunately he seems to have had very little intention of keeping to the spirit of the October Manifesto, having agreed to it only because he had no choice. The *First Duma* (1906) was not democratically elected, for although all classes were allowed to vote, the system was rigged so that landowners and middle classes would be in the majority. Even so, it put forward far-reaching demands such as confiscation of large estates, a genuinely democratic electoral system and the right to approve the tsar's ministers. This was far too drastic for Nicholas who had the *Duma* dispersed by troops after only ten weeks. The *Second Duma* (1907) suffered the same fate, after which Nicholas changed the franchise, depriving peasants and urban workers of the vote. The *Third and Fourth Dumas* were much more conservative and therefore lasted longer, covering the period 1907 to 1917. Though on occasion they criticised the government, they had no real power, since the tsar controlled the ministers and the secret police. Some foreign observers were surprised at the ease with which Nicholas ignored his promises and dismissed the first two *Dumas* without provoking another general strike. The fact was that the revolutionary impetus had subsided for the time being, and many leaders were either in prison or exile.

This, together with the improvement in the economy beginning after 1906, has given rise to some controversy about whether or not the 1917 revolutions were *inevitable*.

(a) One theory is that given time plus gradually improving living standards, the **chances of revolution would fade**, and that if Russia had not become disastrously involved in the *First World War*, the monarchy might have survived; three areas of evidence *support this view*:

   (i) *Peter Stolypin*, prime minister from 1906 to 1911, made determined efforts to win over the peasants believing that given twenty years of peace there would be no question of revolution. Redemption payments were abolished and peasants encouraged to buy their own land (about 2 million had done so by 1916 and another 3.5 million had emigrated to Siberia where they had their own farms). As a result there emerged a class of comfortably-off peasants (called *kulaks*) whom, Stolypin hoped, the government could rely on for *support against revolution*.

   (ii) As more factories came under the control of inspectors, there were signs of improving working conditions, and as industrial profits increased, the first signs of a more *prosperous workforce* could be detected. In 1912 a workers' sickness and accident insurance scheme was introduced.

   (iii) At the same time the *revolutionary parties seemed to have lost heart*: they were short of money, torn by disagreements, and their leaders were still in exile.

(b) The other view is that, given the tsar's deliberate flouting of his 1905 promises, there was **bound to be a revolution sooner or later** and the situation was deteriorating again long before the First World War. The evidence to support this view seems *more convincing*:

(i)   By 1911 it was becoming clear that Stolypin's *land reforms* would *not have the desired result*, partly because the peasant population was growing too rapidly (at the rate of 1.5 million a year) for his schemes to cope with, and because farming methods were too inefficient to support the growing population comfortably. The *assassination* of Stolypin in 1911 removed one of the few really able tsarist ministers and perhaps the only man who could have saved the monarchy.

(ii) There was a wave of *industrial strikes* set off by the shooting of 270 strikers in the Lena goldfields (April 1912). In all there were over 2000 separate strikes in that year, 2400 in 1913, and over 4000 in the first seven months of 1914 – *before* war broke out. Whatever improvements had taken place, they were obviously not enough to remove all the pre-1905 grievances.

(iii) Apart from one or two exceptions there was little relaxation of the government's *repressive policy*, as the secret police rooted out revolutionaries among university students and professors and deported masses of Jews, thereby ensuring that both groups were firmly anti-tsarist. The situation was thus particularly dangerous since peasants, industrial workers and intelligentsia were all alike discontented.

(iv) As 1912 progressed, the fortunes of the various *revolutionary parties*, especially the Bolsheviks and Mensheviks, *revived*. Both groups had developed from an earlier movement, the Social Democrat Labour Party, which was Marxist in outlook. (Karl Marx (1818–83) was a German Jew whose political ideas were set out in *The Communist Manifesto* (1848) and *Das Kapital* (1867). He believed that economic factors are the real cause of historical change, and that workers (proletariat) are everywhere exploited by capitalists (middle-class bourgeoisie), which must inevitably lead to revolution and the setting up of 'the dictatorship of the proletariat'.) One of the leaders was *Vladimir Lenin* who helped to edit the revolutionary newspaper *Iskra* (The Spark). It was over an election to the *Iskra* editorial board in 1903 that the party had split into the Lenin supporters, the *Bolsheviks* (the Russian for 'majority') and the rest, the *Mensheviks* (minority). Both believed in strikes and revolution, but the Bolsheviks felt it was essential to win the support of peasants as well as industrial workers, whereas the Mensheviks, doubting the value of peasant support, favoured close co-operation with the middle class; Lenin was strongly opposed to this. In 1912 appeared the new Bolshevik newspaper *Pravda* (Truth), which was extremely important as a means of publicising Bolshevik ideas and giving political direction to the already developing strike wave.

(v)   The *royal family* was *discredited by a number of scandals*. It was widely suspected that Nicholas himself was a party to the murder of Stolypin, who was shot by a member of the secret police in the tsar's presence during a gala performance at the Kiev Opera; nothing was ever proved, but Nicholas and his right-wing supporters were probably not sorry to see the back of Stolypin, who was becoming too liberal for their comfort. More serious was the royal family's association with Rasputin, a self-professed 'holy man', who made himself indispensable to the Empress Alexandra by his ability to help the ailing heir to the throne, Alexei. This unfortunate child had inherited haemophilia from his mother's family, and Rasputin had the power, apparently through hypnosis, to stop the bleeding whenever Alexei suffered a haemorrhage. Eventually Rasputin became a real power behind the throne, but attracted public criticism by his drunkenness and his numerous affairs with court ladies. Alexandra preferred to ignore the scandals and the *Duma's* request that Rasputin be sent away from the court (1912).

According to Richard Freeborn, there was a 'growing agitation among the workers, which, in July 1914, in St Petersburg, had assumed the proportions of incipient revolution with street demonstrations, shootings and the building of barricades'. However, the government still controlled the army and police and may well have been able to hold on even if a full-scale revolution had developed. What historians are sure about is that Russian *failures in the war made revolution certain* and caused troops and police to mutiny so that there was nobody left to defend autocracy. The war revealed the incompetent and corrupt organisation and the shortage of equipment; it caused tremendous social upheaval with the recruitment of 15 million peasants and ruined the economy, bringing rising prices and chronic food shortages. Nicholas made the mistake of appointing himself *supreme commander* (August 1915) and thus drew upon himself the blame for all future defeats, and for the high death rate, which destroyed the morale of the troops. Even the *murder of Rasputin* by a group of aristocrats (December 1916) could not save the monarchy.

3.2 THE TWO REVOLUTIONS: MARCH AND NOVEMBER 1917

The revolutions are still known in Russia as the February and October Revolutions. This was because the Russians were still using the old *Julian* calendar which was *13 days behind* the Gregorian calendar used by the rest of Europe. Russia adopted the Gregorian calendar in 1918.

(a) **The first revolution began spontaneously on 8 March** when bread riots broke out in Petrograd (St Petersburg). The rioters were quickly joined by thousands of strikers from a nearby armaments factory, and when troops were ordered to open fire they refused and joined in the demonstrations. Mobs seized public buildings, released prisoners from jails and took over police stations and arsenals. Some of his senior generals told Nicholas, who was on his way back to Petrograd, that he

illus 3.1 *Street fighting in Petrograd, 1917*

would have to renounce the throne; on 15 March, in the imperial train standing in a siding near Pskov, the tsar *abdicated* in favour of his brother, the *Grand Duke Michael*; when he refused the throne, the Russian monarchy was at an end. There had been nothing organised about this first revolution; it was simply a *spontaneous reaction to the chaotic situation which the imperial government had allowed to develop.*

(b) The provisional government. The *Duma*, struggling to take control, set up a mainly liberal *provisional government* with *Prince George Lvov* as prime minister; in July, he was replaced by Alexander Kerensky, a moderate socialist. The new government was just as perplexed by the enormous problems facing it as the tsar had been, and in November a *second revolution* took place which *removed the provisional government and installed the Bolsheviks.*

(c) Why did the provisional government fall from power so soon?

(i) It took the unpopular decision to continue the war, but the *June offensive*, Kerensky's idea, was another disastrous failure, causing a complete collapse of army morale and discipline and sending hundreds of thousands of *deserting troops streaming home*.

(ii) The government had to share power with the *Petrograd soviet*, an elected committee of workers' and soldiers' representatives which tried to govern the city. Other soviets appeared in Moscow and all the provincial cities and when the Petrograd soviet ordered all soldiers to obey only the soviet, it meant that in the last resort the provisional government could *not rely on the support of an army*.

(iii) Kerensky delayed the meeting of a *Constituent Assembly* (parliament) which he had promised and did nothing about land reform. This lost him support on all sides.

(iv) Meanwhile, thanks to the new political amnesty, *Lenin* was able to *return from exile* in Switzerland (April). The Germans allowed him to travel through to Petrograd in a special 'sealed' train, in the hope that he would cause further chaos in Russia. After a rapturous welcome he urged that the *soviets should cease to support* the provisional government.

(v) In the midst of general chaos, Lenin and the Bolsheviks put forward a realistic and attractive policy. He demanded *all power to the soviets*, and promised in return an end to the war, all land to be given to the peasants, and more food. By October the Bolsheviks were in control of both the *Petrograd* and *Moscow* soviets, though they were still in a *minority over the country as a whole*.

(vi) On *20 October*, urged on by Lenin, the Petrograd soviet took the crucial decision to attempt to *seize power*. Leon Trotsky, chairman of the soviet, made most of the plans, which went off without a hitch. During the night of *6–7 November*, Bolshevik Red Guards occupied all key points and later *arrested the provisional government ministers* except Kerensky who managed to escape. It was almost a *bloodless coup*, enabling Lenin to set up a new soviet government with himself in charge. The coup had been successful because Lenin had judged to perfection the moment of maximum hostility towards the Kerensky government, and the Bolsheviks, who knew exactly what they wanted, were *well disciplined* and *organised*, whereas all other political groups were in disarray.

3.3 LENIN AND THE BOLSHEVIKS TAKE POWER 1917

The Bolsheviks were in control in Petrograd as a result of their coup, but elsewhere the takeover was not so smooth. Fighting lasted a week in Moscow before the soviet won control and it was the *end of November* before other cities were brought to heel. *Country areas* were much more

illus 3.2 *Lenin addressing a crowd, 1917; the man in the left foreground has been identified as Trotsky*

difficult to deal with, and at first the peasants were lukewarm towards the new government, which very few people expected to last long because of the complexity or the problems facing it. As soon as the other political groups recovered their composure, there was bound to be determined opposition to the Bolsheviks, who had somehow to extricate Russia from the war and then set about repairing the shattered economy while at the same time keeping their promises about land and food for the peasants and workers.

3.4 HOW SUCCESSFUL WERE LENIN AND THE BOLSHEVIKS IN DEALING WITH THESE PROBLEMS (1917–24)?

(a) **The Bolsheviks had nothing like majority support** in the country as a whole; the problem was how to *keep themselves in power* once the public realised what a Bolshevik government involved. One of Lenin's first decrees therefore *nationalised all land* so that it could be redistributed among the peasants; this increased support for the Bolsheviks and was a great help in their fight with the *Constituent Assembly*. Lenin knew that he would have to allow elections, having criticised Kerensky so bitterly for postponing them, but he realised that a Bolshevik majority in the Assembly was highly unlikely. Elections were held (the only completely free and democratic elections ever to take place in Russia), but the Bolsheviks won only *168* seats out of about 700 while the right Social Revolutionaries had 380, a clear anti-Bolshevik majority. This would not do for Lenin who was aiming for a '*dictatorship of the proletariat*', by which he meant that he and the Bolshevik party working through the soviets would run the country on behalf of the workers and peasants. There was no room in the scheme for any other party. Accordingly, after some anti-Bolshevik speeches at its first meeting (January 1918), the Assembly was *dispersed* by Bolshevik Red Guards and never met again. Armed force had triumphed for the time being, but opposition was to lead to civil war later in the year.

(b) The next pressing problem was how to withdraw from the war; an *armistice* between Russia and the Central Powers had been agreed in December 1917, but long negotiations followed, during which Trotsky tried without success to persuade the Germans to moderate their demands. The *Treaty of Brest-Litovsk (March 1918)* was cruel, Russia losing Poland, Estonia, Latvia and Lithuania, the Ukraine, Georgia and Finland; this included a third of Russia's farming land, a third of her population, two-thirds of her coalmines and half her heavy industry. A terrible price indeed, but Lenin insisted that it was worth it, pointing out that Russia needed to sacrifice space in order to gain time to recover. He probably expected to get the land back anyway when, as he hoped, the *revolution spread to Germany*.

(c) By April 1918 armed opposition to the Bolsheviks was breaking out in many areas leading to *civil war*. The *Whites* were a mixed bag, including Social Revolutionaries, Mensheviks, ex-tsarist officers and any other groups which did not like what they had seen of the Bolsheviks; they were not aiming to restore the tsar, but simply to set up a *parliamentary government* on western lines. In Siberia *Admiral Kolchak*, former Black Sea Fleet commander, set up a White government; *General Denikin* was in the Caucasus with a large White army; most bizarre of all the *Czechoslovak Legion* of about 40,000 men had seized long stretches of the Trans-Siberian Railway in the region of Omsk. These troops were originally prisoners taken by the Russians from the Austro-Hungarian army, who had later fought against the Germans under the Kerensky government. After Brest-Litovsk the Bolsheviks gave them permission to leave Russia via the Trans-Siberian Railway to Vladivostock, but then decided to disarm them in case they co-operated with the Allies, who were already showing interest in the destruction of the new Bolshevik government. The Czechs resisted with great spirit and their control of the railway was a serious embarrassment to the government.

The situation was complicated by *foreign intervention to help the Whites* with the excuse that they wanted a government which would continue the war against Germany. When intervention continued even after the defeat of Germany, it became clear that the aim was to destroy the Bolshevik government which was now advocating *world revolution*. The USA, Japan, France and Britain sent troops, with landings at Archangel, Murmansk and Vladivostock. The situation seemed grim for the Bolsheviks when early in 1919 Kolchak (whom the Allies intended to head the next government) advanced with three armies towards Moscow, the new capital. However *Trotsky*, now *Commissar for War*, had done a magnificent job creating the well-disciplined *Red Army*, based on conscription and including thousands of experienced officers from the old tsarist armies. Kolchak was forced back, and later captured and executed by the Reds; the Czech legion was defeated and Denikin, advancing from the south to within 250 miles of Moscow, was forced to retreat; he later escaped with British help. By the end of 1919 it was clear that the Bolsheviks (now calling themselves communists) would survive, though *1920* saw an *invasion of the Ukraine* by Polish and French troops which forced the Russians to hand over part of the Ukraine and White Russia (*Treaty of Riga 1921*). From the communist point of view, however, the important thing was that they had won the civil war. The communist victory was achieved because:

(i) The *Whites were not centrally organised*; Kolchak and Denikin failed to link up, and the nearer they drew to Moscow the more they strained their lines of communication. They lost the support of many peasants by their *brutal behaviour* and because peasants feared a White victory would mean the loss of their *newly acquired land*.

illus 3.3 *The Red Army in the Crimea during the civil war, 1918*

(ii) The *Red Armies* had *more troops* plus the inspired leadership of *Trotsky*.

(iii) Lenin took decisive measures, known as *war communism*, to control the economic resources of the state: all factories of any size were nationalised, all private trade banned, and food and grain seized from peasants to feed town workers and troops. This was successful at first in that it enabled the government to survive the civil war, but it had disastrous results later.

(iv) Lenin was able to present the Bolsheviks as a *nationalist government* fighting against foreigners; and even though war communism was unpopular with peasants, the Whites became even more unpopular because of their foreign connections.

(d) From early 1921 Lenin had the formidable task of **rebuilding an economy shattered by the First World War and then by civil war**. War communism had been unpopular with the peasants who, seeing no point in working hard to produce food which was taken away from them without compensation, simply produced enough for their own needs. This caused *severe food shortages* aggravated by *droughts* in 1920–1. In addition industry was almost at a standstill. In March 1921 a serious *naval mutiny* occurred at Kronstadt, suppressed only through prompt action by Trotsky, who sent troops across the ice on the Gulf of Finland.

This mutiny seems to have convinced Lenin that a new approach was needed to win back the faltering support of the peasants; he put into operation what became known as the *New Economic Policy (NEP)*. Peasants were not allowed to keep *surplus produce* after payment of a tax representing a certain proportion of the surplus. This, plus the reintroduction of *private trade*, revived incentive and food production increased. On the other hand heavy industry was left under state control, though some smaller factories were handed back to private ownership; Lenin also found that often the old managers had to be brought back, as well as such capitalist incentives as bonuses and piece-rates. Lenin saw NEP as a temporary compromise – a return to a certain amount of private enterprise until recovery was assured; his long-term aim remained *full state control* of industry, and of agriculture (through *collective farms*). Gradually the economy began to recover, though there were recurrent food shortages for many years.

(e) Political problems were solved with typical efficiency. Russia was now the world's first *communist state*, the Union of Soviet Socialist Republics (USSR) with power held by the communist party (no other parties were allowed). In March 1921 Lenin banned groups who criticised his policies within the party, and during the rest of that year about one-third of the party members were 'purged' or expelled with the help of the ruthless *secret police* (OGPU). Control by Lenin and the party was complete. (For his successes in foreign affairs see Section 13.3(a) and (b).)

In May 1922 Lenin had his first stroke; after this he gradually grew weaker, suffering two more strokes until he died in January 1924 at the early age of 53. A. J. P. Taylor sums up his career well: 'Lenin did more than any other political leader to change the face of the twentieth-century world. The creation of Soviet Russia and its survival were due to him. He was a very great man and even, despite his faults, a very good man.'

QUESTIONS

1. Russia 1905–17
Study the Sources below, and then answer the questions that follow.

Source A
From Tsar Nicholas II's October Manifesto, 17 October 1905.
Our unchangeable will and desire is:

1. To grant to the population the right of free citizenship, based on the principles of freedom of person, conscience, speech, assembly and union.
2. To include in the work of the Duma those classes that have been until now entirely deprived of the right to vote, and to extend in the future the principles of the general right of election.
3. To establish as an unbreakable rule that no law shall go into force without its approval by the State Duma.

Source: R. Wolfson, *Years of Change* (Arnold, 1978, adapted).

Source B
From Tsar Nicholas II's Manifesto to better the conditions of the peasants, 3 November 1905

The troubles that have broken out in villages fill our heart with deep sorrow. Violence and crime do not, however, help the peasant and may bring much sorrow and misery to the country. The only way to better permanently the welfare of the peasant is by peaceful means; and to improve his condition has always been one of our first cares. We have decided:

1. To reduce by half, from 1 January 1906, and to discontinue altogether from 1 January 1907, payments due from peasants for land which before emancipation, belonged to large landowners.
2. To make it easier for the Peasant Land Bank, by increasing its resources and by offering better terms for loans, to help the peasant who has only a little land to buy more.

Source: R. Wolfson, *Years of Change* (Arnold, 1978, adapted).

Source C
From Tsar Nicholas II's dismissal of the First Duma, 21 July 1906.

We summoned the representatives of the Nation, confidently antici-
pating benefits for the country from their labours. We have always
devoted our greatest care to the removal of the burdens of the people
by improving the conditions of agricultural work.

A cruel disappointment has befallen us. The representatives of the
Nation have strayed into spheres beyond their competence. They have
been making enquiries into the acts of local authorities established by
us, and have been making comments on the faults of our laws, which
can only be changed by our imperial will. In short, they have
undertaken illegal acts. The peasants, disturbed by these happenings,
and seeing no hope of improvement in their lot, have turned to open
violence. But we shall not permit illegal acts, and we shall therefore
impose our will on the disobedient; we therefore dissolve the Duma.

Source: R. Wolfson, *Years of Change* (Arnold, 1978, adapted).

Source D

(i)   Number of strikes per annum

       1910 – 222
       1911 – 466
       1912 – 2032
       1913 – 2404
       1914 – 4098 (Jan.–Jul.)

(ii) Industrial growth rate 1880–1914 (average per annum, %)

    Russia   3.5%
    Germany   3.75%
    USA   2.75%
    UK   1.00%

(iii) Industrial production in millions of tons (1913).

	Russia	*France*	*Germany*	*USA*	*UK*
Coal	36	40	190	517	292
Pig Iron	4.8	5.2	16.8	31	10.4
Steel	5.2	4.6	18.3	31.8	7.8

Source: R. Wolfson, *Years of Change* (Arnold, 1978).

Source E

What had happened? Only a month or three weeks ago no thinking
Russian individual had doubted the fact that the ruler of Russia was a
vile individual, unworthy of serious mention; no one would have

dreamt of quoting him except as a joke. Yet in a matter of days everything had changed. People would gather with serious faces around the advertisement pillars, and the Tsar's long string of pompous titles, simply because they were printed on these massive cylindrical slabs, did not strike them as ridiculous at all. People would read out in loud, clear voices: 'At the call to arms Russia has risen to meet the enemy, not for military ambition, but for a just cause – to defend the safety of our divinely-protected empire.'

Source: Alexander Solzhenitsyn's novel *August 1914* (1972), quoted in R. Brown and C. Daniels (eds) *Twentieth Century Europe* (Macmillan, 1981).

Source F
From a Petrograd police report, October 1916.

Military defeats brought the masses a clearer understanding of the problems of war – unfair distribution of foodstuffs, an immense and rapid increase in the cost of living, and inadequacy in sources of supply. These factors show that neglect of the home front is the prime cause of the disorganisation of the huge machine of state, and that a terrible crisis is on the way. Everywhere there are exceptionally strong feelings of hostility and opposition to the government because of the unbearable burden of the war and the impossible conditions of everyday life. The situation is serious enough to deserve immediate attention.

Source: R. Brown and C. Daniels (eds), *Twentieth Century Europe* (Macmillan, 1981, adapted).

(a)   (i) In what ways do Sources A and B suggest that the situation in Russia might have improved after the 1905 Revolution?

    (ii) What evidence is there in Source B to show what the Tsar's feelings were towards the peasants?   **4(a)**

(b)   (i) How do Sources C and D suggest that many people were likely to be dissatisfied with the rate of progress in Russia before the outbreak of the First World War in 1914?   **4(a)**

    (ii) Do you think the Tsar's statements in Source C contradict what he had said in Sources A and B? Give reasons for your answer.   **4(a,c)**

(c)   (i) What evidence is there in Source E that people's feelings towards the Tsar changed in 1914? What was the reason for this change?

    (ii) According to Source F, why was the situation in October 1916 'serious enough to deserve immediate attention'?   **4(a)**

(d) How useful do you think Sources D, E and F are to a historian trying to decide what caused the downfall of the Tsar in 1917?

  4(b)

(e) Explain whether or not, in your opinion, the Sources support the statement that 'after the 1905 Revolution another revolution was inevitable sooner or later in Russia'. **4(a,b,c)**

2. You are a factory worker in Petrograd, and you became involved in the events that led to the fall of Tsar Nicholas.
   (a) Explain why you were opposed to the Tsar and welcomed the setting up of the Provisional Government.
   (b) Why, by the autumn of 1917, had you become an opponent of the provisional Government and a strong supporter of the Bolsheviks? **1,2,3**

3. Russia under Lenin and the Bolsheviks
Study the Sources below, and then answer the questions that follow.

Source A
From Lenin's Instructions for Harvesting Grain and for Grain Requisitioning Detachments (i.e., War Communism), August 1918.

1. All Soviets of Workers' and Peasants' Deputies, all committees of the poor and trade unions are to form detachments.
2. The tasks of the detachments are:

   (a) Harvest winter grain in former landlord-owned estates.
   (b) Harvest grain in front line areas.
   (c) Harvest grain on the land of kulaks or rich people
   (d) Help in harvest everywhere.

3. Grain for the poor must be stored locally, the rest must be sent to grain collection centres.
4. Every food requisition detachment is to consist of not fewer than 75 men and two or three machine guns.

Source B
Reports from British refugees on conditions in Russia, October 1918.

These people are unanimous in describing conditions as unbearable, owing to the rule of the Bolsheviks, as well as to the appalling economic conditions brought about by Lenin's regime.

The Russian nation is groaning under the tyranny of the Bolsheviks. Workers and peasants are compelled to work under threat of death. Since only the Red Guards have weapons, a rising of the people is not possible.

Famine is widespread. The peasants refuse to sell food but will only barter it. Unless people have about 1000 roubles (£100) a month they have to starve. It is possible to buy food from the Red Guards who are well fed. Lenin and his colleagues are living in luxury.

Source C
Russian production figures.

	1913	1921	1923
Grain (million tons)	81.6	37.6	56.6
Pig iron (million tons)	4.8	0.1	0.3
Steel (million tons)	5.2	0.2	0.7
Cotton fabrics (million metres)	2582	105	691
Electricity (million Kwh)	1.9	0.5	1.1

Source: R. Wolfson, *Years of Change* (Arnold, 1978).

Source D
From Lenin's decree introducing the New Economic Policy (NEP), March 1921.

In order to ensure an efficient and untroubled economic life on the basis of a freer use by the farmer of the products of his labour, in order to strengthen the peasant economy and raise its productivity, requisitioning, as a means of state collection of food supplies and raw material, is to be replaced by a tax in kind. It will be in the form of a percentage or partial deduction from the products raised by the peasant. All the reserves of food, raw material and fodder which remain with the peasants after the tax has been paid may be used by them as they wish – for improving their holdings, for increasing personal consumption and for exchange for products of factory and hand-industry.

Source: W. H. Chamberlin, *The Russian Revolution 1917–1921* (Macmillan, 1935, adapted).

(a) Explain what had happened between 1913 and 1921, apart from the Revolutions of 1917, to bring about the state of the Russian economy in 1921, as revealed in Source C.   **4,1,2**

(b) (i) Why do you think Lenin felt it necessary to issue his Grain Requisitioning Programme described in Source A?   **4,1**

  (ii) In what ways does Source A indicate that the Bolshevik government had difficulties in obtaining grain?   **4(a)**

  (iii) How does Source D suggest that the Grain Requisitioning Programme may not have been completely successful?   **4(a)**

(c) (i) What criticisms of the Bolshevik rule are made in Source B?   **4(a)**

  (ii) In what ways do Sources A and C support or contradict these criticisms?   **4(c)**

(d) (i) According to Source D, why did Lenin introduce his New Economic Policy (NEP)?   **4(a)**

    (ii) Explain in your own words what important changes from previous practice were brought in by NEP.   **4(a)**

    (iii) What evidence does Source C provide to suggest whether or not NEP was successful?   **4(c)**

(e) What doubts might a historian have about accepting the evidence provided by Sources B and C?   **4(b)**

[Reproduced by permission of the Midland Examining Group.]

4. **(a)** Explain why there was a civil war in Russia from 1918 to 1920.

    (b) Show how and why the Bolsheviks won the civil war.

    (c) How well did Lenin deal with the problems of Russia once the civil war was over?   **1,2**

CHAPTER 4

BRITAIN: 1918–39

SUMMARY OF EVENTS

Between the two wars Britain was faced with a great array of problems: disturbances in Ireland, declining industries, social unrest, the general strike of 1926, mass unemployment during the world economic crisis of the early 1930s, and threats to peace from the aggressive dictators Mussolini and Hitler. Politically the most important developments were the blossoming of the *Labour Party* which formed two short governments; the sharp decline of the *Liberals*, still suffering from the split between Asquith and Lloyd George factions; and the often unhappy experience of coalition governments. In spite of all the problems progress was made in the field of social welfare, education and housing.

When the armistice was signed on *11 November 1918*, Lloyd George was still prime Minister of the wartime coalition, supported by his own section of the Liberal party and most of the Conservatives. He decided to hold an immediate election (14 December 1918) which resulted in an *overwhelming victory* for the *coalition*. Lloyd George remained Prime Minister until 1922 when his coalition fell apart and the country returned to party governments: Conservative (1922–4), Labour (January to October 1924), Conservative (1924–9), Labour (1929–31). Labour's failure to deal with the economic crisis led to the formation of another coalition, known as the *National government* (1931–40).

4.1 THE LLOYD GEORGE COALITION 1918–22

(a) **The election** which returned Lloyd George to power was the first since December 1910, and the first to be fought under the *Representation of the People Act* (August 1918) which gave the vote to all men over 21 and to most women over 30.

The coalition won an *easy victory*, mainly because of Lloyd George's great popularity as the man who had led Britain to victory, and his promises to create a 'fit country for heroes to live in' and to make Germany pay 'the whole cost of the war'. The coalition won 484 seats, made up of 338 Conservatives, 136 Lloyd George Liberals, and 10 Labour and other supporters. The main opposition consisted of 59 Labour members, 26 Asquith Liberals and 48 Conservatives who refused to support the coalition. There were also 73 Sinn Feiners, but they refused to take their seats at Westminster and set up their own parliament in Dublin.

(b) What problems faced Lloyd George, and how successful was he in dealing with them?

The situation in the aftermath of the war was *chaotic*, and needed all Lloyd George's brilliance:

(i) Difficulties arose with *demobilisation* when the government began to release holders of key civilian jobs first, leaving the ordinary rank-and-file troops until last. Some alarming protest demonstrations broke out and the government smartly changed its tactics, adopting a 'first in, first out' policy. This worked well, and by the autumn of 1919 over four million troops had been successfully 'demobbed'. Most of them found jobs, thanks to the *post-war boom* – an encouraging beginning.

(ii) There was a sudden period of *inflation* at the end of the war, partly caused by the removal of government wartime controls on prices, profits and guaranteed wage levels. Prices and profits rose, but wages lagged behind. Trade unions were determined to protect their members, and during 1919 and 1920 there were over 2000 *strikes*. It was not simply a matter of higher wages though; there were other causes of labour unrest: there was a terrible *disillusionment* among the working class caused by their experiences in the trenches, and this seemed to emphasise the gulf between workers on the one hand and on the other capitalists and profiteers who had done well out of the war. The Russian revolution (1917) gave tremendous publicity to *nationalisation* and *worker control*, and some of the strikes in 1919 threw the government into a panic in case they developed into a revolution. In February and March 1919 a strike of Clydeside engineers and shipbuilders demanding a 40-hour week seemed ominously like the start of a revolution: huge demonstrations, rioting and a red flag hoisted in George Square, Glasgow, caused the government to move in troops and tanks. Order was quickly restored and two of the leaders, Willy Gallacher and Emmanuel Shinwell, were sent to jail. The Miners' Federation threatened a national strike if their demands for a six-hour day, a 30 per cent wage increase and continued government control of mines through nationalisation were not accepted. This time Lloyd George avoided a confrontation and played for time: he offered a *seven-hour day*, continued government control for the time being, and a *Royal Commission* (the Sankey Commission) to investigate the problem; the miners accepted his offer.

(iii) A *slump* which began early in 1921 threw about two million people out of work by the end of the year and the unemployment figure never fell below a million until the Second World War. Already in 1920 the government had extended the 1911 National Insurance Act so that *unemployment payments* were made, for not more than 15 weeks in any one year, to all workers earning less than £250 a year (except agricultural labourers, domestic servants and civil servants). At that point boom conditions still applied, and mass unemployment was not expected. When it came in 1921 the new scheme could not cope: payments to the unemployed far outweighed contributions. However, having once conceded the principle of state benefit for the unemployed, the government could hardly do a U-turn simply because unemployment increased. During 1921 therefore, benefit was extended to two 16-week periods in the year with a gap between. Much of this was financed by straight 'gifts' from the treasury and these became known as the 'dole'. Extra payments were introduced for wives and children. The government aid probably eased the situation and may even have prevented revolution; nevertheless it was criticised by Labour because it treated only the *symptoms* and did nothing to remove unemployment. Labour MPs claimed that the benefits were too low and were 'mocking the poor', while Conservatives condemned them on the grounds that they would demoralise the workers.

(iv) The trouble in the *coal industry* over whether it should remain under government control or be returned to private ownership had been simmering since the appointment of the Sankey Commission. Matters came to a head on *1 April 1921*, when the *entire industry came out on strike*. This was because the Sankey Commission had been unable to agree on a solution to the problems. Some members recommended nationalisation and others the return of the mines to private ownership. This bitterly disappointed the miners who wanted nationalisation, and gave Lloyd George the opportunity to avoid permanent nationalisation. The government announced that mines and railways would be handed back to private control on 1 April. Mine-owners informed the men that wages would be reduced because of the slump in exports. For a time the miners' strike threatened to develop into a general strike, but on 15 April the miners' allies in the *Triple Alliance* (the railwaymen and transport workers) decided to abandon the idea, which the miners regarded as a betrayal. The miners persisted and their strike lasted three months; but without support their position was hopeless and they had to give way on all points. Soon afterwards workers in other trades (engineering, shipbuilding, building, docks, textiles, printing and railways) had to accept *wage reductions*.

Lloyd George had solved this problem insofar as the strike had failed and a general strike had been averted, but he was fast losing his popularity with the workers.

(v) There was a *reduction in government revenue* (money flowing into the Treasury from taxation). This was caused partly by the general falling-off of business during the slump and partly by the enormous expense of unemployment benefits. A committee under Sir Eric Geddes recommended drastic cuts, many of which were carried out by the government, saving £64 million. They became known as the *Geddes Axe* and involved greatly reduced expenditure on the army, navy, education, health services, and council house building. The economy measures were successful, but highly unpopular with the working class who criticised the government for 'making the children pay while the ladies of Mayfair spend extravagantly on dresses'.

(vi) Trouble flared up in *Ireland* immediately after the election when the 73 Sinn Fein MPs (who wanted Ireland to be independent from Britain) set up their own parliament (*Dail*) in Dublin and proclaimed the Republic of Ireland. The IRA began a campaign of *terrorism* against the police and the government retaliated by using the Black and Tans. Although Lloyd George found a temporary settlement by *partitioning Ireland* (see Section 11.2(a)), he had made enemies in doing so: many Liberals resented his use of the Black and Tans, whereas the Conservatives were furious at the way in which the union between Britain and Ireland had been destroyed. This was serious for Lloyd George because the *survival of his coalition* depended on continued Conservative support.

(vii) Problems in *foreign affairs* also played a part in ruining Lloyd George's reputation. The *intervention in Russia* to try and destroy the new Bolshevik government was an expensive failure and lost him support among the working class, who thought he was too much under the thumb of the Conservatives (see Section 13.2); the Genoa Conference (1922) was another failure (see Section 13.1(c)). Most damaging of all was the *Chanak incident (1922)* which occurred when the Turks threatened to break the Versailles settlement by moving troops into a neutral zone, thereby clashing with the British occupying force based at Chanak on the Straits (see Section 2.10). Lloyd George took a strong line and warned the Turks to keep out. Eventually a compromise was reached and the crisis passed; but though it was something of a triumph for Lloyd George, many Conservatives thought he had acted too rashly, and that the problem could have been solved equally well with more tactful handling and consequently less risk of war.

(c) The coalition found time for some improvements in **domestic affairs:**

(i) The Sex Disqualification Removal Act (1919) allowed *women to stand for Parliament*

(ii) The Addison Housing Act (1919), the work of Christopher Addison, the Minister of Health, provided *subsidies* for local authorities to organise the building of 'homes fit for heroes'; 213,800 council houses were built in England and Wales by the end of 1922. Though this was not enough to solve the housing shortage, and the scheme suffered from the Geddes Axe, the principle had been established that housing was a *social service*, and later on local authorities continued Addison's work.

(iii) The extension of unemployment insurance already mentioned meant that an extra nine million workers had at least some cover against unemployment and though the amounts paid were often inadequate, again an important principle had been accepted: it was the *state's respcnsibility to protect workers* from the effects of industrial variations.

(iv) The Rent Act (1920) *protected working-class tenants* against *exorbitant rent increases.*

(d) The fall of the Lloyd George coalition (October 1922)

Unfortunately for Lloyd George his achievements were not enough to save the coalition. He had been losing working-class support steadily and it was significant that *Labour won 13 by-elections* between 1918 and 1922. Much depended on whether the Conservative MPs would continue to support him at the next general election which he intended to hold fairly soon. A meeting of Conservative MPs was held at the *Carlton Club* (29 October), and the vote was 187 to 87 in favour of ending their support of Lloyd George. The main anti-Lloyd George speech which swayed the meeting was made by *Stanley Baldwin*. Lloyd George immediately resigned and *Andrew Bonar Law* became Prime Minister of a Conservative government. Lloyd George was never again to hold an important political office. The Conservatives decided to abandon him partly because of a combination of their resentment at his solution of the Irish problem, his failure at the Genoa Conference, plus what they considered to be his tactless handling of the Chanak incident, and because they feared that if they supported him much longer, he would split the Conservative party in the same way that he had already split the Liberals (by the way in which he had manoeuvred Asquith into resigning in December 1916). They criticised him because he allowed the *sale of knighthoods* and other honours to unsuitable candidates. This is why Baldwin in his Carlton Club speech spoke of his desire for a return to 'clean government'.

4.2 CONSERVATIVE INTERLUDE: OCTOBER 1922 TO JANUARY 1924

The *Conservatives* won a *clear victory at the general election* held in *November 1922*, with 347 seats, a majority of 88 over all other parties combined. It was a *disaster for the Liberals*, who fought the election in two separate groups: Asquith Liberals won 60 seats, Lloyd George Liberals 57. The combined Liberal total of 117 seats was well behind Labour's 142, and it was clear that *Labour had emerged as the main opposition party* to the Conservatives.

However, the new Conservative government did not last long. After Bonar Law's resignation through ill health in May 1923, *Stanley Baldwin* became Prime Minister. After only a few months in office he decided that *another election* was necessary even though the Conservatives still had their overall majority. His reason was that he had decided to reintroduce *tariffs* (import duties) and since Bonar Law had earlier promised that this was exactly what the Conservatives would not do, Baldwin felt it only fair for the electorate to decide *for or against protection*. Tariffs would make foreign goods more expensive in Britain and thus give a much-needed boost to British industry; the *growing unemployment problems* would thus be solved. The two sections of the Liberal party reunited under Asquith's leadership and campaigned for *free trade*, a traditional Liberal policy. Together with Labour they argued that continued free trade and foreign imports would keep down the cost of living for the workers. The results were: Conservatives 258, Labour 191 and Liberals 158, a clear *defeat for protection* and a further confirmation that Labour had replaced the Liberals as the alternative party to the Conservatives. The Conservatives could not remain in government, because although they were still the largest single party they had *lost their overall majority*, and both Liberals and Labour were against their policy of protection. Labour, the second largest party, therefore formed a government, with a promise of Liberal support in the Commons. In January 1924 the first Labour government took office, with *James Ramsay MacDonald* as Prime Minister.

4.3 WHY DID THE LIBERAL PARTY CONTINUE TO DECLINE?

At the time of the great Liberal victory of 1906 very few people could have foreseen that within less than 20 years the Liberals would be on the way out and Labour would be forming a government. Suggested explanations are:

(a) Even before 1914 there were signs of a **split in the party** between the left (in favour of state action to bring about social reform) and the right (which viewed such ideas with distaste); the party may well have broken up even if the First World War had not accelerated the process.

(b) **Lloyd George split the party** by the way in which he manoeuvred Asquith into resigning in 1916. Asquith's supporters never forgave Lloyd George for this 'betrayal' and the party remained divided until the election of November 1923, just as *Labour was presenting a strong challenge*.

(c) It was always possible as more of the working class got the vote (as they did in 1884, 1918 and 1928) that Labour, projecting itself as the party of the working people, might **entice them away from the Liberals**. Towards the end of the war, local Labour Party organisations were set up in every constituency, and Sydney Webb of the Fabian Society wrote a new programme – 'Labour and the New Social Order' – which included the nationalisation of coal, land, railways, and electricity, plus a levy on capital. In the elections of 1918 and 1922 Labour thus seemed better organised than the Liberals; in 1922 for the first time Labour *won more seats than both groups of Liberals combined* (142 to 117).

(d) Asquith did not provide inspiring leadership and no constructive ideas were put forward on either economic or foreign affairs. Unfortunately for the Liberals he did not retire from the leadership until 1926 when it was too late for the party to recover.

(e) The Liberals were beginning to lose **right-wing support** as many wealthy businessmen switched to the Conservatives as the surest way of keeping Labour out. This was serious because it removed much of the Liberals' *financial support*; three elections between 1918 and 1923 left the party short of funds while Labour was able to rely on trade union cash.

(f) Once Labour had formed a government in 1924 without the expected social revolution, *Liberal election prospects faded*; anti-Conservatives began to vote Labour as the only way to keep the Tories out.

(g) The Liberals were at a disadvantage because of the **electoral system**. With three parties contesting many seats, a high proportion of MPs were returned on a *minority vote*; many Liberals came second and their votes were not reflected in the Commons. In 1922, Liberals polled slightly more votes than Labour, yet won only 117 seats to Labour's 142. (Hence the Liberal agitation ever since for some sort of *proportional representation*.)

(h) The 1929 election is usually regarded as the Liberals' last chance; Lloyd George led a united party with an attractive programme, but they managed only 59 seats to Labour's 288. There was a lack of confidence in Lloyd George and a feeling that Baldwin and MacDonald, though less spectacular, were more *solid and reliable*.

Perhaps the neatest conclusion is that given the circumstances in the years after the First World War, with the Conservatives firmly established as the party of the propertied classes and the ratepayers, and Labour in alliance with the trade unions as the party of the workers, there was *no remaining interest group large enough* to keep the liberals going as a serious contender for power.

4.4 THE FIRST LABOUR GOVERNMENT: JANUARY TO OCTOBER 1924

This Labour government, like the one of 1929–31, was a *disappointment* to its supporters.

(a) Why were they not more successful?

(i) Both were minority governments *lacking an overall majority*, and dependent on Liberal votes to stay in office. They had therefore to pursue *moderate policies*, and it was out of the question to introduce nationalisation and disarmament, even if MacDonald had wanted to. This meant that their policies were very little different from those of Liberal governments.

(ii) Labour had difficulty in projecting itself as a *truly national party*, since from the beginning it had claimed to be the party of the industrial workers and was closely tied to the trade unions. It was distrusted by people of property who feared nationalisation and the link with militant trade unionism.

(iii) Labour could not break its ties with the trade unions because they provided the majority of its funds. In return the unions expected to be able to control the party which caused serious friction because union leaders were preoccupied with furthering the interests of their members. They gave very little support to the 1924 Labour government and made no allowances for its dependence on Liberal support, criticising it for its 'half-measures'. Almost immediately there was a *dockers' strike* in support of a demand for an extra two shillings a day. This was organised by Ernest Bevin, general secretary of the Transport and General Workers' Union. Following the success of this strike London transport workers also came out, and the situation became serious enough for MacDonald to proclaim a *state of emergency*, enabling the government to use armed lorries for moving essential supplies. In the end this was not necessary because the employers gave way and made an acceptable wage offer, but it was embarrassing for the government and left its relationship with the unions strained.

(iv) It proved impossible to work out a joint plan of action between the *parliamentary Labour party* and the *trade unions*. When some Labour intellectuals suggested that the two should co-operate to avoid a repetition of the 1924 fiasco, Bevin dismissed the idea; according to him such theorists did not understand the working class.

(v) Both governments were unfortunate enough to have to deal with *serious economic problems*: a million unemployed in 1924 and the world economic crisis in 1930–1. Labour had no answer beyond nationalisation, and since that was out of the question they were helpless.

(b) Achievements of the first Labour government

The 1924 government managed a few achievements, in spite of the disappointments:

(i) *Wheatley's Housing Act* provided grants of £9 million a year to local authorities for the building of council houses. By 1933 when the subsidy was abolished, 521,700 houses had been built which did much to relieve the housing shortage.

(ii) *Old age pensions and unemployment benefit* were increased and the gap between the two 16-week benefit periods was removed.

(iii) The number of *free places in grammar schools* was increased and state scholarships to universities brought back.

(iv) Sir Henry Hadow was appointed to work out the needs of education. Although his report did not appear until 1926 the Labour Minister of Education, C. P. Trevelyan, must take the credit for the initiative. The Hadow Report was an important milestone in English education, introducing the break between primary and secondary education at 11, and recognising the principle that the *whole population was entitled to some secondary education*.

(v) There were some notable achievements in *foreign affairs* where MacDonald turned out to be something of an expert (he was Foreign Secretary as well as Prime Minister): he played an important part in drawing up the *Dawes Plan* (see Section 13.1(d)), began a policy of friendship towards the *USSR* (see Section 13.2(a)), and strongly supported the *League of Nations*.

(c) The fall of the first Labour government (October 1924)

The end of the government came rather suddenly over the *Campbell Case*. J. R. Campbell, editor of the communist *Workers' Weekly* was arrested and charged with incitement to mutiny (he had written an article urging soldiers not to fire on their fellow workers in the event of a strike). However, the Labour Attorney-General withdrew the prosecution, and both Conservatives and Liberals, already alarmed by MacDonald's opening of relations with Russia, accused the government of being *sympathetic towards communists*. The Liberal demand for an inquiry into the matter was carried by 364 votes to 198; MacDonald took this as a vote of no confidence and resigned. The following election was complicated by the affair of the *Zinoviev Letter*. This appeared in the *Daily Mail* four days before polling and claimed to be from the Russian communist leader Zinoviev to the British Communist Party. It was marked 'very secret' and contained instructions on how to *organise a revolution*. The fact that the Foreign Office protested to the Russians about this interference in British affairs made the letter appear genuine, though it seems fairly certain that it was a *forgery*. But it caused a sensation at the time and was taken to show that Labour sympathy towards Russia was encouraging the British communists. Labour dropped to 151 seats, Liberals lost disastrously winning only 42 seats, while the Conservatives emerged triumphant with 419 seats.

Labour blamed their defeat on the Zinoviev Letter, but historians seem to agree that the Conservatives would have won anyway. Although short, the first Labour government was not without significance; it proved that a *Labour government could work*, and it won respect both at home and abroad for its handling of foreign affairs.

4.5 STANLEY BALDWIN'S CONSERVATIVE GOVERNMENT 1924–9

(a) Conservative achievements

The split in the party was now fully healed and even Winston Churchill drifted back to become Chancellor of the Exchequer after 20 years as a Liberal. It was a fairly uneventful five years with one startling exception: the *1926 general strike*. Baldwin was a moderate Conservative who liked to project himself as the plain and honest man, puffing at his pipe. He was a very able politician and a much better manager of people than Lloyd George. His government introduced a mass of useful legislation; Neville Chamberlain, the Minister of Health, was himself responsible for 21 bills passing the Commons.

(b) Acts passed and bodies set up

(i) The Widows, Orphans and Old Age Contributory Pensions Act (1925) provided a *pension* of 10s. a week for widows with extra for children, and 10s. a week for insured workers and their wives at 65. Both workers and employers contributed to the scheme which was compulsory (the non-contributory pension at 70 still continued).

(ii) The *vote was extended to women at the age of 21*. Labour objected strongly because the *plural vote* (the right enjoyed by owners of business premises to vote in the constituencies where their premises were as well as where they lived) was not abolished.

(iii) The Local Government Act of 1929 was Chamberlain's greatest achievement, providing a *complete overhaul of local government organisation, rates and provision for the poor*: Poor Law Unions and their boards of guardians who had provided relief for the poor since 1834 were abolished, and their function taken over by county and county borough councils. Agricultural land and farm buildings were to be exempt from payment of rates, and industrial property and railways were to pay only one-quarter of the previous rate. This was designed to encourage farmers and industrialists to expand operations and provide more jobs. Local councils would receive a *block grant* from the government to cover the costs of services to the poor and of other functions such as public health, slum clearance, roads, and town and country planning. This was a much fairer system because expenses were being shared by the whole body of taxpayers in the country, instead of poor areas with high unemployment having to foot the bill from rates collected locally. However, the Labour party protested bitterly that it was an attack on the *independence of local councils*, since the government could now cut off grants to councils which did not follow their wishes.

(iv) The Central Electricity Board appointed by the Minister of Transport was made responsible for the *distribution of electricity*.

The National Grid was started with its thousands of pylons connecting the generating stations; it was completed by 1933.

(v) The British Broadcasting Company became a *public corporation*, to be controlled by governors appointed by the Postmaster-General.

(vi) The *Locarno Treaties* (October 1925) were taken at the time to be a triumph for Austen Chamberlain, the Foreign Secretary, but later this opinion was revised (see Section 13.1(e)).

(vii) The way was prepared for the Statute of Westminster (eventually signed in 1931) which *defined the relationship between Britain and the rest of the commonwealth* (see Section 11.1(b)).

4.6 THE GENERAL STRIKE (4–12 MAY 1926)

(a) Causes of the General Strike:

(i) In the background was the *post-war economic depression*, with falling exports and mass unemployment.

(ii) On the whole, industrialists failed to promote greater efficiency and more mechanisation which would have enabled them to *compete better* with other countries. They tended to blame declining profits on higher wages, and their attempts to reduce wages caused strained relations with their workforces.

(iii) The problems of the *coal industry* were important because it was here that the strike began. Coal sales were probably worse hit than those of any other industry, partly because more gas, electricity and oil were being used, and because there was stiff competition from Germany and Poland which had modern mechanised pits. In 1925 only 20 per cent of British output was by coal-cutting machines, the rest was by hand-picks.

(iv) The government had *refused to nationalise the mines*, though it was widely believed that only government control could bring about the essential modernisation that would enable the industry to survive. Mine-owners were unwilling to take any initiative.

(v) The *return to the gold standard* in April 1925 worsened the export position of all British industries, not just coal. According to the economist J. M. Keynes, the Chancellor of the Exchequer, Churchill, had over-valued the pound by 10 per cent, making *British exports* that much more *expensive*.

(vi) The situation worsened in June 1925 when there was a sudden *drop in coal exports*, following a brief revival while the German mines in the Ruhr were closed during the French occupation. The owners announced that they would have to lower wages and increase hours. The miners protested but Baldwin saved the situation for the time being by providing a *subsidy* for nine months to keep wages at the existing levels, and by appointing a Royal Commission under Sir Herbert Samuel to try and find a solution.

(vii)   Meanwhile the TUC made it clear that they would *support the miners*, because if their wages were reduced it was likely that those of other workers would soon follow. This stiffened the attitude of the miners.

(viii) Everything hinged on whether the Samuel Report could find a solution. It appeared in *March 1926* and was an eminently sensible document. It recommended that mine-owners should press ahead with reorganisation and modernisation, should *not insist on longer hours* (which would lead to over-production) and should *not reduce wages* (which would enable them to avoid reorganisation). The government should *not continue the subsidy*. For the time being until the crisis passed, miners must accept some wage reductions. *Neither the owners nor the miners would accept the report*, though the TUC welcomed it and tried to keep negotiations going because they were not prepared for a general strike. The government made no attempt to force its acceptance even though one moderate mine-owner, Sir Alfred Mond, urged Baldwin to do so.

(ix)   The mine-owners brought a showdown one step nearer by announcing that wages would be reduced on 30 April to which the miners replied that they would strike on 1 May. The owners got in first and staged a *lockout* on Friday 30 April. The coal strike had begun. Ernest Bevin announced that a *general strike would begin on 3 May* if *a settlement was not reached*.

(x)   The TUC was still trying to find a solution but was thwarted by circumstances. Negotiations between cabinet and TUC were hampered all through 2 May because the miners' leaders had gone home, leaving the TUC to handle the talks. Baldwin heard that the *Daily Mail* compositors had refused to print an article which claimed that a general strike would be a revolutionary action. He described this as an 'overt act', a sign that the General Strike had begun, whereas in fact it was an unofficial action. Baldwin *called off the negotiations* and the *general strike followed*.

(b) Course of the General Strike

The strike itself was an *impressive show of working-class solidarity*. In the industries called out (road, rail, docks, printing, gas and electricity, building, iron, steel and chemicals), the response was almost 100 per cent, which seemed to show how alienated the workers had become from employers and government. However, by 11 May there was no sign that the government would give way. Baldwin took the view that the strike was an *attack on the constitution* and not an ordinary industrial dispute; therefore no negotiations could begin until the strike was called off. He concentrated on operating *emergency plans* prepared months earlier, and these worked efficiently. Volunteers kept food supplies moving, unloaded ships and drove trains and buses. Food convoys were guarded by armoured cars, while the navy manned power stations. When Sir Herbert

illus 4.1 *A food convoy guarded by armoured cars during the General Strike, 1926*

Samuel offered to act as mediator, the TUC accepted. He produced the *Samuel Memorandum* suggesting a short-term renewal of the subsidy to maintain wage levels, no wage reductions until reorganisation was assured, and a National Wages Board.

On *12 May* the *TUC called off the General Strike*, hoping that the memorandum would be accepted, though it was strictly unofficial and Baldwin had given no guarantees. The strike itself lasted unofficially until 14 May, but the *miners refused to go back*. Since the mineowners refused to compromise, the coal strike dragged on until December, but in the end the miners had to give way and go back to *longer hours* and *lower wages*. There was much bitterness about the TUC 'betrayal'. The TUC called off the strike so soon for several reasons: there was no sign of a softening in the government's attitude – in fact, the cabinet extremists were talking of 'unconditional surrender'; the TUC, completely unprepared for a general strike anyway, was anxious to end it before provocative government actions caused events to take a more violent turn; there were doubts about the legal position; Sir John Simon (a Liberal lawyer) said in the Commons that the strike was 'an illegal proceeding', not an industrial dispute, and that the leaders were liable to be *sued for damages and gaoled*. The Labour party's attitude was unhelpful and the strike was proving expensive – the TUC had already used £4 million out of their total strike fund of £12.5 million.

(c) Results of the General Strike

(i)   There was a good deal of *working-class disillusionment* with the TUC for its 'betrayal' of the miners. Membership dropped from over eight million to well under five million the following year.

(ii) The *TUC turned against the idea of a general strike*, convinced that one could never succeed.

(iii) There was *no solution to the coal industry problems* and no modernisation; the industry continued in slow decline with *exports falling steadily*.

(iv) The government introduced the *Trade Disputes Act* (1927) designed to make *another general strike impossible*. Sympathetic strikes and intimidation were illegal. Trade union members were not required to contribute to the union's political fund (the political levy paid to the Labour party) unless they chose to do so and gave written notice of their intention. This was known as 'contracting-in' which now replaced 'contracting-out' introduced by the 1913 Trade Union Act. The new act *placed the onus on the member*; many did not bother to contract in, hence a fall of over 25 per cent in the Labour party's income.

  The act seems to have been largely unnecessary since the TUC had had enough of general strikes, and it was bitterly resented by the Unions. It was not repealed until 1946.

(v)   The working class realised that only by *parliamentary action* could their aims be achieved and this, plus bitterness at the Trade Disputes Act and unemployment standing at over a million, caused an increase in Labour party support and a *Labour victory in the 1929 general election*.

4.7 THE SECOND LABOUR GOVERNMENT (1929–31) AND THE GREAT DEPRESSION

The most impressive achievements of this government were in *foreign affairs* where Ramsay MacDonald and Arthur Henderson, the new Foreign Secretary, added to their reputation by playing an important part in drawing up the *Young Plan* and supporting the League of Nations (see Section 13.1(g)). In home affairs the government achieved little beyond the 1930 Housing Act which renewed the subsidy for council house building and organised the speeding up of slum clearance, and the Coal Mines Act (1930) reducing the miners' working day from eight hours to seven and a half. Labour suffered the same disadvantages as in 1924: it was still a *minority government* with 287 seats to the Conservatives' 261; since the Liberals had 59, Labour needed Liberal support so that again *socialist legislation* was out of the question. The government was brought down prematurely by the world economic crisis ushered in by the *Wall Street Crash* of *October 1929* (see Section 7.2). By May 1931 Britain was feeling the full impact of the depression, with unemployment at over 2.5 million. Payment of unemployment benefit was placing a severe strain on government finances, and events moved rapidly to cause the government's resignation (August 1931). The May Report (the result of Sir George May's committee of enquiry) appeared at the end of July and forecast that by April 1932 there would be a government deficit of £120 million. It proposed a 20 per cent reduction in unemployment benefit to stave off the crisis. This caused foreign investors to conclude that Britain must be on the verge of bankruptcy and they rushed to *withdraw gold*, plunging the country into a *deeper financial crisis*. The Bank of England informed the government that immediate economies were needed to restore foreign confidence, while French and American bankers demanded economies before further loans could be made. When MacDonald proposed a 10 per cent reduction in unemployment benefit there was fierce argument within the cabinet, and 10 out of the 21 members would not agree.

MacDonald claimed that there was nothing else for it but to *resign*; he handed in the government's resignation, but to the amazement of almost the whole of the Labour party he stayed on as Prime Minister of what was called a *National government* with a cabinet consisting of Conservatives, Liberals and just three other Labour men. The formation of the National government was a highly controversial event. The Labour party blamed MacDonald bitterly for deserting them and branded him a traitor, claiming that he had been planning to ditch them for some time; but David Marquand believes that George V and Baldwin persuaded him to stay on as Prime Minister of a coalition government as the best way of *restoring confidence*.

4.8 **THE NATIONAL GOVERNMENT; FINANCIAL PROBLEMS AND RECOVERY**

A number of measures were introduced to try and restore confidence, including *raising income tax* from 4/6 to 5s. in the pound, *reducing salaries* of public employees and *unemployment benefits* by 10 per cent. These did not produce the desired effect and foreigners continued to withdraw funds from Britain. Nor was the situation helped by the *Invergordon Mutiny* (September 1931) when naval crews protested against proposed salary cuts, though this soon petered out when the government assured them that cuts would not exceed 10 per cent. In the end the government *went off the gold standard*, so that the value of the pound fell by about one-quarter on the foreign exchanges. After a general election in October 1931, in which National government supporters won 521 seats, the country gradually began to recover from the depression. However, it was a very gradual recovery due more to favourable circumstances than to any efforts of the government, though it did attempt to help.

(a) Government action

Free trade was abandoned by Neville Chamberlain's *Import Duties Act* (1932), placing a 10 per cent duty on most imports, except those from the empire. This, as well as increasing sales of British goods at home, brought in extra revenue, so that Chamberlain was able to avoid raising the income tax again. Defence expenditure and interest on war loans were reduced. Some attempt was made to reorganise iron and steel, shipbuilding, textiles and coal, and to persuade new industry to move into areas of high unemployment though without much success (see Section 4.9(c)). Remaining off the gold standard made British goods *cheaper abroad* and led to an *increase in exports. Bank rate was reduced* from 6 per cent to 2 per cent mainly to reduce debt charges; however many local authorities took advantage of low interest rates to borrow money for house building. This provided *extra jobs* not only for builders but for all the allied trades, including gas and electricity.

These measures helped to *stabilise the financial situation* and to increase sales at home and abroad, though it can be argued that foreign manufacturers, deprived of markets in Britain by the new import duties, became competitors in export markets.

(b) Favourable circumstances

These would probably have occurred whatever action the government had chosen to take:

(i) As prices of all products (both British and imported) fell during the depression, the cost of living also fell and, even with wage reductions, there was an *increase in real wages* (what one could actually buy with the cash available).

(ii) This enabled people to spend their extra cash on British consumer goods and even on luxuries such as radios and holidays, which *stimulated the creation of jobs.*

By *1936*, it was clear that Britain had *recovered from the depression*, and probably undeservedly the National government took the credit. For a long time it had been a rather thinly disguised Conservative government, and when Baldwin became Prime Minister in 1935, on MacDonald's retirement, the Conservatives easily won the election of the following October, though they still kept the 'National' label. Two problems with which they did not deal successfully were the dilemma of whether and by how much to *rearm*, and the *persistent unemployment* in certain depressed areas.

4.9 UNEMPLOYMENT IN THE 1930s

Unemployment was not a general phenomenon during the 1930s; it was confined to *certain trades* and *certain areas*. The total unemployed in Britain were (in millions):

illus 4.2 *The Jarrow Crusade – unemployed men marching from Jarrow to London in 1936 in protest against lack of work*

1927 – 1.1	1931 – 2.7	1935 – 2.0
1928 – 1.3	1932 – 2.8	1936 – 1.7
1929 – 1.2	1933 – 2.5	1937 – 1.4
1930 – 1.9	1934 – 2.1	1938 – 1.9

The main industries affected were *shipbuilding* (30.6 per cent of workers in that industry were unemployed in 1936), *steel, coalmining* (25 per cent), *shipping* (22.3 per cent) and *textiles* (13.2 per cent). The areas where these industries were situated were greatly depressed; they included the whole of Scotland, the Tyne-Tees area, Cumberland, Lancashire, and also Northern Ireland and South Wales. In some towns the individual figures were startling: *Jarrow* had *68 per cent* of its total workforce unemployed in 1934; in Merthyr Tydfil the figure was 62 per cent, while in St Albans at the same time it was only 3.9 per cent. The midlands and the south were much better off because they had *new industries* such as motor cars, aircraft, and chemicals.

(a) Why were the depressed areas so bad?

(i) They contained the *older export industries* which had been successful until the 1880s but had then begun to decline. Their decline was accelerated after the First World War because many countries which found *alternative sources of supply during the war* did not resume buying British after 1918. They suffered *fierce competition* from more highly mechanised and more efficient foreign industries and cheaper foreign goods, such as Japanese and east European textiles; India, the main British market for textiles before the war, was rapidly developing her own industry. Coal exports were badly hit by cheap coal from Germany and Poland. Very little attempt was made to modernise these industries to make them more competitive.

(ii) There would have been unemployment therefore even without the world economic crisis, but after 1930 this *made the situation worse* in the depressed areas and caused temporary unemployment elsewhere.

(iii) It is also argued that Chamberlain's *import duties* worsened the export position of the old industries (see Section 4.8(a)).

(iv) The depressed areas had concentrated exclusively on the old industries so that there was *no alternative employment* to be had, and since the majority of unemployed could not afford to move elsewhere, they had to stay put.

(b) Suggested remedies

(i) *J. M. Keynes* (the Liberal economist) suggested that the government should *spend its way out of the depression* by investing in order to stimulate new industries, while at the same time organising the contraction of the declining industries. The government should also give financial aid to enable people to move out of depressed areas.

(ii) 'Peace and Reconstruction', a document produced in 1935 by a group of young Conservative MPs led by *Harold Macmillan* (MP for Stockton-on-Tees) set out detailed schemes such as road-building, electrification, housing and national parks which could be organised by government and local authority expenditure, using cash which would have been spent on unemployment benefit.

(c) Government action

The government's response was *unimaginative* and its measures *failed to get to the root* of the problem.

(i) The Unemployment Act (1934) set up the *National Unemployment Assistance Board* whose branches in every part of the country would pay out benefit after an unemployed man ran out of the normal period of insurance benefit. The way in which this act was applied caused great bitterness among the unemployed since it was based on the *'means test'* introduced in 1931. This took into account the total family income and savings of an unemployed man when assessing the amount of relief he should receive, and caused *demoralisation* when it appeared that the *careful and thrifty* were being penalised.

(ii) The Special Areas Act (1934) appointed two unpaid commissioners and provided them with £2 million to try to revive Scotland, west Cumberland, Tyneside and South Wales. This had little effect because employers *could not be compelled* to move into the depressed areas. Later the government offered rates, rent and income tax remission to encourage firms to move in, which resulted in the setting up of *trading estates* such as the ones at Treforest (South Wales), North Hillington and Larkhall (near Glasgow); but these provided only a few thousand jobs, many of them for women.

(iii) The Bank Rate reduction mentioned in the previous section helped the housing boom and encouraged local authorities to embark on road-building. But the government partially defeated its own ends by continually warning local authorities to *economise*, revealing that it only imperfectly understood the workings of economics.

(iv) An attempt was made to *revive the steel industry* by imposing a tariff on foreign steel and setting up the British Iron and Steel Federation. Government pressure resulted in the building of two new steel works at Ebbw Vale and Corby, but the federation was bitterly criticised for refusing to allow one to be built at Jarrow. However, the steel industry was showing signs of revival.

(v) *Loans were provided to encourage* shipbuilding, including the completion of the *Queen Mary*.

(vi) From 1936 onwards the *rearmament programme* helped in the creation of extra jobs.

Although by the end of 1937 total unemployment had fallen to 1.4 million, there had been little improvement in the depressed areas where most of the 1.4 million were concentrated. In spite of plenty of available advice the government had failed to produce any positive strategy for curing long-term unemployment in these areas, largely because it refused to accept that the problem could be solved.

QUESTIONS

1. The General Strike
Study the Sources below and then answer the questions that follow.

Source A
The Samuel Commission Report, 11 March 1926.

The coalmining industry has come upon difficult times. This change of fortune is the result of powerful economic forces. It is wrong to blame it on the restriction of output among the miners or to inefficiency in the day to day management of the mines. Recommendations:

1. The subsidy should be stopped and never repeated.
2. We do not accept the proposal of the Mineowners' Association to increase the working day by an hour and to reduce miners' wages.
3. Miners should accept a reduction in wages because these were fixed in 1924 at a time of temporary prosperity. The reduction should last until the mines have been reorganised and modernised.

Source: J. H. Bettey (ed.), *English Historical Documents* (Routledge & Kegan Paul, 1967, adapted extracts).

Source B

It is difficult to see what excuse now existed for the government, the mineowners, the miners or the TUC to allow either a coal strike or a national strike to take place; but of all the interested parties only the TUC tried to take the Samuel Report seriously, because they alone lacked the will to fight. The miners were determined to fight against any wage reductions and were not really interested in reorganisation either. This would mean the closing down of a number of uneconomic pits and they took it for granted that nothing would be done for the miners made redundant except to send them to join the dole queue. The mineowners clearly wanted a showdown and so they ignored the Samuel Report and demanded lower wages. The government tried to escape responsibility by announcing, in terms of the utmost vagueness, that it would do what it could to carry out the Samuel Report, provided both sides agreed to it.

Source: L. C. B. Seaman, *Post-Victorian Britain 1902–1951* (Methuen, 1966).

Source C
Letter from Sir Alfred Mond (a coalmine owner) to Stanley Baldwin, 22 April 1926.

I had last night a dinner of representative coal-owners of practically the entire country. If the government expresses itself strongly on the matter and insists on the Samuel Report, I am confident that something can be achieved. I can assure you that the whole country is looking most anxiously to you to force a settlement. Among all the coal-owners present themselves last night, the opinion was that the attitude of their representatives in the negotiations was quite unreasonable, and they merely do not speak out, as they do not want to hamper their side. The industrial community is looking forward with interest to a solution being found, but I think it will have to be imposed. If the responsibility was taken off the shoulders of the two opposing parties, they would be pleased.

Source: C. Farman, *The General Strike* (Granada, 1974).

Source D
Extract from *The British Gazette* (the official government newspaper) 6 May 1926.

The General Strike is in operation, expressing in no uncertain terms a direct challenge to ordered government. It would be useless to attempt to minimise the seriousness of such a challenge, which is an effort to force upon some 42 million British citizens the will of less than 4 million others engaged in the vital services of this country. The strike is intended as a direct hold-up of the nation to ransom. The nation must stand firm in its determination not to give way.

Source: J. H. Bettey (ed.), *English Historical Documents* (Routledge & Kegan Paul, 1967).

Source E
Extract from *The British Worker* (the official strike newspaper of the TUC) 7 May 1926.

The General Council [of the Trades Union Congress] does not challenge the constitution, and does not want to undermine our parliament. The sole aim of the council is to secure for the miners a decent standard of life. The Council is engaged in an industrial dispute. There is no constitutional crisis. The Council struggled hard for peace. They are anxious that an honourable peace be found as soon as possible. They are not attacking the constitution. They are not fighting the community. They are defending the mineworkers against the mine-owners.

Source: J. H. Bettey (ed.), *English Historical Documents* (Routledge & Kegan Paul, 1967).

(a)   (i) According to Source A, who or what was to blame for the problems of the coalmining industry?   **4(a)**
   (ii) What do you think the 'powerful economic forces' were which the Report (Source A) mentions?   **1,4(a)**
(b) Study Source B carefully and then explain:
   (i) What the TUC thought about the Samuel Report, and why.
   (ii) Why the miners did not like the Samuel Report.
   (iii) What the mine-owners did about the Samuel Report, and why.
   (iv) What the government's attitude was towards the Samuel Report.   **4(a)**

(c) Do you think that Source C supports or contradicts what Source B has to say about the mine-owners? Explain your answer fully. **4(c)**

(d) (i) How do the opinions about the General Strike in Sources D and E differ from each other? **4(c)**

(ii) Using the evidence of the Sources and your own knowledge, explain why you think Sources D and E differ so much in what they say about the General Strike. **1,4(b)**

(e) From the evidence provided by the Sources and your own knowledge, try to explain how much blame can be put on each of the four involved groups (miners, mine-owners, Trades Union Congress and government) for causing the General Strike.

1,2,4(a)

(f) How was the General Strike brought to an end? **1,2**

(g) What important results did the General Strike have? **1,2**

2. The formation of the National Government, 1931

Study the Sources below, and then answer the questions that follow.

Source A
Extract from *The Times*, 25 August 1931.

The country awakens this morning to find Mr MacDonald still Prime Minister, with the prospect of a small cabinet representing all three parties. The former cabinet resigned yesterday afternoon. The new cabinet would be formed for the specific purpose only of carrying through a very large reduction of expenditure . . . On Sunday night it had already become clear that the courageous determination of Mr MacDonald to adopt such a policy of retrenchment, including especially cuts in the dole, had made an unbridgeable gulf between two sections in the Socialist cabinet . . . All concerned are to be warmly congratulated on the formation of a National Government. The Prime Minister and the colleagues of his own party who have followed him deserve the utmost credit for their decision to carry through a policy of retrenchment.

Source: J. H. Bettey (ed.), *English Historical Documents* (Routledge & Kegan Paul, 1967, adapted).

Source B
Extract from the *New Statesman*, 29 August 1931.

Mr MacDonald's decision to form a cabinet in partnership with the Liberals and Tories seems to us a mistake. For he must inevitably find himself at war with the whole of organised labour; and he will find himself opposed by all those, in all classes, who believe that the policy of reducing people's purchasing power to meet a situation of over-production is silly economics.

Source: J. H. Bettey (ed.), *English Historical Documents* (Routledge & Kegan Paul, 1967, adapted).

(a)   **(i)**   In Source A, which were the 'three parties' referred to?

                                                                          1,4(a)

      (ii)   'The former cabinet resigned.' What party did the members of this cabinet belong to?   **1**

(b)   **(i)**   According to Source A, what policy would the new cabinet carry through?   **4(a)**

      (ii)   What is meant by 'retrenchment'?   **1,4(a)**

(c)   **(i)**   Describe the circumstances which led to MacDonald's decision (Source B).   **1,2,4(a)**

      (ii)   How does the *New Statesman* show that it does not like this decision?   **4(b)**

     (iii)   What evidence is there in the extracts to show why 'organised labour' would oppose MacDonald's new policies?   **4(c)**

(d)   How do the two reports differ in their comments about Mac-Donald's decision to form a National Government?   **4(a,b)**

(e)   **(i)**   What policies did the National Government introduce in 1931?   **1,2**

      (ii)   How did these policies 'reduce people's purchasing power'?

                                                                          1,2

(f)   Many of the later policies of the National Government were aimed at reviving the economy and increasing purchasing power once more. How successful had the National Government been in these aims by 1939?   **1,2**

    [Southern Examining Group, Specimen Question, adapted.]

3. Britain had two Labour governments before the Second World War – one in 1924 and the other from 1929 to 1931.

    (a)   Describe their achievements.

    (b)   Explain how and why the First Labour government fell in October 1924.

    (c)   Explain what problems the two governments faced with: (i) The trade unions and (ii) The economy.

    (d)   Why did the Second Labour government fall in August 1931?

                                                                          1,2

4. It is October 1922, and you are a Conservative MP. Write a short memorandum or note about Lloyd George, to be circulated among all Conservative MPs. In it, you explain why, although you still admire Lloyd George in many ways, and although he has many achievements to show, you feel the time has come for the Conservatives to withdraw from his Coalition government.

                                                                                        1,2,3

CHAPTER 5

FRANCE IN DECLINE

1918–40

SUMMARY OF EVENTS

The history of France between the wars makes sad reading; though victorious in the First World War, the Third Republic seemed completely exhausted by the effort and drained both by the loss of 15 per cent of her male population either killed or incapacitated and by the enormous financial demands of the war effort. As before 1914, the Republic continued to be *politically unstable*, with constantly changing coalition governments. The years 1919–24 saw a right-wing coalition (*Bloc National*) in power with *Raymond Poincaré* as Prime Minister for part of the time. After his failure over the French occupation of the Ruhr in 1923 (see Section 13.2(c)) a left-wing coalition took over (*Cartel des Gauches*) for a short time, only to be replaced after a serious financial crisis by another right coalition (*Union Nationale*) from 1926 to 1932. This was followed by six different left coalitions, all of which failed to solve France's economic crisis and culminated in riots organised by fascists and royalists (6 February 1934). After another right coalition (1934–6) had failed both to restore the economy and to prevent the Italian seizure of Abyssinia (see Section 14.2(b)), the famous *Front Populaire* came to power (1936–8). This was a coalition of mainly socialists and communists with *Leon Blum* as Prime Minister, which managed some long-overdue reforms before it was brought down by yet another financial crisis. From then until the outbreak of war *Edouard Daladier* headed what was known as a Government of National Defence.

As successive governments came and went it became clear that one of the most serious problems, apart from economic and financial difficulties, was the *widening division between right and left*; at times, this became so bitter that France seemed on the verge of civil war. When Hitler came to power in Germany (January 1933) France was in no state to make decisive anti-Nazi stand, and when war came in 1939 she scarcely managed to present a united front. When the Germans invaded in *May 1940* everything went wrong for the French: within six weeks they had been defeated and the Third Republic was at an end.

5.1 WHAT WERE THE PROBLEMS FACING FRENCH GOVERNMENTS, AND WITH WHAT SUCCESS DID THEY ATTEMPT TO SOLVE THEM?

(a) **The impossibility of one political party ever winning an overall majority** was one basic problem left over from before the war. The right-wing or conservative groups included representatives of industry and banking, Roman Catholics, royalists, and later, fascists; slightly left-of-centre were the radical-socialists who were not actually socialists at all, but represented, as Shirer puts it, the 'solid, middle-of-the-road, small-town bourgeoisie and well-off peasantry'. On the left were the socialists and, from 1920, the communists. All governments were *unstable coalitions*, because both right and left depended on support from the radical-socialists, whose policies unfortunately were rather vague. They were against drastic changes, since being the party of small farmers, small factory owners and small shopkeepers, they were quite happy for the economy to stay as it was – backward. According to Cobban, 'they believed in reducing government to a minimum, which was a recipe for failure at a time when political and social problems were urgently demanding positive action'. Yet this party was able to bring down the *Cartel des Gauches* in 1926 by withdrawing support, and then (having switched sides) to set up a right-wing coalition; in 1938 they ruined the *Front Populaire* when they grew tired of co-operating with the communists. Thus with the exception of Poincaré's ministry (1926–9) French governments tended not to be in power long enough to pursue successful policies.

(b) **France was still economically backward** in a number of ways:

(i) There was the old problem of the *population expanding more slowly* than in any other state in Europe. By 1939 the total population was still only about what it had been in 1913 (40 million compared with at least 80 million Germans).

(ii) Agriculture remained backward because the *smallness* of most farms made it impossible to introduce *mass production methods*. The government's protective tariffs kept agricultural prices high (in 1939 the price of wheat was three times higher than in Britain), which removed the incentive to *modernise*, and kept the cost of living much higher than it needed to be. Yet no government would interfere because of the risk of *losing the farmers' votes*.

(iii) Industrial production lagged well behind that of the other industrial states, again because of the smallness of factories and workshops and also because of the damage suffered to industrial areas during the war. But there were some signs of progress in industry: when factories were rebuilt new modern equipment could be installed, and government investment encouraged modernisation in the metallurgical, engineering and chemical industries. The most impressive development was the rapid expansion of the *motor car industry* in firms such as Renault, Citroën and Peugeot.

(c) There were constant financial problems which caused the value of the franc to fall and prices to rise (inflation):

(i) *Massive borrowing* had taken place to finance the war effort and the reconstruction after the war, and these debts now had to be repaid.

(ii) The government was relying on *German reparations payments* to enable some of their debts to be paid off; unfortunately the Germans paid very little, and the French attempt to force them by occupying the Ruhr (1923) failed; nor was the Dawes Plan (1924) helpful to France, saying in effect that Germany need pay only what she could afford until she had recovered.

(iii) The situation was always more unstable when a left-wing government was in power, because big business tried to *discredit* them by withdrawing capital from the economy and investing it abroad, causing a shortage of capital, and a fall in the value of the franc. Between May 1924 and July 1926 when the *Cartel des Gauches* was in power, the franc fell from 70 to 250 to the pound. When the Bank of France refused to make any further loans to the Treasury, confidence in the government was so shaken that it had to resign. In fact, however, there was no real shortage of money in the country; it was simply that people with money to invest, including small property-owners, *chose not to invest it* because they were suspicious of what a socialist-dominated government might do with their money. When the right-wing Poincaré took over with special powers to ignore parliament and rule by decree, confidence was immediately restored and the franc began to recover almost before he had taken any action.

(d) The world economic crisis had unfortunate effects on France. Although this began in 1929, the worst effects reached France only in 1933. As exports of French luxury goods fell sharply, *unemployment rose*, standing at 1.3 million by the summer of that year. To make matters worse, although Germany paid no more reparations after 1931, the Americans demanded that France should continue to repay her war debts to the USA. It was unfortunate for the left that they had just won the elections of 1932, for they seemed totally incapable of dealing with the problems. One measure which might have helped was the *devaluation of the franc*, making French goods cheaper abroad and possibly boosting exports; but there was so much opposition to this from the capitalist classes that it was out of the question. No decisive action was taken beyond reducing civil servants' salaries by 6 per cent in order to cut government expenditure. No fewer than six different left-wing cabinets came and went between May 1932 and February 1934, as the socialists and radicals squabbled over what to do next.

(e) **There was a lack of first-rate politicians**. By the early 1930s all the strong men of French politics such as Clemenceau and Briand were dead; even Poincaré, the saviour in 1926, had retired in 1929. Herriot and Daladier, the leading men of the 1930s, were shrewd and competent but somehow, as Cobban puts it, 'they lacked a cutting edge', while the socialist leader Blum, perhaps the most able of all, was in power for only just over a year, and being a Jew had to endure the most shameful verbal and physical attacks in the growing atmosphere of anti-Semitism.

(f) As the republic showed itself more and more incapable of decisive action, there was a corresponding **growth of left- and right-wing extremists** who believed that something much more authoritarian than the democratic republic functioning through parliament was needed. On the *left the communists* drew support from workers disillusioned with their lot – long hours, fall in real wages, and lack of any effective bargaining power through trade unions. *The right-wing extremists* formed themselves into *leagues* such as *Action Française* which wanted to restore the monarchy, *Solidarité Française* (founded by François Coty, the millionaire perfume manufacturer) and *Croix de Feu* which were both in favour of some sort of fascist government like the one in Italy. Often anti-Semitic in character, like the German Nazis, the leagues drew support from business and professional classes, and from property-owners – even quite modest businessmen and shopkeepers – who thought their *property was threatened by the communists*. These groups combined in an *attack on parliament* on the evening of *6 February 1934*, but were beaten off by police and mounted guards. Historians disagree about whether the leagues actually hoped to seize power (as the communists believed) or whether they were simply trying to topple Daladier's government (which they succeeded in doing), but it was an unpleasant incident, 15 people being killed and over 300 injured. Shortly before the 1936 elections Blum was beaten up and almost killed in the street by *Action Française* members. The rift between left and right was widening bitterly.

All the problems and weaknesses which plagued the republic were demonstrated in 1936–8 during the unfortunate *Front Populaire* government. It was hailed as the dawn of a new era, a united front of radicals and socialists, supported for the first time by the communists (acting under orders from Moscow in order to put up a strong anti-fascist front). It began well with Blum persuading employers to make concessions (the *Matignon agreement*); these included wage increases averaging 11 per cent, a 40-hour week, an annual 2-week holiday with pay and the right of trade unions to negotiate on behalf of the workers; to stimulate exports, the franc was devalued by 25 per cent. Then things began to go wrong: businessmen, still suspicious of the left, preferred to invest abroad, reserves dwindled, the franc dropped in value and inflation ruined the benefit of the wage increases; unemployment persisted at well over a million and there were massive strikes during 1936 and on into 1937 which the right claimed were communist-inspired. The leagues, supported by most of the daily papers, viciously attacked parliament and

illus 5.1 *Street fighting during a demonstration in Paris, 1934*

Blum in particular because he was Jewish; slogans such as 'better Hitler than Blum' were commonplace. Thus when it came to dealing with the problems of foreign affairs and the deteriorating international situation (see Section 14.4), France was so *bitterly divided* that no decisive action could be taken. In April 1938 Blum was brought down when the senate threw out his proposal to halt the continual drift of capital out of the country. Some of the *Front Populaire*'s achievements survived, but most of France's major problems remained *unsolved* on the eve of the Second World War.

5.2 WHY DID FRANCE COLLAPSE SO RAPIDLY IN 1940?

(a) The weaknesses explained in the previous section meant that France was *economically and psychologically unprepared for war*. Bitterly divided between right and left, the French public at least agreed on one thing: *they did not want another war*. The right was fascist in sympathy and favoured an agreement with Hitler, the destruction of the weak Third Republic and its replacement by a strong semi-fascist regime on the German model. Following the non-aggression pact between Germany and Russia (see Section 14.5(b)), the communists were against the war, and ironically criticised Daladier's government as 'fascist' when it arrested many communist deputies.

(b) French morale was damaged by Hitler's subtle tactics in not invading France until May 1940, seven months after the war began which, according to Bury, 'soon had a disintegrating effect' on the French. He argues that the best thing that could have happened for the French would have been a *massive German attack in 1939*; only that could have produced the same spirit of national unity which had triumphed in 1914. The long period of inaction allowed time for a peace party to develop on the right, headed by *Laval*, who argued that there was no point in continuing the war now that Poland, whom they were supposed to be helping, had been defeated. The communists lost no opportunity to undermine the morale of the troops; both extremes urged a deal with Hitler, which made it difficult for Daladier to resist when Hitler put out peace feelers.

(c) There were serious military weaknesses which hampered the French from the beginning, even though the initial mobilisation went smoothly:

(i) She was deprived of the advantage of Germany facing war on two fronts, which had been vitally important in the years 1914–17; Poland succumbed so swiftly in 1939 that France had to face the full weight of an *undivided German offensive* in 1940.

(ii) The French High Command was obsessed with the idea of defence and intended to sit tight behind the *Maginot Line*, a line of defences stretching from the Swiss to the Belgian frontiers. Unfortunately the Maginot Line did not continue along the frontier between France and Belgium, partly because that might have offended the Belgians and because Pétain believed the Ardennes would be a sufficient barrier; but this was exactly where the Germans *broke through*.

(iii) Although France had as many tanks and armoured vehicles as Germany, the generals had ignored advice from experts such as Charles de Gaulle that all vehicles should be *concentrated in completely mechanised units* allowing greater speed, instead of being split up so many to an infantry division which slowed them to the speed of marching infantry. On the other hand the Germans had self-contained armoured divisions supported by combat planes, another area neglected by the French.

(d) The French generals, including the Commander-in-Chief, Gamelin, **made fatal mistakes:**

(i) No attempt was made to help Poland by *attacking Germany in the west*, though military experts believe that such an attack in early September 1939 would have had an excellent chance of success.

(ii) They failed to act quickly enough when the Germans broke through at *Sedan* on the Meuse (13 May 1940). Troops should have been moved from Belgium and from the Maginot Line forts (most of which were completely inactive). But Gamelin did neither, and German motorised divisions moved across France with incredible speed, forming the southern arm of an enormous pincer movement, sweeping up towards the Belgian coast to encircle close on half a million French, Belgian and British troops at Dunkirk (4 June). Although a brilliant evacuation was conducted saving 330,000 Allied troops, vast amounts of equipment were lost; it was a *disastrous defeat for France*.

(e) Meanwhile, as other German divisions advanced rapidly on Rouen and Paris, **organisational problems contributed to the collapse**; there was poor communication between army and air force, so that air defence to drive German bombers off usually failed to arrive; movement of reinforcements was far too slow; relations with their British ally were far from good, the French being convinced that Britain could have done more to help.

(f) **Military defeats gave the fascist defeatist elements** which had opposed the war from the beginning the chance to *come out into the open*. Tremendous pressure was brought on the Prime Minister, Paul Reynaud, by Laval and by the socialist and communist pacifists to ask for an armistice. Reynaud was a fighter and was determined to continue the struggle even if it meant withdrawing the government to North Africa. However, when even General Weygand, the new Commander-in-Chief, and the 84-year-old Marshal Pétain, hero of Verdun in 1916, urged peace, *Reynaud resigned. Pétain became Prime Minister* and on 22 June an *armistice* was signed, in the same railway coach at Compiègne in which the Germans had signed their armistice in 1918. The right felt that military defeat was a reasonable price to pay for the destruction of the hated Third Republic.

QUESTIONS

1. The Fall of France, June 1940
Study the Sources below, and then answer the questions that follow.

Source A

The battle of France was won by superior skill and not by the crushing weight of numbers. In the vital department of tanks the Germans were numerically the weaker with some 2700 against nearly 3000 French and 200 British. The quality of tanks on the two sides was about the same. But in tactics and leadership the French were outclassed. The German army was more open to new ideas: mobility and the idea that armoured vehicles could provide this mobility in place of the horse; the idea that tanks could be used in massed ranks, separate from the other parts of the military service. With this combination of speed, weight and numbers, their main purpose was to penetrate the enemy's lines and communications. This was the Blitzkrieg and it revolutionised the whole concept of war. The collapse of France in 1940 was first and foremost a military defeat . . . the French forces were badly equipped, badly trained and badly led. They had not been modernised after the First World War.

Source: P. Calvocoressi and G. Wint, *Total War* (Allen Lane/Penguin, 1972, adapted).

Source B

Evidence given by Edouard Daladier (Prime Minister of France, April 1938–March 1940) to a Commission of Enquiry about why France went to war (1947).

For my part, I believed then, as I do now, and I shall try to get you to share this belief, that France was capable of resisting, if not of invading and defeating Germany. I feared that we might have been pushed back in some areas of the front; but I did not for a moment foresee the possibility of military collapse. In my mind this collapse was due to faulty military ideas and even more to the difference between the ideas of the two armies. It was also due to the tremendous strategic surprise which was sprung at the time. If you study the campaign you will see that our General Staff expected the attack to come through Holland and Belgium, which is why our largest and best equipped divisions were moved in that direction. But the surprise was that the bulk of the German army attacked not on the left bank of the Meuse, but on the right bank from Namur to Sedan, to the rear of the French forces that had moved forward.

Source: S. M. Osgood, *The Fall of France* (Harrap, 1975, adapted extracts).

Source C

Speech by Marshal Pétain when he was Prime Minister – October 1940.

Four months ago France suffered one of the most thorough defeats in her history. This defeat was caused by many factors . . . in truth the disaster was simply the reflection of the weaknesses and defects of the former governments . . . which were incapable of thinking up and carrying out a foreign policy worthy of France. This war was all but lost in advance. We had been equally incapable of avoiding or of preparing for it.

Source: S. M. Osgood, *The Fall of France* (Harrap, 1975, adapted extracts).

Source D

Extracts adapted from a book by Paul Reynaud (Prime Minister March–June 1940) published in 1947.

'Parliament led the country to ruin', said Marshal Pétain on the radio . . . but let us suppose for a moment that France had been ruled by a monarchy with Pétain as king. Would we have had a tank corps? Pétain did not even want a single armoured division. Would we have had a single air attack wing? Pétain discounted the role of air power in battle. By leaving entirely to our top soldiers the task of thinking up and carrying out our military policy, the politicians deprived the country of a statesmanlike strategy.

Source: S. M. Osgood, *The Fall of France* (Harrap, 1975).

(a)   **(i)**   What evidence does Source A provide about the respective strengths of the French and German forces?
      (ii)   According to Source A what was new about the German Blitzkrieg method of warfare?   **4(a)**

(b)   **(i)**   What chance did Daladier (Source B) think France had of winning the war?   **4(a)**
      (ii)   Why do you think Daladier blames 'faulty military doctrines' for France's defeat?   **4(b)**

(c)   **(i)**   What chance did Pétain (Source C) think France had of winning the war?   **4(a)**
      (ii)   How does Pétain differ from Daladier in his opinions about who was to blame for France's defeat?   **4(c)**
      (iii)   What reasons can you think of for this difference of opinion between Daladier and Pétain?   **1,4(b)**

(d)   Do you think the evidence provided by Reynaud (Source D) supports Daladier or Pétain?   **4(c)**

(e)   Using the evidence from the Sources, and your own knowledge, explain why you think France was defeated by Germany in June 1940.   **1,2,4**

2. The riots of 6 February 1934
Study the Sources below, and then answer the questions that follow.

Source A
Membership of the Chamber of Deputies after the election of 1932 (Fig. 5.1).

Fig. 5.1

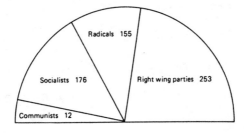

Source: R. Brown and C. Daniels (eds) *Twentieth Century Europe* (Macmillan 1981).

Source B

Speech by Leon Blum (socialist leader and Prime Minister 1936–7) made in 1946.

The sixth of February was a formidable attempt against the Republic. I think that there can be no doubt for anyone who was a witness to these events that the uprising had within the Chamber itself both representatives and leaders. Their tactics were, I believe, to bring about the fall of the cabinet and to ask the Chamber to disperse. A provisional government would have been proclaimed. I do not know what the relations of Marshal Pétain may have been with the organisers of the riot. But I do believe that his name would have been found on the list of the government.

Source: R. Brown and C. Daniels (eds), *Twentieth Century Europe* (Macmillan, 1981, adapted extracts).

Source C

On 6 February, the day on which Daladier [the new Radical Prime Minister] was to meet the Chamber, a series of demonstrations was called for by the different right-wing groups. The columns of Action Française and Solidarité Française showed every intention of pressing on across the bridge to the Chamber. Hoses which were used against them were seized and turned against the police. The rioters got right up to the barricade and then the Guards lost their nerve and fired in self-defence. Later there was a direct attack on the bridge causing new panic among its defenders. Some of the police fired once more. Between midnight and one o'clock the crowds dispersed and the demonstrations came to an end. They had lasted almost 9 hours. The casualties were: rioters, 14 killed, 236 taken to hospital; police, one killed and 92 taken to hospital. In conclusion one must admit that the rioters may have had little leadership and no clear plans for the seizure of power.

Source: Max Beloff, *The Sixth of February* (St Antony's papers No. 5; St Antony's College, Oxford, 1959, adapted extracts).

(a)   (i)   Using the evidence of the diagram in Source A, explain why the period following the 1932 election was likely to be one of unsettled government.   **4(a)**

      (ii)   Which groups actually formed governments after the election?   **1,4**

(b)   (i)   What does Leon Blum (Source B) think were the aims of the rioters?   **4(a)**

      (ii)   Using the evidence of the Sources and your own knowledge, suggest reasons why Blum may have held this opinion.   **1,2,4(b)**

(c)   (i)   In Source C, what were *Action Française* and *Solidarité Française*, and what policies did they stand for?   **1,4(a)**

    (ii) Does the evidence in Extract C support Blum's opinion about the riots or not?   **4(a,c)**

(d) Explain:
    (i) What were the causes of the riots and demonstrations of 6 February 1934;
    (ii) What were the results of the riots for Daladier and his government?   **1,2**

3. The Third French Republic had to deal with several major problems between 1919 and 1939. These included:
    (a) weaknesses of the constitution;
    (b) economic and financial difficulties;
    (c) opposition from right and left-wing extremist parties;
Describe each of the problems and show how successfully the governments managed to deal with them.   **1,2**

4. **(a)** As a socialist member of the Chamber of Deputies, write a speech to be made in June 1936, explaining why you think a Popular Front government should be formed and what its policies will be.
    (b) As a reporter for a right-wing newspaper, write an article (June 1937) setting out your criticisms of Leon Blum and his Popular Front government.   **1,2,3**

CHAPTER 6

ITALY 1918–45: THE FIRST APPEARANCE OF FASCISM

SUMMARY OF EVENTS

The new state of Italy was far from being a great success in the years before 1914; the strain of the First World War on her precarious economy and the bitter disappointment at her treatment by the Versailles treaties caused growing discontent. Between 1919 and 1922 there were five different governments, all of which were incapable of taking the decisive action that the situation demanded. In *1919 Benito Mussolini* founded the *Italian fascist party* which won 35 seats in the 1921 elections. At the same time there seemed to be a real danger of a *left-wing* seizure of power; in an atmosphere of strikes and riots, the fascists staged a *'march on Rome'* which culminated in King Victor Emmanuel III inviting Mussolini *to form a government* (October 1922); he remained in effective power until *July 1943*. Gradually Mussolini took on the powers of a *dictator* and attempted to control the entire way of life of the Italian people. At first it seemed as though his authoritarian regime might bring lasting benefits to Italy, and he won popularity by his adventurous and successful *foreign policy* (see Section 14.2). Later, however, he made the fatal mistake of entering the Second World War on the side of Germany (June 1940) even though he knew that Italy could ill afford involvement in another war. After the Italians suffered defeats by the British who captured her African possessions and occupied Sicily, they turned against Mussolini. He was deposed and arrested (July 1943) but rescued by the Germans in September, and set up as a ruler in northern Italy backed by German troops. In April 1945, as British and American troops advanced northwards through Italy towards Milan, Mussolini tried to escape to Switzerland but was captured and shot dead by his Italian enemies (known as partisans).

6.1 WHY WAS MUSSOLINI ABLE TO COME TO POWER?

(a) There was a general atmosphere of disillusionment and frustration in Italy by the summer of 1919, caused by a combination of factors:

(i) *Disappointment at her gains from the peace settlement*: when she entered the war the Allies had promised her Trentino, the south Tyrol, Istria, Trieste, part of Dalmatia, Adalia, some Aegean islands, and a protectorate over Albania. Although she received the first four areas, the rest were awarded to other states, mainly Yugoslavia (Albania was to be independent). They felt *cheated* in view of their valiant efforts during the war and the loss of close on 700,000 men. Particularly irritating was their failure to get *Fiume* (given to Yugoslavia) even though it had not been promised to them. Gabriele D'Annunzio, a famous romantic poet, marched with a few hundred supporters and occupied Fiume before the Yugoslavs had time to take it; he held it for 15 months and was applauded as a national hero until he was chased out by Italian government troops.

(ii) *The disastrous effect of the war on the economy and the standard of living.* The government had *borrowed heavily*, especially from the USA, and these debts now had to be repaid; as the lira declined in value (from 5 to the dollar in 1914 to 28 to the dollar in 1921) the cost of living increased accordingly by at least 5 times. There was *massive unemployment* as heavy industry cut back its wartime production levels, and 2.5 million ex-servicemen had difficulty finding jobs.

(iii) *Growing contempt for the liberal parliamentary system.* Manhood suffrage and proportional representation were introduced for the 1919 elections, but this made it difficult for any one party to gain an overall majority and *coalition governments* were inevitable. As a result of the election of May 1921, for example, the groups represented included the old pre-war liberals, nationalists, socialists, communists, the Catholic popular party and the fascists. No consistent policy was possible as five different cabinets with shaky majorities came and went. The general frustration among all classes led to industrial unrest.

(b) There was a wave of strikes in 1919 and 1920, accompanied by violence, looting of shops and occupation of factories by workers. In Turin, factory councils reminiscent of the Russian soviets were appearing; in the south socialist leagues of farm workers seized land from proprietors and set up co-operatives. The government's prestige sank even lower because of its failure to *protect property*, and many property-owners were convinced that the revolution was at hand. In fact, the chances of revolution were receding as the strikes and factory occupations fizzled out (although workers in some factories tried to maintain production, claiming union control of the factories, this proved impossible without engineers and managers). But the fear of a communist revolution remained strong.

(c) Mussolini and the fascist party were attractive to many sections of society because, as he said himself, he aimed to *rescue Italy from feeble government*. Mussolini (born 1883), the son of a blacksmith in the

Romagna, had a varied early career, working for a time as a stone-mason's mate and then as a primary school teacher. Politically he was a socialist and began to make a name for himself as a journalist, becoming editor of the socialist newspaper *Avanti*. He fell out with the socialists because they were against Italian intervention in the war, and started his own paper *Il Popolo d'Italia*. In 1919, he founded the *fascist party* with a socialist and republican programme and showed sympathy with the factory occupations of 1919–20. The local party branches were known as *fasci di combattimento* (fighting groups) – the word *fasces* meant the bundle of rods with protruding axe which used to symbolise the authority and power of the ancient Roman consuls. As the factory occupations began to fail, Mussolini altered course and came out as the defender of private enterprise and property, thus attracting much-needed financial support from wealthy business interests. Beginning in late 1920 black-shirted squads of fascists regularly attacked and burned down local socialist headquarters and newspaper offices and beat up socialist

illus 6.1 *Mussolini addressing a crowd*

councillors. By the end of 1921, even though his political programme was vague in the extreme, he had gained the support of property-owners in general, because they saw him as a *guarantee of law and order* (especially after the formation of the communist party in January 1921). Having won over big business Mussolini began to make conciliatory speeches about the Roman Catholic Church so that Pope Pius XI swung the *Church* into line behind Mussolini, seeing him as an anti-communist weapon. When Mussolini announced that he had dropped his republican ambitions (September 1922) even the *king* became well-disposed towards him.

(d) The anti-fascist groups failed to co-operate with each other and made no determined effort to keep the fascists out. The communists refused to co-operate with the socialists, and Giolitti (liberal Prime Minister from June 1920 to June 1921) held the elections of May 1921 so that the fascists, still unrepresented in parliament, might win some seats and then support his government. He was willing to overlook their violence in the hope that they would become more responsible once they were in parliament. However they won only 35 seats whereas the socialists had 122, so that there should have been no question of a fascist takeover, though the number of fascist squads throughout the country was increasing rapidly. The socialists must take much of the blame for refusing to work with the government to curb fascist violence, causing Giolitti to resign in despair; instead they tried to further their own ends by calling a *general strike* in the summer of 1922.

(e) The attempted general strike played right into the hands of the fascists who were able to use it by announcing that if the government failed to quell the strike, they would crush it themselves; when the strike failed Mussolini was able to pose as the *saviour of the state from communism*, and by October 1922 the fascists felt confident enough to stage their march on Rome. As about 50,000 blackshirts converged on the capital while others occupied important towns in the north, the Prime Minister, *Luigi Facta*, was prepared to resist. But King Victor Emmanuel III refused to declare a state of emergency and instead invited Mussolini, who had remained nervously in Milan, to come to Rome and form a new government, which he obligingly did, arriving by train. Afterwards the fascists fostered the myth that they had seized power heroically, but it had been achieved legally by the mere threat of force, while the army and the police stood aside. The *role of the king* was important: he made the crucial decision not to use the army to stop the blackshirts, though many historians believe that the regular army would have had little difficulty in dispersing the disorderly and poorly armed squads, many of which arrived by train. The march was an *enormous bluff which came off*. The reasons why the king decided against armed resistance remain something of a mystery since he was apparently reluctant to discuss them; suggestions include lack of confidence in Facta, doubts about whether the army with its fascist sympathies could be relied on to obey orders, and fears of a prolonged civil war if it failed to crush the fascists quickly. There is no

illus 6.2 *Mussolini and supporters shortly after the March on Rome*

doubt that he had a certain amount of sympathy with the fascist aim of
providing strong government and was also afraid that some of the
generals might force him to abdicate in favour of his cousin, the Duke of
Aosta, who openly supported the fascists. Whatever his motives the
outcome was clear: Mussolini became the *first-ever fascist premier* in
history.

6.2 WHAT DID THE TERM 'FASCISM' STAND FOR?

It is important to try and define what the term 'fascist' stood for because
it was later applied to other regimes and rulers such as Hitler, Franco
(Spain), Salazar (Portugal) and Peron (Argentina) which were sometimes quite different from the Italian version of fascism. Nowadays there
is a tendency among the left to label as 'fascist' anybody who holds
right-wing views. The fact that fascism never produced a great theoretical
writer who could explain its philosophies clearly in the way that Marx did
for communism makes it difficult to pin down exactly what was involved.
Mussolini's constantly changing aims before 1923 suggest that his main
concern was to *acquire power*; after that he seems to have improvised his
ideas as he went along. However after a few years it became clear that
fascism as Mussolini tried to put it into practice did involve *certain basic
principles*:

(a) Extreme nationalism: an emphasis on building up the greatness and prestige of the state, with the implication that one's own nation is *superior* to others.

(b) A totalitarian system of government, that is a complete way of life in which the government attempted to control and organise with strong discipline as many aspects of people's lives as possible. This was necessary to promote the *greatness of the state*, which was more important than the *interests of the individual*.

(c) A one-party state was essential; there was no place for democracy. Fascism was particularly hostile to *communism*, which accounts for much of its popularity. The fascist party members were the élite of the nation and great emphasis was placed on the cult of the *leader/hero* who would win mass support with thrilling speeches and skilful propaganda.

(d) Economic self-sufficiency (*autarchy*) was vitally important in developing the greatness of the state; the government must therefore *direct the economic life of the country* (though not in the Marxist sense of the government owning factories and land).

(e) Military strength and violence were an integral part of the way of life. Mussolini himself remarked, 'Peace is absurd: fascism does not believe in it'. Hence they fostered the myth that they had *seized power* by revolution, they allowed the violent treatment of *opponents and critics*, and pursued an *aggressive foreign policy*.

6.3 MUSSOLINI INTRODUCES THE FASCIST STATE

There was no sudden change in the system of government and state institutions; Mussolini was merely the Prime Minister of a coalition cabinet in which only four out of twelve ministers were fascists and he had to move cautiously. Beginning in the summer of 1924 by a mixture of *violence and intimidation* and aided by hopeless divisions among his opponents, he gradually developed Italian government and society along fascist lines, and at the same time consolidated his own hold over the country. This was largely complete by 1930.

(a) All parties except the fascists were suppressed. Persistent opponents of the regime were either exiled or murdered, the most notorious cases being those of the socialists Giacomo Matteotti and Giovanni Amendola, both of whom were beaten to death by fascist thugs. However, the Italian system was never as brutal as the Nazi regime in Germany, and after 1926 when Mussolini felt more secure, violence was much reduced. Although parliament still met, all important decisions were taken by the fascist Grand Council which always did as Mussolini told it; in effect Mussolini, who adopted the title *Il Duce* (the leader), was the dictator.

(b) In local government elected town councils and mayors were abolished and towns run by officials appointed from Rome. In practice the local fascist party bosses, known as *ras*, often had as much power as the government officials.

(c) A strict press censorship was enforced in which anti-fascist newspapers were either suppressed or their editors replaced by fascist supporters. *Radio, films* and the *theatre* were similarly controlled.

(d) Education in schools and universities was closely supervised, teachers had to wear uniforms, and new textbooks were written to glorify the fascist system. Children were encouraged to criticise teachers who seemed to lack enthusiasm for the party. Children and young people were forced to join the government youth organisations which indoctrinated them with the brilliance of the *Duce* and the glories of war.

(e) The government tried to promote **co-operation between employers and workers** and to end class warfare in what was known as the *Corporate State*. Fascist-controlled unions had the sole right to negotiate for the workers and both unions and employers' associations were organised into *corporations* and were expected to co-operate to settle disputes over pay and working conditions. *Strikes and lockouts were not allowed.* By 1934 there were 22 corporations each dealing with a separate industry, and in this way Mussolini hoped to control the workers and direct production. To compensate for their loss of freedom, workers were assured of such benefits as free Sundays, annual holidays with pay, social security, sports and theatre facilities and cheap tours and holidays.

(f) An understanding was reached with the pope by the *Lateran Treaty (1929)*. The Papacy had been hostile to the Italian government since 1870 and, though sympathetic towards Mussolini in 1922, Pope Pius XI disapproved of the increasing totalitarianism of fascist government (the fascist youth organisations, for example, clashed with the Catholic scouts). Mussolini, though something of an atheist himself, was well aware of the power of the Roman Catholic Church, and put himself out to win over Pius XI who, as the *Duce* well knew, was obsessed with the fear of communism. The result was the Lateran Treaty by which Italy recognised the Vatican City as a sovereign state, paid the pope a large sum of money as compensation for all his losses, accepted the Catholic faith as the official state religion and made religious instruction compulsory in all schools. In return the Papacy recognised the kingdom of Italy. Some historians see the ending of the long breach between church and state as Mussolini's most *lasting and worthwhile achievement*.

(g) How totalitarian was Mussolini's system?
It seems clear that in spite of his efforts Mussolini did not succeed in creating a completely totalitarian state in the fascist sense of there being 'no individuals or groups not controlled by the state', nor like the Nazis

did in Germany. He never completely eliminated the influence of the king or the pope, and the latter became highly critical of Mussolini when he began to persecute Jews in the later 1930s. The historian Benedetto Croce and other university professors were constant critics of fascism and yet they survived, apparently because Mussolini was afraid of *hostile foreign reaction* if he had them arrested. Even fascist sympathisers admitted that the corporative system was not a success in controlling production. According to Elizabeth Wiskemann, 'on the whole the big industrialists only made gestures of submission and in fact bought their freedom from the fascist state by generous subscriptions to fascist party funds'. As far as the mass of the population was concerned, it seems that they were prepared to tolerate fascism while it appeared to bring benefits, but soon grew tired of it when its *inadequacies* were revealed by its failures during the Second World War.

6.4 WHAT BENEFITS DID FASCISM BRING FOR THE ITALIAN PEOPLE?

The acid test of any regime is not whether it is fully totalitarian but whether its policies are *effective*. Did Mussolini rescue Italy from weak government as he had promised, or was he, as some of his critics alleged at the time, just a windbag whose government was as corrupt and inefficient as previous ones?

(a) A promising beginning
Though cautious at first, he was determined and quite decisive in setting up fascist institutions, even though his efforts were not wholly successful:

(i) He encouraged industry with *government subsidies* where necessary, so that iron and steel production doubled by 1930 and artificial silk production increased tenfold. By 1937 production of hydro-electric power had doubled.

(ii) The 'Battle of Wheat' encouraged farmers to concentrate on wheat production as part of the drive for *self-sufficiency*; by 1935, wheat imports had been cut by 75 per cent.

(iii) A programme of *land reclamation* was launched involving the draining of marshes, irrigation, and afforestation of mountains, again as part of the drive to improve and increase agricultural yield. The great showpiece was the reclaimed *Pontine Marshes* near Rome.

(iv) An impressive *public works programme* was designed, among other things to reduce unemployment. It included the building of motorways, bridges, blocks of flats, railway stations, sports stadiums, schools and new towns on reclaimed land; a start was made on electrifying main railway lines.

(v) To promote the image of Italy as a great power a *virile foreign policy* was carried out (see Section 14.2).

(b) Unsolved problems

Even before Italy became involved in the Second World War, however, it was clear that Mussolini *had not solved her problems*:

(i) Little had been done to remedy her *basic shortages of raw materials* – coal and oil – whereas much more effort could have been made to develop hydro-electric power. As an iron and steel producer Italy was not in the same league even as France. Although the 'Battle of Wheat' was a victory, it was achieved only at the expense of dairy and animal farming, whose output fell; the climate in the south is much better suited to grazing and orchards than growing wheat and this would have been much more lucrative for the farmers. As a result agriculture remained *inefficient* and farm labourers the poorest class in the state. The attempt at self-sufficiency was a dismal failure.

(ii) Mussolini *revalued the lira far too high* at 90 to the pound instead of 150 (1926) in an attempt to show that Italy had a strong currency. Unfortunately this made exports more expensive on the world market and led to reduced orders especially in the cotton industry. Many factories were on a three-day week and workers suffered wage reductions of between 10 and 20 per cent – before the world economic crisis.

(iii) The great depression beginning in 1929 with the Wall Street Crash (see Section 7.2) worsened matters. Exports fell further, unemployment rose to 1.1 million, and yet the *Duce* refused to devalue the lira until 1936. Instead wages and salaries were cut, and although the cost of living was falling because of the depression, wages fell more than prices, so that workers suffered a *fall in real wages*. Particularly galling for industrial workers was that they had no means of protesting, since *strikes were illegal and the unions weak*.

(iv) Another failing of the regime was in the area of *social services*, where there was nothing approaching a 'welfare state'. There was no official government health insurance until 1943 and only an inadequate unemployment insurance, which was not improved even during the depression.

(v) The fascist regime was *inefficient and corrupt* so that many of its policies were not fully carried out. For example, in spite of all the publicity about the land reclamation, only about one-tenth of the programme had been carried out by 1939 and work was at a standstill even before the Second World War began. Immense sums of money disappeared into the pockets of corrupt officials.

The conclusion must be therefore that the average Italian can have felt little benefit from the regime and *disenchantment* had probably set in by the end of 1937. When Mussolini began to discriminate against Jews in 1938 by sacking them from important jobs, many Italians disapproved because they felt he was being dragged along by Hitler and they resented Italy's becoming a German satellite. The Italian entry into the war was disastrous for Mussolini both because the majority of Italians were against the idea and because defeats soon showed up the *superficialities* of his entire system and the country's *economic weaknesses*; there were high prices, food shortages and, after November 1942, bombing raids on major cities. By July 1943 many of the fascist leaders themselves realised the lunacy of trying to continue the war. The king was called on to dismiss Mussolini and nobody lifted a finger to save him. Fascism disappeared and most of its work along with it; the only achievements remaining at the end of the war were the agreement with the Church and the public works, and even they, as Elizabeth Wiskemann suggests, could just as well have been achieved by a democratic government.

QUESTIONS

1. Mussolini and Fascism
Study the Sources below, and then answer the questions that follow.

Source A
Extract from *The Times*, 25 May 1934.

> The corporations contemplated in the Italian Labour Charter and in the law of April 3rd 1926, are now on the eve of coming into force . . . thus there will not be, for example, a corporation of furniture makers, but a timber corporation, including the whole cycle through which the tree of the forest is transformed into a piece of furniture or worked wood or materials for other industries [building, shipbuilding, etc.]. In other words, the corporations will be bodies in which all those who are engaged in a given cycle of production will be represented. In every corporation employers and workers are represented in equal numbers, together with experts having the function of advisers, and three representatives of the Fascist Party who are expected to see that the decisions taken are in the general interest of the State. The corporation will be presided over by the Minister of Corporations (Signor Mussolini) or by vice-presidents chosen from among the Fascist members of each corporation. The representatives of the employers and workers will be appointed by their respective federations and syndicates, but their appointment must be approved by the head of the government.

Source B
Extract from Mussolini's autobiography.

> Instead of the old trade unions we substituted Fascist corporations . . . We have solved a series of problems of no little importance: we have abolished all the perennial troubles and disorder and doubt that poisoned our national soul. We have given a rhythm, a law and a protection to work: we have found in the collaboration of classes the

reason for our possibilities, for our future power. We do not lose time in troubles, in strikes, which, while they vex the spirit, imperil also our own strength and the solidarity of our economy. We consider conflict as a luxury for the rich. We must save strength.

Source: D. Gregory, *Mussolini and the Fascist Era* (Arnold, 1968).

Source C
Extract from Mussolini's book *The Doctrine of Fascism* (1941).

Being anti-individualistic, the Fascist system of life stresses the importance of the state and recognises the individual only in so far as his interests coincide with those of the State, which stands for the consciousness and universality of man as an historic entity . . . Fascism stands for liberty and for the only liberty worth having, the liberty of the State and of the individual within the State. The fascist conception of the State is all-embracing; outside it no human or spiritual values may exist, much less have any value. Thus understood Fascism is totalitarian and the Fascist state, as a synthesis and a unit which includes all values, interprets, develops and lends additional power to the whole life of the people.

Fascism, in short, is not only a lawgiver and a founder of institutions, but is an educator and a promoter of spiritual life. It does not merely aim at remoulding the forms of life, but also their content, man, his character and his faith. To achieve this purpose it enforces discipline and makes use of authority, entering into the mind and ruling with undisputed sway. Therefore it has chosen as its emblem the Lictor's rods, the symbol of unity, strength and justice.

Source: D. Gregory, *Mussolini and the Fascist Era* (Arnold, 1968).

Source D
Extract from a letter written by Pope Pius XI, to be read in all Roman Catholic churches (29 June 1931).

A conception of the State which makes the rising generations belong to it entirely, without any exception, from the tenderest years up to adult life, cannot be reconciled by a Catholic either with Catholic doctrine or with the natural rights of the family. It is not possible for a Catholic to accept the claim that the Church and the Pope must limit themselves to the external practices of religion (such as Mass and the Sacraments) and that all the rest of education belongs to the State . . .

Source: D. Gregory, *Mussolini and the Fascist Era* (Arnold, 1968).

Source E
A British cartoon, *Punch*, January 1925.
(a) (i) According to Sources A and B, what were the corporations and how did they work?

(ii)   What were the problems mentioned by Mussolini in Source B, and how did he think the corporations had solved them?

4(a)

(b) Using Source C, summarise in your own words what Mussolini thought were the main features of the Fascist system of life.

4(a)

(c) Using Source D, explain how and why the Pope was disagreeing with Mussolini's ideas in Source C about the Fascist system.

4(a,c)

(d)   (i)   What point do you think the cartoonist in Source E (Fig. 6.1) is trying to put over?   **4(a)**

Fig. 6.1

PUNCH. OR THE LONDON CHARIVARI. – January 14. 1925.

A "SIEGE PERILOUS."

The Volcano (*to Signor Mussolini. who is trying to suppress its activities*). "THIS WILL HURT YOU MORE THAN IT HURTS ME

      (ii) Do you think the cartoonist approves or disapproves of Mussolini's action? Give reasons for your answer.   **4(b)**

(e) Using the Sources and your own knowledge, make a list of evidence which could be used to disprove Mussolini's statement in Source C that 'Fascism stands for liberty'.   **1,2,4**

2. Study the election statistics below carefully, and then answer the questions that follow.

Results of the Italian general election held on 15 May 1921

Extreme Nationalists	10	184	Government bloc (right wing)
Fascists	35		
National Bloc (Giolitti)	139		
Radicals (Liberal Democrats)	68	175	Possible opposition group from parties in the centre
Popolari (Catholic party)	107		
Reformists	29	176	Left-wing opposition
Socialists	123		
Communists	15		
National minorities	9		

(a) What evidence do these statistics give you about how strong and how influential the Fascists were in the parliament that met after the election?   **4(a)**

(b) Giovanni Giolitti served as Prime Minister of the right-wing coalition government from May to July 1921. From the evidence of these statistics and your knowledge, explain what you think some of his difficulties would have been.   **1,2,4**

(c) Explain how it happened that Mussolini and the Fascists, in spite of having only 35 seats in parliament, were able to come to power in October 1922.   **1,2**

3. Study the extract from *The Times*, 29 October 1928 below and answer the questions that follow.

A special number of the party 'Order Sheet' was issued this morning with a message to the Blackshirts. In this message, which strikes the keynote to the celebrations and is being read out publicly throughout Italy, Signor Mussolini says that '2082 public works will be formally opened in order to celebrate with deeds, and in silence, the great undertaking which, in October 1922, freed the Italian Republic and created a regime new in Italy and in the world. There are 566 road works, 337 scholastic buildings, 399 hydraulic works, 65 works of land reclamation, 63 maritime works, 79 works of health, 371 public buildings and 860 various works of minor importance'.

These dry figures, which presumably refer to activities extending over several years and only now brought to completion, will, says the Duce, silence hostile criticism at home and abroad . . .

Special interest attaches to the new motor road also opened today connecting Rome and Ostia and called 'The Road to the Sea', which has been made as far as possible in a straight line, and will, when the full scheme has been completed, be supplemented by two tracks for the use of slower vehicles. The road will be illuminated by special lamps which will eliminate dazzling headlights. A medal has been struck by the Governor of Rome in commemoration of the event.

(a) What evidence does this article provide to suggest that the Italian people benefited under Mussolini's government? **2,4(a)**

(b) Describe what happened in October 1922 which had 'freed the Italian Republic'. **1,2,4(a)**

(c) In what ways had Mussolini 'created a new regime' in Italy? **1,2**

(d) Why do you think Mussolini was suffering 'hostile criticism at home' in 1928? **1,2**

4. As a political opponent of Mussolini:

(a) Draft a speech to be given in the Italian parliament criticising Mussolini.

(b) Write a letter to be smuggled out of your prison cell (in 1937) explaining why you are continuing to oppose Mussolini. **1,2,3**

5. As editor of *Il Popolo d'Italia*, write a leading article dated 29 October 1932 to celebrate the tenth anniversary of the March on Rome. **1,2,3**

CHAPTER 7

THE USA AND THE WORLD ECONOMIC CRISIS

SUMMARY OF EVENTS

The USA has a *federal system of government* with each state having its own legislature for internal affairs, while the Federal Congress in Washington looks after foreign affairs, defence, and matters of war and peace. *Congress* consists of the *Senate* and the *House of Representatives*; its function is to make the laws. The President is elected for four years. There are two main parties, Republicans and Democrats, both of which contain people of widely differing views. The *Republicans* have mostly been the party of the north, supported by big business, and have tended to be the more conservative of the two; the *Democrats* have been able to rely on support from the south and from immigrants, and have tended to be more progressive in home affairs than the Republicans.

When the First World War ended, *Woodrow Wilson* (Democrat) was still President and remained so until the end of 1920, though, after a stroke early in October 1919, he was an invalid. He had worn himself out at the Versailles conference and on an exhausting speaking tour of the USA trying to persuade the American people to accept Versailles and the League of Nations. The ailing President suffered two bitter blows in 1920: in March the *Senate rejected the Versailles treaties and the League*, and in the November presidential election the Democrat candidate, James M. Cox, was easily defeated by the Republican Warren Harding. Wilson died a disappointed man in February 1924.

Following Wilson came three Republican Presidents: *Harding* (1921–3), who died in office, *Calvin Coolidge* (1923–9) and *Herbert C. Hoover* (1929–33). Until 1929 the country enjoyed a period of great prosperity, though not everybody shared in it; the boom ended suddenly with the *Wall Street Crash* (October 1929), which led to the *great depression* or *world economic crisis* only six months after the unfortunate Hoover's inauguration. The effects on the USA were catastrophic: by 1933 almost 14 million were out of work and Hoover's attempts to end the depression failed. Not surprisingly the Republicans lost the elections of November 1932; the new Democrat President, *Franklin D. Roosevelt*, set about solving the problems energetically. Whereas the Republican Presidents had followed a policy of *laissez-faire* (allowing private individuals to run industry with as little government regulation and direction as possible), Roosevelt took the view that the seriousness of the crisis called for a large measure of government direction to put the country on the road to recovery. His policy was known as the *New Deal*. Though not entirely successful, the New Deal achieved enough, together with the circumstances of the Second World War, to keep Roosevelt in the White House until his death in April 1945. He was the only President to be elected for a fourth term.

7.1 THE GREAT BOOM OF THE 1920s

After a slow start, as the country returned to normal after the war, the economy began to *expand* again: industrial production increased to unprecedented levels, and so did sales, profits and wages. There was a great variety of new things to be bought – radio sets, refrigerators, washing machines, vacuum cleaners, smart new clothes, motorcycles and, above all, motorcars; at the end of the war there were already 7 million cars in the USA, but by 1929 there were close on 24 million; Henry Ford led the field with his Model T. Perhaps the most famous of all the new luxuries was the Hollywood film industry which made huge profits and exported its products all over the world.

(a) What caused the boom?

(i) In a sense, it was the climax of the *great industrial expansion of the late nineteenth century*, when the USA had overtaken her two greatest rivals Germany and Britain. The war gave American industry an enormous boost: countries whose industries and imports from Europe had been disrupted bought American goods, and continued to do so when the war was over. The USA was therefore the *real economic victor of the war*.

(ii) The Republican governments' economic policies contributed to the prosperity in the short term. Their approach was one of *laissez-faire*, but there were two significant actions: the Fordney-McCumber tariff (1922) raised import duties on goods coming into America to the highest level ever, thus *protecting American industry* and *encouraging Americans to buy home-produced goods*; a general lowering of income tax rates in 1926 and 1928 left people with more *cash to spend on such goods*.

(iii) As profits increased so did *wages* (though by nothing like so much); between 1923 and 1929 the average wage for industrial workers rose by 8 per cent. Though this was not spectacular it was enough to enable some workers to buy, often on credit, the new consumer luxuries, encouraged by the vast development of advertising and radio commercials. Mechanisation, especially the moving assembly line, helped to increase productivity and satisfy demand.

(iv) The motorcar itself stimulated expansion in a number of *allied industries* – road-building, tyres, batteries, petroleum for petrol, garages and tourism.

(b) Problems behind the prosperity

Perceptive observers realised that although the boom was impressive, there were at the same time some less pleasant features, but in the heady optimism of the 1920s the majority could afford to ignore such tiresome details as these:

(i) *Farmers were not sharing in the general prosperity.* They had done well during the war, but during the 1920s prices of farm produce gradually fell; farmers' profits dwindled and farm labourers' wages in the middle west and the agricultural south were often less than half those of industrial workers in the north-east. The cause of the trouble was simple – farmers with their new combine harvesters were producing *too much food*, more than the home market would take; this was at a time when European agriculture was recovering from the war and when there was strong competition from Canada, Russia and Argentina on the world market, so that not enough could be exported. The government with its *laissez-faire* outlook did little to help; even when Congress passed the McNary–Haugen Bill, by which the government would have bought up farmers' surplus crops, Coolidge twice vetoed it (1927 and 1928) on the grounds that it might encourage farmers to increase production and thus worsen the problem.

(ii) *The black population was left out of the prosperity.* In the south where the majority of Negroes lived, white farmers always laid off black labourers first; about three-quarters of a million moved north during the 1920s looking for jobs in industry, but they almost always had to make do with the lowest paid jobs, worst conditions at work and slum housing. They also had to suffer the persecutions of the *Ku Klux Klan*, the notorious white-hooded anti-Negro society which had about five million members in 1924. Assaults, whippings and lynchings were common, and although the Klan gradually declined after 1925, prejudice and discrimination against the Negro and against other coloured and minority groups still remained.

(iii) *There was an increase in gang violence and crime*, partly because of *Prohibition* (the banning of the manufacture, import and sale of all alcoholic liquor, introduced in 1919). This was the result of the efforts of a well-meaning pressure group during the First World War which believed that a 'dry' America would mean a more efficient and moral America. But it proved impossible to eliminate bootleggers (manufacturers of illegal liquor), who protected their premises from rivals with hired gangs who shot each other up in gunfights. *Gangsters* became part of the American scene, especially in Chicago where Al Capone made himself a fortune, much of it from bootlegging. In 1933 the government admitted failure by abandoning Prohibition and thereafter the crime rate declined since bootlegging was no longer necessary.

(iv) *Industry became increasingly monopolised by large trusts or super-corporations*, so much so that by 1929 the wealthiest 5 per cent of corporations took over 84 per cent of the total corporation income. Although trusts increased efficiency there is no doubt that they kept wages lower and prices higher than was necessary; they were able to keep the trade unions weak by forbidding workers to join. Again the Republicans, pro-business and *laissez-faire*, did nothing to limit the growth of the super-corporations because the system seemed to be working well. Unfortunately prosperity based on those foundations could not last: 'America the Golden' was about to suffer a profound shock.

7.2 THE GREAT DEPRESSION ARRIVES: OCTOBER 1929

In September 1929 the buying of shares at the Stock Exchange in *Wall Street*, New York, began to slow down, and as rumours spread that the boom might be over, people rushed to sell their shares before prices fell too far. By 24 October the rush to sell reached panic proportions and share prices fell dramatically; thousands who had bought their shares when prices were high were *ruined*. This disaster is always remembered as the *Wall Street Crash*. Its effects spread rapidly; so many people in financial difficulties rushed to the banks to draw out their savings that thousands of banks had to close; as demand for goods fell away, factories had to close and unemployment rose alarmingly. The great boom had suddenly turned into the great depression which rapidly affected not only the USA but also foreign countries all over the world, so that it became known as the *world economic crisis*. However, the Wall Street Crash did not cause the depression; it was just a *symptom of a problem whose real causes lay much deeper*.

(a) What caused the great depression?

(i) American industrialists, encouraged by high profits and aided by increased mechanisation, were producing *too many goods for the home market to absorb* (in the same way as American farmers). This was not apparent in the early 1920s, but as the 1930s approached unsold stocks of goods began to build up, and manufacturers produced less; since fewer workers were required, men were laid off; and as there was no unemployment benefit, these men and their families bought less. And so the vicious circle continued.

(ii) There was a *maldistribution of income*, which means that the enormous profits made by industrialists were not being shared evenly enough among the workers. The average wage for industrial workers rose by about 8 per cent between 1923 and 1929 but during the same period industrial profits increased by 72 per cent. An 8 per cent increase in wages meant that there was not enough buying power in the hands of the general public to sustain the boom: they could manage to absorb production for a time with the help of credit but by 1929 they were fast approaching the limit. Unfortunately manufacturers, usually in the form of the super-corporation, were not prepared to reduce prices or to increase wages substantially, and so the *glut of consumer goods* built up. This refusal by the manufacturers to compromise was shortsighted to say the least; at the beginning of 1929 there were still millions of Americans who had no radio, no electric washer and no car because they could not afford them. If employers had been content with rather less profit there is no reason why the boom could not have continued for several more years while its benefits were more widely shared. Even so, a slump was still not inevitable provided the Americans could export their surplus products.

(iii)   However, exports began to fall away, partly because foreign countries were reluctant to buy American goods when the USA herself put up tariff barriers to protect her industries from foreign imports. Thus it became clear that although the Fordney–McCumber tariff (1922) was helping to keep foreign goods out, at the same time it was preventing foreign states, especially those in Europe, from making much-needed profits from trade with the USA. Without those profits European states would be able neither to buy American goods nor to pay in full their war debts to the USA. To make matters worse many states *retaliated* by introducing *tariffs* against American goods. A slump of some sort was clearly on the way.

(iv)   The situation was worsened by the great rush of *speculation on the stock market* which began to gather momentum about 1926. 'Speculation' is the buying of shares in companies; people with cash to spare like to do this with two possible aims in mind – to get the dividend (the annual sharing-out of the company's profits, assuming that it has made any) or to make a quick profit by selling the shares again for more than they have paid for them. In the mid-1920s the second aim most attracted investors: as profits of companies increased, more people began to buy shares, thus rapidly *forcing up share prices* and offering plenty of chances for a quick profit from buying and selling shares. The average value of a share rose from 9 dollars in 1924 to 26 dollars in 1929; share prices of individual companies often rose spectacularly: for example the stock of the Radio Corporation of America stood at 85 dollars a share early in 1928 and had risen to 505 dollars in September 1929, and that was a company which did not pay dividends.

    Promise of quick profits encouraged all sorts of rash moves: quite poor people spent their savings or borrowed money to buy a few shares; stockbrokers sold shares on credit; banks speculated in shares using the cash deposited with them. It was all *something of a gamble* but there was enormous confidence that prosperity would continue indefinitely. This confidence lasted well into 1929, but when the first signs appeared that sales of goods were beginning to slow down, better informed investors decided to sell their shares while prices were still high. This caused suspicion to spread – more people than usual were trying to sell shares – something must be wrong! Confidence in the future began to waver for the first time and more people decided to sell their shares while the going was good. And so a process of what economists call *self-fulfilling expectations* developed. This means that by their own actions investors actually caused the dramatic collapse of share prices which they were afraid of. By October 1929 there was a flood of people rushing to sell shares, but because confidence had been shaken, far fewer people wanted to buy; share prices tumbled and unfortunate investors had to accept whatever they could get; one particularly bad day was *24 October* – Black Thursday – when nearly 13 million shares were 'dumped' on the stock market at depressingly low prices. By mid-1930 share prices were down to about 25 per cent of the peak level, and even after that they continued to fall, reaching rock bottom in 1932. By then the whole of the USA was in the grip of depression.

(b) How did the depression affect people?

(i) To begin with, the stock market crash *ruined millions of investors* who had paid high prices for their shares. If investors had bought shares on credit with borrowed money, as millions had, their creditors lost heavily too, since they had no hope of receiving payment.

(ii) Banks were in a shaky position, having themselves speculated unsuccessfully; when, added to this, millions rushed to withdraw their savings in the belief that the cash would be safer at home, many banks were overwhelmed and had to close down for good. There were over 25,000 banks in the country in 1929, but by 1933 there were fewer than 15,000, which meant that lots of ordinary people who had had nothing to do with the speculation were ruined as their *life savings disappeared*.

(iii) As demand for goods of all types fell away, *men were laid off* and *factories closed*. Industrial production in 1933 was only half the 1929 total, while unemployment stood at around 14 million: about a quarter of the total workforce was without jobs, and one in eight farmers lost all their property. There was a drop in living standards, with bread queues, charity soup kitchens, evictions when tentants could not afford the rent, and near starvation for many; the 'great American dream' of prosperity for all had turned

illus 7.1 *A soup kitchen for down-and-outs*

into a nightmare. In the words of Donald McCoy, 'the American people were affected as though a war had been fought from coast to coast'. And there were no unemployment and sickness benefits to help out. Outside every large city homeless people lived in camps, nicknamed 'Hoovervilles' after the President who was blamed for the depression.

(iv) Many states outside the USA, especially Germany, were also affected because their prosperity depended to a large extent on *loans* from America. As soon as the crash came there were no further loans, and the Americans *called in the short-term loans* they had already made; by 1931 most of Europe was in a similar economic plight. The depression had *political results*, too, for in many states, including Germany, Austria, Japan and Britain, *right-wing governments* came to power when the existing regimes failed to cope with the situation.

(c) Who was to blame for the disaster?

At the time, it was fashionable to blame the unfortunate President Hoover, but this is unfair: the origins of the trouble obviously go much further back, and the Republican party as a whole must share the blame. There were several measures the government could have taken to control the situation: encouraging big business to lower prices and substantially increase wages; encouraging foreign countries to buy more American goods by lowering American tariffs instead of raising them, and it should have taken decisive action in 1928 and 1929 to limit the amount of credit which the stock market was allowing speculators. But their *laissez-faire* approach would allow no such interference with private affairs.

(d) What did Hoover's government do to ease the depression?

Hoover tried to solve the problem by encouraging employers not to reduce wages and lay off workers, by lending money to banks, industrialists and farmers to save them from bankruptcy, by beginning work schemes to relieve unemployment and in 1931 declaring a one-year moratorium on war debts (foreign governments could miss one instalment of their debts to the USA) to encourage them to import more American goods. This came too late to have much effect – American exports in 1932 were less than a third of the 1929 figure. Altogether Hoover's policies made little impact on the depression. Even in a crisis as serious as this one he was against relief payments to individuals because he believed in self-reliance and 'rugged individualism'. It was no surprise when the Democrat Franklin D. Roosevelt, the governor of New York, *easily beat Hoover* in the presidential election of November 1932.

7.3 ROOSEVELT AND THE NEW DEAL

The 51-year-old Roosevelt came from a wealthy New York family; educated at Harvard, he entered politics in 1910 and was Assistant Secretary to the Navy during the First World War. It seemed as though his career might be over when at the age of 40 he was stricken with polio (1921), which left his legs completely paralysed. With tremendous determination he overcame his disability, though he was never able to walk unaided; and now be brought the same determination to bear in his attempts to drag America out of the depression. He was dynamic, full of vitality and brimming with new ideas: he was a brilliant communicator – his radio talks (which he called his fireside chats) inspired confidence and won him great popularity. During the election campaign he had said, 'I pledge you, I pledge myself, to a new deal for the American people', and he kept his word. The phrase stuck and his policies have always been remembered as the New Deal. Right from the beginning, he brought new hope when he said in his inauguration speech, 'Let me assert my firm belief that the only thing we have to fear is fear itself'.

illus 7.2 *The winner and the loser. Franklin D. Roosevelt waves acknowledgement to the cheering crowds, while defeated candidate Herbert Hoover looks downcast during their ride through Washington in March 1933*

(a) What were the aims of the New Deal?
Basically Roosevelt had three aims: *relief* (to give direct help to the poverty-stricken millions without food and homes); *recovery* (to reduce unemployment, stimulate demand for goods and get the economy moving again); and *reform* (to prevent a repeat of the economic disaster). It was obvious that drastic measures were needed and Roosevelt's methods were a complete change from those of the *laissez-faire* Republicans – he was prepared to *interfere as much as possible* and to spend government cash to pull the country out of the depression, a step the Republicans were reluctant to take.

(b) What did the New Deal involve, and how successful was it?
The measures that go to make up the New Deal were strung out over the years 1933 to 1940.

(i) It was important to get the *banking and financial system* working properly again; this was achieved by the government taking over the banks temporarily and guaranteeing that depositors would not lose their cash if there was another financial crisis. This restored confidence and money began to flow into the banks again. The *Securities Exchange Commission* (1934) reformed the stock exchange and, among other things, insisted that buyers of shares on credit must make a down-payment of at least 50 per cent instead of only 10 per cent.

(ii)   The *Farmers' Relief Act* (1933) tried to help farmers, whose main problem was that they were still producing too much, thereby keeping prices and profits low. Under the act the government paid compensation to farmers who *reduced output*, thereby raising prices. This had some success – by 1937 the average income of farmers had almost doubled.

(iii) The *Civilian Conservation Corps* (CCC) was a popular Roosevelt idea to provide jobs for young men in conservation projects in the countryside. By 1940 about 2.5 million had 'enjoyed' a six-month spell in the CCC which gave them a small wage (30 dollars a month of which 25 had to be sent home to the family) as well as food, clothing and shelter.

(iv)   The most important part of the recovery programme was the *National Industrial Recovery Act* (1933) which tried to get people back to work permanently, so that they would then be able to buy more, thus stimulating industry to function more normally. The act introduced the Public Works Administration (PWA) which organised and provided cash for the building of *useful works* – dams, bridges, roads, schools, hospitals, airports and government buildings – providing several million extra jobs. Another section of the act set up the *National Recovery Administration* (NRA) which abolished child labour, introduced an eight-hour day and a minimum wage, and thus helped to create more employment. Although these were not compulsory, employers were pressured to accept them; those who did were privileged to use an official sticker on their goods showing a blue eagle and the letters NRS, and the public was encouraged to boycott firms which refused to co-operate. The response was tremendous, with well over two million employers accepting the new standards.

(v)   Further relief and recovery were provided by the *Federal Emergency Relief Administration* which provided 500 million dollars for dole money and soup kitchens. The *Works Progress Administration* (WPA), founded in 1935, financed a variety of projects such as roads, schools and hospitals (similar to the PWA but smaller-scale projects) and the Federal Theatre Project provided jobs for playwrights, artists, actors, musicians and circus people, as well as increasing public appreciation of the arts. The *Social Security Act* (1935) introduced old age pensions and unemployment insurance schemes, to be jointly financed by federal and state governments, employers and workers. However, this was not a great success at the time, because payments were usually much less than generous; nor was any provision made for sickness insurance. The USA was lagging well behind countries such as Germany and Britain in social welfare.

(vi) Two acts encouraged trade unions and helped improve working conditions. The *Wagner Act* (1935), the work of Senator Robert F. Wagner of New York, gave unions a proper legal foundation and the right to *bargain for their members* in any dispute with management. It also set up the National Labour Relations Board to which workers could appeal against unfair practices by management. The *Fair Labour Standards Act* (1938) introduced a maximum 45-hour working week as well as a minimum wage in certain low-paid trades, and made most child labour illegal.

(vii) Also included in the New Deal were such measures as the *Tennessee Valley Authority* (TVA) which revitalised a huge area of ruined rural America by building dams to provide cheap electricity and organising conservation, irrigation and afforestation to stop soil erosion. There were loans for householders in danger of losing their homes because they could not afford mortgage repayments; slum clearance and building of new houses and flats; increased taxes on the incomes of the wealthy; trade agreements which at last reduced American tariffs in return for tariff reductions by the other party to the treaty (in the hope of increasing American exports); one of the very first measures was the end of prohibition, for as 'FDR' himself remarked, 'I think this would be a good time for beer.'

It was inevitable that such a far-reaching programme should arouse *opposition*; businessmen objected strongly to the growth of trade unions, the regulation of hours and wages and increased taxation; there was resentment at the extent to which the federal government was interfering with the rights of the separate states; the Supreme Court claimed that FDR was assuming too much power, and ruled a good many measures (including NRA) as unconstitutional, thus holding up their operation. However, the Supreme Court grew more amenable during the President's second term after he had appointed five more co-operative judges to replace those who had died or resigned. There was also opposition from socialists who felt that the New Deal was not drastic enough and still left too much power in the hands of big business. But Roosevelt was tremendously popular with the millions of *ordinary Americans*, the 'forgotten men' as he called them, who had benefited from his policies, so that even though the forces of the right gathered themselves to remove him in 1936 and 1940, he won two comfortable victories.

(c) What did the New Deal achieve?

It has to be said that it did not achieve all that FDR had hoped. Some of the measures failed completely or were only partly successful, such as the Farmers' Relief Act which certainly helped farmers but threw many *farm labourers* out of work. Although unemployment was reduced (it was down to under eight million by 1937), it was still a serious problem. Part of the failure was due to the Supreme Court's opposition; but another reason for it was that though bold in many ways, Roosevelt was too cautious in the *amounts of money he was prepared to spend* to stimulate industry. In 1938, he reduced government spending, causing a *recession* (a period when sales of industrial products fall) which sent unemployment up to 10.5 million. The New Deal therefore did not rescue the USA from the depression: it was only the *war effort* that brought unemployment below the million mark in 1943.

Still, in spite of this, it achieved much: in the early days its chief success was in *relief for the destitute and jobless*, and in the provision of millions of extra jobs; confidence was restored in the government and some historians believe it may even have prevented a violent revolution. The public works schemes and the Tennessee Valley Authority provided services of lasting value, and much of the rest initiated long-term developments – welfare benefits, national direction of resources, collective bargaining between workers and management – which are all now accepted as normal. Never before had an American government *intervened so directly* in the lives or ordinary people; never before had so much attention been focused on an American president. Roosevelt's achievement was to rescue what might be termed the American middle way – democracy and free enterprise – at a time when other crisis-ridden states were going over to *fascism and communism*.

QUESTIONS

1. The Great Depression
Study the Sources below, and then answer the questions that follow.

Source A
Unemployment in the USA (Fig. 7.1). The number at the head of each bar represents % of civilian labour force.

Source: H. Ward, *World Powers in the 20th Century* (Heinemann–BBC, 1978).

Source B

Economic experts have since said that the basic trouble was that by the end of the 1920s not enough people were buying the products of America's greatly expanded industries. One reason for this was that too small a share of the increased national wealth of the 'twenties had been finding its way into the hands of the workers as wages. The result was that while the production of consumer goods of many kinds had grown rapidly, the number of people able to buy such goods had increased comparatively slowly. Manufacturers of all kinds thus found

Fig. 7.1

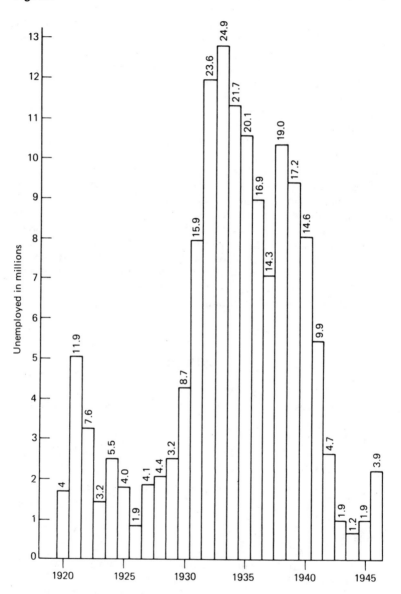

Source: Daniel Snowman, *USA: The Twenties to Vietnam* (Batsford. 1968).

it increasingly difficult to sell their products. After the Wall Street Crash the situation became even more difficult, for the uncertain future made many people decide to save their money instead of spending it on such things as new cars or radios.

As people ceased to buy, the wheels of American industry began to turn more and more slowly. Factory owners were forced to dismiss workers and reduce production as their goods began to pile up unsold in the warehouses. As months passed and things still did not improve, some were forced to close down their factories entirely.

Source: D. B. O'Callaghan, *Roosevelt and the USA* (Longman, 1966).

Source C

On October 24th 1929, blocks of shares went down the river in ten- and twenty thousand lots. Five days later came the deluge . . . caused by legions of small-timers who had no margins to speak of . . . In 1929 you could buy a dollar stock with ten cents in your hand; today it would have to be sixty to sixty-five cents. The federal government regulates investing and insures accounts and even the smallest bank deposits. But none of these safeguards existed in the 1929 casino of the stock market . . . Somebody had to take the blame, and it fell on the unlucky President Herbert Hoover . . . [he] was simply the football coach whose players lost the big game, and his bitter memorial was the shanty-towns of the unemployed down by the rivers of scores of cities.

Source: Alistair Cooke, *America* (BBC, 1973, extracts).

Source D
Yip Harburg, the songwriter, talking to Studs Terkel.

I was walking along the street at that time, and you'd see the bread lines [queues]. The biggest one in New York City was owned by William Randolph Hearst. He had a big truck with several people on it, and big cauldrons of hot soup, bread. Fellows were lined all around Columbus park for blocks and blocks waiting . . . I wrote 'Brother, Can You Spare a Dime';

> Once in khaki suits,
> Gee, we looked swell,
> Full of that Yankee Doodle-de-dum.
> Half a million boots went sloggin' through Hell,
> I was the kid with the drum.
> Say, don't you remember, they called me Al –
> It was Al all the time.
> Say, don't you remember I'm your pal –
> Brother, can you spare a dime.

It was not just a song of despair. In the song the man is really saying:

I made an investment in this country. Where the hell are my dividends?

Source: S. Terkel, *Hard Times* (Pantheon Books, 1983).

(a) Using the diagram in Source A (Fig. 7.1) for information, describe how the number of unemployed changed between 1925 and 1945.

4(a)

(b) **(i)** Using Sources B and C, explain in your own words why unemployment was so high in 1932 and 1933. 4(a)

    (ii) Why was unemployment much lower in 1937 and lower still in 1944? 1,2

(c) **(i)** Why does the author of Source C describe the stock market in 1929 as a 'casino'? 1,4

    (ii) Why does he describe Hoover as 'unlucky'? 1,4

    (iii) Explain why Hoover was the man blamed for the depression. 1,2

(d) **(i)** What was the 'Hell' referred to in the fourth line of the song in Source D? 1,4

    (ii) What do you think Yip Harburg meant when he makes the man in the song say: 'I made an investment in this country. Where the hell are my dividends?' 1,2,4

    (iii) What evidence do the Sources provide to suggest why Harburg wrote 'a song of despair' in the early 1930s? 4

2. The New Deal 1933–9

Historians and others have long debated how far the New Deal, introduced by President Roosevelt, in his first term of office, can be judged a success. The following extracts illustrate some aspects of social and economic life in the USA during the 1930s. Study them, and then answer the questions that follow.

Source A

This extract is taken from a novel, 'The Grapes of Wrath', which recounts the struggle of a farmer from Oklahoma who is trying to reach California after he has been ruined by the dust bowl. It was first published in 1939.

He drove his car into a town. He scoured the farms for work. Where can we sleep the night?

Well there's Hooverville on the edge of the river. There's a whole raft of Okies there.

He drove his old car to Hooverville. He never asked again, for there was a Hooverville on the edge of every town.

The rag town lay close to the water; and the houses were tents, and weed-thatched enclosures, paper houses, a great junk pile. The man drove his family in and became a citizen of Hooverville – always they were called Hooverville. The man put up his own tent as near to the water as he could get; or if he had no tent, he went to the city dump and brought back cartons and built a house of corrugated paper.

Source: J. Steinbeck, *The Grapes of Wrath* (Penguin edition, 1951).

Source B

A *Saturday Evening Post* reporter visits a working-class area of the city of Boston in order to see why Roosevelt had polled so many votes there in the 1940 election:

William J. Galvin, the Democratic ward leader, has a simple explanation for the Roosevelt vote: 'Probably no section in the country gained more under the New Deal'. Out of the population of 30,000, hundreds got pay rises under the wage-hour law; hundreds of seasonal workers are having slack months cushioned by unemployment insurance benefits. The NYA is helping 300–500 youths: at the worst of the depression thousands held WPA jobs; 600 old people received old-age assistance; another 600 are on direct relief and get aid for dependent children. Charlestown is a depressed area; the WPA improved its bathing beach; a new low-cost housing project will relieve some of the area's overcrowding.

Nearly one half of those of voting age are under forty. Their economic memories begin with Hoover. Galvin's two younger brothers left school and went into CCC camps during the depression. They are now working as labourers in the nearby Boston Navy Yard, which has quadrupled its employment in recent months.

Source C

The historian Barton J. Bernstein argues that the New Deal was less successful, in some ways, than many Americans had accepted:

The New Deal neglected many Americans – sharecroppers, tenant farmers, farm labourers and migratory workers, unskilled workers and the unemployed Negroes. They were left outside the new order.

Source: Barton J. Bernstein, *Towards a New Past* (Pantheon Books, 1969).

Source D

National income 1929–41 (Fig. 7.2).

(a) (i) In Source B, what do the initials WPA and CCC stand for?

1

(ii) In Source A, why are the shanty towns called Hooverville?

1,4(a)

Fig. 7.2

(b) **(i)** Study the graph in Source D (Fig. 7.2) carefully. In which year was there the greatest increase in National Income? **4(a)**

(ii) What information is given in Source B which helps to explain such an increase in National Income? **4(a)**

(c) **(i)** To which two groups listed in Source C might the man in Source A have belonged? **4(c)**

(ii) Why did the first four groups listed in Source C not benefit from the Farmers' Relief Act? **1,4(a)**

(d) 'The Newspaper report (Source B) is a much more valuable source to the historian as evidence of social life than is Source A taken from a novel.' Do you agree with the above statement? Explain your answer briefly. **4(b,c)**

(e) Using information from the Sources, and your own knowledge, explain why Roosevelt's New Deal was not completely successful in solving the social and economic difficulties facing the USA in the 1930s. **1,2,4**

[Reproduced by permission of the Midland Examining Group, adapted.]

4. Write the scripts for two of Franklin D. Roosevelt's radio 'fireside chat' broadcasts ('a man talking to his friends', as he described them):

(a) One in March 1933 explaining the New Deal, and how he hoped it would work:

(b) One in 1938, as he looks back over the success (or otherwise) of his policies. **1,2,3**

CHAPTER 8

GERMANY 1918–39: THE WEIMAR REPUBLIC AND HITLER

SUMMARY OF EVENTS

As Germany drew towards defeat in 1918 public opinion turned against the government, and in October the *Kaiser*, in a desperate bid to hang on to power, appointed Prince Max of Baden as Chancellor. He was known to be in favour of a more democratic form of government in which parliament had more power. But it was too late: in November revolution broke out, the *Kaiser* escaped to Holland and abdicated, and Prince Max resigned. Friedrich Ebert, leader of the Social Democrat party, became head of the government. In January 1919 a general election was held, the *first completely democratic one* ever to take place in Germany. The *Social Democrats* emerged as the largest single party and *Ebert* became first President of the Republic. They had some Marxist ideas but believed that the way to achieve socialism was through parliamentary democracy.

However, the new government was by no means popular with all Germans: even before the election the *communists* had attempted to seize power (January 1919) in the *Spartacist Rising*. In 1920 right-wing enemies of the republic occupied Berlin (the *Kapp Putsch*). The government managed to survive these threats and several later ones, including Hitler's *Munich Beer Hall Putsch* (1923).

By the end of 1919 a new constitution had been agreed by the National Assembly (parliament), meeting at *Weimar* because Berlin was still torn by political unrest. This Weimar constitution (sometimes called the most perfect democracy of modern times, at least on paper) lasted until 1933 when it was destroyed by Hitler. During its short life it was extremely unstable, except for the period from the end of 1923 to the end of 1929, when *Gustav Stresemann* was the leading politician. Thanks to the *Dawes Plan* of 1924 by which the USA provided huge loans, Germany seemed to be recovering from her defeat and was enjoying an industrial boom, but this was short-lived. The world economic crisis, beginning with the Wall Street Crash in October 1929, soon had disastrous effects on Germany, producing six and a half million unemployed. The government was unable to cope with the situation and by the end of 1932 the Weimar Republic seemed on the verge of collapse.

Meanwhile *Adolf Hitler* and his *National Socialists* (Nazis) had been carrying out a great propaganda campaign blaming the government for all the ills of Germany and setting out Nazi solutions to the problems. In January 1933 President Hindenburg appointed Hitler as Chancellor, and soon afterwards Hitler saw to it that democracy ceased to exist; the Weimar Republic was at an end, and from then until April 1945, Hitler was the dictator of Germany.

8.1 WHY DID THE WEIMAR REPUBLIC COLLAPSE?

(a) **It began with a number of disadvantages** which hampered it right from the beginning:

(i) It had accepted the humiliating and unpopular *Versailles Treaty* (see Section 2.8), with its arms limitations, reparations and war guilt clause, and was thus always associated with defeat and dishonour. German nationalists could never forgive it for that.

(ii) There was a traditional *lack of respect for democratic government* and a great admiration for the army and the 'officer class' as the rightful leaders of Germany. In 1919, the view was widespread that the army had not been defeated: it had been betrayed – 'stabbed in the back' – by the democrats who had needlessly agreed to the Versailles Treaty. What most Germans did not realise was that it was *Ludendorff* who had asked for an armistice while the *Kaiser* was still in power (see Section 2.6(b)). However, the 'stab in the back' legend was eagerly fostered by all enemies of the republic.

(iii) The parliamentary system laid down in the new Weimar constitution had weaknesses, the most serious of which was that it was organised on a system of *proportional representation* so that all political groups would have a fair representation. Unfortunately there were so many different groups that no party could ever win an overall majority. For example in 1928 the *Reichstag* (lower house of parliament) contained at least eight groups of which the largest were the Social Democrats (153), conservatives or nationalists (78), and the Catholic Centre Party (62). The communists had 54 seats, while the smallest groups were the Bavarian People's Party (16) and the National Socialists (12). A succession of coalition governments was inevitable, with the Social Democrats having to rely on co-operation from left-wing liberals and Catholic Centre; no party was able to carry out its programme.

(iv) The political parties had very little experience of how to operate a democratic parliamentary system, because before 1919 the *Reichstag* had not actually controlled policy: the *Chancellor had had the final authority*. Under the Weimar constitution the Chancellor was responsible to the *Reichstag*, but it usually failed to give a clear lead because the parties refused to compromise. The communists and conservatives/nationalists did not believe in the republic anyway and refused to support the Social Democrats. Disagreements became so bitter that almost every party organised its own *private army*, increasing the threat of *civil war*. The combination of these weaknesses led on to more general outbreaks of violence.

(b) Outbreaks of violence which the government seemed incapable of preventing and managed to control only with great difficulty.

(i) In January 1919 the *Spartacist Rising* occurred (Spartacus was a Roman who led a revolt of slaves in 71 BC) in which the *communists*, inspired by the success of the Russian Revolution and led by *Karl Liebknecht* and *Rosa Luxemburg*, occupied almost every major city in Germany. In Berlin, President Ebert found himself besieged in the Chancellery. The government managed to defeat the communists only because it accepted the help of the *Freikorps* (independent volunteer regiments raised by anti-communist ex-army officers). It was a sign of the government's weakness that it had to depend on forces which it did not itself control. The two communist leaders did not receive a fair trial – they were simply clubbed to death by *Freikorps* members.

(ii) The *Kapp Putsch* (March 1920) was an attempt to seize power by *right-wing elements* sparked off when the government tried to disband the *Freikorps*. They refused to disband and declared *Dr Wolfgang Kapp* Chancellor. Berlin was occupied by a *Freikorps* regiment and the cabinet fled to Dresden. The German army (the *Reichswehr*) took no action against the *Putsch* and in the end the workers of Berlin came to the aid of the Social Democrat government by calling a general strike which paralysed the capital. Kapp resigned and the government regained control. However, it was so weak that nobody was punished except Kapp himself who was imprisoned, and it took two months to get the *Freikorps* disbanded. Even then, their members remained *hostile to the republic* and many later joined Hitler's private armies.

(iii) A series of *political assassinations* took place mainly by ex-Freikorps members. Those murdered included Walter Rathenau (the Jewish Foreign Minister) and Gustav Erzberger (leader of the armistice delegation). When the government sought strong measures against such acts of terrorism, there was great opposition from the right-wing parties, who sympathised with the criminals. Whereas the communist leaders had been brutally murdered, the courts allowed right-wing offenders off lightly and the government was unable to intervene. In fact throughout Germany the legal and teaching professions and the civil service, as well as the *Reichswehr*, tended to be anti-Weimar, which was a *crippling handicap* for the republic.

(iv) Another threat to the government occurred in *November 1923* in *Bavaria*, at the time when there was much public annoyance at the French occupation of the Ruhr (see Section 13.2(c)) and the disastrous *fall in the value of the mark* (see below). Hitler, helped by General Ludendorff, aimed to take control of the Bavarian state government in Munich and then lead a national revolution to overthrow the government in Berlin. However, police easily broke up Hitler's march and the *Beer Hall Putsch* (so called because the march set out from the Munich beer hall in which Hitler had announced his 'national revolution' the previous evening) fizzled out. Hitler was sentenced to five years' imprisonment but served only nine months (which shows how sympathetic the Bavarian authorities were to his aims).

(v) The violence died down during the period 1924 to 1929, but as unemployment grew in the early 1930s the *private armies expanded* and regular street fights occurred between Nazis and communists; all parties had their political meetings broken up by rival armies. The police seemed powerless to prevent it happening.

Again, therefore, the government was shown to be incapable of keeping law and order, and respect for it dwindled. An increasing number of people began to favour a return to strong, authoritarian government, which would maintain strict public order.

Probably the crucial cause of the collapse of the Weimar Republic was the economy.

(c) **The Weimar Republic** was constantly plagued by **economic problems**, which the government failed to solve permanently:

(i) In 1919 Germany was *close to bankruptcy* because of the enormous expense of the war which had lasted for longer than most people had expected.

(ii) Her attempts to pay *reparations instalments* made matters worse. In August 1921, after paying the £50 million due, she requested permission to *suspend payments* until her economy recovered. France refused and in 1922 Germany could not manage the full annual payment.

(iii) In January 1923 French troops *occupied the Ruhr* (an important German industrial area) in an attempt to seize goods from factories and mines. The German government ordered the workers to follow a policy of *passive resistance*, and German industry in the Ruhr was paralysed. The French had failed in their aim, but the effect on the German economy was catastrophic and the *mark collapsed*. The normal rate of exchange was 4 marks to the dollar, but even before the Ruhr occupation reparations difficulties had caused the mark to fall in value so that by 1922 a dollar would buy 191.8 marks. By July 1923, with the Ruhr at a

illus 8.1 *Inflation in Germany. Boys making kites out of worthless banknotes in the early 1920s*

standstill, a dollar would buy 160,000 marks, and at the end of November 1923 the mark was completely worthless at 4,200,000 million to the dollar. Its value was falling so rapidly that a worker paid in mark notes had to spend them immediately; if he waited until the following day his notes would be valueless. It was only when the new Chancellor, Gustav Stresemann, introduced a new currency known as the Rentenmark, in 1924, that the financial situation finally stabilised.

This financial disaster had *profound effects on German society*: the working classes were badly hit; wages failed to keep pace with inflation and trade union funds were wiped out. The middle classes and small capitalists lost their savings and many began to look towards the *Nazis* for improvement. On the other hand landowners and industrialists came out of the crisis well, because they still owned their material wealth – rich farming land, mines and factories. This strengthened the control of *big business* over the German economy. Some historians have even suggested that the inflation was deliberately engineered by wealthy industrialists with this aim in mind. However, this accusation is impossible to prove one way or the other, though the currency and the economy recovered remarkably quickly.

The economic situation improved dramatically in the years after 1924, largely thanks to the *Dawes Plan* of that year which provided an immediate loan from the USA equivalent to £40 million, relaxed the fixed reparations payments and in effect allowed Germany to pay what she could afford; *French troops withdrew from the Ruhr*. The currency was stabilised, there was a boom in such industries as iron, steel, coal, chemicals and electricals, and wealthy landowners and industrialists were quite happy with the republic. Germany was even able to pay her reparations instalments under the Dawes Plan. The work of the Dawes Plan was carried on a stage further by the *Young Plan* agreed in October 1929. This reduced the reparations total from £6600 million to £2000 million, to be paid in annual instalments over 59 years. There were other successes for the republic in foreign affairs, thanks to the work of *Stresemann* (see Section 13.1). But behind this success there was a fatal weakness.

(iv) The prosperity was much more dependent than most people realised *on American loans*. If the USA were to find herself in financial difficulties so that she stopped the loans – or worse still wanted them paid back quickly – the German economy would be shaken again. Unfortunately such a situation developed in 1929.

(v) Following the *Wall Street Crash* (October 1929) the world economic crisis developed (see Section 7.2). The USA stopped any further loans and began to call in many of the short-term loans already made to Germany. This shook the currency and caused a run on the banks, many of which had to close. The industrial boom had led to worldwide over-production, and German exports, along with those of other countries, were severely reduced. Factories had to close, and by the middle of 1931 *unemployment was approaching four million*. Sadly for Germany, Gustav Stresemann, the politician best equipped to deal with the situation, died of a heart attack in October 1929 at the early age of 51.

(vi) The government of *Chancellor Brüning* (Catholic Centre Party) reduced social services, unemployment benefit, and salaries and pensions of government officials, and stopped reparations payments. High tariffs were introduced to keep out foreign foodstuffs and thus help German farmers, while the government bought shares in factories hit by the slump. However, these measures did not produce quick results: unemployment continued to grow and by the spring of 1932 it stood at over six million. The government came under criticism from *almost all groups in society*, especially industrialists and the working class who demanded more decisive action. The loss of *working-class support* because of increasing unemployment and the reduction in unemployment benefit was a serious blow to the republic. By the end of 1932 the Weimar

illus 8.2 *Hitler with a crowd of young admirers*

Republic had thus been brought to the verge of collapse. Even so it might have survived if there had been *no other options.*

(d) As it happened, however, Hitler and the Nazi party offered what seemed to be an attractive alternative just when the republic was at its most incapable. The fortunes of the Nazi party were linked closely to the economic situation: the more unstable the economy, the more seats the Nazis won in the *Reichstag*:

March	1924 –	32 seats	(economy still unstable after 1923 inflation);
December	1924 –	14 seats	(economy recovering after Dawes Plan);
	1928 –	12 seats	(comparative prosperity);
	1930 –	107 seats	(unemployment mounting – Nazis second largest party);
July	1932 –	230 seats	(massive unemployment – Nazis largest single party).

There is no doubt that the rise of Hitler and the Nazis, fostered by the economic crisis, was one of the most important factors in the downfall of the republic. (Note that the same factors to some extent explain both the decline of the republic and the rise of Hitler.)

(e) What was it about the Nazis that made them so popular?

(i) They offered *national unity, prosperity and full employment* by ridding Germany of what they claimed were the real causes of the troubles – Marxists, the 'November criminals' (those who had agreed to the armistice in November 1918 and later the Versailles Treaty), Jesuits, Freemasons and, above all, Jews. Great play was made in Nazi propaganda with the 'stab in the back' myth.

(ii) They promised to *overthrow the Versailles settlement*, so unpopular with most Germans, and to build Germany into a great power again. This would include bringing all Germans (in Austria, Czechoslovakia and Poland) back into the *Reich*.

(iii) The *Nazi private army*, the SA (*Sturmabteilung* – Storm Troopers), was attractive to young people out of work; it gave them a small wage and a uniform.

(iv) Wealthy landowners and industrialists encouraged the Nazis because they feared a *communist revolution* and they approved of the Nazi policy of hostility to communists. There is some controversy among historians, though, about how far this support went. Some German Marxist historians claim that from the early 1920s the Nazis were financed by industrialists as an anti-communist force, that Hitler was in effect 'a tool of the capitalists'. But Joachim Fest believes that the amounts of money involved have been greatly exaggerated, and that though some industrialists were quietly in favour of Hitler becoming Chancellor, it was only *after* he came to power that funds began to flow into the party coffers from big business.

(v) Hitler himself had *extraordinary political abilities*. He possessed tremendous energy and will power and a remarkable gift for public speaking which enabled him to put forward his ideas with great emotional force. Large numbers of Germans began to look towards him as some sort of Messiah figure. A full version of his views and aims was set out in his book *Mein Kampf* (My Struggle) which he wrote in prison after the Beer Hall *Putsch*.

(vi) The striking contrast between the governments of the Weimar Republic and the Nazi party impressed people: the former were cautious, respectable, dull and unable to maintain order, the latter promised *strong, decisive government* and the *restoration of national pride* – an irresistible combination.

(vii) Without the *economic crisis* though, it is doubtful whether Hitler would have had much chance of attaining power; it was the widespread unemployment and social misery which gained the Nazis mass support, not only among the working classes but also among the lower-middle classes – office workers, shopkeepers, civil servants, teachers and small-scale farmers.

In July 1932 then, the Nazis were the largest single party, but Hitler could not become Chancellor, partly because the Nazis still lacked an overall majority (they had 230 seats out of 608 in the *Reichstag*), and because he was not yet quite 'respectable'. Given these circumstances, was it *inevitable* that Hitler would come to full power? This is still a matter for disagreement among historians. Some feel that nothing could have saved the Weimar Republic and that consequently nothing could have kept Hitler out; others believe that already the first signs of economic improvement could be seen, and that it should have been possible to block Hitler's progress. In fact Brüning's policies seem to have started to pay off, though he himself had been replaced as Chancellor by *Franz von Papen* (Conservative/Nationalist) in May 1932. This theory seems to be supported by the election results of November 1932 when the Nazis lost 34 seats and about 2 million votes, a serious setback. Perhaps the republic was weathering the storm and the Nazis would fade. However, at this point a further influence came into play, which killed off the republic by letting Hitler into power legally.

(f) A small clique of right-wing politicians with support from the Reichswehr decided to bring Hitler into a coalition government with the conservatives and nationalists. The main conspirators were Franz von Papen and General Kurt von Schleicher. Their reasons for this momentous decision were:

(i) They were afraid of the Nazis *attempting to seize power* by a *Putsch*.

(ii) They believed they could control Hitler better *inside* the government than if he remained outside it.

(iii) The Nazi votes in the *Reichstag* would give them a *majority*, which might make possible a restoration of the monarchy, and a return to the system which had existed under Bismarck (Chancellor 1870–90), in which the *Reichstag* had much less power. Though this would destroy the Weimar Republic, they were prepared to go ahead because it would give them a better chance of *controlling the communists*.

There was some complicated manoeuvring involving Papen and Schleicher who persuaded President Hindenburg, now completely senile, to dismiss Chancellor Brüning and appoint Papen himself as Chancellor. They hoped to bring Hitler in as Vice-Chancellor, but he would settle for nothing less than himself as Chancellor. In January 1933, therefore, they persuaded Hindenburg to invite Hitler to become Chancellor with Papen as Vice-Chancellor, even though the Nazis had by then lost ground in the elections of November 1932. Papen still believed Hitler could be controlled and remarked to a friend: 'In two months we'll have pushed Hitler into a corner so hard that he'll be squeaking.'

(g) In fact, therefore, **Hitler was able to come to power legally** because all the other parties including the *Reichswehr* failed to recognise the danger from the Nazis and therefore failed to unite in opposition. It ought to have been possible to keep the Nazis out – they were losing ground and had nowhere near an overall majority. But instead of uniting with other parties to exclude them the conservatives made the fatal mistake of inviting Hitler into power.

In conclusion, according to J. W. Hiden: though there were signs of economic improvement by the late summer of 1932, it was perhaps inevitable that the Weimar Republic would collapse, since the powerful conservative groups and the army were prepared to destroy it. But it was *not inevitable that Hitler should take its place*: that need not have happened; Papen, Schleicher and Hindenburg must take the blame for inviting him to become Chancellor.

8.2 WHAT DID NATIONAL SOCIALISM STAND FOR?

What it did *not* mean was nationalisation and the redistribution of wealth. The word 'socialism' was included only to attract the support of the German workers, though it has to be admitted that Hitler did promise a better deal for the workers. In fact it bore marked similarities to Mussolini's fascism (see Section 6.2).

The movement's *general principles* were:

(a) It was more than just one political party among many, **it was a way of life**. All classes in society must be united to make Germany a great nation again and restore national pride. It followed therefore that *communists and other political groups would be eliminated.*

(b) Great emphasis was laid on the **ruthlessly efficient organisation of all aspects of life** under the central government in order to achieve greatness, with violence and terror if necessary. The state, therefore, was supreme; the interests of the individual must be subordinated to the good of the state, that is a *totalitarian state.*

(c) Since it was likely that greatness could be achieved only by war, **the entire state must be organised on a military footing**.

(d) The **race theory** was that mankind could be divided into two groups, *Aryans* and *non-Aryans*. The Aryans were the Germans, ideally tall, blond and handsome; they were the master race, destined to rule the world. All the rest, such as Slavs, coloured peoples and particularly Jews were inferior and were destined to become the slave races of the Germans.

All the various facets and details of the Nazi system sprang from these four basic concepts.

8.3 HITLER CONSOLIDATES HIS POWER

Hitler was an Austrian, the son of a customs official in Braunau-am-Inn on the border with Germany. He had hoped to become an artist but failed to gain admittance to the Vienna Academy of Fine Arts, and afterwards spent six down-and-out years living in Vienna dosshouses and developing his hatred of Jews. In Munich he had joined Anton Drexler's tiny German Workers' party (1919) which Hitler soon took over and transformed into the National Socialist Party. Now, in January 1933, he was Chancellor of a coalition government of National Socialists and conservatives/nationalists, but he was not yet satisfied with the amount of power he possessed: Nazis held only three out of eleven cabinet posts. He therefore insisted on a general election in the hope of winning an overall majority for the Nazis.

(a) The election of 5 March 1933
The election campaign was an *extremely violent one*. The Nazis, now in power, were able to use all the apparatus of state, including press and radio, to try and whip up a majority. Senior police officers were replaced with reliable Nazis, and 50,000 auxiliary policemen were called up, most of them from the SA and the SS (*Schutzstaffel* – Hitler's second private army). They had orders to avoid hostility to the SA and SS but to show no mercy to communists and other 'enemies of the state'. Meetings of all parties except Nazis and nationalists were wrecked and speakers beaten up, while the police looked the other way.

(b) The *Reichstag* fire
The climax of the election came on the night of 27 February when the *Reichstag* was badly damaged by a fire apparently started by a young half-witted Dutch anarchist called van der Lubbe, who was arrested, tried and executed for his pains. It has been suggested that the SA knew about van der Lubbe's plans, but allowed him to go ahead and even started fires of their own elsewhere in the building with the intention of blaming it on the communists. There is no conclusive evidence of this, but what is certain is that Hitler used the fire to *stir up fear of communism and as a pretext for the banning of the party*. However, in spite of all their efforts, the Nazis still failed to win an overall majority. With almost 90 per cent of the electorate voting, the Nazis won 288 and the nationalists 52 out of 647 seats, almost 40 short of an overall majority. Hitler was still dependent on the support of Papen and Hugenberg (leader of the nationalists). As it turned out this was the Nazis' best performance in a 'free' election: they never won an overall majority. It is worth remembering that even at the height of their electoral triumph the Nazis were supported by only *44 per cent* of the voting electorate.

8.4 HOW WAS HITLER ABLE TO STAY IN POWER FOR THE NEXT 12 YEARS?

(a) The legal basis of his power was the **Enabling Law** which was forced through the *Reichstag* on 23 March 1933. This stated that the government could introduce laws without the approval of the *Reichstag* for the next four years, ignore the constitution and sign agreements with foreign countries. All laws would be drafted by the Chancellor and come into operation the day they were published.

(i)   This meant that Hitler was to be the *complete dictator* for the next four years, but since his will was now law he would obviously be able to extend the four-year period indefinitely. He no longer needed the support of Papen and Hindenburg; the Weimar constitution had been abandoned. Such a major constitutional change needed approval by a two-thirds majority, yet the Nazis lacked a simple majority.

(ii) *How was it achieved?* The method was typical of the Nazis. The Kroll Opera House (where the *Reichstag* had been meeting since the fire) was surrounded by black-shirted SS troops, and MPs had to push their way through solid ranks to get into the building. The 81 communist MPs were simply not allowed to pass (many were in jail already). Inside the building rows of brown-shirted SA troops lined the walls. It took courage to vote against the bill in such surroundings with the SS outside chanting 'We want the bill, or fire and murder'. When the Catholic Centre Party decided to vote in favour, the result was a foregone conclusion: it passed by 441 votes to 94 (all Social Democrats).

(b) Hitler followed a policy *of Gleichschaltung (forcible coordination)* which turned Germany into a **totalitarian or fascist state**. As many aspects of life as possible were totally controlled by the government using a huge police force and the notorious *Gestapo (Geheime Staatspolizei* – Secret Police). It became dangerous to criticise or oppose the government in any way. The *main features* of the Nazi totalitarian state were:

(i)   All political parties except the National Socialists were banned so that Germany became a *one-party state* (like Italy and USSR).

(ii)   The separate state parliaments (*Länder*) still existed but lost all power. Most of their functions were taken over by a *Nazi Special Commissioner* appointed in each state by the Berlin government, who had complete power over all officials and affairs within his state. There were no more state, provincial or municipal elections.

(iii) The *civil service was purged*: all Jews and other suspected 'enemies of the state' were removed until it was fully reliable.

(iv) *Trade unions*, a likely source of resistance, were *abolished*, their funds confiscated and their leaders arrested. They were replaced by the *German Labour Front* to which all workers had to belong. The government dealt with all grievances and strikes were not allowed.

(v)   The *education system* was closely controlled so that children could be indoctrinated with Nazi opinions. School textbooks were often rewritten to fit in with Nazi theory, the most obvious examples being in history and biology. History was distorted to fit in with Hitler's view that great things could be achieved only by force. Human biology was dominated by the Nazi race theory. Teachers, lecturers and professors were closely watched to make sure they did not express opinions which strayed from the party line, and many lived in fear lest they be reported to the *Gestapo* by children whose parents were convinced Nazis.

      The system was supplemented by the *Hitler Youth* which all boys had to join at 14; girls joined the *League of German Maidens*. They all learned that 'the *Führer* is always right' and that their first duty was to obey him. They were even encouraged to betray their parents to the *Gestapo*, and many did so.

(vi) All *communications* were controlled by the *Minister of Propaganda, Dr. Joseph Goebbels*. Radio, newspapers, magazines, books, theatre, films, music and art were all supervised. By the end of 1934 about 4000 books were on the forbidden list because they were 'un-German'. It was impossible to perform the plays of Bertolt Brecht (a communist) or the music of Felix Mendelssohn and Gustav Mahler (they were Jewish). Writers, artists and scholars were harassed until it became impossible to express any opinion which did not fit in with the Nazi system. By these methods, public opinion could be moulded and mass support assured.

(vii) The *economic life* of the country was closely organised. Although the Nazis (unlike the Bolsheviks) had no special economic ideas, they did have two main aims: to *remove unemployment* and *to make Germany self-sufficient* by boosting exports and reducing imports (known as autarky). Nazi policies involved:
– Telling industrialists *what to produce*, depending on what the country needed at that moment; closing factories down if their products were not required.
– *Moving workers about the country* to places where jobs existed.
– *Controlling food prices and rents.*
– Manipulating *foreign exchange rates* to avoid inflation.
– Introducing vast schemes of *public works* (slum clearance, land drainage and *Autobahn* (motorway building).
– *Forcing foreign countries to buy German goods* either by refusing to pay cash for goods bought from those countries so that they had to accept German goods instead (often armaments), or by refusing permission to foreigners with bank accounts in Germany to withdraw their cash, so that they had to spend it in Germany on German goods.
– Manufacturing *synthetic rubber and wool* and experimenting to produce petrol from coal in order to reduce dependence on foreign countries.

(viii) *Religion* was brought under state control, since the churches were a possible source of opposition. At first Hitler proceeded cautiously with both Roman Catholics and Protestants:
– *The Roman Catholic Church*
In 1933 Hitler signed an agreement (known as a *Concordat*) with the Pope in which he promised not to interfere with German Catholics in any way; in return they agreed to dissolve the Catholic Centre party and take no further part in politics. But relations soon became strained when the government broke the Concordat by dissolving the Catholic Youth League because it rivalled the Hitler Youth. When Catholics protested their schools were closed down. By 1937 Catholics were completely disillusioned with the Nazis and Pope Pius XI issued an *Encyclical* (a letter to be read out in all Roman Catholic churches in Germany) in which he condemned the Nazi government for being 'hostile to Christ and his Church'. Hitler was unimpressed, however, and thousands of priests and nuns were arrested and sent to concentration camps.
– *The Protestant Churches*
Since a majority of Germans belonged to one or other of the various Protestant groups, Hitler tried to organise them into a '*Reich* Church' with a Nazi as the first *Reich* bishop. But many pastors (priests) objected and a group of them led by *Martin Niemöller* protested to Hitler about government interference and about his treatment of the Jews. Again the Nazis were completely ruthless – Niemöller and over 800 other pastors were sent to

concentration camps. (Niemöller himself managed to survive for eight years until he was liberated in 1945.) Hundreds more were arrested later and the rest were forced to swear an oath of obedience to the *Führer*.

Eventually the persecutions appeared to bring the churches under control, but resistance survived and the churches were the only organisations to keep up a quiet protest campaign against the Nazi system.

(ix) Above all Germany was a *police state*. All opposition was ruthlessly sought out by the police, helped by the SS and the *Gestapo*. The law courts were not impartial: 'enemies of the state' rarely received a fair trial, and the *concentration camps* introduced by Hitler in 1933 were full. The main ones before 1939 were Dachau near Munich, Buchenwald near Weimar and Sachsenhausen near Berlin. They contained 'political' prisoners – communists, Social Democrats, Catholic priests, Protestant pastors and, above all, Jews.

It would be wrong though to give the impression that Hitler hung on to power by terrorising the entire nation. In fact this was not the case at all as far as the great majority of Germans were concerned. Provided you did not mind losing freedom of speech and thought, and did not happen to be a Jew, you could usually exist quite happily under the Nazi system. It was only if you began to protest that you ran into trouble. There can be no doubt that once Hitler was in power he soon won solid support.

(c) Hitler's policies were popular with many sections of the German people

(i) His arrival in power in January 1933 caused a great wave of enthusiasm and anticipation after the weak and indecisive governments of the Weimar Republic. Hitler seemed to offer *promise of action and a great new Germany*. He took care to foster this enthusiasm by military parades, torchlight processions and firework displays, the most famous of which were the great rallies held every year in *Nuremberg* which seemed to appeal to the masses.

(ii) Hitler was successful in *eliminating unemployment*. This was probably the most important reason for his popularity with the masses. When he came to power the unemployment figure still stood at over six million but as early as July 1935 it had dropped to under two million and by 1939 it had disappeared completely. How was this achieved? The *public works schemes* provided thousands of extra jobs. A large party *bureaucracy* was set up now that the Nazi party was expanding so rapidly, providing thousands of extra office and administrative posts. There were *purges* of Jews and anti-Nazis from the civil service and many other jobs connected with law, teaching, journalism, broadcasting, the theatre and music, leaving large numbers of vacancies. *Conscrip-*

illus 8.3 *Hitler and the Sturmabteilung during the Nuremberg rally, 1938*

tion was reintroduced in 1935. *Rearmament* was begun in 1934 and gradually speeded up. Thus Hitler had provided what the unemployed had been demanding in their 1932 marches: work and bread (*Arbeit und Brot*).

(iii) Care was taken to *keep the support of the workers* once it had been gained by the provision of jobs. This was important because the abolition of trade unions still rankled with many of them. The Strength through Joy Organisation (*Kraft durch Freude*) provided benefits such as subsidised holidays in Germany and abroad, cruises, ski-ing holidays, cheap theatre and concert tickets and convalescent homes. Other benefits were holidays with pay and the control of rents.

(iv) Wealthy industrialists and businessmen were delighted with Hitler and the Nazis in spite of the government's interference with their industries, partly because they now felt *safe from a commun-*

ist revolution and were *pleased to be rid of trade unions* which had constantly pestered them with demands for shorter working hours and increased wages. In addition they were able to buy back at low prices the shares which they had sold to the state during the crisis of 1929–32, and there was promise of great *profits* from the public works schemes, rearmament and the orders which the government placed with them.

(v) Farmers, though not impressed at first, gradually warmed towards the Nazis as soon as it became clear that they were in a specially favoured position in the state because of the avowed Nazi aims of *self-sufficiency* in food production. Prices of agricultural produce were fixed so that they were assured of a reasonable profit. Farms were declared to be hereditary estates, and on the death of the owner had to be passed on to his next of kin. This meant that a farmer could not be forced to sell or mortgage his farm to pay off his debts, and was welcomed by many farmers who were heavily in debt as a result of the financial crisis.

(vi) Hitler gained the support of the *Reichswehr* which was crucial if he was to feel secure in power. The *Reichswehr* was the one organisation which could have removed him by force. Yet by the summer of 1934 Hitler had won it over:

– The officer class was well-disposed towards Hitler because of his declared aim of setting aside the restrictions of the Versailles Treaty by *rearmament* and *expansion of the army* to its full strength.

– There had been a steady infiltration of *National Socialists* into the lower ranks and this was beginning to work through to the lower officer classes.

– The army leaders were greatly impressed by Hitler's handling of the troublesome SA in the notorious *Röhm Purge* (*Night of the Long Knives*) of 30 June 1934.

The background to this was that the SA, under their leader Ernst Röhm, a personal friend of Hitler from the early days of the movement, was becoming an embarrassment to the new Chancellor. Röhm wanted his brown-shirts to be merged with the *Reichswehr* and himself made a general. Hitler knew that the aristocratic *Reichswehr* generals would not hear of either; they considered the SA to be little more than a bunch of gangsters, while Röhm himself was known to be a homosexual and had criticised the generals in public for their stiff-necked conservatism. Röhm persisted in his demands, forcing Hitler to choose between the SA and the *Reichswehr*.

Hitler's solution to the dilemma was typical of Nazi methods – ruthless but effective. Röhm and other SA leaders were murdered by SS troops and Hitler seized the opportunity to have a number of other enemies and critics murdered who had no connection with the SA. For example, two of Papen's assistants were shot dead by the SS because ten days earlier Papen had made a speech at Marburg criticising Hitler. Papen himself was probably saved only by the fact that he was a close friend of President Hindenburg. It is thought that at least 400 people were murdered during that one night or soon afterwards. Hitler justified his actions on the grounds that they were all plotting against the state.

The purge had *important results*: the *Reichswehr* were relieved to be rid of the SA and impressed by Hitler's decisive handling of the problem. When President Hindenburg died only a month later, the *Reichswehr* agreed that Hitler should become President as well as Chancellor. (He preferred to use the title *Führer* – leader.) The *Reichswehr* took an oath of allegiance to the *Führer*.

(vii) Hitler's *anti-Semitic* (anti-Jewish) policy was popular with many Germans to begin with. There were only just over half a million Jews in Germany, a tiny proportion of the population, but Hitler decided to use them as scapegoats for everything – the humiliation at Versailles, the depression, unemployment and communism – and claimed that there was a world Jewish plot. Lots of Germans were in such a desperate situation that they were prepared to accept the propaganda about the Jews and were not sorry to see thousands of them removed from their jobs as lawyers, doctors, teachers and journalists. The campaign was given legal status by the *Nuremberg Laws (1935)*, which *deprived Jews of their German citizenship*, forbade them to marry non-Jews (to preserve the purity of the Aryan race) and ruled that even a person with only one Jewish grandparent must be classed as a Jew.

Later the policy became *more extreme*. Jews were harassed in every possible way; their property was attacked and burnt, shops looted, synagogues destroyed, and they themselves herded into concentration camps. Eventually the terrible nature of what Hitler called his 'final solution' of the Jewish problem became clear: he intended to *exterminate the entire Jewish race*. As the Germans occupied countries such as Czechoslovakia, Poland and western Russia, he was able to lay his hands on non-German Jews as well. It is believed that by 1945, out of a total of nine million Jews living in Europe at the outbreak of the Second World War, six million had been murdered, most of them in the gas chambers of the Nazi extermination camps.

(viii) Finally, Hitler's *foreign policy* was a brilliant success. With each successive triumph, more and more Germans began to think of him as infallible (see Section 14.3).

8.5 NAZISM AND FASCISM

(a) Hitler's Nazi state was in many ways similar to **Mussolini's system** (see Section 6.3). **Both:**

(i)   Were intensely *anti-communist* and because of this drew a solid basis of support from all classes.

(ii) Attempted to organise a *totalitarian state*, controlling industry, agriculture, and the way of life of the people, so that personal freedom was limited.

(iii) Attempted to make the country *self-sufficient*.

(iv) Emphasised the *close unity of all classes* working together to achieve these ends.

(v)   Emphasised the *supremacy of the state*, were intensely nationalistic, glorified war, and the cult of the leader.

(b) But there were some important differences:

(i)   Fascism never seemed to take root in Italy as *deeply* as it did in Germany.

(ii) The Italian system was not as *efficient* as that in Germany. They never came anywhere near self-sufficiency and never eliminated unemployment; in fact unemployment rose.

(iii) The Italian system was not as *ruthless and brutal* as that in Germany and there were no mass atrocities, though there were some unpleasant incidents (for example, the murder of Matteotti).

(iv) Italian fascism was not particularly *anti-Jewish* until 1938 when Mussolini adopted the policy to emulate Hitler.

(v)   Mussolini was more successful than Hitler with his *religious policy* after his agreement with the Pope in 1929.

(vi) Finally their *constitutional positions* were different: the monarchy still remained in Italy, and though Mussolini normally ignored Victor Emmanuel, the king proved useful in 1943 when Mussolini's critics were able to turn to him as the head of state. He was able to announce Mussolini's dismissal and order his arrest. There was nobody in Germany who could dismiss Hitler.

8.6 HOW SUCCESSFUL WAS HITLER IN DOMESTIC AFFAIRS UP TO 1939?

There are conflicting views about this.

(a) One school of thought claims that the Nazis were **extremely successful** and provided many benefits of the sort mentioned above in Section 8.4(c). If only Hitler had managed to keep out of war, all would have been well and his Third *Reich* might have lasted a thousand years (as he boasted it would).

(b) The other view is that Hitler's policies were **only superficially successful** and could not stand the test of time; even the superficial success was achieved by methods unacceptable in a modern civilised society:

(i) Full employment was achieved only at the cost of a *brutal anti-Jewish campaign* and a massive *rearmament* programme.

(ii) Self-sufficiency was not possible unless Germany was able to *take over and exploit large areas of eastern Europe* belonging to Poland, Czechoslovakia and Russia.

(iii) Permanent success therefore depended on *success in war*, thus there was no possibility of Hitler keeping out of war (see also Section 14.3(a)).

The conclusion must therefore be, as Alan Bullock wrote in his biography of Hitler: 'Recognition of the benefits which Hitler's rule brought to Germany needs to be tempered by the realisation that for the *Führer* – and for a considerable section of the German people – these were by-products of his true purpose, the creation of an instrument of power with which to realise a policy of expansion that in the end was to admit no limits.'

QUESTIONS

1. Economic problems in the Weimar Republic
Study the Sources below, and then answer the questions that follow.

Source A
Inflation in the Weimar Republic.

Date		Marks required in exchange for £1
November	1918	20
February	1922	1000
June	1922	1500
December	1922	50,000
February	1923	100,000
November	1923	21,000,000,000
	1924	Rentenmark introduced

Source B
Konrad Hieden on life in 1923.

On Friday afternoons long lines of workers waited outside pay windows, slowly advancing until at last they reached the window and received a bag full of paper notes . . . which amounted to seven hundred thousand or 500 million or 3800 billion marks – the figures rose from week to week. With their bags they dashed to the nearest food store . . . The printing presses of the government could no longer keep pace. Life was madness, nightmare, desperation, chaos.

Source C
War debts and reparations 1924–9 (Fig. 8.1).

Fig. 8.1

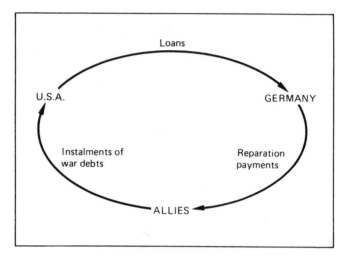

Source D
An American writer in 1929:

The money was merely going round in circles.

(a) By how many times had the mark devalued between the armistice and February 1923? **4(a)**

(b) If you had been a German citizen in 1918 and left your money in the bank, how would you have been affected by the inflation by November 1923?
With the help of Source A and your own knowledge, explain your answer. **1,2,4(a)**

(c) If you had borrowed one million marks in 1918 to buy a factory, how would you have been affected by 1923? Use Source A to explain your answer. **4(a)**

(d) Explain the behaviour of the German workers in Source B.
1,2,4(a,c)

(e) Explain the effect of the German Government printing more money. **1,2,4(a,c)**

(f) The Munich Putsch took place in November 1923. Why might Hitler have chosen this time for the Putsch? **1,2,4(a,c)**

(g) What was done to solve the problem of inflation? **1,2,4(a)**
(h) Explain fully Source C. **1,2,4(a)**
(i) Why might the writer from the USA have said that 'Money was merely going round in circles'? Use Sources C and D for your answer. **4(a,c)**
(j) What new plan was introduced in 1924, and how did this help German recovery? **1,2**
(k) Why did this German recovery end in 1929? **1,2**
[Northern Examining Association, Specimen Question, adapted.]

2. The Nazis gain control of Germany
Study the Sources below, and then answer the questions that follow.

Source A

These meetings brought profit to me in that I slowly became an *orator* at mass-meetings and that the *pathos* and gesture, acquired in large halls holding a thousand people, became a matter of second nature to me. Our first meetings were distinguished by the fact that there were tables covered with leaflets, papers and pamphlets of every kind. But we relied chiefly on the spoken word. And in fact the latter is the sole force capable of producing really great revolutions of *sentiment* . . . Mass assemblies are necessary because whilst attending them the individual . . . submits himself to the magic influence of what we call 'mass-suggestion'. The desires, longings and indeed the strength of thousands is accumulated in the mind of each individual present.

Orator – public speaker
pathos – power of arousing feeling
sentiment – feeling or opinion

Source: Adolf Hitler, *Mein Kampf* (1962 edition).

Source B
A Nazi rally (illus 8.4).

Source C
From *The Times*, March 1933.

The 'seizure of power' by Herr Hitler's government is almost complete. Bavaria, Baden, Wurttemberg and Saxony are virtually governed by Nazi dictators or Reich commissioners with almost unlimited powers. The smaller states have been forcibly converted into Hitlerite *citadels*. In Prussia the council elections have gone in favour of the Nazi–Nationalist combination which now has a majority in most of the local administrations. In the great cities of the Rhineland the tide has turned against the centre and the left. The 'purging' of the police and the civil service is still continuing, but this is no more than an incident

illus 8.4

in the swift advance of the government of the Reich to power over its states and citizens.

Unfortunately the change has been accompanied by indiscriminate violence and persecution. The whole history of the Nazi movement made excesses probable and indeed inevitable.

citadels – strongholds

Source D

On 14 July 1933, a new law destroyed the German people's democratic right to disagree openly with those who ruled them.

Law Against the New Formation of Parties

July 14, 1933

Article 1

The sole political party existing in Germany is the National Socialist German Workers' Party.

Article 2

Whoever shall undertake to maintain the organisation of another party, or to found a new party, shall be punished with a sentence of hard labour of up to three years, or of prison between six months and three years, unless other regulations provide for heavier punishment.

Source E

A cartoon from *Punch*, 1936 (Fig. 8.2).

Fig. 8.2

THE GOOSE-STEP.
—GOOSEY GOOSEY GANDER
WHITHER DOST THOU WANDER'
'ONLY THROUGH THE RHINELAND—
PRAY EXCUSE MY BLUNDER'

(a) **(i)** Who was the German politician standing at the front of the platform in Source B? **1,4**

(ii) What name is given to the symbol on the flags and banners shown in Sources B and E? **1,4**

       (iii)   Why has the cartoonist in Fig. 8.2 shown a goose and referred to 'a goose-step' in Source E?   **1,4**

(b)   **(i)**   Sources C and E (Fig. 8.2) mention the Rhineland. Why was the Rhineland an important news story in March 1936?   **1**

       (ii)   What point is the cartoonist trying to make in Source E (Fig. 8.2)?   **1,4**

      (iii)   What details in the cartoon (Fig. 8.2) suggest that it is anti-German?   **4(a,b)**

(c)   'The Nazis feared little opposition inside Germany in the 1930s.' Is this view supported or contradicted by the evidence in Sources B, C and D? Give reasons for your answer.   **4(a,c)**

(d)   What are the advantages or disadvantages of the following Sources for the historian trying to write about Nazi Germany:

       (i)   memoirs or other books by politicians (as in Source A);

      (ii)   photographs (as in Source B);

     (iii)   newspaper reports (as in Source C)?   **4(a,b)**

(e)   Using evidence from all these Sources, explain the various methods used by the Nazis to gain political control over Germany in the 1930s.   **4(a,c)**

[Reproduced by permission of the Midland Examining Group, adapted.]

3. Germany under the Nazis

Study these extracts from the diary of William L. Shirer, an American journalist working in Germany, and then answer the questions that follow.

Source A
Nuremberg, 4 September 1934.

About 10 o'clock tonight I got caught in a mob of ten thousand hysterics who jammed in front of Hitler's hotel shouting: 'We want our Führer'. I was a little shocked at the faces, especially those of the women, when Hitler finally appeared on the balcony for a moment. They had crazed expressions, and they looked up at him as if he were a Messiah, their faces transformed into something positively inhuman. If he had remained in sight for more than a few minutes, I think many of the women would have swooned from excitement.

Source B
5 September 1934.

I'm beginning to understand, I think, some of the reasons for Hitler's astounding success. Borrowing a technique from the Roman Catholic Church, he is restoring pageantry and colour to the drab lives of twentieth century Germans. This morning's meeting was more than a gorgeous show: the hall was a sea of brightly coloured flags. Even

Hitler's arrival was dramatic: the band stopped playing. There was a hush over the 30,000 people packed in the hall. Then the band struck up a very catchy tune, used only, I'm told, when Hitler makes his big entries. Hitler appeared in the back of the auditorium, and followed by Göring, Goebbels, Hess and Himmler, he strode slowly down the long centre aisle while 30,000 hands were raised in salute. Great lights played on the stage where Hitler sat. In such an atmosphere no wonder that every word dropped by Hitler seemed like an inspired Word from on high. 'Germany has done everything possible to assure world peace', he proclaimed. 'If war comes to Europe it will come only because of Communist chaos.' Later he referred to the fight now going on against his attempt to Nazify the Protestant church.

Source C
7 September 1934.

Another great pageant tonight. Two hundred thousand party officials with their 21,000 flags unfurled in the searchlights like a forest of weird trees . . . Von Papen arrived today and stood alone in a car behind Hitler tonight, the first public appearance he has made since he narrowly escaped being murdered by Göring on June 30 (the Night of the Long Knives). He did not look happy.

Source D
10 September 1934.

After seven days of ceaseless goose-stepping, speech-making and pageantry, the party rally came to an end tonight . . . And now the half million men who have been here during the week will go back to their towns and villages and preach the new gospel with new fanaticism – as Hitler told the reporters in explaining his technique.

Source E
Berlin, 16 August 1936.

The Olympic Games finally came to an end today. Hitler, Göring and the others showed up for the finale which dragged on until after dark . . . I'm afraid the Nazis have succeeded with their propaganda. First they have run the games on a lavish scale never before experienced and second, they have put up a very good front for the general visitor, especially the big business-men. We met some of the American ones who said frankly that they were favourably impressed by the Nazi set-up.

Source: W. L. Shirer, *Berlin Diary* (Hamish Hamilton, 1941).

(a)   (i)   In Source A, what does the word 'Führer' mean?   **1**

       (ii)   Why was Shirer shocked at people's faces?   **4(a)**

(b) **(i)** Using evidence from Sources B, D and E, explain what techniques Hitler used to make himself popular with the masses. **4(a,c)**

  (ii) What policies did the Nazi government introduce during the 1930s which helped to make them popular with large sections of the German public? **1,2**

  (iii) How was Hitler trying to Nazify the Protestant church (Source B), and what was the 'fight now going on' against his policy? **1**

  (iv) How successful was Hitler in his policy towards the churches in Germany? **1**

(c) In Source C:

  (i) Who was Von Papen? **1,4**

  (ii) What was the Night of the Long Knives, and why did it take place? **1,4**

  (iii) Why had Von Papen almost been a victim on 30 June, and why had he escaped? **1,4**

  (iv) Why do you think Von Papen 'did not look happy'? **1,2**

(d) From the evidence of these diary extracts, do you think Shirer admired Hitler and the Nazis or not? Quote examples to support your answer. **4(a,b,c)**

4. As a German shop-keeper, explain:

(a) Why your experiences from 1919 to 1924 led your support for the Weimar Republic to waver, and why it became strong again from mid-1924 until 1929;

(b) Why in 1933 you had become a strong supporter of Hitler;

(c) Why, during the years 1934–6, you believed you had much to thank Hitler for, but had also begun to have doubts about him. **1,2,3**

[Southern Examining Group, Specimen Question.]

5. You are a German who left Germany in 1938 and became a refugee in Britain. You meet a Londoner who two years earlier had visited Berlin for the Olympic Games and had been very impressed by what he had seen in Germany. Explain to the Londoner how you think he might have obtained his impression and why you decided to leave Germany. **1,2,3**

[Southern Examining Group, Specimen Question.]

6. Describe the main events of each of the following, and explain how *each* of them helped Hitler to increase his power in Germany:

  (a) The Reichstag Fire and the election, February–March 1933;

  (b) The passing of the Enabling Act by the Reichstag, March 1933;

  (c) The Röhm Purge (Night of the Long Knives) June 1934.

CHAPTER 9

STALIN AND THE USSR
1924–39

SUMMARY OF EVENTS

Russia during this period was dominated by one man – *Joseph Stalin* – who, as dictator until his death in 1953 at the age of 73, wielded as much power as ever the tsars had done before him. When Lenin died in January 1924 it was widely expected that *Trotsky* would take over as leader, but a complex power struggle developed from which Stalin had emerged triumphant by the end of 1929. Immense problems faced communist Russia, still only a few years old: industry and agriculture were backward and inefficient, there were constant food shortages, pressing political and social problems – and, many Russians thought, the danger of another attempt by *foreign capitalist powers* to destroy the new communist state. Stalin made determined efforts to overcome all these problems: there were the *Five Year Plans* to revolutionise industry, the *collectivisation* of agriculture and the introduction of a *totalitarian regime* which was, if anything, more ruthlessly efficient than Hitler's system in Germany. Yet brutal though Stalin's methods were, they seem to have been successful, at least to the extent that when the dreaded attack from the west eventually came in the form of a massive German invasion in June 1941, the Russians were able to hold out and eventually end up on the winning side, though admittedly at a terrible cost.

9.1 HOW DID STALIN MANAGE TO GET TO SUPREME POWER?

Joseph Djugashvili (he took the name 'Stalin' – man of steel – some time after joining the Bolsheviks in 1904) was born in 1879 in the small town of Gori in the province of Georgia; his parents were poor peasants; in fact his father, a shoemaker, had been born a serf. Joseph's mother wanted him to become a priest and he was educated for four years at Tiflis Theological Seminary, but he hated its repressive atmosphere and was expelled in 1899 for expounding socialist principles. He became a Bolshevik about 1904 and after 1917, thanks to his brilliance as an administrator, he was quietly able to build up his own position under

illus 9.1 *Joseph Stalin*

Lenin. When Lenin died in 1924 Stalin was Secretary-General of the
communist party and a member of the seven-man *Politburo*, the committee which decided government policy. At first it seemed unlikely that
Stalin would become the dominant figure; Trotsky called him 'the party's
most eminent mediocrity', and Lenin thought him stubborn and rude,
and suggested in his will that Stalin be removed from his post. The most
obvious successor to Lenin was Trotsky, an inspired orator, an intellectual, and the organiser of the Red Armies. However, circumstances
arose *which Stalin was able to use to eliminate his rivals*:

(a) Trotsky's brilliance worked against him by arousing **envy and resentment** among the other *Politburo* members who combined to prevent his
becoming leader: collective action was better than a one-man show.

(b) The *Politburo* members **underestimated** Stalin, seeing him as nothing
more than a competent administrator; they ignored Lenin's advice.

(c) As Secretary-General of the party, Stalin had **full powers of appointment and promotion**, which he used to place his own supporters in key

positions while at the same time removing the supporters of others to distant parts of the country.

(d) Stalin used the **disagreements in the Politburo over policy** to his own advantage. These arose partly because Marx had never described in detail exactly *how the new communist society should be organised* and even Lenin was vague about it, except that 'the dictatorship of the proletariat' would be established – that is, workers would run the state and the economy in their *own interests*.When all opposition had been crushed, the ultimate goal of a *classless society* would be achieved in which, according to Marx, the ruling principle would be: 'from each according to his ability, to each according to his needs'. With NEP (the New Economic Policy: see Section 3.3(d)) Lenin had departed from socialist principles, though this would only be a temporary measure until the crisis passed. Now the right, led by *Bukharin*, and the left, whose views were most strongly put by *Trotsky*, fell out about what do do next:

(i) Bukharin wanted to continue NEP, even though it was causing an increase in numbers of *kulaks*. His opponents wanted to abandon NEP and concentrate on rapid industrialisation at the expense of the peasants.

(ii) Bukharin thought it important to consolidate soviet power in Russia, based on a prosperous peasantry and with a very gradual industrialisation – *'socialism in one country'*, as it became known. Trotsky believed that they must work for revolution outside Russia – *'permanent revolution'*; when this was achieved the industrialised states of western Europe would help Russia with her industrialisation.

Stalin, quietly ambitious, apparently had no strong views either way at first, but he supported the right simply to isolate Trotsky. Later, when a split occurred between Bukharin and two other *Politburo* members, Zinoviev and Kamenev, who were feeling unhappy about NEP, Stalin supported Bukharin, and one by one Trotsky, Zinoviev and Kamenev were voted off the *Politburo* by Stalin's yes-men and expelled from the party (*1927*). The following year Stalin decided that NEP must go – the *kulaks* were holding up agricultural progress; when Bukharin protested, he too was expelled (*1929*) and *Stalin was left supreme*. Having reached the pinnacle, Stalin attacked the many problems facing Russia, which fell into three categories: economic, political and social, and foreign (see Section 13.3).

9.2 WHAT WERE THE ECONOMIC PROBLEMS, AND HOW SUCCESSFUL WAS STALIN IN SOLVING THEM?

(a) The problems

(i) Although Russian industry was recovering from the effects of the war, *production from heavy industry was still surprisingly low*; in

1929 for example, France, not a major industrial power, produced more coal and steel than Russia, while Germany, Britain and especially the USA were streets ahead. Stalin believed that a rapid expansion of heavy industry was essential so that Russia would be able to survive the attack which he was convinced would come sooner or later from the Western capitalist powers who hated communism. Industrialisation would have the added advantage of increasing support for the government, because it was the *industrial workers* who were the communists' greatest allies: the more industrial workers, the more secure the communist state would be. One serious obstacle to overcome, though, was *lack of capital* to finance expansion, since foreigners were unwilling to invest in a communist state.

(ii) *More food* would have to be produced, both to feed the growing industrial population and to provide a surplus for export which would bring in foreign capital and profits for investment in industry. Yet the primitive agricultural system was incapable of providing such increases.

(b) The approach

Although he had no economic experience whatsoever, Stalin seems to have had no hesitation in plunging the country into a series of dramatic changes designed to overcome the problems in the shortest possible time. In a speech in February 1931 he explained why: 'We are 50 or 100 years behind the advanced countries. We must make good this distance in 10 years. Either we do it, or we shall be crushed.' NEP had been permissible as a temporary measure, but must now be abandoned: both industry and agriculture must be taken under government control.

(i) *Industrial expansion* was tackled by a series of *Five Year Plans*, the first two of which (1928–32 and 1933–7) were said to have been completed a year ahead of schedule, though in fact neither of them reached the full target. The first plan concentrated on *heavy industry* – coal, iron, steel, oil and machinery (including tractors), which were scheduled to triple output; the two later plans provided for some increases in consumer goods as well as in heavy industry. It has to be said that in spite of all sorts of mistakes the plans were a remarkable success: by 1940 the USSR had overtaken Britain in iron and steel production, though not yet in coal, and she was within reach of Germany:

Table 9.1
Industrial expansion in Russia: production in
millions of tons

	1900	1913	1929	1938	1940
Coal	16.0	36.0	40.1	132.9	164.9
Pig iron	2.7	4.8	8.0	26.3	14.9
Steel	2.5	5.2	4.9	18.0	18.4

Industrial production in Russia compared with
other great powers in 1940 (in millions of tons)

	Pig Iron	Steel	Coal	Electricity (in billion kilowatts)
USSR	14.9	18.4	164.6	39.6
USA	31.9	47.2	395.0	115.9
Britain	6.7	10.3	227.0	30.7
Germany	18.3	22.7	186.0	55.2
France	6.0	16.1	45.5	19.3

Hundreds of *factories* were built, many of them in new towns east of the Ural Mountains where they would be safer from invasion. Well-known examples are the iron and steel works at Magnitogorsk, tractor works at Kharkov and Gorki, a hydro-electric dam at Dnepropetrovsk and the oil refineries in the Caucasus.

How was it achieved? The cash was provided almost entirely by the Russians themselves, with no foreign investment; some came from grain exports, some from charging peasants heavily for use of government equipment and the ruthless ploughing back of all profits and surplus. Hundreds of *foreign technicians* were brought in and great emphasis placed on expanding education in technical colleges and universities and even in factory schools, to provide a whole new generation of skilled workers. In the factories the old capitalist methods of piecework and pay differentials between skilled and unskilled workers were used to encourage production; medals were given to workers who achieved record output; these were known as Stakhanovites after Alexei Stakhanov, a champion miner who in August 1935, supported by a well-organised team, managed to cut 102 tons of coal in a single shift (by ordinary methods even the highly efficient miners of the Ruhr in Germany were managing only 10 tons per shift). Ordinary workers were ruthlessly disciplined: there were severe punishments for bad workmanship, accusations of being a 'saboteur' when targets were not met and often a spell in a forced labour camp. Primitive housing conditions and a severe shortage of consumer goods (because of the concentration on heavy industry) on top of all the regimentation must have made life grim for most workers. As Richard Freeborn points out: 'It is probably no exaggeration to claim that the First Five Year Plan represented a declaration of war by the state machine against the workers and peasants of the USSR who were subjected to a greater exploitation than any they had known under capitalism.' However, by the mid-1930s things were improving as benefits such as education, medical care and holidays with pay became available.

(ii) *The problems of agriculture* were dealt with by the process known as *collectivisation*. The idea was that the small farms and holdings belonging to the peasants should be merged to form large collective farms jointly owned by the peasants. There were two main reasons for Stalin's decision to collectivise:

– *The existing system of small farms was inefficient*, whereas large farms, under state direction and using tractors and combine harvesters, would vastly increase grain production.

– He wanted to *eliminate the class of prosperous peasants* (*kulaks* or nepmen) which NEP had encouraged because, he claimed, they were standing in the way of progress. But the real reason was probably political: Stalin saw the *kulak* as the enemy of communism. 'We must smash the *kulaks* so hard that they will never rise to their feet again.'

The policy was launched in earnest in *1929*, and had to be carried through by sheer brute force, so determined was the resistance in the countryside. It was a complete disaster from which, it is probably no exaggeration to claim, Russia has not fully recovered even today. There was no problem in collectivising landless labourers, but all peasants who owned any property at all, whether they were *kulaks* or not, were hostile and had to be forced to join by armies of party members who urged poorer peasants to seize cattle and machinery from the *kulaks* to be handed over to the collectives. *Kulaks* often reacted by *slaughtering cattle* and *burning crops* rather than allow the state to take them. Peasants who refused to join collective farms were *arrested and deported to labour camps or shot*; when newly collectivised peasants tried to sabotage the system by producing only enough for their own needs, local officials insisted on *seizing* the required quotas, resulting in large-scale *famine* during 1932–3, especially in the Ukraine. Yet one and three-quarter million tons of grain were exported during that period while over five million peasants died of starvation. Some historians have even claimed that Stalin welcomed the famine, since, along with the 10 million *kulaks* who

illus 9.2 *Russian peasants admire the first tractor in their village, 1926*

were removed or executed, it helped to break peasant resistance. In this way, well over 90 per cent of all farmland had been collectivised by 1937. In one sense, Stalin could claim that collectivisation was a success; it allowed *greater mechanisation*, which gradually increased grain output until by 1940 it was over 80 per cent higher than in 1913. On the other hand, so many animals had been slaughtered that it was 1953 before livestock production recovered to the 1928 figure and the cost in *human life and suffering* was enormous.

9.3 POLITICAL AND SOCIAL PROBLEMS, AND STALIN'S SOLUTIONS

(a) The problems were to some extent *of Stalin's own making*; he obviously felt that under his totalitarian regime, political and social activities must be controlled just as much as economic life; he aimed at complete and unchallenged power for himself and became increasingly suspicious and intolerant of criticism.

(i) Starting in 1930, there was growing opposition within the party which aimed to slow down industrialisation, allow peasants to leave collective farms, and remove Stalin from the leadership if necessary. However, Stalin was equally determined that political opponents and critics must be *eliminated* once and for all.

  (ii) A *new constitution* was needed to consolidate the hold of Stalin and the communist party over the whole country.

  (iii) *Social and cultural aspects of life* needed to be brought into line and harnessed to the service of the state.

(b) Stalin's methods were typically dramatic.

  (i) Using the *murder of Sergei Kirov*, one of his supporters on the *Politburo (December 1934)*, as an excuse, Stalin launched what became known as *the purges*. It seems fairly certain that Stalin himself organised Kirov's murder, 'the crime of the century', as Robert Conquest calls it, 'the keystone of the entire edifice of terror and suffering by which Stalin secured his grip on the Soviet peoples', but it was blamed on Stalin's critics. Over the next four years hundreds of important officials were arrested, tortured, made to confess to all sorts of crimes of which they were largely innocent (such as plotting with the exiled Trotsky or with capitalist governments to overthrow the soviet state) and forced to appear in a series of 'show trials' at which they were invariably found guilty and sentenced to death or labour camp. Those executed included all the 'Old Bolsheviks' – Zinoviev, Kamenev, Bukharin and Radek – who had helped to make the 1917 revolution, the Commander-in-Chief of the Red Army, Tukhachevsky, thirteen other generals and about two-thirds of the top officers; millions of innocent people ended up in labour camps (Conquest puts the figure at about eight million by 1938). Even Trotsky was sought out and murdered in exile in Mexico City, though he managed to survive until 1940. The purges were successful in eliminating *possible alternative leaders* and in *terrorising the masses into obedience*, but the consequences were serious: many of the *best brains* in the government, the army and in industry had disappeared, and in a country where the highly educated class was still small, this was bound to *hinder progress*.

  (ii) In 1936, after much discussion, a new and apparently more democratic constitution was introduced in which everyone was allowed to vote by secret ballot for members of a national assembly known as the *Supreme Soviet*. However, this met for only about two weeks in the year, when it elected a smaller body, the *Praesidium*, to act on its behalf, and when it also chose the Union Soviet of Commissars, a small group of ministers of which Stalin was the Secretary, and which wielded the real power. In fact the *democracy was an illusion*: the constitution merely underlined the fact that Stalin and the party ran things, and though there was mention of freedom of speech, anybody who ventured to criticise Stalin was quickly 'purged'.

  (iii) *Writers, artists and musicians* were expected to produce works of realism glorifying soviet achievements; anybody who did not conform was persecuted, and even those who tried often still fell foul of Stalin. The young composer *Shostakovich* was condemned when his new opera, *Lady Macbeth of Mtsensk*, failed to please Stalin, even though the music critics had at first praised it. Further performances were banned with the result, according to the American ambassador, that 'half the artists and musicians in Moscow are having nervous prostration and the others are trying to imagine how to write and compose in a manner to please Stalin'. *Education* like everything else was closely watched by the secret police, and although it was compulsory and free it tended to deteriorate into indoctrination; but at least literacy was increased, which along with the improvement in social services, was an unprecedented achievement. Finally an attempt was made to clamp down on the *Orthodox Church*: churches were closed and clergy persecuted; but this was one of Stalin's failures: in 1940 probably half the population were still convinced believers, and during the war the persecution was relaxed to help maintain morale.

9.4 WAS THE STALIN APPROACH NECESSARY?

Historians have failed to agree about the extent of Stalin's achievement, or indeed whether he achieved any more with his brutality than could have been managed by less drastic methods. Stalin's defenders, who include many soviet historians, argue that the situation was so *desperate* that only the pressures of brute force could have produced such a rapid industrialisation together with the necessary food; for them, the supreme justification is that thanks to Stalin Russia was strong enough to defeat the Germans. The opposing view is that Stalin's policies, though superficially successful, actually *weakened* Russia: ridiculously high targets for industrial production placed unnecessary pressure on the workers and caused slipshod work and poor quality products; the brutal enforcement of collectivisation vastly reduced the amount of meat available and made peasants so bitter that in the Ukraine the German invaders were welcomed; the purges slowed economic progress by removing many of the most experienced men, and almost caused military defeat during the first months of the war by depriving the army of all its experienced generals; in fact Russia won the war *in spite of Stalin*, not because of him.

Whichever view one accepts, a final point to bear in mind is that many Marxists outside Russia feel that Stalin betrayed the idealism of Marx and Lenin: instead of a new classless society in which everybody was free and equal, ordinary workers and peasants were just as exploited as under the tsars, whereas skilled workers were an élite; the party had taken the place of the capitalists, and enjoyed all the privileges – the best houses, country retreats and cars. Instead of Marx's 'dictatorship of the proletariat' there was merely the *dictatorship of Stalin*.

QUESTIONS

1. Stalin and the Five Year Plans

Study the Sources below, and then answer the questions that follow.

Source A

From Stalin's statement about industrialisation, June 1931.

> It is sometimes asked whether it is not possible to slow down the tempo of industrialisation a bit. No, comrades, it is not possible! The tempo must not be reduced. On the contrary, we must increase it as much as is within our powers. This is dictated to us by our obligation to the workers and the peasants of the USSR.
>
> To slacken the tempo would mean falling behind. And those who fall behind get beaten. But we do not want to be beaten. No, we refuse to be beaten! In the past Russia was beaten for her backwardness by British and French capitalists and by Japanese barons. That is why Lenin said: 'Either perish, or overtake and outstrip the advanced capitalist countries'.
>
> We are 50 or 100 years behind the advanced countries. We must make good this distance in 10 years. Either we do it, or we shall be crushed.

Source: J. V. Stalin, *Works* (Lawrence & Wishart, 1953).

Source B

A Russian poster (Fig. 9.1) depicting Stalin as the creator of a powerful industrialised Russia through the success of the Five Year Plan and against the opposition of internal critics and external foes.

Source: British Museum.

Fig. 9.1

Source C
Achievement of targets in Stalin's Five Year Plans (in percentages of target).

	First Five Year Plan 1928–32	Second Five Year Plan 1933–37
Industrial production		
Official Soviet estimate	100.7	103.0
Nutter's estimate	59.7	93.1
Agricultural production		
Official Soviet estimate	57.8	76.9
Nutter's estimate	50.7	69.0

Source: M. McCauley, *Stalin and Stalinism* (Longman, 1983).

(a)   (i)   What clue is given in Source A as to why Stalin issued this statement in 1931?   **4(a)**

    (ii)   According to Source A, why did Stalin think it was so important for Russia to continue to industrialise quickly?   **4(a)**

    (iii)   Name *three* industries which were developed under the First Five Year Plan and explain why these were considered so important.   **1,2,4**

(b)   (i)   The people on the left of the poster (Source B) (Fig. 9.1) represent opponents of the Five Year Plan. From the evidence of the poster, and your own knowledge, suggest what types of people these opponents were likely to be.   **1,4**

    (ii)   What evidence can you find in the poster to suggest that it was intended as a piece of propaganda?   **4(b)**

(c)   Describe briefly the methods used by Stalin in his attempt to achieve:
    (i)   industrial expansion through the Five Year Plans;
    (ii)   collectivisation of agriculture.   **1,2**

(d)   Source C shows estimates of how close the Russians came to achieving the targets set for economic expansion. Warren Nutter is a western economist.
    (i)   Explain why you think the two sets of estimates differ. **1,2,4**
    (ii)   Which estimates, the official Soviet ones or Nutter's, do you think are likely to be more accurate? Explain your answer.   **4(b)**
    (iii)   Using the evidence from Source C and your own knowledge, explain whether or not you think the Five Year Plans were successful   **1,4**

[Northern Examining Association, Specimen Question, adapted.]

2. Stalin

Study the Sources below, and then answer the questions that follow.

Source A

From a letter written by Lenin in December 1922.

> Stalin is too rude, and this shortcoming, though bearable in internal relations amongst us communists, becomes quite unbearable in a General Secretary. I therefore suggest to you, Comrades, that you remove Stalin from his post and replace him with someone else who is superior to Stalin in this respect; namely, is more tolerant, more loyal, more polite, and more attentive to the needs of the comrades, etc. This may seem a trifling detail. But as regards avoiding a split in the party and as regards the relations between Stalin and Trotsky, this is not a mere detail, but a detail which might one day acquire decisive importance.

Source: S. Hendel, *The Soviet Crucible* (Van Nostrand, 1959, adapted).

Source B

> The disagreements between Trotsky and Stalin, and then between Stalin and Zinoviev and Stalin and Bukharin, were genuine disagreements about policy, about economic organization, about the problems of increasing agricultural production. In Lenin's day these would have been hammered out among the party leaders. Though lenin's personality was such that his views usually were finally accepted, people who had spoken and voted against him were not penalised. Now, however, the debate was not just about policy, but about who should control the party. Stalin had begun to establish himself as a total dictator whom nobody dared to oppose . . . in the mid-1930s Stalin was engaged in a ruthless purge of his party and setting in motion the machinery of a reign of terror which, it has been estimated, sent some eight million people to labour camps and condemned about a million to death. Trotsky found refuge in Mexico where he was murdered in 1940 by an agent of the Soviet secret police.

Source: James Joll, *Europe Since 1870* (Penguin, 1973, adapted).

Source C

Osip Mandelstam's poem about Stalin, November 1933 (Mandelstam was arrested in May 1934 for writing this poem and he eventually died in a labour camp).

> We live, deaf to the land beneath us,
> Ten steps away no-one hears our speeches,
>
> All we hear is the Kremlin mountaineer,
> The murderer and peasant-slayer.

His fingers are fat as grubs
And the words, final as lead weights, fall from his lips.

His cockroach whiskers leer
And his boot tops gleam.

Source: N. Mandelstam, *Hope against Hope* (Collins, 1971, excerpts).

Source D
A. O. Audienko's poem about Stalin, published in *Pravda*, August 1936.

O Great Stalin, O leader of the peoples,
Thou who broughtest man to birth.
Thou who makes the earth bear fruit,
Thou who restores the centuries,
Thou who makes bloom the spring,
Thou who makes vibrate the musical chords . . .
Thou, splendour of my spring, O Thou,
Sun reflected by millions of hearts.

Source: T. H. Rigby, *Stalin* (Prentice-Hall, 1966, excerpts).

(a)   **(i)** Explain briefly why, according to Source A, Lenin thought it was so important to get rid of Stalin from his post.   **4(a)**

     (ii) Why do you think Lenin chose that particular time to write the letter?   **1,4**

     (iii) Why was Lenin's advice not carried out?   **1**

(b)   **(i)** How does Source B show that some of the things Lenin hoped to avoid, actually happened?   **4(a,c)**

     (ii) According to Source B, how did Stalin differ from Lenin in his treatment of opponents?   **4(a)**

(c) Using your own knowledge, and the evidence of the Sources, explain why you think Osip Mandelstam (Source C) uses the following phrases to describe Stalin:

     (i) Kremlin mountaineer;

     (ii) murderer and peasant-slayer.   **1,4(a)**

Apart from these two phrases, what other evidence is there in the poem that Mandelstam does not like Stalin?   **4(b)**

(d)   **(i)** How does the poet in Source D differ from the one in Source C in his feelings about Stalin?   **4(c)**

     (ii) What reasons can you think of to explain how there can be such widely differing views of the same man at roughly the same time?   **1,4(b)**

(e) Using the evidence provided by Sources A and B, and your own knowledge, explain which of the two poems (Sources C and D) seems to present the more accurate picture of Stalin.   **1,2,4**

3. You are the editor of:
   (a) *Pravda*;
   (b) the *Washington Post*.

In each case, write an obituary notice for Stalin, which would be suitable for inclusion in your paper (he died in 1953).   **1,2,3**

4. Describe how and with what success Stalin:
    (a) Tried to develop industry;
    (b) Tried to increase agricultural production;
    (c) Dealt with political opponents;
    (d) Tried to control the arts.   **1,2**

CHAPTER 10

TURKEY, JAPAN

AND SPAIN

BETWEEN THE WARS

SUMMARY OF EVENTS

These three countries are interesting in their own ways because each illustrates a different reaction to the problems which faced most countries during the 1920s and 1930s, though all three found themselves with undemocratic nationalist governments. *Turkey* provides a good example of a government achieving success with a minimum of fuss and violence; Mustafa Kemal, President of the Turkish republic from 1923 until his death in 1938, became so popular that in 1934 he was able to take the title or surname of Ataturk (father of Turks). The other two countries were much less successful: in *Japan* the government, increasingly embarrassed by economic, financial and political problems, fell under the influence of the military in the early 1930s, with unfortunate consequences for the rest of the world. In *Spain* an incompetent parliamentary government was replaced by General Primo de Rivera who ruled from 1923 until 1930 as a sort of benevolent dictator; the world economic crisis brought him down, and in an atmosphere of growing republicanism *King Alfonso XIII abdicated (1931)*. Various republican governments failed to solve the array of problems facing them and the situation deteriorated into a *civil war (1936–9)* which was won by the right-wing nationalists; their leader, *General Franco*, became head of the government, a position he held until his death in 1975.

10.1 TURKEY

(a) **In 1919 Turkey was a defeated nation**, further humiliated by the *Treaty of Sèvres*, which compelled them to hand over large areas of the country to the Allies (see Section 2.10). This provoked a strong nationalist reaction especially among the educated classes and the army; the lead was taken by *Mustafa Kemal*, a young general who had made a reputation for himself as the commander who beat the British at *Gallipoli* in 1915. He and his supporters were determined not to accept defeat, and denouncing the Sultan and his government at Constantinople

(Istanbul) as 'prisoners of the Allies', they set up a *rival government* at Ankara with Kemal as president. By September 1922 all foreign occupying troops had been removed though the crisis at *Chanak* almost caused war with Britain (see Section 4.1(b)(vii)), the Sultan fled, the monarchy was abolished and the *Treaty of Lausanne (1923)* allowed Turkey more favourable terms. In October 1923 Kemal, leader of the Republican People's Party which he had himself created, was elected *first president* of the Turkish republic.

(b) What were the problems facing the new president, and how successfully did he deal with them?

The fundamental problem was that Turkey was backward in almost every conceivable way, and though Kemal believed in democracy, the necessary reforms were so drastic that serious opposition was bound to occur.

illus 10.1 *Kemal Ataturk reviewing troops, 1922*

This obliged him to rule as a *dictator* for most of his presidency; his policies had considerable success:

(i) As soon as the drastic nature of Kemal's proposed reforms became known, there was strong opposition both inside and outside the National Assembly (parliament), especially from Muslim clerics. A rebellion broke out in 1925 led by a conservative sheikh; Kemal swiftly suppressed it and used it as an excuse to *ban all political parties except his own* and to *take control of the press*. This enabled the first batch of reforms to be carried through successfully. By 1929, Kemal was ready to relax controls and an opposition party was allowed to form; unfortunately after several demonstrations organised by the new party had deteriorated into riots, Kemal decided that his experiment in democracy was premature, and he again banned all opposition parties. Not until 1946 were the Turks allowed another attempt at democracy. However, Kemal's dictatorship, though strict, was *not brutal or aggressive.*

(ii) The country was *backward socially and legally* because of the influence of the Muslim (Islamic) religion which pervaded all aspects of Turkish life including education and law, and held up Turkey's development into a modern state. To bring Turkey into the twentieth century meant an attack on the powers of Islam and the introduction of western methods and customs. After 1928 *Islam was no longer the state religion* and played no part in politics; Turkey was a *secular state* (one free from religious control). New codes of civil and criminal law, the Roman alphabet, western calendar and the weekend were introduced; thousands of new schools were built. The status of women was much improved: polygamy was prohibited, the wearing of the veil discouraged, civil marriage and divorce made legal and in 1934 women were given the vote. Another law compelled Turks to wear western-style clothes, banned the fez and required that all men's hats must have brims. The burden of taxation on the peasants was reduced and primary education made free and compulsory.

(iii) To cure Turkey's *economic weaknesses* Kemal adopted a policy known as *statism* – state interference in as many areas as possible. *Farmers* were encouraged with government subsidies to use the latest techniques and equipment and to join co-operatives; during the great depression of the early 1930s they were directed to produce those crops which were still exportable; consequently peasant farmers came through the depression reasonably well. The *government took over railways, harbours and shipping* and provided funds to expand industries such as textiles, mining, iron and steel, paper, glass and sugar; again, with the help of tariffs and state control of foreign exchange, Turkish industry weathered the depression bettter than most European countries.

By a curious mixture of measures which his critics variously denounced as communist or fascist and by a *foreign policy* which aimed at *friendship with all*, Kemal transformed Turkey. Of course there was still a long way to go: in 1938 she could hardly be classed as a wealthy industrial state, and her farming remained largely primitive. But his achievement was threefold: he had rid Turkey of the ineffective monarchy, restored her national pride, and brought her part of the way along the road to being a modern, westernised state. It is no exaggeration to call him 'the father of modern Turkey'.

10.2 JAPAN

(a) In 1918 Japan was in a strong position in the Far East; she had a powerful navy, a great deal of influence in China, and had benefited economically from the First World War, while the states of Europe were pre-occupied with fighting each other. Japan took advantage of the situation both by providing the Allies with shipping and other goods, and by stepping in to supply orders, especially in Asia, which the Europeans could not fulfil. During the war years her exports of cotton cloth almost trebled, while her merchant fleet doubled in tonnage. Politically the course seemed set fair for democracy when in 1925 all adult males were given the vote. Hopes were soon dashed: at the beginning of the 1930s the army assumed control of the government.

(b) Why did Japan become a military dictatorship?
During the 1920s problems developed, as they did in Italy and Germany, which *democratically elected governments seemed incapable of solving*:

(i) From the beginning democracy was not popular with many *influential groups* in Japanese society, such as the *army* and the *conservatives* who were strongly entrenched in the upper house of parliament (the Peers) and in the Privy Council. They seized every opportunity to discredit the government, criticising for example Baron Shidehara Kijuro (Foreign Minister 1924–7) for his conciliatory approach to China, which he thought was the best way to strengthen Japan's economic hold over that country. The army was itching to interfere in China, which was torn by civil war, and considered Shidehara's policy to be 'soft'. They were strong enough to bring the government down in 1927 and reverse his policy.

(ii) *Many politicians were corrupt* and regularly accepted bribes from big business; sometimes fighting broke out in the lower house (the Diet) as charges and counter-charges of corruption were flung about. The system was not one to inspire confidence and parliamentary prestige suffered accordingly. Neither (i) nor (ii) made military dictatorship inevitable, but when *economic problems* were added to the political ones the situation became serious.

(iii) The great trading boom of the war years lasted only until the middle of 1921 when Europe began to revive and recover lost markets. Unemployment and industrial unrest developed, and at the same time farmers were hit by the rapidly falling price of rice caused by a series of bumper harvests. When farmers and industrial workers tried to organise themselves into a political party, they were ruthlessly suppressed by the police. Thus the workers, as well as the army and the right, gradually became hostile to a parliament which *posed as democratic but allowed the left to be suppressed and accepted bribes from big business*.

(iv) The *world economic crisis beginning* in 1929 (see Section 7.2) affected Japan severely; her exports shrank disastrously and other countries introduced or raised tariffs against her to safeguard their own industries. One of the worst affected trades was the export of *raw silk* which went mostly to the USA. The period after the Wall Street Crash was no time for luxuries, and the Americans drastically reduced their imports of raw silk, so that by 1932 the price had fallen to less than one-fifth of the 1923 figure. This was a further blow for Japanese farmers, since about half of them relied for their livelihood on the production of raw silk as well as rice. There was desperate poverty, especially in the north, for which peasants and factory workers blamed the government and big business. Most of the army recruits were peasants; consequently the rank-and-file as well as the officer class were disgusted with what they took to be weak parliamentary government. Many officers, attracted by fascism, were as early as 1927 planning to seize power and introduce a *strong nationalist government*.

(v) Matters were brought to a head in *1931* by the situation in *Manchuria* where the Chinese were trying to squeeze out Japanese trade and business, which would have been a severe blow to a Japanese economy already hard hit by the depression. To preserve their economic advantages Japanese army units *invaded and occupied Manchuria (September 1931)* without permission from their government. When Prime Minister Inukai criticised extremist action he was *assassinated* by a group of army officers (*May 1932*); his successor felt he had to support the army's actions. For the next 13 years the army more or less ran the country, introducing similar measures to those adopted in *Germany* and *Italy*: ruthless suppression of Marxists, assassination of opponents, tight control of education, a build-up of armaments, and an aggressive foreign policy which aimed to capture territory in Asia as markets for Japanese exports. This led to an attack on *China (1937)* and participation in the Second World War in the Pacific (see Section 15.2(c)). Some historians blame the Emperor Hirohito who, though he deplored the attack on Manchuria, refused to become involved in political controversy, afraid to risk his orders for a withdrawal being ignored. Richard Storry claims that 'it would have been better for Japan and for the world if the risk had been taken'; he believes that Hirohito's prestige was such that the majority of officers would have obeyed him if he had tried to restrain the attacks on Manchuria and China.

10.3 SPAIN

(a) **The constitutional monarchy** under Alfonso XIII (king since 1885) was never very efficient and reached rock bottom in 1921 when a Spanish army sent to put down a revolt led by Abd-el-Krim in Spanish Morocco was massacred by the Moors. In *1923 General Primo de Rivera seized power in a bloodless coup*, with Alfonso's approval, and ruled for the

illus 10.2 *Japanese troops invade Manchuria, 1931*

next seven years. The king called him 'my Mussolini', but though Primo was a military dictator, he was not a fascist. He was responsible for a number of public works – railways, roads and irrigation schemes; industrial production developed at three times the rate before 1923; most impressive of all, he managed to end the war in *Morocco* (*1925*). When the world economic crisis reached Spain in 1930 unemployment rose, Primo and his advisers bungled the finances, causing depreciation of the peseta, and the army withdrew support, whereupon Primo resigned. In April *1931* municipal elections were held in which the *republicans* won all the large cities; as huge crowds gathered on the streets of Madrid, Alfonso decided to abdicate to avoid bloodshed, and a *republic was proclaimed*. The monarchy had been overthrown without bloodshed, but unfortunately the slaughter had merely been *postponed until 1936*.

(b) Why did civil war break out in Spain?

(i) The new republic was faced by a number of *serious problems*: Catalonia and the Basque provinces wanted independence; the Roman Catholic Church was bitterly hostile to the republic, which in return disliked the church and was determined to reduce its power; it was felt that the army had too much influence in politics and might attempt another coup; there were the additional problems caused by the depression: agricultural prices were falling, wine and olive oil exports declined, land went out of cultivation and peasant unemployment rose; in industry iron production fell by a third and steel production by almost half; it was a time of falling wages, unemployment and falling standards of living. Unless it could make some headway with this final problem, *the republic was likely to lose the support of the workers*.

(ii) The left's solutions to these problems were not acceptable to the right, which became increasingly alarmed at the prospect of *social revolution*. The dominant group in the *Cortes* (parliament) the socialists and middle-class radicals, began energetically: *Catalonia* was allowed some *self-government*; an attack was made on the *church* (church and state were separated, priests would not be paid by the government, Jesuits were expelled, other orders could be dissolved, and religious education ceased); a large number of *army officers* were compulsorily retired; a start was made on the *nationalisation of large estates*; and attempts were made to *raise industrial wages*. Each of these measures infuriated one or other of the right-wing groups (church, army, landowners and industrialists); in 1932 some army officers tried to overthrow the Prime Minister, *Manuel Azana*, but the rising was easily suppressed, as the majority of the army remained loyal at this stage. A new right-wing party, the *Ceda*, was formed to defend the church and the landlords.

(iii) The republic was further weakened by opposition from two powerful *left-wing groups*, the *anarchists* and the *syndicalists* (certain powerful trade unions) who favoured a general strike and the overthrow of the capitalist system; they despised the socialists for co-operating with the middle-class groups. They organised strikes, riots and assassinations; matters came to a head in *January 1933* when government guards set fire to some houses in the village of *Casas Viejas* near Cadiz, to smoke out some anarchists; 25 people were killed, which lost the government much working-class support, and caused even the socialists to withdraw support from Azana, who resigned. In the following elections (*November 1933*) the right-wing parties won a majority, the largest group being the new Catholic *Ceda* under its leader *Gil Robles*.

(iv) The actions of the new right-wing government aroused the left to fury: they cancelled most of Azana's reforms, interfered with the working of the new Catalan government and refused to allow the Basques self-government, a serious error since the Basques had supported the right in the elections, but now switched to the left. As the government moved further right, the left-wing groups (socialists, anarchists, syndicalists and now communists) drew closer together to form a *Popular Front*. Revolutionary violence grew: anarchists derailed the Barcelona–Seville express killing 19 people; there was a general strike in 1934, as well as rebellions in Catalonia and Asturias. The miners of Asturias fought bravely but were crushed ruthlessly by troops under the command of General Franco. In the words of Hugh Thomas, 'after the manner in which the revolution had been quelled, it would have required a superhuman effort to avoid the culminating disaster of civil war. But no such effort was forthcoming'. Instead, as the financial situation deteriorated as well as the political one, the right fell apart, and in the elections of February 1936 the *Popular Front* emerged victorious.

(v) The new government turned out to be *ineffective*, since the socialists decided not to support it, hoping to seize power when the middle-class republican government failed. The government seemed incapable of keeping order, the climax coming in *July 1936*, when *Calvo Sotelo*, the leading right-wing politician, was *murdered* by police. This terrified the right and convinced them that the only way to restore order was by a *military dictatorship*. A number of generals conspiring with the right, especially with the new fascist *Falange* party of *José Antonio de Rivera* (Primo's son), had already planned a military takeover. Using Calvo Sotelo's murder as an excuse, they began a revolt in Morocco, where *General Franco* soon assumed the leadership. *The civil war had begun.*

(c) The civil war 1936–9

By the end of July 1936, the *right* (calling themselves *nationalists*) controlled most of the *north*, while the *republicans* controlled most of the *south*, including Madrid. The following struggle was a bitter one in which both sides committed terrible atrocities. The *nationalists* were helped by *Italy* and *Germany* who sent arms and men; the *republicans* received some help from *Russia* but France and Britain refused to intervene, merely allowing volunteers to fight in Spain. The war ended in *March 1939*, when the nationalists captured *Madrid*.

(i) *Reasons for the nationalist victory* were that Franco was extremely skilful in holding together the various right-wing groups (army, church, monarchists and Falangists); the republicans were much less united (anarchists and communists actually fought each other for a time in Barcelona). The extent of *foreign help* was probably *decisive*: this included 60,000 Italian troops, a large Italian air force, and hundreds of German planes and tanks. One of the most notorious actions was the German bombing of the defenceless Basque town of *Guernica*, in which over 1600 people were killed.

(ii) Franco, taking the title *Caudillo* (leader) set up a government on the *fascist model*, marked by repression and at first mass executions; he was shrewd enough to remain neutral in the Second World War, and consequently survived his supporters, Hitler and Mussolini. He ruled until his death in 1975.

QUESTIONS

1. The bombing of Guernica, 26 April 1937
Study the Sources below, and then answer the questions that follow.

Source A
Extracts from en eye-witness account of the bombing.

> Until the past week, thought IGNACIA OZAMIZ, with the exception of food shortages and the dead being brought from the front for burial, the war had hardly affected Guernica. Lying to the north-east of Bilbao, Guernica, a town of 6000 inhabitants, was a symbol of liberty and tradition for the Basques. In a few hours it became the universal symbol of fascist terror. They hadn't taken adequate precautions against air-raids, though there were some crude shelters. First a solitary Heinkel flew over and dropped half a dozen bombs. Then she saw another nine planes appear, flying low, and she threw herself on the ground as the first bombs fell. Some crashed on the nearby hospital. Then fighters dived down and machine-gunned people trying to flee. After the high explosive bombs, successive waves of planes dropped incendiaries. The town was beginning to burn, the wooden rafters catching alight and a pall of smoke was rising into the sky . . . when we left the shelfter we saw that our house and everything in sight was burning . . . How could they say the Reds had done it when they hardly had a single plane, poor souuuls?

Source: Ronald Fraser, *Blood of Spain* (Penguin, 1979, extracts).

Source B

The Nationalists maintained that Guernica had been blown up by Basques themselves, in order to discredit the blameless nationalists. A later version said that Republican planes dropped bombs to detonate charges of dynamite placed in the sewers. Twenty years later it was still a crime in Franco's Spain to say that Guernica had been destroyed by the Nationalists.

Source: David Mitchell, *The Spanish Civil War* (Granada, 1971).

Source C
A statement by Juana Sangroniz, a Nationalist.

Our consciences were uneasy about it. After living through the raid we knew only too well that the destruction had come from the air. The Reds had hardly any planes, we knew that too. Amongst our own, we'd admit the truth: our side had bombed the town and it was a bad thing. 'But what can we do about it now?' we'd say. It was better simply to keep quiet.

Source: Ronald Fraser, *Blood of Spain* (Penguin, 1979).

Source D

A Nationalist officer admitted to a reporter from the *Sunday Times* in August [1937] that Guernica had been bombed by his side . . .Years later, the German air ace, Adolph Galland, admitted that the Germans were responsible. He argued that the attack was an error, caused by bad bomb sights and lack of experience. The Germans, he said, were trying for the bridge over the river, missed it completely, and by mistake, destroyed the town. The Germans said the wind caused the bombs to drift westwards. In fact Guernica was a military target, being a communications centre close to the battle line. Retreating republican soldiers could only escape with any ease through Guernica because the bridge across the river was the last one before the sea. But if the aim of the [German] Condor Legion was to destroy the bridge why did they not use their supremely accurate Stuka bombers? At least part of the aim must have been to cause maximum panic and confusion among civilians as well as soldiers. The use of incendiary bombs proves that some destruction of buildings and people other than the bridge must have been intended.

Source: Hugh Thomas, *The Spanish Civil War* (Penguin, 1977, 3rd edn).

(a)   (i)   According to Source D, what was the name of the group of German planes which attacked Guernica?   **4(a)**

     (ii) Why was Guernica important to the Basques, according to Source A?   **4(a)**

(b) **(i)** From the evidence of Source A, how badly had Guernica felt the effects of the civil war up to the time of the bombing?

$$4(a)$$

    (ii) Using the evidence in Source A, describe in your own words the various different phases of the attack on Guernica. **4(a)**

(c) **(i)** According to Source B, who was responsible for the attack?

$$4(a)$$

    (ii) How did the two methods of attack mentioned in Source B differ from each other? **4(a)**

    (iii) Why do you think there were two different Nationalist versions of the attack? **4(a,b)**

(d) How does the evidence in Sources A, C and D contradict the claims made in Source B about who was responsible for the attack?

$$4(a,c)$$

(e) **(i)** According to Adolph Galland in Source D, what was the target of the attack? **4(a)**

    (ii) What reasons does Hugh Thomas (Source D) suggest for this choice of target? **4(a)**

    (iii) What evidence does Hugh Thomas give to support his claim that the real aim of the attack was something different? **4(a)**

    (iv) What extra piece of evidence (not mentioned in Source D) does Source A provide which supports Hugh Thomas's claim?

$$4(a,c)$$

(f) Of the four Sources A, B, C and D, which do you think is the most valuable to the historian trying to find out who was to blame for the attack on Guernica? Explain your choice. **4(a,b)**

2. The Shenyang Incident, September 1931

Study the Sources below, and then answer the questions that follow.

Source A

Extract adapted from the official report of the Chinese Provincial Government of Liaoning, 19 September 1931:

> At 10 o'clock last night, Japanese railway guards picked a quarrel by blowing up a section of the South Manchurian Railway at Huangutun, and subsequently accused the Chinese military of having done this. The Japanes troops immediately staged a surprise attack upon Beidaying, bombarding the place at random . . . at 5.30 a.m. large groups of Japanese soldiers began entering the city of Shenyang (Mukden) and immediately occupied all government buildings.

Source: A. C. Morales, *East Meets West 1920–1980* (Macmillan, 1986).

Source B

Extracts adapted from an official Japanese statement on Manchuria, 24 September 1931.

The conduct of Chinese officials for some years past has been such that our national sentiment has frequently been irritated. In particular, unpleasant incidents have taken place one after another in the regions of Manchuria and Mongolia. Amidst the atmosphere of anxiety thus created, a detachment of Chinese troops destroyed the tracks of the South Manchurian Railway in the vicinity of Shenyang and attacked our railway guards at midnight on September 18. In order to forestall an imminent disaster, the Japanese army had to act swiftly . . . It may be unnecessary to repeat that the Japanese government has no plans to take over Manchurian territory.

Source: A. C. Morales, *East Meets West 1920–1980* (Macmillan, 1986).

Source C

After the Second World War, new evidence revealed that Japanese military extremists planned the whole incident so that it could be used as an excuse for direct military action against China to resolve the Manchurian issue. The plotters were led by two senior officers. Only a few weeks before the explosion, one of them informed Major-General Tatekawa of the General Staff Headquarters in Tokyo, and General Honjo, of plans to create an incident to be used as an excuse for the takeover of Manchuria.

The two generals raised no objections at that time. Tatekawa was, however, later sent by Tokyo to Manchuria with a message allegedly ordering Honjo to cancel whatever plans had been drawn up for military action against China. But he failed to deliver this message. Fighting began that night. Shenyang and other strategic points were soon occupied by Japanese troops, and the conquest of Manchuria began.

Source: A. C. Morales, *East Meets West 1920–1980* (Macmillan, 1986, extracts).

(a)   (i)   What differences are there between Sources A and B about the timing of the Shenyang incident?   **4(a,c)**

    (ii)   Explain in your own words the ways in which Source B differs from Source A in its explanation of how the fighting began.   **4(a,c)**

(b)   (i)   According to the evidence in Source C, which of the two versions (Source A or B) seems to be the correct one?   **4(a,b,c)**

    (ii)   What evidence in Source C seems to suggest that the statement in the last sentence of Source B was false?   **4(a,c)**

    (iii)   What does the evidence in the second paragraph of Source C suggest to you about the Japanese leadership?   **4(a)**

(c)   (i)   Explain why Japan was so interested in Manchuria.   **1,2**

    (ii)   What events happened in Japan itself as a result of the Japanese attack on Manchuria?   **1,2**

    (iii) What was the attitude of the Emperor Hirohito to the Japanese attack? **1,2**

(d)   **(i)** What did the League of Nations do about the Japanese invasion? **1,2**

    (ii) Why was no international action taken to remove Japanese troops from Manchuria? **1,2**

(e) Describe the relations between Japan and China during the ten years following the attack on Manchuria. **1,2**

3. It is 1938, and Turkey is mourning the death of Mustafa Kemal, known since 1934 as 'Ataturk' (father of Turks). Write a sympathetic obituary to appear in a newspaper, mentioning among other things:
   (a) Mustafa Kemal's rise to prominence and his overthrow of the monarchy;
   (b) his election as president and his handling of the 1925 rebellion:
   (c) his successful social and legal policy;
   (d) his policy of statism. **1,2,3**

4. **(a)** Describe how Japan benefited from the First World War.
   (b) Why did Japan become a military dictatorship in the early 1930s?
   (c) Explain how Japan became involved in war, first with China and then with the allies in the Second World War. **1,2**

5. **(a)** Describe the events which led to the abdication of King Alfonso XIII of Spain in 1931.
   (b) Explain why a civil war broke out in 1936.
   (c) Why did the Nationalists defeat the Republicans? **1,2**

CHAPTER 11

THE EMPIRES BETWEEN THE WARS

SUMMARY OF EVENTS

Most of the states of Europe had *overseas empires*, built up during the nineteenth century or earlier, of which the greatest in area was the British empire; it included vast tracts of Africa, Malaya, India, Burma, the West Indies, and a special feature which no other empire could boast – the white dominions – Canada, Australia, New Zealand and South Africa. *France* had the second largest empire, with territories in Africa, Indo-China and the West Indies. Both empires had been swelled by the mandates taken from Germany and Turkey in the *peace settlement at the end of the First World War* (see Sections 2.8 and 2.10). Other important empires were those of *Holland* (East Indies), *Belgium* (Congo), and *Portugal* (Mozambique, Angola and Guinea). Italy and Spain also had territory in Africa (see Fig. 2.4).

After 1918 *nationalist movements* aiming at independence developed in many of these empires. Britain had trouble in India, Egypt, the Arab mandates and Ireland; even the white dominions were unhappy about exactly what the term 'dominion status' involved, and pressed for a clear definition. France faced revolutionary nationalism in Indo-China and the Arab mandates as did the Dutch in the East Indies. On the whole Africa remained quiet between the wars and nationalism scarcely existed in the Belgian Congo and the Portuguese colonies; however, the Spanish had to deal with a troublesome revolt in Morocco led by Abd-el-Krim. All these territories eventually gained *independence*, a few before 1939, but most of them after the Second World War.

It is interesting to compare the *attitudes* of the three main colonial powers to the growth of nationalism. *Britain compromised*, claiming that her territories would be allowed to proceed to independence in gradual stages; and indeed southern Ireland was granted dominion status (1922), Egypt semi-independence (1922) and Iraq full independence (1932); the Statute of Westminster (1931) satisfied the dominions about their relationship with Britain and saw the formation of the British commonwealth; however, progress in India was far too gradual for the nationalists' liking. *France* took quite a different view and *refused to make any concessions* to nationalist feeling which was ruthlessly suppressed in Syria and Indo-China. The *Dutch attitude lay somewhere between*: there was talk of independence for the Dutch East Indies, but when slow progress caused revolts in Java (1926–7), determined repression followed. Finally against the general trend, when nineteenth-century-style imperialism was out of fashion, two countries, *Italy* (in Abyssinia) and *Japan* (in China), were trying to *extend their overseas empires during the 1930s*.

11.1 BRITAIN AND THE COMMONWEALTH

(a) **Britain's white dominions**, Canada, Australia and New Zealand, as well as South Africa, and the Irish Free State (since 1922), were already *self-governing* as far as *internal* affairs were concerned, but had to act along with Britain for foreign policy, which was one of the reasons why they all fought on Britain's side in the *First World War*. By the end of the war a desire to run their own foreign affairs had developed, partly because the war had made them more aware of their importance as separate nations (together they had put over a million men in the field); in addition they were encouraged by *Woodrow Wilson*'s support for the principle of *national independence*, and they were worried in case Britain should drag them into another war. Consequently Canada and South Africa refused to help Britain during the Chanak incident (see Section 4.1(b)(vii)), and they all refused to sign the treaties of Lausanne in 1923 (see Section 2.10) and Locarno in 1925 (see Section 13.1(e)). South Africa in particular became increasingly hostile to Britain and seemed determined to leave the empire. Clearly some initiative was needed, and happily for the future of the *commonwealth*, as it was beginning to be called, this was taken.

(b) **The Imperial Conference of 1926**. Under the chairmanship of *Balfour* the former Conservative Prime Minister, the conference showed that Britain was prepared to conciliate the dominions. Balfour produced a famous formula which *defined the dominions as free countries*, equal to each other and to Britain, and in complete control of their own internal and foreign affairs; they were to be 'freely associated as members of the British Commonwealth of Nations'. This satisfied the dominions (even South Africa for the time being) and was passed through the British parliament as the *Statute of Westminster (1931)*. The commonwealth was a unique experiment in international organisation but because of the degree of independence enjoyed by the dominions, the achievements of the new 'white man's club', as it was described, were often something of a disappointment. There was no commonwealth parliament or other set machinery for co-operation to take place, though during the depression of the 1930s some trading agreements were made. In addition the Irish Free State under de Valera was unco-operative.

11.2 BRITAIN AND IRELAND 1916–39

In the summer of 1914 the Third Irish Home Rule Bill, which would have given *self-government* to Ireland, was about to become law. Unfortunately this was no solution to the problems of Ireland since Ulster in the north (with its Protestant majority) wanted to remain with Britain, and it was only the outbreak of war in 1914 which put the situation on ice for the time being. The operation of the act was postponed until the end of the war. The British government hoped that Ireland would remain quiet for the duration of the war, but their hopes were dashed when violence broke out again at *Easter 1916*.

(a) What were the problems in Ireland between 1916 and 1923, and how did British governments try to solve them?

(i) Though the majority of the Irish seemed prepared to wait until the war was over for Home Rule (thousands actually volunteered to fight for Britain against the Germans), a minority, mainly a group called *Sinn Fein* (meaning 'ourselves alone' – freedom from British rule), hoped to seize *independence* while Britain was preoccupied with the war. In 1916 they launched the *Easter Rebellion* proclaiming a republic and seizing several strong points in Dublin, including the General Post Office, in the hope that the rest of the country would rise in sympathy and force the British to withdraw. However, *no sympathetic rising* took place and British troops soon put an end to the rebellion which was militarily a total failure.

(ii) Though the rebellion was over within a few days, *British treatment of the rebels* caused a wave of disgust throughout Ireland and the USA with its large Irish population. Fifteen of the leaders were shot; one of them, James Connolly, was already dying of gunshot wounds and, being unable to stand, was shot sitting in a chair. This caused many more people to want a complete break with Britain, not just Home Rule, and there was a rush of support for *Sinn Fein*, which set about organising the powerful *IRA* (Irish Republican Army).

(iii) There was still a chance that the Irish might be pacified if Home Rule could be introduced immediately. Lloyd George got the Ulstermen and Home Rule supporters together (1917) and persuaded them to agree to a Home Rule scheme, thus detaching the Home Rulers from *Sinn Fein*. Unfortunately the British Conservatives (Unionists) who were against Home Rule and wanted the Irish to be repressed refused to accept the scheme; consequently what was probably the last chance of settling the Irish problem peacefully was lost.

(iv) The problem developed a stage further when in the British general election of December 1918 *Sinn Fein* won 73 out of the 105 Irish seats, but instead of going to the British parliament at Westminster they proclaimed an *independent Irish Republic* with their own parliament (*Dail Eireann* – Assembly of Ireland) in Dublin, and elected *Eamonn de Valera* as leader. He was one of the few surviving leaders of the Easter Rising and became the symbol of Irish republicanism. Together with Michael Collins and Arthur Griffith, he organised an effective government which ignored the British and ran the country in its own way, collecting taxes and setting up law courts. The British Prime Minister, Lloyd George, hoped that the Government of Ireland Act (February 1920) would win moderate support back to the British. This was a revised version of the original Home Rule Bill of 1912, delayed by the Lords and then by the war; this time Ireland was *partitioned*, with one parliament for the south at Dublin and another for the six counties of Ulster at Belfast. The Belfast parliament was for the benefit of the Ulster Protestants, who still refused to be ruled by a Dublin-based Roman Catholic government. Although Ulster reluctantly accepted their parliament, *Sinn Fein* rejected the entire act, because it gave them control only of certain domestic matters, whereas they were determined on a complete break with Britain; also they wanted control of Ulster.

(v)   Violence continued as the IRA pursued a campaign of *terrorism* against the police (Royal Irish Constabulary). Lloyd George retaliated by letting loose the notorious *Black and Tans* (recently demobilised British soldiers) against the IRA, and both sides committed terrible atrocities. By the summer of 1921 Lloyd George realised that such a situation could not continue; under pressure from Labour, from many Liberals and from King George V, who hated the British campaign of violence and pleaded for peace and common sense, Lloyd George decided to try negotiations. The IRA, close to exhaustion, responded, and Lloyd George managed to persuade both *Sinn Fein* and the British Conservatives to sign a treaty (*December 1921*). *Southern Ireland* became *independent* with the same status as the dominions, and accepted membership of the commonwealth; the British navy was to be allowed to use three ports.

(vi) The troubles were still not over: a section of *Sinn Fein*, led by *de Valera*, *refused to accept the settlement* because of the partition and the remaining connection with Britain, and *civil war* broke out between the two *Sinn Fein* factions. This ended in *April 1923* with a victory for supporters of the treaty. *The Irish Free State came into existence officially in December 1922.*

(b) The relationship between Britain and the Irish Free State after 1923 continued to change gradually. De Valera formed a new party, *Fianna Fail* (Soldiers of Destiny) which won the election of 1932, mainly because the slump and unemployment had made the government of William Cosgrave highly unpopular. De Valera, Prime Minister for the next 16 years, set about *destroying the links with Britain*, though without taking the final step of declaring a republic. The oath of allegiance to the British

illus 11.1 *Sinn Feiners held up at pistol point by the Black and Tans, 1920*

monarch was ignored and in *1937* a *new constitution* was introduced making Eire *completely independent in practice*. Neville Chamberlain, the British Prime Minister, made concessions in the hope of winning Eire's friendship. Debts amounting to £100 million still owing by Eire were written off, and the three naval bases handed back. However, Eire remained unco-operative: de Valera would never be satisfied until he controlled Ulster. Consequently Eire took *no part in the commonwealth*, remained *neutral* during the Second World War, and in *1949* finally declared itself an *independent republic*.

11.3 THE INDIAN STRUGGLE FOR INDEPENDENCE

(a) **Indian nationalism** began in the late nineteenth century when many middle-class Indians, having received a British-style education, often at Oxford or Cambridge, felt frustrated that their country continued to be run by the British while they were allowed *no say in government* and only a very *minor role in local affairs*. They founded a party called the *Indian National Congress (1885)* to press for greater participation by Indians in government, in response to which the British introduced the 1909 *Morley–Minto reforms* (Morley was the Secretary of State for India, Lord Minto the Viceroy, who ruled India on behalf of the King). Indians were allowed to sit on the executive councils which advised the provincial governors, and for the time being the Indians seemed satisfied. After 1914 nationalist feeling intensified, probably encouraged by the *important contribution made by Indians to the war effort*, and perhaps by the successful revolutions in Russia and by Woodrow Wilson's talk of self-determination for subject peoples.

(b) **How did the British government deal with the demands for Indian independence?**
The British were slowly coming round to the idea that India would have to be given a *measure of self-government*; in 1917 the Indians were promised 'the gradual development of self-governing institutions with a view to the progressive realisation of responsible government in India as an integral part of the British Empire'. However, many Conservatives, including Winston Churchill and Lord Birkenhead (Secretary of State for India from 1924 to 1928) were utterly opposed to the idea, although the pace was far too slow for the impatient nationalists, whose leaders, *Mahatma Gandhi* and *Jawaharlal Nehru*, both lawyers educated in London, organised the *anti-British campaign*. There were four stages in the gradual move towards independence before the Second World War broke out.

  (i) In 1918 Montagu (Secretary of State for India) and Lord Chelmsford (Viceroy), put forward plans which eventually became the *government of India Act (1919)*. There was to be a *national parliament* with two houses; about five million of the wealthiest Indians were given the vote; in the provincial governments the ministers of education, health and public works could now be Indians; a commission would be held ten years later to decide whether India was ready for further concessions. Congress was bitterly disappointed because the British kept complete control of the *central government* and of the *key provincial ministries* such as law and order and taxation. Moreover the Indians were enraged at the slowness with which the British put even these limited advances into operation. Rioting broke out and at *Amritsar* in the Punjab, after 5 Europeans had been murdered, General Dyer dispersed an excited crowd of over 5000 Indians with machinegun fire, killing 379. Order was soon restored, but the Amritsar massacre was an important turning point: it provoked so much fury that *Congress was transformed from a middle-class party to a mass movement.* 'After Amritsar', writes Martin Gilbert, 'no matter what compromises and concessions the British might suggest, British rule would ultimately be swept away.' By this time *Gandhi* was the leading figure of Congress. He believed in non-violent protest and the equality of the classes. Always dressed as a simple peasant, he somehow managed by sheer force of personality to persuade Indians to refuse to work, stage sit-down strikes, fast, stop paying taxes and boycott elections. Unfortunately he was unable to control his more extreme supporters and *violence* often developed; in 1922 he called off his first non-co-operation campaign.

(ii) The next British move, apart from putting Gandhi in gaol, was to appoint the *Simon Commission* (1928), as mentioned in the 1919 Act. In 1930 this proposed self-government for the provinces but was treated with contempt by the Indians, who were not even represented on the commission and who were demanding immediate *dominion status.* As soon as he was out of gaol Gandhi began his second civil disobedience campaign by breaking the law that only the government could manufacture salt. After a sym-

illus 11.2 *Mahatma Gandhi addressing a crowd in Bombay*

bolic 250-mile march to the sea, he produced salt from seawater; but again violent incidents developed and again Gandhi was arrested.

(iii) *Lord Irwin* (Viceroy 1926–31) was a humane and enlightened politician, sympathetic to the Indians; before the Simon Report appeared in 1930 he had expressed the view that dominion status must come, so that the Indians felt even more let down when the report made no mention of it. Irwin was convinced that negotiations must take place and consequently two *Round Table Conferences* (1930 and 1931) were held in London. The first was unsatisfactory because, although the Indian princes were represented and accepted the idea of an Indian federation, no Congress representatives were there: most of them were in prison. Irwin had them released and prevailed upon Gandhi to travel to London to attend the second conference, much to the horror of Churchill who described Gandhi as 'this malignant and subversive fanatic'. Again little progress was made, this time because of disagreements about *Muslim representation* in an independent Indian parliament.

(iv) A major step towards independence was the *Government of India Act (1935)*, introduced as a result of co-operation between MacDonald and Baldwin, and in spite of bitter opposition from Churchill. The *elected Indian assembly* was to have a say in *everything except defence and foreign affairs*; the *eleven provincial assemblies* were to have *more or less full control over local affairs*. The nationalists were still not satisfied: the act fell short of dominion status (the white dominions controlled their own defence and foreign policies), and the princes who still ruled certain areas of India refused to co-operate; thus their areas remained outside the system. Another failure of the act was that it ignored the *religious rivalry* between *Hindus and Muslims*. Roughly two-thirds of the Indians were Hindus and the next largest group, the Muslims (who believed in the Islamic religion) were afraid that in a democratic India they would be dominated and unfairly treated by the Hindus. When Nehru's Congress party, which was overwhelmingly Hindu, won control of eight out of the eleven provinces in the 1937 elections, the Muslim League under its leader *M. A. Jinnah* demanded a separate state of their own called *Pakistan*, while Congress and Gandhi were determined to preserve a united India. No further developments took place before the Second World War, but mounting Hindu/Muslim hostility boded ill for the future, and provided some justification for the British reluctance to grant full self-government.

11.4 BRITAIN AND HER MIDDLE EAST MANDATES

In *1916* the *Arabs in the Turkish empire rose in revolt*, and helped by the British Colonel T. E. Lawrence (Lawrence of Arabia) and later by

British troops under Allenby, they played an important part in liberating the Arab territories from Turkish control. As a bribe to win Arab support against Turkey, the British had made vague promises that when the war was over, the Arabs would be allowed to set up independent states; but about the same time (1916) doubtless under the pressures of war, the British had also made the contradictory Sykes–Picot agreement with France, whereby Turkey's Arab lands would be divided between the two of them. In 1919 therefore, to their intense disappointment, the Arabs found their territories handed over as mandates (to be 'looked after' and prepared for self-government) to Britain (Iraq, Transjordan and Palestine) and France (Syria and Lebanon). Again Britain was reluctant to sever all connections with her mandates because of the Middle East *oil resources*, particularly in Iraq, and wanted to be allowed to station troops there to guarantee a sure source of oil. On the other hand the British dared not offend the Arabs too deeply or oil supplies might equally be threatened. Consequently *steady progress towards independence* was made in *Iraq* and *Transjordan*, though with strings attached; however the situation in *Palestine* was complicated by the *Jewish/Arab problem*.

(a) **In Iraq**, after some initial nationalist rioting, the British set up an Iraqi national government in which each minister had a British adviser. The *Amir Feisal* (who had just been driven out of Syria by the French) was accepted as king. Although extreme nationalists did not approve, this set-up was agreed by the Anglo-Iraqi Treaty of 1922 and worked well. An elected parliament was introduced in 1924 and Feisal, a man of great personal charm and political ability, proved to be an excellent ruler. With British help, industry and agriculture were organised and an efficient administrative system introduced; the British won Iraqi support by successfully opposing Turkish claims to the province of Mosul with its vast oil resources. In *1932 Iraq became fully independent*, though Britain was allowed to keep two air bases; according to one Arab nationalist, George Antonius, 'the modern state of Iraq owes its existence largely to the efforts and devotion of its British officials'.

(b) **In Transjordan** the British set up Feisal's brother Abdullah as king, and allowed him to run the country's internal affairs, which he did competently. However, Transjordan was a poor state, lacking in resources and with no oil, and was therefore dependent on Britain for subsidies and for defence. In *1946* it was given *complete independence*, though Abdullah kept on the British officers who led his army.

(c) **Palestine** proved to be the most troublesome mandate because of the growing hostility between *Jews* and *Arabs*. The problem originated about two thousand years earlier in AD 71 when most of the Jews were driven out of Palestine, their homeland, by the Romans. In fact small communities of Jews remained behind in Palestine and over the following seventeen hundred years there was a gradual trickle of Jews returning from exile, though until the end of the nineteenth century there were never enough to cause the Palestinian Arabs to feel threatened. However, in 1897 some European Jews founded the *World Zionist Organisation* at Basle in Switzerland, an event which was to be of profound importance for the Middle East. Greatly disturbed by the recent persecution of Jews in Russia, Germany and France, the Zionists demanded a *Jewish national home in Palestine*. Even before they received the mandate over Palestine, the British had become involved in the controversy and must take much of the blame for the chaos that followed, especially after 1945.

(d) How did Britain become involved, and how did the situation develop up to 1939?

(i) During the First World War the British had made three contradictory promises, which were bound to lead to frustration and hostility. There were the two already mentioned: independent states for the Arabs and the partition of the Arab territories between Britain and France; the third was the *Balfour Declaration (November 1917)* in which the British Foreign Minister pledged British support for a Jewish 'national home' in Palestine. The British motive, apart from genuine sympathy with the Zionists, was a belief that the Jews would help to *safeguard the Suez Canal* and provide a *buffer between the canal zone and the French in Syria.*

(ii) Faced with bitter Arab protests both against the British failure to grant independence and against the arrival of increasing numbers of Jews, the British government stated (*1922*) that there was no intention that the Jews should occupy the whole of Palestine and that there would be no interference with the rights of the Arabs in Palestine. The British hoped to persuade Jews and Arabs to live together peacefully in the same state and they *failed to understand the deep religious gulf between the two.*

(iii) Jews continued to arrive complete with Zionist money, bought land from Arabs who were at first willing to sell, started industries and reclaimed land. It was soon clear that they intended to develop not just a national home but a *Jewish national state*; by 1928 there were 150,000 of them. The Arabs rioted and began murdering Jews and consequently in 1930 the British Labour government decided that Jewish immigration must cease for the time being. Now it was the turn of the Zionists to rage against the British to such an extent that MacDonald felt obliged to allow immigration to continue.

(iv) The situation took a turn for the worse after Hitler came to power in Germany (1933): Nazi persecution caused a flood of refugees until by 1935 about a *quarter of the total population of Palestine was Jewish*. Arabs again began to attack Jews while British troops struggled to keep order.

(v) In 1937, the British *Peel Commission* suggested dividing Palestine into two separate states, one Jewish, one Arab, but the Arabs rejected the idea.

(vi) As war loomed in 1939 the British felt the need to win Arab support, and in a White Paper they agreed to limit Jewish immigration to 10,000 a year and promised to set up an independent Arab state in ten years, thus guaranteeing an Arab majority in the new state. At this point, with nothing resolved, the British hoped to *shelve the problem until after the war* (see Chapter 26).

QUESTIONS

1. The Indian Struggle for Independence
Study the Sources below, and then answer the questions that follow.

Source A
From a speech by Gandhi in 1920.

> Those who realise their responsibility and the seriousness of the cause, will not act independently, but together with the committee. Success depends entirely upon disciplined and concerted non-cooperation and the latter is dependent upon strict obedience to instructions, calmness and absolute freedom from violence.

> [Reproduced by permission of the Midland Examining Group.]

Source B
From the 'Declaration of Independence' issued by Congress in India, January 1930.

> We hold it to be a crime against man and God to submit any longer to a rule that has caused disaster in our country. We recognise, however, that the most effective way of gaining our freedom is not through violence.

> [Reproduced by permission of the Midland Examining Group.]

Source C

> Lord Irwin's Viceroyalty (1926–31) is now seen to have been a masterpiece of character and understanding. He followed a humane and realistic policy. The demand for Dominion Status was now being overtaken by the campaign for complete independence. While maintaining law and order and acting firmly in the face of civil disobedience, Irwin realised that negotiation would have to come. He decided that there should be a conference attended by representatives from Britain, the Indian States and British India. This was announced in the 'Indian Gazette' on 31 October 1929. In a separate letter in the

same issue, Irwin stated that the granting of Dominion Status was contained in the 1917 declaration.

Source: R. R. James, *Churchill: a study in Failure* (Weidenfeld & Nicolson, 1970, adapted).

Source D
Extracts from speeches by Churchill, 1929–35.

The rescue of India from ages of barbarism, internal war and tyranny, and its slow but ceaseless march forward to civilisation constitutes the finest achievement of our history. It is therefore the duty of public men to make it plain without delay that the extension of Dominion Status to India is not practicable at the present time and that any attempt to secure it will meet the resistance of the British nation.

We have 45 millions in this island, a very large proportion of whom are in existence because of our world position – economic, political, imperial – we are dependent for our daily bread on our trade. If, guided by advice of madness and cowardice disguised as false benevolence, you troop home from India, you will leave behind you a bloody chaos. You will find famine to greet you when you return home, and at least a third of our population must vanish speedily from the face of the earth. We must hold our own or lose our all.

Source: R. R. James, *Churchill: a study in Failure* (Weidenfeld & Nicolson, 1970, adapted).

Source E
Extracts adapted from the Simon Commission Report, 1930.

No one of either race ought to be so foolish as to deny the greatness of the contribution which Britain has made to Indian progress. It is a tremendous achievement to have brought to India impartial justice and the rule of law, equal rights for all classes and religious groups and an impartial and honest civil service, free from corruption. These are essential elements in any state which is advancing towards self-government.

Source: J. H. Bettey (ed.), *English Historical Documents* (Routledge & Kegan Paul, 1967).

(a)   (i) How did Gandhi carry out his policy of non-cooperation mentioned in Source A?   **1,4(a)**

    (ii) Did his followers always obey his instructions about non-violence?   **1**

(b) Who or what was 'Congress' who issued the Declaration in Source B?   **1,4(a)**

(c)   (i) According to Source C, how had the situation in India changed by 1929?   **4(a)**

  (ii) From the evidence of Source C, in what ways did Irwin pursue a 'humane and realistic policy'?   **4(a)**

  (iii) What success did Irwin's policies have?   **1**

(d) (i) What is meant by 'Dominion Status' mentioned in Sources C and D?   **1**

  (ii) In Source D, what was Churchill's opinion about giving Dominion Status to India?   **4(a)**

  (iii) What reasons does he give to justify his opinion?   **4(a)**

  (iv) Why did Churchill think there would be 'a bloody chaos' if the British left India?   **1,4(a)**

  (v) How did Churchill's views about India differ from those of Lord Irwin (Source C)?   **4(c)**

(e) (i) According to the Simon Commission Report (Source E) what benefits had British rule brought to India?   **4(a)**

  (ii) How does Source B seem to contradict Source E?   **4(c)**

  (iii) Why did the Indians not approve of the Simon Commission, or its Report?   **1,4**

  (iv) What are the weaknesses of Sources B, D and E for the historian?   **4(b)**

(f) (i) What main changes were introduced by the Government of India Act (1935)?   **1,2**

  (ii) Why were the Indians not satisfied with these changes?   **1,2**

2. The Dublin Easter Rising, 1916

Study the Sources below, and then answer the questions that follow.

Source A

The Irish extremists sought German assistance, as the Ulster rebels had done before them. In Germany, Sir Roger Casement, formerly a British consul, attempted unsuccessfully to recruit an Irish legion from among prisoners of war. A rising, with German backing, was planned for Easter Sunday 1916. The plans miscarried. The Germans had never meant their promises seriously, and when Casement landed from a German submarine on Good Friday, it was with a warning to call off the rising, not with German arms or German soldiers. In any case he was captured within a few hours of landing. In Dublin, John MacNeill, chief-of-staff of the Irish Volunteers, cancelled the plans for mobilisation. On Easter Sunday, the Volunteers stayed at home. On Easter Monday, a group in Dublin, unsupported in the rest of the country, seized the General Post Office and proclaimed the Irish Republic. A hundred British soldiers and 450 Irish were killed in the four days of fighting that followed. On the Friday after Easter the first Provisional Government of the Irish Republic surrendered.

Source: A. J. P. Taylor, *English History 1914–1945* (Penguin, 1965, extracts).

Source B
The 1916 Proclamation of the Provisional Government of the Irish Republic.

> The Irish Republican Brotherhood, the Irish Volunteers and the Irish Citizen Army have waited for the right moment and now seize that moment, supported by their exiled children in America and by gallant allies in Europe, to attack in full confidence of victory.
>
> The Republic promises civil and religious liberty, equal rights and equal opportunities to all its citizens and declares its determination to pursue the happiness and prosperity of the whole nation, looking after all members of the nation equally, and forgetting the differences carefully encouraged by a foreign government, which have divided a minority from the majority in the past.
>
> Signed on behalf of the provisional Government:
> Thomas J. Clarke, Sean MacDiarmida, P. H. Pearse, James Connolly, Thomas MacDonagh, Eamonn Ceannt, Joseph Plunkett.

Source: R. Brown and C. Daniels (eds), *Twentieth Century Britain* (Macmillan, 1981, adapted extracts).

Source C
Speech in the House of Commons by John Dillon, an Irish Nationalist MP, 1916.

> I admit they were wrong. I know they were wrong; but they fought a clean fight with superb bravery and skill. As a matter of fact the great bulk of the population were not favourable to the rising, and the rebels themselves, who had confidently counted on a rising of the people in their support, were absolutely disappointed. They got no popular support whatever. What is happening is that thousands of people in Dublin, who ten days ago were bitterly opposed to the whole of the Sinn Fein movement and to the rebellion, are becoming infuriated against the government on account of these executions . . . We who speak for the vast majority of the Irish people, we who have risked a great deal to win people to our side in this great crisis of your Empire's history, and we who have tried, and successfully tried to make sure that the Irish in America shall not go into alliance with the Germans in that country – we, I think, were entitled to be consulted before this bloody course of executions was entered upon in Ireland.

Source: R. Brown and C. Daniels (eds), *Twentieth Century Britain* (Macmillan, 1981).

Source D

In the early days of May, morning after morning, the leaders of the rising were shot in Kilmainham jail, stunning with repeated shocks the minds of a population who had known these men . . . although Catholic and nationalist Irish, 200,000 of them, fought and many died at the Somme, at Gallipoli, at Passchendaele and at other places with names of terror, their sacrifice seemed, by the turn Irish history now took, irrelevant . . . In Northern Ireland Catholics are Blacks who happen to have white skins. Catholics and Protestants are not quarrelling with each other because of matters of religion . . . it is a colonial problem, and the 'racial' distinction between the colonists and the natives is simply expressed in terms of religion. But it goes much deeper: the difference has to be maintained in order to keep the colony as a colony.

Source: Liam de Paor, *Divided Ulster* (Penguin, 1971, adapted extracts).

(a) (i) From the evidence of Sources A and C, what chance do you think the Easter Rising had of success? **4(a,c)**

    (ii) Why did the Irish expect to get help from Germany in their struggle for freedom? **1,4**

(b) (i) In what ways does Source A disagree with Source B? **4(c)**

    (ii) Using Source B, explain in your own words what the Irish Republican Government promised to the Irish people. **4(a)**

    (iii) What did the Proclamation (Source B) mean by the phrase 'a foreign government', near the end? **1,4(a)**

    (iv) Who were the 'minority' and the 'majority' referred to at the end of Source B? **1,4(a)**

(c) (i) In Source C, why does Dillon admit that the rebels were wrong? **1,4(a)**

    (ii) What was the 'Sinn Fein' movement referred to by Dillon, and how was it different from Dillon's party, the Irish Nationalists? **1,4(a)**

    (iii) Who were the people being executed (look at Sources B, C and D)? **4(a,c)**

    (iv) From the evidence of Source C, what effect did the executions have? **4(a)**

(d) (i) What was 'the great crisis of your Empire's history' mentioned in Source C? **1,4(a)**

    (ii) Using evidence from Sources C and D, describe how the Irish had helped the British in their crisis. **4(a,c)**

    (iii) Do you think the writer of Source D is a supporter of the British or the Irish? Give reasons for your answer. **4(a,b)**

(e) Explain how the problems in Ireland were solved temporarily in the years 1920–3. **1,2**

(f) Of the four Sources, which one do you think is most valuable to a historian trying to decide how much support there was for the Easter Rising in Ireland? Give reasons for your answer. **4(a,b)**

3. Jews and Arabs in Palestine

Study the Sources below, and then answer the questions that follow.

Source A
Letter from Arthur Balfour (Foreign Secretary) to Lord Rothschild (President of the English Zionist Federation). The letter is known as the Balfour Declaration (1917).

I have much pleasure in conveying to you, on behalf of His Majesty's Government, the following declaration of sympathy with Jewish Zionist aspirations, which has been submitted to, and approved by, the Cabinet. HM Government views with favour the establishment in Palestine of a national home for the Jewish people, and will use their best endeavours to facilitate the achievement of this object, it being clearly understood that nothing shall be done which may prejudice the civil and religious rights of existing non-Jewish communities in Palestine. I should be grateful if you would bring this declaration to the knowledge of the Zionist federation.

Source: P. F. Speed, *Modern World History* (Arnold–Wheaton, 1985).

Source B

It was not at all clear from the declaration whether a Jewish state was envisaged or whether the Jews were simply to be encouraged to go to Palestine and regard it as their natural habitat . . . The situation was complicated by the promise given by T. E. Lawrence and others that the Arabs would be granted their independence once they had played a part in overthrowing the Turkish Empire. The part had been played and the promises had to be honoured, but it was difficult to reconcile them with the Sykes–Picot agreement. The Balfour Declaration also had to be taken into account, for it was already clear [in 1919] that the Arabs were not happy about the idea of a national home for Jews.

Source: Peter Rowland, *Lloyd George* (Barrie & Jenkins, 1975, adapted extracts).

Source C
Table showing population statistics for Palestine.

Year	Arabs/Moslems	Jews	Christians
1922	486,000	84,000	71,000
1931	693,000	175,000	89,000
1935	770,000	355,000	105,000
1940	881,000	464,000	121,000

Source: *Chambers Encyclopaedia* (1963).

(a)   **(i)** What were the Zionists mentioned in Source A, and what did they want?   **1,4(a)**

     (ii) What did Balfour promise the Jews in his declaration (Source A)?   **4(a)**

     (iii) How did Balfour try to make his declaration accceptable to non-Jews?   **2,4(a)**

(b)   **(i)** From the evidence provided in Source B, why do you think there was some disagreement about the exact meaning of Balfour's promise?   **4(a)**

     (ii) Who was T. E. Lawrence, and what promises, according to Source B, had he given the Arabs?   **1,4(a)**

     (iii) What was the 'Sykes–Picot agreement' mentioned in Source B, and why was it difficult to reconcile it with Lawrence's promises?   **1,2,4(a)**

(c)   **(i)** From the evidence of the statistics in Source C, by roughly how many times had the Jewish population of Palestine increased between 1922 and 1940?   **4(a)**

     (ii) Which of the three groups was increasing most slowly, and which was increasing most quickly?   **4(a)**

     (iii) Using the statistics in Source C to help you, explain why the Arabs in Palestine had good reason to be 'not happy about the idea of a national home for Jews', as Source B puts it.   **2,4**

(d) Why did the situation in Palestine get worse after Hitler came to power in Germany in 1933?   **1,2**

(e) The British government made two attempts to solve the problems in Palestine: The Peel Commission (1937) and the White Paper (1939).

     (i) What did the Peel Commission suggest, and why did this not work?   **1,2**

     (ii) What did the White Paper propose, and what were the effects of these proposals?   **1,2**

4. As an Indian nationalist and a member of Congress, write four letters to the *Times of India*, outlining your criticisms of:

   (a) The Government of India Act (1919);

   (b) The Simon Commission Report (1930);

   (c) Round Table Conferences (1930–1);

   (d) The Government of India Act (1935).   **1,2,3**

5. As an Irish *Sinn Fein* member and supporter of de Valera, write a letter to a cousin in the USA, explaining:

   (a) Why you joined the Easter Rising of 1916, and what happened to you during and after the rebellion;

   (b) Why you would not accept the Government of Ireland Act (1920) or the 1921 treaty;

   (c) Why, during the 1930s, you wanted a complete break with Britain.   **1,2,3**

CHAPTER 12

THE LEAGUE

OF

NATIONS

SUMMARY OF EVENTS

The League of Nations formally came into existence on *10 January 1920*, the same day that the Versailles Treaty came into operation. With headquarters at Geneva in Switzerland, one of its main aims was to settle international disputes and so prevent war from ever breaking out again. After some initial teething troubles, the League seemed to be functioning successfully during the 1920s: not only did it solve a number of *minor international disputes*, it also achieved valuable *economic and social work*, such as helping thousands of refugees and former prisoners of war to find their way home again. In 1930 supporters of the League felt optimistic about its future; indeed the South African statesman, Jan Smuts, was moved to remark that 'we are witnessing one of the great miracles of history'. However, during the 1930s the *authority of the League* was several times *challenged*, first by the Japanese invasion of Manchuria (1931) and later by the Italian attack on Abyssinia (1935). Both aggressors ignored the League's orders to withdraw, and for a variety of reasons it proved impossible to force them to comply. After 1935 respect for the League declined as its weaknesses became more apparent. In Germany's disputes with Czechoslovakia and Poland which led on to the Second World War the League was not consulted, and it was unable to exert the slightest influence to prevent the outbreak of war. After December 1939 it did not meet again and it was dissolved in 1946 – a *total failure, at least as far as preventing war was concerned*.

12.1 WHAT WERE THE ORIGINS OF THE LEAGUE?

The League is often spoken of as being the brainchild of the American president Woodrow Wilson. Although Wilson was certainly a great supporter of the idea of an international organisation for peace, the League was in reality the result of a *coming together of similar suggestions* (made during the First World War) by a *number of world statesmen*. Lord Robert Cecil of Britain, Jan Smuts of South Africa and Léon

Bourgeois of France put forward detailed schemes as to how such an organisation might be set up; Lloyd George referred to it as one of *Britain's war aims*, and Wilson included it as the *last of his 14 points* (see Section 2.7(a)). Wilson's great contribution was to insist that the League Covenant (the list of rules by which the League was to operate), which had been drawn up by an international committee including Cecil, Smuts and Bourgeois as well as Wilson himself, should be included in *each of the separate peace treaties*. This ensured that the League actually came into existence instead of merely remaining a topic for discussion.

The League had *two main aims*:

(a) To maintain peace through **collective security**: if one state attacked another, the member states of the league would act together, collectively, to *restrain the aggressor*, either by *economic* or by *military sanctions*.

(b) To encourage **international co-operation** in order to solve economic and social problems.

12.2 HOW WAS THE LEAGUE ORGANISED?

There were *42 member states* at the beginning and 55 by 1926 when Germany was admitted. Its main organs were:

(a) The General Assembly: this met *annually* and contained representatives of *all the member states*, each of which had *one vote*. Its function was to decide *general policy*: it could, for example, propose a revision of peace treaties, and it handled the finances of the League. Any decisions taken had to be unanimous.

(b) The Council: this was a much smaller body which met more often, *at least three times a year*, and contained *four permanent* members – Britain, France, Italy and Japan (USA was to have been a permanent member but declined to join the League) – and *four other* members to be elected by the Assembly for periods of *three years*. The number of non-permanent members had increased to nine by 1926. It was the Council's task to deal with specific political disputes as they arose and again decisions had to be unanimous.

(c) The Permanent Court of International Justice: this was based at the Hague in Holland and consisted of *15 judges* of different nationalities; it dealt with *legal disputes* between states, as opposed to political ones.

(d) The Secretariat: this looked after all the *paperwork*, preparing agendas, and writing resolutions and reports for carrying out the decisions of the League.

(e) In addition there were a number of **commissions and committees** to deal with *specific problems*. The main *commissions* were those which handled the mandates, military affairs, minority groups and disarmament, while there were *committees* for international labour, health, economic and financial organisation, child welfare, drug problems and women's rights.

(f) In its function of **peace-keeping** it was expected that the League would operate as follows: all disputes threatening war would be submitted to the league and any member which resorted to war, thus breaking the covenant, would face *action by the rest*; the council would recommend 'what effective military, naval or air force the members should contribute to the armed forces'.

12.3 THE SUCCESSES OF THE LEAGUE

(a) **It would be unfair to dismiss the League as a total failure**; in fact, many of the commissions and committees achieved valuable results and much was done to foster international co-operation. One of the most successful was the *International Labour Organisation* (ILO) under its French socialist director, Albert Thomas. Its purpose was to *improve conditions of labour all over the world* by persuading governments to fix a maximum working day and week, specify adequate minimum wages and introduce sickness and unemployment benefit and old age pensions. It collected and published a vast amount of information and many governments were prevailed upon to take action. The *Refugee Organisation* led by Fridtjof Nansen, the Norwegian explorer, solved the problem of thousands of former prisoners of war marooned in Russia at the end of the war; about half a million were returned home. After 1933 valuable help was given to thousands fleeing from the Nazi persecution in Germany. The *Health Organisation* did good work in investigating the causes of epidemics and was particularly successful in combating a typhus epidemic in Russia which at one time seemed likely to spread across Europe. The *Mandates Commission* supervised the government of the territories taken from Germany and Turkey, while yet another commission was responsible for administering the *Saar*, which it did most efficiently, concluding by organising the 1935 plebiscite in which a large majority voted for the Saar to be returned to Germany. Not all were successful, however; the *Disarmament Commission* made no progress in the near impossible task of persuading member states to reduce armaments, though they had all undertaken to do so when they agreed to the covenant.

(b) **Several political disputes were referred to the League** in the early 1920s; in all but two the *League's decisions were accepted*. For example in the quarrel between Sweden and Finland over the *Aaland Islands*, the verdict went in favour of Finland (1920); over the rival claims of

Germany and Poland to the important industrial area of *Upper Silesia*, the League decided that it would be partitioned between the two (1921); when the *Greeks invaded Bulgaria* after some shooting incidents on the frontier, the League swiftly intervened: Greek troops were withdrawn and damages paid to Bulgaria (1925). When *Turkey claimed the province of Mosul*, part of the British mandated territory of Iraq, the League decided in favour of Iraq. Even further afield, squabbles were settled between *Peru and Colombia* and between *Bolivia and Paraguay*. It is significant, however, that none of these decisions went against a major state, which might have challenged the League's verdict. In fact during this same period the League twice found itself *overruled* by the Conference of Ambassadors based in Paris, which was intended to deal with problems arising out of the Versailles treaties. There were first the rival claims of Poland and Lithuania to *Vilna* (1920) followed by the *Corfu Incident*, a quarrel between Italy under Mussolini and Greece (1923). The fact that the League seemed unable or unwilling to respond to these affronts was not a promising sign.

12.4 WHY DID THE LEAGUE FAIL TO PRESERVE PEACE?

At the time of the Corfu Incident in 1923, many people wondered what would happen if a *powerful state were to challenge the League* on a matter of major importance, for example, by invading an innocent country. How effective would the League be then? Unfortunately several such challenges occurred during the 1930s, and on every occasion the League *was found wanting*.

(a) An initial disadvantage was that it was **too closely linked with the Versailles treaties**, giving it the air of being an organisation for the benefit of the victorious powers. In addition it had to defend the peace settlement which was far from perfect. Some of its provisions were bound to cause trouble – for example, the disappointment of Italy and the inclusion of Germans in Poland and Czechoslovakia.

(b) The League was dealt a serious blow in March 1920 when the **United States Senate rejected both the Versailles Settlement and the League**. The reasons behind their decision were varied: many Americans wanted to return to a policy of isolation and feared that membership of the League might cause them to be embroiled in another war; the Republicans, now in a majority in the Senate, strongly opposed Woodrow Wilson (a Democrat), but Wilson refused to compromise one iota over either the terms of the Treaties or the League Covenant. Indeed he was so obstinate that many of his own party lost patience and deserted him. The League was *deprived of a powerful member* whose presence would have been of great *psychological and financial benefit*.

(c) **Germany was not allowed to join until 1926** and the USSR became a member only in *1934* (when Germany left), so that for the first few years of its existence the League was deprived of three of the world's most important powers.

(d) In the early years the Conference of Ambassadors in Paris was an embarrassment. It was intended to function only until the League machinery was established, but it lingered on, and on several occasions took precedence over the League. In 1920 the League supported Lithuania in her claim to Vilna which had just been seized from her by the Poles, but then allowed the Ambassadors to award Vilna to *Poland*. A later example was the *Corfu Incident* (1923) which arose from a boundary dispute between Greece and Albania, in which three Italian officers working on the boundary commission were killed. Mussolini blamed the Greeks, demanded huge compensation and bombarded and occupied the Greek island of Corfu. Greece appealed to the League, but Mussolini *refused to recognise its competence* to deal with the problem and threatened to withdraw from the League, whereupon the Ambassadors ordered Greece to pay the full amount demanded. At this early stage, however, supporters of the League dismissed these incidents as teething troubles.

(e) There were serious weaknesses in the covenant, making it difficult to ensure that *decisive action* was taken against any aggressor. It was difficult to achieve *unanimous decisions*; the League had no military force of its own, and though Article 16 expected member states to supply troops if necessary, a resolution was passed in 1923 that each member would decide for itself whether or not to fight in a crisis. This clearly made nonsense of the idea of collective security. Several attempts were made to strengthen the covenant but these failed because a unanimous vote was needed to change it and this was never achieved. The most notable attempt was made in 1924 by the British Labour Prime Minister, Ramsay MacDonald, in a resolution known as the *Geneva Protocol*, which pledged members to accept arbitration and help any victim of unprovoked aggression. With supreme irony, the Conservative government which followed MacDonald informed the League that they could not agree to the Protocol; they were reluctant to commit Britain and the dominions to the defence of all the 1919 frontiers. Unfortunately this left the League, as its critics remarked, 'lacking teeth'.

(f) The continued absence of the USA and the USSR plus the hostility of Italy made the League very much a **Franco-British affair**, but as their rejection of the Geneva Protocol showed, the British Conservatives were never enthusiastic about the League and preferred to sign the *Locarno Treaties (1925)* outside the League instead of conducting negotiations within it (see Section 13.1(e)). None of these weaknesses necessarily doomed the League to failure, however, provided all the members were prepared to refrain from aggression and accept League decisions; between 1925 and 1930 events ran fairly smoothly.

(g) But the **world economic crisis which began in 1929** contributed to the League's decline. It brought unemployment and falling living standards to most countries, and caused extreme right-wing governments to come to power in Japan and Germany; together with Mussolini, they refused to keep to the rules and pursued a series of actions which *revealed the league's weaknesses.*

(h) In 1931 Japanese troops invaded the Chinese territory of Manchuria (see Section 14.1); China appealed to the League which condemned Japan and ordered her troops to be withdrawn. When Japan refused the League appointed a commission under Lord Lytton which decided (1932) that there were faults on both sides and suggested that Manchuria be governed by the League. However, Japan *rejected this and withdrew from the League (March 1933).* The question of economic sanctions let alone military ones was not raised, because Britain and France had serious economic problems and were reluctant to apply a trade boycott of Japan in case it led to war, which they were ill-equipped to win, especially without American help. *Japan had successfully defied the League,* and its prestige was damaged, though not yet fatally.

(i) The failure of the World Disarmament Conference (1932–3) which met under the auspices of the League was a grave disappointment. The Germans asked for equality of armaments with France, but when the French demanded that this should be postponed for at least eight years, Hitler was able to use the French attitude as an excuse to *withdraw Germany from the conference and later from the League.*

(j) The most serious blow was the **Italian invasion of Abyssinia** in *October 1935* (see Section 14.2(b)). The League condemned Italy and introduced economic sanctions which, however, did not include a ban on exports of oil, coal and steel to Italy. So half-hearted were the sanctions that Italy was able to complete the conquest of Abyssinia without too much inconvenience (*May 1936*). A few weeks later sanctions were abandoned and *Mussolini had flouted the League.* Again Britain and France must share the blame for the League's failure. Their motives were the desire not to antagonise Mussolini too much so as to keep him as an ally against the real danger – Germany. But the results were disastrous: Mussolini was annoyed by the sanctions anyway and began to draw closer to Hitler; small states lost all faith in the League; and Hitler himself was encouraged to break the Versailles treaties. *After 1935, therefore, the League was not taken seriously again.*

The real explanation for the failure of the League was simple: when aggressive states such as Japan, Italy and Germany defied it, the League members, especially Britain and France, were not prepared to support it either by *decisive economic measures* or *by war.* The League was only as strong as the *determination of its leading members to stand up to aggression;* unfortunately determination of that sort was sadly lacking during the 1930s.

QUESTIONS

1. The League and its problems

Study the Sources below, and then answer the questions that follow.

Source A

The Covenant of the League of Nations, signed 1919.

In order to promote international co-operation and to achieve peace and security, by the acceptance of obligations not to resort to war, and by the firm observance of international law as the rule of conduct among governments, and by the maintenance of justice and a scrupulous respect for all treaty obligations, the member states agree to this Covenant of the League of Nations.

Article 16 – Should any member of the League resort to war in disregard of its covenants, it shall be deemed to have committed an act of war against all other members of the League, which hereby undertake immediately to subject it to the severance of trade or financial relations . . . It shall be the duty of the Council in such case to recommend to the several governments concerned what effective military, naval or air force the members of the League shall contribute to the armed forces to be used to protect the covenants of the League.

Article 23 – Members of the League:

(a) will endeavour to secure and maintain fair and humane conditions of labour, both in their own countries and abroad, and for that purpose will establish international organizations.

(b) will endeavour to take steps in matters of international concern for the prevention and control of disease.

Source: J. H. Bettey (ed.), *English Historical Documents* (Routledge & Kegan Paul, 1967, adapted extracts).

Source B

British cartoon (overleaf) of 1931.

Source C

A speech by Sir Samuel Hoare (British Foreign Secretary) to League of Nations at Geneva, 11 September 1935.

I do not suppose that in the history of the Assembly there was ever a more difficult moment for a speech. When the world is stirred to excitement over the Abyssinian controversy, I will begin by re-affirming the support of the League by the government that I represent and the interest of the British people in collective security. On behalf of the Government of the United Kingdom, I can say that they will be second to none in their intention to fulfil within the measure of their capacity, the obligations which the Covenant lays upon them. The League stands, and my country stands with it, for the collective

illus 12.1

maintenance of the Covenant, especially to all acts of unprovoked aggression.

Source: J. H. Bettey (ed.), *English Historical Documents* (Routledge & Kegan Paul, 1967, extracts).

Source D

Manchuria demonstrated that the League was toothless. Collective security depended on the readiness of the great powers to defend the status quo. Although Britain, France and the USA had much to lose in the Far East, Japanese expansion was not yet seen as a direct threat to western trading and colonial interests. Western governments were busy with problems of economic recovery and disarmament negotiations. However, the blow to the League was not a mortal one and the decisive test came two years later in the Abyssinian crisis . . . The Italian attack on Abyssinia, a League member, seemed an open-and-shut case of aggression. Yet the League sanctions imposed in November 1935 were mild and did not include an oil embargo. Six months later the Italian conquest of Abyssinia was complete. Why did Britain and France allow Italy to overrun it? These were their major reasons: the desire to retain Italy as an ally against Germany, military considerations, and divided opinion in Britain and France . . . The Abyssinian crisis delivered a death blow to the League. It was already weakened by the departure of Japan in March 1933 and Germany in

October. Italy left in 1937. While Britain and France were distracted, Hitler made his first major territorial move, sending a force of 22,000 men into the demilitarised Rhineland.

Source: A. P. Adamthwaite, *The Making of the Second World War* (Allen and Unwin, 1977, adapted extracts.

(a) (i) What was the Covenant of the League of Nations, and when was it drawn up? **1,4(a)**

(ii) What other agreements did it form part of? **1**

(b) Explain in your own words:

(i) What, according to Source A, was the main aim of the League? **4(a)**

(ii) How, according to Source A, it was hoped to achieve this. **4(a)**

(c) (i) According to Article 16, what would the members think about a member which attacked another state? **4(a)**

(ii) What immediate action were members expected to take against an aggressor? **4(a)**

(iii) What further action might be taken if the League Council recommended it? **4(a)**

(iv) What phrase in the second sentence of Source C describes the League's method of keeping the peace? **4(a)**

(d) Describe what actions resulted from the two points made in Article 23, and how successful they were. **1,2,4(a)**

(e) (i) In the cartoon (Source B) (illus 12.1) why is 'Geneva' written on the pillar on the right? **1,4(a)**

(ii) The figure kneeling on the right in illus 12.1 represents Britain. Which country do you think the man entering the building represents? **1,4(a)**

(iii) What points is the cartoonist in illus 12.1 trying to make? Use Source D to help you decide. **1,2,4**

(iv) Which of the participants in the Manchuria crisis do you think the cartoonist in illus 12.1 most sympathises with? **4(b)**

(f) (i) According to Source D, why did the League fail to take strong action against the Japanese invasion of Manchuria? **4(a)**

(ii) How does Source D show that Britain did not fully carry out its obligations to the League mentioned in Source C? **4(c)**

(iii) What were the reasons for this weak action, according to Source D? **4(a)**

(iv) From the evidence of Source D, which crisis dealt the more serious blow to the League, Manchuria or Abyssinia? Explain your answer. **4(a)**

(g) From the evidence of the Sources, and your own knowledge, explain why the League failed to preserve peace in the 1930s. **1,2,4**

2. Membership of the League of Nations, 1919–39
Study the diagram below, and answer the questions that follow.

illus 12.2

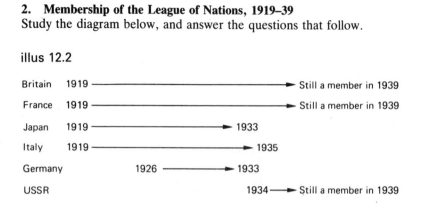

(a) What were the special circumstances of the year 1919, that led to the forming of the League of Nations?
(b) (i) Why did Germany not become a member until 1926?
    (ii) Why did Germany leave the League in 1933?
(c) Why did the Soviet Union not become a member until 1934?
(d) The diagram in illus. 12.2 shows that Japan left the League in 1933 and Italy left in 1935. How far were the circumstances of these two events similar?
(e) Why were Britain and France so important for the success of the League? **1,2**

[Southern Examining Group, Specimen Question.]

3. (a) Explain how the League of Nations came into existence and who helped to set it up.
    (b) Choose *two* of its activities which you think were successful, and describe what happened. **1,2**

CHAPTER 13

FOREIGN AFFAIRS AND INTERNATIONAL RELATIONS 1919–33

SUMMARY OF EVENTS

International relations between the two world wars fall into two distinct phases with the division at *January 1933*, the fateful month in which Adolf Hitler came to power in Germany. Before that there seemed a good chance that world peace could be maintained, in spite of the failure of the League of Nations to curb Japanese aggression in Manchuria; once Hitler was firmly in control there seemed little chance of preventing a war of some sort, either limited or full-scale, depending on one's interpretation of Hitler's intentions (see Section 14.3). The first phase can be divided roughly into three:

(a) 1919 to 1923. In the aftermath of the First World War, relations were disturbed by problems arising from the Paris peace settlement, while the newborn League of Nations struggled to sort things out. Both *Turkey* and *Italy* were *dissatisfied with their treatment*, Turkey being prepared to defy the settlement (see Section 2.10). The Italians, soon to come under the rule of Mussolini (1922), showed their resentment first by the seizure of Fiume which had been awarded to Yugoslavia and then in the Corfu Incident; later Italian aggression was turned against Abyssinia (1935). The problem of *German reparations* and whether or not she could afford to pay caused strained relations between France and Britain, on account of their differing attitudes towards German recovery. Lloyd George's attempt to reconcile France and Germany at the 1922 Genoa Conference failed miserably, and relations deteriorated still further in 1923 when French troops occupied the *Ruhr* (an important German industrial region) in an attempt to seize what the Germans were refusing to pay in reparations; this succeeded only in bringing about the *collapse of the German currency*. Meanwhile the *USA*, though choosing to remain politically isolated, exercised considerable economic influence on Europe by, among other things, insisting on *full payment of European war debts*. The *USSR*, now communist, was viewed with suspicion by the western countries, several of which, along with Japan, intervened against the Bolsheviks in the *civil war* which ravaged the USSR during 1918–20.

(b) 1924 to 1929 saw a *general improvement in the international atmosphere* brought about partly by changes in political leadership. In France Edouard Herriot and Aristide Briand, in Germany Gustav Stresemann and in Britain Ramsay MacDonald came to power, and all were keen to improve relations. The result was the *Dawes Plan* worked out in *1924* with American participation, which eased the situation with regard to German reparations. *1925* saw the signing of the *Locarno Treaties* which guaranteed the frontiers in western Europe fixed at Versailles; this seemed to remove French suspicions of German intentions. *Germany* was allowed to *join the League in 1926* and two years later 65 nations signed the *Kellogg–Briand Pact renouncing war*. The *1929 Young Plan* reduced German reparations to a more manageable figure; all seemed set fair for a peaceful future.

(c) 1930 to 1933. Towards the end of 1929 the world began to run into *economic difficulties* which helped to cause a deterioration in international relations. It was partly for economic reasons that Japanese troops invaded the Chinese province of Manchuria in 1931; mass unemployment in Germany played an important role in enabling Hitler to come to power. In this unpromising climate the World Disarmament Conference met (1932) only to break up in failure when the German delegates walked out (1933). With such a complex period, it will be best to treat the various themes separately.

13.1 WHAT ATTEMPTS WERE MADE TO IMPROVE INTERNATIONAL RELATIONS, AND HOW SUCCESSFUL WERE THEY?

(a) The League of Nations played an important role, settling a number of international disputes and problems (see Section 12.3). However, its authority tended to be weakened by the fact that many states seemed to prefer signing agreements *independently of the League*, which suggests that they were not brimming with confidence at the League's prospects.

(b) The Washington Conferences (1921–2) tried to *improve relations between the USA and Japan*. The USA was increasingly suspicious of growing Japanese power in the Far East and of Japanese influence in China, especially as during the First World War Japan had seized Kiaochow and all the German islands in the Pacific. To prevent a naval building race, it was agreed that the Japanese navy would be limited to three-fifths the size of the American and British navies; Japan also agreed to withdraw from Kiaochow and the Shantung province of China which she had occupied since 1914. In return she was allowed to keep the former German Pacific islands as mandates, and the western powers promised not to build any more naval bases within striking distance of Japan. In addition, the USA, Japan, Britain and France agreed to guarantee the neutrality of China and to respect each other's possessions in the Far East. At the time the agreements were regarded as a great success and relations between the powers involved improved. In reality, however, *Japan was left supreme in the Far East*, possessor of the world's *third largest navy*, which she could concentrate in the Pacific, whereas the navies of Britain and the USA, though larger, were spread more widely. This was to have unfortunate consequences for China in the 1930s when the USA refused to become involved in checking Japanese aggression.

(c) The Genoa Conference (1922) was the brainchild of the British Prime Minister, Lloyd George, who hoped it would solve the pressing problems of Franco-German hostility (the Germans were threatening to stop paying reparations), European war debts to the USA, and the need to resume proper diplomatic relations with Soviet Russia. Unfortunately the *conference failed*: the French refused all compromise and insisted on full reparations payments; the Americans refused even to attend, and the Germans and Russians withdrew and signed a mutual agreement at *Rapallo*. When, the following year, the Germans failed to pay the amount due, French troops occupied the Ruhr, and deadlock quickly developed when the Germans replied with passive resistance.

(d) It was in an attempt to break this deadlock that the **Dawes Plan** was drawn up and finally accepted at a conference in *London (1924)*. The three newcomers to international politics, Ramsay MacDonald, Edouard Herriot and Gustav Stresemann, were eager for reconciliation; the Americans were persuaded to take part and the conference was chaired for part of the time by the American representative, General Dawes. No reduction was made in the total amount Germany was expected to pay, but it was agreed that she should pay *annually only what she could reasonably afford* until she became more prosperous; a foreign loan of 800 million gold marks, mainly from the USA, was to be made to Germany; France, now assured of at least some reparations from Germany, agreed to *withdraw her troops from the Ruhr*. The plan was successful: the German economy began to recover on the basis of the American loans and international tensions gradually relaxed, preparing the way for the next agreements.

(e) The Locarno Treaties (1925) were a number of different agreements involving Germany, France, Britain, Italy, Belgium, Poland and Czechoslovakia. The most important one was that *Germany, France and Belgium promised to respect their joint frontiers*; if one of the three broke this agreement, Britain and Italy would assist the state which was being attacked. Germany signed agreements with Poland and Czechoslovakia providing for arbitration over possible disputes, but Germany would not guarantee her frontiers with Poland and Czechoslovakia. It was also agreed that France would help Poland and Czechoslovakia in the event of a German attack. The agreements were greeted with wild enthusiasm all over Europe, and the reconciliation between Germany and France was referred to as the 'Locarno honeymoon'. Later, historians were not so enthusiastic about Locarno; there was one notable omission from the agreements – no guarantees were given by Germany or Britain about *Germany's eastern frontiers with Poland and Czechoslovakia*. By ignoring this problem, Britain gave the impression that she might not act if Germany attacked Poland or Czechoslovakia. For the time being, though, as the world enjoyed a period of great economic prosperity, such uneasy thoughts were pushed into the background, and *Germany was admitted to the League in 1926* and Stresemann and Briand (French Foreign Minister from 1925 to 1932) met regularly and had friendly discussions; often Austen Chamberlain (British Foreign Minister from 1924 until 1929) joined them. This 'Locarno spirit' culminated in the next piece of paper signing.

(f) **The Kellogg–Briand Pact (1928)** originated in an idea of Briand who proposed that France and the USA should sign a pact *renouncing war*. Frank B. Kellogg, the American Secretary of State, proposed that the whole world should be involved; eventually 65 states signed, agreeing to renounce war as an instrument of national policy. This sounded impressive, but was completely useless because no mention was made of *sanctions against any state which broke its pledge*. Japan, for example, signed the pact, but was not prevented from waging war against China only three years later.

(g) **The Young Plan (1929)** aimed to settle the remaining problem of reparations – the Dawes Plan had left uncertain the *total amount payable*. In the improved atmosphere the French were willing to compromise, and a committee chaired by an American banker, Owen Young, decided to reduce reparations from £6600 million to £2000 million, to be paid on a graded scale over the *next 59 years*. This was the figure that Keynes had urged at Versailles, and its acceptance ten years later was an admission of error by the Allies. The plan was welcomed in Germany, but before there was time to put it into operation a series of events following in rapid succession destroyed the fragile harmony of Locarno: the death of Stresemann (October 1929) removed one of the outstanding 'men of Locarno'; the Wall Street Crash in the same month soon developed into the great depression, and by 1932 there were over six million unemployed in Germany. Hope was kept alive by the *Lausanne Conference (1932)* at which Britain and France released Germany from most of her remaining reparations payments. However, in January 1933 Hitler became German Chancellor and after that, international tension mounted.

(h) **The World Disarmament Conference (1932–3)** met at *Geneva* to try and work out a formula for scaling down armaments, which all members of the League had undertaken to do when they accepted the covenant. In fact Germany was the only state to disarm, as Stresemann regularly pointed out, but the rest shrank from being the first to reduce armaments. If no progress could be made during the Locarno honeymoon, there was little chance of success in the disturbed atmosphere of the early 1930s. The French, alarmed at the rapid increase of support for the Nazis in Germany, refused either to disarm or to allow Germany equality of armaments. Hitler, knowing that Britain and Italy sympathised with Germany, *withdrew from the conference (October 1933) which was dead from that moment*; a week later Germany also withdrew from the League.

In retrospect it could be seen that the statesmen of the world had only a limited success in improving international relations; even the 'Locarno spirit' proved illusory because so much depended on *economic prosperity*; when this evaporated, all the old hostilities and suspicions surfaced again, and authoritarian regimes which were prepared to risk aggression came to power.

13.2 HOW DID FRANCE TRY TO DEAL WITH THE PROBLEM OF GERMANY BETWEEN 1919 AND 1933?

As soon as the First World War ended, the French, after all they had suffered in two German invasions in less than 50 years, wanted to make sure that the Germans *never again violated the sacred soil of France*; this remained the major preoccupation of French policy throughout the inter-war period. At different times, depending who was in charge of foreign affairs, the French tried several different methods of dealing with the problem: trying to keep Germany economically and militarily weak, signing alliances with other states to isolate Germany, and extending the hand of reconciliation and friendship. In the end, *they all failed*.

(a) **At the Paris peace conference** the French premier, Clemenceau, insisted on a *harsh settlement*; in order to strengthen French security, the German army was to number no more than 100,000 men and there were to be severe limitations on armaments (see Section 2.8(a)). The *German Rhineland was to be demilitarised* to a distance of 50 kilometres east of the river, and *France* was to have the use of the *Saar* for 15 years. Britain and the USA promised to help France if the Germans attacked her again. Although many Frenchmen were disappointed (Foch, for example, wanted France to be given the whole of the German Rhineland west of the river but they were allowed to occupy it only for 15 years), it looked at first as though security was guaranteed. Unfortunately French satisfaction was short-lived: when the *Americans rejected the entire peace settlement (March 1920)* they abandoned their guarantee of assistance; the British used this as an excuse to cancel their obligations and the French felt betrayed.

(b) Clemenceau also demanded that the **Germans should pay reparations** (money to help repair damages). The figure was fixed in 1921 at *£6600 million*, payment of which, it was thought, would keep Germany *economically weak for the next 66 years* (the period over which reparations were to be paid in annual instalments) and make another attack on France less likely. However, financial troubles in Germany soon caused the government to fall behind with its payments, and the French, who needed reparations to balance their budget and pay their own debt to the USA, became desperate.

(c) The next Prime Minister, the anti-German Raymond Poincaré, decided that **drastic methods were needed to force the Germans to pay**. *French and Belgian troops occupied the Ruhr* (the main German industrial area which includes the cities of Essen and Dusseldorf), but the Germans replied with *passive resistance, strikes and sabotage*. A number

illus 13.1 *French troops occupy a factory in the Ruhr, 1923*

of nasty incidents between troops and civilians resulted in the deaths of over a hundred people; although the French managed to extract goods worth about £40 million, the whole episode caused galloping inflation and the collapse of the German mark, which by November 1923 was completely valueless. It also revealed the basic difference between the French and British attitudes towards Germany: while France adopted a hard line and wanted a Germany permanently crippled, Britain now saw moderation and reconciliation with Germany as the best security and believed that an *economically healthy Germany would be good for the stability of Europe* (as well as for British exports). Consequently the British government strongly disapproved of the Ruhr occupation and sympathised with Germany.

(d) At the same time the French tried to **increase their security by building up a network of alliances,** first with *Poland (1921),* and later with *Czechoslovakia (1924), Rumania (1926)* and *Yugoslavia (1927).* This network, known as the 'Little Entente', though impressive on paper, did not amount to much because the states involved were *comparatively weak;* what was needed was a renewal of the *old alliance with Russia,* which had served the French well during the First World War, but this seemed out of the question now that Russia had become communist.

(e) The French worked for a strong League of Nations, with the victorious powers acting as a military police force compelling aggressive states to behave themselves. However, in the end it was the much more vague Wilson version of the League that was adopted. French disappointment was bitter when Britain took the lead in *rejecting the Geneva Protocol* which might well have strengthened the League; clearly there was no point in expecting much guarantee of security from that direction.

(f) By the summer of 1924 when the failure of Poincaré's Ruhr occupation was obvious, the new premier Herriot was **prepared to accept a compromise solution** to the still pressing problem of German reparations. This was the *Dawes Plan* (see previous section).

(g) During the Briand era (he was Foreign Minister in eleven successive governments between 1925 and 1932), the French approach to the German problem was one of **reconciliation.** Briand persevered with great skill to build up genuinely good relations with Germany, as well as to improve relations with Britain and strengthen the League. Fortunately Stresemann, who was in charge of German foreign policy from November 1923 until 1929, believed that the best way to foster German recovery was by co-operation with Britain and France; the result was the *Locarno Treaties,* the *Kellogg–Briand Pact,* the *Young Plan* and the cancellation of most of the remaining reparations payments (see previous section). There is some debate among historians about how genuine this apparent reconciliation between France and Germany really was. Taylor suggests that though Briand and Stresemann were sincere, 'they did not carry their peoples with them', so strong was nationalist feeling in the two countries that both men were limited in the concessions they could offer. The fact that Stresemann was privately determined to get the frontier with Poland redrawn to Germany's advantage would have caused friction later, since Poland was France's ally; he was equally determined to work for union with Austria and a revision of the Versailles terms.

(h) Even before that happened though, the death of Stresemann, the world economic crisis and the subsequent growth of support for the Nazis alarmed the French, **causing their attitude towards Germany to harden.** When in 1931 plans were produced for an *Austro-German customs union* to ease the economic crisis, the French insisted that the matter be referred to the Court of International Justice at the Hague on the grounds that it was a *violation of the Paris peace agreements*. Though it made economic sense, the court ruled against it, and the plan was blocked. At the *World Disarmament Conference (1932–3)* relations worsened (see previous section) and when, with Hitler in power, the Germans walked out of the conference and the League, all Briand's work was ruined. The German problem was as far from solution as ever.

13.3 HOW DID RELATIONS BETWEEN THE USSR AND BRITAIN, GERMANY AND FRANCE DEVELOP BETWEEN 1919 AND 1933?

For the first three years after the Bolsheviks came to power (November 1917) relations between the new government and the western countries *deteriorated to the point of open war*. This was mainly because the Bolsheviks tried to spread the revolution further, especially in *Germany*. As early as December 1917 floods of propaganda attempted to turn the masses against their capitalist masters; after the Russian defeat Karl Radek, one of the Bolshevik leaders, went secretly to Berlin to plan the revolution, while other agents did the same in Austria and Hungary; it was hoped that world-wide revolution would follow. This sort of behaviour did not endear the communists to the western governments, Britain, France, Czechoslovakia and the USA, who (together with Japan) tried rather half-heartedly to destroy the Bolsheviks by intervening in the *civil war* to help the *Whites* (see Section 3.5(c)). Nor were the Russians invited to the Versailles conference in 1919. By the middle of 1920, however, circumstances were gradually changing: the interventionist countries had acknowledged failure and withdrawn their troops; communist revolutions in Germany and Hungary had failed; and Russia was too exhausted by the civil war to contemplate stirring up any more revolutions for the time being. The way was open for communications to be re-established.

(a) USSR and Britain

Relations blew hot and cold according to which government was in power in Britain; the two Labour governments (1924 and 1929–31) were much more sympathetic to Russia than the others.

(i) After the interventionist fiasco, Lloyd George (British Prime Minister from 1916 to 1922) was prepared for *reconciliation*, and this corresponded with Lenin's desire for improved relations with the west in order to acquire foreign trade and capital. The result was an *Anglo-Russian trade treaty (March 1921)* which was important for Russia not only commercially but also because Britain was the first of the powers to *acknowledge the existence of the Bolshevik government*; it was to lead to similar agreements with other countries and to full political recognition. The new rapprochement was soon shaken, however, when at the Genoa conference (1922) Lloyd George suggested that the Bolsheviks pay war debts incurred by the tsarist regime. The affronted Russians left the conference and signed the *Treaty of Rapallo with the Germans*; this greatly alarmed Britain and France who could see no good coming from what Lloyd George called this 'fierce friendship'.

(ii) Relations improved briefly in 1924 when Ramsay MacDonald and the new labour government gave *full diplomatic recognition to the communists*, signed another trade treaty and proposed a British loan. However, this was unpopular with British Conservatives and Liberals who soon brought MacDonald's government down.

(iii) Under the Conservative government (1924–9) relations with Russia *deteriorated*. British Conservatives had no love for the communists, even less after the affair of the *Zinoviev Letter* (see Section 4.4(c)). There was evidence that Russian propaganda was responsible for part of the trouble in India. Police raided the British Communist Party headquarters in London (1925) and the premises of Arcos, a soviet trading organisation based in London (1927), and claimed to have found evidence of Russian plotting with British communists to overthrow the system. The government expelled the mission and broke off diplomatic relations with the Russians, who replied by arresting some British residents in Moscow.

(iv) Matters took a turn for the better in 1929 when Labour, encouraged by the new pro-western Foreign Minister, Maxim Litvinov, *resumed diplomatic relations* with Russia and signed another trade agreement the following year; but the improvement was only short-lived.

(v) The Conservative-dominated National government cancelled the trade agreement (1932) and in retaliation the Russians arrested four Metropolitan-Vickers engineers working in Moscow; they were tried and given sentences ranging from two to three years for 'spying and wrecking'. However, when Britain placed an embargo on imports from Russia, Stalin released them (June 1933). By this time Stalin was becoming *nervous about the possible threat from Hitler* and was therefore *prepared to take pains to improve relations with Britain*.

(b) USSR and Germany

Russian relations with Germany were more consistent and more friendly than with Britain. This was because the Germans saw certain advantages to be gained from exploiting friendship with the USSR, and because the Bolsheviks were anxious to have *stable relations with at least one capitalist power*.

(i) A *trade treaty was signed (May 1921)* followed by the granting of Russian trade and mineral concessions to some German industrialists.

(ii) The *Rapallo Treaty signed on Easter Sunday 1922*, after both Germany and Russia had withdrawn from the Genoa conference, was an important step forward. Full diplomatic relations were resumed and mutual claims for reparations cancelled. Thereafter both enjoyed advantages from the new friendship: they could co-operate to keep Poland weak, which was in both their interests; Russia had Germany as a buffer against any future attack from the west; the Germans were allowed to build factories in Russia for the manufacture of aeroplanes and ammunition, enabling them to get round the Versailles disarmament terms; German officers trained in Russia in the use of the new forbidden weapons.

(iii) *The Treaty of Berlin (1926)* renewed the Rapallo agreement for a further five years; it was understood that Germany would remain neutral if Russia were attacked by another power and neither would use economic sanctions against the other.

(iv) About 1930 relations began to *cool somewhat* as some Russians expressed concern at the growing power of the recovered Germany: the German attempt at a customs union with Austria in 1931 was taken as an ominous sign of increasing German nationalism. Russian concern changed to alarm at the growth of the *Nazi party* which was strongly anti-communist, and though Stalin and Litvinov tried to continue the friendship with Germany, they also began approaches to Poland, France and Britain. In January 1934 Hitler abruptly ended Germany's special relationship with the soviets by signing a non-aggression pact with Poland (see Section 14.5(b)).

(c) USSR and France

The Bolshevik takeover in 1917 was a serious blow for France because Russia had been an important ally whom she relied on to *keep Germany in check*. Now her former ally was calling for revolution in all capitalist states and could only be regarded as a menace to be destroyed as soon as possible. The French sent troops to help the *Whites* in the *civil war*, and it was because of French insistence that the Bolsheviks were not invited to Versailles. The French also intervened in the war between Russia and Poland in 1920: troops commanded by General Weygand helped to drive back a Russian advance on Warsaw, and afterwards the French government claimed to have stemmed the westward spread of Bolshevism. The subsequent alliance between *France and Poland (1921)* seemed to be directed as much against Russia as against Germany. Relations improved in 1924 when the moderate Herriot government resumed diplomatic relations, but the French were never enthusiastic especially as the French Communist Party was under orders from Moscow not to co-operate with other left-wing parties. Not until the early 1930s did the *rise of the German Nazis* cause a change of heart on both sides.

13.4   UNITED STATES FOREIGN POLICY 1919–33

The USA had been deeply involved in the First World War and when hostilities ceased she seemed likely to play an important role in world affairs. President Woodrow Wilson was a crucial figure at the Paris peace conference; his great dream was the *League of Nations* through which the USA would maintain world peace. However, the American people, tired of the war and suspicious of Europe, rejected Wilson and his League of Nations. From 1921 until early 1933 the USA was ruled by Republican governments which believed in a policy of *isolation*: she *never joined the League* and she tried to avoid political disputes with other states and the signing of treaties. Some historians still blame the failure of the League on the absence of the USA. In spite of this desire for isolation, the Americans found it impossible to avoid some involvement in world affairs, because of overseas trade, investment and the thorny problem of European war debts and reparations.

(a) During the prosperous years of the 1920s, Americans tried to **increase trade and profits by investment abroad**, in Europe, Canada and in Central and South America, and it was inevitable that the USA should take an interest in what was happening in these areas. There was, for example, a serious dispute with *Mexico* whose government was threatening to seize American-owned oil wells, but a compromise solution was reached.

(b) President Harding called the **Washington Conferences (1921–2)** because of concern at Japanese power in the Far East (see Section 13.1).

(c) **Allied war debts to the USA caused much ill-feeling**. During the war the American government had organised loans to Britain and her allies amounting to almost 12 billion dollars at 5 per cent interest. The Europeans hoped that the Americans would cancel the debts since the USA had done well out of the war (by taking over former European markets) but both Harding and Coolidge insisted that repayments be made in full. The Allies claimed that their ability to pay depended on whether Germany paid her reparations to them, but the Americans would not acknowledge any connection between the two. Eventually Britain was the first to agree to pay the full amount, over 62 years at the reduced interest rate of 3.3 per cent. Other states followed, the USA allowing much lower interest rates depending on the poverty of the country concerned: Italy, for example, got away with 0.4 per cent but this caused strong objections from Britain.

(d) **With the German financial crisis of 1923**, the Americans had to change their attitude and *admit the connection between reparations and war debts*; they agreed to take part in the Dawes and Young Plans (1924 and 1929) which enabled Germany to pay reparations. However, this caused the ludicrous situation in which America lent money to Germany so that she could pay reparations to Britain, France and Belgium, so that they could pay their war debts to the USA. The whole set up, together with the American insistence on keeping high tariffs, was a contributory cause of the world economic crisis (see Section 7.2), with all its far-reaching consequences.

(e) The Kellogg–Briand Pact (1928) was another notable though useless American foray into world affairs.

(f) Relations with Britain were uneasy, not only because of war debts but also because the Conservatives resented the limitations of British naval expansion imposed by the earlier Washington agreement. MacDonald, anxious to improve relations, organised a conference in London (1930), attended also by the Japanese, at which the three states reaffirmed the 5:5:3 ratio in cruisers, destroyers and submarines agreed at Washington. This was successful in re-establishing friendship between USA and Britain, but the Japanese soon exceeded their limits.

(g) The USA reverted to a policy of strict isolation when the Japanese invaded Manchuria in 1931. Although Hoover condemned the Japanese action, he refused to join in economic sanctions or make any move which might lead to war with Japan. Consequently Britain and France felt unable to act and the League was shown to be helpless. Throughout the 1930s, though acts of aggression mounted, the Americans remained determined not to be drawn into a conflict.

13.5 THE TROUBLE-MAKERS: POLAND, ITALY AND JAPAN

(a) It is perhaps unfair to describe **Poland** as a trouble-maker, sandwiched as she was between Germany and Russia, both of which bitterly resented the loss of their territory to make up the new state of Poland in 1919. However, the Poles had grievances arising from Versailles: they believed they ought to have been awarded the important industrial area of *Teschen* (given to Czechoslovakia) and parts of *Lithuania* and the *Ukraine*; they were determined to be as uncompromising as possible in relations with Germany and Russia and to seize every opportunity of furthering their interests:

(i) They took advantage of Bolshevik exhaustion at the end of the civil war to *invade the Ukraine*, and though close to disaster as the Russians counter-attacked the Poles, thanks to French help, were able to force the Russians to sign the *Treaty of Riga (1921)* ceding a large slice of the Ukraine to Poland. The west ignored it because it was a blow at communism.

(ii) They *seized the city of Vilna from Lithuania (1920)* and hung on to it even though the League of Nations believed it should be returned to Lithuania. In 1923 the Conference of Ambassadors reluctantly agreed that Vilna should remain Polish. The French particularly were anxious to strengthen Poland as much as possible to take the place of Russia as her eastern ally against Germany.

(b) Italy also felt cheated by Versailles, and though many Italians were tired of war, nationalists felt that violent gestures were needed for the sake of *national pride*:

   (i)   In September *1919 d'Annunzio occupied Fiume* (see Section 6.1(a)); by an agreement signed at Rapallo in 1920 Fiume was to be a free city, but Italy was given the Istrian peninsula instead.

   (ii) Mussolini (who came to power October 1922) believed that aggression paid dividends. In *1923 Fiume was occupied again*, and the following year the Yugoslavs agreed that it should remain Italian. 1923 also saw the *Corfu Incident*, another example of Italian aggression (see Section 12.4(d)). After 1923 both Poland and Italy calmed down and it was Japan which took over the role of aggressor-in-chief.

(c) Japan had emerged from the First World War in a strong position but after 1929 she was severely affected by the world economic crisis, which led the army to *occupy the Chinese province of Manchuria* (see Section 10.2). The League of Nations failed to control the Japanese (see Section 12.4(h)) who withdrew from the League in 1933. It was clear that international relations were moving into a new phase dominated not by the Locarno spirit but by *major acts of aggression and violence*.

QUESTIONS

1. Foreign policy of Weimar Germany
Study the Sources below, and then answer the questions that follow.

Source A
Letter from Gustav Stresemann to the former German Crown Prince, September 1925.

> In my opinion there are three great tasks that confront German foreign policy in the immediate future –
>
> In the first place the solution of the reparations question in a way acceptable to Germany, and the assurance of peace.
>
> Secondly the protection of Germans abroad, those 10 to 12 million of our kindred who now live under a foreign yoke in foreign lands.
>
> The third is the readjustment of our eastern frontiers; the recovery of Danzig, the Polish corridor, and a correction of the frontier in Upper Silesia.

Hence the Locarno Pact which guarantees us peace and makes England, as well as Italy, guarantors of our western frontiers.

I would utter a warning against any ideas of flirting with Bolshevism; we cannot involve ourselves in an alliance with Russia though an understanding is possible on another basis. When the Russians are in Berlin, the red flag will at once be flown from the castle, and in Russia, where they hope for a world revolution, there will be much joy at the spread of Bolshevism as far as the Elbe. The most important thing for German policy is the liberation of German soil from any occupying force. On that account German policy must be one of finesse and avoidance of great decisions.

Source: E. Sutton, *Gustav Stresemann; His Diaries, Letters and Papers* (Macmillan, 1935, adapted).

Source B

Memorandum by General von Seeckt, Head of the German Army (Reichswehr), September 1922.

Poland's existence is intolerable, incompatible with the survival of Germany. For Russia, Poland is even more intolerable than for us; no Russian can allow Poland to exist. Russia and Germany within the frontiers of 1914 should be the basis of reaching an understanding between the two . . . We aim at two things: first a strengthening of Russia in the economic and political, and thus also in the military field, and so indirectly a strengthening of ourselves, by strengthening a possible ally of the future. We further desire a direct strengthening of ourselves by helping to create in Russia an armaments industry which in case of need will serve us.

Source: F. L. Carsten, *The Reichswehr and Politics 1918–1933* (Oxford, 1966, adapted).

Source C

British cartoon of 1925 (Fig. 13.1), about the Locarno Agreements.

Source D

Also at Locarno, Germany signed arbitration treaties with France, Belgium, Czechoslovakia and Poland. By these the powers promised to submit further frontier disputes and claims for land to arbitration. However, Germany would not agree to mutual frontier guarantees with Czechoslovakia and Poland. Instead their boundaries were secured by treaties of mutual assistance with France. By these Poland and Czechoslovakia promised France assistance if she was attacked by Germany, and France promised them aid if they were attacked by Germany. Herein lay the fatal flaws of Locarno – while Germany's western borders were agreed and guaranteed by Britain, France, Belgium and Italy, her eastern borders were left less secure, since they

Fig. 13.1

Source: *Evening Standard*, trustees of David Low.

were not the subject of a revised agreement . . . Nevertheless Germany's relations with the rest of Europe did seem to be improving. Under the guidance of Stresemann she seemed to be following a more peaceful policy. In the Spring of 1925, French troops left the Ruhr, thanks to the Dawes Plan, and in September 1926 Germany was admitted to the League of Nations.

Source: R. Wolfson, *Years of Change* (Arnold, 1978).

(a) (i) According to Source A, what does Stresemann think the main aims of German foreign policy should be? **4(a)**

   (ii) How does he think they can best be achieved? **4(a)**

  (iii) From the evidence of Source A, describe in your own words, Stresemann's attitude towards the USSR. **4(a)**

(b) (i) In Source B, what does von Seeckt think Germany ought to be aiming for in foreign affairs? **4(a)**

   (ii) What differences can you find between the ideas of Stresemann and von Seeckt? **4(a,c)**

  (iii) How were some of von Seeckt's ideas about Russia soon carried out? **1,4(a)**

(c) The cartoon, Source C (Fig. 13.1), shows from left to right, the foreign ministers of France, Britain and Germany at Locarno:

   (i) What are the names of the three men? **1,4(a)**

   (ii) What points do you think the cartoonist is trying to make? Note the boxing-glove hidden behind the Frenchman's back. **4(b)**

(d) **(i)** According to Source D, which states were represented at Locarno in 1925? **4(a)**

  (ii) What was agreed about Germany's western frontiers? **1,4(a)**

  (iii) What was agreed about Germany's frontiers with Czechoslovakia and Poland? **1,4(a)**

  (iv) What, according to the writer of Source D, were the 'fatal flaws' in the Locarno Agreements? Explain in your own words what he meant, and why the flaws were fatal. **1,2,4(a)**

(e) **(i)** Why had the French troops mentioned in Source D, gone into the Ruhr? **1,2,4(a)**

  (ii) Which countries were involved in the Dawes Plan (Source D) and what were its proposals? **1,2,4(a)**

  (iii) What promising signs for future peace can you find in Source D? **4(a)**

(f) Using evidence from all the Sources, explain why the prospects for future peace were not as good as many people thought in 1925.

4(a,c)

2. Describe and explain the following attempts to improve international relations between 1919 and 1933:
   (a) Washington Conferences, 1921–2;
   (b) Dawes and Young Plans, 1924 and 1929;
   (c) Locarno Treaties, 1925:
   (d) Kellogg–Briand pact, 1928;
   (e) Disarmament Conference, 1932–3. **1,2**

3. Describe Anglo-Soviet and Franco-Soviet relations, using the following material: British intervention in the Russian civil war, 1918–20; recognition of Soviet regime by Britain, 1924; Zinoviev Letter, 1924; the Arcos Affair, 1925; French intervention in war between Russia and Poland, 1920; Franco-Soviet relations resumed, 1924. **1,2**

4.
(a) As a German factory workers in the Ruhr, write a letter to a relative living in another part of Germany, in early 1925, describing:
   (i) What happened when French troops occupied your factory in 1923;
   (ii) How the cost of living was affected and how you coped with the situation;
   (iii) How and why the occupation came to an end;
   (iv) Why you think the French action was wrong.

(b) **(i)** As a supporter of French Prime Minister Poincaré, draft a short speech to be given in 1923, explaining why you think the Ruhr occupation is necessary;

  (ii) As a supporter of French Prime Minister Herriot, draft a short speech to be given in 1924, explaining why, reluctantly, you think the Ruhr occupation must be called off. **1,2,3**

5. American foreign policy after the First World War has often been described as 'isolationist'.
   (a) What is meant by an 'isolationist' policy?
   (b) Why did many Americans want to follow such a policy?
   (c) Was American foreign policy isolationist in the 1920s? Explain your answer. **1,2**
   [Southern Examining Group, Specimen Question.]

CHAPTER 14

FOREIGN AFFAIRS AND INTERNATIONAL RELATIONS 1933–9

SUMMARY OF EVENTS

This short period is of crucial importance in world history because it culminated in the Second World War. Economic problems caused the Locarno spirit to evaporate and the new rule seemed to be each country for itself. Affairs were dominated by the three arch-aggressors – Japan, Italy and Germany – whose extreme nationalism led them to commit so many acts of violence and breaches of international agreements that in the end the world was plunged into the ordeal of total war.

Japan became the first aggressor, as we have already seen, with her successful invasion of *Manchuria (1931)*; both Hitler and Mussolini took note of the failure of the League to curb Japanese aggression. Hitler, much the most subtle of the three, began cautiously by announcing the reintroduction of conscription (March 1935). This breach of Versailles caused Britain, France and Italy to draw together briefly in suspicion of Germany. At a meeting held at *Stresa* (on Lake Maggiore, northern Italy) they condemned Hitler's action and soon afterwards in May the French, obviously nervous, signed a treaty of *mutual assistance with Russia*. However the Stresa Front, as it was called, was only short-lived: it was broken in June 1935 when the British, ignoring their two partners, signed the Anglo-German Naval Agreement allowing the Germans to build submarines – another breach of Versailles. This astonishing move by Britain disgusted France and Italy and destroyed any trust which had existed between the three of them. Mussolini, encouraged by Japanese and German successes, now followed suit with his successful invasion of *Abyssinia (October 1935)* which met only half-hearted resistance from the League and from Britain and France.

March 1936 saw Hitler sending troops into the *Rhineland* which had been demilitarised by the Versailles treaties: Britain and France again protested but took no action to expel the Germans. An understanding then followed (October 1936) between Germany and Italy, Mussolini having decided to throw in his lot with Hitler; it was known as the *Rome–Berlin Axis*. The following month Hitler signed the *Anti-Comintern Pact* with *Japan*. (The Comintern or Communist International was an organisation set up in 1919 by Lenin with the aim of starting communist parties in other countries to work for revolution.) During the summer of 1936 the Spanish Civil War broke out and quickly developed an international significance when both Hitler and Mussolini, flexing their militarty muscles, sent help to Franco, while the republicans received soviet help. Predictably Britain and France refused to intervene and by 1939 Franco was victorious.

In 1937 the Japanese took advantage of Europe's preoccupation with events in Spain to embark on a full-scale invasion of northern China. The resulting Sino-Japanese War eventually became part of the Second World War.

By this time it was clear that the League of Nations working through collective security was totally ineffective: consequently Hitler, now assured of Italian acquiescence, carried out his most ambitious project to date – the *annexation of Austria* (known as the *Anschluss – March 1938*). Next he turned his attentions to Czechoslovakia and demanded the *Sudetenland*, an area containing three million Germans adjoining the frontier with Germany. When the Czechs refused Hitler's demands, the British Prime Minister, Chamberlain, anxious to avoid war at all costs, took up Hitler's invitation to a conference at Munich (September 1938) at which it was agreed that Germany should have the Sudetenland, but no more of Czechoslovakia. War seemed to have been averted. However, the following March Hitler broke this agreement and sent German troops to occupy Prague, the Czech capital. At this Chamberlain decided that Hitler had gone too far and must be stopped. When the Poles rejected Hitler's demand for Danzig, Britain and France promised to help Poland if the Germans attacked. Hitler was not sufficiently impressed by these British and French threats and grew tired of waiting for Poland to negotiate. Having first secured a *non-aggression pact with Russia (August 1939)*, the *Germans invaded Poland on 1 September*. Britain and France accordingly declared war on Germany.

14.1 RELATIONS BETWEEN JAPAN AND CHINA

We have already seen (see Section 10.2(b)) the motives behind the Japanese invasion of Manchuria in 1931: it was essential to keep control of the province as a valuable trade outlet; China seemed to be growing stronger under the rule of Chiang Kai-shek and the Japanese feared this might result in their being excluded from Manchuria. In fact it is possible to present a good defence of Japanese actions, as indeed Sir John Simon, the British Foreign Minister, did at the League of Nations. Japan had been involved in the province since the 1890s and was given Port Arthur and a privileged position in south Manchuria as a result of the Russo-Japanese War. Since then the Japanese had invested millions of pounds in Manchuria in the development of industry and railways. By 1931 they controlled the south Manchurian Railway and the banking system, and could not stand by and see themselves gradually squeezed out of such a out of such a valuable province with a population of 30 million, especially when they were suffering economic hardship because of the great depression. Although nobody was fooled when the Japanese announced that they had turned Manchuria into the independent state of *Manchukuo* under Pu Yi, the last of the Chinese emperors, no action was taken against them. However, what followed could not be justified and could only be described as flagrant aggression.

(a) **In 1933 the Japanese began to advance from Manchuria into the rest of north-eastern China** to which they had no claim whatsoever. By the end of 1935 a large area of China as far as Peking had fallen under Japanese political and commercial control, while the Chinese themselves were torn by civil war between Chiang Kai-shek's *Kuomintang* government and the communists led by Mao Tse-tung (see Section 17.2).

(b) **After signing the Anti-Comintern Pact with Germany (1936)**, the Japanese army seized the excuse provided by an incident between Chinese and Japanese troops in Peking to begin an invasion of other parts of *China (July 1937)*. Although the Prime Minister, Prince Konoye, was against such massive intervention, he had to bow to the wishes of General Sugiyama, the War Minister. By the autumn of 1938 the Japanese had captured the cities of Shanghai, Nanking (Chiang Kai-shek's capital) and Hankow, committing terrible atrocities against Chinese civilians. However, complete victory eluded the Japanese: Chiang had reached an understanding with his communist enemies whereby both co-operated against the invaders; a new capital was established well inland at Chungking and spirited Chinese resistance was mounted with help from the Russians.

(c) **Japanese troops landed in the south of China** and quickly captured Canton, but Chiang still refused to surrender or accept Japanese terms.

Meanwhile the League of Nations had again condemned Japanese aggression but was powerless to act, since Japan was no longer a member and refused to attend a conference about the China situation. Britain and France were too preoccupied with Hitler to take much notice of China, and the Russians did not want full-scale war with Japan. The USA, the only power capable of effectively resisting Japan, was still bent on isolation. Thus, on the eve of the Second World War, the Japanese were in control of most of eastern China (though outside the cities their hold was shaky) while Chiang held out in the centre and west.

14.2 MUSSOLINI'S FOREIGN POLICY

To begin with, Italian foreign policy was somewhat confused: Mussolini knew what he wanted, which was 'to make Italy great, respected and feared', but he was not sure how to achieve it, beyond agitating for a revision of the 1919 peace settlement in Italy's favour. At first as we have already seen, he seemed to think an adventurous policy was his best line of action, hence the *Corfu Incident* and the *occupation of Fiume in 1923*. After these early successes he became more cautious, perhaps alarmed by Italy's isolation at the time of Corfu. After 1923 his policy falls roughly into two phases:

(a) 1923–34. At this stage Mussolini's policy was determined by rivalry with the French in the Mediterranean and the Balkans, where Italian relations with Yugoslavia, France's ally and protégé, were usually strained. Another factor was the Italian fear that the weak state of Austria along her north-eastern frontier might fall too much under the influence of Germany; Mussolini was nervous about a possible German threat via the Brenner Pass. He tried to deal with both problems mainly by *diplomatic* means:

   (i)   He attended the *Locarno Conference (1925)* but was disappointed when the agreements signed did not guarantee the Italian frontier with Austria.
   (ii) He was *friendly towards Greece, Hungary and especially Albania*, the southern neighbour and rival of Yugoslavia. Economic and defence agreements were signed with the result that Albania was virtually controlled by Italy, which now had a strong position around the Adriatic.
   (iii) *He cultivated good relations with Britain*: he supported her demand that Turkey should hand over Mosul province to Iraq and in return the British gave Italy a small part of Somaliland.
   (iv) Italy became the first state after Britain to *recognise the USSR* and signed a non-aggression pact with her in September 1933.
   (v)   He tried to *bolster up Austria against the threat from Nazi Germany* by supporting the anti-Nazi government of Dollfuss and by signing trade agreements with Austria and Hungary. When Dollfuss was murdered by Austrian Nazis (July 1934) the *Duce* sent three Italian divisions to the frontier in case the Germans invaded Austria; consequently the Nazis called off their attempt to seize power in Austria. This decisive anti-German stand improved relations between Italy and France. However, though he was highly respected abroad, Mussolini was growing impatient; his successes were not spectacular enough.

(b) After 1934 he gradually drifted from extreme suspicion of Hitler's designs on Austria to grudging admiration of Hitler's achievements and a desire to *imitate him*. After their first meeting (June 1934) Mussolini described Hitler contemptuously as 'that mad little clown', but he later came to believe that there was more to be gained from friendship with Germany than with Britain and France. The more he fell under Hitler's influence, the more aggressive he became. His changing attitude is illustrated by events:

(i)   When Hitler announced the reintroduction of conscription (March 1935), Mussolini joined the British and French in condemning the German action and guaranteeing Austria (the Stresa Front, April 1935). Both the British and French carefully avoided discussion of the Abyssinian crisis which was already brewing, and Mussolini took this to mean that they would turn a blind eye to an Italian attack on Abyssinia, regarding it as a bit of old-fashioned colonial expansion. The *Anglo-German Naval Agreement (June 1935)*, which broke the Stresa Front, only served to convince Mussolini of British cynicism and self-interest.

(ii) *The invasion of Abyssinia (October 1935)* was the great turning point in Mussolini's career. Italian involvement in the country, the only remaining independent state left in Africa, went back to 1896 when an Italian attempt to colonise it had ended in ignominious defeat at Adowa, Mussolini's motives for the 1935 attack were obvious: Italy's existing colonies in East Africa (Eritrea and Somaliland) were not rewarding, and his attempts (by a treaty of friendship signed in 1928) to reduce Abyssinia to the position of Albania had failed. The Emperor Haile Selassie had strongly resisted falling under Italian economic domination. In addition Italy was suffering from the *depression*, and a victorious war would divert attention from internal troubles, provide a new market for Italian exports, please the nationalists and colonialists, and boost Mussolini's sagging popularity. The Italian victory over the ill-equipped and unprepared Ethiopians was a foregone conclusion. Its real significance was how it demonstrated the *ineffectiveness of collective security*. The League condemned Italy as an aggressor and applied economic sanctions, but these were useless because they did not include preventing sales of *oil and coal* to Italy, even though the resulting oil shortage would have seriously hampered the Italian war effort. The League's prestige suffered a further blow when it emerged that the British Foreign Secretary, Hoare, had made a *secret deal with Laval*, the French prime Minister (*December 1935*) to hand over a large section of Abyssinia to Italy; this was more than the Italians had managed to capture at the time. Public opinion in Britain and France was so outraged that the idea was dropped. Reasons for this *weak stand against Italy* were that Britain and France were economically and militarily unprepared for war and were anxious to avoid any action (such as oil sanctions) which might provoke Mussolini into declaring war on them; both were hoping to resurrect the Stresa Front and use Italy as an ally against the real threat to European peace – Germany; hence their aim was to appease Mussolini. Unfortunately the *results were disastrous*: the League and the idea of collective security were discredited; Mussolini was annoyed by the sanctions and began to be drawn towards friendship with Hitler, who had not criticised the invasion and refused to apply sanctions; in return Mussolini dropped his objections to a German takeover of Austria; Hitler took advantage of the preoccupation with Abyssinia to send troops into the Rhineland.

(iii) When the Spanish Civil War broke out in 1936 Mussolini sent extensive help to Franco in the hope of establishing a *third fascist state in Europe* and of gaining naval bases in Spain from which he could threaten France; his excuse was that he wanted to prevent the spread of communism.

(iv) An understanding was reached with Hitler known as the *Rome–Berlin Axis*, around which, in the *Duce's* words, 'all European states that desire peace can revolve', and in 1937 Italy joined the Anti-Comintern Pact with Germany and Japan, in which all three pledged themselves to stand side by side against Bolshevism. When the Germans occupied Austria (March 1938) Mussolini accepted it without protest. This reversal of his previous policy and his friendship with Germany were not popular in Italy, and disillusionment with Mussolini spread rapidly.

(v) His popularity revived temporarily with his part in the Munich settlement (September 1938) which seemed to have secured peace, but Mussolini failed to draw the right conclusions from his people's relief and committed another act of aggression.

(vi) In *April 1939* Italian troops suddenly occupied *Albania* with very little resistance. This was a pointless operation since Albania was already under Italian economic control, but Mussolini wanted a triumph to imitate Hitler's recent occupation of Czechoslovakia.

(vii) Carried away by his successes, Mussolini signed a *full alliance with Germany*, the *Pact of Steel (May 1939)*, in which Italy promised full military support if war came. Mussolini was committing Italy to deeper and deeper involvement with Germany, which would in the end ruin him.

14.3 WHAT WERE HITLER'S AIMS IN FOREIGN POLICY, AND HOW SUCCESSFUL HAD HE BEEN BY THE END OF 1938?

(a) Hitler aimed to make Germany into a great power again and this he hoped to achieve by destroying the hated Versailles settlement, building up the army, recovering lost territory such as the Saar and the Polish Corridor, and bringing all Germans within the *Reich*. This last aim would involve the annexation of Austria and the acquisition of territory from Czechoslovakia and Poland, both of which had large German minorities as a result of Versailles. There is some disagreement about what, if anything, Hitler intended beyond these aims. Most historians believe that the annexation of Austria and parts of Czechoslovakia and Poland was only a beginning, to be followed by the seizure of the rest of Czechoslovakia and Poland and by the conquest and permanent occupation of Russia as far east as the Ural Mountains. This would give him what the Germans called *Lebensraum* (living space) which would provide food for the German people and an area in which the excess German population could settle and colonise. An additional advantage was that communism would be destroyed. However, not all historians agree about these further aims; A. J. P. Taylor, for example, claims that Hitler never intended a major war and at most was prepared only for a limited war against Poland.

(b) Whatever the truth about his long-term intentions, Hitler began his foreign policy with a **series of brilliant successes** (one of the main reasons for his popularity in Germany). By the end of 1938 almost every one of the first set of aims had been achieved, without war and with the approval of Britain. Only the Germans of Poland remained to be brought within the *Reich*. Unfortunately it was when he failed to achieve this by peaceful means that Hitler took his fateful decision to *invade Poland*.

(i) Given that Germany was still militarily weak in 1933, Hitler had to move cautiously at first. He *withdrew Germany from the World Disarmament Conference* and from the *League of Nations* on the grounds that France would not agree to German equality of armaments. At the same time he insisted that Germany was willing to disarm if other states agreed to do the same, and that he wanted only peace. This was one of his favourite techniques: to act boldly while soothing his opponents with the sort of conciliatory speeches he knew they wanted to hear.

(ii) Next Hitler signed a ten-year *non-aggression pact with the Poles (January 1934)*, who were showing alarm in case the Germans tried to take back the Polish corridor. This was something of a triumph for Hitler: Britain took it as further evidence of his

Fig. 14.1 *Hitler's gains before the Second World War*

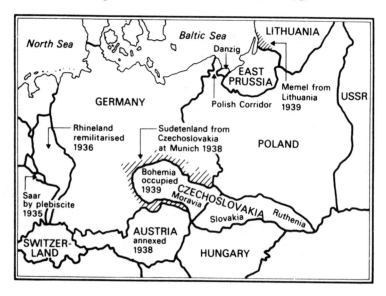

peaceful intentions; it ruined the French Little Entente which depended very much on Poland; and it guaranteed Polish neutrality whenever Germany should move against Austria and Czechoslovakia. On the other hand it improved relations between France and Russia, who were both worried by the apparent threat from Nazi Germany.

(iii) July 1934 saw Hitler suffer a setback to his ambitions of an *Anschluss* (union) between Germany and Austria. The Austrian Nazis, encouraged by Hitler, staged a revolt and murdered the Chancellor, Engelbert Dollfuss, the protégé of Mussolini. However, when Mussolini moved Italian troops to the Austrian frontier and warned the Germans off, the revolt collapsed; Hitler, taken aback, had to accept that Germany was not yet strong enough to force the issue and *disclaimed responsibility* for the actions of the Austrian Nazis.

(iv) *The Saar was returned to Germany (January 1935)* after a plebiscite resulting in a 90 per cent vote in favour. Though the plebiscite had been provided for at Versailles, Nazi propaganda made the most of the success, and Hitler announced that now all causes of grievance between France and Germany had been removed.

(v) Hitler's first successful breach of Versailles came in *March 1935* when he announced the *reintroduction of conscription*. His excuse was that Britain had just announced air force increases and France had extended conscription from 12 to 18 months (their justification was German rearmament). Much to their consternation, Hitler told his startled generals and the rest of the world that he would build up his peacetime army to 36 divisions (about 600,000 men). The generals need not have worried: although the Stresa Front condemned his violation of Versailles, no action was taken, the League was helpless, and the Front collapsed anyway as a result of Hitler's next success.

(vi) Shrewdly realising how frail the Stresa Front was, Hitler detached Britain by offering to limit the German navy to 35 per cent of the strength of the British navy. Britain eagerly accepted in the resulting *Anglo-German Naval Agreement (June 1935)* apparently believing that since the Germans were already breaking Versailles by building a fleet, it would be as well to have it limited. Without consulting her two allies, Britain had condoned German rearmament, which proceeded with gathering momentum. By the end of 1938 the army stood at 51 divisions (about 800,000 men) plus reserves, there were 21 large naval vessels (battleships, cruisers and destroyers), many more under construction, and 47 U-boats. A large air force of over 2000 aircraft had been built up.

(vii) Meanwhile, encouraged by his successes, Hitler took the calculated risk of *sending troops into the demilitarised zone of the Rhineland (March 1936)* – a breach of both Versailles and Locarno. Though the troops had orders to withdraw at the first sign of

French opposition, no resistance was offered beyond the usual protests. At the same time, well aware of the mood of pacifism among his opponents, Hitler soothed them by offering a peace treaty to last for 25 years.

(viii) Later in 1936 Hitler consolidated Germany's position by reaching an understanding with Mussolini (the *Rome–Berlin Axis*) and by signing the *Anti-Comintern Pact with Japan* (also joined by Italy in 1937). Germans and Italians gained military experience helping Franco to victory in the Spanish Civil War, one of the most notorious exploits being the bombing of the defenceless Basque market town of Guernica by the German Condor Legion.

(ix) The *Anschluss with Austria (March 1938)* was Hitler's greatest success to date. Matters came to a head when the Austrian Nazis staged huge demonstrations in Vienna, Graz and Linz, which Chancellor Schuschnigg's government could not control. Realising that this could be the prelude to a German invasion, Schuschnigg announced a plebiscite about whether or not Austria should remain independent. Hitler decided to act before this took place, in case the vote went against union; German troops moved in and Austria became part of the Third *Reich*. It was a triumph for Germany: it revealed the weaknesses of Britain and France who again did no more than protest, it demonstrated the value of the new understanding with Italy, and it dealt a severe blow to Czechoslovakia which could now be attacked from the south as well as from the west and north. All was ready for the beginning of Hitler's campaign to acquire the German-speaking Sudetenland, a campaign which ended in triumph at the *Munich Conference* in *September 1938*. Before examining the events of Munich and after, we must pause to consider why it was that Hitler was allowed to get away with these violations of the Versailles treaties. The reason can be summed up in one word – *appeasement*.

14.4 WHAT IS MEANT BY THE TERM 'APPEASEMENT'? HOW COULD SUCH A POLICY BE JUSTIFIED, AND WHAT PART DID IT PLAY IN INTERNATIONAL AFFAIRS BETWEEN 1935 AND 1939?

(a) Appeasement was the policy followed by the British and later by the French of **avoiding war with aggressive powers such as Japan, Italy and Germany**, by giving way to their demands provided these were not too unreasonable. There were *two distinct phases* of appeasement:

(i) From the mid-1920s until 1937 there was a vague feeling that war must be avoided at all costs, and Britain and sometimes France drifted along accepting the various *faits accomplis* (Manchuria, Abyssinia, German rearmament, Rhineland reoccupation).

illus 14.1 Enthusiastic crowds greet Adolf Hitler during his first visit to the ceded Sudetenland, 1938

(ii) When Neville Chamberlain became British Prime Minister in May 1937 he gave appeasement new drive; he believed in taking the initiative: he would find out what Hitler wanted and show him that reasonable claims could be met by *negotiation rather than by force*.

The origins of appeasement can be seen in British policy during the 1920s with the Dawes and Young Plans, which tried to conciliate the Germans, and also with the Locarno Treaties and their significant omission: Britain did not agree to guarantee Germany's eastern frontiers, which even Stresemann, the 'good German', said must be revised. When Austen Chamberlain, the British Foreign Minister (and Neville's half-brother), remarked at the time of Locarno that no British government would ever risk the bones of a British grenadier in defence of the Polish Corridor, it seemed to the Germans that Britain had turned her back on eastern Europe. Appeasement reached its climax at *Munich*, where Britain and France were so determined to avoid war with Germany that they made Hitler a present of the Sudetenland and so set in motion the destruction of Czechoslovakia. Even with such concessions as this, appeasement failed.

(b) At the time appeasement was being pursued, however, there seemed much to commend it and the appeasers, who included MacDonald, Baldwin, Simon and Hoare as well as Neville Chamberlain were **convinced of the rightness of their policy:**

(i) It was essential to avoid war which was likely to be more devastating than ever before, as the horrors of the Spanish Civil War demonstrated. Moreover Britain, still in the throes of the economic crisis, could not afford vast rearmament and the crippling expenses of a major war. British governments seemed to be supported by a strongly *pacifist public opinion*. In February 1933 the Oxford Union voted that it would not fight for King and Country, and Baldwin and the National government won a huge victory in November 1935 shortly after he had declared: 'I give you my word of honour that there will be no great armaments.'

(ii) Many felt that *Italy and Germany had genuine grievances*: Italy had been cheated at Versailles, Germany treated too harshly. Therefore Britain should react with sympathy and with regard to Germany, try to revise the most hated clauses of Versailles. This would remove the need for German aggression and lead to Anglo-German friendship.

(iii) Since the League of Nations seemed to be helpless, Chamberlain believed that the only way to settle disputes was by *personal contact between leaders*; in this way, he would be able to control and civilise Hitler, and Mussolini into the bargain, and bring them to respect international law.

(iv) *Economic co-operation* between Britain and Germany would be good for both; if Britain helped the German economy to recover, the internal violence would die down.

(v) *Fear of communist Russia* was great especially among British Conservatives, many of whom believed the communist threat to be greater than the danger from Hitler. Many British politicians were willing to overlook the unpleasant features of Nazism in the hope that Hitler's Germany would be a guarantee against communist expansion westwards; in fact many admired Hitler's drive and achievements.

(vi) Underlying all these feelings was the belief that Britain ought not to take any military action in case it led to a full-scale war which Britain was *totally unprepared for*; at the same time, the USA was for isolation and France was weak and divided. Chamberlain speeded up British rearmament so that 'nobody should treat her with anything but respect'. The longer appeasement lasted, the stronger Britain would become and the more this would deter aggression.

(c) Appeasement had a profound effect on the way international relations developed. Although it might have worked with some German governments, with Hitler it was doomed to failure. Some historians believe that it convinced Hitler of the complacency and weakness of Britain and France to such an extent that he was willing to risk attacking Poland, thereby starting the Second World War. It is important to emphasise that appeasement was primarily a British policy, with which the French did not always agree. Poincaré stood up to the Germans (see Section 13.2(c)) and although Briand was in favour of conciliation, even he drew the line at a proposed Austro-German customs union in 1931. Louis Barthou, Foreign Minister for a few months in 1934, believed in firmness towards Hitler and aimed to build up a strong anti-German group which would include Italy and Russia. To this end he was largely responsible for *Russia's entry into the League of Nations (September 1934)*; he told the British that France 'refused to legalise German rearmament' contrary to the Versailles treaties. Unfortunately Barthou was assassinated in October 1934 along with King Alexander of Yugoslavia who was on a state visit to France. They were both shot by Croat terrorists shortly after the king had arrived in Marseilles. Barthou's successor, Pierre Laval, signed an alliance with Russia in May 1935, though it was a weak affair – there was no provision in it for military co-operation, since Laval distrusted the communists. He pinned his main hopes on friendship with Mussolini, but these were dashed by the failure of the Hoare–Laval pact. After this the French were so deeply split between left and right that no decisive foreign policy seemed possible, and since the right admired Hitler, France fell in behind the British. Six examples of *appeasement at work* were:

(i) *No action was taken to check the obvious German rearmament*; Lord Lothian, a Liberal, had a revealing comment to make about this after visiting Hitler in January 1935: 'I am convinced that Hitler does not want war . . . what the Germans are after is a strong army which will enable them to deal with Russia.'

(ii) *The Anglo-German Naval Agreement* condoning German naval rearmament was signed without prior consultation with France and Italy. This broke the Stresa Front, gravely shook French confidence in Britain, and encouraged Laval to look for understandings with Mussolini and Hitler.

(iii) There was only *half-hearted British action against the Italian invasion of Abyssinia.*

(iv) The French, though disturbed at the German reoccupation of the Rhineland (March 1936), *did not mobilise*; they were deeply divided, ultra-cautious and received no backing from the British, who were impressed by Hitler's offer of a 25-year peace. Indeed Lord Londonderry (a Conservative and Secretary of State for Air from 1931–5) was reported to have sent Hitler a telegram congratulating him on his success, while Lord Lothian remarked that the German troops had merely entered their own 'back garden'.

(v) *Neither Britain nor France intervened in the Spanish Civil War*, though Italy and Germany sent decisive help to Franco. Britain tried to entice Mussolini to remove his troops by recognising Italian possession of Abyssinia (April 1938); however, Mussolini failed to keep his side of the bargain.

(vi) Though both Britain and France protested strongly at the *Anschluss* between Germany and Austria (March 1938), many in Britain saw it as the *natural union of one German group to another*. But British passivity encouraged Hitler to make demands on Czechoslovakia, which brought forth Chamberlain's supreme act of appeasement and Hitler's greatest triumph to date: Munich.

14.5 MUNICH TO THE OUTBREAK OF WAR: SEPTEMBER 1938 TO SEPTEMBER 1939

This fateful year saw Hitler waging two pressure campaigns: the first against *Czechoslovakia*, the second against *Poland*.

(a) **It seems likely that Hitler had decided to destroy Czechoslovakia** as part of his *Lebensraum* (living space) policy and because he hated the Czechs for their democracy as well as for the fact that their state had been set up by the Versailles Treaty. His excuse for the opening propaganda campaign was that 3.5 million Sudeten Germans under their leader Konrad Henlein were being discriminated against by the Czech government, though in fact they were not being seriously inconvenienced. The Nazis organised huge protest demonstrations in the Sudetenland and clashes occurred between Czechs and Germans. The Czech President, Beneš, feared that Hitler was fomenting the disturbances so that German troops could march in 'to restore order'. Chamberlain and Daladier, the French Prime Minister, feared the same and that war might break out. They determined to go to almost any lengths to avoid war and put tremendous pressure on the Czechs to make concessions to Hitler. Chamberlain twice flew to Germany to confer with Hitler, but no progress could be made. When it seemed that war was inevitable Hitler invited Chamberlain and Daladier to a *four-power conference* which met at *Munich (29 September 1938)*. Here a plan produced by Mussolini (but drafted by the German Foreign Office) was accepted. The *Sudetenland was to be handed over to Germany immediately*, but Germany along with the other three powers guaranteed the remainder of Czechoslovakia. Neither the Czechs nor the Russians were invited to the conference; the Czechs were told that if they resisted the Munich decision they would receive no help from Britain or France, even though the latter had guaranteed the Czech frontiers at Locarno. When Chamberlain arrived back in Britain he received a rapturous welcome from the public which thought war had been averted. Chamberlain himself remarked: 'I believe it is peace for our time'.

However, not everybody was so enthusiastic: Churchill called Munich 'a total and unmitigated defeat' and Duff Cooper, the First Lord of the Admiralty, resigned from the cabinet saying that Hitler could not be trusted to keep the agreement. They were right: Czechoslovakia was crippled by the loss of *70 per cent of her heavy industry and almost all her fortifications* to Germany. Slovakia began to demand semi-independence, and when it looked as though the country was about to fall apart, Hitler pressurised President Hacha into requesting German help 'to restore order'. Consequently in *March 1939 German troops occupied the rest of Czechoslovakia*. Britain and France protested but took no action: according to Chamberlain, the guarantee of Czech frontiers did not apply because technically Czechoslovakia had not been invaded: German troops had entered by *invitation*. However, the German action caused a great rush of criticism: for the first time even the appeasers were unable to justify what Hitler had done; he had broken his promise and seized non-German territory. Even Chamberlain felt that this was going too far and his attitude hardened.

(b) After taking over the Lithuanian port of Memel (which was admittedly peopled largely by Germans), Hitler turned his attentions to *Poland*. The Germans resented the loss of Danzig and the Polish Corridor at Versailles, and now that Czechoslovakia was safely out of the way, Polish neutrality was no longer necessary. In April 1939 Hitler demanded the *return of Danzig and a road and railway across the corridor*. This demand was, in fact, not unreasonable since Danzig was largely German-speaking; but coming so soon after the seizure of Czechoslovakia, the Poles were convinced, probably rightly, that the German demands were only a prelude to invasion. Already fortified by a British promise of help 'in the event of any action which clearly threatened Polish independence', the Foreign Minister, Colonel Beck, rejected the German demands and refused to attend a conference, no doubt afraid of another Munich. British pressure on the Poles to surrender Danzig was to no avail, and the British were so slow in

illus 14.2 *Chamberlain and Hitler in Munich, September 1938*

pursuing negotiations for an alliance with Russia, the only way in which their promise of help to Poland could be made effective, that Hitler got in first and signed a *non-aggression pact with the USSR*. Also agreed was a *partition* of Poland between Germany and the USSR (24 August). Hitler was convinced that with Russia neutral, Britain and France would not risk intervention; when the British ratified their guarantee to Poland Hitler took it as a bluff. When the Poles still refused to negotiate, a *full-scale German invasion began early on 1 September*. Chamberlain had still not completely thrown off appeasement and suggested that if German troops were withdrawn, a conference would be held – there was no response from the Germans. Only when pressure mounted in parliament and in the country did Chamberlain send an ultimatum to Germany. When this expired at 11 a.m. on 3 September, Britain was at war with Germany. Soon afterwards, France also declared war.

14.6 WHY DID WAR BREAK OUT? WAS HITLER OR WERE THE APPEASERS TO BLAME?

The debate is still going on about who or what was responsible for the Second World War. The Versailles treaties have been blamed for filling the Germans with bitterness and the desire for revenge; the League of Nations and the idea of collective security have been criticised because they failed to secure general disarmament and to control potential aggressors; the world economic crisis has been mentioned, since without it Hitler would probably never have come to power. While these factors no doubt helped to create the sort of tensions which might well lead to war, something more was needed. It is worth remembering also that by the end of 1938 *many of the German grievances had been removed*: reparations were largely cancelled, the disarmament clauses had been ignored, the Rhineland was remilitarised, Austria and Germany were united, and 3.5 million Germans had been recovered from Czecho-slovakia. Britain had even offered some compensation for lost German colonies. Germany was, in fact, a great power again. What went wrong?

(a) During and immediately after the war **there was general agreement outside Germany that Hitler was to blame.** By attacking Poland on all fronts instead of merely occupying Danzig and the corridor, Hitler showed that he intended not just to recover the Germans lost at Versailles, but to *destroy Poland*. Martin Gilbert argues that his motive was to remove the stigma of defeat in the First World War; 'for the only antidote to defeat in one war is victory in the next'. Hugh Trevor-Roper and many other historians believe that Hitler intended a major war right from the beginning; they argue that he hated communism and wanted to conquer Russia and control it permanently, and this could be achieved only by a major war; the destruction of Poland was an essential preliminary to the invasion of Russia; the non-aggression pact with Russia was simply a way of lulling Russian suspicions and keeping her neutral until Poland had been dealt with. Their evidence for this theory is taken from statements in Hitler's book *Mein Kampf* (My Struggle) and from the Hossbach Memorandum, a summary made by Hitler's adjutant, Colonel Hossbach, of a meeting held in November 1937, at which Hitler explained his plans to his generals. If this theory is correct, appeasement can be discounted as a cause of war, except insofar as it made Hitler's job easier; *war was inevitable anyway sooner or later*.

(b) Other historians claim that **appeasement was equally to blame**; Britain and France should have taken a firm line with Hitler before Germany had become too strong: an Anglo-French attack on western Germany in 1936 at the time of the Rhineland occupation would have taught Hitler a lesson. By giving way to him the appeasers increased his prestige at home; as Alan Bullock writes, 'success and the absence of resistance tempted Hitler to reach out further, to take bigger risks'. He may not have had any definite plans for war, but after the surrender at Munich he was so convinced that Britain and France would remain passive again that he decided to gamble on war with Poland. Chamberlain has also been criticised for choosing the *wrong issue* over which to make a stand against Hitler. It is argued that German claims for Danzig and routes across the corridor were more reasonable than her demands for the Sudetenland (which contained almost a million non-Germans);

Poland was difficult for Britian and France to defend and was militarily much weaker than Czechoslovakia. Chamberlain ought therefore to have made his stand at Munich and backed the Czechs. Chamberlain's defenders claim that his main motive at Munich was to give Britain time to *rearm* for an eventual fight against Hitler, but his critics argue that if Chamberlain had genuinely intended to curb Hitler, it would have been better to have fought alongside Czechoslovakia, which was militarily and industrially strong and had excellent fortifications.

(c) Characteristically A. J. P. Taylor has produced the most controversial theory about the outbreak of the war. He believes that **Hitler did not intend to cause a major war, and expected at the most a short war with Poland**. According to Taylor, Hitler's *aims* were similar to those of previous German rulers – Wilhelm II and Stresemann; only his *methods* were more ruthless. Hitler was a brilliant opportunist taking advantage of the mistakes of the appeasers and of events such as the crisis in Czechoslovakia in February 1939, the German occupation of which was not the result of a sinister long-term plan; 'it was the unforeseen by-product of events in Slovakia' (the Slovak demand for more independence from the Prague government). Whereas Chamberlain miscalculated when he thought he could make Hitler respectable, Hitler misread the minds of Chamberlain and the British; how could he be expected to foresee that the British and French would be so inconsistent as to support Poland (where his more reasonable claim lay) after appeasing him over Czechoslovakia (where his case was much less valid)? Thus for Taylor, Hitler was *lured into the war almost by accident*, after the Poles had called his bluff.

(d) **The USSR has been accused of making war inevitable by signing the non-aggression pact with Germany**. It is argued that she ought to have allied with the west and with Poland, thereby *frightening Hitler into keeping the peace*. On the other hand, the British were most reluctant to ally with the Russians; Chamberlain distrusted them, as did the Poles, and believed them militarily weak. Russian historians justify the pact on the grounds that it gave the USSR time to prepare their defences against a possible German attack.

What is the unfortunate student to believe then if historians cannot agree? It has to be said that the majority view is that Hitler was largely responsible. Perhaps it is appropriate to allow the German historian, Joachim Fest, the final word: 'There can be no question about whose was the guilt . . . Hitler's urge to bring things to a head so shaped events that any wish to compromise on the part of the western powers was bound to come to nothing. His entire career was orientated towards war.'

QUESTIONS

1. The Munich Agreement 1938
Study the Sources below, and answer the questions that follow.

Source A
The Munich Agreement, 29 September 1938.

Germany, the United Kingdom, France and Italy, taking into consideration the agreement which has already been made in principle for the handing to Germany of the Sudetenland, have agreed on the following terms:

1. The evacuation will begin on 1st October.
2. The United Kingdom, France and Italy agree that the evacuation of territory shall be completed by 10th October without any existing installations having been destroyed.
3. The occupation by stages of the predominantly German territory by German troops will begin on 1st October.

Source: *History of the 20th Century* (Purnell–BPC Publishing, 1969, adapted extracts).

Source B
A House of Commons speech on the Munich Agreement by Neville Chamberlain, 3 October 1938.

When the House met last Wednesday, we were all under the shadow of a great menace; war in a form more stark and terrible than ever before, seemed to be staring us in the face. Before I sat down a message had come which gave us new hope that peace might yet be saved, and today, only a few days after, we all meet in joy and thankfulness that the prayers of millions have been answered . . . M. Daladier had in some respects the most difficult task of all four of us, because of the special relations uniting his country and Czechoslovakia, and I should like to say that his courage, his readiness to take responsibility, his pertinacity and his unfailing good humour were invaluable throughout our whole discussions . . . My main purpose has been to work for the pacification of Europe, for the removal of those suspicions and animosities which have so long poisoned the air. The path which leads to appeasement is long and bristles with obstacles. The question of Czechoslovakia is the latest and perhaps the most dangerous. Now that we have got past it, I feel that it may be possible to make further progress along the road to sanity.

Source: J. H. Bettey (ed.), *English Historical Documents* (Routledge & Kegan Paul, 1967, extracts).

Source C
A House of Commons speech by Winston Churchill on the Munich Agreement, 5 October 1938.

If I do not begin this afternoon by paying the usual tributes to the Prime Minister for his handling of this crisis, it is certainly not from any lack of personal regard. But I will say the most unpopular thing, namely, that we have sustained a total and unmitigated defeat, and that France has suffered even more than we have . . . I believe the Czechs, left to themselves, would have been able to make better terms than they have got – they could hardly have worse. I think that in future the Czechoslovak State cannot be maintained as an independent entity. You will find that in a period of time which may be measured by years, but may be measured only by months, Czechoslovakia will be engulfed in the Nazi regime. But our loyal brave people should know the truth: that there has been gross neglect and deficiency in our defences; that we have sustained a defeat without a war.

Source: J. H. Bettey (ed.) *English Historical Documents* (Routledge & Kegan Paul, 1967, extracts).

Source D
Russian cartoon (Fig. 14.2) about Munich, 1938: Chamberlain and Daladier act as traffic policemen. The sign-post reads 'Left: Western Europe, Right: USSR'.

Source E
An article by a Russian historian, A. O. Chubaryan.

To the Soviet Union, the Munich Agreement constituted a direct threat. In the first place by conquering the Sudeten region and soon after the whole of Czechoslovakia, the German armies drew near to the very frontiers of the USSR. Secondly Munich showed that Britain and France preferred an agreement with the aggressor to the formation of an alliance against him. After Munich the Soviet Union was directly confronted with the danger of isolation, of being left to face German fascism on its own, and with the prospect of an alliance between Britain, France, Italy and Germany.

Source: *History of the 20th Century* (Purnell–BPC Publishing, 1969, adapted extract).

Source F
An article by a French historian, Maurice Baumont.

Controversy raged fiercely in France. Some felt that France simply did not have the military potential to carry out her promises to Czechoslovakia. The French, remembering the horrors of 1914–18, and disillusioned with the following peace, were in no mood for another war. The

Fig. 14.2

chief of the French air force estimated that it would be wiped out after only eight days in action against Germany . . . The more optimistic considered that Czechoslovakia, France and Russia alone were stronger than Germany and that an easy victory would follow any outbreak of war. Germany was unprepared; the Siegfried line was not complete. Czechoslovakia had over 40 divisions under arms on 23 September, a number Hitler could only just match. Czechoslovakia's strength was increased by her protective fortifications. In the aftermath of Munich, the principles of the agreement were condemned. Suddenly Munich appeared a disaster. War had been averted but there grew a feeling of shame that so much had been yielded for the sake of peace. To Hitler the Agreement was no more than a scrap of paper – less than six months after its signature he was to march into Prague.

Source: *History of the 20th Century* (Purnell–BPC Publishing, 1969, adapted extract).

(a) **(i)** Which four powers signed the Munich Agreement? **4(a)**

  (ii) Which other state involved in the crisis was not allowed to be represented in the discussions? **4(a)**

  (iii) Explain briefly in your own words what was agreed at Munich (study Source A). **4(a)**

  (iv) How soon was the agreement due to be put into operation and how soon was it expected to be completed? **4(a)**

(b) **(i)** According to Source B, what was the 'great menace' referred to by Chamberlain? **1,4(a)**

  (ii) What was the message that came to Chamberlain? **1,4(a)**

  (iii) Why does Chamberlain say that the Commons were meeting 'in joy and thankfulness'? **1,4(a)**

  (iv) Why would the Czechs not agree with Chamberlain that it was a time of joy? (Look at Source A). **1,4(a)**

  (v) What were the 'special relations' (mentioned in Source B) which Daladier's country had with Czechoslovakia and why had this made his job at Munich difficult? **1,2,4(a)**

  (vi) According to Source B, what was Chamberlain's main aim in foreign policy? What word towards the end of Source B sums this policy up well? **4(a)**

(c) **(i)** Explain in your own words why Churchill (Source C) does not like the Munich Agreement. **4(a)**

  (ii) Which one of the British politicians – Chamberlain or Churchill – was right about the future of Czechoslovakia? **1,4(a)**

(d) **(i)** In the cartoon in Fig. 14.2 (Source D) which figure represents Chamberlain and which Daladier? **1,4(a)**

  (ii) After studying Sources D and E, explain what point the cartoonist is trying to make. **4(b,c)**

  (iii) How far did the Russian fears expressed in Source E, become reality? **1,4(a)**

(e) **(i)** From the evidence of Source F, why did France not keep its promises to Czechoslovakia? **4(a)**

  (ii) What evidence can you find in Source F to support Churchill's claim in Source C that, left to themselves, the Czechs would have been able to make better terms? **4(c)**

(f) Using the information from the Sources, and your own knowledge, make out a case to support the opinion that the Munich Agreement was a defeat for France and Britain, as well as for Czechoslovakia. **1,2,4(a,c)**

2. Mussolini and Abyssinia: *The Times*, 1 August 1935

Study the Source below, and then answer the questions that follow.

Describing the 'historical objectives' of Italy in Africa to an assembly of leading Fascists, Signor Mussolini said that above all Italy could civilise Africa and her position in the Mediterranean gave her this right and placed this duty upon her. These words show the Italian attitude towards colonial expansion and in particular towards Abyssinia. Italy's need for expansion is an old theme which has become increasingly insistent in recent years . . . Italy, faced with a rapidly growing population, has long felt stifled within her narrow boundaries. It is calculated that by 1950 or even sooner, there will be 50 million Italians living in a country one half the size of France, without prime raw materials, prisoners in an enclosed sea, the outlets from which are in the hands of other powers. 'I think for Italy', said Mussolini, 'like the great Englishmen who have made the British Empire have fought for England, like the great French colonizers have thought for France'.

(Adapted extract.)

(a)   **(i)**   According to the article, why did Mussolini want to take Abyssinia?   **4(a)**

    (ii)   What right did he think Italy had to land in Africa?   **4(a)**

    (iii)   Explain in your own words what Mussolini meant in the last sentence of the article.   **1,2,4(a)**

(b)   **(i)**   When did Italian troops invade Abyssinia?   **1**

    (ii)   Who was the ruler of Abyssinia at the time?   **1**

(c)   What were the reactions of:

    (i)   Great Britain;

    (ii)   France:

    (iii)   The League of Nations;

  to the Italian invasion?   **1,2**

(d)   What important effects did the Abyssinian War have on international relations?   **1,2**

(e)   **(i)**   Describe how Mussolini's policy towards Germany changed between 1934 and 1939.   **1,2**

    (ii)   What unfortunate results did this change of policy have for Italy?   **1,2**

3. The Nazi–Soviet Pact, August 1939

Study the Sources below, and then answer the questions that follow.

Source A

Cartoon (Fig. 14.3) from the *Evening Standard*, 1939.

Source B

From 'The Soviet–German Treaty', an article published in 1969.

The treaty with Germany was a step which the USSR was forced to take in the difficult situation that had come about in the summer of 1939. The Soviet government did not deceive itself regarding Hitler's aims. It understood that the treaty would not bring the USSR lasting peace but only a more or less lengthy breathing-space. When it signed the treaty with Germany the Soviet government undertook the task of using the time thus gained to carry through the political and military measures needed in order to ensure the country's security and strengthen its capacity for defence.

Source: History of the 20th Century (Purnell–BPC Publishing, 1969).

Fig. 14.3

Source C
From 'Directing Hitler Westwards', an article published in 1969)

The Soviet authorities knew that Hitler was preparing to attack the West if he could not frighten them off – and he expected the signing of the Nazi–Soviet Pact to do this. Yet no serious evidence has been produced which would show that British policy was directed to attempting to procure a German attack on the Soviet Union. If the Soviet leadership believed this to be the aim of British policy, they would appear to have been influenced by a major misjudgement.

The real defence of Soviet policy in 1939 is that the British were casting them in a role which if it succeeded in restraining Hitler would be to the credit of Great Britain, whereas if it failed, the Soviet Union would have to bear the burden of fighting on land. Great Britain had no forces available for a major land offensive in Europe and the French saw no point in abandoning their fortifications.

Source: *History of the 20th Century* (Purnell–BPC Publishing, 1969).

Source D
From 'The Brutal Courtship', by David Floyd, published in 1969.

In reply to a question about the military situation in western Europe in the spring of 1940, Stalin said with a smile:

'Daladier's government in France and Chamberlain's government in Britain don't want to get seriously involved in war with Hitler. They are still hoping to push Hitler into war with the Soviet Union.'

In March 1941 the Russian military asked Stalin to agree to the call-up of reserves for re-training. Stalin refused on the grounds that 'it might provide the Germans with an excuse for provoking war'. At this time German reconnaissance planes were making daily flights over Soviet territory and providing the Germans with detailed pictures of the Russian defences. Stalin issued strict orders that the planes were not to be fired on.

In the period 1939–1941, Russian industry was not put on to a war footing: many types of new weapons, tanks, and aircraft, which had already been tested and were superior to their German equivalents, were not put into production; some proven weapons, such as the 44-mm. anti-tank gun, were actually withdrawn from service; the reorganisation of armoured units was not carried through; troop training was still on a peacetime basis.

Source: *History of the 20th Century* (Purnell–BPC Publishing, 1969).

(a) Name Figures A and B in the cartoon in Fig. 14.3 (Source A).
   1,4(a)

(b) Sources A, B and C come from either British or Russian documents. Which of the Sources do you think are more likely to be British and which are more likely to be Russian? Give reasons for your answer.
   4(a,b)

(c) 'Russia should not have made the Pact with Germany in 1939.' Using the Sources, explain how far you agree with this opinion.
   4(a,c)

(d) After this Pact had been signed, the German leader said, 'Now I have the world in my pocket.' What do you think he meant by this?
   1,2,4

(e) Does the evidence in Source D support the views expressed in Source B? Give reasons for your answer.   **4(a,c)**

(f) From the Sources, give *one* piece of primary evidence and *one* piece of secondary evidence which tells us about people's views at the time of the Nazi–Soviet Pact. Explain why the examples you have chosen are regarded as being primary or secondary sources. **4(a,c)**

(g) Choose *one* of these Sources and comment on its reliability to the historian.   **4(a,b)**
   [Northern Examining Association. Specimen Question.]

4. (a) What were Hitler's aims in foreign policy?
   (b) Describe how far these aims had been achieved up to March 1939.
   (c) Explain why Hitler was so successful up to that point.
   (d) How far do you think Hitler was to blame for the Second World War?   **1,2**

5. You are a British supporter of appeasement who keeps a detailed diary about international events. Give extracts from your diary –

(a) explaining your reactions to the Anglo-German naval Agreement (1935), and also explaining why you support appeasement;

(b) giving your feelings about the German occupation of the Rhineland (1936), the Anschluss and Munich (1938);

(c) explaining why you began to change your mind about appeasement after German troops entered Prague (1939);

(d) describing your reactions to Hitler's demands on Poland.

1,2,3

CHAPTER 15

THE SECOND WORLD WAR 1939–45

SUMMARY OF EVENTS

Unlike the 1914–18 war, the Second World War was a war of *rapid movement* and was altogether a more complex affair with major campaigns taking place in the Pacific and the Far East, in North Africa and deep in the heart of Russia, as well as in central and western Europe and the Atlantic. The war falls into *four fairly clearly defined phases*:

(a) Opening moves: September 1939 to December 1940. By the end of September the Germans and Russians had occupied *Poland*; after a five-month pause (known as the 'phoney war') the Germans occupied *Denmark and Norway* (April 1940). In May attacks were made on Holland, Belgium and France, who were soon defeated, leaving Britain alone to face the dictators (Mussolini had declared war in June, just before the fall of France). Hitler's attempt to bomb Britain into submission was thwarted in the *Battle of Britain* (July to September), but Mussolini's armies invaded Egypt and Greece.

(b) The Axis offensive widens: 1941 to the summer of 1942. The war now began to develop into a *world-wide conflict*. First Hitler, confident of victory over Britain, launched an invasion of *Russia (June 1941)*, breaking the non-aggression pact signed less than two years previously; then the Japanese forced the USA into the war by attacking the American naval base at *Pearl Harbor (December 1941)* and proceeded to occupy territories such as the Philippines, Malaya, Singapore and Burma, scattered over a wide area. At this stage of the war there seemed to be no way of stopping the Germans and Japanese, though the Italians were less successful.

(c) The offensives held in check: summer 1942 to summer 1943. This phase of the war saw three important battles in which Axis forces were defeated. In June 1942 the Americans drove off a Japanese attack on *Midway Island*, inflicting heavy losses. In October the Germans, under Rommel and advancing towards Egypt, were halted at *El Alamein* and later driven out of North Africa. The third battle was in Russia where by *September 1942* the Germans had penetrated as far as *Stalingrad*. Here the Russians put up such a fierce resistance that the following February the German army was surrounded and compelled to surrender. Meanwhile the war in the air continued with both sides bombing enemy cities, and at sea where, as in the First World War, the British and Americans gradually got the better of the German submarine menace.

(d) The Axis powers defeated: July 1943 to August 1945. The enormous power and resources of the USA and the USSR combined with an all-out effort from Britain and her empire slowly but surely wore the Axis powers down. *Italy* was eliminated first and this was followed by an Anglo-American invasion of *Normandy (June 1944)* which liberated France, Belgium and Holland and crossed the Rhine to capture Cologne. In the east the Russians drove the Germans out and advanced on *Berlin* via Poland. *Germany surrendered in May 1945* and *Japan in August* after the Americans had dropped *atomic bombs* on *Hiroshima* and *Nagasaki*.

15.1 OPENING MOVES; SEPTEMBER 1939 TO DECEMBER 1940

(a) The Poles were defeated swiftly because of the German *Blitzkrieg* (lightning war) which they were ill-equipped to deal with. It consisted of rapid thrusts by motorised divisions and tanks (*Panzers*) supported by air power: the *Luftwaffe* (the German air force) put the Polish railway system out of action and destroyed the Polish air force. Polish resistance was heroic but pathetic: they had no motorised divisions and attempted to stem the German advance by massed cavalry charges. Britain and France did little to help their ally directly because French mobilisation procedure was slow and out-of-date and it was difficult to transport sufficient troops to Poland to be effective. When the *Russians invaded eastern Poland* resistance collapsed. On *29 September Poland was partitioned* between *Germany* and *Russia* (as agreed in the August pact).

(b) Very little happened in the west for the next five months; in the east the *Russians absorbed Estonia, Latvia and Lithuania and invaded Finland (November 1939)*, forcing her to hand over certain territories which would enable the Russians to defend themselves better against any attack from the west. Meanwhile the French and Germans manned their respective defences – the Maginot and Siegfried Lines. Hitler seems to have hoped that the pause would weaken the resolve of Britain and France and encourage them to negotiate a settlement; in addition it pleased his generals who were not convinced that the German army was strong enough to attack in the west. It was the American press which described this period as the 'phoney war'.

(c) The apparent calm of the 'phoney war' was rudely shattered in April 1940 when **Hitler's troops occupied Denmark and landed at the main**

Fig. 15.1 *main German thrusts in 1940*

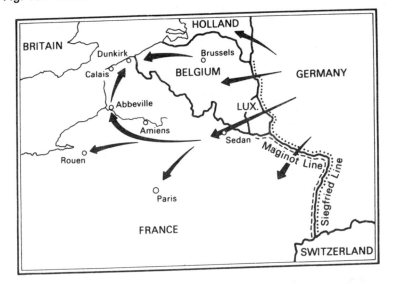

Norwegian ports. *Control of Norway* was important for the Germans because Narvik was the main outlet for Swedish iron ore to Germany, which was vital for her *armaments industry*. The British were interfering with this trade by mining Norwegian coastal waters, and the Germans were afraid that they might occupy some of Norway's ports, as they were indeed planning to do. Admiral Raeder, the German navy chief, realised that the fjords would be excellent naval bases from which to attack Britain's trans-Atlantic supply lines. When a British destroyer chased the German vessel *Altmark* into a Norwegian fjord and rescued 300 British prisoners, Hitler decided it was time to act. On *9 April* the Germans landed at Oslo, Kristiansand, Stavanger, Bergen and Trondheim, and although British and French troops arrived a few days later, they were unable to dislodge the Germans who were already well-established. After a temporary success at Narvik, all allied troops were withdrawn by early June because of the growing threat to France itself. The Germans were successful because the Norwegian forces were *not even mobilised*, and local Nazis under their leader *Vidkun Quisling* gave the invaders every assistance. In addition the British had *no air support*, whereas the German air force constantly harassed the Allies. This Norwegian campaign had *important results*: Germany was assured of her bases and her iron ore supplies, but had lost three cruisers and ten destroyers, which rendered the navy less effective at Dunkirk than it might have been. The campaign also showed the incompetence of Chamberlain's government; he was forced to resign and *Winston Churchill* became Prime Minister. Although there has been criticism of Churchill's mistakes there is no doubt that he supplied what was needed at the time – drive, a sense of urgency and the ability to make his coalition cabinet work well together.

(d) **The attacks on Holland, Belgium and France** were launched simultaneously on 10 May and again *Blitzkrieg* methods brought swift victories. The Dutch, shaken by the bombing of Rotterdam which killed almost a thousand people, surrendered after only four days. Belgium held out longer but her surrender at the end of May left the British and French troops in Belgium perilously exposed as German motorised divisions swept across northern France; only Dunkirk remained in Allied hands. The British navy played the vital role in evacuating over 338,000 troops, two-thirds of them British, from Dunkirk between 27 May and 4 June. Dunkirk was a remarkable achievement in the face of constant *Luftwaffe* attacks on the beaches; it would perhaps have been impossible if Hitler had not ordered the advance towards Dunkirk to halt (24 May) probably because the marshy terrain and numerous canals were unsuitable for tanks. The events at Dunkirk were important: *a third of a million troops were rescued to fight again* and Churchill used it for *propaganda purposes* to boost British morale with the 'Dunkirk spirit'. In fact it was a serious blow for the Allies: the armies at Dunkirk had lost all their arms and equipment so that it became impossible for Britain to help France. The Germans now swept southwards; *Paris* was captured on *14 June* and *France surrendered* on 22 June. At Hitler's insistence the armistice was signed at *Compiègne* in the same railway coach which had been used for the 1918 armistice (for a full explanation of the French defeat see Section 5.2). The Germans occupied northern France and the Atlantic coast, giving them valuable *submarine bases*, and the French army was demobilised. Unoccupied France was allowed its own government under *Marshall Pétain* at *Vichy*, but it had no real independence and collaborated with the Germans.

(e) **The Battle of Britain (12 August to 30 September)** was fought in the air when Goering's *Luftwaffe* tried to destroy the RAF as a preliminary to the *invasion of Britain*. The Germans bombed harbours, radar stations, aerodromes, munitions factories, and in September London itself (in retaliation for a British raid on Berlin). The RAF inflicted heavy losses on the *Luftwaffe* (1389 German planes were lost as against 792 British) and when it became clear that British air power was far from being destroyed, Hitler called off the invasion. The British success was partly due to their *chain of radar stations* which gave plenty of warning of approaching German attackers, and partly because the German bombers were poorly armed. In addition, though the British fighters (Spitfires and Hurricanes) were not significantly better than the German Messerschmitts, the Germans were hampered by *limited range* (they could stay in the air only about 90 minutes). The switch to bombing London was a bad mistake because it *relieved pressure on the air fields* at the critical moment. The Battle of Britain was probably the *first major turning point of the war*: for the first time, the Germans had been checked; they were not invincible. Britain was able to remain in the struggle, thus facing Hitler (who was about to attack Russia) with the *fatal situation of war on two fronts*. As Churchill remarked as he paid tribute to the British fighter pilots: 'Never in the field of human conflict was so much owed by so many to so few.'

(f) Not to be outdone by Hitler, **Mussolini sent an army from the Italian colony of Libya which penetrated about 60 miles into Egypt** (*September 1940*) while another army *invaded Greece* from *Albania* (*October*). However, the British soon drove the Italians out of Egypt, pushed them back deeply into Libya and defeated them at Bedafomm, capturing 130,000 prisoners and 400 tanks. They seemed poised to take the whole of Libya. British naval aircraft sank half the Italian fleet in harbour at Taranto and occupied Crete. The Greeks forced the Italians back and invaded Albania. Clearly Mussolini was going to be an embarrassment to Hitler.

15.2 THE AXIS OFFENSIVE WIDENS: 1941 TO THE SUMMER OF 1942

(a) Hitler's first moves in 1941 were to help out his faltering ally. In February he sent Erwin Rommel and the Afrika Korps to Tripoli, and together with the Italians they cleared the British out of Libya; after much advancing and retreating, by June 1942 the Germans were in Egypt

Fig. 15.2 *North Africa and the Mediterranean*

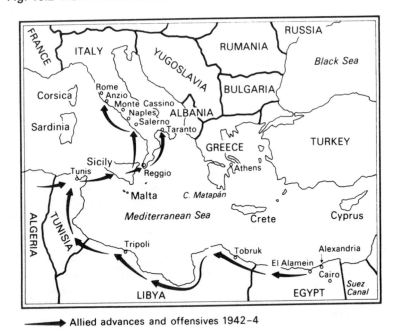

⟶ Allied advances and offensives 1942–4

approaching El Alamein, only 70 miles from Alexandria. In April 1941 Hitler's forces invaded Greece, the day after 60,000 British, Australian and New Zealand troops had arrived to help the Greeks. The Germans soon captured Athens, forcing the British to withdraw, and after bombing Crete launched a parachute invasion of the island; again the British were forced to evacuate (May 1941). The campaigns in Greece and Crete had important effects: it was depressing for the Allies who lost some 36,000 men; many of the troops had been removed from North Africa, thus weakening British forces there just when they needed to be at their most effective against Rommel. More important in the long run was that Hitler's involvement in Greece and Yugoslavia (which the Germans invaded at the same time as Greece) may well have delayed his *attack on Russia* (originally planned for 15 May) by five weeks. If the invasion had taken place in May, the Germans might well have taken Moscow before the winter set in.

(b) The German invasion of Russia (Operation Barbarossa) began on *22 June 1941*:

(i) *Hitler's motives seem to have been mixed*: fear that the Russians might attack Germany while she was still occupied in the west; hope that the Japanese would attack Russia in the Far East; the more powerful Japan became, the less chance there was of the USA entering the war (or so Hitler thought). But above all there was his hatred of communism and his desire for *Lebensraum*. According to Bullock, 'Hitler invaded Russia for the simple and sufficient reason that he had always meant to establish the foundations of his thousand-year *Reich* by the annexation of the territory lying between the Vistula and the Urals'. It has sometimes been suggested that the attack on Russia was Hitler's greatest mistake, but in fact, as Hugh Revor-Roper has pointed out, 'to Hitler the Russian campaign was not a luxury: it was the be-all and end-all of Nazism; it could not be delayed. It was now or never.'

(ii) The attack was *three-pronged: in the north towards Leningrad, in the centre towards Moscow and in the south through the Ukraine*. It was *Blitzkrieg* on an enormous scale involving close on 3.5 million men, and 3550 tanks supported by 5000 aircraft. Important cities such as Riga, Smolensk and Kiev were captured; the Russians had been caught off guard, still re-equipping their army and air force, and their generals, thanks to Stalin's purges, were inexperienced. However, the Germans failed to capture Leningrad and Moscow. They were severely hampered by the heavy rains of October which turned the Russian roads into mud and by the severe frosts of November and December when in some places the temperature fell to minus 38° Centigrade. The Germans had inadequate winter clothing because Hitler had expected the campaigns to be over before winter. Even in the spring of 1942 no progress was made in the north and centre as Hitler decided to concentrate on a *major drive south-eastwards towards the Caucasus to seize the oil-fields*.

(c) The USA was brought into the war by the Japanese attack on Pearl Harbor (their naval base on the Hawaiian Islands) on *7 December 1941*. Until then the Americans, still intent on isolation, had remained neutral, though after the *Lend-Lease Act (April 1941)* they had provided Britain with massive *financial aid*.

(i) *Japanese motives for the attack were tied up with her economic situation*. The government believed they would soon run short of raw materials and cast longing eyes towards territories such as Britain's *Malaya* and *Burma* which had rubber, oil and tin, and the *Dutch East Indies*, also rich in oil. Since both Britain and Holland were in no state to defend their possessions, the Japanese prepared to attack, but would probably have preferred to avoid war with the USA. However, relations between the two states deteriorated steadily. The Americans assisted the Chinese who were still at war with Japan; when the Japanese persuaded Vichy France to allow them to occupy French Indo-China (where they set up military bases), President Roosevelt demanded their withdrawal and placed an *embargo on oil supplies* to Japan (26 July 1941). Long negotiations followed in which the Japanese tried to persuade the Americans to lift the embargo, but stalemate was reached as the Americans insisted on a Japanese withdrawal both from Indo-China and China itself. When the aggressive *General Tojo* became Prime Minister (16 October) war seemed inevitable.

(ii) *The attack was brilliantly organised by Admiral Yamamoto*. There was no declaration of war: 353 Japanese planes arrived undetected at Pearl Harbor and in 2 hours destroyed 350 aircraft, 5 battleships and 3700 men. Roosevelt called 7 December 'a date which will live in infamy'. Pearl Harbor had important results: the *Japanese now controlled the Pacific* and by May 1942 had captured Malaya, Singapore, Burma, Hong Kong, the Dutch East Indies, the Philippines, and two American possessions, Guam and Wake Island. *It caused Hitler to declare war on the USA*. This was perhaps his most serious mistake: he need not at this stage have committed himself to war with the USA, in which case the Americans might well have concentrated on the Pacific War. As it was, Germany was now faced with the immense potential of the USA which, together with the vast resources of the USSR and the British commonwealth, meant that the longer the war lasted, the less chance there was of an Axis victory. It was essential for them to deliver swift knock-out blows before the American contribution became effective.

illus 15.1 *Pearl Harbor, 7 December 1941. US warships lie in ruins after the Japanese air attack*

(d) The behaviour of both Germans and Japanese in their conquered territories was ruthless and brutal. The Nazis treated the peoples of eastern Europe as sub-humans, fit only to be slaves of the German master race. Jews were even lower – they were to be exterminated. As William Shirer puts it: 'Nazi degradation sank to a level seldom experienced by man in all his time on earth. Millions of decent, innocent men and women were driven into forced labour, millions more tortured in the concentration camps and millions more still (including nearly six million Jews) were massacred in cold blood or deliberately starved to death and their remains burned.' Not only was this immoral, it was also *bad tactics*; in the Baltic states and the Ukraine the soviet government was so unpopular that decent treatment would have turned the people into allies of the Germans. The Japanese treated prisoners of war and the Asian peoples badly. Again this was ill-advised: many of the Asians, in Indo-China for example, welcomed the Japanese who were freeing them from European control. The Japanese hoped to organise their new territories into a great economic empire known as a *Greater East Asia Co-prosperity Sphere*, which would be defended by sea and air power. However, harsh treatment by the Japanese soon turned the Asians against rule from Tokyo, and determined resistance movements began, usually with communist involvement.

15.3 THE OFFENSIVES HELD IN CHECK: SUMMER 1942 TO SUMMER 1943

In three separate theatres of war, Axis forces were *defeated and began to lose ground.*

(a) **At Midway Island (June 1942)** in the Pacific the Americans beat off a powerful Japanese attack, which included 5 aircraft carriers, nearly 400

Fig. 15.3 *the war in the Pacific*

aircraft, 17 large warships and an invasion force of 5000 troops. The Americans, with only three carriers and 233 planes, destroyed four of the Japanese carriers and about 330 planes. There were several reasons for the American *victory against heavier odds*: they had broken the Japanese radio code and knew exactly where and when the attack was to be launched; the Japanese were over-confident and made two fatal mistakes; they split their forces, thus allowing the Americans to concentrate on the main carrier force, and they attacked with the aircraft from all four carriers simultaneously, so that when they were all rearming the fleet was extremely vulnerable. At this stage, the Americans launched a counter-attack by dive-bombers which swooped unexpectedly from 19,000 feet, sinking two of the carriers and all their planes. *Midway proved to be a crucial turning point* in the battle for the Pacific: the loss of their carriers and strike planes seriously weakened the Japanese, and from then on the Americans maintained their lead in carriers and aircraft, especially dive-bombers. Although the Japanese had far more battleships and cruisers, they were mostly ineffective: the only way that war could be waged successfully in the vast expanses of the Pacific was by *air power operating from carriers*. Gradually the Americans under General MacArthur began to recover the Pacific islands beginning in August 1942 with landings in the Solomon Islands. The struggle was long and bitter and continued through 1943 and 1944 by a process known as 'island hopping'.

(b) At El Alamein in Egypt (October 1942) Rommel's *Afrika Korps* were driven back by Montgomery's Eighth Army. This great battle was the culmination of several engagements fought in the El Alamein area: first the Axis advance was temporarily checked (July); when Rommel tried to break through he was halted again at Alam Halfa (September); finally seven weeks later in the October battle, he was chased out of Egypt for good by the British and New Zealanders. The Allies were successful partly because during the seven-week pause *massive reinforcements* had arrived so that the Germans and Italians were heavily outnumbered (80,000 men and 540 tanks against 230,000 troops and 1,440 tanks); in addition Allied *air power* was vital, constantly attacking the Axis forces and sinking their supply ships crossing the Mediterranean, so that by October there were serious shortages of food, fuel oil and ammunition; at the same time the air force was strong enough to protect the Eighth Army's own supply routes. Montgomery's skilful preparations probably clinched the issue, though he has been criticised for being over-cautious and for allowing Rommel and half his forces to escape into Libya. However, there is no doubt that the El Alamein victory was another *turning point in the war*: it *prevented Egypt and the Suez Canal from falling into German hands* and ended the possibility of a link-up between the Axis forces in the Middle East and those in the Ukraine. More than that, it led on to the *complete expulsion of Axis forces from North Africa*: it encouraged landings of American and British troops in the French territories of Morocco and Algeria to threaten the Germans and Italians from the west while the Eighth Army closed in on them from Libya. Trapped in Tunisia, 275,000 Germans and Italians were forced to surrender (May 1943) and the Allies were well-placed for an *invasion of Italy*. The desert war had been a serious drain on German resources which could have been used in Russia where they were badly needed.

(c) At Stalingrad the German southern attack which had penetrated deeply through the Crimea, capturing *Rostov*, was finally checked. The Germans had reached *Stalingrad* at the end of August 1942, and though they more or less destroyed the city, the Russians refused to surrender. In November they counter-attacked ferociously, trapping the Germans whose supply lines were dangerously extended in a larger pincer movement cutting off their retreat. On 2 February 1943 the German commander von Paulus had no reasonable alternative but to *surrender with about 100,000 men*. If Stalingrad had fallen, the supply route for Russia's oil from the Caucasus would have been cut off, and the Germans had

Fig. 15.4 *the Russian Front*

- - - - Line of the German advance in December 1941

········ German line in November 1942

hoped to advance up the River Don to attack Moscow from the south-east. This plan had to be abandoned but more than that was at stake: the defeat was a catastrophe for the Germans; it shattered the myth that they were invincible and boosted Russian morale. They followed up with more counter-attacks forcing the Germans to abandon the siege of Leningrad and to retreat from their position west of Moscow. It was only a matter of time before the Germans, now heavily outnumbered and short of tanks and guns, were cleared out of Russia.

15.4 WHAT PART WAS PLAYED BY ALLIED NAVAL FORCES IN THE WAR?

We have already seen how the combination of sea and air power was the key to success in the Pacific War and how, after the initial shock at Pearl Harbor, the Americans were gradually able to build up that superiority in both departments which was to lead to the eventual defeat of Japan. At the same time the British navy, as in the First World War, had a vital role to play; this included protecting merchant ships bringing food supplies, sinking German submarines and surface raiders, blockading Germany, and transporting and supplying the Allied troops fighting in North Africa and later in Italy. At first success was mixed, mainly because the British failed to understand the importance of air support in naval operations and had few aircraft carriers. Thus they suffered defeats in Norway and Crete where the Germans had strong air superiority. In addition the Germans had numerous naval bases in Norway, Denmark, France and Italy. In spite of this the British had some *successes*:

(a) **Aircraft from the carrier *Illustrious* sank half the Italian fleet at Taranto** (*November 1940*); the following March five more warships were destroyed off Cape Matapan.

(b) **The threat from surface raiders** was removed by the sinking of the *Bismarck*, Germany's only battleship at the time (May 1941).

(c) **The navy destroyed the German invasion transports** on their way to Crete (May 1941), though they could not prevent the landing of parachute troops.

(d) **They provided escorts for convoys carrying supplies to help the Russians**; these sailed via the Arctic to Murmansk in the far north of Russia. Beginning in September 1941 the first twelve convoys arrived without incident, but then the Germans began to attack them, until convoy 17 lost 23 ships out of 36 (June 1942). After this disaster Arctic convoys were not fully resumed until November 1943, when stronger escorts could be spared. Altogether 40 convoys sailed: 720 out of a total of 811 merchant ships arrived safely, with valuable cargo for the Russians including 5000 tanks and 7000 aircraft as well as thousands of tons of canned meat.

(e) Their most important contribution was their victory in *the Battle of the Atlantic*. This was the struggle against *German U-boats* attempting to deprive Britain of food and raw materials. At the beginning of 1942 the Germans had 90 U-boats in operation and 250 being built; in the first six months of that year the Allies lost over 4 million tons of merchant shipping and destroyed only 21 U-boats; losses reached a peak of 108 ships in March 1943, almost two-thirds of which were in convoy. However after that the number of sinkings began to fall, while U-boat losses increased; by July 1943 the Allies could produce ships at a faster rate than the U-boats could sink them, and the situation was under control. The reasons for the *Allied success* were that *more air protection* was provided for convoys by long-range Liberators, both escorts and aircraft protection improved with experience, and the British introduced the new *centimetric radar sets* which were small enough to be fitted into aircraft, so that submarines could be detected in poor visibility and at night. The victory was just as important as Midway, El Alamein and Stalingrad: Britain could not have continued to sustain the losses of March 1943 and remained in the war.

15.5 WHAT CONTRIBUTION DID AIR POWER MAKE TO THE DEFEAT OF THE AXIS?

(a) The first significant achievement was in the Battle of Britain (1940) when the RAF beat off the *Luftwaffe* attackes, causing Hitler to abandon his invasion plans (see Section 15.1).

(b) In conjunction with the British navy, aircraft played a varied role: the successful attacks on the Italian fleet at Taranto and Cape Matapan, the sinking of the German battleship *Tirpitz* by heavy bombers in Norway (November 1943), the protection of convoys in the Atlantic, and anti-submarine operations. In fact in May 1943 Admiral Doenitz, the German navy chief, complained to Hitler that since the introduction of the new radar devices, more U-boats were being destroyed by aircraft than by naval vessels.

(c) The American air force together with the navy played a vital part in **winning the Pacific War against the Japanese**. Dive-bombers operating from aircraft carriers won the *Battle of Midway Island in June 1942* (see Section 15.3). Later, in the 'island-hopping' campaign, attacks by heavy bombers prepared the way for landings by marines, for example at the Mariana Islands (1944) and the Philippines (1945). American transport planes kept up the vital flow of supplies to the Allies during the campaign to recapture *Burma*.

(d) The RAF took part in specific campaigns which would have been hopeless without them; for example, during the desert war, operating from bases in Egypt and Palestine, they constantly bombed Rommel's supply ships in the Mediterranean and his armies on land.

(e) British and Americans later flew in parachute troops to aid the landings in Sicily (July 1943) and Normandy (June 1944) and provided air protection for the invading armies. (However, a similar operation at Arnhem in September 1944 was a failure.)

(f) The most controversial aspect was the Allied bombing of German and later Japanese cities. The Germans themselves had bombed London and other important cities and ports during 1940 and 1941, but these raids dwindled after the German attack on Russia which required all the *Luftwaffe*'s strength. The British and Americans retaliated with a 'strategic air offensive' – massive attacks on military and industrial targets in order to hamper the German war effort. The Ruhr, Cologne, Hamburg and Berlin all suffered badly. Sometimes raids seem to have been carried out purely to undermine *civilian morale*, as when about 40,000 people were killed during a single night raid on Dresden (February 1945). Early in 1945 the Americans launched a series of devastating raids on Japan from bases in the Mariana Islands. In a single raid on Tokyo (March) 80,000 people were killed and a quarter of the city destroyed. There has been argument about how effective the bombing was in hastening the Axis defeat, beyond merely causing inconvenience.

The conclusion now seems to be that the campaign against Germany was not effective until the autumn of 1944. Industrial production continued to increase until as late as July 1944. After that, thanks to the increasing accuracy of the raids, synthetic oil production fell rapidly, causing acute fuel shortages; in October the vital Krupp armaments factories at Essen were put out of action permanently, and the war effort ground to a halt in 1945. By June 1945 the Japanese had been reduced to the same state. In the end, therefore, after much wasted effort early on, the Allied strategic air offensive was one of the decisive reasons for the Axis defeat: besides *strangling fuel and armaments production* and *destroying railway communications*, it caused the *diversion of many aircraft from the eastern front*, thereby helping the Russian advance into Germany.

15.6 THE AXIS POWERS DEFEATED: JULY 1943 TO AUGUST 1945

(a) The fall of Italy was the first stage in the Axis collapse. British and American troops landed in Sicily from sea and air (10 July 1943) and quickly *captured the whole island*. This caused the *downfall of Mussolini* who was dismissed by the king. Allied troops crossed to Salerno, Reggio and Taranto on the mainland and captured Naples (October 1943) by which time Marshal Badoglio, Mussolini's successor, had *signed an armistice* and brought Italy into the war on the *Allied side*. However the Germans, determined to hold on to Italy, rushed troops through the Brenner Pass to occupy Rome and the north. The allies landed a force at

Anzio, 30 miles south of Rome (January 1944) but bitter fighting followed before Monte Cassino (May) and Rome (June) were captured; Milan in the north was not taken until April 1945. The campaign could have been finished much earlier if the Allies had been less cautious in the early stages and if the Americans had not insisted on keeping many divisions back for the invasion of France. Nevertheless the elimination of Italy did contribute towards the final victory: it provided *air bases for the bombing of the Germans in Central Europe and the Balkans* and kept German troops occupied when they were needed to resist the Russians.

(b) The invasion of France (known as the Second Front) began on 'D-Day', *6 June 1944*. It was felt that the time was ripe now that Italy had been eliminated, the U-boats controlled and Allied air superiority achieved; the Russians had been urging the Allies to start this second front ever since 1941 to relieve pressure on them. The landings took place from sea and air on a 60-mile stretch of Normandy beaches between *Cherbourg* and *Le Havre*. There was strong German resistance, but at the end of the first week, aided by prefabricated 'Mulberry'

illus 15.2 *D-Day. US assault troops landing in Normandy*

harbours and by PLUTO (pipelines under the ocean) carrying motor fuel, 326,000 men with tanks and heavy lorries had landed safely; eventually over three million Allied troops were landed. Within a few weeks most of northern France was liberated (*Paris on 25 August*), putting out of action the sites from which the German V1 and V2 rocket missiles had been launched with devastating effects on south-eastern Britain. Brussels and Antwerp were captured in September.

(c) The assault on Germany itself followed, but the end was delayed by desperate German resistance and disagreements between the Americans and British. Montgomery wanted a rapid thrust to reach Berlin before the Russians, but the American General Eisenhower favoured a cautious advance along a broad front. The *British failure at Arnhem* in Holland (September 1944) seemed to support Eisenhower's view, though in fact the Arnhem operation (an attempt by parachute troops to cross the Rhine and outflank the German Siegfried Line) might have worked if the troops had landed nearer the two Rhine bridges.

Consequently Eisenhower had his way and Allied troops were dispersed over a 600-mile front, with unfortunate results: Hitler was able to launch a last offensive through the weakly defended Ardennes towards Antwerp; the Germans broke through the American lines and advanced 60 miles, causing a huge bulge in the front line (December 1944).

Fig. 15.5 *the Western Front 1944–5*

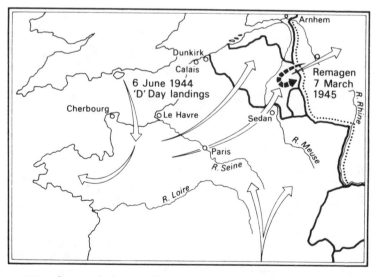

 German Ardennes offensive checked (December 1944), Battle of the Bulge

⟶ Allied advances 6 June 1944 – 7 March 1945

·········· Siegfried Line

Determined British and American action stemmed the advance and pushed the Germans back to their original position. But the *Battle of the Bulge*, as it became known, was important because Hitler had risked everything on the attack and had lost 250,000 men and 600 tanks, which at this stage could not be replaced. Early in 1945 Germany was being invaded on both fronts; the British still wanted to push ahead and take Berlin before the Russians, but supreme commander Eisenhower refused to be hurried, and Berlin fell to Stalin's forces in April. *Hitler committed suicide and Germany surrendered.*

(d) **The defeat of Japan** was still to be achieved. On 6 August 1945 the Americans *dropped an atomic bomb on Hiroshima*, killing 84,000 people, and one on *Nagasaki* three days later which killed another 40,000, after which the Japanese government surrendered. The dropping of these bombs was perhaps the most controversial action of the whole war: President Truman's justification was that he was saving American lives, since the war might otherwise drag on for another year. Many historians believe that this bombing was not necessary since, in fact, the Japanese had already put out peace feelers in July via Russia. Liddell-Hart suggests that the real reason was to end the fighting swiftly before the Russians (who had promised to enter the war against Japan) gained too much territory which would entitle them to share the occupation of Japan.

15.7 WHY DID THE AXIS POWERS LOSE THE WAR?

The reasons can be summarised briefly:

(a) **A basic weakness was shortage of raw materials:** both Italy and Japan had to import supplies and even Germany was short of rubber, cotton, nickel and, after mid-1944, oil. These need not have been fatal, but success depended on a swift end to the war, which indeed seemed likely at first thanks to the speed and efficiency of the German *Blitzkrieg*. However, the survival of Britain in 1940 was important because it kept the western front alive until the USA entered the war.

(b) **The Allies soon learned from their early failures:** by 1942 they knew how to check *Blitzkrieg* attacks and appreciated the importance of air support and aircraft carriers. Consequently they built up an air and naval superiority which won the battles of the Atlantic and the Pacific and slowly starved their enemies of supplies.

(c) **The Axis simply took on too much:** Hitler did not understand that war against Britain would involve her empire as well, and that his troops were bound to be spread too thinly – on the Russian front, on both sides of the Mediterranean, and on the western coastline of France. Japan made the same mistake: as Liddell-Hart puts it, 'they became stretched out far beyond their basic capacity for holding their gains. For Japan was a small island state with limited industrial power'. In Germany's case Mussolini was partly to blame: Italian incompetence was a constant drain on Hitler's resources.

(d) The combined resources of the USA and the USSR, not to mention the British empire, were so great that the longer the war lasted the less chance the Axis had of victory. The Russians rapidly moved their industry east of the Ural Mountains and so continued production even though the Germans had occupied vast areas in the west. By 1944 they had four times as many tanks as the Germans and could put twice as many men in the field. When the American war machine reached peak production it could turn out over 70,000 tanks and 120,000 aircraft a year, which the Germans and Japanese could not match.

(e) In addition the Axis made serious tactical mistakes which they could not afford. The Japanese failed to learn the lesson about the importance of aircraft carriers and concentrated too much on producing battleships. Hitler failed to provide for a winter campaign in Russia and became obsessed with the idea that the Germans must not retreat; this led to many disasters in Russia, including Stalingrad, and left his troops badly exposed in Normandy (1944). Perhaps most serious of all was Hitler's decision to concentrate on producing V-rockets when he could have been developing jet aircraft which might well have restored German air superiority and prevented the devastating bomb attacks of 1944 and 1945.

15.8 WHAT WERE THE EFFECTS OF THE WAR?

(a) There had been immense destruction of lives, homes, industries and communications both in Europe and Asia. At least 30 million people were killed, over half of whom were Russians; a further 21 million had been uprooted from their homes (taken to Germany as labourers, placed in concentration camps or forced to flee before invading armies) leaving the victorious governments with the problem of how to *repatriate* them. However, it can be argued that the cost was worth it, since it rid the world of Nazism, which among other atrocities had deliberately murdered six million Jews and hundreds of thousands of non-Jews in extermination camps.

(b) There was no all-inclusive peace settlement of the type reached at Versailles at the end of the First World War; this was mainly because the suspicion and distrust, which had re-emerged between Russia and the west in the final months of the war, made a comprehensive settlement impossible. The results of a number of separate treaties can be summarised briefly: *Italy* lost her African colonies and renounced her claims to Albania and Abyssinia (Ethiopia); *Russia* took the eastern tip of

illus 15.3 *The devastation of war. Women salvage their personal belongings after a mass air-raid on London*

Czechoslovakia, the Petsamo district and the area round lake Ladoga from Finland and held on to Estonia, Latvia, Lithuania and eastern Poland which had been occupied in 1939. Russia also took Bessarabia and northern Bukovina from Rumania, who recovered northern Transylvania which the Hungarians had occupied during the war. *Trieste,* claimed by both Italy and Yugoslavia, was declared *free territory protected by the United Nations.* Later at San Francisco (1951) *Japan* agreed to surrender all territory acquired during the previous 90 years, which included a complete withdrawal from China. The Russians refused to agree to any settlement over Germany and Austria beyond that they should be occupied by Allied troops (see Section 16.2(a)), and that East Prussia should be divided between Russia and Poland.

(c) The war stimulated rapid social and scientific developments, the two most quoted examples being the Beveridge Report (1942), a British plan for introducing a welfare state (see Section 21.2(a)), and the production of nuclear weapons, which have a potential so horrifying that they must have acted as a deterrent from another total war.

(d) Other long-term effects which were to set the pattern of world events for the remainder of the century were:

(i) *European domination of the world*, already in decline before 1939, was *now seen to be over*; the USA (which had suffered relatively little from the war), and Russia (almost as much an Asian as a European power) became the leading states, with China and Japan (which recovered remarkably quickly) also playing an important role in world affairs.

(ii) Instead of fostering a long period of friendship, the Soviet–American victory was followed by an intensification of their previous suspicions and distrust which became known as the *Cold War* (see Chapter 16). The rivalry of these two super-powers has been the most important feature of international relations since 1945, and apparently a constant threat to world peace.

(iii) The occupation by the Japanese of European controlled territories such as Malaya and Singapore, French Indo-China and the Dutch East Indies ended the tradition of European invincibility. It could hardly be expected that having fought to rid themselves of the Japanese, the Asiatic peoples would willingly return to the pre-war status quo. Gradually they achieved *full independence*, though not without a struggle in many cases. This in turn intensified independence demands in Africa and the Middle East, which resulted in the 1960s in a vast array of new states. The leaders of many of these newly emerging nations met in conference at Algiers (1973) and made it clear that they regarded themselves as a *Third World*. By this they meant that they wished to remain neutral or non-aligned in the struggle between the other two worlds – communism and capitalism. Usually poor and underdeveloped industrially, the new nations were often intensely suspicious of the motives of both communism and capitalism and resented their own economic dependence on the world's wealthy powers.

(iv) The *United Nations Organisation* (UNO) emerged as the successor to the League of Nations to try and maintain world peace; on the whole it has been more successful than its unfortunate predecessor (see Chapter 20).

QUESTIONS

1. Japan and the USA during the Second World War
Study the Souces below, and then answer the questions that follow.

Source A

By the summer of 1941 opinion in Japan had veered around to the view that Japan should strike south. There lay the vastly rich resources of oil, tin, rubber and other valuables. This was the area of colonies: British, Dutch, French and American. If it seized them Japan could hope for three results: it would make itself free from the economic pressure of the western countries which had the nerve to threaten it with economic sanctions in order to control Japanese expansion; it would make China ask for peace; and it would build up a great Japanese empire overseas, to be called 'The Greater East Asia Co-Prosperity Sphere' . . . The Japanese people responded to this policy; quite sincerely they saw themselves, in opposing western activity in Asia, as fighting a battle against imperialism . . . In December 1940 the American government, disturbed by the increasing warlike tone of Japan, placed a ban on the sales of scrap iron and war materials to Japan. This action was an attempt to halt Japan's military activity against China. In July 1941, when the Japanese extended their political control of Indo-China from the north to the south, Roosevelt responded firmly – he froze Japanese assets and announced a ban on Japanese trade in oil and steel.

Source: P. Calvocoressi and G. Wint, *Total War* (Allen Lane/Penguin, 1972, adapted extracts).

Source B
By Howard Zinn, an American historian.

Pearl Harbor was presented to the American public as a sudden, shocking, immoral act. Immoral it was, like any bombing, but not really sudden or shocking to the American government . . . In initiating economic sanctions against Japan, the USA undertook actions that were widely recognised in Washington as carrying grave risks of war . . . One of the judges in the Tokyo War Crimes Trial after World War II, disagreed with the general verdict against Japanese officials and argued that the USA had clearly provoked the war with Japan and expected Japan to act. The records show that a White House Conference two weeks before Pearl Harbor anticipated a war and discussed how it should be justified. A State Department memorandum, a year before Pearl Harbor, did not talk of the independence of China or the principle of self-determination [as reasons for American action].

Source: Howard Zinn, *A People's History of the United States* (Longman, 1980, adapted extracts).

Source C
American State Department memorandum, December 1940 (referred to in Source B above).

Our general diplomatic and strategic position would be weakened – by our loss of Chinese, Indian and South Seas markets (and by our loss of Japanese markets for our goods, as Japan would become more and more self-sufficient), as well as by insurmountable restrictions on our access to the rubber, tin, jute and other vital materials of the Asian and Oceanic regions.

Source: Howard Zinn, *A People's History of the United States* (Longman, 1980, extracts).

Source D

And then on August 6, 1945, came the lone American plane in the sky over Hiroshima, dropping the first atomic bomb, leaving perhaps 100,000 dead, and tens of thousands more slowly dying from radiation poisoning. Three days later a second atomic bomb was dropped on the city of Nagasaki, with perhaps 50,000 killed . . . The justification for these atrocities was that it would end the war quickly, making unnecessary an invasion of Japan. Such an invasion would cost a huge number of lives, the government said – a million according to Secretary of State Byrnes; half a million Truman claimed.

Source: Howard Zinn, *A People's History of the United States* (Longman, 1980, adapted extracts).

Source E
Statements by two American admirals soon after the war.

The naval blockade alone would have starved the Japanese into submission, through lack of oil, rice and other essential materials, had we been willing to wait. – Admiral King.

The use of this barbaric weapon at Hiroshima and Nagasaki was of no material assistance in our war against Japan. The Japanese were already defeated and ready to surrender because of the effective sea blockade and the successful bombing with conventional weapons . . . The scientists and others wanted to make this test because of vast sums that had been spent on the project – two billion dollars. – Admiral Leahy.

Source: B. H. Liddell-Hart, *History of the Second World War* (Cassell, 1970).

Source F

Stalin's demand at Potsdam to share in the occupation of Japan was very embarrassing, and the US government was anxious to avoid it happening. The atomic bomb might help to solve the problem. The Russians were due to enter the war on August 6th. As Churchill wrote [if the war ended in a few days] 'we should not need the Russians. The end of the Japanese war no longer depended upon the pouring in of their armies. We had no need to ask favours of them'.

Source: B. H. Liddell-Hart, *History of the Second World War* (Cassell, 1970, adapted extracts).

Source G
Remarks of President Truman.

> If this bomb explodes, as I think it will, I'll have a hammer on those boys [the Russians] . . . Force is the only thing the Russians understand.

Source: D. S. Clemens, *Yalta* (Oxford University Press, 1970).

(a)   (i)   According to Source A, what lay to the south of Japan which the Japanese wanted to get their hands on?   **4(a)**

    (ii)   What did the Japanese hope to achieve by striking south?   **4(a)**

    (iii)   When and how had the war with China, referred to in Source A, started?   **1,4(a)**

    (iv)   According to Source A, what economic measures against Japan were taken by the USA?   **4(a)**

(b)   (i)   Why does the judge mentioned in Source B think the USA provoked the war with Japan?   **4(a)**

    (ii)   According to Sources B and C, what were the American motives for the economic sanctions against Japan?   **4(a)**

    (iii)   What differences can you find between the reasons suggested in Sources B and C for the American action, and those suggested in Source A?   **4(a,c)**

(c)   From the evidence of Sources A, B and C, and your own knowledge, do you think the USA or Japan was most to blame for the outbreak of war between the two states? Explain your answer fully.   **1,2,4**

(d)   (i)   According to Source D, how many people were killed in the atomic bombings?   **4(a)**

    (ii)   Do you think the writer of Source D approves or disapproves of the bombings? Give reasons for your answer.   **4(b)**

(e)   (i)   Explain what is meant by the phrase 'sea blockade' in Source E.   **1,2,4(a)**

    (ii)   In Source F, why do you think the American government found Stalin's request 'very embarrassing'?   **1,2,4(a)**

(f)   Using the evidence from Sources E, F and G, make a list of reasons why the Americans dropped the atomic bombs on Japan.   **4(a,c)**

(g)   How does Source D disagree with Sources E, F and G about:
    (i)   The strength of Japan just before the atomic bombings;
    (ii)   American motives for the bombings.   **4(a,c)**

(h)   (i)   How successful were the Japanese in creating 'The Greater Asia Co-Prosperity Sphere' up to June 1942?   **1,2**

    (ii)   Describe and explain the stages, from the Battle of Midway Island (June 1942) until July 1945, in which the Japanese were brought towards defeat.   **1,2**

2. The Normandy landings, June 1944

Study the Sources below and then answer the questions that follow.

Source A

Map of the invasion area (Fig. 15.6).

[Southern Examining Group.]

Fig. 15.6

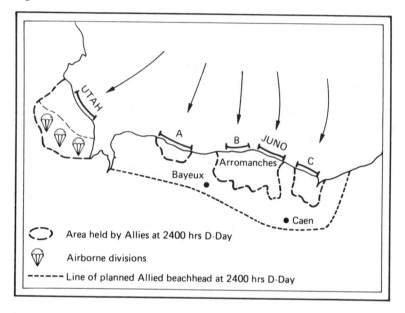

Source B

The Allied troops had to disembark on a coast that the enemy had occupied for four years, with ample time to fortify it. For the defence the Germans had 58 divisions. The Allies were hampered by the fact that they had to cross the sea and by the number of landing craft available. They could disembark only six divisions in the first seaborne lift, together with three airborne, and a week would pass before they could double the number ashore . . . The Allies had complete supremacy in the air – by smashing most of the bridges over the Seine in the east and the Loire in the south, they isolated the Normandy battle zone, and German reserves, having to make long detours, suffered endless delays. In addition there was a conflict of ideas on the German side – between Hitler and his generals and among the generals themselves.

Source: B. H. Liddell-Hart, *History of the Second World War* (Cassell, 1970, adapted extracts).

Source C

Extracts from evidence given after the war by General Blumentritt, one of Hitler's commanders in France.

Very little reliable news came out of England. Intelligence gave us reports of where British and American forces were assembling in Southern England, but nothing we learnt gave us a definite clue where the invasion was actually coming.

As early as 4 a.m. [on D-Day] I telephoned Hitler's headquarters and asked for the release of the Panzer division which lay north-west of Paris – to strengthen Rommel's punch against the Americans. But Jodl, speaking for Hitler, refused to allow it. He doubted whether the landings in Normandy were more than a sham attack, and was sure that the major landing was coming east of the Seine.

Source: B. H. Liddell-Hart, *History of the Second World War* (Cassell, 1970).

(a) Why was it vitally important for the allies to keep their invasion plans as secret as possible? **4(a,c)**

(b) (i) From the evidence of the map (Fig. 15.6), how successful had the Allies been in achieving their objectives by midnight on D-Day? **4(a)**

    (ii) From the information provided by the map (Fig. 15.6) where do you think the heaviest fighting was likely to be? **4(a)**

(c) What evidence can you find in Source C which:
    (i) tells you how successfully the Allies kept their invasion plans secret; **4(a)**
    (ii) supports the statement in Source B that 'there was a conflict of ideas on the German side'? **4(a,c)**

(d) Using the evidence provided by the Sources, and any other information you have, explain why the Normandy landings succeeded. **1,2,4**

(e) How important were the Normandy landings in deciding the final outcome of the war? **1,2**

3. The German attack on Russia, June 1941

Study the Sources below, and then answer the questions that follow.

Source A
Report sent to Stalin by a Russian spy working in Japan, 2 May 1941.

Hitler has resolved to begin war and destroy the USSR in order to utilize the European part of the Union as a raw materials and grain base. The critical term for the possible beginning of war . . . completion of the spring sowing. The decision regarding the start of the war will be taken by Hitler in May.

Source B
Announcement by *Tass*, the Soviet News Agency, 13 June 1941.

In view of the persistent rumours, responsible circles in Moscow have thought it necessary to state that they are a clumsy propaganda manoeuvre of the forces arrayed against the Soviet Union and Germany which are interested in the spread and intensification of the war. In the opinion of Soviet circles the rumours of the intention of Germany to break the Non-Aggression pact and to launch an attack against the Soviet Union are completely without foundation. The recent movement of German troops to the eastern parts of Germany must be explained by other motives which have no connection with Soviet–German relations. As a result, all the rumours according to which the Soviet Union is preparing for a war with Germany are false and provocative.

Source C

Extract from the diary of General Halder, Hitler's Chief of Staff, 23 June 1941.

The offensive of our forces caught the enemy with tactical surprise. Evidence of the complete unexpectedness for the enemy of our attack is the fact that units were captured quite unawares in their barracks, aircraft stood on the airdromes secured by tarpaulins, and forward units, attacked by our troops, asked their commanders what they should do.

Source D

Extracts from a work by an American writer.

In the view of Admiral Kuznetsov, Stalin unquestionably expected war with Hitler. Stalin regarded the Nazi–Soviet Pact as a time-gaining stop-gap, but the time-span proved much shorter than he anticipated. His chief mistake was in underestimating the period he had available for preparation. 'The suspiciousness of Stalin towards England and America made matters worse', concluded Kuznetsov. 'He doubted all evidence about Hitler's activities which he received from the English and the Americans and simply threw it on one side' . . . On June 6 he approved a plan for the shift-over of Soviet industry to war production; this timetable called for the completion of the plan by the end of 1942 . . . When the Soviet commander at Kiev ordered some of his troops to occupy sections of the frontier fortifications which had not yet been completed, he received the following order telegraphed from Moscow: 'Your action may quickly provoke the Germans to armed clash with serious consequences. You are ordered to reverse it immediately.'

Source: H. E. Salisbury, *The 900 Days: the Siege of Leningrad* (Macmillan, 1969, adapted extracts).

(a) (i) According to Source A, why did Hitler want war with the USSR?   **4(a)**
     (ii) What other important reasons might he have had for wanting to attack the USSR?   **1,2**

(iii) Why do you think 'completion of the spring sowing' was a likely time for the Germans to attack? **1,2,4(a)**

(b) **(i)** In Source B, who do you think Tass meant by 'responsible circles in Moscow'? **1,4(a)**

(ii) What was the Non-Aggression Pact referred to in Source B? When and by whom was it signed, and what did it say? **1,4(a)**

(iii) Who did *Tass* mean by 'the forces arrayed against the Soviet Union and Germany'? **4(a)**

(c) **(i)** In Source D, why do you think Stalin was suspicious of England and America? **1,4(a)**

(ii) According to Source D, what action did the Kiev commander take, and why was he ordered to reverse it? **4(a)**

(d) **(i)** How do Source B, C and D differ from each other in the evidence they provide about whether or not Stalin expected war with Germany? **4(a,c)**

(ii) How reliable do you think the *Tass* announcement (Source B) is as an accurate source of information? Give reasons for your answer. **4(a,b)**

(e) Using evidence from Sources B, C and D, assess how well prepared the USSR was for the German attack. **4(a,c)**

(f) **(i)** How close did Hitler get towards achieving his aim, referred to in Source A, of destroying the USSR? **1,2**

(ii) Describe how the German invasions of Russia were checked, and then driven back. **1,2**

(iii) Explain why the USSR was able to defeat Germany. **1,2**

4. Describe *three* of the following campaigns or battles of the Second World War, and show how *each* of these three contributed to the defeat of the Axis Powers (Germany, Italy and Japan):

(a) The Battle of Britain.

(b) The Battle of El Alamein.

(c) The Battle of Stalingrad.

(d) The Battle of Midway Island.

(e) The Normandy landings. **1,2**

5. It is the end of June 1940. France has fallen to the successful German army and most of France has been occupied. Many newspapers from neutral countries have their own correspondents in France, reporting on these events.

You are the correspondent of an American newspaper and have recently interviewed a middle ranking German officer who has served in the campaign. Write an article for your newspaper in which you

(a) give an outline account of the German advance in May and June 1940;

(b) use the material obtained from the interview to help explain the rapid German success in Western Europe. **1,2,3**

[Southern Examining Group, Specimen Question.]

6. You are one of Hitler's generals given a gaol sentence at Nuremberg in 1946. With plenty of time on your hands, you set about writing down your thoughts on the campaigns of the Second World War. Give extracts from your writings explaining

    (a) why the German armies were completely successful up to about September 1941;

    (b) why the war ended in total defeat for Germany and her allies.

                                                  1,2,3

CHAPTER 16

THE COLD WAR: PROBLEMS OF INTERNATIONAL RELATIONS AFTER THE SECOND WORLD WAR

SUMMARY OF EVENTS

Towards the end of the war the harmony that had existed between the USSR, the USA and the British empire began to evaporate and all the old suspicions came to the fore again. Relations between soviet Russia and the west soon became so difficult that although no actual armed conflict took place directly between the two opposing camps, the decade after 1945 saw the first phase of the *Cold War* which continued, in spite of several 'thaws', into the 1980s. This means that instead of allowing their mutual hostility to express itself in open fighting, the rival powers confined themselves to attacking each other with *propaganda* and *economic measures* and with a general policy of non-co-operation. Both super-powers gathered allies about them: between 1945 and 1948 the USSR drew into its orbit most of the states of *eastern Europe*, as communist governments came to power in Poland, Hungary, Rumania, Bulgaria, Yugoslavia, Albania, Czechoslovakia and East Germany (1949). A communist government was established in North Korea (1948) and the communist bloc seemed to be further strengthened in 1949 when Mao Tse-tung was at last victorious in the long-drawn-out civil war in China. On the other hand the USA hastened the recovery of *Japan* and fostered her as an ally and worked closely with Britain and 14 other European countries as well as with Turkey, providing them with vast economic aid in order to build up an anti-communist bloc. Whatever one bloc suggested or did was viewed by the other as having only ulterior and aggressive motives; thus, for example, there was a long wrangle over where the frontier between *Poland and Germany* should be, and no permanent settlement for *Germany and Austria* could be agreed on. Then in the mid-1950s after the death of Stalin (1953), the new Russian leaders began to talk about 'peaceful co-existence' and the icy atmosphere between the two blocs began to thaw. It was agreed to remove all occupying troops from Austria (1955); however, relations did not warm sufficiently to allow agreement on Germany.

16.1 WHAT CAUSED THE COLD WAR?

The basic cause lay in the *differences of principle* between the communist states and the capitalist or democratic states which had existed ever since the communists had set up a government in Russia in 1917. Only the need for self-preservation had caused them to sink their differences and as soon as it became clear that the defeat of Germany was only a matter of time, both sides, Stalin in particular, began to plan for the post-war period.

(a) Stalin's foreign policies contributed to the tensions: his aim was to take advantage of the military situation to strengthen Russian influence in Europe; this involved occupying as much of Germany as possible as the Nazi armies collapsed and acquiring as much territory as he could get away with from other states such as Finland, Poland and Rumania. In this, as will be seen, he was highly successful but the west was alarmed at what seemed to be Russian aggression. *Was Stalin to blame then* for the Cold War? The motives behind Stalin's aims are still a subject of controversy among historians:

(i) Many western historians still believe, as they did at the time, that Stalin was either continuing the traditional expansionist policies of the tsars or, worse still, was determined to *spread communism* over as much of the world as possible now that 'socialism in one country' had been established.

(ii) The Russians themselves, and since the mid-1960s some western historians as well, claim that Stalin's motives were purely *defensive*: he wanted a wide buffer zone to protect Russia from any further invasion from the capitalist west. There had been much to arouse his suspicions that the USA and Britain were still as keen to destroy communism as they had been at the time of their intervention in the civil war (1918–20): their delay in opening the second front against the Germans in France seemed deliberately calculated to keep most of the pressure on the Russians and bring them to exhaustion. Stalin was not informed about the existence of the atomic bomb until shortly before its use on Japan, and his request that Russia should share in the occupation of Japan was rejected. Above all, the west had the atomic bomb and Russia did not. Unfortunately it is impossible to be sure which motive was uppermost in Stalin's mind.

(b) Leading American and British politicians were deeply hostile to the soviet government as they had been since 1917. *Harry S. Truman*, who became US President in April 1945 on the death of Roosevelt, was much more suspicious of the Russians than Roosevelt who was inclined to trust Stalin. Churchill's views were well known: towards the end of the war he had wanted the British and Americans to make a dash for Berlin before the Russians took it; and in May 1945 he had written in a letter to Truman: 'What is to happen about Russia? Like you I feel deep anxiety . . . an iron curtain is drawn down upon their front.' Both were prepared to take a hard line.

Historians must try to ignore their own bias and be guided only by the evidence; the conclusion has to be that *both sides* were to some extent to blame for the Cold War. If somehow mutual confidence could have been created between the two sides, the conflict might have been avoided, but given their entrenched positions and deep suspicion of each other, perhaps it was inevitable. In this atmosphere almost every international act could be interpreted in two different ways: what was claimed as necessary for self-defence by one side was taken by the other as evidence of aggressive intent, as the events described in the next section show. But at least open war was avoided because the Americans were reluctant to use the atomic bomb again unless attacked directly, while the Russians dare not risk such an attack.

16.2 HOW DID THE COLD WAR DEVELOP BETWEEN 1945 AND 1953?

(a) The Yalta Conference (February 1945) held in the Crimea was attended by Stalin, Roosevelt and Churchill. At the time it was generally thought to be a success, agreement being reached on several points: the United Nations Organisation should be set up; Germany was to be divided into *zones* – Russian, American and British (a French zone was included later) – while Berlin (which would be in the Russian zone) would be split into corresponding zones; similar arrangements were to be made for Austria; free elections would be allowed in the states of eastern Europe; Stalin promised to join the war against Japan on condition that Russia received the whole of Sakhalin Island and some territory in Manchuria. However, there were ominous signs over Poland: when the Russians swept through Poland, pushing the Germans back, they had set up a communist government in Lublin, even though there was a Polish government-in-exile in London. It was agreed at Yalta that some members (non-communists) of the London-based government should be allowed to join the Lublin government, while in return Russia would be allowed to keep the strip of eastern Poland which she had occupied in 1939; but Roosevelt and Churchill refused to agree to Stalin's demands that Poland should be given *all German territory east of the Rivers Oder and Neisse.*

(b) The Potsdam Conference (July 1945) revealed a distinct cooling-off in relations. The main representatives were Stalin, Truman and Churchill

Fig. 16.1 *Europe after 1945*

Land taken by Poland from Germany: territory east of the *Oder–Neisse* Line and part of East Prussia

Land acquired by the USSR during the war

Occupation zones in Germany and Austria:
1 Russian	3 French
2 British	4 American

(replaced by *Clement Attlee* who became British Prime Minister after Labour's election victory). The war with Germany was over but no agreement was reached about her long-term future beyond what had been decided at Yalta (it was understood that she should be disarmed, the Nazi party disbanded and its leaders tried as 'war criminals'). Moreover Truman and Churchill were annoyed because Germany east of the Oder–Neisse Line had been occupied by Russian troops and was being run by the pro-communist Polish government which expelled some five million Germans living there; this had not been agreed to at Yalta! Truman did not inform Stalin about the nature of the atomic bomb, though Churchill was told about it during the conference. A few days after the conference closed the two atomic bombs were dropped on Japan and the war ended quickly on 10 August without the need for Russian aid (though the Russians declared war on Japan on 8 August and invaded Manchuria). Though they annexed south Sakhalin as agreed at Yalta they were allowed no part in the occupation of Japan.

(c) Churchill's 'Iron Curtain' speech (March 1946) was made at Fulton, Missouri (USA) in response to the spread of communism in eastern Europe. By this time pro-communist coalition governments had been established under Russian influence in Poland, Hungary, Rumania, Bulgaria and Albania. In some cases their opponents were imprisoned or murdered; in Hungary, for example, the Russians allowed free elections and, though the communists won less than 20 per cent of the votes (November 1945), they saw to it that a majority of the cabinet were communists. Repeating the same phrase that he had used earlier, Churchill declared: 'From Stettin in the Baltic to Trieste in the Adriatic an *iron curtain* has descended across the continent'; claiming that the Russians were bent on 'indefinite expansion of their power and doctrines', he called for a *western alliance* which would stand firm against the communist threat. The speech helped to widen the rift between east and west: Stalin was able to denounce Churchill as a warmonger while over a hundred British Labour MPs signed a motion criticising the Conservative leader; but he was only expressing what most leading American politicians felt.

(d) Undeterred by the Fulton Speech the **Russians continued to tighten their grip on eastern Europe**; by the end of 1947 every state in that area with the exception of Czechoslovakia had a fully communist government. Elections were rigged, non-communist members of the coalition governments were expelled, many being arrested and executed, and eventually all other political parties were dissolved; all this took place under the watchful eyes of secret police and Russian troops. In addition Stalin treated the *Russian zone of Germany* as if it *belonged to Russia*, allowing only the communist party and draining it of vital resources. (Yugoslavia did not quite fit the pattern: the communist government of *Marshal Tito* had been legally elected in 1945. He had immense prestige as a leader of the anti-German resistance; it was Tito's forces, not the Russians, who had liberated Yugoslavia from the Nazi occupation, and Tito resented Russian interference.) The west was profoundly irritated by Russia's attitude, which seemed to disregard Stalin's promise of free elections made at Yalta; the Russians could argue that friendly governments in her neighbouring states were essential for self-defence, that these states had never had democratic governments anyway and that communism would bring much-needed progress to backward countries. Even Churchill had agreed with Stalin in their 1944 discussions that much of eastern Europe should be a Russian 'sphere of influence'.

(e) The next major development was the appearance of the **'Truman Doctrine' which soon became closely associated with the Marshall Plan.**

(i) The *'Truman Doctrine'* sprang from events in Greece where communists were trying to overthrow the monarchy. British troops, who had helped liberate Greece from the Germans in 1944, had restored the monarchy but were now feeling the strain of supporting it against the communists who were receiving help from Albania, Bulgaria and Yugoslavia. Ernest Bevin, the British Foreign Minister, appealed to the USA and Truman announced (*March 1947*) that the USA would 'support free peoples who are resisting subjugation by armed minorities or by outside pressures'. *Greece* immediately received massive amounts of arms and other supplies and by 1949 the communists were defeated. *Turkey*, which also seemed under threat, received aid worth about 60 million dollars. The 'Truman Doctrine' made it clear that the US had no intention of returning to isolation as she had after the First World War; she was committed to a policy of *containing the spread of communism*, not just in Europe but throughout the world, including Korea and Vietnam.

(ii) The *Marshall Plan* (announced *June 1947*) was an economic extension of the 'Truman Doctrine'. American Secretary of State George Marshall produced his *European Recovery Programme (ERP)* which offered economic and financial help wherever it was needed. 'Our policy', he declared, 'is directed not against any country or doctrine but against hunger, poverty, desperation and chaos.' Its aim was to promote the *economic recovery of Europe*, thus ensuring markets for American exports; in addition, *communism was less likely to gain control* in a prosperous western Europe. By September 16 nations (Britain, France, Italy, Belgium, Luxembourg, Netherlands, Portugal, Austria, Switzerland, Greece, Turkey, Iceland, Norway, Sweden, Denmark, and the 3 western zones of Germany) had drawn up a joint plan for using American aid; over the next four years over 13,000 million dollars of Marshall Aid flowed into western Europe, fostering the recovery of agriculture and industry which in many countries were in chaos as a result of war devastation. The Russians on the other hand were well aware that there was more to Marshall Aid than benevolence. Although aid was in theory available to eastern

Europe, Molotov, the Russian Foreign Minister, denounced the whole idea as 'dollar imperialism', seeing it as a blatant American device for gaining control of western Europe – and, worse still, for interfering in eastern Europe, which Stalin considered to be in the Russian 'sphere of influence'. Russia rejected the offer and neither her satellite states nor Czechoslovakia, which was showing interest, were allowed to take advantage of it. The 'iron curtain' seemed a reality and the next development only served to strengthen it.

(f) The Cominform was set up by Stalin (*September 1947*). This was an organisation to draw together the various European communist parties. All the satellite states were members and the French and Italian communist parties were represented. Stalin's aim was to tighten his grip on the satellites: to be communist was not enough; it must be *Russian-style communism*. Eastern Europe was to be industrialised, collectivised and centralised; states were expected to trade primarily with Cominform members and all contacts with non-communist countries were discouraged. Only Yugoslavia objected, and was consequently expelled from the Cominform in 1948, though she remained communist. In 1949 the *Molotov Plan* was introduced, offering Russian aid to the satellites, and another organisation known as *Comecon* (Council of Mutual Economic Assistance) was set up to co-ordinate their economic policies.

(g) The communist takeover in Czechoslovakia (February 1948) came as a great blow to the western bloc, because it was the only remaining democratic state in eastern Europe. There was a coalition government freely elected in 1946. The communists had won 38 per cent of the votes and held a third of the cabinet posts. The Prime Minister, Klement Gottwald, was a communist; President Beneš and Foreign Minister Jan Masaryk were not, and they hoped that Czechoslovakia with its highly developed industries would remain as a *bridge between east and west*. However, a crisis arose early in 1948. Elections were due in May and all the signs were that the communists would lose ground: they were blamed for the Czech rejection of Marshall Aid which might have alleviated the continuing food shortages. The communists decided to act before the elections; already in control of the unions and the police, they seized power in an armed coup, while thousands of armed workers paraded through Prague. All non-communist ministers, with the exception of Beneš and Masaryk, resigned. A few days later Masaryk's body was found under the windows of his offices; his death was described officially as suicide, but Dubcek's (see Section 18.2(f)) opening of the archives in 1968 proved it was murder. The elections were duly held in May but there was only a single list of candidates – all communists. Beneš resigned and Gottwald became President. The western powers and the UN protested but could hardly take any action because they could not prove Russian involvement; the coup was purely an internal affair. However, there can be little doubt that Stalin, disapproving of Czech connections with the west and of their interest in Marshall Aid, had prodded the Czech communists into action; nor was it just coincidence that several of the Russian divisions occupying Austria were moved up to the Czech frontier. The bridge between east and west was gone; the 'iron curtain' was complete.

(h) The Berlin blockade and airlift (June 1948–May 1949) brought the Cold War to its first climax. The crisis arose out of disagreements over the treatment of *Germany*:

(i) At the end of the war, as agreed at Yalta and Potsdam, Germany and Berlin were each *divided into four zones*. While the three western powers set about organising the economic and political recovery of their zones, Stalin, determined to make the Germans pay for the damage inflicted on Russia, continued to treat his zone as a *satellite, draining its resources away to Russia.*

(ii) Early in 1948 the three western zones were *merged* to form a *single economic unit* whose prosperity, thanks to Marshall Aid, was in marked contrast to the poverty of the Russian zone. At the same time the west began to prepare a constitution for a self-governing West Germany, since the Russians had no intention of allowing complete German reunification. However, the Russians were alarmed at the prospect of a strong independent West Germany which would be part of the American bloc.

(iii) When in June 1948 the west introduced a new currency and ended price controls and rationing in their zone and in West Berlin, the Russians decided that the situation in Berlin had become impossible. Already irritated by the island of capitalism deep in the communist zone, they felt it impossible to have two different currencies in the same city and were embarrassed by the contrast between the prosperity of West Berlin and the poverty of the surrounding area.

The Russian response was immediate: *all road, rail and canal links between West Berlin and West Germany were closed*; their aim was to force the west to withdraw from West Berlin by reducing it to starvation point. The western powers, convinced that a retreat would be the prelude to a Russian attack on West Germany, were determined to hold on; they decided to fly supplies in, rightly judging that the Russians would not risk shooting down the transport planes. Over the next 10 months 2 million tons of supplies were airlifted to the blockaded city in a remarkable operation which kept the 2.5 million West Berliners fed and warmed right through the winter. In May 1949 the Russians admitted failure by lifting the blockade. The affair had important results: the outcome provided a great *psychological boost* for the western powers, though it brought relations with Russia to their worst ever; it caused the western powers to *co-ordinate their defences by the formation of NATO*. In addition it meant that since no compromise seemed possible, Germany was doomed to be *permanently divided*.

(i) The formation of NATO (North Atlantic Treaty Organisation) took place in *April 1949*. The Berlin blockade demonstrated the west's military unreadiness and frightened them into making definite preparations. Already in *March 1948* Britain, France, Belgium, Holland and Luxembourg had signed the *Brussels Defence Treaty*, promising military collaboration in case of war. Now they were joined by the USA, Canada, Portugal, Denmark, Ireland, Italy and Norway. All signed the *North Atlantic Treaty*, agreeing to regard an attack on any one of them as an attack on them all, and placing their defence forces under a joint NATO Command Organisation which would co-ordinate the defence of the west. This was a highly significant development: the Americans had abandoned their traditional policy of 'no entangling alliances' and for the first time had pledged themselves *in advance* to military action. Predictably Stalin took it as a challenge, and tension remained high, especially when it became known in September 1949 that the Russians had developed their own atomic bomb.

(j) The two Germanies. Since there was no prospect of the Russians allowing a united Germany, the western powers went ahead alone and set up the *German Federal Republic*, known as West Germany (*August 1949*). Elections were held and *Konrad Adenauer* became the first Federal Chancellor. The Russians replied by setting up their zone as the *German Democratic Republic* or East Germany (*October 1949*). Even in the 1980s Germany remains divided, and it is difficult to imagine the circumstances in which she could become united again.

(k) Though tension remained high in Europe, the Cold War spotlight now shifted to the **war in Korea (1950–3)** (see Section 17.2), at the end of which tensions began to relax and it was possible to talk of a 'thaw' in the Cold War.

16.3 WHY WAS THERE A 'THAW' IN THE COLD WAR AFTER 1953, AND WHAT FORM DID IT TAKE?

(a) The death of Stalin (March 1953) was probably the starting point of the 'thaw', because it brought to the forefront new leaders – Malenkov, Bulganin and Khrushchev – who wanted to improve relations with the USA. Their reasons were possibly connected with the fact that by August 1953 the Russians as well as the Americans had developed the hydrogen bomb: the two sides were now so finely balanced that international tensions had to be relaxed if nuclear war was to be avoided. *Nikita Khrushchev* explained the new policy in a famous speech (*February 1956*) in which he criticised Stalin and said that 'peaceful co-existence' with the west was not only possible but essential: 'there were only two ways – either peaceful co-existence or the most destructive war in history. There is no third way.' This did not mean that Khrushchev had given up the idea of a communist-dominated world; this would still come,

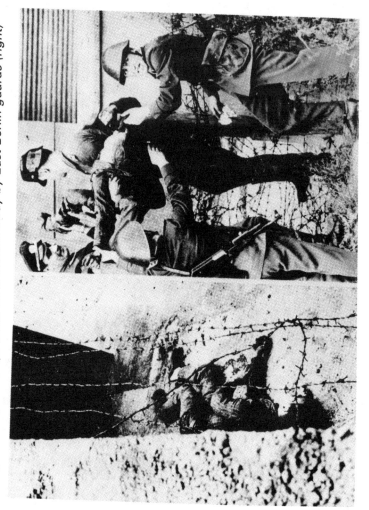

Illus 16.1 *The Berlin Wall – an eighteen-year-old East Berliner lies dying after being shot during an escape attempt (left); he is carried away by East Berlin guards (right)*

but would be achieved when the western powers *appreciated the superiority of the soviet economic system*, not when they were defeated in war. In the same way, he hoped to win neutral states over to communism by *lavish economic aid*.

(b) The 'thaw' showed itself in several ways: in a sense the *ending of the Korean War in 1953* and of the *war in Indo-China* the following year (see Section 17.4(a)) were the earliest signs. In 1955 the Russians agreed to give up their military bases in Finland, Bulganin attended a summit meeting in Geneva where he met US President Eisenhower, and in December the Russian veto on the admittance of 16 new member states to the United Nations was lifted. The *quarrel with Yugoslavia was healed* when Khrushchev paid a visit to Tito and the Cominform was abandoned, suggesting more freedom for the satellite states (April 1956). Most satisfying of all, at least for the west, was that agreement was at last reached over Austria by the *Austrian State Treaty (May 1955)*. At the end of the war in 1945, the country was divided into four occupied zones with the capital, Vienna, in the Russian zone, but unlike Germany she was allowed her own government, because she was viewed not as a defeated enemy but as a *state liberated from the Nazis*. The Austrian government had only limited powers, and the problem was similar to the one in Germany: whereas the three western occupying powers set about organising the recovery of their zones, the Russians insisted on squeezing reparations, mainly in the form of food supplies, from theirs. No permanent settlement seemed likely, but early in 1955 the Russians unexpectedly became co-operative, possibly because they feared a merger between West Germany and western Austria, and agreement was reached. *All occupying troops were withdrawn* and Austria became independent with her 1937 frontiers. She was not to unite with Germany, her armed forces were strictly limited and she was to remain neutral in any dispute between east and west, which meant that she joined neither NATO nor the European Economic Community. Since then the country has developed successfully though the Austrians were not happy about the loss of the German-speaking people in the *south Tyrol*, which *Italy* was allowed to keep.

(c) In fact, though, **the 'thaw' was only partial:** Khrushchev's policy was a curious mixture which western leaders often found difficult to understand. While making the apparently conciliatory moves just described, he was quick to respond to anything which seemed to be a **threat to the east** and had no intention of relaxing his overall grip on the satellites, as the *Hungarians* discovered to their cost when a rising in *Budapest* was ruthlessly crushed by Russian tanks *(1956)* (see Section 18.2(c)). Sometimes he seemed prepared to see how far he could push the Americans before they stood up to him, as when he made the provocative move of installing *soviet missiles in Cuba (1962)*.

(i) *The Warsaw Pact (1955)* was signed between Russia and her satellite states shortly after West Germany was admitted to

NATO. The pact was a mutual defence agreement which the west took as a gesture against German membership of NATO.

(ii) *The Russians continued to build up nuclear armaments*: by 1957 they had successfully tested an intercontinental ballistic missile and had also launched the first *space satellite, Sputnik 1*, none of which made the west feel any more secure.

(iii) The *situation in Berlin caused more tension*. In 1958, perhaps encouraged by Russia's apparent lead in the nuclear arms race, Khrushchev announced that Russia no longer recognised the rights of the western powers in West Berlin; when the Americans made it clear that they would resist any attempt to push them out, Khrushchev did not press the point. In 1960 it was Khrushchev's turn to feel aggrieved when an American U-2 spy plane was shot down over a thousand miles inside Russia. President Eisenhower declined to apologise, defending America's right to make reconnaissance flights and the affair ruined the summit conference which was about to begin in Paris. In 1961 Khrushchev again suggested, this time to the new American President John F. Kennedy that the *west should withdraw from West Berlin*. The communists were embarrassed at the large numbers of refugees escaping from East Germany into West Berlin – these averaged about 200,000 a year and totalled over 3 million since 1945. When Kennedy refused, the *Berlin Wall* was erected (*August 1961*), a 28-mile-long monstrosity across the entire city effectively blocking the escape route.

(iv) The *Cuban missile crisis (1962)* was the most tense incident of the entire Cold War. It occurred when Kennedy demanded the removal of Russian missiles from Cuba, which is less than 100 miles from the American coast. The two powers seemed on the brink of nuclear war, but Khrushchev agreed to remove the missiles (see Section 17.3(b)). The crisis had *important results*: the enormity of what might have happened seemed to bring both sides to their senses and produced a marked relaxation of tension. A telephone link (the '*hot line*') was introduced between Moscow and Washington to allow swift consultations, and in July 1963, Russia, USA and Britain signed a *Nuclear Test Ban Treaty* agreeing to carry out nuclear tests only underground to avoid polluting the atmosphere. (For further developments in east–west relations see Chapter 17.)

QUESTIONS

1. The beginning of the Cold War
Study the Sources below, and then answer the questions that follow.

Source A
From a speech by Winston Churchill, March 1946.

From Stettin in the Baltic to Trieste in the Adriatic, an iron curtain has descended across the continent. Behind that line lie all the capitals of the ancient states of Central and Eastern Europe – Warsaw, Berlin, Prague, Vienna, Budapest, Belgrade, Bucharest and Sofia. All these famous cities and the populations around them lie in the Soviet Sphere and all are subject in one form or another, not only to Soviet influence but to a very high and increasing measure of control from Moscow.

Source: M. Gilbert, *Winston S. Churchill* (Heinemann, 1986).

Source B
Map (Fig. 16.2) showing the post-war frontiers of Central and Eastern Europe.

Source C
From a speech made by President Truman of the United States, 1947.

One way of life is based upon the will of the majority with free institutions, elected government, free elections, guarantees of individual liberty, freedom of speech and religion, and freedom from political oppression.

The second way of life is based upon the will of the minority forced upon the majority. It relies upon terror and oppression, a controlled press and radio, fixed elections, and the suppression of personal freedoms.

I believe that it must be the policy of the United States to support free peoples who are resisting the attempt by armed minorities or by outside pressures to control them.

I believe that our help should be primarily through economic and financial aid which is essential to economic stability and orderly political processes.

[Adapted.]

Source D
From a speech made by George C. Marshall, American Secretary of State, 5 June 1947.

The physical destruction of much of Europe's cities, factories, mines and railroads is probably less important than the dislocation of the economy. The town and city industries are not producing enough goods to exchange with the food-producing farmer. Raw materials and fuel are in short supply. Machinery is lacking or worn out.

The truth of the matter is that for the next three or four years Europe's need for foreign food and other essential products – principally from America – is so much greater than her present ability to pay that she

Fig. 16.2

must have considerable additional help, or face economic, social and political decline of a very grave character.

[Adapted.]

Source E

The Marshall Plan of 1947 was anti-communist in so far as its motive was the American wish to help European countries struggling with post-war conditions, and thus discourage the spread of communism, which was believed to occur in conditions of social distress. The USSR delegation to the talks staged a walk-out led by Molotov, and Soviet pressure prevented Czechoslovakia from joining.

Source: J. N. Westwood, *Russian History, 1812–1971* (Oxford University Press, 1977).

Source F
A British cartoon (Fig. 16.3) in the *Evening Standard*, 1947.

Fig. 16.3

Marshall   Molotov
'WHICH HAND WILL YOU HAVE, COMRADE?'
17 JUNE 1947

(a) (i)   Source A refers to Soviet influence or control over the countries of Eastern Europe. Name *two* of the countries Churchill referred to in his speech as 'the ancient states'.
                                                                    1,4(a)

  (ii) What reason for the Soviet interest is suggested by the map in Fig. 16.2 (Source B)?   **4(a)**

  (iii) How does Source C suggest the Russians were bringing about the 'high and increasing measure of control' to which Churchill (Source A) referred?   **4(a,c)**

  (iv) Which other Source directly supports Churchill's view of the course of events in Eastern Europe? In what way does it do so?   **4(a,c)**

(b) President Truman (Source C) refers to 'the policy of the United States to support free peoples'. How would Truman expect his policy to work? **4(a)**

(c) **(i)** What according to Marshall (Source D) were the main reasons why Europe was facing economic difficulties? **4(a)**

(ii) Why, according to Source E, did the Soviet Union object to the proposals that Marshall was introducing in his speech?

4(a)

(d) **(i)** The cartoon in Fig. 16.3 (Source F) suggests a choice is being offered. With reference to other sources, what kind of alternatives were being offered and what 'choice' was made?

4(a,c)

(ii) How trustworthy is the view given by the cartoon of United States' policy towards the Soviet Union? Explain your answer.

4(a,b)

(e) Explain whether or not, in your opinion, the Sources support the following statements:

(i) American economic support for European countries was an act of considerable generosity. **4(a,c)**

(ii) Marshall Aid was part of an American policy of hostility towards the Soviet Union. **4(a,c)**

[Southern Examining Group, Specimen Question.]

2. Berlin and the German problem

Study the Sources below, and then answer the questions that follow.

Source A

Map of Berlin (Fig. 16.4).

Source: H. Ward, *World Powers in the 20th Century* (Heinemann–BBC, 1978).

Source B

A speech by President Kennedy, July 1961.

Our presence in West Berlin and our access thereto cannot be ended by any act of the Soviet government . . . For West Berlin, lying exposed 110 miles inside East Germany, surrounded by Soviet troops, has many roles. It is more than a showcase of liberty, a symbol, an island of freedom in a Communist sea, an escape hatch for refugees. West Berlin is all of that, But above all it has now become, as never before, the great testing place of Western courage and will . . . We cannot and will not permit the Communists to drive us out of Berlin, either gradually or by force.

Source: University of London Board, 1984, adapted extracts.

Fig. 16.4

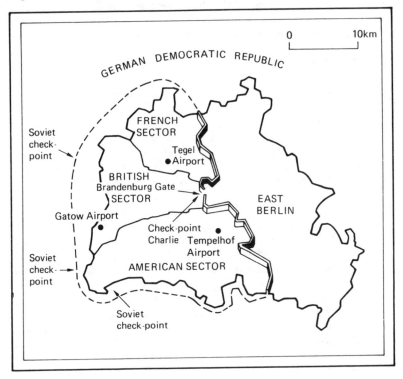

Source C

The government of the German Democratic Republic was threatened with collapse. Its citizens were escaping from it at the rate of 1000 a day, which was ruinous economically and in other ways. Its boss, Walter Ulbricht, had to act urgently in order to maintain his regime. Khrushchev probably decided that if he did not support Ulbricht, the crisis in the German Democratic Republic would lead to a war in Germany. He therefore gave his consent to the erection of a wall between the eastern sector and the western sector in Berlin, so that the eastern sector would become part of the German Democratic Republic and the west sector might be made too uncomfortable for continued western occupation. In the night of 12–13 August the wall was built and the flow of refugees virtually stopped . . . the building of the wall was a provocative act which the United States accepted.

Source: Peter Calvocoressi, *World Politics Since 1945* (Longman, 1982, 4th edn).

(a)   (i)   Explain when and how Berlin came to be divided in the way shown on the map (Fig. 16.4).   **1,2,4(a)**

    (ii)   Using the evidence of the map in Fig. 16.4 (Source A) and Source B, explain why the western powers seemed to be in a weak position in West Berlin. **4(a,c)**

    (iii)   What information does the map in Fig. 16.4 tell you about the Berlin Wall? **4(a)**

(b)   (i)   In what ways did the USSR try to get the western powers out of Berlin in 1948–9? **1**

    (ii)   Why did the USSR want the west to withdraw from Berlin? **1,2**

    (iii)   How did the western powers manage to remain in Berlin? **1**

    (iv)   What important results did the 1948–9 Berlin crisis have for east–west relations, and for Germany itself? **1,2**

Sources B and C are concerned with a later crisis in Berlin, which resulted in the building of the Berlin Wall in August 1961.

(c)   (i)   Using Source B as your evidence, make a list of the reasons why President Kennedy thought the western presence in Berlin was necessary. **4(a)**

    (ii)   From the evidence of Source C, why was the East German government unhappy about the situation in Berlin? **4(a)**

    (iii)   What do the words 'an escape hatch for refugees' (Source B) and 'its citizens were escaping' (Source C) suggest to you about life in East Germany? What does the use of these words tell you about the writers of the two sources? **4(a,b,c)**

(d)   (i)   Who was Walter Ulbricht referred to in Source C? **1,4(a)**

    (ii)   Why did Khrushchev feel he had to support him? **4(a)**

(e)   (i)   According to Source C, what did the East Germans hope to achieve by building the Berlin Wall? **4(a)**

    (ii)   Did the wall achieve what they wanted? **1,4(a)**

    (iii)   'The Berlin Wall was a defeat for Kennedy and the western powers.' Using evidence from Sources B and C, explain whether or not you agree with this statement. **4(a,c)**

(f)   Explain why Germany continued to be divided into two separate states into the 1980s. **1,2**

3. The communist takeover in Czechoslovakia, 1948.

Study the Source below, and then answer the questions that follow.

An eye-witness account of the Communist takeover in Czechoslovakia, 1948, by Howard K. Smith, a western observer.

For pure craftsmanship this coup d'état was stunning. With a minimum of fuss and no bloodshed the Czech Communist Party succeeded in taking over the country with only the sympathetic supervision and advice of the Soviet embassy. There seemed to be hardly any opposition. When the Nazis marched into the country, the Czechs wept as they lined the streets and cursed their oppressors openly. While walking the streets from dawn till dusk for all five days of the crisis, I saw no single person weeping, nor, in fact, any expression of anger. The walls remained clean of chalked slogans for or against the coup.

Source: H. K. Smith, *The State of Europe* (Cresset Press, 1950, adapted).

(a)   **(i)**   Explain what is meant by the phrase 'coup d'état'.   **1**

     (ii)   How long did the crisis in Czechoslovakia last, according to the eye-witness?   **4(a)**

    (iii)   How much help did the Czech Communists get from the USSR, according to the extract?   **4(a)**

(b)   The passage describes how the Czechs wept when the Nazis entered the country:

     (i)   Explain when this Nazi entry took place.   **1**

    (ii)   Describe the circumstances which led up to the Nazi entry.   **1,2**

   (iii)   Explain why the Czechs wept at this time.   **1,2**

(c)   Describe the situation in Czechoslovakia from 1946 to 1948, and explain why the Communists thought a coup was necessary.   **1,2**

(d)   After reading the extract carefully, do you get the impression that the writer approves or disapproves of the Communist takeover?   **4(a,b)**

(e)   What reasons can you think of to explain why the Czechs wept when the Nazis entered Czechoslovakia, but did not weep when the Communists took over?   **1,2,4**

(f)   Why did the western countries disapprove strongly of the Communist takeover in Czechoslovakia?   **1,2**

4.   **(a)**   Explain what is meant by the phrase the 'Cold War'.

    (b)   Describe briefly how each of the following helped to cause the Cold War:

       (i)   Stalin's distrust of Truman and Truman's distrust of Stalin;

      (ii)   the Potsdam Conference (July 1945);

     (iii)   the Truman Doctrine and the Marshall Plan;

     (iv)   the formation of the Cominform (September 1947);

      (v)   the Berlin blockade and airlift (June 1948–May 1949).   **1,2**

CHAPTER 17

THE SPREAD OF COMMUNISM OUTSIDE EUROPE AND ITS EFFECT ON INTERNATIONAL RELATIONS

SUMMARY OF EVENTS

Communism was not confined to Europe: several other communist states emerged each with its own particular brand of Marxism. As early as 1921, encouraged by the Russian Revolution, the *Chinese Communist Party* (CCP) had been founded. At first it co-operated with the *Kuomintang* (KMT), the party trying to govern China and control the generals who were struggling among themselves for power. The *Kuomintang* leaders were Dr Sun Yat-sen and, after his death in 1925, *General Chiang Kai-shek*. As the KMT established its control over more of China, it felt strong enough to dispense with the communists and tried to destroy them. The communists reacted vigorously and, after escaping from surrounding KMT forces, embarked on the famous 6000-mile *Long March* (1934–5) to form a new power base in northern China. *Civil War* dragged on, complicated by Japanese interference which culminated in the *full-scale invasion of 1937*. When the Second World War ended in the defeat and withdrawal of the Japanese, Chiang, with American help, and the communists under their leader Mao Tse-tung were still fighting it out. At last in 1949 *Mao triumphed*, and *Chiang and his supporters fled* to the island of *Taiwan* (Formosa); the second major country had followed Russia into communism.

Meanwhile communism had also gained a hold in *Korea*, which had been controlled by Japan since 1910. After the Japanese defeat in 1945 the country was divided into *two zones*: the *north occupied by Russians, the south by Americans*. The Russians set up a *communist government* in their zone, and since no agreement could be reached on what government to have for the whole country, Korea, like Germany, remained divided into two states. In *1950 communist North Korea invaded South Korea*. United Nations forces (mostly American) moved in to help the south, while the Chinese helped the north. After much advancing and retreating, the war ended in 1953 with South Korea still non-communist.

In *Cuba* early in 1959 *Fidel Castro* ousted the corrupt dictator, *Batista*. Although Castro was not a communist to begin with, the Americans soon turned against him, particularly when they discovered in 1962 that Russian missiles were based on the island; these were later removed after a tense Cold War crisis which brought the world to the brink of nuclear war. In *Vietnam* a similar situation to that in Korea occurred after the Vietnamese had won their independence from the French (*1954*): the country was divided, temporarily it was thought, into *north (communist)* and *south (non-communist)*; when a rebellion broke out in the south against a corrupt government, communist North Vietnam gave military assistance to the rebels and the Americans became heavily involved supporting the South Vietnamese government to stop the spread of communism. In 1973 the Americans withdrew from the struggle, following which the South Vietnamese forces rapidly collapsed, and the whole country became united under a *communist government (1975)*. Before the end of the year neighbouring *Cambodia and Laos* had also become communist.

In South America, which had a tradition of right-wing military dictatorships, communism made little headway, except in *Chile*, where in *1970* a *Marxist* government was democratically elected, with *Salvador Allende* as President. This was an interesting but short-lived experiment, since in *1973 the government was overthrown by the army and Allende killed*. Africa saw the establishment of governments with strong Marxist connections in *Mozambique (1975)* and *Angola (1976)* both of which had just succeeded in winning independence from Portugal. In December *1979* the Russians intervened in an already disturbed *Afghanistan* in support of a communist government, a move which caused a recurrence of the Cold War.

17.1 CHIANG OR MAO? TROUBLED YEARS IN CHINA 1918–49

(a) **Soon after a republic was proclaimed (1911)** China had dissolved into the chaos known as the *Warlord Era (1916–28)*, during which a number of generals seized control of different provinces, so that China seemed about to break up into many separate empires. The main hope for the survival of a united China lay with *Dr Sun Yat-sen* and his National People's Party or *Kuomintang* (formed 1912) which succeeded in setting up a government at Canton in southern China (1917). The *Kuomintang* was not a communist party, though it was prepared to co-operate with the communists and developed its own party organisation along communist lines as well as building up its own army. Sun himself summarised his aims as the *Three Principles*: nationalism (to rid China of foreign influence and build her into a strong and united power respected abroad), democracy (China should be ruled not by warlords, but by the people themselves after they had been educated to equip them for

Fig. 17.1 *China after the First World War*

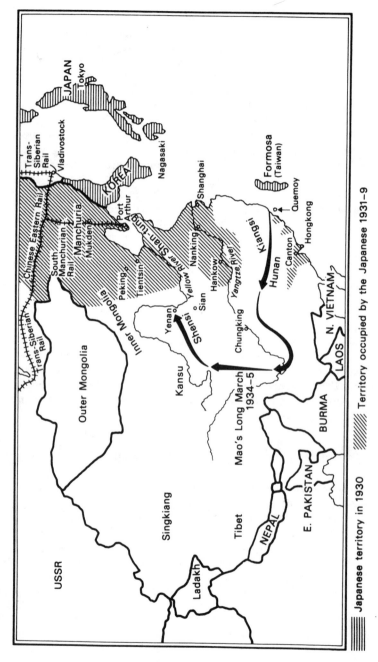

Japanese territory in 1930 [vertical line pattern] Territory occupied by the Japanese 1931–9 [diagonal line pattern]

democratic self-government) and land reform, sometimes known as 'the people's livelihood' (this was vague: although Sun announced a long-term policy of economic development and redistribution of land to the peasants and was in favour of rent restraint, he was opposed to the confiscation of landlords' property). Sun gained enormous respect as an intellectual statesman and revolutionary leader, but when he died in 1925 little progress had been made towards achieving the three principles, mainly because he was not himself a general; until the KMT armies were built up, he had to rely on alliances with sympathetic warlords and had trouble exercising any authority outside the south.

(b) General Chiang Kai-shek became leader of the KMT after Sun's death. He had received his military training in Japan before the First World War, and being a strong nationalist, joined the KMT. At this stage the new Russian soviet government was providing help and guidance to the KMT in the hope that nationalist China would be friendly to Russia. In 1923 Chiang spent some time in Moscow studying the organisation of the communist party and the Red Army; the following year he became head of the Whampoa Military Academy (near Canton) which was set up with Russian cash, arms and advisers to train officers for the KMT army. However, in spite of his Russian contacts, Chiang was not a communist; in fact he was more right-wing than Sun Yat-sen and became increasingly anti-communist, his sympathies lying with businessmen and landowners. Soon after becoming party leader he removed all left-wingers from leading positions in the party though for the time being he continued the KMT alliance with the communists. In 1926 he set out on the *Northern March* to destroy the warlords of central and northern China. Starting from Canton, the KMT and the communists had captured Hankow, Shanghai and Nanking by 1927. Peking was taken in 1928. Much of Chiang's success sprang from *massive local support* among the peasants attracted by communist promises of land; the capture of *Shanghai* was helped by a *rising of industrial workers* organised by *Chou En-lai*, a member of the KMT but also a communist. By April 1927 Chiang decided that the communists were becoming too powerful; in areas where communists were strong, landlords were being attacked and land seized; it was time to destroy an embarrassing ally. All communists were expelled from the KMT, and a terrible 'purification movement' was launched in which thousands of communists, trade union and peasant leaders were massacred; some estimates put the total murdered as high as 250,000. The communists had been checked, the warlords were under control and Chiang was the military and political leader of China. The *Kuomintang* government proved to be a great disappointment for the majority of Chinese. Chiang could claim to have achieved Sun's first principle, nationalism, but relying as he did on the support of wealthy landowners, no moves were made towards democracy or land reform though there was some limited progress with the building of more schools and roads.

(c) Meanwhile Mao Tse-tung and the Chinese Communist Party (CCP) concentrated on survival as Chiang carried out five 'extermination campaigns' against them between 1930 and 1934. The party had been officially founded in 1921, and at first consisted mostly of intellectuals with no military strength, which explains why they were willing to join the KMT. Mao, who was present at the founding meeting, was born in Hunan province (1893) in south-east China, the son of a prosperous peasant farmer. After some time working on the land, Mao trained as a teacher, and then moved northwards to Peking where he worked as a library assistant at the University, a centre of Marxist studies. Later he moved back to Hunan and built up a reputation as a skilful trade union and peasant association organiser. After the communist breach with the KMT, Mao was responsible for changing the party's strategy: they would concentrate on winning *mass support among the peasants* rather than trying to capture industrial towns where several communist insurrections had failed because of the strength of the KMT. In 1931, Mao was elected chairman of the Central Executive Committee of the party, and from then on he gradually consolidated his position as the *real leader of Chinese communism*. During the extermination campaigns Mao and his supporters took to the mountains between Hunan and Kiangsi provinces and concentrated on building up the Red Army. However, early in 1934 Mao's base area was surrounded by KMT armies poised for the final destruction of Chinese communism. Mao decided that the only chance of survival was to break through Chiang's lines and found another power base elsewhere. In October 1934 the breakthrough was achieved and almost 100,000 communists set out on the remarkable *Long March* which was to become part of Chinese legend. They covered about 6000 miles in 368 days and, in the words of Edgar Snow, 'crossed 18 mountain ranges, 5 of which were snow-capped, and 24 rivers. They passed through 12 different provinces, occupied 62 cities, and broke through enveloping armies of 10 different provincial warlords, besides defeating, eluding, or out-manoeuvring the various forces of government troops sent against them.' Eventually the 20,000 survivors found refuge at *Yenan* in Shensi province, where a new base was organised. Mao was able to control the provinces of Shensi and Kansu. During the next 10 years the *communists continued to gain support while Chiang and the KMT steadily lost popularity*.

(d) Why did Mao and the communists gain support?

(i) The basic opportunity for them to win support was provided by the *inefficiency and corruption of the KMT in government*. They had little to offer in the way of reform, spent too much time looking after the interests of industrialists, bankers and land-owners, and made no effective attempts to organise mass support.

(ii) There was *little improvement in factory conditions*, in spite of laws designed to remove the worst abuses such as child labour in textile mills. Often these laws were not applied: there was widespread bribery of inspectors and Chiang himself was not prepared to offend his industrialist supporters.

(iii) There was *no improvement in peasant poverty*. In the early 1930s there was a series of *droughts and bad harvests* which caused widespread *famine* in rural areas; at the same time there was often plenty of rice and wheat being *hoarded in the cities by profiteering merchants*. In addition, there were *high taxes and forced labour*. In contrast, the land policy followed in areas controlled by the communists was much more attractive: at first in the south they seized the estates of rich landlords and redistributed them among the peasants; after the temporary truce with the KMT during the war with Japan, the communists compromised and confined themselves to a policy of restricting rents and making sure that even the poorest labourers got a small piece of land. This less drastic policy had the advantage of winning the support of the *smaller landowners as well as the peasants*.

(iv) The crucial factor was that the KMT put up *no effective resistance to the Japanese*, who occupied Manchuria in 1931 and were obviously working to bring the neighbouring provinces of northern China under their control. Chiang seemed to think it was more important to destroy the communists than to resist the Japanese, and moved into south Shensi to attack Mao (1936). Here a remarkable incident took place: Chiang was taken prisoner by some of his own troops, mostly Manchurians, who were incensed at the Japanese invasion. They demanded that Chiang turn against the Japanese, but at first he was unwilling. Only after the prominent communist Chou En-lai came to see him at Sian did he agree to a fresh alliance with the CCP and a national front against the Japanese. The new alliance brought great advantages to the CCP: the KMT extermination campaigns ceased for the time being and consequently the CCP was secure in its Shensi base; when full-scale war broke out with Japan in 1937, the KMT forces were quickly defeated and most of eastern China was occupied by the Japanese as Chiang retreated westwards to Chungking; this enabled the communists, undefeated in Shensi, to present themselves as *patriotic nationalists*, leading an *effective guerrilla campaign* against the Japanese in the north. This won them *massive support among peasants and middle classes*, who were appalled at Japanese brutality and arrogance. Whereas in 1937 the CCP had 5 base areas controlling 12 million people, by 1945 this had grown to 19 base areas and 100 million people.

(e) The communist victory in 1949 was still not inevitable, though all the points examined in (d) contributed to it. When the Japanese were defeated in 1945, the KMT and the CCP became *locked in the final struggle for power*. Many observers, especially in the USA, hoped and expected that Chiang would be victorious. The Americans helped the KMT to take over all areas previously occupied by the Japanese, except

Manchuria which had been captured by the Russians a few days before the war ended. Here the Russians obstructed the KMT and allowed CCP guerrillas to move in. In fact the *apparent strength of the KMT was deceptive*: in 1948, the ever-increasing communist armies were large enough to abandon their guerrilla campaign and challenge Chiang's armies directly. As soon as they came under direct pressure, the KMT armies began to disintegrate. In January 1949 the communists took Peking, and later in the year Chiang and what remained of his forces fled to the island of Taiwan, leaving *Mao Tse-tung in command of mainland China.*

There were *several reasons for the CCP triumph*: the communists continued to win popular support by their restrained land policy which varied according to the needs of particular areas – some or all of a landlord's estates might be confiscated and redistributed among the peasants, or there might simply be rent restriction; communist armies were well-disciplined and communist administration was honest and scrupulously fair. On the other hand, the *KMT administration was inefficient and corrupt*, much of its American aid finding its way into the pockets of officials; its policy of paying for the wars by printing extra money resulted in *galloping inflation* which caused hardship for the masses and ruined many of the middle class. Its *armies were poorly paid and were allowed to loot the countryside*; subjected to communist propaganda, they gradually became disillusioned with Chiang and began to desert to the communists. The KMT tried to terrorise the local populations into submission, but this only alienated more areas. Towards the end, Chiang also made some tactical blunders: like Hitler he could not bear to order retreats and consequently his scattered armies were surrounded and often, as at Peking and Shanghai, surrendered without resistance, totally disillusioned. Finally the CCP leaders, Mao Tse-tung and Chou En-lai, were shrewd enough to take advantage of KMT weaknesses and were completely dedicated; the communist generals Lin Piao, Chu Teh and Ch-en Yi, had prepared their armies carefully and were more competent tactically than their KMT counterparts.

17.2 WAR IN KOREA 1950–3

Soon after the communist victory in China *civil war broke out in Korea*. Its origins lay in the fact that the country had been divided into two zones in 1945 at the end of the Second World War.

(a) Korea was divided into two at the 38th parallel by agreement between the USA and the USSR for purely military reasons – so that they could organise the *surrender of the occupying Japanese forces*; it was not intended to be permanent political division. The United Nations wanted free elections for the whole country and the Americans agreed, believing that since their zone, the south, contained two-thirds of the population,

Fig. 17.2 *the war in Korea*

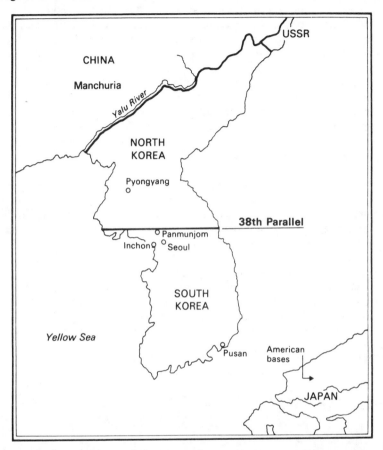

the communist north would be outvoted. However the unification of Korea, like that of Germany, soon became part of *Cold War rivalry* and no agreement could be reached. Elections were held in the south, supervised by the UN, and the independent *Republic of Korea (ROK)* or South Korea was set up with *Syngman Rhee* as president and its capital at *Seoul (August 1948)*. The following month the Russians created The *Democratic People's Republic of Korea* or North Korea under the communist government of *Kim Il Sung*, with its capital at *Pyongyang*. In 1949 Russian and American troops were withdrawn, leaving a potentially dangerous situation: most Koreans bitterly resented the artificial division forced on their country by outsiders, but both leaders claimed the right to rule the whole country. Without warning, *North Korean troops invaded South Korea in June 1950*.

(b) There is some controversy about the origins of the attack. It is still not clear whether it was Kim Il Sung's idea, perhaps encouraged by General

MacArthur's statement in 1949 that Korea was no longer part of the US defence perimeter in the Pacific; or he may have been egged on by the new Chinese communist government who were at the same time massing troops in Fukien province facing Taiwan, as if they were about to attack Chiang Kai-shek; perhaps the Russians were responsible: they had supplied the North Koreans with tanks, planes and other equipment; a communist takeover of the south would strengthen the Russian defensive position in the Pacific and provide a splendid gesture against the Americans to make up for Stalin's failure to squeeze them out of West Berlin. The communists claimed that South Korea had started the war, when troops of the 'bandit traitor' Syngman Rhee had crossed the 38th parallel.

(c) American and UN involvement. President Truman was convinced that the attack on South Korea, coming so soon after Cold War events in Europe, was part of a *vast Russian plan to advance communism* wherever possible in the world, and believed it essential for the *west to take a stand by supporting South Korea.* American troops in Japan were ordered to South Korea before the UN had decided what action to take. The UN Security Council called on North Korea to withdraw her troops, and when this was ignored asked member states to send assistance to South Korea. This decision was reached in the absence of the Russian delegation, who were boycotting meetings in protest against the UN refusal to allow Mao's new Chinese regime to be represented, and who

illus 17.1 *US Marines guard North Korean prisoners, stripped so that their clothes can be searched for hidden arms*

would certainly have vetoed such a decision. In the event, the USA and 14 other countries (Australia, Britain, Canada, New Zealand, Nationalist China (Chiang), France, Netherlands, Belgium, Colombia, Greece, Turkey, Panama, Philippines and Thailand) sent troops, though the vast majority were Americans. All forces were under the command of MacArthur.

Their arrival was none too soon: by *September communist troops had overrun the whole of South Korea* except the south-east, around the port of Pusan. UN reinforcements poured into Pusan and on 15 September American marines landed at Inchon, near Seoul, two hundred miles behind the communist front lines. Then followed an incredibly swift collapse by North Korean forces: by the end of September UN troops had entered Seoul and cleared the south of communists. Instead of calling for a ceasefire now that the original UN objective had been achieved, Truman ordered an *invasion of North Korea*, with UN approval, aiming to unite the country and hold free elections. Chou En-lai had warned that China would resist if UN troops entered the north, but the warning was ignored; by the end of October UN troops had captured Pyongyang, occupied two-thirds of North Korea, and reached the *Yalu River*, the frontier between North Korea and China.

The Chinese government was seriously alarmed: the Americans had already placed a fleet between Taiwan and the mainland to prevent an attack on Chiang, and remembering the assistance given to the KMT during the civil war, the Chinese feared an American invasion of Manchuria. In November they launched a massive counter-offensive with over 300,000 troops described as 'volunteers'; by *mid-January 1951* they had *driven the UN troops out of North Korea and crossed the 38th parallel*; Seoul was captured again. MacArthur was shocked at the strength of the Chinese forces and argued that the best way to beat them and stop the spread of communism was to attack Manchuria, with atomic bombs if necessary. However, Truman felt this would cause a large-scale war, which the USA did not want, and decided to settle for merely 'containing' communism; MacArthur was removed from his command. In June UN troops cleared the communists out of South Korea again and fortified the frontier; peace talks at Panmunjom lasted for two years, ending in *July 1953* with an agreement that the frontier should be *roughly along the 38th parallel*.

(d) The results of the war were wide-ranging. For Korea herself it was a disaster: the country was devastated, about four million Korean civilians and soldiers had been killed and five million were homeless. The division seemed permanent; both states remained intensely suspicious of each other and heavily armed, and there were constant ceasefire violations. The USA could take satisfaction from having contained communism and could claim that this success, plus American rearmament, dissuaded world communism from further aggression. The United Nations had exerted its authority and *reversed an act of aggression* (something which the League of Nations had never achieved). On the other hand, the communist world denounced the UN as a capitalist tool. The military performance of communist China was impressive; she had prevented the unification of Korea under American influence and was now clearly a *world power*; the fact that she was still denied a seat in the UN seemed even more unreasonable. The conflict brought a *new dimension to the Cold War*: American relations now seemed permanently strained with China as well as with Russia; the familiar pattern of both sides trying to build up alliances appeared in Asia as well as Europe. China supported the Indo-Chinese communists in their struggle for independence from France and at the same time offered friendship and aid to under-developed 'third world' countries in Asia, Africa and Latin America; 'peaceful co-existence' agreements were signed with India and Burma (1954). Meanwhile the Americans tried to encircle China with bases: in 1951 defensive agreements were signed with Australia and New Zealand and in 1954 these three states together with Britain and France set up the South East Asia Treaty Organisation (SEATO); however, the USA was disappointed when only three Asian states – Pakistan, Thailand and the Philippines – joined SEATO. It was obvious that many states wanted to keep clear of the Cold War and remain uncommitted.

Relations between the USA and China remained poor, mainly because of the Taiwan situation. The communists still hoped to capture the island and destroy Chiang Kai-shek and his Nationalist party for good, but the Americans were committed to defend Chiang and wanted to keep Taiwan as a military base.

17.3 CUBA: WHY DID FIDEL CASTRO COME TO POWER, AND HOW WERE CUBA'S FOREIGN RELATIONS AFFECTED?

(a) The situation which resulted in Fidel Castro coming to power in January 1959 had built up over a number of years:

(i) There was a long-standing resentment among many Cubans of *American influence*, which dated back to 1898 when the USA had helped wrest Cuba from Spanish control. Although the island became an independent republic, American troops were needed from time to time to maintain stability, and American financial aid and investment kept the Cuban economy ticking over. In fact there was some truth in the claim that the *USA controlled the Cuban economy*: American companies held controlling interests in all Cuban industries (sugar, tobacco, textiles, iron, nickel, copper, manganese, paper and rum), owned half the land, about three-fifths of the railways, all electricity production and the entire telephone system. The USA was the main market for Cuba's exports, of which sugar was by far the most important.

Small wonder that the American ambassador in Havana was usually referred to as the second most important man in Cuba. The American connection need not have been so much resented if it had resulted in an efficiently run country, *but this was not so.*

(ii) Though Cuba was prosperous compared with other Latin American countries, she was too *dependent on the export of sugar*, and the wealth of the country was concentrated in the hands of a few. *Unemployment* was an insoluble problem: it varied from about 8 per cent of the labour force during the 5 months of the sugar harvest to over 30 per cent during the rest of the year. Yet there was no unemployment benefit, and the trade unions, dominated by workers who had all-the-year-round jobs in sugar mills, did nothing to help. The poverty of the unemployed was in stark contrast to the wealth in Havana, the capital, and in the hands of corrupt government officials; consequently *social tensions were high.*

(iii) *No effective democratic political system* had been developed. In 1952 *Fulgencio Batista*, who had been in the forefront of politics since 1933, seized power illegally and began to rule as a dictator. He introduced no reforms and according to Hugh Thomas, 'spent a lot of time dealing with his private affairs and his foreign fortunes, leaving himself too little time for affairs of state'. As well as being corrupt, his regime was also brutal.

(iv) Since there was no prospect of a peaceful social revolution, the feeling grew that *violent revolution* was necessary. The leading exponent of this view was *Fidel Castro*, a young lawyer from a middle-class background. Before he came to power, Castro was more of a liberal nationalist than a communist: he wanted to rid Cuba of Batista and corruption and to introduce limited land reforms so that all peasants should receive some land. After an unsuccessful attempt to overthrow Batista in 1953, which earned him two years in gaol, Castro began a campaign of *guerrilla warfare and sabotage* in the cities. The rebels soon controlled the mountainous areas of the east and north and won popular support there by carrying through Castro's land reform policy.

(v) *Batista's reaction* played into Castro's hands. He took *savage reprisals* against the guerrillas, torturing and murdering suspects, which polarised the struggle; even many of the middle class began to support Castro as the most likely way of ousting a brutal dictator. Morale in Batista's poorly paid army began to crumble in the summer of 1958 after an unsuccessful attempt to destroy Castro's forces. The USA began to feel embarrassment at Batista's behaviour and cut off arms supplies, a serious blow to the dictator's prestige. In September a small rebel force under *Che Guevara*, an Argentinian supporter of Castro, gained control of the main road across the island and prepared to move on Santa Clara. On *1 January 1959 Batista fled from Cuba*, and a liberal government was set up with Castro at its head.

(b) Cuban relations with the USA did not deteriorate immediately; Castro was thought to be, at worst, a social democrat, and consequently most Americans were prepared to give him a chance. Before long, however, he had outraged the USA by *nationalising American-owned estates and factories*. President Eisenhower threatened to stop importing Cuban sugar, forcing Castro to sign a *trade agreement with Russia*. In July 1960, when the Americans carried out their threat, the USSR promised to buy Cuba's sugar, and Castro confiscated all remaining American property. As Cuba's relations with the USA worsened, those with Russia improved: in January 1961 the USA broke off diplomatic relations with Cuba, but the Russians were already supplying economic aid. Convinced that Cuba was now a communist state in all but name, the new American president, John F. Kennedy, approved a plan by a group of Batista supporters to *invade Cuba from American bases in Guatemala*. The American Central Intelligence Agency (CIA), a kind of secret service, was deeply involved. The small invading force landed at the *Bay of Pigs* in April 1961, but the operation was so badly planned and executed that Castro's forces and his two jet planes had no difficulty in crushing it. Later the same year Castro announced that he was a *Marxist* and that *Cuba was now a socialist country*.

The *missile crisis (1962)* brought Cuba into the Cold War forefront and the world to the brink of nuclear war. During the summer *Russia supplied Cuba with large quantities of arms* and on 22 October Kennedy announced that U-2 spy planes had photographed Russian missile bases being built in Cuba; he alerted American troops, began a blockade of Cuba to keep out further arms (several Russian ships carrying missiles were en route for Cuba) and demanded that Russia withdraw the missiles. On 28 October Khrushchev agreed to remove the offending missiles and in return Kennedy promised not to invade Cuba. The crisis had passed and thereafter the Cold War thawed somewhat (see Section 16.3(c)). but relations between Cuba and the USA remained cool. The attitude of other Latin American states, most of which had right-wing governments, was one of extreme suspicion; in 1962 they expelled Cuba from the Organisation of American States (OAS), which only made her more *dependent on Russia*.

17.4 CASTRO'S PROBLEMS, MEASURES, SUCCESSES AND FAILURES

(a) Some of Castro's most serious difficulties were *special to Cuba*: how would the other Latin American states (and above all the USA) react to this new socialist threat on their doorsteps? Cuba was dependent on the USA's taking most of her sugar exports; the economy relied far too heavily on the sugar industry and was at the mercy of fluctuations in world sugar prices. The whole of government and administration was riddled with corruption and in addition there was serious unemployment and poverty.

(b) Castro had the help of *Ernesto 'Che' Guevara*, an Argentinian Marxist who had played an important part in the revolution and was a member of Castro's government until 1965. (Guevara believed, wrongly as it turned out, that the peasants of South America were ready to burst out into revolution. He became an expert in guerrilla warfare and wrote a book about it which had a great impact on Latin America, stirring up guerrilla campaigns in a number of states. He soon became frustrated in government and, believing that his real mission was to organise further revolutions, he left Cuba in 1965 and was killed by troops of the Bolivian government in 1967.)

The new government set about the problems with *enthusiasm* and *dedication*; David Harkness writes that during his first ten years Castro took this poor and backward country by the scruff of the neck and shook it into new and radically different patterns of life. Agricultural land was taken over by the government and collective farms introduced; factories and businesses were nationalised; attempts were made to modernise sugar production and increase output, and to introduce new industries to reduce Cuba's dependence on sugar. Social reforms included attempts to improve education, housing, health, medical facilities and communications; there was equality for negroes and more rights for women; there were touring cinemas, theatres, concerts and art exhibitions. Castro himself seemed to have boundless energy, constantly touring the island, making speeches and urging people to greater efforts.

(c) The government could claim considerable success, especially in the sphere of *social reform*: all children were now receiving some education, instead of fewer than half before 1959; sanitation and hygiene were much improved, unemployment and corruption reduced, and there was a greater sense of equality and stability than ever before. At the end of its first decade in power the government seemed to be popular with the vast majority of people.

On the other hand there were some *significant failures*: the attempt to *diversify industrial and agricultural output* met with very little success; consequently the island's economy still depended dangerously on the quality of the sugar harvest, the world price of sugar, and the willingness of the USSR and her satellites to absorb her exports. In the late 1970s sugar production actually began to decline and in 1980 the crop was further reduced by a fungus infection, while the tobacco crop was also seriously affected by another fungus. This plunged the country into an economic crisis, unemployment rose again, and thousands of people began to emigrate to the USA. Food rationing was in operation and the whole economy was being heavily subsidised by the Soviet Union.

It is probably too early to write Castro's regime off as a failure, but after a promising start, its progress is certainly faltering.

17.5 THE WARS IN VIETNAM: 1946–54 AND 1961–75

(a) **From 1946 until 1954 the Vietnamese were fighting for independence from France.** Vietnam together with Laos and Cambodia made up Indo-China which had been part of the French empire since the late nineteenth century. During the Second World War the area was occupied by the Japanese; resistance to both Japanese and French was organised by the *League for Vietnamese Independence* (Vietminh), led by the communist *Ho Chi Minh* who had spent many years in Russia learning how to organise revolutions. The Vietminh, though led by communists, was an alliance of all shades of political opinion which wanted to see the end of foreign control. At the end of the war in 1945 Ho Chi Minh declared the whole of Vietnam independent; when it became clear that the French had no intention of agreeing to full independence, the Vietminh attacked the French in Hanoi, beginning an eight-year struggle which ended with the *French defeat at Dien Bien Phu (May 1954)*. The Vietminh were successful partly because they were masters of *guerrilla tactics* and had massive support from the *Vietnamese people* and because the French, still suffering the after-effects of world war, *failed to send enough troops*. The decisive factor was probably that from 1950 the *new Chinese communist government supplied the rebels with arms and equipment*. The USA also became involved: seeing the struggle as part of the Cold War and the fight against communism, she supplied the French with military and economic aid; but it was not enough. By the *Geneva Agreement (1954)* Laos and Cambodia were to be independent; Vietnam was temporarily divided into two states at the 17th parallel: Ho Chi Minh's Vietminh government was recognised in North Vietnam; South Vietnam was to have a separate government for the time being, but elections were to be held by 1956 for the whole country, which would then become united. Ho Chi Minh was disappointed at the partition, but was confident that the communists would win the national elections. As it turned out the elections were never held and a repeat performance of the Korean situation seemed likely. A *civil war* gradually developed in South Vietnam which involved the north and the USA.

(b) What caused the war, and why was the USA involved?

(i) The South Vietnamese government under *President Ngo Dinh Diem* (chosen by a national referendum in 1955) refused to make preparations for the elections for the whole of Vietnam, and the USA, which was backing his regime, did not press him for fear of a communist victory if the elections were held.

(ii) Although Diem began energetically, his government *soon lost popularity*: he came from a wealthy Roman Catholic family, whereas three-quarters of the population were Buddhist peasants who thought themselves discriminated against; they demanded land reform of the type carried through in China and North Vietnam, but none was forthcoming. He also gained a reputation,

Fig. 17.3 *the wars in Vietnam*

...... Ho Chi Minh Trail

■ American bases

perhaps not wholly deserved, for *corruption* and was unpopular
with nationalists who thought he was *too much under American
influence.*

(iii) In *1960* various opposition groups, which included many former
communist members of the Viet Minh, formed the *National
Liberation Front (NLF).* They demanded a democratic national
coalition government which would introduce reforms and negotiate peacefully for a *united Vietnam.* A *guerrilla campaign* was
started, attacking government officials and buildings, while
Buddhist monks had their own special brand of protest, committing suicide in public by setting fire to themselves. Diem's
credibility declined further when he dismissed all criticism and

opposition as communist inspired whereas the communists were only one section of the NLF; he also introduced harsh security measures. He was *overthrown and murdered by an army coup (1963)* and the country was ruled by a series of generals of which *President Nguyen Van Thieu* survived longest (1967–75). The removal of Diem left the basic situation unchanged and the guerrilla war continued.

(iv)   When it became clear that Diem could not cope with the situation the *USA decided to increase her military presence in South Vietnam.* Under Eisenhower she had been supporting the regime since 1954 with economic aid and military advisers and accepted Diem's claim that communists were behind all the trouble. Kennedy and Johnson saw it as another *Korea*: if a strong enough stand were made, South Vietnam could be saved from communism.

(v)   The Americans were strengthened in their determination by the knowledge that the *Vietcong* (as the guerrillas were now known) were receiving supplies, equipment and troops from *North Vietnam.* Ho Chi Minh believed that such aid was justified: given South Vietnam's refusal to agree to the national elections, *only force could unite the two halves of Vietnam.*

(c) The phases of the war correspond to successive American presidencies which each saw the introduction of new policies:

(i)   *Kennedy (1961–3)* tried to keep American involvement down to an *anti-guerrilla campaign.* He sent about 16,000 advisers plus equipment and helicopters and introduced the *'safe village' policy,* in which local peasants were moved en masse into fortified villages, leaving the Vietcong isolated outside. This was a failure because most of the Vietcong were peasants who simply continued to operate inside the villages.

(ii)   *Johnson (1963–9)* was not deterred by reports from American advisers in 1964 that the Vietcong and the NLF controlled about 40 per cent of South Vietnamese villages and that the peasant population seemed to support them. He assumed that the Vietcong were controlled by Ho Chi Minh and decided to *bomb North Vietnam (1965)* in the hope that he would call off the campaign. Over the next seven years North Vietnamese cities suffered an even greater tonnage of bombs than the Germans during the Second World War. In addition over half a million American troops arrived in the south. In spite of these massive efforts the Vietcong still managed to unleash an offensive in February 1968 which captured something like 80 per cent of all towns and villages; although much ground was lost later, this offensive convinced many Americans of the hopelessness of the situation, and *great pressure was brought on the government to withdraw from Vietnam.* This Johnson had no intention of doing, though he did suspend the bombing of North Vietnam (March 1968).

(iii) *Nixon (1969–74)* realised that a new approach was needed since public opinion would hardly allow him to commit any more American troops (early in 1969 there were 500,000 Americans, 50,000 South Koreans and 750,000 South Vietnamese against 450,000 Vietcong plus perhaps 70,000 North Vietnamese). His new idea was *Vietnamisation*: the Americans would rearm and train the South Vietnamese army to look after the defence of South Vietnam; this would allow a gradual withdrawal of American troops (in fact about half had been sent home by mid-1971). On the other hand Nixon began the heavy bombing of North Vietnam again and also began to bomb the Ho Chi Minh Trail through Laos and Cambodia along which supplies and troops came from North Vietnam. All was to no avail: *at the end of 1972 the Vietcong controlled the entire western half of the country*. By now Nixon was under pressure both at home and from world opinion to withdraw; apart from the terrible bombing of North Vietnam, the use of chemicals to destroy jungle foliage and of inflammable napalm jelly which burned people alive, plus the deaths of thousands of innocent civilians, caused a revulsion of feeling against continuing the war. Even Russia and China who were helping the Vietcong with supplies and equipment were looking round for a way out. Consequently a *cease-fire was arranged for January 1973*. It was agreed that all American troops would be withdrawn from Vietnam and both north and south would respect the frontier along the 17th parallel. However, the Vietcong continued their campaign and without the Americans, President Thieu's government in Saigon soon collapsed. In *April 1975 Saigon was occupied by the North Vietnamese and Vietcong*; at last Vietnam was united and free from foreign intervention – under a communist government. In the same year, communist governments were also established in *Laos and Cambodia*. American policy of preventing the spread of communism in south-east Asia had ended in *complete failure and humiliation*.

(d) Why did the Americans fail?

(i) The main reason was that the Vietcong and the NLF had *widespread support among ordinary peasants* who had genuine grievances against an inefficient government which failed to introduce necessary reforms. When the NLF was formed in 1960 the communists were only one of several opposition groups; by ignoring the rightness of the NLF case and choosing instead to prop up such an obviously deficient regime in their obsession with the fight against communism, the Americans actually encouraged the spread of communism in the south.

(ii) The Vietcong, like the Vietminh before them, were *experts at guerrilla warfare and were fighting on familiar territory*; the Americans found them much more difficult to deal with than the conventional armies they had faced in Korea: with no distinguishing uniform, guerrillas could easily merge into the local peasant population. It proved impossible to stop supplies and reinforcements moving down the Ho Chi Minh Trail.

(iii) The Vietcong received *important help from North Vietnam* in the *way of troops*, while *China and Russia supplied arms*. After 1970 the Russian contribution was vitally important and included rifles, machineguns, long-range artillery, anti-aircraft missiles and tanks.

(iv) *The North Vietnamese were dedicated to eventual victory and the unification of their country*, and showed amazing resilience; in spite of appalling damage and casualties during the bombings, they responded by evacuating city populations and rebuilding factories outside the cities.

The *effects of the war were wide-reaching*: Vietnam was united but the problems of *reconstruction* were enormous, and the new government's policies had unpleasant aspects such as concentration camps for opponents, and loss of freedom of speech. As well as being a blow to American prestige, her failure had a profound effect on American society: involvement in the war was seen in many circles as a terrible mistake and this, together with the Watergate scandal (see Section 22.1(f)) which forced *Nixon to resign (August 1974)*, shook confidence in a political system which could allow such things to happen. Future American governments would have to think carefully before committing themselves so deeply to any similar situation. The war was a victory for the communist world, though both the Russians and Chinese reacted with restraint and did not boast about it to any great extent, indicating perhaps that they wanted to relax international tensions; however, the communist world now had another powerful military force in the Vietnamese army.

17.6 CHILE UNDER SALVADOR ALLENDE 1970–3

In September 1970 Salvador Allende, a Marxist doctor of medicine from a middle-class background, won the presidential election as the leader of a left-wing coalition of communists, socialists, radicals and social democrats; it called itself Unidad Popular (UP). It was a narrow victory, Allende gaining 36 per cent of the poll against the 35 per cent of his nearest rival. But it was enough to make him president, *the world's first Marxist president to be voted in through a democratic election*. Although it lasted only three years Allende's government is worth looking at in some detail because it is still the only one of its kind and it illustrates the problems faced by a Marxist government trying to function within a democratic system.

(a) How did Allende come to be elected?

Chile, unlike most other South American states, had a *tradition of democracy*. There were three main parties or groups of parties: the

Unidad Popular on the left, the Christian Democrats (also left-inclined) and the National Party (a liberal/conservative coalition). The army played little part in politics and the democratic constitution (similar to that of the USA except that the president could not stand for re-election immediately) was usually respected. The election of 1964 was won by *Eduardo Frei*, leader of the Christian Democrats, who believed in social reform. Frei began vigorously: *inflation was brought down* from 38 per cent to 25 per cent, the rich were made to pay their taxes instead of *evading them*, 360,000 new houses were built, the number of schools was more than doubled and some limited land reform introduced: over 1200 private holdings which were being run inefficiently were confiscated and redistributed to landless peasants. He also took over about half the holdings in the American-owned Chilean copper mines, with suitable compensation. The American government admired his reforms and poured in lavish *economic aid*.

By 1967, however, the tide was beginning to turn against Frei: the left thought his land reforms too cautious and wanted *full nationalisation* of the copper industry (Chile's most important export), whereas the right thought he had gone too far as it was. In 1969 there was a serious drought in which a third of the harvest was lost; large quantities of food had to be imported, causing *inflation to soar again*. There were strikes of copper miners demanding higher wages and several miners were killed by government troops. Allende made skilful use of this ammunition during the 1970 election campaign, pointing out that Frei's achievements fell far short of his promises. Allende's coalition had a much better campaign organisation than the other parties and could get thousands of supporters out on the streets. *Allende himself* inspired confidence: elegant and cultured, he appeared the very opposite of the violent revolutionary; appearances were not deceptive: he believed that communism could succeed without a violent revolution. In the 1970 election 36 per cent of the voters were in favour of trying his policies.

(b) Allende's problems and policies. The problems facing the new government were enormous: *inflation* was running at over 30 per cent, *unemployment* at 20 per cent, *industry was stagnating*, and 90 per cent of the population lived in such poverty that half the children under 15 suffered from *malnutrition*. Allende believed in a redistribution of income, which would enable the poor to buy more and thereby stimulate the economy. All-round wage increases of about 40 per cent were introduced and firms were not allowed to increase prices. The remainder of the copper industry, textiles and banks were nationalised, and Frei's land redistribution speeded up. The army was awarded an even bigger pay rise than anybody else to make sure of retaining its support. In foreign affairs, he restored diplomatic relations with Castro's Cuba, China and East Germany. Whether Allende's policies would have succeeded in the long run is open to argument. Certainly he retained his popularity sufficiently for the UP to win 49 per cent of the votes in the 1972 municipal elections and to increase slightly their seats in the 1973 congressional elections. However, the Allende experiment came to an *abrupt and violent end in September 1973.*

(c) Why was he overthrown?

Criticism of the government gradually built up as Allende's policies began to cause problems: land redistribution caused a fall in agricultural production, mainly because farmers whose land was due to be taken stopped sowing and often slaughtered their cattle (like the Russian *kulaks* during collectivisation); this caused food shortages and further inflation. Private investors were frightened off and the government became short of funds to implement social reforms (housing, education, social services) as rapidly as it would have liked. Copper nationalisation was disappointing: there were long strikes for higher wages, production fell, and the world price of copper fell suddenly by about 30 per cent causing a further drop in government revenue. Some communists who wanted a more drastic Castro-style approach to Chile's problems grew impatient with Allende's caution, refusing to make allowances for the fact that he did not have a stable parliamentary majority; they founded the Movement of the Revolutionary Left (MIR) which embarrassed the non-violent UP by seizing farms and evicting the owners. In addition the USA disapproved strongly of Allende's policies and other South American governments were nervous in case the Chileans tried to export their 'revolution'.

Looming above all else was the question of what would happen in September 1976 when the next presidential election was due; under the constitution Allende would not be able to stand, but no Marxist regime had ever allowed itself to be voted out of power. The opposition feared, perhaps with justification, that Allende was planning to change the constitution. As things stood, any president finding his legislation blocked by congress could appeal to the nation by means of a referendum. With sufficient support Allende might be able to use the referendum device to postpone the election. It was this fear, or so they afterwards claimed, that caused the opposition groups to draw together and take action before Allende did. They organised a massive strike and having won the support of the army, the *right staged a military coup* organised by leading generals, and set up a military dictatorship in which *General Pinochet* came to the fore. Left-wing leaders were murdered or imprisoned; Allende himself was killed in the coup. It has been suggested that the *American CIA*, helped by the Brazilian government (a repressive military government), played an important role in the preparations for the coup as part of its policy of preventing the spread of communism in Latin America. The new regime provoked great criticism from the outside world for its brutal treatment of political prisoners; however the American government, which had greatly reduced its economic aid while Allende was in power, stepped up its assistance again. The Pinochet government had some economic success and by 1980 had brought the annual inflation rate down from around 1000 per cent to manageable proportions.

17.7 *DÉTENTE*: INTERNATIONAL RELATIONS IN THE 1970s

The world '*détente*' is used to mean a *permanent relaxation* of international tensions, rather than just a 'thaw' in the Cold War. The first signs of real *détente* between east and west came in the early 1970s, stimulated probably by the continuing fear of nuclear war and the horrors of Vietnam.

(a) **The motives of the individual powers** in pursuing *détente* were mixed: the *Chinese* were anxious about their isolation, nervous about American intentions in Vietnam (after what had happened in Korea) and not happy about their worsening relations with Russia. The *Americans* were realising that there must be a better way of coping with communism than the one they were trying in Vietnam; perhaps peaceful co-existence was the way after all. The *Russians* wanted to reduce defence spending so as to devote more energy to bringing living standards up to western levels; nor did they want to be left out when they saw relations between China and the USA improving.

(b) **The USSR and the USA** had already made progress with the 'hot line' telephone link and the agreement to carry out only underground nuclear tests (both 1963); further steps were taken in 1969 with the beginning of *Strategic Arms Limitation Talks (SALT)*. Nixon twice visited Moscow (1972 and 1974) while Brezhnev went to Washington in 1973. The USA began to export wheat to Russia. Most important of all was the *Helsinki Agreement (July 1975)* in which the USA, the USSR, Canada and almost all the European states accepted the European frontiers which had been drawn up after the Second World War (thus recognising the permanent division of Germany). The communist countries undertook to allow their peoples 'human rights' (including freedom of speech and freedom to leave the country).

(c) **China and the USA** had been extremely *hostile towards each other* since the Korean War and seemed likely to remain so while the Americans backed Chiang Kai-shek and the Chinese Nationalists in Taiwan and while the Chinese backed Ho Chi Minh.. However the Chinese made the first move in 1971, and an unlikely one at that: they invited an American table tennis team to visit China, and following the success of that visit the USA responded by *calling off her veto of Chinese entry into the United Nations*. Communist China was admitted in October 1971 and the Nationalist representatives from Taiwan left. Presidents Nixon and Ford both paid successful visits to Peking (1972 and 1975). However, Taiwan still remained to sour the relationship: though Chiang himself died in 1975, the KMT still occupied the island and the communists would not be satisfied until it was brought under their control. Relations improved further in December 1978, when Carter decided to withdraw recognition of Nationalist China; however, this caused a row in the USA where Carter was accused of betraying his ally.

The climax of *détente* between China and the USA came in January 1979 when Carter gave formal recognition of the People's Republic of China, and ambassadors were exchanged.

(d) Relations between the USSR and China, on the other hand, have deteriorated steadily since about 1956. In 1950 they had signed a treaty of mutual friendship and assistance, but later the Chinese disapproved of Khrushchev's policies, particularly his belief in 'peaceful co-existence' and his claim that it was possible to achieve communism by methods other than violent revolution (see Section 18.1). This was not what Lenin had said and consequently the Chinese accused the Russians of '*revisionism*' – revising or reinterpreting the teachings of Marx and Lenin to suit their own ends. They were incensed at Khrushchev's 'soft' line towards the USA. In retaliation the Russians sharply reduced economic aid to China. The ideological argument was not the only source of trouble: there was also a frontier dispute; during the nineteenth century Russia took over large areas of Chinese territory north of Vladivostok and in Sinkiang province which the Chinese were now demanding back, so far without success. Now that China herself was following a 'softer' policy towards the USA it seemed that the territorial problem was the main bone of contention between them. At the end of the 1970s it seemed that both Russia and China were vying for American support against each other in the struggle for the leadership of world communism, in which, to complicate matters further, Vietnam now supported Russia.

17.8   *DÉTENTE* UNDER STRAIN: THE 1980s

(a) *Détente* **falters.** As the world moved towards the 1980s, there were disturbing signs that *détente* was perhaps not going to be permanent. In spite of the Helsinki Agreement, neither free speech nor free travel were allowed in eastern Europe where dissidents (people who ventured to criticise the government) were harassed in all sorts of ways. NATO became nervous at the deployment of 50 of the new Soviet 'Backfire' bombers and some 150 SS20 missiles. By the end of 1979 it was feared that Russia was poised to outstrip America's long range nuclear arsenal and to threaten Europe with her short range nuclear weapons; and all this on top of conventional forces which outnumbered NATO's forces in Europe by an average of about two to one. Consequently NATO took the decision (*December 1979*) to *deploy over 500 Pershing and Cruise missiles in Europe by 1983* as a deterrent to a possible Russian attack on Western Europe. At the same time, the US Senate decided *not to accept a SALT 2 Treaty* which would have limited numbers of missiles.

Most serious of all was the *Russian invasion of Afghanistan* which began on *Christmas Day 1979*. The Russians claimed to be responding to pleas for help from the Marxist government of Afghanistan. However, the President, Hafizullah Amin, was murdered and replaced by another Marxist, Babrak Karmal. There was widespread condemnation of the

Russian action and President Carter reacted angrily, announcing a grain embargo, breaking off SALT talks and calling for a *boycott of the Olympic Games* due to be held in Moscow during the summer of 1980. When *Andrei Sakharov*, the Russian Nobel Prize-winning physicist, dared to voice his criticisms of the invasion, he was *exiled to Gorky*, a city closed to foreigners. All the old western suspicions revived: though the Russians claimed that their real motive was to help a fellow communist government put down some troublesome Islamic fundamentalist guerrillas and thus secure their frontier, was their presence in fact part of the march of world communism, perhaps a move to control the *Persian Gulf*?

After this inauspicious beginning, both sides spent the first half of the 1980s building up their nuclear arsenals. The new American President *Ronald Reagan* (took office *January 1981*) was determined to take a tough line with the Soviets. Although several sets of discussions continued off and on, including Intermediate Nuclear Force (INF) Talks and Strategic Arms Reduction Talks (START), no real progress was made. Instead Cruise and Pershing missiles were *deployed in Britain and West Germany (December 1983)* and by 1984 each side could boast some 7000 nuclear warheads. When the American missiles arrived in Europe the Russians immediately walked out of all the talks, and Reagan made no attempt at a summit meeting either with Brezhnev or with his two elderly successors, Andropov and Chernenko.

However the situation was not one of total gloom. In reality *neither of the superpowers was as secure or as entrenched as it might have seemed.* By 1985 the USSR was seriously embarrassed by its involvement in Afghanistan. Although there were over 100,000 Soviet troops in the country, they found it impossible to subdue the ferocious Islamic guerrillas; it was a drain on their resources and a blow to their prestige. Another worry was the *continuing split in the communist world between the Russian and Chinese blocs* (see below). At the same time, the Americans felt threatened by the *left-wing Sandinista government of Nicaragua* with its Cuban advisers. Perhaps more worrying for the Americans was the strength of the *European peace movements*, which campaigned vigorously against the deployment of American missiles in their homelands, arguing that they raised the possibility of a limited nuclear war confined to Europe, which need not necessarily involve the Americans. Perhaps it was these insecurities (and in the case of the Americans, the imminent presidential elections) which encouraged both sides to start talking again: in September 1984 Reagan met the Soviet Foreign Minister Gromyko in Washington, his first meeting with a senior Russian politician since taking office.

(b) The Gorbachev initiatives. The new Soviet leader, *Mikhail Gorbachev* (took over after Chernenko's death, *March 1985*), was eager to make a significant breakthrough in foreign affairs, particularly in the area of East–West relations. He immediately announced a six-month freeze on the deployment of Soviet missiles in Europe; if NATO responded with a similar freeze on their deployment of Cruise and Pershing missiles in Europe, the Soviet freeze could be extended. He also declared his readiness to meet Reagan as early as possible. The Americans announced that they would continue to keep to the terms of the SALT 2 Treaty, even though it had not been ratified. In August, on the 40th anniversary of the dropping of the atomic bomb on Hiroshima, the Russians declared a *unilateral moratorium on nuclear testing*. During a visit to France (October), Gorbachev made tempting proposals: in return for suitable concessions, the Russians were prepared to consider a 50 per cent reduction in strategic nuclear weapons, direct talks with France and Britain about their nuclear weapons, and a continuing freeze on the deployment of Soviet intermediate range nuclear weapons in Europe.

US–Soviet relations improved when Gorbachev had a three day *summit meeting with Reagan in Geneva (November)* where they discussed cultural and scientific exchanges as well as arms control. Although nothing specific was agreed, the atmosphere was cordial, and in the euphoria which followed both leaders delivered televised New Year messages to each other's peoples. Gorbachev proposed a 15 year timetable for a 'step-by-step process for ridding the earth of nuclear weapons'. He also extended the moratorium on Soviet nuclear tests for a further three months, and soon afterwards (16 January 1986) the US–Soviet arms negotiations re-opened in Geneva.

Not content merely with cordial discussions, Gorbachev again met Reagan at a hastily arranged *summit at Reykjavik in Iceland (October 1986)*. The Russians offered to halve their land-based Inter-Continental Ballistic Missiles (ICBM), their submarine-based strategic missiles and their air-based missiles; in addition they would reduce their SS20 missiles in Asia to 100 warheads and freeze short-range nuclear missiles in Europe. Impressed by this, the Americans were apparently prepared to eliminate all Cruise, Pershing and SS20 missiles in Europe. The *talks broke down* when it emerged that the Russian offer was *conditional on the Americans abandoning their Strategic Defence Initiative (SDI)*, sometimes called 'Star Wars'. This system is designed to use weapons based in space to destroy ballistic missiles in flight, and though it was only in the research stage, Reagan was not prepared to give it up. The Russians argued that it would violate the Anti-Ballistic Missile (ABM) Treaty signed in 1972, which banned 'development, testing or deployment' of such weapons in space. After the failure of the summit, Reagan faced strong criticism (both at home and in Western Europe) that he had sacrificed the chance of an historic agreement for a system that might not even be feasible. However, there still seemed a good chance of some further agreement, since the Russians insisted that their offer was still on the table and the Geneva talks continued.

The climax came towards the end of 1987 when *the Geneva talks finally produced agreement*. Formally signed by Gorbachev and Reagan in Washington (8 December 1987), this *INF Treaty* was perhaps a turning point in the nuclear arms race. All land-based intermediate range (between 300 and 3000 miles) nuclear weapons were to be scrapped over the next three years. This meant 436 American and 1575 Soviet warheads, and would include all Russian missiles in East Germany and Czechoslovakia and all American Cruise and Pershing missiles based in Western Europe. The treaty also contained *strict verification provisions* so that both sides could check that the weapons were actually being destroyed. However, all this amounted at most to only 4 per cent of existing stocks of nuclear weapons, and there was still the stumbling block of Reagan's 'Star Wars'. But at least it was a beginning, perhaps soon to lead on to a START (Strategic Arms Reductions Treaty).

Meanwhile Gorbachev switched his attention to Afghanistan. The bitterness of the Islamic and nationalist opposition, the hostility of China, the suspicion of Islamic states all over the world, and the repeated condemnations by the UN, all convinced him it was time to pull out. In January 1987, hoping to secure a compromise solution, the Russians announced a *ceasefire for six months*: government and Soviet troops would fire only in self-defence. However the guerrillas were not prepared to accept this, and fighting continued. A year later, in January 1988, the Russians tried again, announcing that they would begin withdrawing their troops from Afghanistan on 1 May 1988 provided the Americans stopped sending military aid to the Afghan resistance movement.

(c) **China and the USA** maintained their *détente* during the 1980s. The Chinese were anxious to maintain good relations because of their continuing conflict with *Vietnam*, Russia's ally, which began in February 1979 (see below). Regular meetings of top politicians were held: Zhao Ziyang, the Chinese premier, paid an official visit to the USA (January 1984) and the following April Reagan had talks with Chinese leaders in Peking. Li Xiannion, the Chinese President, was in New York in July 1985 signing an agreement with Reagan on nuclear co-operation.

(d) **Relations between the USSR and China** took a disastrous plunge in February 1979 when the *Chinese attacked Vietnam*, Moscow's ally. This was partly in retaliation for *Vietnam's invasion of Kampuchea* (formerly Cambodia) (*December 1978*) which overthrew the Khmer Rouge government of Pol Pot, a protégé of China, and partly because of a frontier dispute. With both conflicts dragging on interminably, it was not easy to improve Sino-Soviet relations. Andropov tried to relieve the freeze by calling for an understanding with 'our great neighbour' (November 1982) but it was another two years before it thawed sufficiently for any agreement to be reached. In December 1984 no fewer than three agreements were signed: on economic, trade and scientific matters; but these were merely sideshows and the basic obstacles still remained. The Chinese defined these as: the presence of Soviet troops in Afghanistan, Soviet backing of the Vietnamese troops in Kampuchea and the Soviet troop build-up on the Mongolian and Manchurian frontiers.

Gorbachev was determined to begin a new era in Sino-Soviet relations.
Five-year agreements on trade and economic co-operation were signed
(July 1985). Trade soon began to flourish and regular contacts took place
between the two governments. However, Gorbachev wanted the restoration of full links between the two Communist parties. To encourage this
he announced, in a speech at Vladivostock (July 1986), a reduction in the
numbers of troops in Mongolia and Afghanistan and a proposal to
redraw the frontier in order to transfer to China some islands now
occupied by Russian troops; he had nothing to suggest about the
China–Vietnam–Kampuchea situation. In 1987, heavy fighting was still
going on around the China–Vietnam border and between Khmer Rouge
supporters (in uneasy alliance with two non-communist guerrilla groups)
and Vietnamese troops in Kampuchea. So long as this continued it was
difficult to imagine any major breakthrough in relations. Meanwhile a
further complication arose: in December 1986 the Russians *promised to
supply Kim Il Sung of North Korea with jets, missiles and tanks*, not a
prospect likely to please the Chinese. In January 1988 when Gorbachev,
in the euphoria following the signing of the INF Treaty, proposed a
Sino-Soviet summit, the Chinese rejected the offer, demanding that the
USSR must first use its influence to get Vietnam to withdraw its troops
from Kampuchea.

QUESTIONS

1. The Communist victory in China
Study the Sources below, and then answer the questions that follow.

Source A
Extracts from the works of Edgar Snow, an American who lived in China
for seven years.

> I had to admit that most of the peasants to whom I talked seemed to
> support the communists and the Red Army. Many of them were very
> free with their criticisms and complaints, but when asked whether they
> preferred it to the old days, the answer was nearly always an emphatic
> yes. I noticed also that most of them talked about the Soviets as 'our
> government'. To understand peasant support for the Communist
> movement it is necessary to keep in mind the burden borne by the
> peasantry under the former regime [the Kuomintang]. Now, wherever
> the Reds went there was no doubt that they radically changed the
> situation for the tenant farmer, the poor farmer, and all the 'have-not'
> elements. All forms of taxation were abolished in the new districts for
> the first year, to give the farmers a breathing space. Second, the Reds
> gave land to the land-hungry peasants, and began a reclamation of
> great areas of 'wasteland' – mostly the land of absentee or fleeing
> landlords. Thirdly, they took land and livestock from the wealthy
> classes and redistributed them among the poor . . . However, both the

landlord and the rich peasant were allowed as much land as they could till with their own labour.

Source: Edgar Snow, *Red Star over China* (Penguin, 1938, adapted extracts).

Source B
The eight rules of the Red Army (1928), quoted by Edgar Snow.

1. Return and roll up the straw matting on which you sleep.
2. Be courteous and polite to the people and help them when you can.
3. Return all borrowed articles.
4. Replace all damaged articles.
5. Be honest in all transactions with the peasants.
6. Pay for all articles purchased.
7. Don't take liberties with women.
8. Be sanitary, and, especially, establish latrines a safe distance from people's houses.

Edgar Snow adds:

These eight points were enforced with better and better success, and today [1937] are still the code of the Red Soldier, memorised and frequently repeated by him.

Source: E. Snow, *Red Star over China* (Penguin, 1938).

Source C
Statement by a Red General, P'eng Teh-huai, in 1936.

I remember the winter of 1928 when my forces in Hunan were encircled. The KMT troops burned down all the houses in the surrounding area, seized all the food there, and then blockaded us. We had no cloth, we used bark to make short tunics, we had no quarters, no lights, no salt. We were sick and half-starved. The peasants were no better off and we would not touch what little they had. But the peasants encouraged us. They dug up from the ground the grain which they had hidden from the KMT troops and gave it to us, and they ate potatoes and wild roots. Even before we arrived they had fought the landlords and tax collectors, so they welcomed us. Many joined us, and nearly all helped us in some way. They wanted us to win. Tactics are important, but we could not exist if the majority of the people did not support us. We are nothing but the fist of the people beating their oppressors.

Source: E. Snow, *Red Star over China* (Penguin, 1938).

Source D
Report by an American official to the US State Department, November 1944.

Relying on his dispirited troops, on his decadent and corrupt bureaucracy, and whatever nervous foreign support he can muster, Chiang Kai-shek may plunge China into civil war. He cannot succeed. The Communists are already too strong for him. Chiang's feudal China cannot long exist alongside a dynamic popular government in North China. The Communists are in China to stay. And China's destiny is not Chiang's but theirs.

Source: Howard Zinn, *A People's History of the United States* (Longman, 1980, adapted).

Source E
Extracts from a speech by John F. Kennedy to Congress on the Communist capture of Peking, January 1949.

Over this weekend we have learned the extent of the disaster that has befallen China and the United States. The responsibility for the failure of our foreign policy in the Far East rests squarely with the White House . . . So concerned were our diplomats and their advisers with the imperfection of the democratic system in China after 20 years of war and the tales of corruption in high places, that they lost sight of our tremendous stake in a non-Communist China. This House must now take up the responsibility of preventing the onrushing tide of Communism from engulfing all of Asia.

Source: Howard Zinn, *A People's History of the United States* (Longman, 1980).

(a) **(i)** According to Edgar Snow in Source A, how strong was the support of the Chinese peasants for the Communists? **4(a)**

(ii) What reasons did Snow give to explain why the peasants supported the Communists? **4(a)**

(b) **(i)** What evidence do Sources B and C contain to suggest why the Communists were supported by the peasants? **4(a)**

(ii) According to the speaker in Source C, how did the peasants show their friendliness towards the Communists? **4(a)**

(c) **(i)** What evidence can you find in Sources C, D and E to explain why the KMT were unpopular with the peasants? **4(a,c)**

(ii) How do the two American Sources (D and E) differ from each other in their opinions about the Chinese Communists? **4(a,c)**

(iii) How do you explain this difference? **1,2,4**

(d) **(i)** What signs of bias, if any, can you find in each of the five Sources? **4(b)**

(ii) Using the evidence from the Sources, and your own knowledge, explain why the Communists won the Civil War. **1,2,4(a,c)**

2. The Vietnam War 1961–75

Study the Sources below, and then answer the questions that follow.

Source A

From a secret memorandum of the US National Security Council, June 1952.

> Communist control of all Southeast Asia would render the US position in the Pacific offshore island chain precarious and would seriously endanger fundamental US security interests in the Far East.

(Extract.)

Source B

From a speech given to a group of Detroit businessmen by U. Alexis Johnson, Undersecretary of State to President Kennedy, 1963.

> Why is Southeast Asia desirable and why is it important? First it provides a lush climate, fertile soil, rich natural resources, a relatively sparse population in most areas, and room to expand. It also produces rich exportable surpluses such as rice, rubber, teak, corn, tin, spices, oil and many others.

(Extract.)

Source C

Statement by President Kennedy at a news conference, February 1962.

> As you know, the US, for more than a decade, has been assisting the government and the people of Vietnam, to maintain their independence.

Source D

Extracts from the *New York Times*.

5 June 1965

> As the Communists withdrew from Quangngai last Monday, US jet bombers pounded the hills into which they were headed. Many Vietnamese – one estimate is as high as 500 – were killed by the strikes. The Americans say they were Vietcong soldiers. But three out of four patients seeking treatment in hospital afterwards for burns from napalm or jellied gasoline, were village women.

6th September 1965

> Few Americans realise what their nation is doing to South Vietnam with air power . . . innocent civilians are dying every day in South Vietnam.

Source E

On March 16th, 1968, a company of American soldiers went into the hamlet of My Lai; they rounded up the inhabitants, including old people with infants in their arms. These people were ordered into a ditch, where they were methodically shot to death by American soldiers . . . army investigators later found mass graves at three sites, as well as a ditch full of bodies. It was estimated that between 450 and 500 people – most of them women and children and old men – had been slain and buried there . . . In the summer of 1965, a few hundred people had gathered in Washington to march in protest against the war; the first in the line were splattered with red paint by hecklers. In 1971, twenty thousand came to Washington to express their revulsion against the killing still going on in Vietnam, by trying to tie up Washington traffic.

Source: Howard Zinn, *A People's History of the United States* (Longman, 1980, adapted extracts).

Source F
Extract from Richard Nixon's *Memoirs* (published 1978).

Although publicly I continued to ignore the raging anti-war controversy . . . I knew that after all the protests, American public opinion would be seriously divided by any military escalation of the war.

Source: Howard Zinn, *A People's History of the United States* (Longman, 1980).

(a) (i) Explain briefly why Vietnam was divided into two separate states by the 1956 Geneva Agreement. **1,2**
     (ii) Why did civil war break out between the two Vietnams? **1,2**
(b) (i) From the evidence of Sources A, B and C, what were the reasons for US involvement in the Vietnam War? **4(a)**
     (ii) How do the reasons for US involvement given in Sources A and B differ from those given in Source C? **4(a,c)**

     (iii) Can you suggest any reasons why the statements in Sources A and B were made secretly and privately, while the one in C was made in public? Explain your answers. **4(b)**
     (iv) Which of the three Sources (A, B, C) do you think is likely to be the most accurate statement of US motives? Explain your answer fully. **4(a,b,c)**
(c) (i) In Source D what is meant by 'Vietcong'? **1,4(a)**
     (ii) Using the evidence of Sources D and E, describe the methods used by the Americans in Vietnam. **4(a)**
     (iii) How does the evidence of Sources D and E seem to contradict President Kennedy's statement in Source C? **4(a,c)**

(d) **(i)** Why do you think the protesters in Source E were 'splattered with red paint by hecklers'? **1,2,4(a)**

   (ii) According to Source E, how did Americans show their opposition to the war in Vietnam? **4(a)**

   (iii) How do Sources D and E explain why American public opinion about the war changed between 1965 and 1970? **4(a,b)**

(e) **(i)** From the evidence of Source F, what effects did the protests have on President Nixon? **4(a)**

   (ii) In what ways did Nixon change US policies in Vietnam? **1,2**

(f) **(i)** From the evidence of the extracts, and your own knowledge, explain why American troops were withdrawn from Vietnam in 1973. **1,2,4**

   (ii) What happened in Vietnam betweeen the withdrawal of American troops and April 1975? **1**

   (iii) Why did the Americans fail in Vietnam? **1,2**

   (iv) What effects did the American failure have in the USA and in Southeast Asia? **1,2**

3. The Cuban missile crisis

Study the Sources below, and then answer the questions that follow.

Source A

From a work by Nikita Khrushchev.

> Then I had the idea of installing missiles in Cuba without letting the United States find out they were there until it was too late to do anything about them. The installation of our missiles would, I thought, restrain the US from hasty military action against Castro's government . . . The Americans had surrounded our country with military bases . . . and now they would learn what it feels like to have enemy missiles pointing at you.

Source: N. Khrushchev, *Khrushchev Remembers*.

Source B

From President Kennedy's broadcast of 22 October 1962.

> This urgent transformation of Cuba into an important strategic base – by the presence of these large, long-range, and clearly offensive weapons of sudden mass destruction – constitutes an explicit threat to the peace and security of all the Americas . . .
>
> Acting, therefore, in the defence of our own security and of the entire Western Hemisphere . . . I have directed that the following initial steps be taken immediately.

Source C

From Robert Kennedy's own story of the crisis.

There could be no deal made under this kind of pressure . . .
However, I said, President Kennedy had been anxious to remove these
missiles from Turkey and Italy for a long period of time.

Source D
Kennedy's quarantine action against Cuba (Fig. 17.4).

Fig. 17.4

(a) (i) Study Source A. What does Khrushchev give as his reason for
the installation of missile sites in Cuba? **4(a)**

   (ii) How justified do you think Khrushchev's claims were? **1,2**

(b) (i) Study Source B. What does President Kennedy consider to be
the aims of Khrushchev and the USSR? **4(a)**

   (ii) Describe features from Source D which would support President Kennedy's view. **4(a,c)**

(c) (i) What does Source D show to have been President Kennedy's
initial steps to counteract this threat? **4(a)**

    (ii) What alternative courses of action were open to President Kennedy and why did he *not* choose them?   **1,2**

(d)   **(i)** From Sources A and C what was the *deal* which had been put forward to solve this crisis?   **4(a,c)**

    (ii) Describe the events which led to the settlement of the crisis.   **1,2**

    (iii) What results did the crisis have for east–west relations and for relations between Cuba and other countries?   **1,2**

    [By permission of the London and East Anglian Group.]

4. **(a)** Explain what the term '*détente*' means.

  (b) Why did the USA and the USSR pursue this policy in the 1970s?

  (c) In what ways did relations between the USA and the USSR improve during the 1970s?

  (d) Describe relations between these powers in the late 1970s and 1980s. Would you agree that by 1987, the policy of *détente* had failed?   **1,2**

5. You are an unemployed Cuban worker; explain:

  (a) why you disliked the Batista government;

  (b) why you found Castro and his supporters attractive;

  (c) what your feelings were in April 1961 after the Bay of Pigs affair.   **1,2,3**

CHAPTER 18

INTERNAL AFFAIRS OF THE COMMUNIST STATES OF EASTERN EUROPE

SUMMARY OF EVENTS

The theories of Marx and Lenin are so vague that many different interpretations of them are possible; consequently there is a great deal of variation in what actually happens in communist countries and a communist system of government *need not be identical to the Russian system*. Of course Stalin tried to keep it that way, but after his death in 1953 the states of eastern Europe began to show more independence. *Yugoslavia under Tito* had already developed a more decentralised system in which the communes were an important element. Poland and Rumania successfully introduced variations, but the *Hungarians (1956)* and *Czechs (1968)* went too far and found themselves invaded by Russian troops and brought to heel. In *1980–1* events in *Poland* again provoked Russian intervention, though on this occasion a threat to cut off oil supplies was enough to force the Polish government to clamp down on an *independent trade union movement*. During the 1970s the states of Eastern Europe enjoyed a period of comparative prosperity, but in the 1980s most of them felt the effects of world depression.

18.1 THE USSR

(a) **Joseph Stalin** continued to rule Russia after 1945 for a further eight years until his death in *March 1953*. The western half of European Russian was devastated by the war: roads, railways and industries were shattered and 25 million people were homeless. Stalin was determined that there would be no relaxation of government controls: the economy must be reconstructed. The *Fourth Five Year Plan* was started in 1946 and, incredibly in the circumstances, succeeded in restoring industrial production to its 1940 levels. And then, just as he was about to launch another set of purges, Stalin died, to the immense relief of his close associates.

(b) The rise of Khrushchev 1953–7

With the departure of Stalin, the situation was similar to that after Lenin's death in 1924: there was *no obvious candidate to take over the reins*; Stalin had allowed no one to show any initiative in case he developed into a dangerous rival. The leading members of the *Politburo* or Praesidium (as it was now called) decided to *share power and rule as a group*: Malenkov became Chairman of the Council of Ministers, Khrushchev Party Secretary, and Voroshilov Chairman of the *Praesidium*; also involved were Beria (Chief of the Secret Police), Bulganin and Molotov. Gradually, however, *Nikita Khrushchev* began to emerge as the dominant personality. The son of a peasant farmer, he had worked as a farm labourer and then as a mechanic in a coalmine before going to technical college and joining the communist party. Beria, who had an atrocious record of cruelty as police chief, was executed, probably because the others were nervous in case he turned against them. Malenkov resigned in 1955 after disagreeing with Khrushchev about industrial policies, but it was significant that in the new relaxed climate he was not executed or imprisoned. Khrushchev's position was further strengthened by an amazing speech which he delivered at the *Twentieth Communist Party Congress (1956)* strongly criticising various aspects of Stalin's policies. He *condemned Stalin* for encouraging the cult of his own personality instead of allowing the party to rule, revealed details about Stalin's purges of the 1930s, criticised his conduct of the war, claimed that socialism could be developed in ways other than those insisted on by Stalin, and suggested that *peaceful co-existence with the west was not only possible but essential if nuclear war were to be avoided*. Khrushchev was not quite supreme yet: Molotov and Malenkov believed his speech was too drastic and would encourage unrest (they blamed him for the Hungarian revolution of October 1956); they tried to force him out of office. However as Party Secretary, Khrushchev, like Stalin before him, had been quietly filling key positions with his own supporters, and since he could rely on the army, it was Molotov and Malenkov who found themselves compulsorily retired (June 1957). After that Khrushchev was fully responsible for all Russian policy until 1964; but he never wielded as much power as Stalin; the Central Committee of the party was ultimately in charge and it was the *party which voted him out in 1964*.

(c) Khrushchev's problems and policies

In spite of Russia's recovery during Stalin's last years there were a number of serious problems including the *low standard of living* among industrial and agricultural workers, and the *inefficiency of her agriculture* which was still a long way from providing all Russia's needs. Khrushchev was fully aware of the problems both at home and abroad and was determined to introduce important changes as part of a general *de-Stalinisation policy*:

   (i) *Industry* was still organised on the Five Year Plans but for the first time these concentrated more on light industries producing *con-*

sumer goods (radios, television sets, washing machines, sewing machines) in an attempt to raise living standards. To reduce over-centralisation and encourage efficiency a hundred *Regional Economic Councils* were set up to make decisions about and organise their local industries. Managers were encouraged to make profits instead of merely meeting quotas, and wages depended on output. All this certainly led to an improvement in living standards: a vast housing programme was started in 1958; between 1955 and 1966 the number of radios per thousand of the population increased from 66 to 171, television sets from 4 to 82, refrigerators from 4 to 40, and washing machines from 1 to 77. However, this was way behind the USA which in 1966 could boast per thousand of the population no fewer than 1300 radios, 376 television sets, 293 refrigerators and 259 washing machines. Of course much depends on how one measures progress, but it was Khrushchev himself who had rashly claimed that the gap between Russia and America would be closed within a few years. Another more spectacular piece of technological progress was the *first manned orbit of the earth* by *Uri Gagarin (1961)*.

(ii) In *agriculture* there was a drive to increase food production. Khrushchev's special brainchild was the *virgin lands scheme* (started *1954*) which involved cultivating for the first time huge areas of land in Siberia and Kazakhstan. Peasants on collective farms were allowed to keep or sell crops produced on their private plots and the government increased its payments for crops from the collectives, thus providing *incentives to produce more*. By 1958 total farm output had risen by 56 per cent; between 1953 and 1962 grain production rose from 82 million tons to 147 million. But then things began to go wrong; the 1963 grain output was down to 110 million tons, mainly because of the failure of the virgin lands scheme. The trouble was that much of the land was of poor quality, not enough fertilisers were used, and the exhausted soil began to blow away in dust storms. In general there is still *too much interference in agriculture from local party officials*, and it remains the least efficient sector of the economy; the Russians have to rely on grain imports, often from the USA.

(iii) *Political changes* (the thaw) included the return to party control instead of Stalin's personality cult, a reduction in secret police activities (deposed politicians and officials retired into obscurity instead of being tortured and executed), more freedom for ordinary Russians, more tourism, and a slight relaxation of press controls.

(iv) In *foreign affairs*, following his Twentieth Congress speech, Khrushchev aimed for *peaceful co-existence* and a thaw in the Cold War (see Section 16.3) and seemed prepared to allow different 'roads to socialism' among the satellites. However, these departures from strict Marxist/Leninist ideas (including his encouragement of profit and wage incentives) laid him open to

Chinese accusations of *'revisionism'* (see Section 17.6(d)); moreover, encouraged by his speech, Poland and Hungary tried to break Moscow's grip; Khrushchev's reaction to these attempts showed how *limited his toleration was*.

(d) Khrushchev's fall. In *October 1964* the Central Committee of the party voted Khrushchev into retirement on the grounds of ill health; although he was 70 his health was perfectly good. The real reasons were probably the *failure of his agricultural policy* (though he had been no less successful than previous governments in this), his *loss of prestige over the Cuban missile crisis* and the widening breach with *China* which he made no attempt to heal. Perhaps his colleagues were tired of his extrovert personality (once in a heated moment at the United Nations he took off his shoe and hammered the table with it) and felt he was taking too much on himself (without consulting them he had just tried to win the friendship of President Nasser of Egypt by awarding him the Order of Lenin at a time when he was busy arresting Egyptian communists). Khrushchev was a man of outstanding personality: a tough politician and yet impulsive and full of warmth and humour. He deserves to be remembered for his foreign policy innovations, for the return to comparatively civilised politics (at least inside Russia) and for the improved living standards of the masses.

(e) The Brezhnev era. After Khrushchev's departure, three men, Kosygin, Brezhnev and Podgorny seemed to be sharing power. At first Kosygin seemed to be the dominant figure and was the chief spokesman on foreign affairs, while Breshnev and Podgorny looked after home affairs. In the early 1970s *Kosygin was eclipsed by Brezhnev* after a disagreement over economic policies: Kosygin pressed for more economic decentralisation, but this was unpopular with the other leaders who claimed that it encouraged too much *independence of thought in the satellite states*, particularly Czechoslovakia. Brezhnev established firm personal control by 1977 and he remained leader until his death in *November 1982*. Broadly speaking, their policies were similar to those of the Khrushchev period:

(i) *Economic policies* maintained *wage differentials* and *profit incentives*, some growth took place but the rate was slow. The system remained strongly *centralised*, and Brezhnev was reluctant to take any major initiatives. By 1982, therefore, much of Russian industry was old-fashioned and in need of new production and processing technology. There was concern about the failure of the coal and oil industries to increase output and the building industry was notorious for slowness and poor quality. Low agricultural yield was still a major problem – not once in the period 1980–1984 did grain production come anywhere near the targets set. The 1981 harvest was disastrous and 1982 was only slightly better, throwing Russia into an *uncomfortable dependence on American wheat.* It was calculated that in the USA in 1980 one agricultural worker produced enough to feed 75 people, while his counterpart in Russia could manage only enough to feed 10.

(ii)   The *Eastern Bloc states* were expected to obey Moscow's wishes and to maintain their existing structure. When *liberal trends developed in Czechoslovakia* (especially abolition of press censorship) a massive *invasion* took place by *Russian and other Warsaw pact troops.* The reforming government of *Dubcek* was replaced by a strongly centralised, pro-Moscow regime (*1968*) (see Section 18.2(f)). Soon afterwards Brezhnev declared the so-called *Brezhnev Doctrine*: according to this, intervention in the internal affairs of any communist country was justified if *socialism in that country was considered to be threatened.* This caused some friction with *Rumania*, which had always tried to maintain some independence, refusing to send troops into Czechoslovakia and keeping on good terms with China. The Russian invasion of *Afghanistan (1979)* was the most blatant application of the doctrine, while more subtle pressures were brought to bear on *Poland (1981)* to control the independent trade union movement, *Solidarity* (see Section 18.2(b)).

(iii) On *human rights*, Brezhnev's record was not distinguished; though he claimed to be in favour of the Helsinki Agreement, and appeared to make important concessions about human rights in the USSR, in fact little progress was made. Groups were set up to check whether the terms of the agreement were being kept, but the authorities put them under intense pressure. Their members were arrested, imprisoned, exiled or deported and finally the groups were dissolved altogether (September 1982).

(iv)   In *foreign policy* the Russians worked towards *détente*, but after 1979 relations with the west deteriorated sharply as a result of the *Afghanistan invasion* (see Section 17.7(a)). Brezhnev continued to advocate *disarmament* but presided over a rapid increase in Soviet armed forces, particularly the navy and the new SS20 missiles. He stepped up Soviet aid to Cuba and offered aid to Angola, Mozambique and Ethiopia.

(f) Andropov and Chernenko. After Brezhnev's death Russia was ruled for a short period by two elderly and ailing politicians – Andropov (November 1982–February 1984) and then Chernenko (February 1984–March 1985). Head of the KGB until May 1982, Andropov immediately launched a vigorous campaign to *modernise and streamline the Soviet system.* He began an anti-corruption drive and introduced a programme of continuous economic reform, hoping to increase productivity by encouraging decentralisation. Some of the older party officials were replaced with younger, more go-ahead men. Unfortunately he was dogged by ill-health and died after little over a year in office. The 72-year-old Chernenko was a more conventional type of Soviet politician. There was no relaxation in the treatment of human rights activists:

members of an unofficial trade union, supporters of a group 'for the establishment of Trust between the USSR and the USA' and members of unofficial religious groups were all arrested. Nor was *Dr Sakharov* allowed out of exile in spite of appeals by Western leaders.

(g) Mikhail Gorbachev (came to power *March 1985*) was, at 54, the most gifted and dynamic leader Russia had seen for many years. He was determined to *transform and revitalise the country* after the sterile years following Khrushchev's fall, and talked about *glasnost* ('openness') and *perestroika* (economic and social reform).

(i) In *foreign affairs*, he took initiatives on *détente*, arms control, relations with China and Russian involvement in Afghanistan (see Section 17.7(b) and (d)).

(ii) In *economic affairs*, he introduced *new and profoundly important laws*. In November 1986 he announced that '1987 will be the year for broad applications of the new methods of economic management'. *Small-scale private enterprise* such as family restaurants, family businesses making clothes or handicrafts or providing services such as car and television repairs, painting and decorating and private tuition, *was to be allowed*, and so were *workers' co-operatives* up to a maximum of 50 workers. One motive behind this reform was to provide *competition* for the slow and inefficient services provided by the state in the hope of stimulating a rapid improvement. Another was the need to provide *alternative employment* as patterns of employment changed over the following decade: as more automation and computerisation are introduced into factories and offices, the need for manual and clerical workers will decline. Another important change was that the responsibility for *quality control* throughout industry as a whole was to be taken over by independent state bodies rather than factory management. If these measures are successful there is no doubt that by the year 2000 the USSR will have experienced a profound social and economic transformation.

(iii) *Human rights* was another area in which Gorbachev was prepared to change course. *Several well-known dissidents were released* and the Sakharovs allowed to return to Moscow from internal exile in Gorky (*December 1986*). *Pravda* was even allowed to print an article *criticising Brezhnev* for over-reacting to dissidents. A new law was introduced preventing dissidents from being sent to mental institutions (January 1988).

(iv) In *cultural matters*, there were some startling developments. In May 1986 both the Union of Soviet film-makers and the Union of writers were allowed to sack their reactionary heads and elect more independent minded leaders. Long-banned *anti-Stalinist films* and novels were shown and published and preparations made to publish works by the great poet Osip Mandelstam who died in a labour camp in 1938. Along with this came a new 'openness' (*glasnost*) in the media; in April 1986, for example, when a nuclear reactor at *Chernobyl* in the Ukraine exploded, releasing a massive radioactive cloud which soon drifted across most of Europe, the disaster was discussed with unprecedented frankness. One advantage of this new approach was that the government could use the media to *publicise the inefficiency and corruption* which it was so anxious to stamp out. *Glasnost* was encouraged, provided nobody criticised the party itself.

(v) *Political changes* were introduced in January 1987. After delivering a devastating attack on the *stagnation and corruption of the Brezhnev years*, Gorbachev announced moves towards *democracy*: in the elections for local government there was to be a choice of *candidates* (though not of *parties*) and there were to be secret elections for top party positions. According to one western journalist, 'these changes were greeted with a combination of delight, fascination and disbelief'.

18.2 THE USSR AND THE STATES OF EASTERN EUROPE

When fully communist governments had been established in Russia's satellite states (Poland, Hungary, Czechoslovakia, Rumania, Bulgaria, Albania and East Germany) Stalin set about making them into *carbon copies of Russia* through the *Cominform* and *Comecon* (see Section 16.1(f)). All had the same political and educational systems, and the same Five Year Plans (involving nationalisation of industries and ruthless collectivisation of agriculture); all had to carry out the bulk of their trade with Russia, and their foreign policies and armed forces were controlled by Moscow. Politicians who protested were shot or imprisoned. Once Stalin was dead there was likely to be a reaction against such close control; Khrushchev's Twentieth Congress speech also encouraged the *desire for more independence*.

(a) **Yugoslavia** was the only east European state that refused to be brow-beaten by the Russians. Occupied by the Germans during the war, the Yugoslavs organised a successful *resistance campaign* which liberated the country in 1945. One of the resistance leaders, *Marshal Tito*, who had been head of the Yugoslav Communist Party since 1937, was elected leader of the new republic (1945) and was President from 1953 until his death in 1980. The establishment of communism owed nothing to the Russians; like Mao in China, Tito owed much of his popularity to his successful resistance against a hated enemy. By 1948 he had fallen out with Stalin: he was determined to follow his *own road to communism*, not Stalin's; he was against overcentralisation, and objected to Stalin's plan for the Yugoslav economy and to the constant Russian interference; he wanted to be free to *trade with the west* as well as with Russia. Consequently Stalin expelled Yugoslavia from the Cominform and cut off economic aid, expecting that the country would soon be ruined economically and Tito forced to resign. However, Stalin miscalculated: Tito was much too popular to be toppled by such outside pressures; he continued to apply communism in his own way, which included full contact and trade with the west and the acceptance of aid from the *International Monetary Fund (IMF)*. Relations with Russia remained non-existent until 1955 when Khrushchev visited Belgrade and apologised for Stalin's attitude. The breach was fully healed the following year during Khrushchev's second visit (June 1956) when he gave approval to Tito's successful brand of socialism (with important effects for the Russian satellites).

(i) What was *special about Yugoslav communism*? The Yugoslavs soon realised that the Russian system of control from the centre was too *rigid, too distant and inefficient*; it took away the rights and initiatives of ordinary local people; the officials at the centre became corrupt and workers became bored and apathetic. In 1950, the Yugoslavs began to reverse the process of centralisation: *industries were denationalised* and instead of being state-owned became public property, managed by workers' representatives through councils and assemblies. The same applied in agriculture. The *communes* were and still are the most important unit in the state: these are groups of families (501 of them in 1973) each containing between 5000 and 100,000 people; the elected Commune Assembly takes decisions about and organises matters to do with the economy, education, health, culture and welfare. The whole system is a remarkable example of ordinary people playing a part in making the decisions which closely affect their own lives, both at work and in the community; it has achieved much because workers have a *personal stake* in the success of their firm and their commune. There were some weaknesses, however, such as workers' unwillingness to sack colleagues and a tendency to pay themselves too much (leading to over-employment and high costs and prices). Nevertheless with its capitalist elements (wage differentials and a free market) it was an alternative Marxist system which many developing African states, especially *Tanzania*, found attractive.

(ii) *After Tito's death (May 1980)* the immediate problem was whether the different ethnic groups in Yugoslavia would survive as a *united state*. It consisted of six republics (Macedonia, Bosnia–Herzegovina, Slovenia, Serbia, Croatia and Montenegro) and two provinces (Vojvodina and Kosovo). In *Croatia* there was a strong *separatist movement* which Tito had successfully blocked. It was widely expected that once he was gone, Yugoslavia would pass through a difficult period, with disputes about his successor and perhaps civil war. In the event, this did not happen. Tito had laid plans to avoid such problems, and with some modifications, these were carried smoothly into operation. The country was to be ruled by a *collective presidency* consisting of one representative from each of the six republics and one each from the two provinces; a different president of this council would be elected each year. There were some tensions in Kosovo where many people wanted *union with Albania*, but this was not serious enough to threaten the unity of the state.

The real problem of the 1980s turned out to be something quite different – *the economy*. The weaknesses mentioned earlier seemed to be getting out of hand. *Inflation* (already running at 30 per cent when Tito died) had soared to 90 per cent in 1986. 1984 was a particularly bad year: there were *shortages of food and consumer goods*, partly because of a drought in 1983 which caused a poor harvest and a sharp drop in amounts of hydro-electric power available. By December 1986 unemployment had risen to over a million – 13 per cent of the working population. Inevitably this poor performance provoked criticism which the government answered harshly: according to Amnesty International, since May 1980 over 500 people a year had received prison sentences of up to 15 years for 'hostile propaganda'. The government was hoping to solve its energy problem by building four *nuclear reactors*. However, following the Chernobyl explosion, there was a massive public campaign against the dangers of nuclear energy. The plan was abandoned and it was decided to build another large hydro-electric plant instead. Yugoslavia and its collective leadership were facing a stiff test as the economic crisis deepened.

(b) Poland was the first of the satellite states to come out in open protest against the Russians (except for *East Berlin*, where in *May 1953* 100,000 workers demonstrating for better pay were dispersed by Russian tanks). The Polish communist leader, *Wladyslaw Gomulka*, had been expelled from the party and imprisoned because Stalin disapproved of his support of *Tito* (1948).

(i)   But as soon as Stalin was dead discontent began to build up among the Poles, who had a long tradition of *anti-Russian hostility*. Spurred on by Khrushchev's Twentieth Congress speech, it burst out at *Posen* (Poznan) in *June 1956* in a massive anti-government and anti-Russian demonstration; their banners demanded 'bread and freedom' and they protested against poor living standards, wage restrictions and high taxes; they were *dispersed by Russian tanks*. However, the Russians were prepared to compromise: Khrushchev went to Warsaw for discussions and it was decided that Gomulka should be reappointed as First Secretary of the party and that Polish communism could develop in its own special way provided that the Poles went along with Russia in foreign affairs. The Russians obviously felt that Gomulka *could be trusted not to stray too far*. Relations between the two states were fairly smooth, though Poland was quite 'revisionist' in her application of communism (only about 10 per cent of farmland was collectivised and she traded extensively outside the communist bloc). The Polish government was more susceptible to public opinion than the Russian government: in 1970 Gomulka resigned in favour of Gierek after riots in Gdynia; in 1980 food shortages and industrial unrest again led to strikes in Gdansk (Danzig) and other cities and caused Gierek's resignation; the government was forced to allow the formation of an *independent trade union movement (Solidarity)*. This acted with admirable restraint, insisting on the sacking of corrupt party officials responsible for the country's economic plight (almost bankrupt and heavily in debt to the west) but not demanding an end to press censorship or the introduction of free elections. Nevertheless the situation was extremely delicate; one step too far could mean Russian military intervention.

(ii)   In *September 1980*, the Russians held *large-scale military manoeuvres* along the Polish frontier, but no invasion took place. Perhaps Moscow was unwilling to risk another intervention so soon after Afghanistan, and decided to try political pressure first. This was successful and the government of Stanislaw Kania (who took over from Gierek) was replaced by *General Jaruzelski* who was prepared to take a firmer line with Solidarity and its leader *Lech Walesa*. However, there was no improvement in the economic situation and the continuing crisis came to a head in December 1981 when Solidarity demanded a referendum to demonstrate the strength of its support, which was considerable (it had about 13 million members compared with only about 3 million communist party members). Jaruzelski *declared martial law, banned Solidarity and arrested hundreds of activists*. By July 1983, the government was in firm control and he felt it safe to lift martial law.

(iii) Jaruzelski made a determined effort to do something about one of the *underlying causes* of the unrest – the *economic situation* – and here too he had some success. Official sources claimed that most of the targets for 1983–85 had been attained: industrial output increased by 16 per cent, exports to other communist countries were up by 23 per cent and inflation was down from 23 per cent to under 15 per cent. 1986 promised to be an even better year, but the economy suffered a blow from the Chernobyl nuclear accident (April). Outside the USSR, Poland was probably the country most affected, suffering high radioactivity levels. From May until August her foreign customers refused to buy Polish food exports in case of contamination, and it was estimated that she lost some £35 million in hard currency. On a brighter note, Poland was admitted to *membership of the International Monetary Fund (IMF) and the World Bank (June 1986)*. This was seen as an important step in the return to normal economic relations with western nations following the martial law period. The Five Year Plan for 1986–90 showed signs of the *new thinking* sweeping through much of the eastern bloc: *encouragement for the private sector*, especially in agriculture, *new incentive schemes for industrial workers* and a rapid development of *precision and electronic engineering*. The fact that it was given the seal of approval by Gorbachev during a visit to Warsaw showed that the plan was clearly in line with current Soviet thinking.

(iv) *Jaruzelski received a setback* in November 1987 when a referendum was held (itself a novelty in a Communist state) to seek approval for his policies. Only two thirds of the electorate bothered to vote and 56 per cent of those *voted against the economic reforms*, because of fears that they would cause food prices to double. A later opinion poll (January 1988) suggested that two out of every three Poles thought that there would be 'open social conflict' if the general persisted with his policies.

(c) Hungary, which had fought on Germany's side during the war, was viewed as a defeated enemy by the Russians and treated harshly, being made to pay *reparations*. Although the communists gained less than 20 per cent of the votes in the free elections held in November 1945, the Russians saw to it that communists filled all important posts, and under their leader *Rakosi*, they were soon running the country. When protests developed against the Moscow hard line, Laszlo Rajk, the leading anti-Stalin communist was hanged (1949) and over 200,000 expelled from the party. Rakosi toed the Stalin line, but after Stalin's death he was replaced by *Imre Nagy*, a more moderate communist.

(i) However, Rakosi continued to interfere and overthrew Nagy (1955); from then on resentment steadily built up until it exploded in the *Hungarian Rising (October 1956)*. Its *causes* were many: hatred of Rakosi's brutal and repressive regime which executed at least 2000 people and put 200,000 others in prisons and concentration camps; falling living standards for the masses while hated party leaders were comfortably off; intense anti-Russian feeling; Khrushchev's Twentieth Congress speech and the return to power of Gomulka in Poland stimulated the demonstrators to greater efforts. At first the Russians seemed prepared to compromise and Nagy, ecstatically received, was allowed to become Prime Minister. The demonstrations soon swelled into a national rising against the hated Russians; *Cardinal Mindszenty*, who had been in prison for six years for anti-communist views, was released and plans were afoot to allow other political parties and to withdraw from the Warsaw Pact. At this point the Russian army moved in and blasted Budapest into submission; 20,000 people were killed, a similar number imprisoned and Nagy executed after being promised a safe-conduct; about 20,000 people fled the country. *Janos Kadar*, a reliable communist, was made Prime Minister by the Russians.

(ii) The *rising was important* because it showed how *limited Khrushchev's new tolerance was*: Gomulka could be stomached in Poland because Poland would remain a close Russian ally; but Nagy had gone too far and was threatening Russian control of eastern Europe; if he had his way, Hungary might become non-communist and neutral instead of a Russian ally. The rest of eastern Europe was very quiet after 1956. Although both Rumania and Albania showed some independence there was no fundamental attempt to change relationships with Russia until 1968 in Czechoslovakia. The Russians also took heed of the lesson and allowed the Kadar government to provide more *consumer goods*. In 1962 when Khrushchev suggested that each satellite state should concentrate on a particular commodity, the Hungarians along with the Rumanians and Poles who wanted to develop an all-round economy objected strongly, and the idea was not pressed. After 1966 the government gradually began to *decentralise control of industry*, but not quite so drastically as did the ill-fated Czechs.

(iii) There were incentives, profits and bonuses and workers were given a genuine say in how their factories were run. During the first half of the 1970s wages and the standard of living steadily improved and Hungary began to *import extensively*. Unfortunately this produced a *huge balance of payments deficit*, forcing Kadar to introduce new policies of recentralisation and austerity (*1975*). These had some success, enabling him to relax controls and allow some private enterprise in agriculture. Early in 1982 it was announced that more encouragement would be given to the private sector and by the end of 1984 there were about 25,000 privately owned companies.

(iv) The mid-1980s saw the economy again running into difficulties as Hungary felt the effects of *world recession*. Kadar himself admitted (March 1985) that living standards had fallen over the previous five years, and he blamed poor management, poor organisation and outdated machinery and equipment in the state sector of industry. He announced new measures of *decentralisation* to improve performance. There was to be more encouragement of private sector industry, which with its greater efficiency and better quality products, would stimulate the state sector to greater efforts. *Company councils* were to be set up, representing workers and management to decide on strategy, investment, wages and prices, and to elect the works managers. Unprofitable state enterprises would be reorganised or closed down to eliminate under-employment. Kadar was confident, or so he said, that by 1990 the economy would be healthy and competitive again, though the future looked bleak for many industrial workers facing redundancy as a result of reorganisation. By 1987 there was some conflict in government circles between those who wanted to continue with more reform and those who wanted to return to strict central control. The climax came in May 1988 when, amid dramatic scenes at the party conference, Kadar and eight of his supporters were voted off the Politburo, leaving the progressives in control. Karoly Grosz became the new party leader. Kadar's reign was over and Hungary was in line with Gorbachev's USSR.

(d) In Albania the *communist resistance movement seized power and set up a republic in 1945*, so that as in Yugoslavia the Russians were not responsible for the introduction of communism. Nevertheless they insisted on the Albanian government following their line and executed the communist leader Koze Xoxe when he seemed reluctant to do so.

(i) His successor *Enver Hoxha* was an admirer of Stalin and copied his system faithfully. With Russian aid and their own oil supplies, the Albanians began to *industrialise*, with particular success in *textiles*. After Stalin's death Hoxha did not approve of Khrushchev's revisionist policies, feeling more in sympathy with what was happening in China. Diplomatic relations with Moscow were severed in 1961 and Albania left the Warsaw pact in 1968 after the invasion of Czechoslovakia, which Hoxha denounced as 'fascist aggression'. However, since there was *no question of her ceasing to be communist* (and strict Marxist/Leninist communist at that) and since she had a *powerful ally in China*, The Russians took no action.

(ii) In *1977*, Albania broke with its only ally, China, disapproving of the new Chinese government's *criticisms of Mao*, whom Hoxha admired. Consequently Albania had no major patron anywhere and remained deeply suspicious of foreigners. Hoxha continued to rule as a Stalinist dictator until his death in *1985* at the age of 76.

(iii) Albania under its new leader, *Ramiz Alia*, had much to commend it: self-sufficiency in key food areas, electricity in every household, no taxes, no inflation and no privately owned cars (which made for an unusual peace and quiet). However, many of the basic freedoms such as travel abroad and religion, were denied, and it was still arguably the *poorest country in Europe*: wages for a six day, 48-hour week were miserably low, prices were high and choices for the consumer limited. The debate was slowly but surely getting under way about introducing reforms and incentives and decentralising management in order to boost production.

(e) Rumania provides the best example (apart from Yugoslavia) of a satellite state pushing revisionist policies to the absolute limit that the Russians would accept without military intervention.

(i) Like Hungary she had been *occupied by the Russians in 1945*, forced to pay *reparations* and had a *communist government thrust upon her*. Patrascanu, a communist leader unco-operative to the Russians, was expelled (1949) and later shot, and another, Anna Pauker, removed in 1952. However, in the early 1960s Rumania, a *comparatively prosperous country* with her oil wells, wheatlands and great potential for tourism, took the lead under President Ceauşescu in *opposing the Russian desire to organise the economy of the entire communist bloc*. She insisted on adopting plans for decentralised industrial development whereas the Russians wanted to use Rumania as a source of raw materials and food; she was keen to expand her trade with countries outside the soviet bloc, which the Russians did not encourage; to show their attitude the Rumanians dropped Russian as a compulsory school subject (1962). Although she made it plain that she would remain in the Warsaw Pact she began to cultivate friendship with Yugoslavia, with western states and even with China. The Russians angrily condemned these trends (1963), but since the Rumanians pointed out that they were merely trying to develop their economy in the best national interest and were not threatening the unity of the communist bloc, no military action took place. Unfortunately this was not the case with Czechoslovakia which in 1968 pushed matters too far and found itself occupied by Warsaw pact troops. Ceauşescu condemned the invasion, and although he quietened down after some threatening words from Moscow, he continued to maintain some independence. He visited Peking (1971), entertained President Nixon in Bucharest (1972) and he refused to take any part in Warsaw Pact manoeuvres or to have Soviet troops on his soil. Moscow's attitude only increased Rumanian nationalism and strengthened Ceauşescu's position.

(ii) Economically Rumania's performance throughout the 1970s was reasonably encouraging; by 1975 she was conducting about *half her foreign trade with countries outside Comecon*, in order to increase her trade with the Third World. During the 1980s she suffered the same problems as the rest of Eastern Europe: the more she imported from the West, the more this *fuelled inflation and led to a balance of payments deficit*. By the end of 1982 Rumania owed about £10,000 million to Western banks. Production levels in both agriculture and industry fell well short of the targets set in the Five Year Plan for 1981–85. This was partly because of a decline in the production of crude oil and the refusal of Western banks to lend any more cash, following the crisis in Poland (see above). Even the elements seemed to conspire against the Rumanians: there was a drought in 1983 which caused a reduction in hydro-electric power; the winter of 1984–85 was the coldest for 44 years. Ceauşescu countered with a drastic reduction in imports from the West, power cuts and the sacking of the Power and Mining Ministers; *a state of emergency was declared in the country's energy sector (October 1985)*. By *early 1987* there were signs of *recovery*: the foreign debt was down to less than £4000 million and a Canadian-designed nuclear power station was nearing completion. But much remained to be done – a Western journalist visiting Bucharest in December 1986 sent back a gloomy report: 'endless tins of sardines are the only concession to meat in the capital. There is no milk and butter on sale and many other basic goods are spoken of as in fairy tales. The economy is likely to be the first target for reform when the present era ends.'

(f) Czechoslovakia was the *last of the satellites to go communist, in 1948* (see Section 16.2(g)). This was followed by the usual executions of 'unreliable' communist leaders (Clementis and Slansky) following which she was a fully obedient satellite under Novotny until 1968.

(i) It was in the mid-1960s that *opposition to the government* began to come out into the open. The Czechs, *industrially and culturally the most advanced of the satellites*, objected to the over-centralised Russian control of their economy; it seemed senseless, for example, that they should have to put up with poor quality Siberian iron-ore when they could have been more conveniently using high-grade Swedish ore. Having enjoyed great freedom between 1918 and 1938, they resented the restrictions on *personal liberty*, particularly the press censorship and the loss of freedom of speech; protest marches were brutally suppressed by the police. Matters came to a head in January 1968 when Novotny was forced to resign and *Alexander Dubcek* became First Secretary of the Party with Svoboda as President and Cernik as Prime Minister.

(ii) Then followed what later became known nostalgically as the *Prague Spring*. They had a *completely new programme*: the communist party would no longer dictate policy; industry would be decentralised with factories run by works councils and with independent farming co-operatives encouraged; there were to be wider powers for trade unions, expansion of trade with the west and freedom to travel abroad (the frontier with *West Germany* was immediately thrown open); there was to be freedom of speech and press, and criticism of the government was encouraged. Dubcek believed that although the country would remain communist, the government should earn the right to be in power by responding to the people's wishes; it was what he called 'socialism with a human face'. He was most careful to assure the Russians that Czechoslovakia would stay in the Warsaw Pact and remain a reliable ally. As the spring and summer progressed, the Russians became increasingly disturbed as this programme was carried into operation. In *August a massive invasion of Czechoslovakia* took place by Russian, Polish, Bulgarian, Hungarian, and East German troops. The Czech government decided not to resist and although the Czech people resisted passively for a time, the government was compelled eventually to abandon its reforms; the following year Dubcek was replaced by the more amenable *Husak*.

(iii) Why did the Russians *intervene in Czechoslovakia but not in Rumania*? In fact as we have seen, many similar developments were taking place in Rumania. Where the Czechs went too far for the Russians was in allowing freedom of speech and press, which

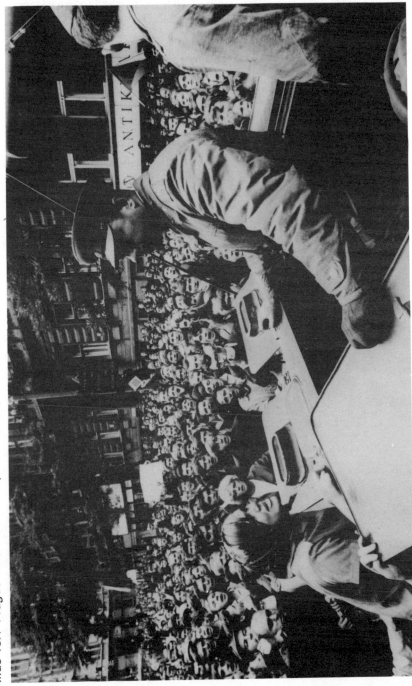

illus 18.1 Prague 1968. Czechs implore and argue with a Russian tank commander

345

was bound to lead to *similar demands throughout the soviet bloc*; this the Russians dare not risk since it might cause the downfall of Kosygin and Brezhnev as well as Novotny. There was pressure for Russian action from other communist leaders, especially Ulbricht of East Germany. The Russians were also suspicious of increasing Czech contact with *West Germany*; Rumania, on the other hand, was geographically relatively safe, having *no common frontier with a Western power*. The invasion was not universally welcomed within the Communist bloc: China, Albania and Yugoslavia all condemned it, while Rumania denounced it as a 'flagrant violation of the national sovereignty of a socialist country'.

(iv)   The Czech *economy* seemed little affected by the events of 1968, and it continued to be *one of the most successful of the satellite states*. She traded extensively with the West and her industry and commerce remained buoyant throughout the 1970s. During the early 1980s, however, the economy was in trouble, mainly because there had been very little attempt to *modernise industry*. While her Comecon neighbours and even the USSR itself were busy decentralising, the over-centralisation of the Husak regime stifled initiative. In August 1985, the Czech human rights group, *Charter 77*, claimed that the government was caught in 'a death-like torpor – 17 years of constant inertia is already too long in a rapidly changing world. That other policies are possible is shown by the reformist efforts in neighbouring countries with similar political systems.' Soon afterwards the Finance Minister, Leopold Ler, who wanted to introduce policies similar to those of Gorbachev in the USSR, resigned after a dispute with the 74-year-old Husak who was unwilling to change anything. The leader approved by Brezhnev had now incurred the displeasure of Gorbachev: during 1986 the Czech Communist Party Congress received a visit from only a junior member of the Russian *Politburo*, whereas Gorbachev himself attended the Polish and East German Congresses; it was reported that Russian speeches calling for reform were being censored in Czechoslovakia – an ironic reversal of the Prague Spring. A Charter 77 spokesman summed up the situation well (in December 1986) when he wrote: 'while Husak lives, political stagnation will reign supreme. Once he has gone, the party will explode.' A year later *Husak resigned*, probably under pressure from Moscow, but there was no immediate 'explosion'. His successor, *Milos Jakes*, did not have a reputation as a reformer and it seemed certain that whatever changes were introduced in Czechoslovakia would be at best cautious.

QUESTIONS

1. The USSR after 1945
Study the Sources below, and then answer the questions that follow.

Source A
A Russian poster of 1952 (illus. 18.2), showing children thanking Stalin for a happy childhood. Stalin was then 72 years old.

Source: *Musée de l'Armée Royale*, Brussels.

Source B

After the end of the war the atmosphere of terror was intensified; Stalin and his associates were determined to suppress any possible criticism or opposition . . . There was plenty of ground for criticism; although the production of heavy industrial products recovered reasonably quickly from the damage caused by the war, consumer good were extremely scarce and housing conditions were very bad. On the land the reimposition of collective farm discipline failed to raise production or to improve the standard of living . . . Stalin himself, always suspicious and tyrannical, had become even more so . . . by the beginning of 1953 it looked as though a renewed purge like that of the 1930s might be under way. A doctors' plot was unearthed, and nine eminent physicians were accused of poisoning Zhdanov and of planning to murder a number of military leaders.

Source: James Joll, *Europe Since 1870* (Penguin, 1973, extracts).

Source C
Table showing distribution of consumer goods in the USSR and the USA.

	Number of each item per thousand of the population		
	USSR, 1955	USSR, 1966	USA, 1966
Radios	66	171	1300
Cars	2	5	398
TV sets	4	82	376
Refrigerators	4	40	293
Washing machines	1	77	259
Sewing machines	31	151	136

Source: J. N. Westwood, *Khrushchev and After*, in Purnell's *History of the Twentieth Century*, vol. 6, ch. 3 (BPC Publishing and Phoebus Publishing, 1968–9).

illus 18.2

Source D
Russian Communist Party Central Committee 50th Anniversary Survey, 1967.

> Socialism does away with exploitation and oppression and creates instead friendships, co-operation and mutual aid . . . socialism has relieved the worker of all anxiety about the next day; there is now no fear of unemployment and no fear of miserable poverty.

Source: D. Harkness, *The Post-War World* (Macmillan, 1974, extract).

Source E

> The Russians are proud of their record in industry, education and welfare, the more so since their successes have been won at the price of immense sacrifice and hardship . . . And yet in spite of all the effort of the Soviet people, serious mistakes were made by their leaders, and their system had produced much inefficiency and waste . . . Individual initiative is stifled and worker productivity is low . . . The most notable area of failure has been agriculture. Productivity in the collective farms has been low, due to a failure in the mechanism for pricing and planning and to an inbuilt discouragement of individual initiative.

Source: D. Harkness, *The Post-War World* (Macmillan, 1974, adapted extracts).

(a) **(i)** What details in Source A tell you that it is a propaganda poster designed to flatter Stalin? **4(a,b)**

  (ii) What is a 'collective farm', mentioned in Source B? **1**

(b) **(i)** What evidence is there in Source B which seems to contradict the impression of Stalin given in Source A? **4(a,c)**

  (ii) How does Source C suggest that Stalin could have done more for his people? **4(a)**

(c) In what ways did Nikita Khrushchev try to improve the Soviet economy after Stalin's death? **1,2**

(d) **(i)** What evidence do Sources C, D and E provide to suggest that Khrushchev's policies had some success? **4(a,c)**

  (ii) According to Source C, which was the only article that the Russians had more of than the Americans? Explain why you think this was so. **4(a)**

(e) **(i)** What evidence is there in Sources C and E which might be said to contradict the claim in Source D that now there was 'no fear of miserable poverty'? **4(a,c)**

  (ii) How reliable do you think Source D is for the historian? Explain your answer. **4(a,b)**

(f) Explain why Khrushchev fell from power in 1964. **1,2**

2. Czechoslovakia 1968

Study the Sources below, and then answer the questions that follow.

Source A

A statement by the Soviet government, 1959.

> Relations between the socialist countries are based on the principle of complete equality, respect for territorial integrity, state independence, and non-interference in each others affairs. All matters can be and are settled through comradely discussion and frank talks.

Source: R. Brooks, *The Modern World since 1870* (Bell and Hyman, 1985, adapted extracts).

Source B

The 'Warsaw Letter', sent by East European countries to the Czech government, July 1968.

> The development of events in your country arouses deep anxiety in us . . . we cannot agree to have hostile forces push your country off the road to socialism and endanger the interests of the entire socialist system. Anti-socialist forces have laid hands on the press, radio and television. A situation has thus arisen which is entirely unacceptable for a socialist country. We believe that a decisive rebuff to the forces of anti-communism in Czechoslovakia is not only your task but ours too.

Source: Sir W. Hayter, *Russia and the World* (Secker and Warburg, 1978, adapted extracts).

(a) Describe in your own words the relationship between the USSR and other socialist countries, according to Source A. **4(a)**

(b) (i) According to Source B, why were the USSR and other East European countries anxious about events in Czechoslovakia? **4(a)**

    (ii) What threat is contained in the last few words of Source B? **4(a)**

    (iii) What contradictions can you find between Source A and B? **4(a,c)**

(c) (i) Why was Novotny forced to resign in January 1968? **1,2**

    (ii) What were the details of Alexander Dubcek's new programme? **1**

    (iii) Why did the USSR believe that the proposed changes would be 'entirely unacceptable for a socialist country', as Source B puts it? **1,2,4(a)**

(d) (i) What were the results of the invasion by Russian and East European troops for Dubcek and for Czechoslovakia? **1,2**

    (ii) How did the Russian intervention in Czechoslovakia differ from their intervention in Hungary in 1956? **1,2**

3. As a supporter of the independent Polish trade union, Solidarity:

    (a) Explain why you were so discontented that you joined Solidarity;

(b) Describe your part in the events of 1980–81 when Solidarity seemed to be successful.

(c) Describe what happened to you during the period of martial law, and how you felt in 1983 when it was lifted.   **1,2,3**

4. (a) Describe briefly relations between the USSR and: (i) Albania, (ii) Hungary, (iii) Rumania, since 1945.

(b) Explain why the USSR intervened militarily in Hungary in 1956, but not in Rumania.   **1,2**

CHAPTER 19

CHINA UNDER THE
COMMUNISTS

SUMMARY OF EVENTS

After the *Communist victory over the Kuomintang in 1949*, Mao Tse-Tung set about rebuilding a shattered China. At first there was Russian advice and aid, but in the late 1950s relations cooled and Russian economic aid was reduced. In 1958 Mao introduced the *Great Leap Forward*, in which communism was adapted – not altogether success-fully – to meet the Chinese situation, with the emphasis on decentralisa-tion, agriculture, communes and contact with the masses. Mao became highly critical of the Russians who, in his view, were straying from strict Marxist–Leninist principles and following the 'capitalist road' in both foreign and domestic affairs. During the 1960s these disagreements caused a serious rift in world communism which had still not healed in the 1980s. With the *Cultural Revolution (1966–9)* Mao tried successfully to crush opposition within the party and to keep China developing along Marxist–Leninist lines.

After Mao's death in *1976*, there was a power struggle within the Communist Party from which by 1981 *Deng Xiaoping* had emerged as undisputed leader. Much less conservative than Mao, Deng was respon-sible for some important policy changes, moderating Mao's hard-line communism and looking towards Japan and the capitalist West for ideas and help. This aroused resentment among the Maoist supporters who accused Deng of straying along the 'capitalist road'. The climax came in 1987 when Deng was forced to *slow down the pace of his reforms*.

19.1 WHAT WERE THE PROBLEMS FACING MAO TSE-TUNG, AND HOW SUCCESSFUL WAS HE IN DEALING WITH THEM?

(a) **The problems facing the People's Republic in 1949** were complex to say the least. The country was *devastated* after the long *civil war* and the war with Japan: railways, roads, canals and dykes had been destroyed and there were chronic food shortages. Industry was backward, agriculture was inefficient and incapable of feeding the poverty-stricken masses, and inflation seemed out of control. Mao had the support of the peasants and many of the middle class, disgusted by the miserable performance of the KMT, but it was essential for him to improve conditions if he were to hold on to their support. To control and organise such a vast country with a population of at least 600 million must have been a superhuman task; yet Mao managed it, and China today, whatever its faults, is his creation. He began by looking closely at Stalin's methods and experimented by a process of trial and error to find which would work in China and where a *special Chinese approach* was necessary.

(b) The constitution of 1950 (officially adopted 1954) included the National People's Congress (the final authority for legislation), whose members were elected for four years by people over 18, the State Council and the Chairman of the Republic (both elected by the Congress), whose function was to make sure that laws were carried out and the administration of the country went ahead; the whole system was, of course, dominated by the communist party. The constitution was important because it provided China with a *strong central government* for the first time for many years, and it has remained more or less unchanged.

(c) Agricultural changes transformed China from a country of small, inefficient private farms into one of *large co-operative farms* like those in Russia (1950–6). In the first stage land was taken from large landowners and redistributed among the peasants, no doubt with violence in places; some sources mention as many as two million people killed, though Jack Gray believes that 'the redistribution of China's land was carried out with a remarkable degree of attention to legality and the minimum of physical violence against landlords'. The next step was achieved without violence: peasants were persuaded (not forced as they were in Russia) to join together in *co-operative (collective) farms* in order to increase food production. By 1956 about 95 per cent of all peasants were in such co-operatives (consisting of between 100 and 300 families) with joint ownership of the farm and its equipment.

(d) Industrial changes began with the government nationalising most businesses; in 1953 it embarked on a Five Year Plan concentrating on the development of *heavy industry* (iron, steel, chemicals and coal). The Russians helped with cash, equipment and advisers, and the plan had some success. Before it was complete, however, Mao began to have grave doubts as to whether China was suited to this sort of heavy industrialisation. On the other hand he could claim that under his leadership the country had recovered from the ravages of the wars: full communications had been restored, inflation was under control and the economy was looking much healthier.

(e) The Hundred Flowers Campaign (1957) seems to have developed to some extent out of industrialisation which produced a vast new class of *technicians and engineers*. The party *cadres* (groups who organised the masses politically and economically; the collectivisation of the farms for example was carried out by cadres) believed that this new class of experts would threaten their authority. The government, feeling pleased with its progress so far, decided that open discussion of the problems might improve relations between cadres and experts or intellectuals; 'let a hundred flowers bloom and a hundred schools of thought contend', said Mao, calling for constructive criticism. Unfortunately he got more than he had anticipated: critics attacked the cadres for incompetence and over-enthusiasm, the government for over-centralisation and the party itself; some suggested that opposition parties should be allowed. Mao hurriedly called off the campaign and clamped down on his critics, insisting that his policies were right. The campaign showed how much opposition there still was to communism and to the uneducated cadres, and convinced Mao that a drive was necessary to *consolidate the advance of socialism*: hence in 1958 he called for the 'Great Leap Forward'.

(f) The **Great Leap Forward** was a policy designed to meet the *Chinese situation* and not based on Russian experience; it involved further important developments in both agriculture and industry, in order to increase output (agriculture particularly was still not providing the required food) and to adapt industry to Chinese conditions. Its most important features were:

(i) The introduction of *communes*, units larger than collective farms, containing up to 75,000 people, divided into brigades and work teams with an elected council. They ran their own collective farms

illus 19.1 *China – building a canal by mass labour*

and factories, carried out most of the functions of local government within the commune and undertook special local projects. One typical commune, for example, in 1965 contained 30,000 people of which a third were children at school or in crèches, a third were housewives or elderly and the rest the workforce (which included a science team of 32 graduates and 43 technicians). Each family received a shareout of profits and also had a small private plot of land.

(ii) A complete change of emphasis in industry: instead of aiming for large-scale works of the type seen in Russia and the west, much *smaller factories* were set up in the countryside to provide machinery for agriculture; Mao talked of 600,000 'backyard steel furnaces' springing up, organised and managed by the communes, which also undertook to build roads, dams, reservoirs and irrigation channels.

At first it looked as though the Great Leap might be a failure: there was some opposition to the communes, a series of *bad harvests (1959–61)* and the withdrawal of all Russian aid following the breach between the two; all this coupled with the lack of experience amoung the cadres caused hardship in the years 1959 to 1963. Even Mao's prestige suffered and he was forced to resign as Chairman of the People's Congress (to be succeeded by Liu Shao-chi) though he remained Chairman of the communist party. However, in the long term the importance of the Great Leap became clear: eventually both *agricultural and industrial production increased substantially*, and China was managing at least to feed its massive population without famine (which rarely happened under the KMT); the commune proved to be a remarkably successful innovation – much more than merely collective farms, they are perhaps the ideal solution to the problem of running a vast country while at the same time avoiding the over-centralisation that stifles initiative; the crucial decision had been taken that China would remain predominantly an *agricultural country* with small-scale industry scattered about the countryside; the economy would be *labour-intensive* (relying on massive numbers of workers instead of introducing labour-saving machines). Given the country's enormous population, this seems sensible, and so far China has avoided the growing unemployment problems of the highly industrialised western nations. Other benefits were the spread of education and welfare services and the improvement of the position of women in society.

(g) The Cultural Revolution (1966–9) was Mao's attempt to keep the revolution and the Great Leap on a pure Marxist–Leninist course. In the early 1960s, when the success of the Great Leap was by no means certain, opposition to Mao grew. Right-wing members of the party believed that more *incentives* (piecework, greater wage differentials and larger private plots, which had been creeping in in some areas) were necessary if the communes were to function efficiently; also there should be an expert managerial class to push forward with industrialisation on the Russian model, instead of relying on the cadres. But to the Maoists this was totally unacceptable; it was exactly what Mao was condemning among the Russians who he dismissed as 'revisionists' taking the capitalist road. The party must avoid the emergence of a privileged class and *keep in touch with the masses*. Between 1963 and 1966 there was a great public debate about which course to follow, between the rightists (who included Liu Shao-chi and Deng Xiaoping) and the Maoists. Mao, using his position as chairman of the party to rouse the young people, launched a desperate campaign to 'save' the revolution. In this Great Proletarian Cultural Revolution, as he called it, Mao appealed to the masses. His supporters, the *Red Guards* (mostly students), toured the country arguing Mao's case, while schools and, later on, factories were closed down. It was an incredible propaganda exercise in which Mao was trying to renew revolutionary fervour and even to create a *new kind of socialist person* whose aim was to serve others. At times fighting broke out between the two factions and the country seemed likely to descend into chaos. In the end the Maoists were successful thanks to the army under the command of Lin Piao; order was restored and the 'revisionists' disgraced (1969). Afterwards the Maoist approach was followed until 1976 when both Mao and his reliable ally Chou En-lai died.

The Cultural Revolution had been a success in the sense that it allowed Mao to have his own way, but the disruption it caused, together with the policies of Mao's final years, had the effect of *delaying China's modernisation*.

19.2 LIFE AFTER MAO

(a) **A power struggle followed the death of Mao.** There were three main contestants: *Hua Guofeng*, named by Mao himself as his successor, *Deng Xiaoping*, who had been sacked from his position as general secretary of the party during the Cultural Revolution for allegedly being too liberal, and a group known as the *Gang of Four*, led by Jiang Jing, Mao's widow, who were extremely militant Mao supporters, more Maoist than Mao himself. At first Hua seemed to be the dominant figure, having the Gang of Four arrested and keeping Deng in the background but Deng soon reasserted himself and for a time seemed to be sharing the leadership with Hua. From the middle of 1978 Deng gradually gained the ascendancy and Hua was forced to resign as party chairman leaving *Deng as undisputed leader (June 1981)*. As a gesture of open criticism of Mao and his policies, the Gang of Four were put on trial for 'evil, monstrous and unpardonable crimes' committed during the Cultural Revolution.

(b) There was a **period of dramatic policy changes** (beginning June 1978) as Deng Xiaoping gained the ascendancy:

(i) Many changes introduced during the Cultural Revolution were *reversed*: the revolutionary committees set up to run local government were abolished and replaced by more democratically elected groups. Property confiscated from former capitalists was returned to survivors and there was more religious freedom and greater freedom for the *intelligentsia* to express themselves in literature and the arts.

(ii) In economic matters Deng and his protégé, Hu Yaobang, wanted *technical and financial help from the west* in order to modernise industry, agriculture, science and technology. Loans were accepted from foreign governments and banks, and contracts signed with foreign companies for the supply of modern equipment. In *1980*, China joined the *IMF* and the *World Bank*. On the home front, state farms were given more control over planning, financing and profits; bonuses, piece-rates and profit-sharing schemes were encouraged and the state paid higher prices to the communes for their produce and reduced taxes in order to stimulate efficiency and output. These measures had some success – grain output reached a record level in 1979.

As so often happens this reform programme led to demands for more radical reform.

(c) Demands for more radical reform: the Democracy Wall. In November 1978 there was a poster campaign in Peking and other cities, often in support of Deng Xiaoping. Soon there were massive demonstrations demanding more drastic changes, and early in 1978 the government felt obliged to ban marches and poster campaigns. However, there still remained the so-called 'Democracy Wall' in Peking, where the public could express itself. During 1979 the posters displayed there became *progressively more daring*, attacking Chairman Mao and demanding a wide range of human rights: the right to criticise the government openly, representation for non-Communist parties in the National People's Congress, freedom to change jobs and travel abroad, and abolition of the communes. This infuriated Deng who had approved Democracy Wall in the first place only because most of the posters criticised the Gang of Four. Now he launched a fierce attack on the leading dissidents, accusing them of *trying to destroy the socialist system*. Several were arrested and given prison sentences of up to 15 years; in November, the Democracy Wall was abolished altogether. Law and order and party discipline were restored. 'Without the party', Deng remarked, 'China will retrogress into divisions and confusions'.

(d) Modernisation and its problems. Following the first flush of reforming zeal and the embarrassment of the Democracy Wall, the pace slowed considerably. But Deng, together with his two protégés Hu Yaobang (Party General Secretary) and Zhao Ziyang (Prime Minister) was determined to press ahead with modernisation as soon as possible. Zhao Ziyang had won a reputation as a brilliant administrator in Sichuan province where he was responsible for an 80 per cent increase in industrial production in 1979; he also began experiments, later extended to the whole country, to *break up the communes* so as to give peasants control of individual plots. In December 1984, Zhao announced that compulsory state purchase of crops was to be abandoned; the state would continue to buy staple products, but in much smaller quantities than previously; prices of surplus grain, pork, cotton and vegetables would be allowed to *fluctuate on the open market*. By this time, however, modernisation was having some unfortunate side-effects. Although exports increased by 10 per cent during 1984, imports increased by 38 per cent leaving a record trade deficit of 1100 million dollars and causing a sharp fall in China's foreign exchange reserves. The government tried with some success to control imports by placing heavy duties on all imported goods except vital raw materials and microchip equipment (80 per cent on cars and 70 per cent on colour televisions and videos). Another unwelcome development was that the *annual rate of inflation began to rise*, reaching 22 per cent in 1986.

(e) The thoughts of Deng Xiaoping. Apparently not unduly worried by these trends, the 82-year-old Deng explained his ideas for the future in a magazine article of November 1986. His main aim was to enable his people to get *richer*. By the year 2000, if all went well, the average annual income per head should have risen from the equivalent of £280 to somewhere near £700, and China's production should have doubled. 'To get rich is not a crime', he added. He was happy with the way agricultural reform was going, but emphasised that in industry, sweeping *decentralisation* was still needed. The party must withdraw from administrative tasks, issue fewer instructions, and allow more initiative at the lower levels. Only capitalist investment could create the conditions in which China could become a prosperous, modernised state. His other main theme was China's *international* role: to lead a peace alliance of the rest of the world against the dangerous ambitions of the USA and the USSR. Nothing, he said, could possibly alter the course he had set for his country.

(f) The political crisis of 1987. No sooner had Deng laid down the course China was to follow up to the year 2000 and beyond, than the government was unexpectedly plunged into a serious political crisis which dealt a severe blow to Deng's ambitions. Beginning in December 1986, there was a series of *student demonstrations* supporting Deng Xiaoping and the 'Four Modernisations' (agriculture, industry, science and defence), but urging a much quicker pace and more democracy. It was a similar situation to the one in 1978–9, and again Deng dare not let it get out of hand for fear of antagonising the conservatives (Maoists). However, the students ignored a new ban on wall posters and a new rule requiring five days' notice for demonstrations, and forced the release of some students arrested in an earlier demonstration. This challenge to party control and discipline aroused the conservatives who were already critical of the economic problems caused by Deng's policies – high inflation, dwindling foreign exchanges and lagging exports. Chen Pixian, a vice-chairman of the National People's Congress, rallied the attack, accusing Deng of *sacrificing socialism in favour of capitalist policies.* 'Some of our comrades have paid little attention to adherence to the four party principles over the past two years', he complained and he went on to explain these basic principles as strict adherence to the socialist road, the people's democratic dictatorship, leadership by the Chinese Communist Party and Marxist-Leninist and Maoist thought.

After two weeks of internal party wrangling it was announced in *mid-January 1987* that *Hu Yaobang* (Party General Secretary) *had resigned* 'for making mistakes'. Instead of confining himself to policies of economic modernisation, he was said to have been too liberal in his political outlook, encouraging intellectuals to demand greater democracy and even some sort of opposition party. The fall of the 71-year-old Hu Yaobang, no doubt forced to resign by conservative pressure, was a serious blow to Deng, though not a complete disaster, since his place was taken by the other leading Deng protégé, the 69-year-old Zhao Ziyang, also an economic reformer, but one who had kept clear of controversial politicial ideas. Zhao soon announced that the government had no intention of abandoning its economic reform programme, and promised new measures to speed up financial reform, and at the same time, a clamp-down on 'bourgeois intellectuals' who threatened party control. This highlighted the dilemma facing Deng and Zhao: was it logical to offer people a choice in the area of buying and selling and yet deny them any choice in other areas such as policies and political parties? Many western observers thought it impossible not to have one without the other, and by the end of January 1987 there were signs that they were right. As expected, order was restored and many intellectuals were expelled from the party for offences such as 'failing to control bourgeois liberalisation in the media' and 'spreading ideas of total westernisation'. More ominously, the *economic reforms were slowing down as well*: Deng admitted that his decentralising reforms begun in 1978–9 had been marked by 'overdemanding and excessive speed'. From now on they would be 'realistic and practical' – a dramatic climbdown from his thoughts of only two months earlier. At the same time, the conservative Maoist victory was emphasised by one of Deng's critics in the National People's Congress. The only way to get the economy right, he argued, was to return to central planning; China should not indulge in consumerism or high consumption; it was vital 'to advocate hard struggle and thrift and to oppose extravagance'. For the time being, the outlook for reformers and intellectuals looked grim. However, Chinese affairs soon took another unexpected turn: at the 13th Party Congress (November 1987), Deng's supporters won control of the Politburo and most of the elderly conservatives were voted off. Deng was still very much in control and China looked set for a period of stability and further reform.

QUESTIONS

1. The Cultural Revolution

Study the Sources below, and then answer the questions that follow.

Source A

Report by an Austrian journalist.

> Years later, Mao was to say of that period between the Great Leap Forward (1957) and the Great Proletarian Cultural Revolution (1966) 'At that time most people disagreed with me. Sometimes I was alone. They said that my views were out of date.' Compared with the quivering tension you feel everywhere today, China in 1957 was almost boring. On 16 July 1966, when Mao emerged from the Yangtze River – or precisely, on 25 July, when the press announced that he had swum nine miles down river in sixty-five minutes thus proving to the world that his health was excellent – he took his place as the leader of his nation.

Source: K. Mehnert, *China Today*.

Source B

The view of the Central Committee of the CCP.

> Although the bourgeoisie has been overthrown, it is still trying to use the old ideas, culture, customs and habits of the exploiting classes to corrupt the masses, capture their minds and endeavour to stage a come-back. The Proletariat must be the exact opposite: it must meet head-on every challenge of the bourgeoisie in the ideological field and use new ideas, culture, customs and habits of the proletariat to change the mental outlook of the whole of society. Since the Cultural Revolution is a revolution, it inevitably meets with resistance. This resistance comes chiefly from those in authority who have wormed their way into the Party and are taking the Capitalist road. It also comes from the force of habits from the old society. What the Central Committee demands of the Party Committee at all levels is to boldly arouse the masses, encourage those comrades who have made mistakes but are willing to correct them to cast off their burdens and join in the struggle.
>
> A most important task is to transform the old education system.

Source: *Peking Review*, August 1966.

Source C

The Red Guards and their Little Red Books (illus. 19.2).

illus 19.2

Source: Camera Press.

Source D
Statement by a Chinese embassy official following the news of the death of Lin Piao.

Lin Piao repeatedly committed errors; and Mao Tse-tung had waged many struggles against him. Sometimes Lin Piao was obliged to quell his arrogance and then was able to accomplish some useful work. But he was not able to give up his underhand nature and during the Cultural Revolution he appeared to support the thought of Mao Tse-tung. He was thus able to hoodwink the masses to become in their eyes the successor to Mao Tse-tung. But he was a double-faced man who was in reality opposed to the revolutionary line of Mao Tse-tung. He undertook anti-party activities in a planned way with the aim of taking over power. Mao Tse-tung unmasked his plot and made efforts to recover him but Lin Piao attempted a coup d'etat and tried to assassinate Mao Tse-tung.

Source: *China Now*, March 1973.

Source E
Comments by a British reporter, based in Singapore.

The power game in China is being played out between not only the moderates and the Maoists, the army and the leftists, but also between Peking and the provinces.

And the military commander is very much the master of the provinces. In almost all the provincial revolutionary committees that now run China the soldiers take the decisions.

Broadly speaking, it can be said that seven military regions out of eleven are in the hands of men who disapproved of the Cultural Revolution and distrusted Mao's impatience for a classless Communist Utopia.

Source: Dennis Bloodworth, *Observer* Foreign News Service, November 1971.

(a) (i) According to Source A, what did Mao do to prove he was in good health? **4(a)**

    (ii) Explain briefly what was the 'Great Leap Forward', mentioned in Source A? **1**

(b) (i) Explain what is meant by the words 'bourgeoisie' and 'proletariat', in Source B. **1,4(a)**

    (ii) What evidence is given in Sources A and B to explain why the writer of Source B made the statement (at the end) that, 'A most important task is to transform the old education system'? **4(a,c)**

    (iii) What clues do Sources B and C give about what methods were used to change the education system? **4(a,c)**

(c) (i) Suggest a possible reason why such a large crowd was gathered in the photograph in illus. 19.2 (Source C). **1,2,4(a)**

    (ii) What information can the historian get from the photograph in illus. 19.2 about the Chinese people and the sort of society to which they belonged at that time? **4(a)**

    (iii) Can you think of any ways in which the photograph in illus. 19.2 might be used as political propaganda? **4(a,b)**

(d) (i) In what ways does the writer of Source D criticise Lin Piao? **4(a)**

    (ii) What part did Lin Piao play in the Cultural Revolution? **1,4(a)**

(e) (i) What clues does Source E provide about how successful the Cultural Revolution was? **4(a)**

    (ii) What doubts might a historian have about the reliability of Sources D and E? Explain your answers fully. **4(a,b)**

(f) Using all the Sources, and your own knowledge, write an account of the part played in the Cultural Revolution by Mao Tse-tung. **1,2,4(a,c)**

[Reproduced by permission of the Midland Examining Group.]

2. The Chinese economy

Study the Sources below, and then answer the questions that follow.

Source A

Chou En-lai's 'Great Leap Forward' speech, January 1959.

Our Socialist countries are marching along the road of Socialist construction. In the past year [1958] a big leap forward in industry and agriculture and a surging movement to set up people's communes took place in China. China's steel output reached over 11 million tonnes, double that of 1957; its grain output reached 375 million tonnes, more than double that of 1957. Actively supported and guided by the Chinese Communist Party and Comrade Mao Tse-tung, the Chinese have created large-scale people's communes which combine industry, agriculture, trade, education and military affairs.

Source: R. Brooks, *The Modern World Since 1870* (Bell & Hyman, 1985, adapted extracts).

Source B
China's population and production.

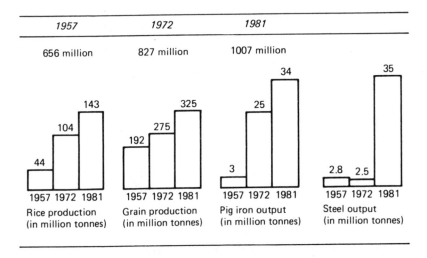

1957	1972	1981
656 million	827 million	1007 million

Rice production (in million tonnes)	Grain production (in million tonnes)	Pig iron output (in million tonnes)	Steel output (in million tonnes)
1957: 44, 1972: 104, 1981: 143	1957: 192, 1972: 275, 1981: 325	1957: 3, 1972: 25, 1981: 34	1957: 2.8, 1972: 2.5, 1981: 35

Source: R. Brooks, *The Modern World Since 1870* (Bell & Hyman, 1985).

Source C
Daily Telegraph article, 10 August, 1978.

The Chinese Communist Party now supports the principle of 'material incentives' – bonus payments – for overtime or extra work on the grounds that they increase productivity and raise the quality of work. Since the Cultural Revolution of the late Sixties, material incentives have been the dirtiest of words. But a dramatic change of attitude has taken place since the disgrace of the radical 'Gang of Four', led by Chiang Ching, the widow of Mao Tse-tung. The *People's Daily* outlined the results of 'material incentives' introduced in a Peking construction unit. It said that the bonuses for overall excellent performance and over-fulfilment of the tasks outlined in the work plan had had an outstanding effect. Their productivity had gone up by 53 per cent compared with last year. The first all-round pay increases last year, plus the new bonus payments are having a tremendous effect on productivity in the drive to modernise industry and agriculture.

(Adapted extracts.)

(a) **(i)** According to Source A, which increased more, industrial or agricultural output? **4(a)**

   (ii) Using your own knowledge, and the information provided in Source A, write a short paragraph explaining what a people's commune was. **1,4(a)**

(b) **(i)** Which product showed the greatest percentage increase between 1957 and 1972 (Source B)? **4(a)**

   (ii) Which product showed the greatest percentage increase between 1972 and 1981 (Source B)? **4(a)**

   (iii) What contradictions can you find between the statistics of grain and steel production given in Source A and those in Source B? **4(a,c)**

   (iv) Which statistics do you think are likely to be more accurate, those in Source A or those in Source B? Explain your answer fully. **4(a,b)**

   (v) From the statistics of food production and population in Source B, would you say that in 1981 the people of China were likely to be better fed than in 1957, or not? Give reasons for your answer. **4(a)**

(c) **(i)** According to Source C, what were 'material incentives', and why were they introduced? **4(a)**

   (ii) Who were the 'Gang of Four' mentioned in Source C, and why had they been disgraced? **1,2,4(a)**

(d) **(i)** What evidence is there in Source C that the policy of giving 'material incentives' was successful? **4(a)**

   (ii) In what ways do the statistics in Source B support or contradict the claims made in Source C? **4(a,c)**

   (iii) From the evidence of Source C, what would you say was one of the main reasons for the failure to increase production in some industries during the Cultural Revolution? **4(a)**

3. Deng Xiaoping and his policies

Study the Sources below, and then answer the questions that follow.

Source A

An article in the *Observer*, November 1986.

Deng Xiaoping, China's 82-year-old leader, has revealed his vision of the early twenty-first century. The Chinese will be ten times richer than they are today. Deng disagrees with those old revolutionaries, and by implication, Mao Tse-tung, who believed that 'poor communism is better than wealthy capitalism'. Deng says, 'To get rich is not a crime' . . . Agricultural reform has progressed well and the new prosperity will be based on sweat, enterprise and capitalist investment, in which communist ideas play virtually no part.

(Extracts.)

Source B
An article in the *Observer*, 25 January 1987.

Last week Communist Party General Secretary Hu Yaobang was forced to 'resign'; a discouraged official said afterwards in Canton: 'It's a tremendous conservative victory. The demonstrations were the spark, but with the economy in trouble, the conservatives would have found another reason to attack the reforms. They believe they can bring in foreign technology and keep everything else out by getting rid of Hu. They will sacrific efficiency for control and order every time.' Sacking Hu, one of his closest supporters for 40 years, loses Deng plenty of face. Last week Deng was forced to confess to the visiting Zimbabwe Prime Minister Robert Mugabe, that the decentralising reforms in agriculture and industry, which began in 1979 were marked by 'excessive speed', and now they would slow down and become 'realistic and practical'. The conservatives [Maoists] are very critical of the economy: inflation is climbing, foreign exchange has drained away, exports lag and are of poor quality, foreign investment is down, and most dangerous of all in a country terrified of a repeat of the sweeping famine of 1959–61, grain harvests have not kept pace with the rest of agricultural production.

(Adapted extracts.)

(a) **(i)** According to Source A, what does Deng expect will happen in China in the early 21st century? **4(a)**

   (ii) How do Deng's ideas differ from those of Mao? **4(a)**

(b) **(i)** Who was Hu Yaobang mentioned in Source B, and what happened to him in January 1987? **4(a)**

   (ii) What were the demonstrations mentioned by the official in Source B, and what did he mean by saying they were 'the spark'? **1,2,4(a)**

(c) **(i)** What evidence is there in Source B to support the claim that the economy was 'in trouble'? **4(a)**

   (ii) Describe in detail the reforms introduced by Deng since 1979. **1,2**

(d) **(i)** What did the conservatives or Maoist supporters hope to achieve by forcing Deng to sack Hu? **4(a)**

   (ii) According to Source B, what was it that many Chinese feared more than anything else? **4(a)**

(e) **(i)** In what ways does the information about the economy given in Source B contradict the claims made in Source A? **4(a,c)**

    (ii)   How do you explain these contradictions, bearing in mind the short time between the publication of the two articles?

                            1,2,4(a,b,c)

(f) Using your own knowledge, and the Sources, explain why the Maoists disapproved of Hu Yaobang and the reforms.   **1,2,4**

4.   When Chinese people want to express their opinions publicly (illus 19.3) they write in large letters on posters which they paste on walls in universities and schools. These Dazibao – 'big character' posters – became a major feature of the Cultural Revolution.

    (a) Write a wall poster (in English) in which, in 1966, you support the ideas of the Cultural Revolution, and describe some of the actions you have taken.

    (b) Write a wall poster (in English) in which, by 1968, you suggest reasons why the Cultural Revolution should be ended.   **1,2,3**

                  [Southern Examining Group, Specimen Question.]

illus 19.3

CHAPTER 20

THE UNITED NATIONS

ORGANISATION

SUMMARY OF EVENTS

The United Nations Organisation (UNO) was formed in *1945* to replace the discredited League of Nations which had failed so dismally. The *United Nations Charter* was drawn up at San Francisco during 1945 based on proposals made at an earlier meeting between Russia, the USA, China and Britain held at Dumbarton Oaks (USA) in 1944. The aim of the UN was to preserve peace and to remove the causes of conflict by encouraging economic, social, educational and cultural progress throughout the world, especially in under-developed nations. It was hoped that the careful framing of the charter would have eliminated some of the weaknesses which dogged the League, but in fact the UN was unable to solve many of the most important problems of international relations, particularly those caused by the Cold War. On the other hand it played an important role in a number of *international crises* by arranging cease-fires, negotiations and peace-keeping forces; its successes in *non-political work* (such as care of refugees, protection of human rights, dealing with health and population problems and economic planning) have been enormous.

20.1 THE STRUCTURE OF THE UNITED NATIONS ORGANISATION

The basic structure of UNO with its *six main organs* (General Assembly, Security Council, Secretariat, International Court of Justice, Economic and Social Council, and Trusteeship Council) looks remarkably similar to that of the League, though the last two did not appear in the same form in the League, and there were important changes of procedure in the Assembly and the Council designed to produce more decisive action.

(a) **The General Assembly** includes representatives from *every member state* and *each member has one vote*. It meets once a year in September but special sessions can be called in times of crisis by the members themselves or by the Security Council. Its function is to *debate and make*

illus 20.1 *The headquarters of the United Nations Organisation, New York*

proposals about international problems, to consider the budget and what amounts each member state should pay, to elect the Security Council members and generally to supervise the work of the many other UN bodies. Decisions do not require a unanimous vote as they did in the League Assembly: sometimes a *simple majority* is enough though on issues which the Assembly deems to be of major importance a *two-thirds majority* is needed.

(b) The Security Council began with *eleven members*, five of them permanent (China, France, Britain, USA and Russia) and the other six elected by the General Assembly for two-year terms; in 1965 the number of non-permanent members was increased to *ten*. The Security Council's function is to deal with crises as they arise, by whatever action seems appropriate, and if necessary by calling on members to take *economic or military action against an aggressor*. Decisions require at least *nine* of the fifteen members to vote in favour, but these must include *all five permanent members*; thus any one of the permanent members can *veto* a decision and prevent action being taken. In practice, it has gradually been accepted that abstention by a permanent member does not amount to a veto, but this had not been written into the charter. In order to secure some action in case of veto, the General Assembly in 1950 (at the time of the Korean War) introduced the '*Uniting for Peace' resolution*, stating that if the Council's proposals were vetoed the Assembly could meet within 24 hours and decide what action to take (even military intervention if necessary); such a decision by the Assembly would require only a two-thirds majority. Again this was not added to the charter, and the Russians, who used the veto more often than any other member, have always maintained that a Security Council veto should take precedence over a General Assembly decision. Nevertheless the Assembly has acted in this way many times.

(c) The Secretariat looks after the administrative work, preparing minutes, translations and information; it is headed by the *Secretary-General*, appointed for a five-year term by the Assembly on the recommendation of the Security Council. He has much greater responsibility and influence than his counterpart in the League had: he has the power to bring before the Security Council any matter he wishes. The UN has been fortunate in having five Secretaries' General of outstanding ability and dedication: Trygve Lie of Norway (1946–52), Dag Hammarskjöld of Sweden (1952–61), U Thant of Burma (1961–71), Kurt Waldheim of Austria (1971–81) and Pérez de Cuellar of Peru (1981–).

(d) The International Court of Justice at the Hague *has fifteen* judges, all of different nationality, elected for three-year terms by the Assembly and Council jointly. It has dealt successfully with a number of disputes that could be *settled judicially*, including a frontier dispute between Holland and Belgium and a disagreement between Britain and Norway over fishing limits.

(e) The Trusteeship Council replaced the League Mandates Commission, its main function being to see that all states looking after trust territories *prepared them as soon as possible for independence*. By 1970 its job was almost completed, but there are still some trouble spots, particularly South West Africa, the territory given to South Africa as a mandate by the Versailles treaties in 1919. South Africa refused to grant independence to the territory (now known as Namibia), though by 1980 there were signs that she was prepared to do so.

(f) The Economic and Social Council has *27 members* elected by the Assembly, with one-third retiring each year; it organises projects concerned with health, education and other social and economic matters. Its task is so enormous that it has appointed *four regional commissions* (for Europe, Latin America, Africa, and Asia and the Far East), as well as commissions on population problems, drugs problems, human rights and the status of women. The Council also supervises and co-ordinates the work of an astonishing array of other commissions and specialised agencies, approaching 30 in all. Among the best known are the *International Labour Organisation (ILO)*, founded originally in 1919, which continues its successful work of trying to secure basic minimum standards of employment; the *World Health Organisation (WHO)* which has achieved excellent results, fighting epidemics, promoting maternal and child welfare, and generally improving living standards, and whose most celebrated breakthrough was the *eradication of smallpox*; and the *Food and Agriculture Organisation (FAO)* which aims to raise living standards by encouraging improvements in agricultural production, and which has had particular success in India and Pakistan. The *United Nations Educational Scientific and Cultural Organisation (UNESCO)* encourages not simply the spread of education but also international co-operation between artists, scientists and scholars in all fields, working on the assumption that the best way of avoiding war is to educate people's minds in the pursuit of peace. The *United Nations Children's Fund (UNICEF)* was founded originally in 1946 to help children left in difficulties by the war; nowadays its scope has widened to include relief work for children suffering as a result of disasters – famine, earthquakes and tornadoes. To deal with the specific problem of Arab refugees from Palestine (see Section 26.2), the *United Nations Relief and Works Agency (UNRWA)* was set up (1950). Its achievement has been remarkable: it began by providing basic food, clothing and shelter, and later went on to provide schools and medical services; it is not difficult to imagine the chaos that would have developed without the work of UNRWA; as it is, although some camps are still unsatisfactory, others are gradually becoming self-supporting. Finally there are a number of financial agencies; the one which the general public hears most about is the *International Monetary Fund (IMF)* which provides short-term loans to countries in financial difficulties to enable them to avoid devaluation, while the *World Bank* provides larger and longer loans to help countries undertake economic development.

20.2 WHAT ARE THE MAIN DIFFERENCES BETWEEN UNO AND THE LEAGUE?

Obviously the *vastly enlarged scope of its activities* (all the specialised agencies mentioned in the previous section, with the exception of the ILO, were founded in 1945 or later) is one of the major differences between UNO and the League. Others already mentioned are the changes in procedure of the Assembly and the Council, and the increased power of the Secretary-General, all designed to secure *more decisive action* than the League achieved. UNO has a much wider membership and is therefore more of a *genuine world organisation* than the League, with all the extra prestige that this entails. Both the USA and the USSR were founder-members of UNO which in 1980 contained over 150 member states whereas the League never had more than 50. Between 1963 and 1968 no fewer than 43 new members joined, mainly the emerging states of Africa and Asia. This meant that the combined *Afro-Asian bloc had a majority in the General Assembly*, making it more difficult for the east–west power blocs to control the voting. The increased importance of the Assembly resulting from the 'Uniting for Peace' resolution meant that these new Third World states could often determine the outcome of important issues. Some of the great powers found this alarming since many of the new members were inexperienced, and the rival blocs began to spend a lot of time and energy *intriguing to win the support of each new member*.

20.3 HOW SUCCESSFUL HAS UNO BEEN AS A PEACE-KEEPING BODY?

Although it has had mixed success, it is probably fair to say that UNO has been rather more successful than the League in its peace-keeping efforts, especially in *crises which did not directly involve the interests of the great powers*, such as the civil war in the Congo and the dispute between Holland and Indonesia over West New Guinea. On the other hand, it has often been just as ineffective as the League in situations – such as the Hungarian and Czech crises – when the interests of one of the great powers, in this case Russia, seemed to be threatened and where the *great power chose to ignore or defy UNO*. The best way to illustrate the organisation's varying degrees of success is to examine some of the major disputes in which it has been involved.

(a) **In 1946 UNO helped to arrange the granting of independence by Holland to the Dutch East Indies** which became *Indonesia* (see Fig. 24.3). However no agreement was reached about the future of *West New Guinea (West Irian)* which both countries claimed. In 1961 fighting broke out; after U Thant had appealed to both sides to reopen negotiations, it was agreed (1962) that the territory should become part of Indonesia. The transfer was organised and policed by a UN force. In this case the UN played a vital role in getting successful negotiations going, though it did not itself make the decision about West Irian's future.

(b) **The problem of the warring Jews and Arabs in Palestine** was brought before the UN in 1947, and the resulting UN investigation decided to partition Palestine, setting up the Jewish state of Israel (see Section 26.2). The UN was unable to prevent a series of wars between Israel and various Arab states (1948–9, 1956, 1967 and 1973) though it did useful work arranging cease-fires and providing supervisory forces while UNRWA cared for the Arab refugees.

(c) The Korean War (1950–3) was the only occasion on which the UN was able to take decisive action in a crisis directly involving the interests of the great powers; when South Korea was invaded by communist North Korea in June 1950, the Security Council immediately passed a resolution condemning North Korea and called on member states to send help to the south. However, this was possible only because of the temporary absence of the Russian delegates who would certainly have vetoed the resolution if they had not been boycotting Council meetings since January in protest against the failure to admit communist China to UN membership. Although the Russian delegates returned smartly, it was too late for them to prevent action going ahead. Troops of 16 countries were able to repel the invasion and preserve the frontier between the two Koreas along the 38th parallel (see Section 17.2). Though this was claimed by the west as a great UN success, it was in fact overwhelmingly an American operation; the vast majority of troops and the commander-in-chief General MacArthur, were American, and the US government had already decided to intervene with force the day before the Security Council decision was taken. Only the absence of the Russians enabled the USA to turn it into a UN operation, a situation not likely to be repeated since the Russians would take good care to be present at all future Council sessions.

The *Korean War had important results for the future of the UN*: one was the passing of the 'Uniting for Peace' resolution which would permit a Security Council veto to be bypassed by a General Assembly vote; another was the launching of a bitter attack by the Russians on Trygve Lie for what they considered to be his biased role in the crisis; as a result his position became impossible so that he eventually agreed to retire early and was replaced by Dag Hammarskjöld.

(d) The Suez Crisis (1956) *showed the UN at its best.* When President Nasser of Egypt suddenly nationalised the Suez Canal, many of the shares in which were British- and French-owned, both these powers protested strongly and sent troops 'to protect their interests' (see Section 26.3). At the same time the Israelis invaded Egypt from the east; the real aim was to *destroy Nasser*. A Security Council resolution condemning force was vetoed by Britain and France, whereupon the matter passed to the Assembly which by a majority of 64 votes to 5 condemned the invasions and called for a withdrawal of troops. In view of the weight of opinion against them the aggressors agreed to withdraw provided the UN ensured a reasonable settlement over the canal and kept the Arabs and Israelis from slaughtering each other. A United Nations Emergency Force of 5000 made up of troops from 10 different countries moved in while British, French and Israelis went home. The prestige of the UN and of Hammarskjöld himself, who conducted the operation with consummate skill, was greatly enhanced, though American and Russian pressure was important in bringing about a cease-fire. However, the UN was not so successful in the 1967 Arab–Israeli conflict (see Section 26.4).

illus 20.2 *United Nations truce supervision in Palestine*

(e) The Hungarian Rising (1956), which occurred at the same time as the Suez Crisis, showed the UN *at its most ineffective*. When the Hungarians tried to exert their independence from Russian control, soviet troops entered Hungary to crush the revolt (see Section 18.2(c)). The Hungarian government appealed to the UN, but the Russians vetoed a Security Council resolution calling for a withdrawal of their forces. The Assembly passed the same resolution and set up a committee to investigate the problem; but the Russians refused to co-operate with the committee and no progress could be made. The contrast with Suez was striking: there Britain and France had been willing to bow to international pressure; the Russians, not so susceptible, *simply ignored the UN*, and nothing could be done.

(f) In the Belgian Congo civil war, which dragged on from 1960 until 1964 (see Section 25.1), the UN mounted its most complex operation so far (excepting Korea). When the Congo (known as *Zaire* since 1971) dissolved into chaos immediately after gaining independence, a UN force numbering over 20,000 at its largest managed to restore some sort of precarious order; a special UN Congo Fund was established to help with the recovery and development of the ravaged country. But the financial cost of the operation was so high that the UN was brought *close to bankruptcy*, especially when Russia, France and Belgium refused to pay their contributions towards the cost of the operations, because they disapproved of the way the UN was handling the situation. The crisis also cost the life of Dag Hammarskjöld who was killed in a plane crash in the Congo.

(g) Cyprus has kept the UN busy since 1964. A British colony since 1878, the island was granted *independence* in *1960*; in *1963 civil war broke out* between the *Greeks*, who made up about 80 per cent of the island's population, and the *Turks*. A UN peace-keeping force arrived in March 1964; an uneasy peace was restored but it required 3000 troops permanently stationed in Cyprus to prevent Greeks and Turks tearing each other apart. Even this was not enough for in 1974 the Greek Cypriots tried to unite the island with Greece; this prompted the Turkish Cypriots, helped by invading Turkish regular troops, to seize the north of the island as their own territory and to expel all the Greeks who happened to be living in that area. Again UN forces achieved a cease-fire and are still *policing the frontier* between Greeks and Turks. However the UN has not been successful in finding an acceptable constitution or any other compromise and dare not risk withdrawing its troops.

(h) In Kashmir the UN found itself in a similar situation to that in Cyprus. After 1947, this large province lying between India and Pakistan (see Fig. 24.2) was claimed by both states. Already in 1948 the UN had negotiated a cease-fire after fighting had broken out. At this point the Indians were occupying the southern part of Kashmir, the Pakistanis the northern part, and for the next 16 years the UN policed the cease-fire line between the two zones. When *Pakistani troops invaded the Indian zone in 1965*, a short war developed between India and Pakistan, but once again the UN successfully intervened and hostilities ceased. The original dispute still remained, though, and by 1980 there seemed little prospect of the UN or any other agency finding a permanent solution.

(i) The Czechoslovakia crisis (1968) was almost a repeat performance of the Hungarian Rising twelve years earlier. When the Czechs showed what Moscow judged to be too much independence, Russian and other Warsaw Pact troops were sent in to enforce obedience (see Section 18.2(f)). The Security Council tried to pass a motion condemning this action but the Russians vetoed it, claiming that the Czech government had asked for their intervention. Although the Czechs denied this, there was nothing the UN could do in view of the Russian refusal to co-operate.

(j) **The Russian invasion of Afghanistan (December 1979)** to replace one communist government with another (that of Babrak Karmal) posed similar problems for the UN: a motion condemning Russian intervention and calling for a withdrawal of troops was predictably vetoed by the Russians in the Security Council (January 1980), and although a similar motion passed the General Assembly with a large majority, Russian troops stayed put; it seemed that yet another satellite had been brought into the soviet orbit.

(k) **Other crises over which the UN failed to register any significant achievements** were the *civil war in the Lebanon (1975–6)* and the frontier struggle which followed in southern Lebanon between Palestinians and Lebanese Christians (aided by the Israelis). The UN Interim Force in Lebanon (UNIFIL) numbered 7000 in 1982 but it was always in difficulties trying to deal with constant battles, assassinations, terrorism and seizing of hostages. During the *Falklands War* between *Argentina and Britain (1982)*, both sides ignored UN attempts to find a negotiated solution, though the war lasted only three months before the British recaptured the islands. Similarly in the *Gulf War* between *Iran and Iraq* which began in 1980, all UN efforts at mediation failed and hostilities dragged on into the eighth year.

20.4 WHAT ARE THE WEAKNESSES OF UNO?

Obviously one of its major problems is the difficulty of prevailing upon great powers to accept its decisions *if they chose to put self-interest first*. This has meant that some states put more faith in their own regional organisations, such as NATO, than in the UN which, among its other weaknesses, is always *short of cash*. There is the problem of exactly when during the course of a dispute the UN should become involved; sometimes it hangs back (as it did in the case of Uganda) too long, so that the problem becomes much more difficult to handle; sometimes it hesitates so long that it scarcely becomes involved at all, which happened with the Vietnam War and the Cuban missile crisis. Another difficulty is that the preponderance of *Third World* members means that only they can be certain of having their resolutions passed and it is increasingly difficult for the other blocs to get resolutions through the General Assembly. Some delegates become disillusioned because member states usually vote by bloc rather than on the merits of each case; for years it proved impossible, for example, to have a motion condemning terrorism passed in the General Assembly: when it appeared in September 1979 such a motion was defeated by the Arab states and their supporters.

The whole organisation was thrown into confusion in *1983* when a row blew up at the UNESCO General Congress. Many western nations, particularly the USA, protested at what they claimed were UNESCO's *administrative inefficiency and unacceptable political aims*. What brought matters to a head was a proposal by some communist states for the internal licensing of journalists. According to the USA, this would lead to a situation in which member states would exercise an effective *censorship* of each other's media organisations. Consequently the Americans announced that they would *withdraw* from UNESCO on 1 January 1985, since it had become 'hostile to the basic institutions of a free society, especially a free market and a free press'. Great Britain and Singapore withdrew in 1986, for similar reasons.

A perennial weakness of the UN throughout its existence was a *shortage of funds*. The organisation was always heavily dependent on the annual contributions of the member states, many of which refused to pay from time to time either because of financial difficulties of their own or as a mark of disapproval of UN policies. 1986 was a particularly bad year financially: no fewer than 98 of its members owed money, chief among them being the USA which withheld more than 100 million dollars until the UN reformed its budgeting system and curbed its extravagance. The Americans wanted the countries who gave most to have more say in how the money was spent, but most smaller members rejected this as undemocratic. As Sri Lanka's delegate put it: 'In our political processes at home, the wealthy do not have more votes than the poor. We should like this to be the practice in the UN as well.'

For these reasons, many observers became *pessimistic about the future of the UN*, pointing out also that as more and more international agreements were reached outside the UN (such as SALT, Vietnam, the Camp David peace between Israel and Egypt and the settlement of the Rhodesia–Zimbabwe problem), the organisation was becoming irrelevant, little more than an arena for propaganda speeches.

Looking on the brighter side, however, there seemed good reason for some optimism in the late 1980s. The UN continued to bring together 159 nations, keeping them talking to each other and providing even the smallest of them with a *world forum*. Though it might not be producing dramatic solutions, it was nevertheless doing valuable work: preventing bloodshed and human suffering by its peace-keeping forces and care of refugees, investigating and reporting on human rights under repressive regimes, and organising conferences on drugs problems and Aids. Even the financial situation was improving: early in 1987 Secretary-General Pérez de Cuellar announced a wide range of austerity measures, the USSR paid part of its annual contribution early to ease the crisis, and the USA promised to pay its arrears. This followed the adoption of new procedures giving what amounted to powers of veto to the 21 members of the programme and co-ordination committee, who could now *fix the budget and the limits on individual items*. This 'historic step' as President Reagan called it, was approved by both the USA and the USSR. It meant that the major financial contributors would have more control over spending, and a more careful and economical approach was soon apparent.

QUESTIONS

1. The United Nations Organisation
Study the Sources below, and then answer the questions that follow.

Source A
From the Charter of the United Nations, 1945.

Article 9: The General Assembly shall consist of all members of the United Nations.

Article 24: In order to ensure prompt and effective action by the United Nations, its members confer on the Security Council responsibility for the maintenance of international peace and security.

Source B

Those who depict the assembly as an anarchic collection of small countries constantly voting down with glee, the great responsible powers are wide of the mark. Most of the small countries have to exercise considerable thought in the way they vote because of their ties with this or that great power.

Source: Conor Cruise O'Brien, *Katanga and Black* (1962).

Source C
From the work of an historian writing in 1984.

It would be easy to list the failures of the UN. There have been many wars in the last thirty years. The great powers have ignored the UN at times, even by-passing it as, for example with the 'hot line'. It failed to play any significant part in the Cuban crisis of 1962, the Vietnam War, the Russian invasion of Afghanistan or the Falklands Crisis. Disarmament has not been achieved.

The success of the UN depends so much on countries acting for an ideal that it fails so often.

(a) Using Sources A and B, and your own knowledge, explain why the United Nations was created in 1945. **1,2,4(a,c)**
(b) What was the 'Charter'? **1**
(c) What do Sources A and B say about the membership and the pattern of voting in the General Assembly? **4(a,c)**
(d) What is the main purpose of the Security Council? How effective has this part of the United Nations been? **1,2,4(a)**
(e) Using Source C, explain the reference to the 'Hot Line'. **1,4(a)**
(f) What reasons can you suggest for the great powers ignoring or by-passing the UN? **1,2,4(a)**

(g) What evidence in Source B suggests that the writer is sympathetic to the United Nations? **4(a,b)**

(h) Why might the historian who wrote Source C be considered a critic of the UN? Give reasons for your answer. **4(a,b)**

(i) Which of the sources A, B, or C do you consider to be the least biased about the United Nations? Give reasons for your answer.

4(a,b,c)

[Northern Examining Association, Specimen Question.]

2. International peace-keeping

Study the extract below, and then answer the questions that follow.

> In 1941 Roosevelt and Churchill met and drew up the Atlantic Charter as the basis of their war aims. Among these they put forward the 'Four Freedoms' – 'Freedom from want, freedom of speech, freedom from fear and freedom of religion'. They also proposed the setting up of a new international peace-keeping organisation to replace the League of Nations. They felt that the idea of the League had been a good one, but there had been faults and weaknesses. They hoped to put these faults right. After further meetings and discussions had taken place, the Charter of the United Nations was signed in 1945 at San Francisco by 51 founder members.

Source: C. Culpin, *Making History* (Collins, 1984, adapted).

(a) Why were the 'Four Freedoms' considered so important when Roosevelt and Churchill met in 1941? **1,2,4(a)**

(b) What main points to do with the United Nations were considered at the 'further meetings and discussions' that took place between 1941 and 1945? **1,4(a)**

(c) In what ways is the United Nations organised in order to try to avoid the 'faults and weaknesses' of the League of Nations? **1,2**

(d) Since the signing of the United Nations Charter at San Francisco, the 51 founder members have been joined by about one hundred new members.

    (i) Why has there been this huge increase in United Nations membership? **1,2**

    (ii) How has the United Nations changed as a result of this increased membership? **1,2**

[Southern Examining Group, Specimen Question.]

3. The UN and its problems

Study the Source below, and then answer the questions that follow.

Guardian, 11 December 1986.

> The problem is that the UN has exhausted its available funds and 98 of its members owe it money. By the beginning of next year it will be 824

million dollars short. The United States is the largest debtor, still owing more than 100 million dollars. The debt is likely to mount because the Americans plan to withhold a large portion of their future payments unless the General Assembly reforms its administration and budgeting so that the UN's chief donor countries have considerably more say in the way its money is spent.

(Adapted.)

(a)   (i)   According to the *Guardian* article, what serious problem was the UN facing?   **4(a)**

    (ii)   Roughly what proportion of the debt was owed by the USA?   **4(a)**

(b)   (i)   What did the USA want the General Assembly to do?   **4(a)**

    (ii)   How do you think the smaller member countries of the UN would react to the American proposals?   **1,2,4(a)**

(c)   How were the problems mentioned in the article temporarily solved early in 1987?   **1,2,4(a)**

(d)   What other weaknesses has the UN suffered from since its beginning in 1945?   **1,2**

(e)   (i)   Choose *one* major area of world crisis where you think the UN acted successfully. Describe what happened, and explain why the UN was successful.   **1,2**

    (ii)   Choose *one* major area of world crisis where you think the UN failed. Describe what happened, and explain why the UN failed.   **1,2**

CHAPTER 21

WESTERN EUROPE
SINCE 1945

SUMMARY OF EVENTS

In 1945, *much of Europe lay in ruins*; it no longer dominated the world and seemed about to be engulfed by the tide of *communism* spreading from Russia. In this situation, many people felt that the continent could be rebuilt and defended only by a common military, economic and political effort; this move towards a *united Western Europe*, which involved the setting up of *NATO* and the *Council of Europe* (both in 1949) as well as the *European Economic Community (EEC) or the Common Market (1957)*, has been the most striking development of the post-war period. In Britain enthusiasm for such co-operation developed more slowly than in other countries through fear that it would threaten British sovereignty. Britain declined to join the EEC in 1957; when she changed her mind in 1961 the French vetoed her entry, and it was *1972* before she finally became a member.

The states of western Europe recovered surprisingly quickly from the effects of the war, thanks to a combination of American aid under the *Marshall Plan* (see Section 16.2(e)), and increase in world demand for European products, technological improvement and careful planning by governments. During the 1960s, however, *inflation* became a serious problem and during the mid-1970s *rising oil prices* worsened inflation and combined with unemployment as Europe began to move into a trade recession (a temporary reduction in demand for goods, but not as serious as a slump).

In *Britain* the *Labour governments (1945–51)* introduced important nationalisation and social welfare measures. Under the *Conservatives (1951–64)* the British people had 'never had it so good', as the Prime Minister, Macmillan, told them; but in fact inflation and a worsening balance of payments (when the value of goods imported is greater than that of goods being exported, causing a drain on gold and foreign currency reserves) caused growing concern. After 1964 governments alternated and all of them wrestled with the same economic problems, apparently without any lasting success.

In *France* the *Fourth Republic (1946–58)* suffered from most of the political weaknesses of the Third; it was further troubled by inflation and by defeat in Indo-China (1954) and was brought down by a rebellion in Algeria. At the height of the crisis General de Gaulle stepped in to become President of the Fifth Republic, under which the President had much more power than before. Though de Gaulle gradually lost much of his popularity and resigned in 1969, the Fifth Republic continued with right-wing governments under Pompidou (1969–74) and Giscard d'Estaing (1974–81) and the Socialist Mitterrand (1981–8).

The *German Federal Republic (West Germany)*, set up in 1949, enjoyed a remarkable economic recovery under the conservative government of *Chancellor Adenauer (1949–63)*, though there were some setbacks and a rise in unemployment under his successors Erhard (1963–6) and Kiesinger (1966–9). From 1969 until 1982 the left-wing Social Democrats were in power, with Liberal support, first under Brandt (1969–74) and then under Schmidt. *Economic difficulties* forced Schmidt to resign and a centre–right coalition led by *Helmut Kohl* took office.

The new *Republic of Italy* began with a period of prosperity and stable government under *de Gasperi (1946–53)* but then many of the old problems of the pre-Mussolini era reappeared; weak coalition governments failed to solve problems of inflation and unemployment so that support for the communist party grew rapidly. Meanwhile *Spain* played little part in European affairs; outwardly quiet, she was kept under the tight fascist rein of Franco who ruled until his death in 1975 whereupon the monarchy was restored under King Juan Carlos. There was a return to democracy as there was in neighbouring Portugal after the overthrow of the fascist regime in 1974.

21.1 THE GROWTH OF UNITY IN WESTERN EUROPE

(a) **In every country in western Europe** there were people from all parts of the political spectrum who believed in **closer co-operation between the states**, while some thought in terms of a *united federal Europe* on the same lines as the United States of America. Their *reasoning was simple*: only by a co-operative effort and a pooling of resources could Europe recover from the ravages of war; the countries were too small to be economically and militarily viable separately in a world dominated by the super-powers, the USA and the USSR; there would be less likelihood of war between the countries; the threat from Russia could be met only by joint action. West Germany especially supported the idea because it would gain her early acceptance as a responsible nation, and *Winston Churchill* was one of its most eloquent advocates: in March 1943 he spoke of the need for a Council of Europe, and in a speech at Zurich in 1946 he argued that only as a United States of Europe could the countries count for anything in the world.

(b) Although federalists have been bitterly disappointed by their failure to achieve complete integration, some progress has been made:

(i)   The *Organisation for European Economic Co-operation (OEEC)* was the first initiative towards unity; it was set up in *1947* in response to the American offer of Marshall Aid (see Section 16.2(e)), with 16 European nations involved. Its first function, successfully achieved over the next four years, was to apportion American aid among its members, after which it went on, again with great success, to encourage trade among its members by reducing restrictions. It was helped by a United Nations *General Agreement on Tariffs and Trade (GATT)* whose function was to reduce tariffs and by the *European Payments Union (EPU)* which encouraged trade by improving the system of payments between member states so that each state could use its own currency. The OEEC was so successful that trade between its members doubled during the first six years; when the USA and Canada joined in 1961 it became the *Organisation for Economic Co-operation and Development* (OECD); later Japan and Australia joined.

(ii) The *North Atlantic Treaty Organisation (NATO)* was established in *1949* (see Section 16.2(i)) as a mutual defence in case one of the member states should be attacked. The Korean war (1950–3) caused the USA to press successfully for the integration of NATO forces under a centralised command; a *Supreme Headquarters Allied Powers Europe (SHAPE)* was established near Paris. Until the end of 1955, NATO seemed to be developing impressively: the forces available for the defence of western Europe had been increased fourfold; it was claimed by some that it had deterred the Russians from attacking West Germany. However, problems soon arose: the French were not happy about the dominant American role; in 1966 *de Gaulle withdrew from NATO* so that French forces and nuclear policy would not be controlled by a foreigner. Moreover, compared with the Warsaw Pact countries, NATO was weak: with 60 divisions in 1980 it fell far short of its target of 96 divisions, whereas the communist bloc boasted 102 divisions and 3 times as many tanks as NATO.

(iii) The *Council of Europe (1949)* was an attempt at *political unity*. By 1971 all the states of western Europe (except Spain and Portugal) had joined and Turkey was included (making 16 members in all). Based at Strasbourg, it consists of the foreign ministers of the member states and an Assembly of representatives chosen by the parliaments of the states. It has *no powers*, however, since several states, particularly Britain, refused to join any organisation which threatened their own sovereignty. It can make recommendations and has achieved useful work *sponsoring human rights agreements*, but it has been a grave disappointment to the federalists.

(iv) The *European Economic Community had the most direct impact* on the majority of ordinary people in Europe.

(c) The European Economic Community (EEC), known in Britain as the *Common Market*, was established by the *Treaty of Rome (1957)*, and in spite of many difficulties it has been the most successful of the attempts at co-operation. The stages in its evolution were:

(i) In 1944 the exiled governments of Belgium, Netherlands and Luxembourg formed the *Benelux Union*, a customs and trading association which came into operation in 1947.

(ii) By the *Treaty of Brussels (1948)* Britain and France joined the three Benelux countries in pledging 'military, economic, social and cultural collaboration'. While the military collaboration eventually resulted in NATO, the next step in economic co-operation was the ECSC.

(iii) The *European Coal and Steel Community (ECSC) (1951)*. This was the brainchild of *Robert Schuman*, the French Foreign Minister, who hoped by involving West Germany to improve Franco-German relations as well as to make European industry more efficient. *Six* countries joined: France, West Germany, Italy, Belgium, Netherlands and Luxembourg. All duties and restrictions on trade in coal, iron and steel between the six were removed, and a High Authority created to administer the community and organise a joint programme of expansion. The only disappointment for the federalists was that Britain refused to join because she objected to *handing over control of her industries to a supranational authority*. Nevertheless the ECSC was such an outstanding success, with steel production rising by almost 50 per cent during the first five years that the six decided to extend it to include all production. The agreements setting up the full EEC were signed in *Rome (1957)* and came into operation on *1 January 1958*.

The six countries would *gradually remove all customs duties and quotas* so that there would be *free competition and a common market*. Tariffs would be kept against non-members, though even these were reduced. The treaty also spoke of improving living and working conditions, expanding industry, encouraging the development of the world's backward areas, safeguarding peace and liberty, and working for a closer union of European peoples; obviously *something much wider than just a common market* was in the minds of the statesmen of the six countries. By 1967 the machinery to run the EEC had been refined to include the Commission (which manages the EEC), the Council of Ministers, an Assembly or Parliament (containing representatives since 1979 directly elected by voters in all member states), a Secretariat and a Court of Justice. Associated with the EEC was EURATOM, an organisation in which the six pooled their efforts towards the development of *atomic energy*. Like the ECSC, the EEC was soon off to a flying start; within five years it was the world's *biggest exporter and buyer of raw materials* and was second only to the USA in steel production. Once again, however, Britain had declined to join.

(d) Why did Britain refuse membership of the EEC? It was ironic that though Churchill (who retired as Prime Minister in 1955) was one of the strongest supporters of a united Europe, both Labour and Conservative governments drew back from committing themselves too far; their main objection was that Britain would no longer be in complete control of her own economy which would be at the mercy of a supranational authority – the EEC Commission in Brussels. There was also the fear that Britain's relationship with the commonwealth might be ruined if she were no longer able to *give preference to commonwealth goods* such as New Zealand lamb and butter; the commonwealth with its population of over 800 million seemed a more promising market than the EEC with its 165 million. Nor did Britain want to risk upsetting her *special relationship with the USA* by becoming too deeply involved in economic integration with Europe which many Europeans wanted to see extended into political integration.

Britain and other countries outside the EEC were worried about being excluded from trade with the six by their high external tariffs. Consequently Britain took the lead in organising the *European Free Trade Area (EFTA) in 1959*. Britain, Denmark, Norway, Sweden, Switzerland, Austria and Portugal agreed gradually to abolish tariffs between each other, but there was no mention of common economic policies. By 1961, however, the British had had a complete change of mind, and Macmillan announced that they *wished to join the EEC*.

(e) Why did the British attitude to the EEC change? In the first place, it was clear that by 1961 the EEC was an outstanding success – without Britain. Since 1953 French production had risen by 75 per cent while German production had increased by almost 90 per cent; Britain's, however, was only 30 per cent up. EFTA had been successful in increasing the trade of its members, but to nothing like the same extent as the EEC. In fact the British economy seemed to be stagnating in comparison with those of the six. The commonwealth, in spite of its size, could not compare with the purchasing power of the EEC, and Macmillan pointed out that there was no clash of interest between Britain's membership of the EEC and trade with the commonwealth: there were signs that the EEC was willing to make *special arrangements* for the commonwealth countries to become associate members and to allow Britain's EFTA partners to join as well. Another argument was that once Britain was in, competition from the other EEC members would stimulate British industry to greater effort and efficiency. Macmillan even made the point that Britain could not afford to be left out if the EEC developed into a political union.

Negotiations opened in October 1961, and though there were some difficulties it came as a shock when in *January 1963 de Gaulle broke off the talks* and announced that Britain was not ready for membership.

(f) Why did the French oppose British entry to the EEC? At the time, de Gaulle claimed that Britain had too many economic problems and would therefore weaken the EEC. Though the French colonies were associate members, he objected to any concessions being made for the commonwealth since this would be a drain on Europe's resources. It was suggested in Britain that de Gaulle wanted to continue dominating Europe; if Britain came in she would be a serious rival, while her close ties with the USA would bring unwelcome American influence producing, as he himself said, 'a colossal Atlantic grouping under American dependence and control'. He was perhaps annoyed that Britain had just agreed to receive American Polaris missiles without first consulting France, while he was determined to prove that France was a great power and in no need of American assistance. Finally there was the problem of French agriculture: the EEC protected its farmers with high tariffs so that prices were much higher than in Britain whose agriculture was highly efficient and subsidised to keep prices relatively low. If this continued after Britain's entry French farmers, with their small and inefficient farms, would be exposed to competition from Britain and perhaps from the commonwealth.

Britain's entry was eventually secured from *1 January 1973* by two factors: after de Gaulle's resignation in 1969, his successor Pompidou was more amenable to Britain while the new British Conservative Prime Minister, Edward Heath, a committed European, negotiated with obstinate determination for British admission. Eire and Denmark also joined. In 1975 a referendum was held in Britain in which *67 per cent of those who voted expressed approval of British membership*.

(g) What have been the EEC's main problems?

The EEC has faced several crises and problems. During the 1960s *de Gaulle* caused tension first by his high-handed attitude towards British entry and later by his hostility to the Commission which was becoming too powerful for his liking. In 1965 he threatened to withdraw from the EEC if the Commission's powers were not reduced. He got his own way but held up progress for almost a decade. There was – and still is – the problem of producing a *common agricultural policy* acceptable to all members. France objected to imports of cheap wine from Italy and lamb from Britain, and on occasion refused them entry, though this was a breach of the community rules. A major crisis blew up in *1980* when Britain protested about her *budget contribution* for that year which seemed unreasonably high at £1209 million compared with £699 million from Germany and only £13 million from France. The difference was so marked because the contribution was calculated partly as a levy on each country's duties received from imports from outside the EEC. Since Britain imported much more from the outside world than the other members, her contribution soared. Fortunately, after some ruthless bargaining by the British Prime Minister, Margaret Thatcher, a compromise was reached whereby Britain's contribution was reduced to a total of £1346 million over the next three years. This was not the end of the problem, though – every year there was a new row about Britain's contribution and about how much rebate she was entitled to. The main

British complaint was that far too much of the EEC budget went on paying inflated prices to farmers who continually *produced more than could be sold.* The dispute was particularly bitter in 1984 when Britain, West Germany and the Netherlands pressed for a top limit to be placed on farm subsidies. Britain blamed France for the failure to find a long-term solution, while the French press savaged Mrs Thatcher for her intransigence and her unwillingness to take 'one small step' towards her EEC partners.

A further complication arose with the admission of *three new members* – Greece (1981) and Spain and Portugal (1986), bringing the total membership to 12 and the community population to over 320 million. Their arrival increased the influence of the *southern, less industrialised countries,* and the pressure to improve the economic balance between wealthy and poor regions.

An encouraging development occurred early in 1986 when all 12 members working closely together, negotiated a reform package which included a move to a *complete common internal market by 1992;* more control over health, safety and environmental and consumer protection; encouragement of scientific research and technology; greater powers for the European Parliament so that measures could be passed with less delay; measures to help backward regions.

Nevertheless, in 1987 the Community was facing a massive *budget crisis* – £3 billion in the red and with debts of £10 billion. The cause was the same old problem – the Common Agricultural Policy (CAP), which was using up two-thirds of the EEC's total spending every year to *subsidise farm prices.* In spite of strict *production quotas* introduced for the first time in 1984, Europe's farmers still produced vast surpluses of milk and butter which could not be sold. By 1987 the 'butter mountain' had reached ludicrous proportions – $1\frac{1}{2}$ million tonnes – enough to supply the entire EEC for a year. There was enough milk powder to last five years and storage fees alone were costing a million pounds a day. Efforts to get rid of the surplus involved selling it off cheaply to the USSR, India, Bangladesh and Pakistan, distributing it free of charge to the poor within the Community, using it to make animal feed, and burning the oldest butter in boilers.

As 1987 progressed, the community made a real attempt to solve the problem by introducing a harsh programme of production curbs and a price freeze to put a general squeeze on Europe's farmers.

21.2 BRITAIN

(a) Labour in power, 1945–51. The Labour Party won an *overwhelming majority* in the General Election of *July 1945,* with 393 seats against 213 Conservatives, 12 Liberals and 22 others. It was the *first time* Labour had won an overall majority. Their victory was surprising after Churchill's success as a war leader, but though Churchill himself was popular, the Conservatives were not – too many people remembered the unemployment of the 1930s, appeasement, and the early disasters in the war;

Labour promised social reform and more housing. The new government faced enormous economic problems in the aftermath of the war, but the Prime Minister, Clement Attlee, though mild in appearance (Churchill once described him as 'a sheep in sheep's clothing'), was shrewd and determined. With its large majority Labour was able to push ahead with a programme of drastic changes amounting to a social revolution. *What were Labour's achievements?*

(i) *A major expansion of the welfare state* based on the *Beveridge Report (1942)*. William Henry Beveridge was a liberal who believed the time was ripe for social revolution. The great evils to be overcome, as the report explained, were want, disease, ignorance, squalor and idleness. The government should fight them with insurance schemes, child allowances, a national health service and a policy of full employment. The wartime coalition government had already made a start with R. A. Butler's *Education Act (1944)* which introduced *free secondary education for all* and raised the leaving age to 15 (from 1947); the government had also introduced *family allowances* at the rate of 5s. a week for each child after the first. The first of Labour's major contributions was the *National Insurance Act (1946)*. This extended the previous schemes so that the *whole adult population was insured* for unemployment and sickness benefit, retirement, widows' and orphans' pensions, and maternity and death grants. As in the original 1911 scheme, all workers and employers as well as the government had to pay weekly contributions. The *National Health Service Act (1946)*, mainly the work of Aneurin Bevan, the Minister of Health, was a remarkable achievement. Most hospitals were brought under state control and everyone was entitled to free medical, dental and ophthalmic treatment including free teeth and spectacles. It was financed partly from taxation and partly from revenue received from National Insurance payments. It resulted in a marked improvement in the health of the working class, while deaths from tuberculosis, pneumonia and diphtheria were greatly reduced. The *National Assistance Act (1948)* gave financial help to those not covered by the National Insurance Act and introduced old people's homes. In the same year the *Children's Act* provided child care officers and the Youth Employment Service. The *Industrial Injuries Act (1946)* set up tribunals to decide the amount of benefit to be paid for *injuries suffered at work*. The government encouraged *council house building*; by 1951 over 800,000 had been completed, though this was well below target (it was estimated in 1945 that there was a shortage of at least a million houses). *New towns* such as Stevenage, Harlow and Hatfield were built and tenants protected by rent controls.

(ii) *Nationalisation* of the Bank of England, the coal industry, civil aviation, railways, canals, road haulage, gas and electricity, and iron and steel. The justification for this was that government control would lead to *more efficient planning* and *better conditions for the workers*. Nationalisation has always been a controversial issue and not everybody – certainly not the Conservatives – would agree that it was an achievement. However, both the coal industry and the railways were inefficient and using obsolete equipment and needed the drastic modernisation that nationalisation was expected to provide. The National Coal Board increased output after the serious coal shortages of 1947, but results in some of the other industries were often disappointing because the government was unwilling to invest in them sufficiently.

(iii) *Help for agriculture*. It was important in a time of world food shortages that farmers produced the maximum amount possible. The government encouraged them by *price guarantees, subsidies* for modernisation, and the National Agricultural Advisory Service to provide the expertise. The results were highly successful: a 20 per cent increase in output between 1947 and 1952 and one of the most mechanised and efficient farming industries in the world.

(iv) *Miscellaneous reforms* included the repeal of Baldwin's 1927 Trade Disputes Act so that sympathetic strikes and the political levy were legal again (see Section 4.6(e)); the reduction of the delaying power of the House of Lords to one year; and the abolition of plural voting.

(v) *Recovery and full employment*. This was not achieved without setbacks such as the serious coal shortage during the bitterly cold winter of 1946–7 when over a million workers had to be laid off for a time, and the 1949 financial crisis which led to a *devaluation of the pound*. However, by the end of 1950 industry was booming: exports were 77 per cent above the 1938 level, the most spectacular success being in the car industry, with tractors, motorcycles, engineering, shipbuilding and chemicals not far behind. Success was achieved by a combination of factors: a high demand for goods at home to repair wartime shortages and damage; Marshall Aid; low interest rates to stimulate house-building and industrial expansion; strict government control of the economy. The Chancellor of the Exchequer, Sir Stafford Cripps, became famous for his 'austerity' policies; he restricted imports, persuaded the trade unions to accept a wage freeze (1948–50), continued wartime rationing and exhorted businessmen to export as much as possible. The devaluation of the pound from 4.03 to 2.80 American dollars made British exports cheaper abroad. Prospects for the future seemed bright in 1950 when there was a healthier balance of payments than at any time since 1918.

Behind the dramatic social revolution and the return to full employment, the government was plagued by the inter-linked problems of *inflation and the balance of payments*. From 1945–7, partly because of high interest payments on loans from the USA and the loss of many overseas assets during the war, the balance was *unfavourable*. The only way to earn was to increase exports which in 1945 stood at less than half the 1938 figure. But this concentration on exports meant a shortage of consumer goods for the home market and consequently rising prices and demands for wage increases which in a time of full employment and even labour shortage, employers were forced to meet. By 1950, as we have seen, the government seemed to have both problems under control, thanks to Cripps's wage freeze and the boom in exports after the devaluation; but this proved to be short-lived: in 1951 the balance was back in the red again mainly because of the Korean War which disrupted trade. As the USA frantically rearmed, prices of raw materials were forced up on the world market so that goods imported by Britain rose sharply in price; when Britain also decided to increase her rearmament programme this caused more economies and shortages. When the new Chancellor, Hugh Gaitskell, tried to save money by the introduction of *charges for spectacles and dental treatment*, Bevan resigned, along with Harold Wilson, the President of the Board of Trade, causing a serious split in the party. As Seaman says, 'the gains so painfully achieved between 1945 and 1950 were almost entirely eclipsed in the public mind, and the Conservatives were returned to power in 1951'. (Labour's overall majority had already been reduced to 7 in the election of 1950.)

(b) The Conservatives in power, 1951–64. The Conservatives won only a *small overall majority* of 15 in the 1951 General Election; this increased to over 60 in 1955 and to over 100 in 1959. Churchill was Prime Minister until his retirement shortly before the 1955 election, when he was replaced by Anthony Eden, who resigned through ill health in 1957 soon after the failure of his Suez policy (see Section 26.3). Harold Macmillan, one of the most progressive of the Conservatives and on the left wing of the party, was Prime Minister from 1957 until 1963 when Sir Alec Douglas-Home took over for the final year.

During the 1950s there was no dramatic change in policies, and the term '*Butskellism*' was coined from the surnames of R. A. Butler (Churchill's Chancellor of the Exchequer) and Hugh Gaitskell of the Labour Party, implying that there was *little to choose between the parties*. This was not strictly true, of course, but certainly the Conservatives accepted most of Labour's nationalisation (only iron and steel and road transport were denationalised), the welfare state and full employment.

There have been widely differing assessments of the 13 years of Tory rule. Some, pointing to the steady increase in living standards – the affluent society – claimed that they were successful years, an attitude summed up by one of the slogans during the 1959 election campaign – 'Life's better under the Conservatives'. Critics dismissed them as years of missed opportunities.

What did the Conservatives *achieve*?

(i) A *marked increase in living standards*. Between 1951 and 1963 wages rose by 72 per cent while prices rose only 45 per cent so that people could afford more consumer goods than ever before: the number of cars rose from under 3 million to 7.5 million and licensed televisions from 340,000 to almost 13 million. The rate of house-building increased from about 200,000 a year under Labour to around 320,000. In 1961 the working week was reduced from 48 to 42 hours.

(ii) Some *important extensions of the welfare state*, including the raising of benefits (though a 2*s* prescription charge was introduced) and the Mental Health Act (1959) by which mental illness was to be regarded no differently from physical illness.

(iii) *Help for agriculture* in the form of grants for improvements so that production continued to rise.

(iv) *Education expansion*, with about 6,000 new schools, 11 new universities and the introduction of colleges of advanced technology.

On what grounds could the Conservatives be *criticised*?

(i) Like Labour before them, the Conservatives did not find a permanent solution to the triple problems of *economic growth, inflation and the balance of payments*. Successive Chancellors tried different methods, sometimes completely reversing the policy of the previous Chancellor, an approach which came to be called '*stop–go*'. Under Butler, the economy was stable: exports boomed and the balance of payments was so favourable that he reduced income tax. By 1955, however, rising wages caused increased demand for goods at home (and therefore *inflation*) which was met by increasing imports; at the same time exports were adversely affected by strikes and consequently the balance of payments (with imports increasing while exports decreased) became *unfavourable*. Butler tried to reduce home demand by raising purchase tax and hire purchase deposits, while his successor, Macmillan, raised the bank rate to 5.5 per cent, making it more expensive to borrow cash. This is known as a *credit squeeze*: an attempt to reduce spending, thereby checking inflation and reducing imports in order to improve the balance of payments. This successfully produced a favourable balance for 1956. Unfortunately this was a 'stop' period after the 'go' of 1952–4; the difficulty with squeezes is that when credit is restricted, investment is reduced and industry cannot expand as rapidly as is necessary to sustain exports. Consequently governments dare not risk continuing 'stop' periods too long because this slows the economic growth rate and industry is in danger of stagnating. The dilemma facing the Tories (and all governments into the 1980s) was how to *maintain the economic growth rate* while at the same time *avoiding inflation and an unhealthy balance of payments*.

This is what led Thorneycroft (Chancellor 1957–8) to relax the squeeze and risk a 'go': taxes and credit restrictions were reduced and an *export boom* followed; but at the same time more cash was available to spend at home, causing an increase in demand and a consequent rise in *prices* and *imports*. Price rises led to wage demands and strikes, so that exports were soon affected and the balance of payments threatened again. The next Chancellor, Heathcoat Amory, tried to hold down wage increases and began a further credit squeeze in 1960, but this was not enough and his successor, Selwyn Lloyd, took tougher measures: he raised interest rates, put 10 per cent on purchase tax and raised import duties. He also tried a new idea – a *pay pause* which managed to hold wages of government employees down for almost a year, but was repeatedly breached after that; this was the first attempt at a definite pay policy: it failed. By the early 1960s the repeated 'stops' were holding back industrial expansion, and Britain was lagging behind her competitors in Europe.

The Conservatives realised that a new approach was needed: first, in 1961, they applied for membership of the EEC, but the application was turned down by France: later the same year they set up the National Economic Development Council (Neddy) followed by a National Incomes Commission (1962) to try and *plan the economy centrally*; finally the latest Tory Chancellor, Reginald Maudling, aimed for growth with another 'go' period: there were generous tax reductions and encouragement for investors.

(ii) The Conservatives can be criticised for *failing to join the EEC* at the outset in 1957, with unfortunate consequences for British production and exports (see Section 21.1(e)).

(iii) *Certain industries declined*, particularly textiles (hampered by competition from Portugal, Japan and India) and shipbuilding (competition from Japan); although other industries were expanding (aircraft, cars and chemicals), production costs were high which often made British goods expensive; in the face of some strong foreign competition, exports did not boom as much as they might; consequently there was a constant struggle to keep costs down. *Unemployment* became more of a problem in the 1960s especially in the north of England and in Scotland; early in 1963 there were almost 900,000 out of work.

(iv) A combination of failure to enter the EEC, economic stagnation and Maudling's final 'go' period which caused a sudden surge of imports, resulted in a *record balance of payments deficit* of £748 million for 1964.

In addition to its economic problems the government's reputation was somewhat tarnished after the War Minister, John Profumo had resigned following a scandal involving call girls and spies, and after a rather unseemly squabble over Macmillan's successor as prime Minister. Labour won a *small overall majority of four (October 1964)* and *Harold Wilson* became Prime Minister.

(c) Labour and Wilson (1964–70) faced a number of serious problems:

(i) Most pressing was the *balance of payments deficit* inherited from the Conservatives. James Callaghan, the Chancellor, borrowed heavily from the International Monetary Fund to replenish dwindling gold reserves (which were being used up to cover the deficit); in yet another squeeze he tried to cut spending by holding wages down and raising import duties. In *1967 the pound was devalued* from 2.80 to 2.40 dollars, making exports cheaper. The next Chancellor, Roy Jenkins, cut government spending by £750 million and tightened the wages policy. These drastic measures gradually worked and by 1969 there was a favourable balance of payments which lasted until 1972. However, by 1970 as the wages policy ended, wages began to rise steeply and so did prices.

(ii) *Unemployment*, which had fallen to under 400,000 in 1964, gradually rose to just over 600,000 in 1970, because of the contraction of coal-mining, shipbuilding, textiles and railways, and increasing automation in other industries.

(iii) The economy was damaged by large numbers of *strikes*, many of which seemed irresponsible; but when Wilson tried to introduce a bill to reform trade unions and curb unofficial strikes, both the Labour party and the TUC rejected it and it was dropped.

(iv) There was *serious violence in Northern Ireland* which had been comparatively calm since Lloyd George's 1922 settlement (see Section 11.2). However, the IRA (Irish Republican Army) would never rest until the North was united with Eire; this the Protestant-dominated Northern Ireland parliament would never agree to. Northern Ireland Catholics (about one-third of the population) were not allowed equal rights with the Protestants: they were discriminated against in jobs, housing and voting. In 1968 the Catholics began to campaign for full equality, but in October, Protestant extremists and the police (Royal Ulster Constabulary) took to breaking up civil rights marches, provoking retaliation by Catholics. By mid-1969 violence had reached alarming proportions and the province seemed on the verge of civil war. In August Wilson *sent troops into Belfast and Londonderry* to restrain the two factions and particularly to protect Catholic areas from attacks by Protestants. This calmed the situation briefly but not for long. (For the Rhodesian problem see Section 25.2.)

In spite of its preoccupation with the economy, the government found time for some *valuable reforms*: rent rebates, votes at 18, abolition of the death penalty, creation of the Ombudsman (to investigate complaints against inefficient administrators) and the Race Relations Act which made it illegal to discriminate in jobs, housing and other areas. More controversial were Labour's *renationalisation of the steel industry* and moves towards *comprehensive schools*.

(d) Heath and the Conservatives (1970–4). The Conservatives won the 1970 election with a *comfortable overall majority of 31* after Edward Heath had conducted a skilful campaign dwelling on Wilson's failures. Heath believed it was possible to escape from the 'stop-go' trap by reducing controls to a minimum and taking Britain into the EEC, which would stimulate British industry. *Very little went right* for the government:

(i) The Chancellor, Anthony Barber, began decisively, cutting taxes and reducing restrictions on hire purchase and credit; Britain's *entry into the EEC* was secured in 1972, Heath's greatest achievement. However, the hoped-for investment in industry failed to materialise and inflation became serious again, causing Heath to introduce a sharp about-turn: a three-stage policy holding wages down, and the return of controls; but there was no rapid improvement: 1973 showed a balance of payments deficit of over £900 million, unemployment hovering at over 850,000 and inflation still rising (partly because of a 70 per cent increase in oil prices imposed by Arab producers).

(ii) The Family Income Supplement and rate and fuel rebates helped poor families but were criticised by many Conservatives as being *too much like socialism.*

(iii) The *Industrial Relations Act (1971)* reformed trade union law in an attempt to cut down strikes and curb extremists. It set up a National Industrial Relations Court and introduced a 'cooling-off period' and ballots for strikes. Although in many quarters this was seen as a moderate and sensible measure, the unions opposed it bitterly with a wave of strikes, the most serious of which was the miners' strike (1974).

(iv) Disturbances continued in *Ireland* where the British army soon found itself in the impossible situation of trying to prevent Catholics and Protestants slaughtering each other while at the same time having to endure attacks from the IRA and another group calling itself the Provisional IRA. The government decided to *suspend the Northern Ireland parliament* and bring the province under direct rule from Westminster. When early in 1974 a new coalition government was set up in which the Catholics had more say than ever before, Protestant extremists organised massive strikes which quickly paralysed the country; after only a few weeks parliament was again suspended. Since then no government has been able to make any progress, and a solution seems as far away as ever.

(v) Heath decided to hold an *election (February 1974)* hoping to win public support for his stand against the miners' wage demands; but Labour with a programme of ending wage policies and reducing taxes won 301 seats against 296 Conservatives, 14 Liberals and 24 assorted Nationalists.

(e) What was wrong with the British economy? The simple fact was that British industry was *not producing enough goods for export at the right prices*; foreign competitors could produce more cheaply and secured a larger share of the market. The reasons for the inefficiency are a matter of controversy: management blamed unions for excessive wage demands;

unions blamed poor management and insufficient investment on new equipment and automation; management were criticised for being so greedy for profit that too little was ploughed back for development. It was also suggested that governments should have spent more on grants to develop industry and less on social services.

(f) Labour in power (1974–9). The new government did nothing to remedy the basic weakness of the economy, and after Wilson allowed the miners' full claim, a rash of other wage increases followed. By 1976 inflation was increasing at a rate of over *20 per cent* a year and 1.3 million people were out of work; the high cost of oil imports contributed to the enormous balance of payments deficit. Labour's main weapon for controlling inflation was to persuade the unions to co-operate and accept limited wage increases; this was known as the '*social contract*'. Under Callaghan, who became Prime Minister in 1976 after Wilson's retirement, Labour's policies, plus the increasing *output of oil from British fields in the North Sea*, began to have an impact, and by the end of 1978 the annual rate of inflation had fallen below 10 per cent. Unfortunately for Callaghan, the unions at this point refused to accept his proposal to extend the social contract for a further period by limiting wage increases to 5 per cent, and a number of damaging strikes followed in what became known as the 'winter of discontent'. In the election of May 1979 the Conservatives won an *overall majority of 43* and their new leader, *Margaret Thatcher*, became Britain's *first woman Prime Minister*.

(g) The first Thatcher government (1979–83). This was the first government since the war to try a *completely new remedy* for Britain's economic ills – the *monetarist approach*. Monetarists believe in keeping a tight hold on the money supply via the Bank of England by maintaining high rates of interest, so that firms and individuals are forced to reduce borrowing. Management must therefore keep costs down by laying off workers and streamlining operations for greater efficiency. There would be no government grants to prop up inefficient firms, so that only those which made themselves *competitive* would survice. Such a policy meant a high unemployment level, but its supporters claimed that it was like a major surgical operation – drastic but effective in the long run: British industry, though much contracted, would be efficient and competitive overseas. With purchasing power reduced as unemployment rose, inflation would be controlled and wage demands moderated accordingly. Another side effect, particularly attractive to the Conservatives, was that *trade unions would be less powerful*: workers, thankful to be in a job, would be less willing to strike.

Thatcher and her Chancellor, Howe, stuck resolutely to this policy with a cripplingly high minimum lending rate of 17 per cent early in 1980 (though this was reduced to 14 per cent by the end of the year) and massive spending cuts affecting housing, education and transport. They confidently predicted that by the end of 1981, the rate of inflation, which had soared to 20 per cent again early in 1980, would be down to 10 per cent and still falling. Their predictions were correct and by June 1983 the inflation rate was down to only 4 per cent. However, the disturbing feature was that monetarism, together with a deepening world recession, sent unemployment soaring past the 3 million mark by the autumn of 1981, the highest level since the great depression of the early 1930s. Many small companies went *bankrupt* and in the summer of 1981 there were riots in London, Liverpool and Manchester. The government was becoming unpopular and lost three by-elections to the newly formed Liberal–SDP Alliance (the social Democrat Party was formed in March 1981).

The *Falklands War (April–June 1982)* transformed the situation. When *Argentinian forces invaded the islands* (2 April) and ignored a UN demand for their withdrawal, Thatcher acted decisively, sending a British task force of some 70 ships and 6000 troops to recapture the islands. During the three weeks it took the force to sail the 8000 miles to the South Atlantic, frantic attempts were made by the USA and the UN to reach a negotiated settlement. However, the British rejected South American charges of colonialism, pointing out that the islanders wished to remain associated with Britain. The Argentinians, in possession of the islands, naturally refused to budge, and the British refused to negotiate unless Argentinian forces were removed. The task force arrived in Falklands waters towards the end of April. The *General Belgrano*, an elderly Argentinian cruiser carrying troops and deadly Exocet missiles, was sunk by a British nuclear submarine, and though *HMS Sheffield* was badly damaged by an Exocet missile, successful British landings were made and *Port Stanley* captured. Argentinian troops surrendered on *14 June* and the recapture of the islands was complete. The war brought forth an outburst of patriotism in Britain such as had not been seen since the Second World War, and the government's waning popularity revived.

The *election of June 1983*. With over three million out of work, Labour ought to have had a good chance of winning; but the 'Falklands factor' was probably the main reason for the *overwhelming Conservative victory* – 397 seats against 209 Labour, 23 for the Alliance and 21 others. The Conservatives also attracted votes because of their success in bringing the inflation rate down to four per cent. The *Employment Act* of October 1982 was popular with critics of the unions: it restricted the operation of closed shops and made trade unions more accountable for their actions; compensation was to be paid to workers who had been dismissed from their jobs for non-membership of a union. Labour's election campaign with its emphasis on unilateral nuclear disarmament and withdrawal from the EEC, failed to arouse sufficient enthusiasm.

(h) The second Thatcher government (1983–7)

Fortified by its huge Commons majority, the government pushed confidently ahead with its programme against a background of continuing monetarism. Its record contained some *major achievements*, though all were highly controversial:

(i) *Privatisation* was strongly advocated on the grounds that it would increase efficiency, encourage more concern for the customer, and enable the general public and employees to become shareholders. Also attractive to the government were the proceeds – £2500 million in 1985–6 and about £4700 million in each of the next three years. By January 1987 no fewer than 14 major companies (including British Aerospace, British Petroleum, British Telecom, Britoil, the Trustee Savings Bank and British Gas) had been sold off to private ownership. This was bitterly attacked by the Labour Party with its belief in nationalisation, and even some Conservatives were uneasy: Lord Stockton (formerly Harold Macmillan) called it 'selling off the family silver'.

(ii) *Strict maintenance of law and order and public security.* The government took a tough line with the trade unions, banning union membership at Government Communications Headquarters (GCHQ) and refusing to compromise in a year-long mineworkers' strike (February 1984–March 1985). This was a bitter struggle which ended in total failure for the miners and seemed to exacerbate the divisions in society. The army and police were used several times to remove peace campaigners from Greenham Common and Molesworth RAF bases; they were protesting against American Cruise missiles being deployed there. The BBC was continually attacked for allegedly being biased against the government; the BBC offices in Glasgow were raided and films said to threaten Britain's security were seized (February 1987). Among them was a programme about Zircon, a new spy satellite for eavesdropping on the Russians.

(iii) *Government and local authority spending was closely controlled.* Top-spending local authorities had a maximum rate placed on them (*rate-capping,*) to force them to economise (February 1986) and the Greater London Council (GLC) and the six other Metropolitan County Councils were abolished on the grounds that they were a costly and unnecessary layer of local government.

(iv) *The Anglo-Irish Agreement (November 1985)* was a new attempt to secure peace and stability in Northern Ireland: any change in the status of the province would only come about with the consent of a majority of the people of Northern Ireland; Britain and Eire would confer regularly about the situation in Northern Ireland and about relations between the two parts of the island. This was seen by many as a statesman-like initiative by Mrs Thatcher and Dr Garret Fitzgerald, the Irish Prime Minister, coming as it did in the wake of IRA outrages such as the bomb explosion which killed five people at the Brighton hotel where Thatcher and most of her cabinet were staying during the Conservative Party conference(*October 1984*). However, amid massive demonstrations, it was immediately denounced by the two main Unionist parties as a sell-out, while Charles Haughey (Irish opposition leader) called it 'a very severe blow to the concept of Irish unity'.

(v)   A *tough stance against international terrorism*. Britain broke off diplomatic relations with Libya after a policewoman was killed by shots fired from the Libyan People's Bureau in London (*April 1984*). In April 1986 Thatcher supported the USA's punitive action against Libya, allowing American F1-11 bombers to fly from bases in Britain to take part in air strikes on Tripoli and Benghazi which killed over a hundred people. The US claimed that they were aiming for 'terrorist-related targets', but the raids aroused world-wide condemnation for causing the deaths of so many innocent civilians. Britain also broke off relations with Syria (October 1986) whose government was allegedly involved in an attempt to blow up a jumbo jet at Heathrow Airport.

(vi) An *agreement was signed with China (1984)* by which Britain promised to *hand over Hong Kong* in *1997* and the Chinese in return offered safeguards, including maintaining the existing economic and social structure for at least 50 years.

Meanwhile the government came under increasing fire from its critics. Unemployment stubbornly refused to come down below 3 million and it seemed that Britain was rapidly becoming 'two nations'. The government's own statistics revealed (1987) that 94 per cent of job losses since the Conservatives took office were in the North while the South was largely thriving and prosperous. Since 1979 there had been a 28 per cent drop in manufacturing and construction jobs, which compared badly with an 8 per cent drop in Germany, a 2 per cent drop in the USA and a 5 per cent increase in Japan. *Inner cities* were neglected and there was a rundown in public services, especially the health service, where in 1986–7 a chronic shortage of beds caused many patients to be turned away and lengthened waiting-lists for operations. In addition the government suffered a number of embarrassments and scandals. A public conflict of attitude between two cabinet ministers (Heseltine and Brittan) over the future of the ailing *Westland Helicopter Co.*, led to the resignation of both and called into question Thatcher's integrity and political judgement (*January 1986*). Early in 1987 there was a scandal on the Stock Exchange when it emerged that some directors of the Guinness Co. had illegally bolstered the price of their own shares during their battle to take over the Distillers' Co.

    A measure of their unpopularity was the fact that the Conservatives lost four by-elections (three to the Alliance and one to Labour) between June 1984 and May 1986, reducing their overall majority from 144 to 136. However, as the next election approached, the Chancellor, Nigel Lawson, suddenly announced extra spending of £7.5 billion for 1987 on education, health and social services. This seemed to be a U-turn away from monetarism, though the government did not admit it. With the inflation rate well under control at only 3 per cent and the promise of good times ahead, opinion polls showed a revival in the Conservatives' popularity.

In the *general election of June 1987 the Conservatives won a third successive victory*, almost as sweeping as the one in 1983. The Conservatives took 380 seats, Labour 229 and the Alliance 22, a Conservative overall majority of 102. The relatively prosperous South and Midlands were apparently well satisfied with Tory rule and were confident that the economic recovery would continue; Labour defence and economic policies seemed to put many voters off. It was clearly *a remarkable achievement by Mrs Thatcher* to lead her party to three successive election victories and in January 1988 she broke Asquith's record as the longest serving British Prime Minister this century. There were two other striking points about the 1987 election: the Conservatives did badly in Scotland, winning only 10 out of the 72 seats, and further entrenching the North–South divide; and over the country as a whole, almost three people in five voted against the Conservatives. Under the existing electoral system, with Labour and Alliance candidates splitting the anti-Tory vote it was difficult to foresee how the Conservatives could ever lose an election.

21.3 FRANCE

As soon as France was liberated in 1944, *General de Gaulle* took over the government. The old constitution, which had produced weak government for so many years, was scrapped, a new one produced and the title changed to the Fourth Republic. De Gaulle resigned in disgust because he felt the president ought to have more power. Though it was born out of the euphoria of liberation the Fourth Republic found its support gradually dwindling until its fortunes reached rock bottom in 1958.

(a) Why did the Fourth Republic lose popularity?

(i) There was constant *inflation* which produced demands for wage increases and in 1947 widespread *strikes*. In fact the economy recovered well from the war, because of Marshall Aid and some efficient government planning (largely the work of Jean Monnet). By 1954 industrial production was 50 per cent higher than in 1938 and the steel industry was now fully modernised. The government had the vision to take *France in the EEC in 1957*. However agriculture still stagnated, and as inflation continued, there was unrest among the small craftsmen, employers, peasants and shopkeepers who did not seem to be sharing in the general progress.

(ii) Governments were still weak since the new constitution retained *proportional representation* and gave the president no more power. There were five major parties; from left to right they were: communists, socialists, radicals, *Mouvement Républicain Populaire* (MRP) – a new party which stood for Christian democratic principles – and de Gaulle's party, *Rassemblement du*

Peuple Français (RPF). The communists and the RPF were hostile to the republic; consequently governments were coalitions made up of ministers from the other three parties; they were constantly changing: in the 12 years which the Fourth Republic lasted there were *25 different governments* which were mostly too weak to rule effectively. It was not a system that inspired confidence, and its ineptness was demonstrated by a number of disasters.

(iii) In the eight-year struggle to hold on to Indo-China the government finally had to admit defeat after the *military disaster at Dien Bien Phu (1954)* (see Section 17.4(a)). Soon afterwards nationalist agitation caused *independence to be given to Tunisia and Morocco.*

(iv) *French intervention in Suez (1956)* turned out to be a fiasco (see Section 26.3).

(v) Troubles in *Algeria* reached a climax in *1958* and the crisis brought de Gaulle back to power. The problem was similar to that in Tunisia and Morocco – the nationalists wanted independence from France and began anti-French riots as early as 1945. By 1954 the National Liberation Front (FLN) led by Ben Bella was ready for a full-scale *military revolt.* Many French people were prepared to give the Algerians independence, but the situation was complicated by the fact that over a million French settlers lived in Algeria who were flatly opposed to any such move. In addition the 400,000 French troops fighting the rebels were determined not to suffer another Dien Bien Phu. When in 1958 it was suspected that the government was about to give way, French troops and civilians occupied government buildings in Algiers in open revolt against the politicians in Paris and demanded that de Gaulle be called in to head a new government. They were convinced that the general, a great patriot, would never agree to Algerian independence. Civil war seemed imminent; the government could see no way out of the deadlock and consequently resigned. President Coty called upon de Gaulle who agreed to become Prime Minister on condition that he could draw up a new constitution. This was *in effect the end of the Fourth Republic.*

De Gaulle soon produced his new constitution (approved in a referendum by almost 80 per cent of the electorate) and was elected *President of the Fifth Republic (December 1958)*, a position he held until his resignation in April 1969.

(b) What were de Gaulle's achievements?

(i) The new constitution was a marked improvement on the previous one since it allowed *strong and decisive government* for the first time since 1871. It transferred the power to make laws from parliament to the *President* who could choose his own Prime Minister and other ministers. The Assembly and the Senate had to agree to laws before they could be carried out, but the President, elected by a national referendum for *seven years*, could *dissolve the Assembly*. He controlled foreign policy and defence and could hold referendums on important questions, thus reducing the influence of parliament. Proportional representation was replaced by single member constituencies in which the winning candidate had to poll half the votes; if he failed, a second ballot was held for which the candidates with fewest votes in the first ballot dropped out, so that votes would switch to one of the other candidates. Although this system worked against left-wing parties and enabled the Gaullists to remain the largest party in the Assembly, it provided France with a period of *much-needed stability*.

(ii) He *settled the Algerian problem*, though not in the way the Europeans and the French army in Algeria had expected. Vicious fighting continued with the FLN and the army both committing atrocities; de Gaulle soon realised that *military victory was out of the question* and opened negotiations with the FLN, offering them independence. When some French generals defied him and seized power in Algeria, de Gaulle, appearing on television in his general's uniform, denounced them, and the rebellion collapsed. Public opinion in France was now sick of the war and when it was agreed (*March 1962*) that Algeria *should become independent*, the decision was approved by a 90 per cent vote in a referendum. The Algerian settlement was probably de Gaulle's greatest achievement after 1945, but it was bitterly resented by the French settlers who felt that the general had betrayed them.

(iii) The *economy continued to expand steadily* between 1958 and 1963 with many new industries established and moves made to modernise agriculture. However, this was due as much to the planning that had taken place under the Fourth Republic as it was to de Gaulle's efforts, and also to France's membership of the EEC.

De Gaulle was at the height of his popularity in 1962 at the end of the Algerian war. By 1965 his prestige was already waning and in that year, although he defeated the socialist *François Mitterrand* in the presidential election, the margin was much smaller than in 1958 – 54 per cent to 46 per cent. This trend continued until in 1969 he *failed to win a referendum and retired into private life*.

(c) Why did de Gaulle lose power?

(i) His *foreign policy aroused criticism*. In his quest to make France a great power again, he pursued an anti-American, anti-NATO and anti-British line, twice vetoing British entry into the EEC. In 1966 he withdrew France from NATO and insisted on having his own nuclear deterrent. Many people were horrified at the vast expense of this policy and realised that it was absurd of France to be developing her defences *in isolation* instead of co-operating with other states in western Europe, especially as France's real weakness had been shown up in Indo-China and Algeria. Moreover his attitude towards the EEC held up its development by a decade (see Section 21.2(f)) and (g)).

(ii) By 1968, *all was not well with the economy*: coal, steel and railways seemed to have expanded too far and were showing deficits; about half a million were unemployed and inflation was increasing more rapidly than in the other EEC countries.

(iii) *Pressing social problems* had been ignored by de Gaulle: there was a serious housing shortage making it almost impossible for young married couples to find homes; very few hospitals and schools had been built.

(iv) In February 1968 there was a *wave of student strikes and demonstrations*; students were objecting to poor accommodation, irrelevancy of courses and the authoritarian and undemocratic nature of the regime. In May, ten million workers joined the students and there seemed a real danger of *revolution* developing. However, de Gaulle was able to weather the storm by promises of wage increases and shorter hours and by playing on the danger of a communist takeover if he fell.

(v) The economic problems and inflation still remained and de Gaulle tried to *revive his prestige* by creating regional assemblies and abolishing the senate. In April 1969 he held a referendum seeking approval of the changes and indicated that he would treat the result as a vote of confidence. Nearly 11 million voted in favour but 12.5 million voted against; consequently the general resigned.

He *died in 1970*, a controversial figure who, as Walter Lacqueur says, 'outlasted his usefulness. By clinging to power too long, he put in question the achievements of the earlier years of his rule.'

(d) After de Gaulle's departure the Fifth Republic continued to provide *stable government* under the next two Presidents. Pompidou, though a Gaullist, was more realistic and more moderate than the general, approving of British entry to the EEC, devaluing the franc, paying more attention to social reform and improving relations with the USA. After Pompidou's death in 1974, Giscard d'Estaing (who called himself a liberal rather than a Gaullist) was very narrowly elected President. Like Pompidou he realised the importance of keeping working-class support and sought this by lowering the voting age to 18 and increasing worker participation in industry. By 1980 France, like the rest of western Europe, was suffering from the *world recession*; there was growing impatience with Giscard's autocratic style of government and the blatant appointment of his supporters as prefects, and in the police and in the media. In May 1981 François Mitterrand, the socialist leader, was elected president in the first left-wing victory since 1956.

(e) The Mitterrand era (1981–)

(i)   Mitterrand and his socialist Prime Minister *Pierre Mauroy* (whose cabinet included some *communists*) did not have an altogether happy time. They soon found themselves struggling against rising unemployment, a declining franc and inflation which reached 14 per cent by June 1982. They were forced to take *unpopular measures* – a four-month wages and prices freeze, followed by increased social service contributions, train fares, and fuel, alcohol and tobacco prices. The communists disapproved of these austerity measures and grumbled at the government's failure to keep its election promises: it had not reduced unemployment, it had not introduced proportional representation, it had not abolished private Roman Catholic schools and it had allowed the gap between rich and poor to widen. When Mauroy resigned (*July 1984*), to be replaced by the 37-year-old *Laurent Fabius*, the communists declined to join his cabinet.

(ii)   An important constitutional change introduced by the Fabius government was *proportional representation (1985)* in elections to the National Assembly and regional councils. The number of seats was increased from 491 to 577, allowing one deputy for 108,000 people. The first election fought under the new system (*March 1986*) was a disappointment for the socialists. Though still the largest single party with 207 seats, they had *lost their overall majority*, and their former allies, the communists, emerged with only 35 seats. On the other hand, the alliance of the Gaullist RPR (Rally for the Republic) and the Centrist UDF (Union for French Democracy) won 277 and the far right National Front 35. The presence of 14 centre and right-wing independents meant that the Gaullist–UDF alliance could always command a small majority. Fabius resigned and *Jacques Chirac*, Gaullist leader and since 1977 mayor of Paris, became Prime Minister. Referred to as 'co-habitation', this was an unprecedented situation: a *socialist president* who still had two years of his seven year term left, had to work with a *conservative prime minister and cabinet*. It was a situation which many thought would prove unworkable.

(iii)   The alliance won the election partly because the *socialists were divided about* how to cope with France's problems and over the merits of proportional representation. The popular Agriculture Minister, Michel Rocard, resigned, complaining that it 'threatened firm and efficient government'. In contrast the alliance had what seemed to be a decisive 'shock programme to re-launch the economy'. This included the reprivatisation of banks and large companies, reduction in maximum rate of income tax, and increased defence spending.

(iv)   The *Chirac government was soon involved in controversy*. Massive student protest demonstrations reminiscent of 1968 soon forced Chirac to drop plans to increase the universities' control over student entry and courses. Faced by a railway strike at the end of

1986, he dropped a plan to promote railwaymen on merit rather than seniority. When he attempted to impose a 2 per cent limit on public sector pay rises, the strike escalated to include the Paris underground, seamen and some miners. By February 1987 he had managed to outrage the primary school teaching profession against proposed increases in the powers of headmasters. It was no real surprise when, in May 1988, Mitterrand was re-elected as President for a further seven years, scoring a comfortable victory over Chirac who immediately resigned as Prime Minister.

21.4 WEST GERMANY

(a) Adenauer in charge (1949–63)

The new *German Federal Republic* came into being in *1949* (see Section (16.2(h) and (j)) with the 73-year-old *Konrad Adenauer* as Chancellor. He had acquired his reputation as a successful *mayor of Cologne* (1919–33) who had been dismissed for opposing Hitler. Under Adenauer's leadership West Germany recovered quickly from the ruin and destruction of the war and was soon enjoying remarkable prosperity. Reasons for the German *success* were:

(i) There was *stable government* because although the new constitution was similar to that of the Weimar Republic, there was one crucial difference: a party had to receive *5 per cent of the total votes* before it could be represented in the *Bundestag* (the lower

illus 21.1 *Konrad Adenauer and Charles de Gaulle, 1963*

house). Thus the trend was towards a *two-party system*: Christian Democrats (CDU – Adenauer's conservative party) and Social Democrats (SPD) with the liberals (FDP) a poor third. The CDU was the dominant party for the first 20 years and Adenauer brought sanity and tranquillity back to German life.

(ii) Guided by the Minister of Economics, Ludwig Erhard, the country enjoyed an 'economic miracle'. It was achieved by a *high rate of investment in new plant and equipment* and the *ploughing of profits back into industry* rather than distributing them as higher dividends or higher wages (which happened in Britain). Through *fear of inflation, unions did not press high wage demands* and therefore *prices were kept under control.* Industrial recovery was so complete that by 1960 West Germany was producing 50 per cent more steel than the united Germany in 1938. All classes enjoyed prosperity; pensions and children's allowances were geared to the cost of living and 10 million new dwellings had been provided.

(iii) Adenauer's *foreign policies were successful and popular* on the whole. The *occupation by foreign troops ended in 1952* and West Germany was recognised as an equal member of *NATO (1955)*. He believed strongly in European unity and took Germany into the *European Coal and Steel Community* and the *EEC*, providing industry with new opportunities for expansion. He worked hard for reconciliation with France and signed a treaty of co-operation with her (January 1963).

During the early 1960s Adenauer was increasingly criticised for his authoritarian methods, his refusal to recognise East Germany and his apparent determination to hang on to power at all costs. In addition there were the first signs of the end of the economic boom. At last he was manoeuvred into retiring at the age of 87.

(b) Erhard (of the CDU) led a coalition with the liberals; problems occurred in 1965 as *domestic orders began to level out and unemployment appeared.* Although this was through no fault of Erhard's, the liberals withdrew support and he was forced to resign (1966). He was replaced by another CDU member, *Kurt Kiesinger*, who headed a coalition, this time with the Social Democrats. This would have been out of the question a few years earlier, but in 1959 the SPD had abandoned its Marxist outlook and was attracting middle-class support. The coalition soon dealt with unemployment, but by *1969* other problems were *causing concern*: *inflation* was developing because full employment caused demand for goods to exceed the capacity of industry to meet it; there were outbursts of *violence* from *left-wing students* protesting against their lack of say in the running of universities, against the materialistic society and against the Germany connection with the *Americans* who were felt to have been discredited by their involvement in Vietnam; a new *extreme right-wing party*, the National Democrats (NDP), also caused anxiety.

(c) The Social Democrats in power (1969–82)

The SPD narrowly defeated the CDU in the 1969 elections but needed liberal support for a majority. *Willi Brandt*, an efficient administrator and mayor of West Berlin, became Chancellor; he introduced several new policies:

(i) He worked for friendly relations with eastern Europe, including East Germany, a policy known as *Ostpolitik*. Treaties were signed with Russia and Poland (1970) renouncing the use of force and recognising Polish possession of the former German lands east of the Oder–Neisse line (see Section 16.2(a) and (b)). In 1971 agreement was reached with Russia that access to Berlin was still a four-power responsibility and that West Berliners could visit relatives over in the east. These were courageous and statesman-like policies which aimed, in the long run, at the reunification of Germany. In the short term, *Ostpolitik* contributed towards *détente* and prepared the way for the Helsinki Agreement of 1975 (see Section 17.6(b)).

(ii) He tried to *control inflation* by revaluing the mark upwards, thereby making more goods available through cheaper imports. This had a fair amount of success but was risky because it made German exports, already expensive because of the strong mark, even more so.

Brandt resigned unexpectedly in 1974 after one of his aides confessed to being an East German spy. In fact Brandt need not have resigned on account of this, since his personal prestige remained high. It is believed that his real motive was his disappointment at the bitter criticism aroused at home by his *Ostpolitik*, his failure to secure educational reforms and the worsening economy.

The SPD remained in power with *Helmut Schmidt* as Chancellor. His main problem was a *sudden surge in unemployment* which reached one million in 1975. Schmidt acted decisively, giving government aid to new firms, and successfully encouraging modest wage increases. Unemployment gradually fell and inflation was kept at no more than 6 per cent. As West Germany moved into the 1980s, she suffered increasingly from the world recession, though less severely than the other states of western Europe. Even so there was an *adverse balance of payments in 1980*, for almost the first time since the Federal Republic's formation. The *Ostpolitik* received a setback late in 1980 when the East Germans suddenly became much less co-operative because of the difficult situation in Poland (see Section 20.2(b)). However, none of these problems was serious enough to prevent Schmidt from being convincingly re-elected as Chancellor in October 1980.

But within a few months, unemployment had soared to around 2 million, and like his fellow socialists in France, Schmidt found himself having to take *unpopular measures*: an increase in VAT and a rise in taxes on undeveloped land, in order to finance youth training schemes and environmental improvements and to subsidise firms so that they could increase exports and create more jobs. The socialists clashed with their coalition partners, the liberals (FDP) over the budget for 1982–3: the SPD favoured *increased spending* to stimulate the economy whereas the more cautious liberals who felt that the budget deficit was already too large, preferred to keep *spending at the same level*. Schmidt failed to win a vote of confidence in the *Bundestag* (lower house of parliament) and resigned (*October 1982*). A new right-wing coalition of Christian Democrats (CDU) and Bavarian Christian Social Union (CSU) was formed with FDP support and the 52-year-old *Helmut Kohl*, the CDU leader, became Chancellor.

(d) Kohl and conservative government (1982–)

Chancellor Kohl soon won a comfortable election victory (*March 1983*) with 244 seats for his CDU/CSU alliance and 34 for his new coalition partners the FDP (which lost ground because many people thought its switch of allegiance the previous October was somewhat treacherous), while the SPD could muster only 193. A significant development was the election of 27 members of the *Green party* who were dedicated to protecting the environment, the first time they had gained representation. The government introduced no dramatic policy changes; Kohl's style, as one observer put it, was 'based on inertia: non-intervention and immobility in the face of crises and criticisms'. Much the most exciting development was a series of scandals which kept the public enthralled throughout the period. Otto Lambsdorff, Kohl's liberal Minister of Economic Affairs, was charged with evading taxes and accepting bribes (December 1983) but did not resign until June 1984; this caused a *damaging loss of credibility* both for the FDP and Kohl's government. Soon afterwards, the speaker of the Bundestag resigned following accusations that he had accepted bribes, while 1985 saw a major espionage scandal when the senior assistant to Martin Bangemann (FDP leader and Kohl's new Economics Minister) turned out to be an East German spy. On top of this, *unemployment* reached 2.3 million and in the autumn of 1985 there were *mass protest rallies* in 17 cities.

Towards the end of 1985 the government's fortunes improved; statistics for 1985 showed a *healthy economic growth rate* of 2.5 per cent, and an *export boom*, much of it to the USA, resulted in a *trade surplus* of DM 73 million. The economic recovery continued during 1986 and lasted long enough to enable the *conservatives to win the election of January 1987*, though with a *reduced majority*. With only 233 seats as against 186 for the SPD, the CDU–CSU alliance was more than ever dependent on support from the FDP (46 seats). The Greens (ecology party) with 42 seats showed most gains, a clear reflection of the *growing concern over damage to the environment* by the Chernobyl nuclear accident, pollution of the Rhine, acid rain, and nuclear energy and weapons.

Early in 1988 it was obvious that *the economic boom was over*, as the USA, struggling with its own dollar crisis (see Section 22.1(h)(ix)), began to reduce its imports from Europe. Unemployment rose to 2.3 million again (about ten per cent of the labour force) and the coalition came under strain as disagreements emerged between Kohl's CDU and the FDP about how to deal with the worsening economic situation.

QUESTIONS

1. The United Kingdom and Europe
Study the Sources below, and then answer the questions that follow.

Source A
A press conference given by Charles de Gaulle, January 1963.

The Treaty signed in 1957 was concluded between six continental states which are economically speaking of the same nature. Moreover they are adjacent and an extension of each other through their communications. Then Britain presented her application to the EEC, after having earlier refused to participate as well as after creating a sort of free trade area of her own. England is insular, maritime, linked through its trade, markets and food supply to very diverse and often very distant countries. The nature and economic situation of England differ profoundly from those of the other states of the continent.

What is to be done so that Britain can join the Common Market? For example, what is to be done about the means by which the people of Britain are fed – the importation of food bought cheaply from the two Americas and the Old Dominions, while at the same time considerable subsidies are given to British farmers. These methods do not fit in with the system set up by the Six.

The question is to know if Britain can at present place itself with the Continent and like it, within a tariff that is truly common, give up all preference with regard to the Commonwealth, stop claiming that its agriculture be privileged, and cancel the commitments it has made with the countries that are part of its free trade area.

Source: G. M. D. Howat, *European History, 1789–1970* (Arnold, 1975, adapted extracts).

Source B
A British cartoon of 1963 (Fig. 21.1), from the *Daily Mirror* showing de Gaulle and Macmillan.

Source C

The decision to apply to 'enter Europe' had been taken slowly and, in fact, dishonestly, as far as Britain was concerned. The motives behind the application were not those of European unity, and Macmillan had no intention of making Britain a 'European power'. The real reason

Fig. 21.1

"VOILA, THIS IS WHAT YOU CALL 'HIT FOR SIX, NON' . . ."

behind the British application was the need to find a theatre in which Britain could act the leading role and thereby increase her reputation on the international stage. Once inside the Common Market, Macmillan planned to organise it into a sort of 'second pillar' of Western defence, and to lead it, in co-operation with America, as part of an extended Atlantic partnership.

Source: A. Sked and C. Cook, *Post-War Britain* (Penguin, 1979, adapted extracts).

(a) (i) What was the 'Treaty signed in 1957' referred to in Source A?
1,4(a)
   (ii) What did de Gaulle mean when he talked about 'the Six'?
1,4(a)
  (iii) What do the letters 'EEC' stand for?
1
  (iv) What factors does de Gaulle think unite the continental states?
4(a)

(b) (i) When and why had Britain 'earlier refused to participate' in the Common Market?
1,2
  (ii) What does de Gaulle mean when he says Britain had created 'a sort of free trade area of her own'?
1,4(a)

(c) (i) What reasons does de Gaulle give for refusing Britain entry to the Common Market?
4(a)
  (ii) What other reasons did de Gaulle have, besides those mentioned in the extract, for not wanting Britain in?
1,2

    (iii) According to Source A, what does de Gaulle think Britain must do before she could be allowed in? **4(a)**

(d) (i) Explain the point which the cartoonist in Fig. 21.1 is trying to put over (Source B). **4(a)**

    (ii) What impression do you think the cartoonist in Fig. 21.1 is trying to give of de Gaulle? **4(a,b)**

    (iii) What impression is he trying to give of Macmillan? **4(a,b)**

(e) (i) What evidence can you find in Source C to suggest that de Gaulle was perhaps right to be suspicious of the British application? **4(a,c)**

    (ii) Do you think the writers of Source C are supporters or critics of Macmillan? Explain your answer fully. **4(a,b)**

(f) Explain how and why Britain was able to enter the Common market in 1973. **1,2**

2. France and de Gaulle

Study the Sources below, and then answer the questions that follow.

Source A

Press statement by Charles de Gaulle, 15 May 1958.

When the state suffers humiliation and disgrace, this inevitably leads to the alienation of the peoples associated with it, to uneasiness in the fighting forces and to national dislocation. For 12 years, France, at grips with problems too difficult for the regime of the parties, has been entangled in this disastrous process. In the past, the country, from its very depth, trusted me to lead it in unity to its salvation. Today, in the face of the crises which mount before it, let the country know that I hold myself to assume the powers of the Republic.

Source: J. Joll, *Europe Since 1870* (Penguin, 1973, adapted extracts).

Source B

Broadcast by de Gaulle, 25 April 1969.

Frenchwomen, Frenchmen – You, to whom I have so often spoken for France, must know that your reply on Sunday is going to determine her destiny, because it is a question of bringing a very considerable change to the structure of our country. It is a great thing to bring about the rebirth of our old provinces, improved for modern times in the form of regions. It is a great thing to unite the Senate and the Economic and Social Council in a single assembly. If I am rejected by a majority of you, my present task as Chief of State would become impossible and I would immediately cease to exercise my functions. How, then, could the situation be mastered? There would be an inevitable return to the play of ambitions, illusions, plots and treasons, and national upheaval . . . On the contrary, if I receive proof of your confidence, I shall continue, with your support, to ensure that whatever happens, progress is maintained, order assured, the currency defended, independence upheld, peace safeguarded, and France respected . . . in what is going to become of France, never has the decision of each one of you weighed so heavily.

Source: E. M. D. Howat, *European History, 1789–1970* (Arnold, 1975, adapted extracts).

(a) **(i)** According to Source A, what was 'the disastrous process' which had brought France to a state of crisis? **4(a)**

    (ii) What 'humiliation and disgrace' had France suffered during the preceding 12 years? **1,2**

(b) **(i)** After he became President in 1958, what changes did de Gaulle make to the constitution of France? **1**

    (ii) Explain how de Gaulle was able to use his new powers to bring the Algerian war to an end. **1,2**

(c) **(i)** What had recently happened in France which caused de Gaulle to want to change 'the structure of our country' (referred to in Source B)? **1,2,4(a)**

    (ii) According to Source B, what changes was de Gaulle hoping to introduce? **4(a)**

    (iii) What methods does de Gaulle use in his speech to try and persuade people to vote for him? **4(a,b)**

    (iv) What disadvantages do you think these two Sources might have for the historian? **4(a,b)**

(d) **(i)** What was the result of the referendum held 'on Sunday' (Source B)? **1,4(a)**

    (ii) What did de Gaulle do after the result was announced? **1**

(e) Explain why a majority of the French people voted for de Gaulle in 1958 but not in 1969. **1,2**

(f) Summarise briefly what you think de Gaulle achieved for France between 1958 and 1969. **1,2**

3. West Germany

Study the Source below, and then answer the questions that follow.

During the formation of the West German state, the Social Democrats were out-manoeuvred by the Christian Democratic Union (CDU), whose leader Konrad Adenauer proved to be one of the shrewdest and toughest statesmen of post-war Europe. In the Weimar Republic he was Mayor of Cologne and a Catholic Centre Party politician who had been spoken of as a possible Chancellor in the late 1920s. He had again become Mayor of Cologne in 1945, but had soon been dismissed by the British military administration, allegedly for incompetence. This experience left him, perhaps justifiably, suspicious about British intentions and policies . . . Under Adenauer's government the Federal Republic made a rapid economic recovery and enjoyed a 14-year period of political stability.

Source: J. Joll, *Europe Since 1870* (Penguin, 1973, extract).

(a) **(i)** In what year was the new Federal German Republic formed?
1

    (ii) What political party did Adenauer belong to during the Weimar Republic (according to the extract)? 4(a)

    (iii) Why did he cease to be Mayor of Cologne in 1933? 1,2

    (iv) What party did he belong to after the Second World War?
4(a)

(b) **(i)** According to the extract, what was Adenauer's attitude towards the British; why did he feel this? 4(a)

    (ii) From the evidence of the extract, and your own knowledge, summarise briefly what was achieved during the 14 years of Adenauer's rule. 1,2,4(a)

    (iii) Explain why Adenauer fell from power in 1963. 1,2

(c) **(i)** What new policies were introduced by Willi Brandt and the SPD, 1969–74, and how successful were they? 1,2

    (ii) Why did Brandt resign in 1974? 1,2

(d) **(i)** What further changes of government and policies have taken place in West Germany since 1974? 1,2

    (ii) Why did Helmut Kohl and the CDU win the election of 1987?
1,2

4. It is October 1964, shortly before the British general election. Write two radio scripts:

    (a) one for a Conservative party political broadcast, setting out the achievements of Conservative governments from 1951 to 1964 and explaining why you think people ought to vote Conservative in the approaching election.

    (b) one for a Labour party political broadcast explaining your criticisms of the '13 wasted years' of Tory government and pointing out why people ought to vote Labour. 1,2,3

5. Imagine yourself to be an Algerian in 1962 when French rule came to an end. Write an account of your life and experiences in the previous ten years. 1,2,3

        [Southern Examining Group, Specimen Question.]

CHAPTER 22

THE USA, THE AMERICAS AND JAPAN AFTER 1945

SUMMARY OF EVENTS

The USA continued to be the world's *largest industrial power* and the world's *richest nation*. In spite of this, the country was racked by serious problems, outlined below, some of which still remain unsolved in the 1980s. There have been unhappy experiences such as the *assassination of President Kennedy (1963)*, the *failure of American policy* in *Vietnam*, and the *forced resignation of President Nixon (1974)* as a result of the *Watergate scandal*, all of which have shaken confidence in American society and values and in the American system. Both political parties have taken turns in power: Democrats (Truman 1945–53), Republicans (Eisenhower 1953–61), Democrats (Kennedy 1961–3 and Johnson 1963–9), Republicans (Nixon 1969–74 and Ford 1974–7), Democrats (Carter 1977–81) and Republicans again (Reagan 1981–9). *Latin America* was by comparison *underdeveloped* both industrially and agriculturally with massive problems of *poverty, illiteracy and unstable political systems*. Revolutions, military coups and assassinations were common and there had been no significant improvement by 1980 when dictators such as Pinochet (Chile) and Videla (Argentina) headed repressive military regimes. The great success story was provided by *Japan* which recovered remarkably swiftly from defeat in 1945 to become one of the world's *leading industrial and exporting powerss*. The USA provided economic aid for both Latin America and Japan, though, as we shall see, her motives were not entirely selfless.

22.1 THE UNITED STATES OF AMERICA

(a) What were the problems?

(i) The USA took upon herself the world role of *preventing the spread of communism*, causing her to become deeply involved in Europe, Korea, Vietnam, Latin America and Cuba (see Chapters 16 and 17).

(ii) At home, many Americans were obsessed with anti-communist feelings which sometimes bordered on hysteria. This was at its most serious from 1949–54 when Republican Senator *Joseph McCarthy* led a campaign to root out suspected communists; unfortunately the operation got out of hand: socialists, liberals, intellectuals, artists, pacifists and anyone whose views did not appear orthodox were liable to be hounded out of their jobs for 'un-American activities' and McCarthy became the most feared man in the country. Even after McCarthy overreached himself and was disgraced in 1954, right-wing extremism continued.

(iii) Ironically in the world's richest country, *poverty* remained a problem. Although the economy was on the whole a spectacular success story with industry flourishing and exports booming, there was constant *unemployment*: in 1960 the figure stood at 5.5 million, about 7 per cent of the labour force. In 1945, social welfare and pensions were still limited: there was, for example, *no national health system*. More people shared in the general prosperity than ever before but as late as 1966 it was calculated that 30 million Americans were living below the poverty line, a large proportion of them over 65.

(iv) The *colour issue* has passed through several phases: in 1977 there were 24 million Negroes in the USA, about 12 per cent of the population. After the war, Negroes were still being treated as second-class citizens, deprived of full civil rights, particularly in the southern states where they were not allowed to vote and were segregated into separate schools, buses, restaurants and other facilities. Although Negroes had the vote in the north and official segregation was much less, they were still under-privileged and discriminated against in employment. There was increasing pressure on the Federal government to grant full civil rights and *Martin Luther King*, a coloured Baptist Minister, emerged as the outstanding leader of the non-violent protest movement. He organised a boycott of buses in Montgomery, Alabama, so that *segregated seating* was abandoned (1955–6). However, progress was so painfully slow that in the mid-1960s some Negroes broke away from the non-violent protest movement to form *militant organisations* such as the Black Panthers, leading to riots, arson and murder. By the mid-1970s (when Negroes had full civil rights, at least by law) the race problem was largely one of poverty: there was still discrimination in jobs and housing which left millions of poor Negroes living in ghettoes in decaying city centres; at the same time thousands of Indians were living a meagre existence on reservations.

(v) In the late 1960s there was a strong reaction against American activities in Vietnam, the power of the state, poverty and what was seen as a moral decline in American society; this led to the *New Left* movement which did not fit in with either of the major parties and expressed itself in demonstrations and student sit-ins.

The following sections examine how the presidents dealt with whichever of these problems loomed largest during their years in office.

(b) Harry S. Truman (1945–53) (Democrat)

(i) Truman, a man of great courage and common sense, once compared by a reporter to a bantam-weight prize fighter, had to face the special problem of *returning the country to normal after the war*. This was achieved though not without difficulties: removal of wartime price controls caused inflation and strikes, and the Republicans won control of Congress in 1946.

(ii) Abroad he took up the *anti-communist crusade*: the Truman Doctrine and Marshall Aid (see Section 16.2(e)), help for the *Kuomintang* in China (see Section 17.1) and intervention in Korea (see Section 17.2).

(iii) In the fight against poverty his programme was known as the *Fair Deal*: a national health scheme, a higher minimum wage, slum clearance and full employment. However, the Republican majority in Congress threw out his proposals, and even passed over his veto the *Taft–Hartley Act (1947)* reducing trade union powers. The attitude of Congress gained Truman working-class support and enabled him to win the 1948 Presidential election together with a Democrat majority in Congress. Some of the Fair Deal then became law (extension of social security benefits and an increase in the minimum wage), but Congress still refused to pass his national health and old age pensions schemes, which was a bitter disappointment. Many southern Democrats voted against Truman because they disapproved of his support for Negro civil rights. Again Congress prevented progress in that direction except that *segregation in the army was ended (1948)*.

(iv) Truman had to face the full impact of McCarthyism, and although he did much to tone down the movement's hysteria, it was an embarrassment when Congress passed over the President's veto the *McCarran Act (1950)* which required organisations suspected of being communist to supply lists of members who were then likely to be dismissed from their jobs – a serious infringement of personal liberties. The pervading attitude which regarded *social welfare as socialism* – only one step removed from communism – helps to explain why much of the Fair Deal failed to pass Congress.

(c) Dwight D. Eisenhower (1953–61) (Republican)

Eisenhower was chosen as Republican candidate because of his popularity as a *victorious general*, although he had no previous party connections. He won a decisive victory, but disappointed the right-wing Republicans who expected him to reverse the New Deal and Fair Deal reforms; in fact he made no attempt to do so and in his affable way often seemed to have more in common with moderate Democrats (who supported his policies in Congress) than with conservative Republicans.

(i) Problems of foreign affairs were mostly handled by Secretary of State *John Foster Dulles*, who continued the *anti-communist stand*. The Korean War was brought to an end but the USA became involved in *Vietnam* with economic aid and military advisers (see Section 17.4(b)). After the death of Dulles (1959) Eisenhower was able to appear more moderate, favouring peaceful coexistence. Unfortunately his summit meeting with Khrushchev (1960) was a failure because of the *U-2 affair* (see Section 16.3(c)).

(ii) McCarthyism reached a climax soon after Eisenhower's election. Though McCarthy had probably won many votes for the Republicans among those who took his wild accusations seriously, he went too far when he began to accuse leading generals of communist sympathies. The Senate condemned him by a large majority and he foolishly attacked the President for supporting the Senate. After that his reputation was ruined; but at least nine million people had been 'investigated', thousands of innocent people had lost their jobs, and an atmosphere of *suspicion and insecurity* had been created.

(iii) For dealing with *poverty Eisenhower had no particular programme*, though some slight progress was made: insurance for long-term disabled, financial help towards medical bills for people over 65, federal cash for housing, and more spending on education to encourage study in science and mathematics (it was feared that Americans were falling behind the Russians who in 1957 launched the first satellite – Sputnik). Farmers faced problems during the 1950s because increased production kept agricultural prices and therefore incomes low. The government spent massive sums paying farmers to take land out of production, but this was not a success: farm incomes did not rise rapidly and poorer farmers hardly benefited at all; many of them sold up and moved into the cities. Much remained to be done, but the Republicans were totally against national schemes such as Truman's health service which smacked of socialism.

(iv) The government itself did a little to ease the *racial problem* by passing two *Civil Rights Acts*: one (*1957*) established a Commission to investigate the denial of voting rights to Negroes; the second (*1960*) provided help for Negroes to register as voters, but this was ineffective. More important than government action were a number of decisions by the *Supreme Court* which showed itself pro-Negro. It ruled that some Negroes must be included on juries, that separate schools for blacks and whites were illegal (1954) and that desegregation in education must take place (1955). The problem was that whites in the southern states refused to carry this out, and to his credit, Eisenhower sent federal troops to escort Negro children into the high school at Little Rock, Arkansas, where the governor had defied the Supreme Court order (1957). This was a symbolic victory, but southern whites continued to defy the law and by 1961 only a tiny fraction of schools and colleges in the south were desegrated. Negroes were already turning impatiently to more violent methods of protest.

(d) John F. Kennedy (1961–3) (Democrat)

Kennedy was the first *Roman Catholic* and, *at the age of 42, the youngest* President ever to be elected. He won because the Republicans were blamed for inflation, unemployment and for their unsatisfactory handling of foreign affairs (particularly the U-2 affair and the Paris summit), and because Kennedy ran a brilliant campaign accusing them of neglecting education and social services. He came over as elegant, articulate, witty and dynamic, and though his margin of victory was very slim, his election seemed to many to be the beginning of a *new era*. He faced enormous problems in foreign affairs, as well as poverty, unemployment and the civil rights situation at home; his policies showed great vigour and promise, but his presidency was tragically cut short after less than three years when he was *shot dead in Dallas, Texas*.

(i) Kennedy's handling of *foreign affairs met with mixed success*: he acted decisively over the Russian threat to Berlin (see Section 16.3(c)) and in the Cuban missile crisis in 1962 (see Section

illus 22.1 *The assassination of John F. Kennedy, 1963. Here the President slumps forward seconds after having been shot*

17.3(b)) but his attempt to keep American involvement in Vietnam to a minimum failed (see Section 17.4(c)). The setting up of the telephone link with Moscow and the *Partial Test Ban Treaty (1963)* were constructive achievements. He began a policy of economic co-operation with Latin America and founded the Peace Corps consisting of skilled volunteers who would work abroad bringing much-needed expertise to underdeveloped countries. His Trade Expansion Act reduced tariffs and encouraged international trade.

(ii) The poverty problem was pressing, with over 4.5 million unemployed when Kennedy took office. He had a *detailed programme*: medical payments for the poor and aged, more federal aid for education and housing, increased unemployment and social security benefits. 'We stand today on the edge of a New Frontier', he said, and implied that only when these reforms were introduced would the frontier be crossed and poverty eliminated. From this his policy became known as the *New Frontier*. Unfortunately for Kennedy, he had to face strong opposition from Congress where many Democrats as well as Republicans viewed his proposals as 'creeping socialism'; hardly a single one was passed without some watering down and many were *rejected altogether*. Congress would allow no extra federal cash for education and rejected his scheme to pay hospital bills for old people. His successes were an extension of social security benefits to each child whose father was unemployed; raising of the minimum wage from a dollar to 1.25 an hour; federal loans to enable people to buy houses; federal grants to the states enabling them to extend the period covered by unemployment benefit. Kennedy's overall achievement was limited: unemployment benefit was only enough for subsistence and even that for a limited period; unemployment still stood at 4.5 million in 1962, and soup kitchens had to be set up to feed poor families.

(iii) The New Frontier also included *full civil rights and equality for Negroes*; just how far there was still to go on this issue was summed up by Kennedy himself when he said (1963) that an American Negro had 'half as much chance of completing high school as a white, one-third as much chance of completing college, twice as much chance of becoming unemployed, one-seventh as much chance of earning 10,000 dollars a year, and a life expectancy which is seven years less'. Kennedy showed his intentions by appointing the *first Negro ambassador* and presenting a *Civil Rights Bill* to Congress; this was delayed at first by the conservative Congress but *passed in 1964* after a debate lasting 736 hours. It was a far-reaching measure, guaranteeing the vote for negroes and making racial discrimination in public facilities (such as hotels, restaurants and stores) and in jobs illegal. Again the act was not always carried out, especially in the south where Negroes were afraid to vote.

(e) Lyndon B. Johnson (1963–9) (Democrat)

Johnson, Kennedy's Vice-President, became President under the terms of the constitution on Kennedy's assassination. Coming from a humble background in Texas, Johnson was just as committed as Kennedy to social reform, and achieved enough in his first year to enable him to win a landslide victory in the 1964 election. In 1963, as well as facing a nation in deep shock, appalled at the growing violence, he inherited all Kennedy's problems.

(i) In Vietnam Johnson decided to commit the USA far more deeply than Kennedy had done and he began the *bombing of North Vietnamese cities* (see Section 17.4(c)). These policies brought no success and eventually ruined his popularity within America.

(ii) In 1964 Johnson's economic advisers fixed an annual income of 3000 dollars for a family of two or more as the *poverty line* and estimated that over 9 million families (30 million people, approaching 20 per cent of the population) were on or below the line. Many of them were Negroes, Puerto Ricans, Red Indians and Mexicans; the problems of poverty and racial discrimination were closely connected. Johnson announced that he wanted to move America towards the *Great Society* where there would be an end to poverty and racial injustice and 'abundance and liberty for all'. Many of his measures became law partly because after the 1964 elections the Democrats had a huge majority in Congress and partly because Johnson was more skilful and persuasive in handling Congress than Kennedy had been. The *Economic Opportunity Act (1964)* provided a number of schemes whereby young people from poor homes could receive job training and higher education. Other reforms were federal money for special education schemes in slum areas, including help in paying for books and transport; financial aid for clearing slums and rebuilding city areas; and the Appalachian Regional Development Act (1965) which created new jobs in one of the poorest regions. Perhaps his most important innovation was the Social Security Amendment Act (1965), also known as *Medicare*: this was a partial national health scheme, though it applied only to people over 65. This is an impressive list and yet the overall results were not as successful as Johnson would have hoped, for a number of reasons: it has been suggested that the whole programme was *under-financed* because of the enormous expenditure on the war in Vietnam; on the other hand there was a lack of public support because of the strong American tradition of *self-help*: it was up to the poor to help themselves and wrong to use the taxpayers' money on such a scheme which would only make the poor lazier; thus many state governments failed to take advantage of federal offers of help.

(iii) *Civil rights* were an important aspect of the Great Society. Johnson began by steering Kennedy's Civil Rights Bill through Congress, and followed it with the *Voting Rights Act (1965)* to try and make sure that Negroes exercised their right to vote, and another *Civil Rights Act (1968)* which made it illegal to discriminate in selling property or letting accommodation. Again the problem was to make sure that these acts were applied in the face of bitter white prejudice; much progress was made especially in the voting field (by 1975 there were 18 Negroes in Congress, 278 in various state governments, and 120 had been elected mayors). However, there can never be full equality until black poverty and the black ghettoes disappear.

(iv) In the mid-1960s *violence seemed to be getting out of hand*: riots in Negro ghettoes where the sense of injustice was strongest; student riots in the universities, protesting, among other things, at Vietnam; political assassinations (President Kennedy in 1963, Martin Luther King and Senator Robert Kennedy in 1968). Between 1960 and 1967 the number of violent crimes rose by 90 per cent. Johnson could only hope that his 'war on poverty' would gradually remove the causes of discontent; beyond that he had no answer to the problem. The general discontent and particularly the student protests about Vietnam (LBJ, LBJ, how many kids have you burnt today?') caused Johnson not to stand for re-election in November 1968, and explain why the *Republicans won, on a platform of restoring law and order*.

(f) Richard M. Nixon (1969–74) (Republican)
Nixon, who had been Eisenhower's Vice-President from 1956 and had narrowly lost to Kennedy in the 1960 election, faced an unenviable task: what to do about Vietnam, poverty, unemployment, violence and the general crisis of confidence that was afflicting America. How successful was he in dealing with these problems?

(i) *Overseas problems, particularly Vietnam, dominated his Presidency* (until 1973 when Watergate took over). After the Democrat-dominated Congress had refused to vote any further credits for the war, Nixon extricated the USA from Vietnam with a *negotiated peace* signed in *1973* (see Section 17.4(c)), to the vast relief of the American people who celebrated 'peace with honour'. Yet in April 1975 South Vietnam fell to the communists; the American struggle to prevent the spread of communism in South East Asia had ended in failure and her world reputation was somewhat tattered. Nixon was responsible for a radical and constructive change in foreign policy when he sought, with some success, to *improve America's relations with Russia and China* (see Section 17.6(b) and (c)).

(ii) *Unemployment* became a problem again with over four million out of work in 1971; their plight was worsened by rapidly rising prices. The Republicans were anxious to cut public expenditure and Nixon reduced spending on Johnson's poverty programme, and introduced a wages and prices freeze. However social security benefits were increased, Medicare extended to disabled people under 65, and a Council for Urban Affairs set up to try and deal with the problems of slums and ghettoes.

(iii) A *financial crisis and a balance of payments deficit* caused Nixon to impose a 10 per cent surcharge on imports and allow a devaluation of the dollar, so that the position improved temporarily.

(iv) *Violence* seemed to present *less of a problem* under Nixon partly because protesters could now see the approaching end of the controversial Vietnam involvement and because students were allowed some say in running their colleges and universities.

By the end of his first term Nixon's achievements seemed, if not spectacular, at least full of promise: he had brought the American people within sight of peace, he was following sensible policies of *détente* with the communist world and law and order had returned. The Americans had enjoyed a moment of glory by putting the *first men on the moon* (Neil Armstrong and Ed Aldrin, 20 July 1969). Nixon won the election of November 1972 overwhelmingly and in January 1973 was inaugurated for a second term. However, his second term was ruined by a new crisis.

(v) The *Watergate scandal* broke in *January 1973* when a number of men were charged with breaking into the Democratic Party offices in the Watergate Building, Washington, back in June 1972 during the presidential election campaign. They had *planted listening devices* and *photocopied important documents*. It turned out that the burglary had been organised by leading members of Nixon's staff, who were sent to gaol. Nixon insisted that he knew nothing about the affair, but suspicions mounted when he consistently refused to hand over tapes of discussions in the White House which, it was thought, would settle matters one way or the other. The President was widely accused of having deliberately 'covered up' for the culprits and he received a further blow when his Vice-President, Spiro Agnew, was forced to resign (December 1973) after facing criminal charges of bribery and corruption. (He was replaced by Gerald Ford, a little-known politician but one with an unblemished record.) Nixon was called on to resign but refused even when it was discovered that he had been guilty of tax evasion. He was threatened with *impeachment* (a formal accusation of his crimes before the Senate, which would then try him for the offences); to avoid this, he *resigned (August 1974)* and Ford became President. It was a sad end to a presidency which had shown positive achievements especially in foreign affairs, but the scandal shook people's faith in politicians and in a system which could allow such happenings. Ford won admiration for the way in which he restored dignity to American politics, but given recession, unemployment and inflation, it was no surprise when he *lost the 1976 election to the Democrat Carter.*

(g) Jimmy Carter (1977–81) (Democrat)

Carter's presidency was a disappointment. He was elected as an outsider (peanut farmer, ex-governor of Georgia, and a man of deep religious convictions), the newcomer to Washington who would restore the public's faith in politicians. He managed some significant achievements: he stopped giving automatic American aid to right-wing authoritarian governments merely in order to keep communism out; he co-operated with Britain to bring about black majority rule in Zimbabwe (see Section 25.2(d)); he signed a second Strategic Arms Limitation Treaty (*SALT II*) with the USSR; and he played a vital role in the *Camp David* talks bringing peace between Egypt and Israel (see Section 26.6).

Unfortunately his lack of experience of handling Congress meant that he had the same difficulties as Kennedy, and he failed to pilot the majority of his reforming programme into law. By 1980 the *world recession was biting deeply*, with factory closures, rising unemployment and oil shortages. Apart from Camp David, Democratic foreign policy seemed unimpressive; there was the American inability to take effective action against the Russian occupation of Afghanistan (see Section 17.6(e)). Just as frustrating was their failure to free a number of American hostages seized in Teheran by Iranian students (November 1979) and held for over a year. The Iranians were trying to force the American government to return the exiled Shah and his fortune, but stalemate persisted even after the Shah's death. A combination of these problems and frustrations resulted in a *decisive Republican victory in the election of November 1980*. Ironically the hostages were set free minutes after the inauguration of Carter's successor (January 1981).

(h) Ronald Reagan (1981–9) (Republican)

Reagan, a former film-star, quickly became the most popular president since the Second World War. He was a reassuring father-figure who won a reputation as 'The Great Communicator' because of his *straightforward and simple way of addressing the public*. Americans particularly admired his determination to stand no nonsense from the Soviets (as he called the USSR); he wanted to work for peaceful relations with them, but from a *position of strength*. He persuaded Congress to vote extra cash to build MX intercontinental ballistic missiles (May 1983) and deployed Cruise and Pershing missiles in Europe (December 1983). He intervened in *Central America*, sending financial and military aid to rebel groups in El Salvador and Nicaragua, whose governments he believed were communist-backed. He continued friendly relations with *China*, visiting Peking in April 1984, but did not meet any top Russian politicians until shortly before the presidential election of November 1984.

On the home front, there was a marked *economic recovery*, America enjoying the most sustained period of economic growth since 1945. Those in work were highly prosperous, but 'Reaganomics', as the president's policies became known, had similarities with Mrs Thatcher's monetarist policies in Britain – they benefited the wealthy but increased the tax burden on the poor and reduced social programmes to help them. According to congressional investigations, taxes took only 4 per cent of the income of the poorest families in 1978 but over 10 per cent in 1984. In April 1984, it was calculated that thanks to successive Reagan budgets since 1981, the poorest families had gained an average of 20 dollars a year from tax cuts but had lost 410 dollars a year in benefits. On the other hand, households with the highest incomes (over 80,000 dollars a year) had gained an average of 8,400 dollars from tax cuts and lost 130 dollars in benefits.

Reagan nevertheless retained his popularity with the vast majority of the American people and won a *sweeping victory in the presidential election (November 1984)* over his Democratic rival, Walter Mondale, who was portrayed by the media, probably unfairly, as an unexciting and old-fashioned politician with nothing new to offer. Reagan took 59 per cent of the popular vote; at 73, he was the oldest person ever to be president.

During his second term in office, everything seemed to go wrong for the president. He was dogged by economic problems, disasters, scandals and controversies:

(i) Congress became increasingly worried by the *rapidly growing federal budget deficit* and the Senate rejected Reagan's 1987 budget for increasing defence spending at a time when they felt it was vital to reduce the deficit. Senators also complained that the cash allowed for Medicare would be 5 per cent short of the amount needed to cover rising medical costs. In the end Reagan was forced to accept roughly an 8 per cent cut in defence spending and to spend more than he wanted on social services (February 1986).

(ii) 1986 was a disastrous year for *America's space programme*. The space shuttle, *Challenger*, exploded only seconds after lift-off, killing all seven crew members (January). A Titan rocket carrying secret military equipment exploded immediately after lift-off (April) and in May a Delta rocket failed, the third successive failure of a major space launch. This seemed likely to delay for many years Reagan's plan to develop a permanent orbital space station.

(iii) The *bombing of Libya (April 1986)* provoked a mixed reaction. Reagan was convinced that Libyan-backed terrorists were responsible for numerous outrages, including bomb attacks at Rome and Vienna airports in December 1985. After Libyan missile attacks on American aircraft, American F1-11 bombers attacked the Libyan cities of Tripoli and Benghazi (see Section 21.2(h)(v)), killing 100 civilians. While the attack was widely applauded in most circles in the USA, world opinion on the whole condemned it as an over-reaction.

(iv) American policy towards *South Africa* caused a row between president and Congress. Reagan wanted only limited sanctions but Congress was in favour of a much stronger package of sanctions to try to bring an end to apartheid, and they managed to overturn the president's veto (September 1986).

(v) The *Reykjavik meeting with Mr Gorbachev (October 1986)* did little to enhance Reagan's reputation. He appeared to have been outmanoeuvred by the Soviet leader. However, failure turned to success in December 1987 with the signing of the *INF Treaty* (see Section 17.8(b)).

(vi) There was a serious *depression in the agricultural mid-west*, which experienced falling prices, falling government subsidies and rising unemployment.

(vii) The growing dissatisfaction was reflected in the mid-term congressional elections (November 1986) when the Republicans lost many seats, leaving the Democrats with an even larger majority in the House of Representatives (260–175) and more important, now in *control of the Senate (54–45)*. With two years of his second term still to go, Reagan was a 'lame-duck' president – a Republican faced with a Democrat Congress. He would have the utmost difficulty in persuading Congress to vote him the cash for policies such as Star Wars (which most Democrats thought impossible) and aid for the Contra rebels in Nicaragua; and under the constitution, a two-thirds majority in both houses could over-rule the president's veto.

(viii) The *Irangate scandal* was the most damaging blow to the president. Towards the end of 1986, it emerged that the Americans had been *supplying arms secretly to Iran* in return for the release of hostages; however, Reagan had always insisted publicly that the USA would never negotiate with governments which condoned terrorism and the taking of hostages. Worse still, it turned out that *profits from the Iranian arms sales were being used to supply military aid to the Contra rebels in Nicaragua*; this was illegal since Congress had banned all military aid to the Contras from October 1984. The findings of the *Tower Commission (February 1987)* were that a group of Reagan's advisers, including his National Security Chief, Donald Regan, had been responsible, with help from the CIA, and that the president himself was only dimly aware of what was going on. It was clear that Reagan was no longer in touch with affairs. Irangate, as it was dubbed, did not destroy Reagan as Watergate did Nixon, but all the main culprits were forced to resign.

(ix) There was a *severe stock market crash (October 1987)*, brought on by the fact that the American economy was in serious trouble. There was a huge budget deficit, mainly because the Reagan administration had more than doubled defence spending since 1981, while at the same time cutting taxes. During the period 1981–7, the national debt had more than doubled – to 2400 billion dollars, and borrowing had to be stepped up simply to pay off the massive annual interest of 192 billion dollars. At the same time there was a *balance of payments deficit*, and industry was slowing down as *America moved into a deep recession*. The first priority was somehow to reduce the budget deficit, but this proved difficult. There was a further serious stock market crash in January 1988, and estimates put the likely budget deficit at 67 billion dollars by January 1989.

22.2 LATIN AMERICA

(a) The area known as Latin America consists of the countries of South America, Central America including Mexico and islands in the Caribbean Sea such as Cuba and Hispaniola (divided into two states, Haiti and the Dominican Republic). These states gained independence from Spain or Portugal in the early nineteenth century and had much in common: *Spanish* is spoken in most of them, though in Brazil Portuguese is the main language; *in the period after 1945 they shared similar problems*:

(i) They were *economically underdeveloped* both industrially and agriculturally. Factory industries did exist (the Second World War

Fig. 22.1 *Latin America*

acted as a stimulus to industrial development because manufactured goods from Europe and the USA were impossible to come by), but for all sorts of reasons Latin American industry is still well below the level of industry in the developed countries of Europe, the USA and Japan: there was *a shortage of capital, equipment and technical knowledge*; home markets were unpredictable because the vast majority of people were too poverty-stricken to provide enough *purchasing power*; and it was difficult to export in competition with advanced industrial nations. Thus states found themselves heavily dependent for exports on a limited range of products, *sometimes even a single commodity*; a fall in the world price of that commodity would be a major disaster: Chile relied on copper, Cuba on sugar and tobacco, Bolivia on tin; in fact 80 per cent of all Bolivian revenue came from tin in the 1950s. Agriculture remained backward because peasant labour was so plentiful and cheap that wealthy estate owners had no need to bother about modernisation; Peru was dominated by huge estates whose owners were all-powerful, ruling their peasants like feudal monarchs.

(ii) There was a *massive rise in population* due mainly to advances in medicine and hygiene and the refusal of the Roman Catholic church to promote birth control. The population is still increasing at a rate of 3 per cent per year, faster than in any other area of the world: between 1945 and 1962 it rose from 130 million to 216 million and by 1980 to over 500 million. Whenever it seemed that a country might be making some progress – for example, by land reform in which a peasant received land of his own – this was neutralised by the population growth. Peasant holdings were too small to support large families; many left for the cities but found jobs hard to come by; almost all the major cities were surrounded by filthy improvised slums without water, sewage disposal or electricity. The *gap between rich and poor grew wider* and little progress was made in eliminating poverty and illiteracy.

(iii) *Latin American political systems* were, for the most part, inadequate for dealing with such enormous problems. There was no tradition of democracy (except in Chile) and states were run by groups of wealthy landowners supporting *caudillos* (military dictators). When democratic systems were introduced in some of the states after the Second World War and governments tried to effect reforms, it was common for the army to intervene on behalf of the disapproving landowners, either to block the reforms or to overthrow the government; this happened in Guatemala (1950), Bolivia (1964), Brazil (1964, after only eight years of democracy), Argentina (1966) and Chile (1973).

(iv) *Heavy investment by foreigners in industry and agriculture* was a problem because *much of the profit was taken out of the countries*: most of the oil in Bolivia and Venezuela (potentially rich countries) is got out by American-owned companies; the US United

Fruit Company was the biggest land-owner in Guatemala; Chilean copper mines and Cuban sugar plantations were also American controlled.

(b) What was done about the problems?

(i) Several *international organisations* were set up: the Organisation of American States (OAS), founded in 1948, included most of the Latin American countries and the USA, and aimed to bring about inter-American co-operation and to settle disputes. The Central American Common Market (1960) had some success in bringing about a reduction of tariffs. However, the Latin American Free Trade Association (LAFTA) formed in 1961 has had little success.

(ii) The *United Nations* helped by sending *technical experts* and by holding conferences to consider how underdeveloped nations might increase exports.

(iii) The *USA has sent massive economic aid.* Kennedy started the 'Alliance for Progress', which aimed to pump billions of dollars into Latin America to enable economic and social reform to be carried out. However, this sort of aid did not always work out for the best, sometimes creating extra problems. American motives were mixed: they hoped, by solving economic problems, to *encourage moderate reforming governments* which would be popular enough to keep communism out. Sometimes the loans were provided on condition that a high proportion was spent on American products, which hardly helped *native industries to develop* and involved governments in large *interest payments.* Often, as with Castro's Cuba and Allende's Chile, aid would be cut short if a government unacceptable to the USA came to power, to be resumed later when the government changed. The USA therefore could exert *political influence via economic control.* Sometimes there was more direct influence: in 1954 Washington supplied arms to Guatemalan rebels who overthrew a reforming government and replaced it with a right-wing military dictatorship; more blatant was US intervention in the Dominican Republic (1965) where 20,000 American troops crushed an attempted come back by former President Bosch who had an extensive programme of social reform and was therefore suspected of being a communist.

(c) The crisis of the 1980s

By the 1980s, it was clear that the problems of Latin America had not been solved. One problem in particular – that of *debt and finance* – had reached crisis proportions. The trouble was that the countries of Latin America (along with those of Asia and Africa – i.e., the Third World) had borrowed massively from foreign banks, many of them in the USA, to develop their industries and amenities. This borrowing was at its height from 1973 until 1982, and in that year the seven largest US banks made 60 per cent of their profits from interest on loans to Third World countries (as against only 22 per cent in 1970). With the doubling of American interest rates in the period 1979–81, the *debtor nations could not even pay the interest*, let alone repay the debts, and the amount of interest they failed to repay each year was added on to the existing debt. They were forced to borrow from new sources merely to keep up the interest payments on the original loans. By 1985, Latin America owed some 368 billion dollars and there was a constant *drain of capital to the USA*, leaving Latin America increasingly impoverished. By 1987, as export earnings steadily declined, the situation was approaching catastrophe. *Brazil*, one of the most prosperous states with its huge natural resources, had debts of over 100 million dollars, and in February, announced that it was *suspending interest payments*. Mexico, which owed almost as much, was considering the possibility of repudiating its debts. As the Mexican President de la Madrid put it: 'We have reached the limit of being able to sustain this net transfer of resources to the rest of the world which violates economic logic and is tremendously inequitable'. The more pessimistic of economists were predicting the collapse of world trade financial systems if Third World countries did begin a mass repudiation of debts.

(d) Venezuela

Venezuela is one of the wealthiest states of Latin America because of its *oil resources*, but until 1945 profits went to *foreign oil companies* (mainly American and British) or to the small group of wealthy people who ran the country through a military dictatorship. The great mass of the population received no benefit and remained poor and illiterate. In 1945 Romulo Betancourt, leader of a progressive left-wing party called *Accion Democratica*, was placed in power by a group of young army officers after fierce fighting in Caracas, the capital, had overthrown the military government. Betancourt introduced a new constitution which allowed full civil rights to all citizens; land reform was started, heavy taxes placed on the foreign oil companies, and plans prepared to exclude the army from politics. These reforms were bitterly opposed by foreign companies and rich landowners and in 1948 Betancourt was driven out by an army coup.

For the next ten years the country was under *ruthless military dictatorship*. American dollars flowed in and some progress was made with the building of steel plants to exploit local iron ore deposits. Iron and steel soon became Venezuela's most valuable export. In 1957 Archbishop Blanco of Caracas publicly condemned the government's wealth and corruption while the majority of Venezuelans lived in sub-human conditions. In 1958 a general strike broke out and a section of the army removed the dictator, Jimenez. Democracy was restored and Betancourt was voted back to power. Immediately he raised Venezuela's share of oil revenues to 60 per cent, but this disappointed the growing communist party who had expected him to nationalise all foreign companies. However, Betancourt proceeded cautiously, not wanting to alienate the USA in case aid was stopped, and although measures were introduced to improve education and health and some land redistributed to peasants, Betancourt's popularity gradually waned. Nevertheless democracy survived, the presidency alternating between *Accion Democratica* and the other main group, the Christian Social Party. Venezuela did well out of oil revenues, being the main supplier for the Central American states and to a lesser extent for the USA.

In the 1980s, though still politically stable, Venezuela was seriously affected by the *fall in the world oil prices* and by difficulties in maintaining the levels of her other main exports – iron and steel. In March 1985, President Lusinchi (*Accion Democratica*, elected 1983) complained about the 'obstinately protectionist policies' of industrialised nations, which 'obstruct our trade possibilities'. He was especially critical of the USA which had just announced that it would reduce imports of Venezuelan steel from 550,000 tonnes a year (about 85 per cent of her total steel export) to 110,000 tonnes for the next five years – a disastrous blow for Venezuelan industry. Like other Latin American states, though to a lesser degree, she was falling into arrears with her debt repayments, and the government was trying to cope by reducing imports and government spending.

(e) Guatemala

In marked contrast to Venezuela, Guatemala is one of the poorest states of Latin America and its history is an *excellent illustration of US involvement*. Largely an *agricultural* state, its economy depended on exports of bananas and coffee. The population consisted mainly of landless peasants and the economy was dominated by American firms, particularly the United Fruit Company. The country's military dictator was overthrown by revolution in 1945, elections were held and the Christian Socialist Juan José Arevalo became President for five years. *Much-needed reforms* were introduced: many foreign estates were confiscated and redistributed to peasants; there was a minimum wage, new houses, hospitals and schools, and landowners were required to provide adequate housing for their workers. The next President, Jacobo Arbenz, took uncultivated land from large estates, to be redistributed among peasants and *legalised the communist party*. This was too much for the USA: *all aid was immediately stopped*, Arbenz was accused of being a communist, and his opponents were supplied with arms and trained in neighbouring Honduras. In 1954 *American-backed forces* led by Castillo Armas *invaded Guatemala* and *overthrew Arbenz*. Armas became military dictator; he was assassinated in 1955 only to be replaced by another dictator, Miguel Ydigoras. *US aid was resumed* and a revolution against Ydigoras was put down in 1960 with American help.

There can be little doubt that the Eisenhower government *overestimated the danger from communism* in Guatemala; it was prepared to sacrifice the reforming government of Arbenz even though it meant violating the principle of non-intervention and souring relations with the rest of Latin America.

Years of military dictatorship followed during which the opposition took to guerrilla attacks and kidnappings. When General Garcia, president from 1978–82, and apparently more liberal than his predecessors, announced that the government intended to distribute uncultivated land in the north to landless peasants, there were violent protests from the right and somehow the land fell into the hands of rich landowners. The country was in a state of *virtual civil war* and it was calculated that in four months (October 1979–January 1980) 3252 political murders had taken place. After the next election, said to have been won by a Garcia nominee, General Guevara, a group of army officers declared that the result had been fixed and put General Rios Montt in power (March 1982). After little more than a year another coup replaced Rios Montt by yet another General, Oscar Mejia (August 1983). Montt complained that the USA had been pressurising him to act against Nicaragua, and that when he refused they had engineered his removal in favour of somebody who would. Soon afterwards Mejia did indeed announce that he saw the Sandinista government of Nicaragua as a threat to the whole of central America (see below). *Mejia promised a return to civilian democracy* and in *November 1985 elections were held* for a legislative assembly. The *Christian Democrats emerged clear winners with 51 out of the 100 seats* and in December, their leader, *Cerezo Arevali*, was elected president for five years. He faced a daunting task, trying to reconcile left-wing guerrillas, right-wing landowners and the baleful presence of the army; at the same time there was a chronic economic crisis, a completely empty treasury, and the fear of US pressure if his reforming policies fell under suspicion of being 'communist'. He began bravely, abolishing the secret police, requesting American help and at the same time opposing American policy in Nicaragua. It was a narrow tightrope to tread.

(f) Nicaragua

Nicaragua had a *long history of US domination*. American troops were stationed there since before the First World War until 1933 and from 1936 until 1979 the country was ruled by the *Somoza family* who co-operated with, and were supported by the USA. On three occasions the USA was able to use Nicaraguan territory or troops for attacks on other Latin American governments which it did not like – Guatemala (1954), Cuba (1961) and the Dominican Republic (1965). The last of the Somozas, Anastasio (1967–79) was so *blatantly corrupt* that he became an embarrassment to the Americans and Carter urged him to reform and pay more attention to human rights. This had little effect and in *1979 Somoza was driven out by the Sandinista National Liberation Front* (called after Augusto Sandinista who had led an unsuccessful revolution in 1933).

The new Sandinista government immediately introduced a programme of *long overdue reforms*: a redistribution of 5 million acres of land (some of it confiscated Somoza property) to about 100,000 families, a literacy drive and health improvements which got rid of polio and reduced other diseases. Although the Sandinistas allowed a mixed economy of state and privately owned business, the *Reagan government* saw them as *dangerous communists and did all it could to bring them down*. The Americans began and encouraged others to join a trade blockade and a credit squeeze against Nicaragua and financed the Nicaraguan Democratic force (FDN), known as the *Contras*, which conducted a damaging guerrilla campaign, blowing up bridges, schools, and health clinics and burning crops. This policy was not popular with most of Nicaragua's neighbours: at a meeting of the Latin American Parliament (founded in 1968) in Guatemala City (April 1986), 16 of the 18 members (El Salvador and Honduras being the exceptions) passed a motion condemning the US attitude. The policy was controversial in the USA itself and in March 1987, following the Irangate scandal (see Section 22.1(h)(viii)), Congress voted that aid to the Contras should be stopped. This provided a ray of hope for embattled Nicaragua and her president *Daniel Ortega* (elected January 1985 for six years). In August 1987 President Arias of Costa Rica persuaded all the Central American Presidents to support his peace plan for the region, an achievement which won him the Nobel Peace Prize. However, the plan proved difficult to carry out, mainly because the Reagan administration was still doing all it could to de-stabilize Nicaragua, and under US pressure, both El Salvador and Honduras declined to co-operate.

22.3 JAPAN

At the end of the Second World War *Japan was defeated*; her *economy was in ruins* with a large proportion of her factories and a quarter of her housing destroyed by bombing. *Until 1952* she was *occupied by allied troops*, mostly American, under the command of General MacArthur. For the first three years the Americans aimed to make sure that Japan *could never again start a war*; she was forbidden to have armed forces and was given a democratic constitution under which ministers had to be members of the *Diet* (parliament). The Americans did not at this stage seem concerned to restore the Japanese economy. During 1948 the American attitude gradually changed: as the Cold War developed in Europe and the *Kuomintang* crumbled in China, they felt the need for a *strong ally in South East Asia* and began to encourage Japanese economic recovery. From 1950 industry recovered rapidly and by 1953 production had reached the 1937 level. *American occupying forces were withdrawn in April 1952* (as had been agreed by the Treaty of San Francisco the previous September) though some American troops remained for defence purposes.

(a) How was Japan's rapid recovery possible?

(i) *American help was vital*: Japanese goods were allowed into American markets on favourable terms and the USA supplied aid and new equipment: an economically healthy Japan meant a strong bulwark against communism in South East Asia.

(ii) The *Korean War (1950–3)* brought orders for military equipment and supplies, and American firms began to co-operate with the Japanese in the development of new industries.

(iii) The alliance with the USA meant that Japan felt well protected and was therefore able to *invest in industry money that would otherwise have gone on armaments.*

(iv) *Profits from exports were ruthlessly ploughed back into industry* and this was helped by keeping wages and government expenditure low. Japanese goods (motorcycles, cars, television and hi-fi equipment and ships) were therefore *highly competitive* on world markets.

(v) Recovery was helped by a series of *stable governments*, mostly conservative in character, which had the solid support of the farmers who benefited from the land reform carried through by the Americans. Enjoying plots of their own for the first time they were afraid that their land would be nationalised if the socialists came to power.

(b) Japanese recovery was not without its problems however. There was a good deal of *anti-American feeling* in some quarters; many Japanese felt inhibited by their close ties with the USA; they felt that the Americans exaggerated the threat from communist China. They wanted good relations with China and the USSR but this was difficult with Japan in the American camp. The renewal of the defence treaty with the USA in 1960 caused strikes and demonstrations. The Japanese gradually restored good relations with Russia and in the early 1970s reached an understanding with their old enemy China. Another problem was working class unrest at low wages and over-crowded living conditions. *Stability* depended on economic prosperity, but as the Japanese economy remained buoyant throughout the 1970s, the situation gradually improved. During the world recession of the early 1980s Japan *coped better than any of the other industrialised countries*, and 1984 saw a record 11 per cent growth in industrial production. Exports continued to increase, particularly to the USA, Canada and the EEC. Inflation was well under control at below 3 per cent and unemployment was relatively low at less than 3 per cent of the working population (1.6 million in 1984). Japan's prosperity caused some problems: there were constant protests from the USA, Canada and Western Europe that the Japanese were flooding foreign markets with their exports while refusing to buy a comparable amount of imports from their customers. In response Japan *abolished or reduced import duties on almost 200 commodities* (1982–3) and agreed to limit car exports to the USA (November 1983); France herself restricted imports of cars, TVs and videos. To compensate for these setbacks the Japanese managed to achieve a 20 per cent increase in exports to the EEC between January and May 1986. The Japanese success story was symbolised by a remarkable engineering feat – a tunnel 54 kilometres long linking Honshu (the largest island) with Hokkaido to the north. Completed in 1985, it had taken 21 years to build, and was the world's longest undersea tunnel.

QUESTIONS

1. Civil rights in the USA
Study the Sources below, and then answer the questions that follow.

Source A
From a speech by Martin Luther King in Washington, 1963.

I say to you today, my friends, that in spite of the difficulties and frustrations of the moment, I still have a dream. I have a dream that one day on the red hills of Georgia the sons of former slaves and the sons of former slaveowners will be able to sit down together at the table of brotherhood. I have a dream that my four little children will one day live in a nation where they will not be judged by the colour of their skin but by the content of their character. I have a dream today.

[Reproduced by permission of the Midland Examining Group.]

Source B
From *Stride Towards Freedom*, by Martin Luther King, written in 1959.

We are too often loud and boisterous and spend far too much on drink. Even the most poverty-stricken among us can purchase a ten-cent bar of soap; even the most uneducated among us can have high morals. By improving our standards we will go a long way towards breaking down the arguments of those who argue in favour of segregation . . . The other part of our programme must be nonviolent resistance to all forms of racial injustice, including state and local laws and practices, even when this means going to jail; and bold action to end the demoralisation caused by the legacy of slavery and segregation, inferior schools, slums and second-class citizenship . . . A new frontal assault on the poverty, disease and ignorance of a people too long ignored by America's conscience will make victory more certain.

Source: M. Luther King, *Stride Towards Freedom* (Harper & Row, 1979 edition, adapted extracts).

Source C
From *Chaos or Community*, by Martin Luther King.

[There is a] remarkable record of achievements that have already come through nonviolent action. The 1960 sit-ins desegregated lunch counters in more than 150 cities within a year. The 1961 'Freedom

Rides' put an end to segregation in interstate travel. The 1956 bus boycott in Montgomery, Alabama, ended segregation on the buses not only of that city but in practically every city of the South. The 1963 Birmingham movement and the climactic March on Washington won passage of the most powerful civil rights law in a century. The 1965 Selma movement brought enactment of the Voting Rights Law. Most significant is the fact that this progress occurred with minimum human sacrifice and loss of life. Fewer people have been killed in ten years of nonviolent demonstrations across the South than were killed in one day of rioting in Watts [the black area of Los Angeles where there were race riots in 1965].

Source: M. Luther King, *Chaos or Community* (Penguin, 1967, adapted extracts).

Source D
Desegregation (illus 22.2): a group of black students leaves a school at Little Rock under escort, 1957.

illus 22.2

Source E
A speech made by Malcolm X, the American (black) Muslim civil rights leader, in 1964.

You'll get freeeedom by letting your enemy know that you'll do anything to get your freedom; then you'll get it. It's the only way you'll get it. When you get that kind of attitude they'll label you as a 'crazy nigger'.

Source: Howard Zinn, *A People's History of the United States* (Longman, 1980, extract).

Source F
The National Advisory Committee Report on Urban Disorders, 1968.

The urban riots of 1967 in the black ghettoes of the country involved Negroes acting against local symbols of white American society. The overwhelming majority of the persons killed or injured in all the disorders were Negro civilians . . . The typical rioter was a young high-school dropout, but somewhat better educated than his non-rioting Negro neighbour, and usually under-employed or employed in a menial job. He was proud of his race and extremely hostile to both whites and middle-class Negroes. White racism is to blame for the explosive mixture which has been accumulating in our cities since the end of World War II: wide-spread discrimination and segregation in employment, education and housing . . . growing concentrations of impoverished Negroes in our major cities, creating a growing crisis of deteriorating facilities and services, and unmet human needs.

Source: Howard Zinn, *A People's History of the United States* (Longman, 1980, adapted extracts).

(a) (i) Who was Martin Luther King (Sources A, B and C)?   1
     (ii) Explain in your own words what his dream was (Source A).
                                                              4(a)
(b) (i) What two methods does King suggest blacks follow to improve their situation (Source B)?   **4(a)**
     (ii) What evidence can you find in Source B of the 'difficulties and frustrations' (beginning of Source A) facing blacks?   **4(a,c)**
(c) (i) From the evidence provided by Sources C and D, what had been achieved by the civil rights movement by the end of 1965?   **4(a,c)**
     (ii) Who was the President at the time of the March on Washington (Source C)?   **1,4(a)**
     (iii) What were the details of 'the most powerful civil rights law in a century' (Source C)?   **1,4(a)**
(d) What advantages and disadvantages do you think Sources C and D have for the historian?   **4(a,b)**
(e) (i) How do Sources E and F show that some blacks preferred different methods of campaigning from those advocated by Martin Luther King?   **4(a,c)**
     (ii) What is meant by the phrase 'black ghettoes' (beginning of Source F)?   **1,4(a)**

(iii) 'The evidence in Source F shows that Martin Luther King's claims of success (in Source C) were false.' Do you agree or disagree with this statement? Explain your answer fully.

4(a,b,c)

(f) (i) Do you think that the author of the Report (Source F) is sympathetic to Negroes or not? Give reasons for your answer.

4(a,b)

(ii) What further progress was made towards civil rights in 1968 under President Johnson? **1,2**

(g) To what extent do you think American Negroes had gained full equality with whites by the 1970s? **1,2**

2. Nicaragua and the Contras

Study the Source below and then answer the questions that follow.

An article in the *Guardian*, 30 October 1986.

The Reagan administration last night stepped up its pressure on the Sandinista regime in Nicaragua. The Defence Secretary, Mr Caspar Weinberger, publicly accused Moscow of providing it with unprecedented quantities of military equipment to further its aim of 'another Cuba' on the American mainland. Mr Weinberger's televised remarks came in the wake of the US veto at the United Nations of a Nicaraguan-inspired resolution condemning US support for the contra rebels.

President Reagan last week signed the one hundred million dollar bill which resumes direct military aid to the contras after a two year breach, and enables the CIA to take back its control of the overall direction of the guerrilla war. The Americans have revealed that large quantities of Soviet military aid, notably helicopter gun-ships, have recently arrived at a Nicaraguan port. 'I have total confidence in the information', Mr Weinberger said. He denied that these Soviet shipments are 'in response' to renewed US aid to the contras, who are trying to overthrow the regime in Managua. The Russian aid, according to Mr Weinberger, is part of a Nicaraguan offensive build-up in the region.

The American Justice Department has confirmed that it is investigating claims that Reagan officials illegally helped the contras during the years when such action was forbidden by Congress. There are signs that thorough investigations would reveal the White House itself was involved.

(Adapted extracts.)

(a) (i) Who was Mr Caspar Weinberger? **4(a)**

(ii) When did the Sandinista regime come to power in Nicaragua?

What regime did it replace and how did the change happen?

1,2,4(a)

    (iii) Who were the contras?   **1,4(a)**

    (iv) What was the CIA?   **1**

(b)   **(i)** What evidence does the article give to suggest why the American government was helping the contras?   **4(a)**

    (ii) Explain why the USA has been so interested in Central and South America since 1945.   **1,2**

(c) Describe briefly two other occasions (apart from Nicaragua) on which the USA has interfered in the internal affairs of a Latin American state with the intention of overthrowing its government.

1,2

(d)   **(i)** What evidence can you find in the article to suggest that not all Americans approve of their government helping the contras?

4(a)

    (ii) What does the writer mean when he says that some Reagan officials acted illegally by sending help to the contras?   **4(a)**

(e)   **(i)** What did the 'thorough investigations' (mentioned at the end of the article) discover about the illegal help sent to the contras?   **1,4(a)**

    (ii) What effects did these discoveries have on the Reagan administration during 1987 and later?   **1,2**

3. Japan after 1945

Study the Sources below, and then answer the questions that follow.

Source A

The new Japanese constitution, introduced 1947.

> Introduction: We, the Japanese people, acting through our duly elected representatives in the National Diet [Parliament], aim and determine that we shall secure for ourselves and our posterity the fruits of peaceful co-operation with all nations and the blessings of liberty throughout this land. We are resolved that never again shall we be visited with the horrors of war through the action of government.
>
> 1. Sovereign power resides with the people. Government is a sacred trust of the people, the authority for which is derived from the people and the powers of which are exercised by the representatives of the people in the Diet, the sole law-making body of the state.
>
> 2. The Emperor is a symbol of state and all acts of the Emperor require the advice and approval of the cabinet, which is itself subordinate to the Diet.
>
> 3. Land, sea and air forces, as well as other war potential, will never be maintained.

4. Everybody will be equal before the law and will enjoy the right to maintain the minimum standards of wholesome and cultured living and to receive an equal education.

(Adapted extracts.)

Source B

Under the 1889 constitution the Emperor was given almost absolute power. His person was sacred. He could dissolve the Diet [parliament] at will, and had the power to make war or peace and sign treaties. In practice therefore it was his advisers who had tremendous power and influence. Japan's military tradition ensured that she had an army second only to Germany's in strength. Though basic human rights were guaranteed by the constitution, they were never exercised fully.

Source: A. C. Morales, *East meets West 1815–1919* (Macmillan, 1986, extract).

Source C

The American occupation ended in 1952. By then the Japanese economy was recovering rapidly and the 1960s and 1970s were boom years. Her economic growth rate was among the highest in the world and her international prestige rose with the holding of the 1964 Olympic Games in Tokyo and the 1970 Osaka International Exposition . . . Japan's industrial achievements have brought many new problems. Industrialisation has caused serious air and water pollution in urban areas while migration to the cities has led to overcrowding. Abroad the USA and Europe have criticised Japan for flooding world markets with her goods while pursuing strongly protectionist policies at home . . . Yet another problem is the almost total dependence of the Japanese economy on natural resources from abroad. She has to rely on imports of oil and ore for her industries.

Source: A. C. Morales, *East meets West 1920–1980* (Macmillan, 1986, adapted extracts).

(a) (i) According to Source C, when did the American occupation of Japan end? **4(a)**

    (ii) Why were American troops in Japan, and how long had they been there? **1,2**

(b) (i) According to the Introduction to the 1947 Constitution (Source A), what three things were the Japanese people determined to achieve? **4(a)**

    (ii) Which 'horrors of war' do you think were likely to be uppermost in the minds of the Japanese people in 1947? **1,2,4(a)**

(c) **(i)** Explain how points 1–4 of the 1947 Constitution (Source A) were designed to achieve the aims referred to in the Introduction. **4(a)**

(ii) Compare Sources A and B carefully and then make a list of differences between the new 1947 Constitution and the way in which Japan was ruled under the old 1889 Constitution.

4(a,c)

(d) **(i)** According to Source C, why did Japanese prestige rise during the 1960s and 1970s? **4(a)**

(ii) What does the writer of Source C mean by the phrase 'strongly protectionist policies'? **1,4(a)**

(iii) Using your own knowledge, explain why the Japanese economy 'was recovering rapidly' in the 1950s. **1,2**

(e) **(i)** According to Source C, what internal problems did Japan's industrial success cause for her? **4(a)**

(ii) What problems did Japan's success cause abroad? **4(a)**

(iii) In the 1980s, what action did the USA and Europe take to try and make Japan take notice of their criticisms? **1,2,4(a)**

(f) From the evidence of the extracts, and your own knowledge, how successful do you think the Japanese have been in achieving the aims mentioned in the Introduction to Source A? **1,2,4(a)**

4. Describe the aims, achievements and failures of:
(a) President John F. Kennedy (1961–3):
(b) President Richard M. Nixon (1969–74).

In *each case*, explain the circumstances which cut short his term of office. **1,2**

5. **(a)** What common problems have the countries of Latin America suffered since 1945?

(b) Explain briefly the problems experienced by *two* of the following countries, and describe how they have tried to deal with their problems: Venezuela, Guatemala, Nicaragua, Chile. **1,2**

6. It is 1951:
(a) Write a letter to a major American newspaper attacking the activities of Senator Joseph McCarthy.
(b) In reply to the first letter, write a second letter in which a supporter of Senator McCarthy defends him against your attack. **1,2,3**

[Southern Examining Group, Specimen Question.]

CHAPTER 23

THE END
OF THE
EMPIRES

SUMMARY OF EVENTS

The 20 years after 1945 saw remarkable changes taking place in Asia and Africa as the European states gradually released their hold over their empires, which *broke free to form a large number of independent states*. The *pace of nationalist aspirations was accelerated by the Second World War*: the prestige of Europe was badly damaged by the failure to defend Asian possessions against the Japanese and the myth of European invincibility was destroyed; Asians in areas such as the Dutch East Indies, French Indo-China and the British territories of Burma and Malaya had no wish to return to the pre-war status quo after stubbornly resisting the Japanese occupation. Their success in gaining independence encouraged similar demands in the Middle East and Africa. Many Africans, who had left their homeland for the first time to fight in the war, were appalled at the contrast between the primitive conditions in Africa and their relatively comfortable existence even in the armed forces. Nationalists were also encouraged by the Russians who constantly denounced 'imperialism'.

The colonial powers had to decide *first whether and then how to grant independence*. The problems involved were often complex; for example in *India* there were *bitter religious differences* to resolve; in some areas large numbers of *whites* had settled (Algeria, Kenya, Uganda, Tanganyika and Rhodesia) who were *relentlessly hostile to independence which would place them under black majority rule*. *Britain* was prepared to concede independence as soon as she felt individual territories were ready for it; by 1964 most of her empire had become independent though the majority of the new states retained a link with Britain by remaining in the commonwealth. The main territories gaining independence (some of which changed their names) were India and Pakistan (1947), Burma and Ceylon (1948), Malaysia (1957), Gold Coast (Ghana, 1957), Nigeria (1960), Cyprus (1960), Tanganyika and Zanzibar (together forming Tanzania, 1961), Uganda (1962), Kenya (1963), Nyasaland (Malawi, 1964), Northern Rhodesia (Zambia, 1964), British Guiana (Guyana, 1964), Malta (1964), Bechuanaland (Botswana, 1966) and Aden (South Yemen, 1967).

The *French* were at first determined to hold on to their empire, but *strong nationalist resistance in Indo-China* (see Section 17.4(a)) and *Algeria* (see Section 21.3) forced a change of heart. They withdrew from Indo-China in 1954, from Morocco and Tunisia in 1956, and by 1962 from most of their other African possessions, including Equatorial and West Africa. *Belgium* granted independence to the *Congo (1960)* with insufficient preparation, leading immediately to a *terrible civil war* (see Section 25.1). The *Dutch* were forced against their will to accept the independence of the *East Indies* (Indonesia, 1949) and the *Spanish* withdrew from *Spanish* Morocco (1956), Ifni (1969) and Spanish Sahara (1978). *Portugal* held out stubbornly against the general trend but the new left-wing government decided to withdraw from her African colonies, Guinea (became Guinea–Bissau, 1974), Mozambique and Angola (1975).

23.1 WHY, AND HOW, WAS INDIA PARTITIONED IN 1947?

By 1945 Indian independence could not be delayed much longer after the long *nationalist campaign* (see Section 11.3). The British had promised to allow *dominion status* once the war was over and the new Labour government was anxious to go ahead. Unfortunately there was more to it than simply granting independence: there were complex problems which resulted in *India being divided into two separate states, India and Pakistan.*

(a) Why was partition necessary?

  (i)   The problem sprang from *religious hostilities between Hindus who made up about two-thirds of the population* and the *rest who were mostly Muslims*. After their victories in the elections of 1937 (see Section 11.3(b)), the Hindu Congress party unwisely called on the Muslim League to merge with Congress; this alarmed the League who were convinced that an independent India would be dominated by Hindus. *Jinnah*, the Muslim leader, demanded a *separate Muslim state of Pakistan.*

 (ii)   Attempts to draw up a compromise constitution acceptable to Hindu leaders (Nehru and Gandhi) and to Jinnah, failed. The British proposed a federal scheme in which the central government would have only limited powers while those of the provincial governments would be extensive; thus provinces with a Muslim majority would be able to control their own affairs, and there would be no need of a separate state. *Both sides accepted the principle but could not agree on details.*

(iii)   *Violence broke out in August 1946* when the Governor-General, Lord Wavell, invited Nehru to form an interim government, still hoping that details could be worked out later. Nehru formed a cabinet which included two Muslims, but Jinnah, convinced that

illus 23.1 *New Delhi, 1947. During a lull in the rioting, victims of the many clashes are removed from the streets*

the Hindus could not be trusted, called for 'direct action' to achieve Pakistan. Fierce rioting followed in Calcutta where 5000 people were killed, and spread to Bengal where Muslims set about slaughtering Hindus. As Hindus retaliated the country seemed on the verge of civil war.

(iv) To try and force the Indians into a more responsible attitude, Attlee announced early in 1947 that the British would leave no later than June 1948. The new Viceroy, Lord Mountbatten, realised that *partition was the only way to avoid civil war* and by this time the majority of Congress (though not Gandhi) agreed with him. Afraid that delay would cause more violence, *Mountbatten advanced the date for British withdrawal to August 1947.*

(b) How was partition carried out?

The *Indian Independence Act* was rushed through the British parliament (*August 1947*) separating the Muslim majority areas (the north-west and north-east India) from the rest of India as the independent state of *Pakistan*, which was in *two sections, over a thousand miles apart*. But it was not easy to operate the act:

(i) It had been necessary to *split the provinces of the Punjab* and *Bengal* which had mixed Hindu/Muslim populations and inevitably millions of people found themselves on the wrong side of the new frontiers.

(ii) Fearing persecution, millions made for the frontier, Muslims trying to get into Pakistan and Hindus into India. Clashes occurred developing into near-hysterical mob violence, especially in the *Punjab*, in which about 250,000 people were murdered. Violence was not quite so widespread in Bengal where Gandhi, still preaching non-violence and toleration, managed to calm the situation.

(iii) Violence began to die down before the end of 1947, but in *January 1948 Gandhi was shot dead by a Hindu fanatic* who detested his tolerance towards Muslims. It was a tragic end to a disastrous set of circumstances, but the shock seemed to bring people to their senses, so that India and Pakistan could begin to think about their other problems.

23.2 MALAYA AND CYPRUS

(a) **Malaya** was *liberated from the Japanese occupation in 1945* but there were two difficult problems to be faced before the British could think of withdrawing:

(i) How could such a complex area be organised? it consisted of *nine states* each ruled by a sultan, *two British settlements*, Malacca and Penang, and *Singapore*, a small island less than a mile from the mainland. The population was *multi-racial*: mostly Malays and Chinese but with Indians and Europeans as well. It was decided to group the states and the settlements into the *Federation of Malaya (1948)* while *Singapore remained a separate colony*. Each state had its own legislature for local affairs, the sultans retained some power, but the central government had firm overall control. Since everybody had the vote, the *Malays*, the largest group, *usually dominated affairs*.

(ii) *Chinese communist guerrillas* who had led the resistance to the Japanese, now began to *stir up strikes and violence against* the *British*, and the situation was serious enough for a *state of emergency* to be declared in *1948*. The British dealt with the problem successfully, though it took time: all Chinese suspected of helping the guerrillas were resettled into specially guarded villages; it was made clear that independence would follow as soon as the country was ready for it; this ensured that the Malays remained firmly pro-British and gave little help to the communists, who were Chinese. Even so, the *emergency remained in force until 1960*.

The move towards independence was accelerated when the Malay party under their able leader Tunku Abdul Rahman, joined forces with the main Chinese and Indian groups to form the *Alliance Party*, which won 51 out of 52 seats in the 1955 elections. This seemed to suggest stability and the British were persuaded to *grant full independence in 1957 when Malaya was admitted to the commonwealth.*

(b) Cyprus

Unlike the Malaya success story, British handling of Cyprus left much to be desired and the island was still *troubled and divided in the 1980s.* The problems were:

(i) The *population was mixed* – about 80 per cent were Greek-speaking Christians of the Orthodox Church, while the rest were Muslims of Turkish origin. The Greek Cypriots wanted union with Greece (*enosis*); the Turks strongly opposed this, but there was no serious trouble until 1954, when:

(ii) Churchill's government produced a new constitution which allowed *Cypriots far less power* than the previous Labour government had envisaged. There were hostile demonstrations, which had to be dispersed by British troops.

(iii) Eden, Churchill's successor, thought Britain needed Cyprus as a *military base* to protect her interests in the Middle East, and announced that Cyprus *must remain permanently British*, though the Greek government promised that they could retain their military bases even if *enosis* took place.

(iv) The Greek Cypriots led by *Archibishop Makarios* pressed their demands while a guerrilla organisation called *Eoka*, led by General Grivas, waged a terrorist campaign against the British who declared a *state of emergency (1955)* and deployed about 35,000 troops to try and keep order. British policy also involved deporting Makarios and executing terrorists.

Eden's successor, Macmillan, adopted a conciliatory approach and appointed the sympathetic and tactful Hugh Foot as governor. He persuaded Makarios to agree to a compromise: the Archibishop dropped *enosis* and in return Cyprus was *granted full independence*: Turkish interests were safeguarded, Britain returned two military bases and, along with Greece and Turkey, guaranteed the independence of Cyprus; Makarios became first president (1960). It seemed a masterly solution, but unfortunately it lasted only until 1963 (see Section 20.3(g)).

23.3 THE BRITISH IN AFRICA

African nationalism spread rapidly after 1945; this was because more and more Africans were being educated, many of them in Britain and the USA where they were made aware of racial discrimination. Colonialism was seen as the humiliation and exploitation of blacks by whites, and working-class Africans in the new towns were particularly receptive to nationalist ideas. They were greatly encouraged by Indian independence (1947) and by the sympathetic attitude of the British labour government (1945–51).

(a) **West Africa** presented comparatively few problems, since the British in that area tended to be *administrators* rather than *permanent settlers with estates to defend.*

(i) In the *Gold Coast, Kwame Nkrumah*, educated in London and America and since 1949 leader of the Convention People's party (CPP), organised the campaign for independence. There were demonstrations, some of which got out of hand, and Nkrumah was twice imprisoned. However, the British soon agreed to allow a new constitution which included the vote for all adults, an elected assembly and an eleven-man Executive Council of which eight were chosen by the assembly. In the 1951 elections, the first under the new constitution, the CPP won 34 out of 38 seats; Nkrumah was released from prison and became Prime Minister in 1952. For the next five years the African politicians gained experience of government under British supervision until in *1957 Ghana*, as it was now known, *became independent.*

(ii) In *Nigeria* the leading nationalist was *Nnamdi Azikiwe*; popularly known as 'Zik', he had been educated in the USA, and after his return to Nigeria in 1937 soon gained enormous prestige. Nigeria was a more difficult proposition than Ghana because of its *great size* and its *regional differences* between the huge Muslim north, the western region (dominated by the Yoruba tribe) and the eastern region (the Ibo tribe). However, after Azikiwe had organised an impressive general strike in 1945, the British gradually began to prepare Nigeria for independence. It was decided that a *federal system* was most suitable; in 1954 a new constitution introduced local assemblies for the three regions with a central (federal) government in Lagos, the capital; the regions assumed self-government first and the *country as a whole became indepen-dent in 1960.*

(b) **East Africa** included Tanganyika, Uganda and Kenya, and here the problems of independence were complicated by the presence of *European and Asian settlers* who were afraid of their future under black African government. The *Tanganyika Africa National Union (TANU) led by Dr Julius Nyerere*, who had been educated at Edinburgh University, insisted that the government must be African, and the British, impressed by Nyerere's ability and sincerity, accepted this view and granted independence (1961). This *marked an important change in British policy*: they had begun in 1945 by thinking that independence was not as necessary in East Africa as in the west, and that when it came it would be under multi-racial governments. By 1960 the British prime Minister, Macmillan, talked of 'the wind of change' in Africa' it was inevitable that Ghana's example would be followed in both East and

Central Africa, and Macmillan dropped the idea of multi-racial govern-ments in favour of *black majority rule*. Independence for *Uganda* was delayed by tribal squabbles; the ruler of the Buganda area (known as the *Kabaka*) objected to the introduction of democracy. Eventually a solution was found in a *federal constitution* which allowed the *Kabaka* to retain some powers in Buganda. Uganda itself *became independent in 1962* with *Dr Milton Obote* as Prime Minister. *Kenya* was the most troublesome area. Here *Jomo Kenyatta* and his Kenya African Union led the struggle for independence and at first made little progress, the only British concession being to allow six Africans on the legislative Council of 54 members. African impatience burst out in a campaign of terrorist attacks on European farms and African workers, organised by the *Mau Mau* secret society. A *state of emergency* was declared in 1952, and Kenyatta and other nationalists were arrested; thousands of British troops were used to flush out the terrorists and by 1960 the emergency was over. By this time, no doubt encouraged by the strength of African feeling, the British change of heart had taken place: *Kenya became independent under a black African government* with *Kenyatta* as Prime Minister (*1963*); this was in spite of bitter resistance from the European settlers, many of whom left the country.

(c) **Central Africa** (Nyasaland, Northern and Southern Rhodesia) was the most difficult area to deal with because this was where the *white settlers* were most strongly entrenched, particularly in Southern Rhode-sia. Alarmed at the spread of African nationalism to the north, the whites, with the approval of Churchill's government, set up the *Central African Federation (1953)*, a union of the three states. Their aim was to preserve the *supremacy of the white minority* (about 300,000 Europeans out of a total population of 8.5 million), and the federal parliament at *Salisbury* (in Southern Rhodesia) was heavily weighted to favour the whites, who hoped the Federation would soon gain full independence from Britain with dominion status. The Africans watched with growing distrust, and as outstanding nationalist leaders emerged, such as Dr Hastings Banda (Nyasaland), Kenneth Kaunda (Northern Rhodesia) and Joshua Nkomo (Southern Rhodesia), they became more militant. As violence spread, states of emergency were declared in Nyasaland and Southern Rhodesia with mass arrests of Africans (1959). However, there was much support for the Africans in Britain, especially in the Labour Party, and the Conservative Colonial Secretary, Iain Macleod, was sympathetic. The *Monckton Commission (1960)* recommended votes for Africans, an end to racial discrimination and the right of territories to leave the Federation. The British introduced new constitutions in Nyasaland and Northern Rhodesia which in effect allowed the Africans their own parliaments (1961–2); both wanted to leave the Federation which was *terminated in December 1963*. The following year *Nyasaland and Northern Rhodesia* became fully independent as *Malawi and Zam-bia*. There still remained the problem of Southern Rhodesia, or Rhode-sia as it was now known. Here the ruling whites, more numerous than in the other two areas, opposed any change in the constitution which would increase African rights; they demanded independence but Harold Wilson, the new British Labour Prime Minister, refused this unless the whites showed a willingness to move towards black majority rule. No compromise could be reached and in 1965 Rhodesia declared itself *independent against the wishes of Britain* (a unilateral declaration of independence or UDI) (see Section 25.2).

23.4 PORTUGAL

The main Portuguese possessions were in Africa: the two large areas of Angola and Mozambique and the small West African colony of Guinea. The Portuguese right-wing government of Dr Salazar for a while blithely ignored nationalist developments in the rest of Africa and their empire seemed likely to survive; it was mainly agricultural, there were few industrial workers, the black populations were almost entirely illiterate, and though nationalist groups were formed in all three colonies in 1956 they remained insignificant. *Several factors changed the situation*: by 1960 the nationalists were greatly encouraged by the large number of other African states winning independence; in alarm the Salazar regime stepped up its repressive policy, but this served only to make the nationalists more resolute. Fighting broke out first in Angola (1961) where Agostinho Neto's MPLA (People's Movement for Angolan Liberation) was the main nationalist movement. Violence soon spread to Guinea where Amilcar Cabral led the resistance and to Mozambique where the Frelimo guerrillas were organised by Eduardo Mondlane. It was an uphill struggle which *succeeded only after the Portuguese dictatorship was overthrown by an army coup in 1974*. The new president Spinola agreed to all demands: *all three states were granted independence in 1975*; the transfer of power went smoothly in Guinea–Bissau and Mozambique but in *Angola civil war flared up* as two rival groups, FNLA (National Front for the Liberation of Angola) and UNITA (National Union for the Total Independence of Angola), tried to seize power from the MPLA. It seems likely that the MPLA had majority support but this did not deter President Mobutu of Zaire, with American backing, from launching an invasion in support of the rival groups; nor did it prevent an invasion by 6000 white South Africans. By March 1976 the MPLA, with the aid of Russian weapons and a Cuban force, had defeated both invasions and Neto was accepted as president of the new state. The end of Portuguese control in Africa was vitally important: it meant that the white minority regimes in Rhodesia and South Africa were more vulnerable than ever before (see Fig. 23.1).

QUESTIONS

1. Decolonisation in Africa
Study the Sources below, and then answer the questions that follow.

Source A
Comments by Iain Macleod, British Colonial Secretary, 1959.

We could not possibly have held by force our territories in Africa. We could not with an enormous force of troops even continue to hold the small island of Cyprus. General de Gaulle could not hold on to Algeria. The march of men towards freedom cannot be halted. It can only be guided. Of course there were risks in moving quickly but there were even bigger risks in moving slowly.

Our task is completed. Our African territories are very different places now from when we arrived. Among other things they have a respect for democratic values.

Source: *Keesing's Contemporary Archives* (1959, extract).

Source B
Comments by Kwame Nkrumah, Prime Minister of Ghana, 1958.

We will welcome the Europeans if they come in a spirit of friendship and co-operation. We do not want them to remain here if they wish to be our rulers. We can rule ourselves. We did this before they came. Why should we not do it now? We did not ask them to come here. They invited themselves. This has always been a civilised country with civilised values. The Europeans have shown us how to make technical progress and we are grateful, but at the same time they have not done this for nothing. They have had their pound of flesh. They have grown fat on the riches of Africa. Now we have freedom and we shall use it. All Ghanaians will be free. All people can speak their mind for or against the government. That is what freedom means.

Source: *Keesing's Contemporary Archives* (1958, extract).

Source C
Comments by Sir James Robertson, former Governor-General of Nigeria, 1979.

I think a great deal is now spoken by people who do not know much about our rule in Africa. When we took over these countries there was very little government, there was very little civilisation, there was a great deal of intertribal warfare. Our policy in Africa was to impose the ways of peace and that is what we did.

One thing our critics forget is that we had no money. The British government gave us nothing for many years. When we came to Africa there were no railways, telegraphs, schools, hospitals, no proper government at all. People had all manner of barbaric practices. When we left there were railways, there was a system of roads, there was a police force, there was an Army, there were hospitals, schools and even universities. All this was done in about fifty years. You could walk more safely in the streets of Africa than you could in the back streets of London. We had set up a civilisation which had not existed before.

Source: Southern Examining Group, Specimen Question.

Source D

Between 1957 and 1977 thirty-nine states south of the Sahara became independent. The process was started by Britain and accelerated by General de Gaulle. The new states were faced with many problems. They were all economically weak. For example, by the time Malawi achieved independence there were only two secondary schools for its three million Africans, no roads to speak of, only one railway line and not a single industrial factory.

The new governments were inexperienced and had few trained administrators. There was a danger that the unity previously imposed by the Europeans would now weaken. Nationalism, created by opposition to the Europeans, could vanish now that they had gone. Tribalism could recur. Many Africans believed that a one-party state was an answer to these difficulties.

Source: R. D. Cornwell, *World History in The Twentieth Century* (Longman, 1982)

Source E
African independence (Fig. 23.1).

(a) Compare the map in Source E (Fig. 23.1) with the map on p. 32. How does Source E show that major political changes took place during the 1950s and 1960s? **4(a,c)**

(b) Consider *each* of the following statements, and then decide whether it is:
certainly true, or
possibly true, or
unlikely to be true.
In each case, give reasons for your decisions by referring to the Sources:
  (i) The Europeans could not prevent African countries from obtaining independence.
  (ii) After the Europeans left the Africans respected democratic values. **4(a,c)**

(c) How does Source B show Nkrumah's bias against colonial rule? **4(b)**

(d) Consider each of the five Sources and state which *one* you think is likely to be the most valuable to a historian trying to obtain an unbiased view of the decolonisation of Africa. **4(a,b)**
Explain why you have chosen this Source as likely to be more valuable than the others.

Fig. 23.1 *Africa becomes independent*

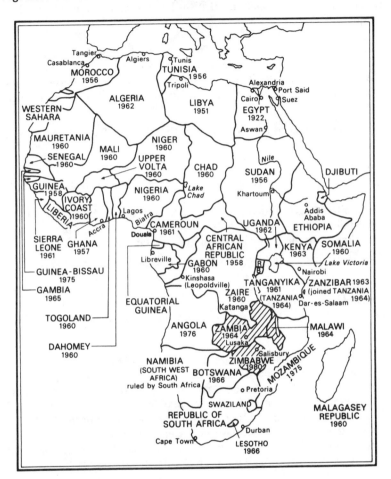

///// The Central African Federation 1953–63
Northern Rhodesia (Zambia) Southern Rhodesia (Zimbabwe)
Nyasland (Malawi)

R Ruanda 1962
B Burundi 1962

(e) 'European rule benefited Africa.'
Explain whether or not, in your opinion, the evidence in Sources A to E justifies this statement. **4(a,b,c)**
[Southern Examining Group, Specimen Question.]

2. Indian independence and partition, 1947

Study the Sources below, and then answer the questions that follow.

Source A

Statement by Hugh Dalton, British Labour Chancellor of the Exchequer, 1946.

If you are in a place where you are not wanted and where you have not got the force to squash those who don't want you, the only thing to do is to come out. I don't believe that one person in a thousand cares tuppence about it, so long as British people are not being mauled about.

[Reproduced by permission of the Midland Examining Group.]

Source B

Statement by Clement Attlee, British Labour Prime Minister, 1947.

The difficulties in India were not due to any fault of this country but to the failure of Indians to agree among themselves . . . There was no weakness and no betrayal, but simply limitations to our powers.

Source: A. Sked and C. Cook, *Post-War Britain* (Penguin, 1979).

Source C

Letter from Nehru to Mountbatten, Governor-General of India, 1 May 1947.

It has been our earnest desire that India should achieve her freedom peacefully. But we have ever been faced with a major difficulty. The policy of the Muslim League, started in August last, has deliberately encouraged violence and disorder and has resulted in murder and looting in many parts of India. Our invitation to the Muslim League to send their representatives to meet ours was not responded to. We repeat our acceptance of the principle of the partition of India in order to avoid conflict, though we are passionately attached to the idea of a United India.

Source: R. Brooks, The *Modern World Since 1870* (Bell & Hyman, 1985, adapted extracts).

Source D

Statement by Lord Mountbatten, Governor-General of India, 3 June 1947. He had decided that the only solution was a partition of India and he had persuaded the Congress and the League to agree.

The solution I put forward is that His Majesty's Government should transfer power to one or two governments of British India, each having Dominion status, as soon as the necessary arrangements can be made. I wish to emphasise that this legislation will not impose any restriction on the power of India as a whole or of the two states if there is a partition.

Source: A. F. Havighurst, *20th Century Britain* (Chicago University Press, 1955).

Source E
Map showing the partition of India (Fig. 23.2).

Fig. 23.2

(a) **(i)** What reasons does Dalton give (Source A) for the British decision to give India independence? **4(a)**

   (ii) What other reasons were there for the British decision? **1,2**

(b) **(i)** Who were the Congress and the League mentioned in Source D? **1,4(a)**

   (ii) According to Sources B and C, who was to blame for the violence in India? **4(a,c)**

   (iii) Do you think Nehru (Source C) would agree with Attlee (Source B) that the problems in India were caused by 'the failure of Indians to agree among themselves'? **1,4(a,b,c)**

(c) **(i)** According to Sources C and D, what major concession was Nehru prepared to make to prevent more violence? **4(a,c)**

(ii) What problems do you think there might be in governing such a state?   **2,4(a)**

(e) Look at all the Sources again. Do you think they provide enough evidence to explain why India was divided into two states? Give reasons for your answer.   **4(a,b,c)**

3. Britain and African nationalism

Study the Source below, and then answer the questions that follow.

Harold Macmillan's 'Wind of Change' speech to the South African parliament in Cape Town, 3 February 1960, at the end of his tour of Africa.

> The most striking of all impressions I have formed since I left London a month ago, is of this African national consciousness. In different places it may take different forms, but it is happening everywhere. The wind of change is blowing through the continent. Whether we like it or not this growth of national consciousness is a political fact, and our national policies must take account of it.

(a) (i) What position did Macmillan hold in 1960?   **1**

(ii) What had struck him most during his tour of Africa?   **4(a)**

(b) (i) What advice does Macmillan give?   **4(a)**

(ii) Why do you think Macmillan decided to make this speech to the South African parliament?   **1,2,4(a)**

(c) (i) What were the reasons for the growth of African nationalism?   **1,2**

(ii) When Macmillan made his speech, the British colonies in West Africa had already been granted independence. Describe and explain how this was achieved in the Gold Coast and Nigeria.   **1,2**

(d) (i) Why did it take longer for the countries of East and Central Africa to achieve independence?   **1,2**

(ii) Describe and explain how Kenya and Northern Rhodesia achieved independence.   **1,2**

(e) Why did Southern Rhodesia not gain independence at the same time as Northern Rhodesia?   **1,2**

4. Study the quotation below and answer the question that follows.

> 'Gandhi's assassin was a fanatical Hindu who disapproved of Gandhi's championship of Muslims. If the assassin had been a Muslim, there would undoubtedly have been a terrible bloodbath in India. Nehru broadcast to his people: "Friends, a light has gone out of our lives and there is darkness everywhere. Our beloved father is dead".' (E. M. Roberts)

Write an account of life in India between 1945 and 1948 as experienced by *either* an ordinary Muslim *or* an ordinary Hindu. Among other material your answer should refer to:

(a) life under the British;
(b) relations between Muslims and Hindus;
(c) Gandhi and independence. **1,2,3**

[Southern Examining Group, Specimen Question.]

CHAPTER 24

THE NEW COMMMONWEALTH STATES

SUMMARY OF EVENTS

Having gained independence, all the former British possessions except Burma and Aden chose to *remain within the Commonwealth*. However, they found that independence was not all plain sailing. Most of them had serious political, social and economic problems. Fighting twice erupted between *India and Pakistan over possession of Kashmir* (1947 and 1965), and *India found herself attacked by China* (1962). *Malaysia* became involved in a *long confrontation with Indonesia* (1963–6) while *Nigeria* suffered a *bloody civil war* (1967–70). Pakistan had a similar experience in *1971 when East Pakistan broke away to become the independent state of Bangladesh. Cyprus* was *torn by strife between Greeks and Turks* and since 1974 a United Nations peace-keeping force has been holding the two factions apart (see Section 20.3(g)). In fact the Commonwealth seemed to be so full of problems of one sort or another that its critics began to question its value.

24.1 WHAT IS THE COMMONWEALTH, AND WHAT USE IS IT?

Originally, an *association of Britain and her dominions* (the 'white man's club') drawn up by the 1931 Statute of Westminster (see Section 11.1(b)), the Commonwealth changed, with the admission of the new Asian and African states, into a *multi-racial organisation*. It is a loose association based on voluntary co-operation in which all member states are *equal partners*. There is very little formal machinery except the Secretariat (set up only in 1965) and the regular *biennial Commonwealth Prime Ministers' Conferences* which discuss pressing problems and plan mutual aid. The Commonwealth has done a good deal of unspectacular but valuable work in the way of economic aid. The Colombo Plan (began 1950) provides grants and advisers for projects in the poorer countries of the Commonwealth (and outside); Canadian engineers helped to build a dam in Pakistan; Australia supplied equipment and teachers to develop Malaysian education. The *Special Commonwealth African Assistance*

Plan (1960) provided financial, technical and educational aid for the emerging African nations; Nigeria, for example, received help to develop hydro-electric schemes and Malawi to set up a university. On average Britain spent somewhere approaching £200 million a year in Commonwealth aid.

On the other hand, *critics* of the Commonwealth have plenty of ammunition: many argue that the rich members could have done far more to help the still poverty-stricken Third World nations of Africa; the Commonwealth was unable to prevent or solve serious problems such as civil wars in Nigeria and Pakistan, while two of its members, India and Pakistan, have actually fought each other. The rest of the Commonwealth was alarmed at Britain's entry into the EEC (1973) and *her special trading relationship with the Commonwealth gradually faded as she traded more with Europe*: Australia, for example, bitterly attacked Britain and the EEC, blaming them for the declining markets for her beef and lamb (October 1980). However, in spite of the *departure of South Africa (1961)* because of disapproval of her racial policies (see Section 25.3), and the Rhodesia upheaval (see Section 25.2(b)) the member states chose to remain in the Commonwealth, which would suggest that it still had something to offer.

During the 1980s one of the main preoccupations of the Commonwealth was what to do about *South Africa*, the other members being indignant at the Thatcher government for refusing to support their proposals for *drastic economic sanctions*.

24.2 INDIA

For all but three years (1977–80) India after independence was ruled by the *Congress party*, first under Nehru (1947–64), then under Lal Bahadur Shastri (1964–6), followed by Nehru's daughter, Mrs Indira Gandhi (1966–77), who was again elected in 1980 following an anti-Congress coalition government. After her *assassination by Sikh extremists (October 1984)*, her son Rajiv Gandhi became Prime Minister. All these governments had to deal with awe-inspiring problems – racial, social, political and foreign.

(a) What were India's domestic problems, and how successfully were they dealt with?

(i) India had been held together only by British rule and as soon as the British left, the *country seemed in grave danger of disintegrating*. There were racial, cultural and language differences and the provinces had no sense of loyalty to the central government. Sikhs and Nagas and some of the native princes like the Nizam of Hyderabad, wanted separate states of their own. Nehru's government refused concessions and insisted on *unity*. The princes were persuaded to surrender their powers and allow their states to be

456

Fig. 24.1 *the Indian subcontinent after 1947*

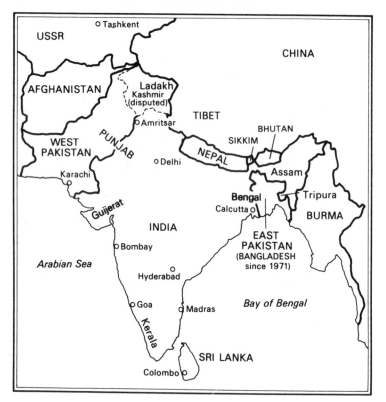

incorporated with the rest of India in return for pensions; by 1952
the initial problem of unity had been solved.

(ii) There were difficulties in *working a democratic constitution* in a
country which had had *no real experience of such government*,
where 80 per cent of the population were illiterate and where
large communist groups, encouraged by Stalin, were intent on
revolution. *Nehru was determined that democracy should be given
a chance*; communist disorders were suppressed and a new
constitution introduced (1950) with a strong central government
at Delhi, two houses of parliament, provincial governments in
each of the states, and votes for all adults. The *system passed an
important test in 1964 when Nehru died* and Shastri was appointed
smoothly and without violence. In the early 1980s there were
tensions between the central and state governments. Three
states – West Bengal, Tripura and Kerala – had *communist*
governments, and in September 1980 Mrs Gandhi, beset by
enormous problems, gave the government wider powers of arrest
and detention without trial, which caused many observers to
conclude that this was an *admission of failure*.

(iii) The *caste system* stood in the way of progress: Hindu society was divided into four main classes – priests, rulers and soldiers, traders and farmers, and artisans (craftsmen). People outside these groups were regarded as 'untouchables' who were discriminated against in all spheres of activity. Nehru, a strong supporter of human rights, was responsible for a *law (1955) banning discrimination against untouchables*; he also gave *women equal rights*; but practices of such long standing would take years to disappear.

(iv) Most serious of all was the *state of the economy*. Agriculture was primitive, cows, sacred to Hindus, were unproductive, industry was very small and poverty immense; there were horrifying slums in the big cities and in 1958 the average income per person was only £27 a year (£425 in Britain and £880 in the USA). Nehru realised that economic progress was vital, especially as communism seemed to be working miracles in neighbouring China. He adopted a *socialist approach involving a series of Five Year Plans*. The *first* one (1951–6) concentrated on *agriculture*, introducing fertilisers, improving seed, stock and irrigation and encouraging land redistribution; it was a striking success, increasing food production by 20 per cent. The *second* and *third plans increased industrial production*. Attempts were made to provide *education for all* and to improve *living conditions in the villages*. Mrs Gandhi continued her father's work: the *fourth plan aimed to provide millions of extra jobs*, though it fell short of its targets. Great progress was made, but despite attempts to encourage birth control, the *entire achievement was threatened by the rapidly growing population*: standing at 356 million in 1951, by 1971 it had reached 550 million and threatens to be around the 1000 million mark by the end of the century. The increases in food production could barely keep pace with the population increase and a poor harvest meant famine; there was a *chronic shortage of capital for industrial expansion* and the economy still remained precarious. Towards the end of 1980 *inflation* was rising steeply, there was industrial stagnation, acute power shortages and widespread flooding. However, during the 1980s the economic problems began to seem more manageable. *Agricultural production increased* thanks to the expanding irrigation network and the need for food imports was almost eliminated. *Oil production increased* so that in 1985 India was supplying 73 per cent of her needs, compared with only 34 per cent in 1980.

(v) *Corruption* was so widespread as to constitute a major problem; in such a poorly paid society, the acceptance of bribes, 'grease money', was common at all levels, and though Mrs Gandhi launched a determined attack, progress was slow.

(vi) The most serious problem after Mrs Gandhi's return to power in 1980 was the *Sikh separatist movement* in the Punjab where all through 1983 there was violence as Sikhs and Hindus attacked each other. Moderate Sikhs (who would be content with *more political autonomy*) were attacked by militants (who would be satisfed with nothing less than an *independent Sikh state*). Over 400 people were killed during the first half of 1984 and the climax came in June when the Indian army fought its way into and gained control of the Golden Temple, the famous Sikh holy place in Amritsar, the main city of the Punjab, which had been occupied by Sikh militants. This outraged many of the Sikh community who saw it as an act of sacrilege. Fierce fighting followed between Sikhs and the army and then in *October 1984 Mrs Gandhi was shot dead by Sikh members of her bodyguard*. The assassination was followed by the worst violence since 1947 as gangs of Hindus attacked Sikhs in retaliation, especially in the Delhi area, where support for Mrs Gandhi was strong.

Rajiv Gandhi, more prepared to compromise than his mother, tried hard to find a solution to the problem, and *signed an agreement (July 1985)* with *the moderate Sikh Akali Dal party*, promising the Sikhs much more say in local self-government and new elections for the Punjab Assembly which had been suspended since 1983. The success of the agreement seemed in grave doubt when a few weeks later, militants assassinated *Sant Longowal*, the leader who had signed it, and urged Sikhs to boycott the forthcoming elections. However, the elections went ahead, the Akali Dal winning 73 of the 117 seats, (September 1985), which was taken as a sign of public support for the July agreement. The militants refused to be reconciled and continued to harass both Hindus and moderate Sikhs.

(b) Foreign affairs

Nehru dominated Indian foreign policy and soon won a reputation as a statesman of international calibre. The *main issues* were:

(i) He was in favour of *non-alignment* – to avoid involvement with either of the power blocs in the Cold War and assume leadership of the world's uncommitted countries; these Third World states would be a powerful force for the maintenance of world peace. Cynics claimed that Nehru merely wanted to receive help from both sides, but in fact his motives seemed genuine. He supported the United Nations and helped to mediate in the Korean War and in Vietnam (1954). Although *India became a republic in 1950*, Nehru *kept her in the Commonwealth* because it would make for better understanding between Europe and Asia, and improve India's chances of qualifying for British aid. When the Indians expelled the Portuguese from their colony of Goa he was strongly criticised, but his action could be defended on grounds of nationalism.

(ii) *Relations with China* deteriorated in the late 1950s over a border dispute in *Ladakh*, a barren and sparsely populated area of

Kashmir. Oddly, Nehru, probably afraid of outraging Indian nationalist feeling, refused to compromise. In 1962 fighting broke out in which Indian troops suffered humiliating defeats, but when it seemed that northern India was open to a full-scale invasion, the Chinese withdrew. Relations continued to be uneasy, however, and the dispute remained unsettled. The incident was important: fear of Chinese attack forced Nehru to accept American military aid, so that strictly speaking, *India was no longer non-aligned*. Nehru's reputation suffered because he was thought to have neglected India's defences.

(iii) *Relations with Pakistan* were tense over a number of issues:
  – There was a dispute about which of them should own the rich province of *Kashmir*, bordering northern India and West Pakistan. Fighting twice broke out (1947 and 1965) (see Section 20.3(h)) and after the second war the Russian Prime Minister, Mr Kosygin, got Shastri and Ayub Khan of Pakistan together at Tashkent (1966) and persuaded them to withdraw their troops to the positions held before the fighting. No permanent solution was found and *Kashmir* remains partitioned.
  – The *Indus River dispute* arose because of *West Pakistan's dependence on this river and its four great tributaries* for her water supply, hydro-electric plants and irrigation. Unfortunately for the Pakistanis these rivers rise in India or the Indian part of Kashmir, and the Indians planned to build a canal to carry water from the rivers to irrigate a large desert area west of Delhi. Afraid of being left without water, the Pakistanis protested strongly; after long negotiations (1951–60), an amicable solution was found (the *Indus Waters Treaty*) for a sharing of the rivers. The *World Bank* helped by organising massive foreign loans for the building of storage dams and irrigation canals.
  – *India intervened in the civil war which broke out in Pakistan in March 1971* when East Pakistan declared itself the independent state of Bangladesh. West Pakistani forces fought savagely to bring Bangladesh back into the fold, but they committed the most terrible atrocities, and millions of refugees flooded over the border into India. *Mrs Gandhi sent Indian troops in support of Bangladesh (December 1971)* so that peace could be restored as soon as possible and the refugees, a serious drain on Indian resources, could be returned home. The Indians soon defeated the West Pakistanis and the independence of Bangladesh was assured.
  – The *Simla Conference (July 1971)* seemed the beginning of a new friendship between India and Pakistan with agreement being reached about withdrawal of troops from Bangladesh and return of prisoners of war. It was also agreed to accept the *1966 cease-fire line in Kashmir as permanent*. There was a temporary hitch when President Bhutto of Pakistan refused to recognise Bangladesh, though it gradually dawned on both governments that they could ill afford to waste their meagre resources fighting each other when

both still had appalling poverty to overcome. An important step in developing co-operation was a *trade treaty signed in 1975*, though neither her improving relations with Pakistan nor her continuing poverty dissuaded India from becoming a *nuclear power* – her first nuclear weapon was exploded in 1974.

– *Relations with Pakistan deteriorated again in 1984*: the Indians claimed that Pakistan was aiding and abetting the Sikh separatists, and they also suspected that Pakistan was on the brink of developing a nuclear weapon. President Zia went to Delhi and an agreement was signed in which both countries promised not to attack each other's nuclear installations and to curb cross-border incidents, especially in Kashmir (*December 1985*). In spite of this, trouble soon flared up again in Kashmir, and the two countries seemed on the brink of war after shelling incidents on the frontier. But neither side wanted war and in March 1987 both agreed to withdraw most of their troops from the frontier. Indian mistrust remained though, especially when it was confirmed a few weeks later that *Pakistan had indeed produced a nuclear bomb*.

24.3 PAKISTAN

Pakistan had a *much less successful history than India*; democratic governments repeatedly found themselves in difficulties and were removed by military coups.

(a) The first 10 years of independence were chaotic; everything seemed to go wrong for the Pakistanis. They soon lost their two most capable leaders: Jinnah died in 1948 and Liaquat Ali Khan was assassinated in 1951. There was no obvious successor and politics deteriorated into a sordid squabble, riddled with corruption from top to bottom. Governments seemed incapable of solving any of the problems facing them; they failed to cope with the *8 million Muslim refugees who flocked in from India*; the country was backward industrially and agriculturally and 85 per cent of the 76 million population were illiterate; although they attempted a Five Year Plan like the Indians, little progress was made because of corrupt politicians. There were the *disputes with India over Kashmir and the Indus* (see Section 24.2(b)), neither of which could be solved. Most serious of all was the difficulty of *holding together the two sections of the country* which were a thousand miles apart and had little in common except the Muslim religion: the west spoke Urdu or Punjabi and relied on wheat production, the east spoke Bengali, grew rice and produced jute, its main export. People in the east felt they were not given equal treatment with people in the west, who dominated the army, the civil service and most other spheres of activity: *discontent simmered*.

(b) Ayub Khan in power (1958–69)
By 1958, parliamentary democracy had become so discredited that the

army seized power and General Auyb Khan headed a new military government. His period in power was the most successful in Pakistan's history; trained at Sandhurst, Ayub turned out to be a first-rate administrator.

(i) His *achievements were impressive*: he removed corrupt politicians and civil servants; he introduced land reform, restricting the size of estates and taking away surplus land from wealthy landowners for redistribution among the peasants; within six months the refugees had been housed and a successful Five Year Plan for the economy was under way. Dams and hydro-electric schemes were built; production of jute, carpets and leather goods expanded, and great emphasis was laid on education. A new constitution was drawn up which would gradually return the country to full democracy, beginning with elections for local councils (1959) whose members were later allowed to elect a central parliament (1962) with limited powers. A successful solution was found to the Indus water problems, though a settlement to the Kashmir dispute eluded even Ayub after the second outbreak of war with India (1965). Apart from that Pakistan maintained *good relations with both sides in the Cold War* and particularly with *China*, India's other enemy.

(ii) *Ayub Khan's fall from power (March 1969)* came quite suddenly. In spite of his many achievements criticism mounted: the land-lords had not forgiven him for land redistribution; there were still food shortages in the east, the leaders of the Muslim religion (mullahs) claimed he was not religious enough, while the politicians, especially *Zulfikar Ali Bhutto*, accused him of corruption and a refusal to return to genuine democracy. As disorders broke out particularly in the east, Ayub resigned and the *army took power again with General Yahya Khan as President.*

(c) Civil war and the loss of Bangladesh (1971)

The well-meaning Yahya Khan was unfortunate enough to *preside over the dissolution of Pakistan*. He promised that as soon as law and order had been restored, democratic elections would be held. He kept his word and elections went ahead with remarkable smoothness (*December 1970*). The results, however, precipitated a crisis: in the west Bhutto's People's Party won a large majority while in the east Sheikh Mujibur Rahman's Awami League did even better, winning all but two of the seats. This meant that when the national parliament met the *Awami League would have an overall majority*, and for the first time the Bengalis would be able to dominate the west. This Bhutto refused to accept even though the election had been perfectly fair and legal, and he announced that his party would boycott the new parliament. After negotiations had failed to find any compromise, *Sheikh Mujib declared East Pakistan the independent republic of Bangladesh (March 1971)*. Yahya tried vainly to preserve the union, arresting Sheikh Mujib and sending troops to the east where the Bengalis resisted desperately. Ten million refugees crossed into India to escape the violence, starvation and disease; with help from India, Bangladesh managed to maintain its independence. Yahya Khan had to admit defeat and when the civil war ended he resigned (December 1971). *Bhutto became President of Pakistan while Sheikh Mujib took over Bangladesh.*

(d) **Bhutto faced dreadful problems**: his country was *humiliated by defeat* and could *ill afford to lose East Pakistan's valuable trade*; the economy was still precarious. Having precipitated the crisis that led to civil war, Bhutto now rashly *took Pakistan out of the Commonwealth* (1972) in protest against the admittance of Bangladesh, just when she needed all the help available. He remained in power and won an election in 1977. However, there were accusations of *corruption* during the election and when violence broke out the *army stepped in again and arrested Bhutto (1977)*. *General Zia ul Haq* became President heading a military government and, in spite of world-wide protests, *Bhutto was executed*. Once again the Pakistanis had been unable to work a democratic system.

Zia continued as president during the 1980s, permitting elections for a new National Assembly in February 1985. However, he had already announced that he would remain president for the next five years whatever the result of the election, so in protest, the Movement for the Return of Democracy boycotted the election.

Zia's main concerns during these years were *Pakistan's relations with India* (see above) and the constant flow of hundreds of thousands of refugees from the *civil war in Afghanistan*, which placed an enormous strain on Pakistan's slender resources. There was also the question of how long he would be able to resist the growing pressure for a *return to genuine democracy*. One of the groups supporting the campaign was the *Pakistan People's Party* under its chairman *Miss Benazir Bhutto*, daughter of the former president. When she returned to Pakistan in April 1986 she was received by an enthusiastic crowd in Lahore, and on Independence Day the following August, there were massive anti-government demonstrations in which thirty people were killed. Nor did the murder of Fazil Rahoo, vice-president of the left-wing Awami National Party (January 1987), allegedly by state intelligence agents, seem calculated to increase General Zia's popularity.

24.4 MALAYSIA

Since independence in 1957 (see Section 23.2(a)) Malaya has been the *most successful of all the former British possessions*, though it too had its problems. The main issues were:

(a) Founding of the Federation of Malaysia (1963)

Malaya seemed stable under the Prime Minister *Tunku Abdul Rahman*. Educated at Cambridge, he retained a high regard for Britain and *chose*

Fig. 24.2 *Malaysia and Indonesia*

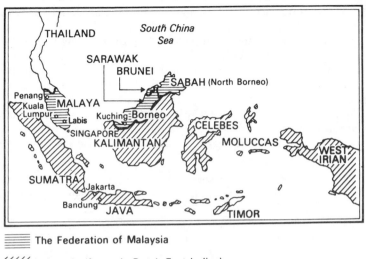

The Federation of Malaysia

Indonesia (formerly Dutch East Indies)

to remain in the Commonwealth. By 1960 the communist threat seemed to have been overcome and the economy, based on *exports of rubber and tin*, was the most prosperous in South East Asia. Thus in 1961 when Abdul Rahman proposed that Singapore and the three British colonies of North Borneo (Sabah), Brunei and Sarawak should join Malaya to form the *Federation of Malaysia*, Britain agreed. Abdul Rahman had something of an ulterior motive: the island of Singapore with its prosperous port would be a valuable acquisition, but since three-quarters of its population were Chinese, the Malays would be outnumbered if union took place just between Malaya and Singapore; if the other three colonies with their predominantly Malay population also joined the federation, the *Malay majority would be preserved.* Singapore, Sabah and Sarawak were in favour but objections came from two quarters:

(i) In *Brunei*, groups of people opposed to joining the federation started a *revolt (December 1962).* Although this was quickly suppressed by British troops flown in from Singapore, the Sultan decided not to join. This was a disappointment for Abdul Rahman since Brunei had *rich oil resources.*

(ii) *President Sukarno of Indonesia* protested because he hoped that Sabah and Sarawak would become part of Indonesia once the British left.

   After a United Nations investigation team reported that a large majority of the populations concerned was in favour of the union, the *Federation of Malaysia* was officially proclaimed (*September 1963*).

(b) Confrontation with Indonesia (1963–6)

Immediately the new state had to face a challenge from Sukarno who had announced a policy of 'confrontation' with Malaysia. His motives were not clear: he may have intended to seize Sabah and Sarawak; perhaps he hoped to manoeuvre the entire federation into becoming part of *Indonesia* as he had with West Irian in 1962 (see Section 20.3(a)); or the campaign may have been a ploy to divert attention away from Indonesia's domestic troubles. 'Confrontation' consisted of propaganda, attempts to stir up racial troubles between Malays and Chinese in Singapore, a boycott of trade with Malaysia, guerrilla attacks on Sabah and Sarawak and an airdrop of paratroops at Labis in Malaya itself. Well before the end of 1965 it was clear that Sukarno's efforts were *not going to cause Malaysia to disintegrate*:

(i)   The *Commonwealth*, particularly Britain, Australia and New Zealand, sent *troops* and their extensive use of helicopters helped them to control the situation.

(ii) The *United Nations condemned Indonesia for aggression* and the *International Monetary Fund stopped giving aid*, while the trade boycott disrupted Indonesia's economy more than Malaysia's.

(iii) *Domestic squabbles between communists and the army* drew Indonesian attention away from Malaysia and Sukarno called off 'confrontation' in June 1966.

(c) Dispute with Singapore

Singapore's membership of the federation was uneasy from the beginning and the feeling rapidly grew that she would be better off going it alone. She had already enjoyed independence from 1959 until 1963 under her energetic Prime Minister, the Cambridge-educated *Lee Kuan Yew*. The mainly Chinese population, though they had voted to join the federation, now felt that their interests were not sufficiently looked after by the Malay-dominated government at Kuala Lumpur (the federal capital); they were annoyed at the tariffs introduced to protect Malaysian industries whereas they, depending for much of their income on the port, wanted free trade to encourage business. Serious *race riots* broke out in Singapore between Chinese and Malays (September 1964) though these were aggravated by Indonesian agents. Tension remained high until in *August 1965 Singapore left the federation and became an independent republic again.*

(d) Problems of racial harmony still remained.
The Malays resented the Chinese minority either because, being involved in business, they became *wealthy*, or because they were *suspected of being communist agents*. Serious anti-Chinese rioting erupted in 1969 which was controlled only with difficulty.

(e) Communist terrorism broke out again in 1974.
Operating from the mountainous jungle near the frontier with Thailand they launched a campaign which culminated in the assassination of Perak state's police

chief. Malaysian and Thai troops co-operated in a flushing-out operation, but the guerrillas had still not been entirely suppressed at the end of 1980; alarm increased after the *communist victory in Vietnam (1975)* and even more so when *communist incursions began to take place into Thailand* from *Kampuchea* (formerly Cambodia).

Abdul Rahman (until his retirement in 1970) and his successor, Abdul Razak, at first worked on the theory that *prosperity was the best way to keep communism* out. Reliance on rubber and tin was reduced by promoting pineapple and rice growing, fishing and livestock farming; Malaysia processed more of its own rubber in the manufacture of tyres; new markets were found in America and Japan, while education and health services were extended. In 1980 a large development programme was started for the neglected north and a new 72-mile east–west highway was due to be opened in 1981 linking Penang to the east coast. In the late 1970s the government also began to build up its military strength, buying 88 Skyhawk planes, 60 tanks and other assorted equipment. By 1984 the army expected to be able to mobilise half a million troops, if the need arose.

(f) Problems during the 1980s. After the prosperity of the 1970s, the economy began to feel the rigours of *world depression*, particularly the *fall in world prices of all Malaysia's main products* – oil, rubber, palm oil and tin – which caused a 7 per cent drop in government income and threw about 8 per cent of the working population out of their jobs by 1985. A problem of quite a different sort was Malaysia's involvement with the *drug trade*; it had become a centre for processing and distributing heroin. Fearing that this presented a threat to national security, the government introduced tough measures (1983), including the death penalty for anyone caught in possession of over 15 grammes of heroin. During the three years following, some 38 people were hanged for drug offences. In spite of some international protest at the execution of two young Australians (July 1986), the government seemed to be getting the situation under control.

24.5 THE AFRICAN NATIONS

(a) Common problems
All the new African nations, not just the former British possessions, faced *similar problems*.

(i)   They each contained a number of *different tribes* which had been held together only by the foreign colonial rulers and had united in the nationalist struggle for freedom from the foreigners. As soon as the Europeans withdrew there was little incentive to stay together and they tended to regard *loyalty to the tribe* as more important than *loyalty to their new nation*. In Nigeria and the Congo (now Zaire) tribal differences became so intense that *civil war* developed.

(ii) Like many other Third World states, they were *economically under-developed*, often relying on one or two commodities for export, so that a fall in the world price of their products was a major disaster. There was a *shortage of capital and of skills of all kinds*, and the *population was growing at a rate of over 2 per cent a year*. Loans from abroad left them *heavily in debt*, and as they concentrated on increasing exports to pay for the loans, food for home consumption became scarcer.

(iii) Faced with such difficulties the politicians, lacking experience of how to work the systems of parliamentary democracy left behind by the Europeans, failed to cope and *governments became corrupt*. This led to the creation of *one-party states* as the only way to achieve progress. In many states such as Kenya and Tanzania, this worked well providing stable and effective government; on the other hand since it was impossible to oppose such governments by legal means, violence was often the only answer and the *military coup* to remove unpopular politicans became common. President Nkrumah of Ghana, for example, was removed by the army in 1966 after two assassination attempts had failed.

(iv) In the 1980s the whole of Africa was beset by *economic and natural disasters*. The *world recession* reduced demand for African exports such as oil, copper and cobalt and there was a severe *drought (1982–5)* which caused crop failures, deaths of livestock, famine and starvation. The drought ended in 1986 and much of the continent had record harvests that year. However, by this time Africa, like the rest of the Third World, was suffering from a severe *debt crisis* (see Section 22.2(c)), while having been forced by the IMF to economise drastically in return for further loans. This often involved *devaluing their currency*, and *reducing food price subsidies*, which *increased food prices* at a time when unemployment was rising, wages falling and social services being cut as part of the austerity programme. Africa was the only area of the world where, in 1987, incomes were, on average, lower than in 1972. At an Addis Ababa summit meeting of the African nations (July 1985), President Nyerere of Tanzania blamed the crisis on the world recession, an unjust international economic system, an unprecedented rise in interest rates, famine and drought. He warned that most of them were unable to keep up their interest repayments, and called on the international community to find a lasting solution.

(b) Ghana

Kwame Nkrumah ruled Ghana from *independence in 1957* until his *removal by the army in 1966*.

(i) *His achievements were impressive to begin with*. He was a *socialist* in outlook and wanted his people to enjoy a higher standard of living that would come from efficient organisation and industrialisation. Production of *cocoa* (Ghana's main export) doubled, forestry, fishing and cattle-breeding expanded and the country's modest deposits of gold and bauxite were more effectively exploited. The *building of a dam on the Volta River* (begun 1961) provided water for irrigation and hydro-electric power, producing enough electricity for the towns as well as for a new aluminium smelting plant. Government money was provided for *village projects* in which local people built roads and schools. Nkrumah also gained prestige *internationally*: he strongly supported the *pan-African movement*, believing that only through a federation of the whole continent could African power make itself felt. As a start an *economic union* was formed with Guinea and Mali, though nothing much came of it. He supported the *Organisation of African Unity (set up 1963)* and usually played a responsible role in world affairs, *remaining in the Commonwealth* while at the same time *forging links with the USSR and China*.

(ii) *Why was Nkrumah overthrown?* He had tried to *introduce industrialisation too quickly* and had *borrowed vast amounts of capital* from abroad, hoping to balance the budget from increased exports. Unfortunately Ghana was still uncomfortably dependent on cocoa exports and a *steep fall in the world price of cocoa* left her with a *huge balance of payments deficit*. There was criticism that too much money was being wasted on unnecessary projects like the 10-mile stretch of motorway from Accra (the capital) to Tema. Probably the most important reason was that Nkrumah gradually began to abandon parliamentary government in favour of a *one-party state* and personal dictatorship. He justified this on the grounds that the opposition parties, which were based on tribal differences, were not constructive and merely wanted more power in their own areas; they had no experience of working a parliamentary system and as Nkrumah himself wrote: 'Even a system based on a democratic constitution may need backing up in the period following independence by emergency measures of a totalitarian kind.' From 1959 opponents could be deported or imprisoned for up to five years without trial. Even the respected opposition leader, J. B. Danqua, was arrested in 1961 and died in prison. In 1964 all parties except his own were banned, and even within his own party no criticism was allowed. He began to build up the image of himself as the 'father of the nation'. Slogans such as 'Nkrumah is our Messiah, Nkrumah never dies' were circulated and numerous statues of the saviour were erected. This struck many people as absurd but again Nkrumah justified it, claiming that the population could identify itself better with a single personality as leader than with *vague notions of the state*. All this, plus the fact that he was believed to have amassed a personal fortune through corruption, was *too much for the army who seized control* when Nkrumah was on a visit to China.

The military government promised a return to democracy as soon as a new constitution could be drawn up, complete with safeguards against a return to dictatorship. The constitution was ready in 1969 and the elections returned Dr Kofi Busia, leader of the Progressive Party, as the new Prime Minister (October 1969).

(iii) *Kofi Busia* lasted only until January 1972 when he too was *overthrown by the army.* An academic who had studied economics at Oxford, Busia illustrates perfectly the difficulties of democratically elected politicians in the African situation. In power in the first place only by permission of the army, he had to produce *quick results.* Yet the problems were enormous – rising unemployment, rising prices and massive debts to be repaid. Canada and the USA were prepared to wait for repayment but other countries, including Britain, were not so sympathetic. Busia, who had a reputation for honesty, tried genuinely to keep up payments, but these were using up about *40 per cent of Ghana's export profits.* In *1971 imports were limited* and the *currency devalued by nearly 50 per cent.* Busia was hampered by the *tribal squabbles* which re-emerged under the free democracy and the economic situation deteriorated so rapidly that in *January 1972 he was evicted, without resistance,* by Colonel Ignatius Acheampong who headed a military government until July 1978. As Ghana continued to flounder amid her economic problems, Acheampong was himself removed from power by General Fred Akuffo, for alleged corruption. In June 1979 a group of junior officers led by *J. J. Rawlings* (of mixed Ghanaian–Scottish parentage) seized power on the grounds that corrupt soldiers and politicians needed to be weeded out before a return to democracy. They launched what was described as a 'house-cleaning' exercise in which Acheampong and Akuffo were executed after secret trials. In July elections were held as a result of which Rawlings returned Ghana to *civilian rule* with Dr Limann as President (September 1979).

(iv) *Jerry Rawlings again.* Limann was no more successful than previous leaders in halting Ghana's economic decline. Corruption was still rife at all levels, and smuggling and hoarding of basic goods were commonplace; during *1981 inflation* was running at *125 per cent*, and there was widespread *labour unrest* as wages remained low. Limann was removed in a military coup (December 1981) and Flight-Lieutenant J. J. Rawlings became chairman of a Provisional National Defence Council. He was rare among military leaders: the army did not want power, he said, but simply to be 'part of the decision-making process' which would change Ghana's whole economic and social system. Though Rawlings remained leader, the PNDC appointed a civilian government of well-known figures from political and academic circles. Ghana suffered badly from the *drought in 1983*, but there was ample rainfall in 1984, bringing a good maize harvest. The *new recovery programme seemed to be working*, production rose by 7 per cent and early in 1985 inflation was down to 40 per cent.

As Ghana celebrated 30 years of independence (March 1987), she was still on course for recovery, and Rawlings and the PNDC, evoking memories of Nkrumah, were running an apparently successful campaign to unite the 12 million Ghanaians solidly behind them.

(c) Nigeria

Superficially Nigeria, which gained independence in 1960, seemed to have advantages over Ghana; it was potentially a wealthy state, extensive *oil resources* having been discovered in the eastern coastal area. The Prime Minister was the capable and moderate Sir Abubakar Tafawa Balewa assisted by the veteran nationalist leader Azikiwe, who was made President when *Nigeria became a republic in 1963*. However, in *1966 the government* was overthrown by a military coup and the following year *civil war broke out* which lasted until *1970*.

(i) *What caused the civil war?* A combination of problems of the type mentioned in Section 24.5(a) led to the outbreak. Nigeria's *tribal differences* were more serious than Ghana's, and although the constitution was a *federal one* in which each of the three regions (north, east and west) had its own local government, the regions felt that the central government in Lagos did not safeguard their interests sufficiently. Balewa came from the north where the Hausa and Fulani tribes were powerful, and the Yorubas of the west and Ibos of the east were constantly complaining about northern domination, even though Azikiwe was an Ibo. To make matters worse there was an *economic recession*. By 1964 prices had risen 15 per cent, unemployment was rising and wages were, on average, well below what had been calculated as the minimum living wage. Criticism of the government mounted and Balewa replied by arresting Chief Awolowo, Prime Minister of the western region, which for a time seemed likely to break away from the federation. The central government was also accused of corruption after blatantly trying to 'fix' the election results of 1964. In January 1966 there was a military coup carried out by mainly Ibo officers, in which Balewa and other politicians were killed. After this the situation deteriorated steadily: in the north there were savage massacres of Ibos who had moved into the region for better jobs and the new leader, General Ironsi, himself an Ibo, was murdered by northern soldiers. When a northerner, *Colonel Yakubu Gowon*, emerged supreme, almost all the Ibos fled from other parts of Nigeria back to the east whose leader Colonel Ojukwu announced that the *eastern region had seceded from Nigeria to become the independent state of Biafra (May 1967)*. Gowon launched what he described as a 'short surgical police action' to bring the east back to Nigeria.

(ii) *The civil war.* It took more than a short police action as the Biafrans fought back vigorously. It was a bitter and terrible war in

illus 24.1 *Biafra – a fifteen-year-old victim of war and famine*

which Biafra lost more civilians from disease and starvation than troops killed in the fighting. Neither the United Nations nor the Commonwealth was able to mediate, and the Biafrans hung on to the bitter end as Nigerian troops closed in on all sides; the *final surrender came in January 1970*. Nigerian unity had been preserved.

(iii) *Recovery after the war* was remarkably swift. There were pressing problems: *famine in Biafra, inter-tribal bitterness, unemployment and economic resources strained by the war*. Gowon showed considerable statesmanship in this difficult situation: he made every effort to reconcile the Ibos and persuaded them to return to their jobs in other parts of the country; he introduced a new federal system of 12 states, later increased to 19, to give more recognition of local tribal differences. Nigeria was able to take advantage of rising oil prices in the mid-1970s which gave her a healthy balance of payments position. In 1975 Gowon was removed by another army group, which probably thought he intended to return the country to civilian rule too early. Nigeria continued to prosper and the *army kept its promise of a return to democratic government in 1979*. Elections were held as a result of which President Shagari became head of a civilian government. With Nigeria's oil much in demand abroad, prosperity seemed assured and prospects for a stable government bright.

(iv) *Unfulfilled promise.* Unfortunately disappointment was soon to follow: during 1981 the economy got into difficulties because of the *fall in world oil prices*, and the healthy trade balance of 1980 became a *deficit in 1983*. Although Shagari was elected for another four-year term (August 1983), he was removed by a military coup the following December. According to the new leader, Major-General Bukhari, the civilian government was guilty of mismanagement of the economy, financial corruption and rigging of the election. Before long Bukhari became the victim of yet another coup carried out by a rival group of army officers who complained that Bukhari had not done enough to reverse the fall in living standards, rising prices, chronic shortages and increasing unemployment. The new president, Major-General Babangida, began energetically, introducing what he called a 'belt-tightening' campaign, and announcing plans to develop the *non-oil side of the economy*. He aimed to expand production of rice, maize, fish, vegetable oil and animal products and to give special priority to steel manufacture and assembly of motor vehicles. Following the example of Jerry Rawlings in Ghana, he declared that his military government would not remain in power 'a day longer than was absolutely necessary'. A committee of academics was set to work to produce a new constitution which could 'guarantee an acceptable and painless succession mechanism', and October 1990 was fixed as the date for a return to civilian rule. Another blow came in 1986 with a *further dramatic fall in oil prices* which in July reached a record low of only 10 dollars a barrel. This was a disaster for the government which had *based its 1986 budget calculations on a price of 23.50 dollars a barrel*. In October, it announced that it could not manage repayments due for goods imported on credit, and was *forced to accept a loan from the World Bank* to enable the recovery programme to go ahead.

Of the new states of East and Central Africa, Uganda followed the pattern of Ghana and Nigeria: President Milton Obote was overthrown by General Idi Amin (1971) who was himself removed after a brutal dictatorship (1979). In 1980 the country was still in a state of chaos, no stable system having emerged. However, the other states managed to avoid such upheavals, mainly because of the skill of their respective leaders.

(d) Kenya

Jomo Kenyatta ruled undisturbed from 1963 until his death in 1978 when his Vice-President, Daniel arap Moi, took over smoothly.

(i) *Problems*. There were the usual *tribal rivalries*: Kenyatta himself came from the largest tribe, the Kikuyus, while other influential ones were Luos, Massais and Hamitics. There were also racial difficulties: out of a population of 10 million, 200,000 were Asians, about 50,000 British and 30,000 Arabs, and non-Africans held most of the dominant positions in the professions and commerce: Kenyatta wanted Africans to fill these jobs. *The economy was too dependent on exports of tea and coffee* and there was hardly any industry and very few resources.

(ii) *Kenyatta's achievements were considerable* in spite of such an unpromising situation. In the first decade of independence he ruled firmly and decisively while managing to avoid the sort of semi-dictatorship adopted by Nkrumah in Ghana. He handled the tribal rivalries skilfully, although there was a crisis in 1969 when his Vice-President Tom Mboya, a Luo, was assassinated in Nairobi by a Kikuyu. Luo tribesmen rampaged through the city smashing up cars and shops in revenge, but violence subsided after the assassin was arrested and hanged. He worked towards *Africanisation* (allowing Africans equal opportunities with other races to achieve top positions) but at the same time aimed for a multi-racial society in which Asians and other non-Africans were welcome provided they took Kenyan citizenship. Pressure was brought to bear on those, *particularly Asians*, who refused and in 1968 over 60,000 of them fled from Kenya to Britain, causing the British government to limit entry to about 5000 Asians a year. After that, Kenyatta relaxed the pressure and allowed Asians to leave gradually under a quota system; over 100,000 Asians remained after taking Kenyan citizenship.

Economic problems were tackled by carefully worked out *Five Year Plans*, the first three of which (1964–79) showed promising results. Tea and coffee output increased and industries such as paper manufacturing and soda production for making glass expanded rapidly. Cotton production increased from 20,000 bales in 1977 to 70,000 in 1979. Foreign investment by governments and firms helped: British Leyland, for example, became a partner in a vehicle assembly plant at Thika. As a result the economy was generally healthy with especially good years in 1976 and 1977 when tea and coffee prices reached record heights.

(iii) *Criticisms can be made of Kenyatta*, however. In the mid-1970s there was a *distinct drift towards a one-party state*, Kenyatta's party, the Kenya African National Union (KANU). There was less tolerance of criticism: in 1975 a prominent Kikuyu politician, Josiah Kariuki was found dead in the bush shortly after condemning corrupt 'get-rich-quick' politicians (in which he included Kenyatta). In spite of the economic boom, too much of the profits went to *foreign shareholders*; and though many African politicians and businessmen made ample profits, the mass of the population felt no benefit whatsoever; it made little difference to them whether Kenya was a British colony or an independent state run by Africans.

(iv) *Daniel arap Moi* was unfortunate in that he became President (August 1978) *just as the economic boom ended*, and there was a sharp fall in the world prices of coffee and tea, which still accounted for 60 per cent of Kenya's exports. The *value of exports fell by 25 per cent* causing an *unfavourable balance of payments*, and there was a serious food shortage and rocketing prices after a poor harvest. This brought to light a glaring example of *inefficiency* and *corruption* among government officials: it was discovered in March 1980 that the maize reserve of two million bags had vanished and it emerged that certain officials had declared the reserves unfit for human consumption and allowed them to be bought at bargain prices by merchants who resold them abroad at a handsome profit. President Moi, a former headmaster with a reputation for honesty, came to power on a wave of goodwill as he freed many political prisoners and promised reform, especially a war on corruption. The *fourth Five Year Plan* was launched in 1979 with the aim of alleviating *poverty*, and it enjoyed a certain amount of success. However, Kenya, like the rest of Africa, was affected by *drought*, especially in *1984–5*. About one-third of the country's 10 million cattle died, while maize production fell 35 per cent. The picture was not all gloom though: exports of tea and coffee remained good and *manufacturing* was the fastest growing part of the economy, increasing by about 4 per cent each year. Important political developments took place, *moving Kenya towards totalitarianism*. In May 1982 the country was declared a *one-party state*: only KANU was allowed, and Oginga Odinga

474

(leader of the Luos) was expelled from KANU for allegedly planning to launch a new socialist opposition party. President Moi was re-elected unopposed for a further term (September 1983) and in December 1986 the constitution was changed, giving him extra powers to appoint and dismiss senior officials and civil servants, and making him and his party supreme over both the elected parliament and the High Court. Church leaders complained that even constructive criticism was becoming impossible and in 1987 Amnesty International protested that large numbers of people, allegedly connected with a secret opposition party called Mwakenya, were being held, tortured and beaten.

(e) Tanzania

Tanganyika became independent in 1961 and was joined in *1964* by the *island of Zanzibar to form Tanzania.* It was ruled continuously by *Dr Julius Nyerere*, leader of the Tanzanian African Nationalist Union (TANU), who had to deal with formidable problems: Tanzania was arguably the *poorest state in the whole of Africa*, with very little industry, few mineral resources and a heavy dependence on *coffee* production; in addition there were the usual tribal and racial problems plus, later, Tanzania's expensive involvement in military operations to oust President Amin of Uganda. Nyerere retired in 1985 (aged 63), and was succeeded by his Vice-President, Ali Hassan Mwinyi.

(i) *Nyerere's approach and achievements.* His approach was different from that of any other African ruler. He began conventionally enough by *expanding the economy*: during the first ten years of independence, production of coffee and cotton doubled and sugar production trebled, while health services and education expanded. But Nyerere was not happy that Tanzania seemed to be developing along the same lines as Kenya, with an ever-widening gulf between the wealthy élite and the resentful masses. His proposed solution to the problem was set out in a remarkable document known as the *Arusha Declaration* published in *1967*: the country must be run on *socialist* lines. All human beings should be treated as equal; the state must have effective control over the means of production and must intervene in economic life to make sure that people were not exploited by other groups, and that poverty, ignorance and disease were eliminated; there must be no great accumulations of wealth or society would no longer be classless; bribery and corruption must be eliminated. According to Nyerere, *Tanzania was at war and the enemy was poverty and oppression*; the way to victory was not through money and foreign aid but through hard work and self-reliance; the first priority was to *improve agriculture* so that the country could be *self-sufficient in food production.*

Nyerere strove hard to put these aims into practice: all important enterprises, including those owned by foreigners, were *nationalised*; five-year development plans were introduced. Village projects were encouraged and given aid by the government; these involved *ujamaa* ('familyhood' or self-help): families in each village pooled resources and farmed collectively using more modern techniques. Foreign loans and investments as well as imports were reduced to a minimum to avoid running into debt. Politically, Nyerere's brand of socialism meant a *one-party state run by TANU*, but elections were still held. It seemed that some elements of genuine democracy existed since voters in each constituency had a choice of two TANU candidates and every election resulted in a large proportion of MPs losing their seats. Nyerere himself provided dignified leadership and with his simple life style and complete indifference to wealth he set the perfect example for the party and the country to follow. The enterprise was a fascinating experiment which *tried to combine socialist direction from the centre with the African traditions of local decision making*; it tried to provide an alternative to western capitalist society with its pursuit of profit, which most other African states seemed to be copying.

(ii) *Success or failure?* Despite Nyerere's achievements, it was clear when he retired in 1985 that his experiment had been, at best, *only a limited success*. At an international conference on the Arusha Declaration (held December 1986) President Mwinyi gave some impressive social statistics which few other African countries could match: 3.7 million children in primary school; two universities with over 4500 students; a literacy rate of 85 per cent; 150 hospitals; 2600 dispensaries; infant mortality down to 137 per thousand; life expectancy up to 52. However, other parts of the Arusha Declaration were not achieved: *corruption* crept in because many officials were not as high-minded as Nyerere himself; there was *insufficient investment in agriculture* so that *production was far below what was expected*; the nationalisation of the sisal estates carried out in the 1960s, was a failure – Nyerere himself admitted that production had declined from 220,000 tonnes in 1970 to only 47,000 tonnes in 1984, and in May 1985 he *reversed the nationalisation*. From the end of 1978 Tanzania was in difficulties because of the *fall in world prices of coffee and tea* (her main exports), *rising oil prices* (which used up almost half of her earnings from exports) and the *expenses of the war against Amin in Uganda* (at least £1000 million). Although oil prices began to fall during 1981, there was soon the further problem of the near collapse of her other exports (cattle, cement and agricultural produce) which left her *without foreign exchange. IMF loans* only brought her the added problem of how to meet the *interest repayments*. Tanzania was *nowhere near being a socialist state*, nor was it *self-reliant* – two major aims of the Declaration. Nevertheless Nyerere was deservedly highly respected both as an African and world statesman, as an enemy of apartheid in South Africa and as an outspoken critic of the world economy and the way it exploited poor countries. His prestige was at its height when he was chosen as chairman of the Organisation of African Unity (OAU) for 1984–5.

(f) Zambia

Formerly Northern Rhodesia, Zambia, like Tanzania, was fortunate in having an outstanding and dedicated President, *Dr Kenneth Kaunda.* The son of a Methodist minister, he cared deeply about his people, was aware of their problems and genuinely tried to build a successful multi-racial society in Zambia. Amid a mass of complex problems he was a major force for good. What were the *problems* and *how successfully* did Kaunda deal with them?

(i) *Tribal rivalry* was more serious than in Tanzania; there were *over 70 different tribes* and Kaunda, himself a Nyanja, tried to include a wide tribal representation in his government. However the Bembas of the north and the Lozis of the north-west wanted to break away, even though Kaunda appointed Simon Kapwepwe, a Bemba, as his Vice-President. In the late 1960s it became increasingly difficult for Kaunda to get his policies accepted, and when a disagreement arose between Kaunda and Kapwepwe, who wanted a harder line towards South Africa (see Section 25.3), the President felt compelled to make a stand, if any progress at all was to be achieved. By 1973 it had turned Zambia into a *one-party state* (the United National Independence Party), and although he was criticised for this outside Zambia, it seemed the only way to prevent the country disintegrating into tribal groups.

(ii) There were *serious racial problems* as thousands of whites stayed on after independence; there were extreme racialists of all colours. Kaunda managed to overcome the extremists with his humane and sensible approach and to make a multi-racial society work. So great was his prestige that even white South Africans working in the copper mines were prepared to risk staying on; provided Kaunda remained in power.

(iii) Zambia had the misfortune to *border onto Southern Rhodesia* which illegally declared itself independent of Britain in 1965 (see Section 25.2). Zambia found herself caught up in the *front line of the struggle to bring down the Smith regime*, and suffered serious inconvenience as a result. When Britain helped by the United Nations imposed economic sanctions on Rhodesia, Zambia, which depended on Rhodesian railways for carrying her oil supplies and her copper exports, was probably worse hit than Rhodesia. The irony of it was that while *Zambia genuinely tried to maintain sanctions, to her own detriment, British and French* companies as well as those of many other nationalities, which considered profit more important, *ignored them* and Rhodesia continued to obtain oil supplies and to sell her products abroad. In desperation Zambia and Tanzania turned to *China*, who agreed to build the *Zam Tan Railway*; started in 1971 this provided a *vital new trade link to the coast through Tanzania*.

When it became clear that sanctions were ineffective, black African nationalists, determined to free *Zimbabwe* (the African name for Rhodesia) from white control, began a *guerrilla campaign operating from bases in Zambia and Mozambique* (after 1975 when Mozambique became independent from Portugal). The Smith government retaliated by *bombing guerrilla bases in Zambia*. A further complication was that other black African states expected Zambia to play a more active role against Rhodesia, but Kaunda was anxious to avoid all-out war; he knew that Zambia could not afford such extravagance, and apart from that Zambia and Rhodesia shared the *Kariba Dam* whose *generating stations were all on the Rhodesian side*; Kaunda dared not risk losing vital electricity supplies. It was the end of a major headache when the Rhodesian problem was apparently solved early in 1980.

(iv) Zambia's economy seemed reasonably healthy for the first few years after independence: *she had more of an industrial base than Tanzania*, having extensive *copper* resources which were mined and exported. Tobacco and cotton were grown and there was a small textile industry. The *weakness was that copper made up 90 per cent of Zambia's exports*; in *1971 a sudden fall in the world price of copper* threw her economy into disarray – she had an unfavourable balance of payments for the first time since independence. Although prices fluctuated after that, they never fully recovered, and Zambia, with her weak bargaining position, tended to get lower prices from wealthy industrial nations than other copper producers did. At the same time certain *foreign companies took advantage of Zambia* (and of other African states as well) by *charging over-inflated prices for vital goods* which could not be obtained elsewhere (spares for tractors for example). For the average Zambian this situation meant a *fall in real wages and growing discontent*.

As Zambia celebrated the twenty-second anniversary of independence (October 1986) President Kaunda was still in power. He had steered his country skilfully through tribal, racial and foreign problems, but had still to find a solution to the economic problems: the need for *self-sufficiency in food production* and the need to *diversify industrial production* in order to reduce dependence on copper and so earn valuable foreign exchange. 1982–3, for example, was a bad year when, because of a fall in world demand for copper, cobalt and lead, Zambia's exports were 7 per cent down on the previous two years. 1983–4 saw an improvement – thanks to a slight increase in world metal prices, the mining industry made a profit for the first time in several years and export earnings were 10 per cent up on the previous year. But 1986 saw Zambia as the typical African victimn of the world economic system. The government was doing its best to carry out a programme of agricultural expansion, but found it was impossible to finance it without *IMF loans*.

These were provided only on condition that a *stringent economic reform package* – currency devaluation, price rises and cuts in food subsidies – was introduced. This had a disastrous effect on an already impoverished population and there were numerous outbreaks of rioting and looting of food shops. A climax came in December when the government announced a 120 per cent rise in the price of refined maize meal, one of the country's staple foods. Four days of widespread rioting followed in the copperbelt and the army had to be sent in to restore order. The situation remained so tense that President Kaunda withdrew the price rise a few days later. An ominous sign during the riots was attacks on the houses of party officials, whish suggested that President Kaunda's rule was likely to face a growing challenge unless the economic situation improved.

QUESTIONS

1. Tanzania since independence

Study the Sources below, and then answer the questions that follow.

Source A

The code of conduct issued for TANU members, 1962.

1. All men are my brothers and Africa is one.
2. Bribery is the enemy of justice; I will never receive or offer a bribe.
3. Leadership is a trust; I will not exploit my position or the position of another for personal advantage.
4. I will educate myself to the extent that I am able and use my knowledge for the benefit of all.

(Extracts.)

Source B

President Nyerere's Arusha Declaration, February 1967.

1. Every citizen is an integral part of the nation and has the right to take equal part in governmment at local, regional and national level; i.e., a socialist government of the people.
2. All citizens together possess all the natural resources of the country in trust for their descendants.
3. In order to ensure economic justice, the State must have effective control over the principal means of production.
4. There must be equal opportunity for all men and women irrespective of race, religion or status, and there must be no accumulation of wealth to an extent which is inconsistent with the existence of a classless society.
5. All resources must be mobilised towards the elimination of poverty, ignorance and disease.

6. Independence means self-reliance; we know what is the foundation and what is the fruit of development; between MONEY and PEOPLE, it is obvious that their foundation is the people and their HARD WORK, especially in agriculture. This is the meaning of self-reliance.

Sources A and B are both quoted in D. Harkness, *The Post-War World* (Macmillan, 1974, adapted extracts).

Source C

President Julius Nyerere is the only African Head os State who has evolved a political system based on African Traditions . . . it seems likely that he will succeed in carrying out his full programme; and if he does, the egalitarian Tanzanian nation which he will have created, cannot fail, by its example, to influence, not only other states in the African continent, but also developing countries in other parts of the world.

Source: Judith Listowel, *Tanzania and her Future* (in Round Table, no. 239, July, 1970, extract).

Source D
A newspaper article of 1987 – 'Africa'a New Dawn in a Poor Light', by Haroub Othman.

On the 20th anniversary of Tanzania's Arusha Declaration this week, Tanzanians have been looking back at the results of one of Africa's most controversial landmarks . . . In some respects it provided the basis for some remarkable achievements, especially in the social services . . . However, the last decade has seen a consistently worsening economic climate; the causes – steep oil prices, the war with Uganda and a fall in trade. The government therefore sought foreign aid and Tanzania now receives a very high level of Western development assistance. Agricultural investment has been low and production is showing a downward curve. Inefficiency and corruption have become the norm, and Tanzania is not anywhere near being a socialist state, as Nyerere himself is quick to remind others.

Source: *Guardian*, 6 February 1987.

(a) (i) What do the initials TANU stand for in Source A? **1**
     (ii) Why do you think President Nyerere decided to issue the code of conduct (Source A)? **1,2,4(a)**
(b) (i) Suggest *one* word which sums up the idea expressed in point 1 of Source B. **1,4(a)**
     (ii) Summarise briefly, in your own words, the aims which are put forward in points 2, 3 and 4 of the Arusha Declaration.
     4(a)

    (iii)   Explain what is meant by the phrase 'self-reliance' in point 6.

                                                                 4(a)

(c)   (i)   According to Source C, what was special about President Nyerere?   **4(a)**

    (ii)   What does the writer of Source C mean by the phrase 'the egalitarian Tanzanian nation'?   **4(a)**

    (iii)   Using your own knowledge, describe how President Nyerere tried to carry out the aims of the Arusha Declaration.

                                                              1,2,4(a)

(d)   'Neither the code of conduct nor the aims of the Arusha Declaration have been achieved to any great extent.' Using your own knowledge and the evidence in Source D, explain fully whether you agree or disagree with this statement.   **1,2,4(a,c)**

(e)   (i)   What are the advantages and disadvantages of *each* of these four Sources, for the historian trying to find out what actually happened in Tanzania?   **4(a,b)**

    (ii)   Which one of the four Sources do you think is most useful? Explain your choice fully.   **4(a,b,c)**

2. India and Pakistan

Study the Sources below, and then answer the questions that follow.

Source A

Kashmir and Pakistan (Fig. 24.3).

Source B

Report in the *Guardian*, 3 February 1987.

New Delhi: The Indian army evacuated 20,000 to 25,000 residents from 100 border villages in Kashmir after Pakistani troops shelled parts of the area over the weekend. A local journalist in Jammu, the summer capital of the state, said there were four incidents of firing across the border over the weekend. He had seen 'Indian tanks taking position on the border'. Indian Defence Ministery sources have said that 220,000 Indian troops were positioned on the frontier. Pakistan's troop strength was not known. One Kashmiri official called the situation 'quite serious' and said that as many as 30,000 people may have fled from the Pargwal district alone, in the south of the state. India and Pakistan have fought three wars since independence in 1947. Two were over Kashmir which both claim as their territory. Since the last war, in 1971, troops of the two countries have held their positions at the time of the ceasefire.

Source C

Report in the *Guardian*, 5 March 1987.

India and Pakistan will begin withdrawing their troops from the border today. About 50,000 men on either side are to be redeployed to their

Fig. 24.3 *the Kashmir and Indus River disputes between India and Pakistan*

——— The 1949 cease-fire line, still being observed

peace-time bases within 15 days. Agreement was reached last night on a balanced sector-by-sector withdrawal designed to defuse the crisis which brought the two countries to the brink of a war neither wanted. The deputy chief of the Indian army staff said that Operation Brass Tacks, the big Indian exercise involving 200,000 troops which provoked Pakistan to move its forces to the border, would 'proceed as planned' during February and March. Both sides have now agreed not to attack each other, to exercise maximum restraint, and to avoid all provocative actions along the border.

(a)   (i)   Using the information provided by Sources A and B, explain why there has been a dispute over Kashmir and how a temporary solution was found in 1949.   **4(a,c)**

     (ii)   According to Source B, how many times have India and Pakistan fought each other since 1947?   **4(a)**

(b)   Source B mentions 'the last war, in 1971'. Explain:
    (i)   why India fought Pakistan in 1971;
    (ii)   how the war was brought to an end;
    (iii)   what results the war had for Pakistan.   **1,2**

(c) Source A also illustrates another dispute between India and Pakistan. Using your own knowledge, and the information provided by Source A, explain:

    (i) why this other dispute arose;

    (ii) how it was eventually settled.   **1,2,4(a)**

(d)   (i) According to Source B, why were people being evacuated from border villages?   **4(a)**

    (ii) Using the evidence in Sources B and C, explain how the 1987 crisis in Kashmir arose.   **4(a,c)**

    (iii) According to Source C, how was this crisis settled?   **4(a)**

    (iv) Why do you think this 1987 Kashmir crisis was settled peacefully whereas those in 1948 and 1965 led to war?   **1,2,4(a)**

(e)   (i) Are Sources B and C primary or secondary sources? Give reasons for your answer.   **4(a,b)**

    (ii) How far do you think Sources B and C provide the historian with a full and accurate picture of what happened in the 1987 Kashmir crisis? Explain your answer fully.   **4(a,b)**

3. Malaysia

Study the Source below, and then answer the questions that follow.

A speech by Sir Robert Menzies, Prime Minister of Australia, to the Australian parliament, 25 September 1963.

> Australia will give military assistance to defend Malaysia in the event of any armed invasion or of any subversive activity inspired from outside Malaysia. So far back as April 1955, the government emphasised the importance of Malaya to the security of the zone in which we live and pointed out that, in consequence, Malayan defence was a matter from which we could not stand aloof . . . Malaysia, the new nation, is here. The processes of its creation have been democratic. The UN Secretary-General reported that the people of North Borneo and Sarawak desired incorporation into Malaysia . . . We publicly support Malaysia which is a Commonwealth country just as our own is.

Source: *Keesing's Contemporary Archives* (October 1963, adapted extracts.)

(a)   (i) What four states joined together to form the Federation of Malaysia in 1963?   **1,4(a)**

    (ii) What other former British colony in the area decided not to join Malaysia?   **1**

    (iii) Why was this decision taken and why did it disappoint the Malaysian government?   **1,2**

(b)   (i) How long was it since the Australian government had first announced its interest in Malaya?   **4(a)**

    (ii) What clues does the speech give as to why Australia was interested in what happened in Malaysia?   **4(a)**

    (iii) What promises does the Australian Prime Minister give in his speech?   **4(a)**

(c)   (i) Explain why the Secretary-General of the UN had become involved in the situation.   **1,2,4(a)**

    (ii) What evidence is there in the speech that the creation of Malaysia had been democratic?   **4(a)**

(d)   (i) Describe how, in the months following this speech, President Sukarno followed a policy of 'confrontation' with Malaysia.   **1,2**

    (ii) What were his motives for this policy?   **1,2**

(e)   (i) Mentioning Australia's contribution, describe and explain how Malaysia was able to survive Indonesia's campaign. **1,2**

    (ii) Explain why Singapore decided to leave the Federation of Malaysia in 1965.   **1,2**

4. **(a)** What problems have the newly independent African nations had to face?

    (b) Choose one of the following African countries and describe how it has tried to deal with its problems: Ghana, Nigeria, Kenya, Zambia.   **1,2**

5. It is 1987, and you are the editor of a government controlled newspaper in Ghana. Write an article celebrating the 30th anniversary of Ghana's independence. Among other things, you should mention:

    (i) the achievements of Kwame Nkrumah;

    (ii) why he was overthrown in 1966 and your feelings about his fall from power;

    (iii) Ghana's problems during the years 1966 to 1981;

    (iv) the part played in Ghana's affairs since 1979 by Flight-Lieutenant J. J. Rawlings.   **1,2,3**

CHAPTER 25

PROBLEMS IN AFRICA

SUMMARY OF EVENTS

Three special problems in Africa were those of the former Belgian Congo, Rhodesia and South Africa. The *Congo*, which became independent in *1960*, was immediately ravaged by a *civil war* which lasted until 1963. This turned out to be a special case because the *United Nations became deeply involved*, mounting one of its largest and most successful operations: the unity of the new state was preserved, though affairs remained chaotic until 1968. The country changed its name to *Zaire* in *1971*. In 1977, problems flared up again and though the government gradually restored order, unity seemed fragile in the early 1980s.

Rhodesia provided a special case in that it was the only British dependency in which the *resident white settlers carried their resistance to black rule to extreme lengths*. The problem became serious in 1965 when the white government, ignoring British pressure to allow black Africans more say in the running of the country, *illegally declared Rhodesia independent of Britain*. After economic sanctions had failed to bring down the illegal white government, pressure from black African states built up and a guerrilla campaign against Rhodesia escalated. In 1979 when it seemed that the whole country might be engulfed in bloodshed, a solution was found: the whites gave way, free elections were held, and power was handed over, relatively peacefully to the black Africans. *Rhodesia became legally independent as Zimbabwe.*

South Africa is very much a special case: it remains the *last bastion of white rule on the continent of Africa*, and the white minority is determined to hold out to the bitter end against black nationalism. In 1948 the government of South Africa, still a British dominion, alarmed at the upsurge of black nationalism, introduced the policy known as *apartheid* – separated development or segregation for the different races in South Africa. This was designed to bolster up white supremacy and was widely condemned outside the country. Opposition at the *1961 Commonwealth Conference* was so bitter that *South Africa left the commonwealth, became an independent republic*, and has since gone its own way, taking little notice of world opinion.

25.1 THE CONGO

(a) Why, and how, did civil war develop?

(i)   The Belgian government made little attempt to prepare the Africans for independence. *African nationalism seemed much less advanced* in the Congo than elsewhere and the Belgians were taken by surprise when there was widespread rioting in the capital, Leopoldville, in January 1959. In fact the rioting was as much in protest against *unemployment* caused by a recent recession as it was against Belgian rule, but the Belgians *agreed to allow independence in June 1960*. This was, to say the least, ill advised. Unlike most other African states, there was *no experienced group of Africans* to which power could be handed over. The Congolese had not been educated for professional jobs, very few had received any higher education and no political parties had been allowed. There was just over a year to make up the deficiencies, but this was not enough.

(ii) There were about *150 different tribes* which would have made the Congo difficult to hold together even with experienced administrators. Violent and chaotic elections were held in which the Congolese National Movement (MNC) led by a former post office clerk, Patrice Lumumba, emerged as the dominant party, but there were over 50 different groups. Agreement of any sort was going to be difficult; nevertheless the Belgians handed power over to a coalition government with Lumumba as Prime Minister, and Joseph Kasavubu, the leader of another group, as President.

(iii) *A mutiny broke out in the Congolese army (July 1960)* only a few days after independence. This was in protest against the fact that all officers were Belgians whereas the Africans expected instant promotion. Lumumba was deprived of the means of keeping law and order and tribal violence began to spread.

(iv) The south-eastern province of *Katanga* which had *rich copper deposits*, was encouraged by the Belgian company (*Union Minière*) which still controlled the copper-mining industry, to *declare itself independent* under Moise Tshombe. This was the wealthiest part of the Congo which the new state could not afford to lose; Lumumba, unable to rely on his mutinous army, appealed to the *United Nations* to help him preserve Congolese unity and a 3000 strong *peace-keeping force* soon arrived.

(b) The civil war and UN involvement

Lumumba wanted to use UN troops to force Katanga back into the Congo but the situation was complex: many Belgians preferred an independent Katanga which would be easier for them to influence; with this in mind the UN Secretary-General, Dag Hammarskjöld, refused to allow a UN attack on Katanga, though at the same time he refused to recognise Katangese independence. In disgust Lumumba appealed for help to the

Russians, but this horrified Kasavubu who, encouraged by the Americans and Belgians, had Lumumba arrested (he was later murdered). As the chaos continued, Hammarskjöld realised that more decisive UN action was needed and, although he was killed in an air crash while flying to Katanga to see Tshombe, his successor U Thant followed the same line. By mid-1961 there were 20,000 UN troops in the Congo; in *September* they *invaded Katanga* and in *December 1962* the province admitted failure and *ended its secession*, while Tshombe went into exile. Though successful, UN operations had been expensive and within a few months all their troops were withdrawn. Tribal rivalries aggravated by unemployment caused disorders to break out again almost immediately and calm was not restored until 1965 when General Joseph Mobuto of the Congolese army, using white mercenaries and backed by the USA and Belgium, crushed all resistance and took over the government himself.

(c) Mobutu in power
It was probably inevitable that if the country were to stay united, a *strong authoritarian government* was required; this Mobuto provided. There was a gradual improvement in conditions as the Congolese gained experience of administration, and the economy began to look healthier after most of the European-owned mines were nationalised. However, in the late 1970s there were more troubles. In *1977* Katanga (now known as *Shaba*) was *invaded by troops from Angola* apparently encouraged by the Angolan government which resented Mobutu's earlier intervention in her affairs (see Section 23.4), and by the USSR which resented American support for Mobutu. Having survived that problem, Zaire found herself in economic difficulties mainly because of *declining world copper prices* and drought which made expensive food imports necessary. Mobutu came under increasing criticism outside Zaire for his authoritarian style of government and his huge personal fortune; in May 1980 Amnesty International claimed that at least a thousand political prisoners were being held without trial and that several hundred had died from torture or starvation during 1978–9.

25.2 RHODESIA

(a) Why did the whites make a unilateral declaration of independence?

(i)   The problem sprang from the determination of the white Rhodesians *never to surrender control of the country to black African rule*. There were 4 million Africans, just over 200,000 whites and about 20,000 Asians, yet even under the relatively progressive constitution introduced by Sir Edgar Whitehead's government in 1961, black voters were allowed to choose only 15 out of the 65 members of parliament. When the Africans protested that the new constitution was unfairly weighted, Whitehead banned the African National Democratic Party; when one of the main African leaders, Joshua Nkomo, began another party, the Zimbabwe African People's Union (ZAPU), that too was banned.

(ii) The right-wing Rhodesian Front Party won the elections of December 1962 and Winston Field, a tobacco farmer, became Prime Minister. The Front was strongly racialist and felt that Whitehead had been too sympathetic towards the blacks. When the Central African Federation broke up in December 1963 (see Section 23.3(c)) and it became clear that Zambia and Malawi would soon be granted independence, Field assumed that Rhodesia would receive the same treatment and put in a formal request for independence. This was refused by the British Conservative government: *independence would be granted only if the constitution was changed to allow Africans at least a third of the seats*, which would enable them to prevent changes in the constitution after independence which might exclude them from government altogether. Field was prepared to go on negotiating, but many whites were beginning to want something more.

(iii) The more aggressive *Ian Smith* took over as Prime Minister from Field (*April 1964*). At first he continued to negotiate but made it plain that the Rhodesian Front would offer no concessions. He argued that continued white rule was essential in view of the problems being faced by the new black governments in other African states, particularly the Congo, and because the Zimbabwe nationalists were divided: a new party had been formed, the Reverend Ndabaningi Sithole's Zimbabwe African National Union (ZANU), which seemed to be involved in constant gang warfare with the rival ZAPU.

(iv) *Harold Wilson*, the new British Labour Prime Minister, *continued to refuse independence*. The British attitude was: no independence without a change in the constitution to prepare the way for rule by the black majority. Smith's attitude was: no change in the constitution; white rule must continue. Since no compromise seemed possible, *Smith unilaterally declared Rhodesia independent* (meaning without approval from Britain, the other party to the dispute). *UDI*, as it became known, took place on *11 November 1965*.

(b) Outside reaction to UDI

(i) *Britain* immediately condemned UDI as an act of rebellion, but, much to the disappointment of the back African states, decided not to use force against the illegal Smith government. It was hoped to bring the country to its knees by *economic sanctions* and Britain stopped buying tobacco and sugar from Rhodesia.

(ii) The *United Nations* also condemned the Rhodesian action and called on all member states to place a complete trade embargo on the country.

(iii) *South Africa*, also ruled by a white minority government, and *Portugal*, which still owned neighbouring Mozambique, were sympathetic to Rhodesia's plight and refused to obey the Security Council resolution so that *Rhodesian trade was able to continue* through these territories. Many other countries, while publicly condemning UDI, privately evaded the embargo: the USA, for example, bought Rhodesian chrome because it was the cheapest available. Companies and businessmen in many countries, including British oil companies, continued to break sanctions, and although the Rhodesian economy suffered to some extent, it was not serious enough to topple the Smith regime.

(iv) The *Commonwealth* was seriously shaken: Ghana and Nigeria wanted Britain to use force and offered to supply troops. Zambia and Tanzania hoped that economic sanctions would suffice and their relations with Britain became extremely cool when it seemed that she was deliberately soft-pedalling sanctions, especially as Zambia was suffering more from them than Rhodesia. When Wilson twice met Smith (aboard HMS *Tiger* in 1966 and HMS *Fearless* in 1968) to put new proposals, there was a howl of protest that he was about to betray the black Rhodesians. Perhaps fortunately for the future of the commonwealth, Smith rejected both sets of proposals, but the African commonwealth members remained deeply distrustful of Britain's intentions. When the Smith government began to discriminate against the blacks even more, especially under the new constitution of 1970, the Zambian government allowed guerrillas to make raids over the border into Rhodesia.

(c) Rhodesia under the Smith regime

African rights were gradually whittled away until the blacks were suffering similar treatment to that experienced by blacks in South Africa under the system of apartheid (see next section). There was a strict press censorship, people could be arrested and imprisoned without trial and almost half the land was reserved for whites, although there were about 18 times more blacks than whites. In *1970* Rhodesia *declared itself a republic* and introduced a new constitution under which whites and non-whites were on separate voting lists, voting only for MPs of their own colour; there was a *built-in guarantee that white MPs would always be in a large majority*. Extra land was allocated to the whites and any Africans who happened to be living in those areas were forcibly removed. Black schools were down-graded so that Africans would have little chance of reaching the educational level enjoyed by whites. In spite of world-wide criticism and some reduction in exports because of sanctions the whites remained unmoved until 1976, but early that year the first signs appeared that they would have to compromise.

(d) Why did the whites give way?

(i) *Mozambique's independence from Portugal (June 1975)* was a serious blow to Rhodesia. The new President, Machel, *applied economic sanctions* and *allowed Zimbabwean guerrillas to operate from Mozambique.* Thousands of black guerrillas were soon active in Rhodesia, straining the white security forces to their limits and forcing Smith to hire foreign mercenaries.

(ii) The *South Africans became less inclined to support Rhodesia* after their *invasion of Angola (October 1975)*, in support of the FNLA which was receiving help from the USSR and Cuba (see Section 23.4), had been called off on American orders.

(iii) The USA which had also backed the FNLA, feared that the USSR and Cuba might become involved in Rhodesia unless some compromise could be found; together with South Africa, she urged Smith to make some concessions to the blacks before it was too late.

(e) The end of white rule

Towards the end of 1976, Smith admitted that black majority rule would have to come within a few years, but he was determined to try every trick he knew to delay it as long as possible. Though a conference to consider possible solutions met at Geneva, it was impossible to pin Smith down to a definite commitment. *He was able to present the divisions between the Zimbabwean nationalist leaders* as his excuse for the lack of progress. This was a genuine problem: ZAPU, the party of the veteran nationalist Joshua Nkomo, and ZANU, Sithole's party, seemed to be bitter enemies; in addition there was Bishop Abel Muzorewa's United African National Council (UANC), as well as supporters of Robert Mugabe, leader of the guerrilla wing of ZANU. However in 1978, with the guerrilla war escalating, Smith at last began concessions, which were soon to lead to the transference of power to the blacks. This happened in *two stages*:

(i) Smith introduced his own scheme which allowed blacks to vote on equal terms. A general election was held in April 1979 for a new parliament in which 72 of the 100 MPs were to be black. Bishop Muzorewa's party won 51 seats, and Smith stepped down for Muzorewa to become Prime Minister. However, this was not a success: ZAPU decided not to fight the election and both Britain and the USA felt that any viable settlement must include Nkomo and Mugabe; Sithole, whose party had won only 12 seats, claimed that the whites had rigged the elections so that the more amenable Muzorewa would win. Both the UN and the Organisation of African Unity (OAU) condemned the elections as invalid. The guerrilla war continued and by November 1979 the patriotic Front (the two main guerrilla groups led by Nkomo and Mugabe) had 15,000 troops in Rhodesia fighting against the Muzorewa government. Smith was forced to concede that his scheme had failed.

(ii) The *Lancaster House Conference (September–December 1979)* convened by Britain and held in London, involved representatives from all parties including the Patriotic Front. After skilful manoeuvring by Lord Carrington, the British Foreign Secretary, the conference agreed on a *constitution for the new republic of Zimbabwe*, arrangements for elections and an end to the guerrilla war. Muzorewa agreed to step down as Prime Minister and Lord Soames was to be governor during the transitional period until elections were held. These were contested by all parties and *Mugabe's ZANU won a sweeping victory* taking 57 out of the 80 seats reserved for Africans in the 100-seat parliament. Nkomo's ZAPU won 27 while Muzorewa's UANC was reduced to 3 seats. With a comfortable overall majority Mugabe, a self-proclaimed Marxist, became Prime Minister and Zimbabwe became officially an *independent republic (April 1980)*. The transference to black majority rule was welcomed by all African and commonwealth leaders as a triumph for common sense and moderation, though some British Conservatives accused the British government of betraying Muzorewa and allowing Zimbabwe to fall to Marxism.

(f) Zimbabwe since independence

Two main themes ran through Zimbabwean affairs during the early years of independence: the *tribal rivalry between ZANU and ZAPU* and the *struggle to overcome economic problems*. The ZANU–ZAPU feud had been healed temporarily during the fight against the Smith regime, and Mugabe included Nkomo and other senior ZAPU members in his first cabinet. However, the rift soon reopened: ZAPU was suspected of plotting a coup and Mugabe expelled them from the cabinet (February 1982). This was followed by weeks of violence in Matabeleland (Nkomo's power base), where at least 200 civilians were killed by alleged ZAPU supporters. Eventually government troops restored order, with some brutality, over a thousand deaths being reported (June 1983). Towards the end of 1986 relations improved and plans were made for a *merger of the two parties*; both Mugabe and Nkomo felt that national unity was vital to enable the economic struggle against South Africa to be carried on effectively. In December 1987 the two parties formally merged and Zimbabwe became a one-party state. Mugabe became the country's first President and brought Nkomo and two other former ZAPU leaders into his new cabinet.

At first Zimbabwe's economy prospered, but from 1982 it suffered from *drought* and *declining world markets*. Recovery came quickly, with good maize harvests in 1984–6; Zimbabwe was able to feed all its people and there was enough left over to export. Another success story was the steadily increasing output of tobacco, groundnuts, soya beans and sunflower oil, much of it produced by small-scale peasant farmers who had received land at independence. Mugabe proceeded cautiously, and did not introduce a wholesale nationalisation programme, probably because he was afraid of upsetting western nations whose capital he needed for development. In 1987, though Marxist observers might be disappointed at what they saw as a lack of progress, there was good reason for optimism both politically and economically.

25.3 SOUTH AFRICA

(a) The Union of South Africa

The Union of South Africa, a *British dominion*, dated from *1910* when the two former Boer republics, Transvaal and Orange Free State, joined Cape Colony and Natal, following the Boer War (1899–1902). Since then power has remained firmly in the hands of the whites, though they formed less than 20 per cent of the population. In 1974 there were almost 18 million black Africans, known as Bantus, 2.3 million Coloureds, 700,000 Asians and 4.2 million whites. Roughly two-thirds of the whites were of Dutch (Boer) origin and known as Afrikaners; the rest were of British origin. With the granting of independence to India and Pakistan in 1947, white South Africans became alarmed at the growing racial equality within the commonwealth and were determined to preserve their supremacy. Most of the whites were against racial equality but the most extreme were the Afrikaner Nationalists led by Dr Malan, who claimed that the whites were a master race and that non-whites were inferior beings. The Dutch Reformed Church (the official state church) supported this view, though the Christian Church in general believes in racial equality. The Nationalists won the 1948 elections with promises to rescue the whites from the 'black menace'; Malan's policy was *apartheid*.

(b) Apartheid in operation

Malan (Prime Minister 1948–54) aimed to *separate* or *segregate* the different races in order to preserve the *racial purity of the whites* and thus their supremacy. Later Prime Ministers, Strijdom (1954–8), Verwoerd (1958–66), and Vorster (1966–78) continued Malan's policy and developed it further. There had been some segregation before 1948; for example Africans were forbidden to buy land outside special reserve areas; but Malan's apartheid was much more *systematic*.

(i) There was *complete separation of blacks and whites as far as possible* at all levels. In country areas, blacks live in special reserves; in urban areas they have separate townships at suitable distances from white residential areas. Whole communities of Africans were uprooted and 're-grouped' in the reserves to make separation as complete as possible. There are separate buses, coaches, trains, park benches, cafés, toilets, shops, hospitals, beaches, sports and even churches. Black children are educated in separate schools and receive a much inferior education. In fact complete separation was impossible because *over half the non-white work in white-owned industries* and other concerns; the economy would collapse if all non-whites were moved to the reserves.

(ii) Every person was given a *racial classification* and an *identity card*; strict *pass laws* demanded that non-whites remain in their reserves and townships except when going to work; otherwise movement was forbidden without police permission.

(iii) *Marriage* and *sexual relations between whites and non-whites were forbidden*, in order to preserve the purity of the white race; police spied shamelessly on anybody suspected of breaking the rules. Verwoerd introduced two new refinements, both in 1959.

(iv) The Bantu Self-Government Act set up seven regions called *Bantustans*, based on the original African reserves. It was claimed that they would eventually proceed to self-government; in 1976 it was announced that the first Bantustan, the Transkei, had become 'independent' with Chief Mantanzima as Prime Minister. However, the outside world dismissed this with contempt since Pretoria (the capital of South Africa) still controlled the Transkei's economy and foreign affairs. The whole policy was criticised because the Bantustan areas cover only about 13 per cent of the total area of the country and into these relatively small areas are crammed over 8 million blacks; vastly overcrowded and unable adequately to support the native populations, they became little more than rural slums. The government continued its policy undeterred and by 1980 two more African 'homelands', Bophuthatswana and Venda, had received 'independence'.

(v) *Africans lost all political rights* and their representation in parliament (by white MPs) was abolished.

(c) Opposition to apartheid

(i) *Inside South Africa*, opposition was difficult. Anyone who objected – including whites – or broke the apartheid laws was accused of being a *communist* and was severely punished under the Suppression of Communism Act. Africans were forbidden to strike and their political party, the African National Congress, was helpless. In spite of this, *Chief Albert Luthuli*, the Congress leader, protested by stopping work on certain days and in 1952 attempted a systematic breach of the laws by entering shops and other places reserved for whites. Over 8000 blacks were arrested and many were flogged; Luthuli was deprived of his chieftaincy and imprisoned for a time, and the campaign was called off. Later Luthuli organised other protests including the *1957 bus boycott*: instead of paying a fare increase on the bus route from their township to Johannesburg ten miles away, thousands of Africans walked to work and back for three months until fares were reduced. Protests reached a climax in 1960 when a large demonstration against the pass laws took place at *Sharpeville*, an African township near Johannesburg. Police fired on the crowd, killing 67 Africans and wounding many more. After this hundreds of Africans were arrested, including Luthuli, and Congress was banned. It was much to the credit of Luthuli and his non-violent methods that the Africans behaved with surprising restraint in the face of such brutal treatment. He was awarded the Nobel Peace Prize in 1961 after publishing his moving autobiography *Let My People Go*, but was killed in 1967; the authorities claimed that he had deliberately stepped in front of a train.

Discontent swelled again in the 1970s because *wages of Africans failed to keep pace with inflation*. In 1976 when the Transvaal authorities announced that Afrikaans (the language spoken by the whites of Dutch descent) was to be used in black African schools, massive demonstrations which included young people of school age took place at *Soweto*, an African township near Johannesburg. Again police fired on the crowds, killing at least 200 Africans, but this time protests did not subside completely: according to Basil Davidson, 'from one month to the next, onwards from May 1976, the silenced multitudes had found their voice, and the voice proved angry and unafraid'.

(ii) Most of the *commonwealth* members were strongly opposed to apartheid; early in 1960 the British Prime Minister, Macmillan, had the courage to speak out against it in Cape Town; he spoke about the growing African nationalism: 'the wind of change is blowing through the continent . . . our national policies must take account of it'. His warning was ignored and shortly afterwards the world was horrified by the Sharpeville massacre. At the 1961 Commonwealth Conference criticism of South Africa was intense and many thought she should be expelled. In the end *Werwoerd withdrew South Africa's application for continued membership* (in 1960 she had decided to become a republic instead of a dominion, thereby severing the connection with the British crown; because of this she had to apply for readmission to the commonwealth) and she ceased to be a member of the commonwealth.

(iii) The *United Nations* and the *Organisation of African Unity* condemned apartheid and were particularly critical of continued South African occupation of *South West Africa*, given her as a mandated territory in 1919 (see Section 2.8(b)). The government ignored repeated UN calls to grant the territory (known as Namibia) independence and extended apartheid to its African population. The UN General Assembly voted to place an economic boycott on South Africa (1962) but this proved useless because not all states supported it. Britain, the USA, France, West Germany and Italy condemned apartheid in public, but took little positive action. Among other things they sold South Africa massive arms supplies, apparently hoping she would prove to be a bastion against the spread of communism in Africa. Consequently Verwoerd (until his assassination in 1966) and his successor Vorster (1966–78) were able to ignore the protests from the outside world until well into the 1970s.

(iv) External pressure became greater in 1975 when the white-ruled Portuguese colonies of Angola and Mozambique fell to the African nationalists, while the African takeover in Zimbabwe (1980) *removed the last of South Africa's white satellites*. She was now surrounded by hostile black states and many Africans have vowed never to rest until their fellow Africans in the republic have been liberated.

(d) First signs of compromise

During 1979 appeared the first glimmer of hope that under increasing internal and external pressures the government might be prepared to relax some aspects of apartheid. In a speech in September 1979 which astonished many of his supporters, the new Nationalist Prime Minister, P. W. Botha, said: 'A revolution in South Africa is no longer just a remote possibility. Either we adapt or we perish. White domination and legally enforced apartheid are a recipe for permanent conflict.' He went on to suggest that the black homelands must be made viable and that unnecessary discrimination must be abolished. The first concrete concession was that blacks were allowed to join trade unions with full rights. In 1981 they were allowed to elect their own *local township councils*, but not to vote at national level; later a new constitution was introduced setting up *two new houses of parliament* – one for Coloureds and one for Indians but weighted so that the Whites kept control.

(e) South Africa in crisis

Far from being won over by these concessions, black Africans were incensed that the new constitution made no provision for them; they saw it not as progress, but as an *entrenchment of apartheid*. A multi-racial alliance, the United Democratic Front (UDF), successfully campaigned for a boycott of the elections; only 30 per cent of Coloureds and 20 per cent of Indians voted. The government arrested most of the UDF leaders, charging them with treason, and widespread violence broke out in black townships. The banned African National Congress (ANC) began a campaign against black councillors and police who were regarded as collaborators with apartheid. Many were assassinated and there were mass resignations of councillors and mayors, making the black local government system unworkable. In January 1985 President Botha offered to release *Nelson Mandela*, leader of the ANC, who had been in gaol since 1964, provided he would renounce violence, but the offer was rejected. Violence escalated with both sides guilty of excesses. The ANC used the 'necklace' (a tyre placed round the victim's neck and set on fire) to murder 'collaborators', while on the 25th anniversary of Sharpeville, police opened fire on a procession of mourners going to a funeral near Uitenhage (Port Elizabeth), killing over 40 (March 1985). Botha gave an important concession by allowing *marriages* and *sexual relations* between people of different races (June 1985), but this was greeted contemptuously by Desmond Tutu (the first black Anglican Bishop of Johannesburg) calling it 'mere tinkering with apartheid'. In

July, a *state of emergency* was declared in the worst affected areas (extended to the *whole country in June 1986*) giving the police the power to arrest without warrants and freedom from all crimiinal proceedings. This failed to quell the violence.

(f) International reaction to the crisis

The international community deplored all the violence, but was particularly critical of the *brutal police methods of crowd control*. A Commonwealth Conference at Nassau in the Bahamas (October 1985) called on South Africa to dismantle the apartheid system and to begin by fulfilling five demands:

   (i)   end the state of emergency;
  (ii)   release Nelson Mandela;
 (iii)   recognise banned political parties;
  (iv)   free political prisoners;
   (v)   begin a dialogue between government and black leaders.

There was no response either to this, or to a joint declaration by the EEC and the six 'front-line' states (Angola, Botswana, Mozambique, Tanzania, Zambia and Zimbabwe), repeating the same demands (February 1986). Sir Geoffrey Howe, the British Foreign Secretary, visited Botha the following July, and tried to persuade him to release Mandela, but the meeting was a failure, Botha retorting that he 'would rather resist threats from the outside world'; nor would he legalise the ANC so long as it remained 'under communist control'.

Meanwhile an international debate dragged on about whether *harsh economic sanctions* should be placed on South Africa to bring the country to its knees, whether sanctions should be mild, merely as a gesture of disapproval or whether there should be any at all. At a Commonwealth meeting in London (August 1986) all except Britain agreed on a strong package of sanctions (no further loans, no sales of oil, computer equipment or nuclear goods to South Africa, and no cultural and scientific contacts; if these were unsuccessful, there would be a ban on airlinks). However, Mrs Thatcher would commit Britain only to a *voluntary ban on investment* in South Africa; her argument was that severe economic sanctions would worsen the plight of black Africans who would be thrown out of their jobs. This caused the rest of the Commonwealth to feel bitter against Britain; Rajiv Gandhi, the Indian Prime Minister, accused Mrs Thatcher of 'compromising on basic principles and values for economic ends'. In September 1986 the USA joined the fray when Congress voted (over President Reagan's veto) to stop American loans, to cut airlinks and to ban imports of iron, steel, coal, textiles and uranium from South Africa.

(g) President Botha's dilemma

There was no denying that Botha found himself in a difficult situation. He was prepared to make further concessions: the *hated pass laws were abolished (July 1986)* and a council was set up to draft plans including blacks in central government – though not, at yet, as members of parliament. In 1987, the ANC went to great pains to present itself as a moderate party and to reassure whites that they would be safe and happy under black majority rule. The party president, Oliver Tambo, condemned the 'necklace' and called for blacks and whites to 'come together in a massive democratic coalition to oppose the racists and to struggle side by side, as equals, for the birth of the new South Africa'. Botha's dilemma was whether he could risk dismantling apartheid any further without provoking a backlash from *right-wing Afrikaners*; the Conservative and Herstigte Nasionale parties were bitterly critical of the concessions already made to blacks. An extreme right-wing group, the Afrikaner Resistance Movement, campaigned for the re-establishment of the white Boer republics of Transvaal and Orange Free State. At the same time the more moderate members of Botha's own National party complained that he seemed to have shelved further reform. Several of them left the party and prepared to fight the approaching election (whites only) as independents on a programme of equal rights, justice and safety for all and the scrapping of all discriminatory laws such as the Group Areas Act which forced blacks and whites to live in separate areas. The election results realised Botha's fears – there was a *swing to the right* as the National Party lost four seats (127 to 123), the Conservatives gained four (18 to 22) and the liberal progressive Federal Party lost eight (27 to 19). None of the independents were elected and the Conservatives took over from the Progressives as the official opposition party. Further reform seemed unlikely and Archbishop Tutu said that the result heralded the 'darkest stage' in South Africa's history.

QUESTIONS

1. Apartheid in South Africa
Study the Sources below, and then answer the questions that follow.

Source A
Report of the Tomlinson Commission set up by the South African Nationalist Government, published 1955.

> The policy of separate development is the only means by which the Europeans can ensure their future existence, and by which increasing race tensions and clashes can be avoided, and by means of which the Europeans will be able fully to meet their responsibilities as guardians of the Bantu population. The Europeans therefore should be prepared to make the necessary sacrifices required to put this policy into effect: for the first ten year programme, an amount of about £104 million will be required to develop the Bantu homelands, so that all rights, privileges, duties and responsibilities can be granted to the Bantu.

Source: D. Harkness, *The Post-War World* (Macmillan, 1974, adapted extracts).

Source B
South African notice.

DEPARTMENT VAN BOSBOU
PIEKNIEKTERREIN VIR BLANKES
TERREIN VIR NIE-BLANKES 3 MYL LAER AF
VURE SLEGS IN VUUR – MAARKPLEKKE TOECELAAT
SWEM VERBODE

DEPARTMENT OF FORESTRY
PICNIC SITE FOR WHITES
SITE FOR NON-WHITE 3 MILES LOWER DOWN
FIRES ALLOWED IN FIRE-PLACES ONLY
SWIMMING PROHIBITED

Source: Southern Examining Group.

Source C
Statement by a South African government official, 1959.

All the Bantu have their permanent homes in the Reserves and
their entry into other areas and into the urban areas is merely of a
temporary nature and for economic reasons. In other words they
are admitted as work seekers, not as settlers.

[Reproduced by permission of the Midland Examining Group.]

Source D
Nelson Mandela speaking at his trial in 1964.

Africans want to be paid a living wage. Africans want to be part of the
general population and not confined to living in ghettoes. African men
want to have their wives and children live with them where they work
and not be forced into an unnatural existence in men's hostels.
Africans want a just share in the whole of South Africa; they want
security and a stake in society.

Source E
Statement by Dr J. Adendort, the Afrikaner General Manager of the
Bantu Investment Corporation, 1968.

At the present rate of development the Bantu homelands will never be
in a position to absorb the increases in Bantu population and assure
decent living standards.

Source: D. Harkness, *The Post-War World* (Macmillan, 1974).

Source F

From *The Transkei – A South African Tragedy*, by Randolph Vigne, a white South African, now living in exile.

The economic outlook is as grim as the political one. The people of the Transkei can expect, if they are the fortunate ones who are allowed to work outside the Transkei, only the lives of migrant labourers who have no rights. For the rest there is ever increasing poverty at home. For many the future can only mean starvation. The projected Bantustans total a mere 13 per cent of South Africa's total area.

Source: D. Harkness, *The Post-War World* (Macmillan, 1974, adapted extracts).

Source G
Population and income

Population of South Africa in 1974	
Black Africans (Bantus)	18 million
Whites	4.2 million
Coloureds	2.3 million
Asians	0.7 million

Average annual income per head in 1968 (South African Rands)	
Whites	1400–1500
Africans working in towns	120–130
Africans in Bantustans	30–35

Source: D. Harkness, *The Post-War World* (Macmillan, 1974).

(a) (i) Using Source A to help you, explain what the word 'apartheid' means. **4(a)**

     (ii) Why did the South African government decide to follow the policy of apartheid, according to Source A? **4(a)**

(b) (i) Using the information provided by Sources A, B, C and D, describe how apartheid has affected the everyday lives of black Africans. **4(a,c)**

     (ii) What other restrictions has apartheid placed on black Africans? **1,2**

(c) (i) Why do you think the author of Source F is now living in exile? **1,2,4(a)**

     (ii) What is the Transkei? **1**

    (iii) In what ways does the evidence in Sources C, E, F and G support the complaints of Nelson Mandela in Source D?

           4(a,c)

(d) From the evidence of the Sources, which of the ideas mentioned in Source A were carried out in South Africa, and which were not?

           4(a,c)

(e)   **(i)** Look again at Sources C, E, D and F. What are the advantages and disadvantages of each one for the historian? **4(a,b)**

    (ii) Which of the four do you think gives the most unbiased view? Explain your answer. **4(a,b)**

(f)   **(i)** Describe the opposition to apartheid both inside and outside South Africa. **1,2**

    (ii) How did the South African governments respond to this opposition up to 1980? **1,2**

2. Southern Rhodesia and Zimbabwe

Study the Sources below, and then answer the questions that follow.

Source A

Ndabaningi Sithole, a nationalist leader, describes a political meeting in Salisbury, 1960.

> The meeting at Salisbury was packed to capacity – over 1000 people inside and many outside. Then they called upon me to speak. In Africa we do not speak from papers. We speak from the heart. If a thing is not in your heart you do not speak. I had my heart, and the thing African freedom – was in it, and so I rose to my feet in the midst of the deafening cheers. In my speech I reminded people that Zimbabwe was our country; that it was important we organised ourselves throughout the country as efficiently as we could; that other African countries won their independence because they worked unflinchingly for it, and that we also would get our independence if we fought with the consuming zeal of freedom fighters. I sat down amid deafening cheers.

Source: Southern Examining Group.

Source B

A cartoon from *Punch*, March 1966 (Fig. 25.1): British Prime Minister Harold Wilson tries to defuse a mine (Rhodesia).

(a)   **(i)** What clue in Source A suggests that, at the time of this speech, it was Britain that ruled Zimbabwe? **4(a)**

    (ii) At the time of the meeting, Zimbabwe was still known as Southern Rhodesia. Why do you think Sithole chose to use the name 'Zimbabwe' in his speech? **1,4(a)**

(b)   **(i)** What was the main message Sithole had to give his audience? **4(a)**

    (ii) How does the Source show that Sithole was a popular leader? **4(a)**

Fig. 25.1

"You're getting nowhere man — let us try."

(c) (i) Why did Southern Rhodesia not gain independence in 1964 along with Malawi and Zambia? **1,2**

    (ii) What happened on 11 November 1965 which caused a crisis between Britain and Rhodesia? **1,2**

(d) (i) What points is the cartoonist in Source B (Fig. 25.1) trying to make? **4(a)**

    (ii) Explain why sanctions were 'getting nowhere'. **1,2**

(e) (i) Describe what happened in the 1970s when the people represented by the man on the left of the cartoon (Fig. 25.1) tried their method of dealing with the problem. **1,2**

    (ii) Explain how, and why, Zimbabwe achieved its independence in 1980. **1,2**

3. Civil War in the Congo

Study the Sources below, and then answer the questions that follow.

Source A

Statement by Mr Eyskens, Prime Minister of Belgium, in the Belgian Senate, 12 July 1960.

Legally, Belgium cannot recognise the independence of Katanga in the present circumstances, but the Congo is independent and can obviously modify the Law which we gave her. It may develop towards a federal constitution. We cannot get ourselves involved in this. But here is a government – Mr Tshombe's government – in Katanga which seems to be taking decisions in certain fields, has a parliamentary majority and is trying to re-establish order. I prefer the presence of such a government to anarchy such as the Communists want.

Source: *Keesing's Contemporary Archives*, 1960.

Source B

Telegram from Mr Lumumba, Prime Minister of the Congolese Republic, to Dr Hammarskjöld, Secretary-General of the UN, asking for UN military help in view of the Belgian action in sending more troops to the Congo, 13 July 1960.

The Belgians have acted in violation of the Treaty of Friendship which said that Belgian troops can only intervene at the express request of the Congolese government. No such request has been made and the Belgian action therefore constitutes an act of aggression against the Congo. The real cause of most of the disorder lies in colonialist provocations. We accuse the Belgian government of having prepared the secession [withdrawal] of Katanga in order to preserve its power over our country. The overwhelming majority of the Katangese population is opposed to secession. Our request for military aid is aimed at the protection of the Congo against the present foreign aggression. We strongly emphasise the extreme urgency of sending UN troops to the Congo.

Source: *Keesing's Contemporary Archives*, 1960.

(a) (i) To which European country did the Congo belong before it became independent? **1,4(a)**
     (ii) When was it granted independence? **1**
     (iii) Why do you think Mr Eyskens (Source A) said that Belgium could not recognise the independence of Katanga? **1,2,4(a)**
(b) (i) According to Source A, who was Mr Tshombe? **4(a)**
     (ii) From the evidence of Source A, do you think Mr Eyskens approves or disapproves of Katanga becoming independent? **4(a)**

502

(c) (i) From the evidence of Source B, how had the Belgians violated the Treaty of Friendship between the Congo and Belgium?
4(a)

(ii) Why does Mr Lumumba want UN troops in the Congo, according to Source B?
4(a)

(d) (i) How do the two Sources differ in their explanations of what was causing the disorders in the Congo?
4(a,c)

(ii) How far do the two Sources give a full explanation of the causes of the civil war?
4(a,b)

(e) (i) How did Dr. Hammarskjöld respond to Mr Lumumba's appeal (Source B), and what were the immediate consequences of his response?
1,2,4(a)

(ii) Explain how the civil war in the Congo was brought to an end in December 1962.
1,2

4. You are a member of the Zimbabwe African National Union. Write brief notes in preparation for a book about Zimbabwe's successful struggle for independence referring, among other things, to:

(a) why you became a strong African nationalist;

(b) Ian Smith and UDI;

(c) your impatience with British governments and their non-violent methods;

(d) your part in the guerrilla campaign of the 1970s;

(e) your joy at the achievement of independence in 1980. **1,2,3**

CHAPTER 26

THE MIDDLE EAST

SUMMARY OF EVENTS

The Arab lands stretch from North Africa through the Middle East to the shores of the Persian Gulf and northwards to the frontier with Turkey. The main Arab states are Morocco, Algeria, Tunisia, Libya, Egypt, the Sudan (about half the population are Arabs), Syria, Lebanon, Jordan, Iraq and Saudi Arabia. The area known as the Middle East includes Egypt and all the Arab lands to the east of Egypt, as well as Turkey (non-Arab) and Iran (not, strictly speaking, an Arab state, though it contains many Arabs in the area at the northern end of the Persian Gulf). The Middle East also contains the *Jewish state of Israel set up in 1948*.

The main Arab concerns since 1945 included attempts to achieve some political and economic unity and problems caused by the fact that outside powers were constantly interfering in the Middle East because of its importance as a strategic *crossroads* and a *source of oil*. However, the dominating issue which united all the Arab states was the desire to *destroy Israel*, the alien within their midst. This desire caused four short and, from the Arab point of view, unsuccessful wars (1948–9, 1956, 1967 and 1973) which Israel survived.

26.1 ARAB UNITY AND OUTSIDE INTERFERENCE

(a) **Since they all share the Arabic language and mostly the Muslim religion** (though about half the Lebanon is Christian) many Arabs want some sort of *union among the Arab states*. As early as 1931 an Islamic conference in Jerusalem announced: 'The Arab lands are a complete and indivisible whole . . . all efforts are to be directed towards their complete independence, in their entirety and unified.' Several attempts were made to promote unity. The *Arab League* founded in 1945 included Egypt, Syria, Jordan, Iraq, Lebanon, Saudi Arabia and Yemen; membership expanded later to include 20 states in 1980. However, it achieved very little politically and was constantly hampered by *internal squabbles*. In the mid-1950s Pan-Arabism seemed to receive a boost with the

504

Fig. 26.1 *the Middle East*

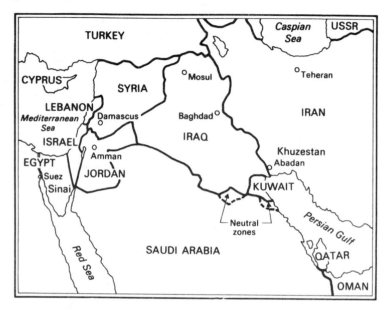

energetic leadership of *Nasser* in Egypt who gained enormous prestige in the Arab world after the *1956 Suez Crisis* (see below Section 26.3). In 1958 Syria joined Egypt to form the *United Arab Republic* with Nasser as President. However, this lasted only until 1961 when Syria withdrew because of resentment at Nasser's attempts to dominate the union. After Nasser's death in 1970, his successor President Sadat organised a loose union between Egypt, Libya and Syria, the *Federation of Arab Republics*, but it never amounted to much, and there seems little chance of any more progress being made towards full Arab unity. There are too many points at issue between the various states; for example Jordan and Saudi Arabia are still ruled by fairly conservative royal families who were often criticised for being too pro-British by the governments of Egypt and Syria which were pro-Arab nationalist as well as socialist. The whole Arab world was thrown into disarray in 1979 when *Egypt*, the leading Arab state, reached a *separate peace agreement with Israel at Camp David* (see below Section 26.6), whereupon *Egypt was expelled from the Arab League*.

(b) Outside interference in the Middle East was probably inevitable given the fact that the area produces *over a third of the world's oil supplies* and stands at the *crossroads between the communist world and Africa*. Disunity among the states invited interference, which in turn often bred more disunity.

(i) *Iran* (Persia) came in for attention from the USSR which in 1945 tried to set up a communist government in northern Iran and demanded an oil concession. The western-educated Shah Reza Pahlevi resisted and signed a defence treaty by which the USA provided economic and military aid including tanks and jets (1950). Matters were complicated by anti-British feeling on account of the British controlling interest in the Anglo-Iranian Oil Company and its refinery at Abadan. It was widely felt that the British were taking too much of the profits and in 1951 premier Mussadiq nationalised the company. However, most of the world boycotted Iranian oil exports, bringing Mussadiq down, and in 1954 a compromise was reached in which British Petroleum was allowed 40 per cent of the shares. Iran now took 50 per cent of the profits which the Shah was able to use for a *cautious modernisation and land reform programme*. This was not enough for the left and for radical Islam supporters who resented the Shah's close ties with the USA and the large slice of the national wealth which found its way into his private fortune. In January 1979 he was forced to leave the country and an *Islamic republic* was set up under a religious leader, the *Ayatollah Khomeini*, who wanted *non-alignment*.

(ii) Britain and France tried to maintain their influence in the area against that of the USSR, and to this end Britain joined the *Baghdad Pact* (1955) which also included Iraq, Iran, Turkey and Pakistan. Egyptian hostility to this contributed towards the 1956 Suez Crisis and the pro-British policy of King Feisal and Premier Nuri-es-Said of Iraq caused a revolution in which they were both murdered (1958). The new government was sympathetic towards Egypt and withdrew from the Baghdad pact which was replaced by the Central Treaty Organisation (CENTO), now defunct, sponsored by the USA as a buffer against the spread of communism.

(iii) The *Russians seized the chance to intervene during the Suez Crisis* with strong support for Egypt. Friendship with the Arab world would provide a useful link for the Russians with Africa and might enable them to threaten the west's oil supplies. This prompted the USA to issue the *Eisenhower Doctrine (1957)* offering aid to any Arab states which wanted to resist 'communist aggression'.

(iv) The USA was *committed to support Israel against the Arab states*, another reason for the Russians to work for an Arab alliance.

During the 1970s both east and west became much more cautious in their attitudes towards the Middle East; the west particularly took care not to offend the Arab states in case oil supplies were cut off.

26.2 THE CREATION OF ISRAEL AND THE ARAB–ISRAELI WAR OF 1948–9

(a) What caused the war?

(i) The trouble began soon after the First World War when *large numbers of Jews began to settle in Palestine*, a British mandate, hoping to set up a Jewish 'national home' (see Section 11.4(c)). The Arabs in Palestine were implacably hostile to the idea of a separate Jewish state in what they considered to be their homeland. In order to retain Arab friendship and their own oil supplies the British limited Jewish immigration to 10,000 a year (1939).

(ii) The Second World War intensified the problem with *hundreds of thousands of Jewish refugees from Hitler's Europe looking for somewhere to go*. In 1945 the USA pressed Britain to admit 100,000 of them into Palestine; this demand was echoed by David Ben Gurion, one of the Jewish leaders, but the British refused, not wanting to offend the Arabs.

(iii) The Jews, after all that their race had suffered at the hands of the Nazis, were determined to fight for their 'national home'. They began a *terrorist campaign* against both Arabs and British, the most spectacular incident of which was the blowing up of the King David Hotel, the British headquarters in Jerusalem, with the loss of 91 lives (1946). The British responded by arresting Jewish leaders and by turning back ships such as the *Exodus* crammed with intending immigrants.

(iv) The British, weakened by the war, were unable to cope; Ernest Bevin, the Foreign Secretary, invited the *United Nations* to deal with the problem, and in *November 1947 the UN voted to partition Palestine*, setting aside roughly half of it to form an independent Jewish state.

(v) *Early in 1948 the British abandoned the mandate and withdrew their troops*, though fighting was already taking place between Jews and Arabs, who bitterly resented the loss of half of Palestine. In *May 1948 Ben Gurion declared the new state of Israel independent*. It was immediately attacked by Egypt, Syria, Jordan, Iraq and Lebanon.

(b) The war and its results

Against apparently overwhelming odds, the Israelis managed to survive and even to capture more of Palestine including the port of *Eilat* on the Red Sea, seized from Egypt. The UN played an important part in bringing the fighting to an end. Israeli success was due partly to their own desperate resistance and to the fact that the Arabs were divided amongst themselves and poorly equipped; King Abdullah of Jordan was less than enthusiastic about the war because the partition gave him the chance to seize the section of Palestine west of the River Jordan (known as the West Bank). The most tragic result of the war was the plight of the

Palestinian Arabs who found themselves inside the new state of Israel.
After Jewish terrorists had slaughtered the entire population of an Arab
village, nearly a million Arabs fled into Egypt, Lebanon, Jordan and
Syria where they lived in miserable refugee camps. Jerusalem was
divided between Israel and Jordan, and although the USA, Britain and
France guaranteed Israel's frontiers, the Arab states did not regard the
cease-fire as permanent; this was only the first round in the struggle to
destroy Israel and liberate Palestine.

26.3 THE SUEZ WAR 1956

(a) The causes of the war were complex: partly the Arab–Israeli conflict,
partly the result of the struggle between Arab nationalism and the British
and French who wanted to prolong their influence in the Middle East,
and an episode in the Cold War between the USA and the USSR.

(i)   *Colonel Gamal Abdel Nasser*, the new ruler of Egypt (who came
to power in *1954* soon after the overthrow of the unpopular King
Farouk), was *aggressively in favour of Arab unity and independence* including the liberation of Palestine from the Jews.

(ii) He *organised guerrilla bands (fedayeen*: self-sacrificers) to sabotage and murder inside Israel and blockaded the Gulf of Aqaba
leading to the Israel port of Eilat.

(iii) He insisted that *Britain evacuate her base at Suez* (the agreement
signed in 1936 allowing her to keep the base expired in 1956), sent
aid to the Algerian Arabs in their struggle against France,
prodded the other Arab states into opposing the British-
sponsored Baghdad Pact and forced King Hussein of Jordan to
dismiss his British chief of staff.

(iv) In September 1955 Nasser signed an *arms deal with Czechoslovakia* for Russian fighters, bombers and tanks, and soviet experts
went to train the Egyptian army.

(v)   The *Americans saw this as a Russian attempt to 'move into' the
Middle East* and cancelled a promised grant of 56 million dollars
towards the building of a dam at Aswan (July 1956); the intention
was to force Nasser to abandon his new links with the communists.

(vi) Nasser immediately retaliated by *nationalising the Suez Canal*,
intending to use its revenues to finance the dam; share-owners, a
majority of whom were British and French, were promised
compensation. However, British Prime Minister Anthony Eden
believed that Nasser was on the way to forming a united Arabia
under Egyptian control and communist influence which could cut
off Europe's oil supplies at will. This must be prevented at all
costs.

(vii) *Secret negotiations took place between Britain, France and Israel
who agreed on a joint attack on Egypt.* The British and French

508

illus 26.1 *President Nasser of Egypt acclaimed by wildly cheering crowds in Cairo after proclaiming the nationalisation of the Suez canal*

hoped to bring down Nasser while the Israelis wanted to stop *fedayeen* raids and open the Gulf of Aqaba.

(b) The war began with an Israeli invasion of Egypt (29 October) which within a week had *captured the entire Sinai peninsula*. Meanwhile the British and French bombed Egyptian airfields and landed troops at Port Said at the northern end of the Suez Canal. The attacks caused an outcry from the rest of the world, and the Americans, who were afraid of alienating the Arabs and forcing them into closer ties with the USSR, refused to support Britain although they had earlier hinted that support would be forthcoming. At the United nations Americans and Russians joined in demanding a cease-fire (see Section 20.3(d)); with the pressure of world opinion against them, Britain, France and Israel agreed to withdraw, while UN troops moved in to police the frontier between Egypt and Israel.

(c) The results of the war were important. It was a *complete humiliation for Britain and France* who achieved none of their aims and were shown to be weak. They failed to topple Nasser whose prestige as leader of Arab nationalism against European interference was greatly increased. The Egyptians blocked the canal, the Arabs reduced oil exports to western Europe, where petrol rationing had to be introduced for a time, and Russian aid replaced that from America. British action seriously embarrassed Premier Nuri-es-Said of Iraq who now came under increasing attack from other Arabs for his pro-British attitude; he was murdered in 1958. The Algerians were encouraged in their struggle for independence from France which they achieved in 1962. From Israel's point of view the war was something of a success: although she had been compelled to hand back all captured Egyptian territory, she had inflicted heavy losses on Egypt in men and equipment which took several years to make good. For the time being *fedayeen* raids ceased and Israel had a *breathing-space in which to consolidate*.

26.4 THE SIX DAY WAR 1967

(a) Background to the war

(i) Iraq, after the murder of Nuri-es-Said, had an *aggressive nationalist government* prepared to co-operate with Egypt. President Aref announced (1 June 1967): 'Our goal is clear – to wipe Israel off the map.'

(ii) Political upheavals in Syria brought to power the *left-wing Ba'ath Party (1966)* which supported El Fatah, the Palestine Liberation Movement, a more effective guerrilla force than the *fadayeen*. The Syrians also bombarded Jewish settlements from the Golan Heights overlooking the frontier.

(iii) Nasser was now immensely popular in Egypt because of his leadership of the Arab world and his attempts to improve conditions inside the country with his *socialist* policies, which included limiting the size of farms to 100 acres and redistributing the surplus land to peasants. Attempts were made to *industrialise* the country and over a thousand new factories were built, almost all under government control. The Aswan Dam project was vitally important, providing electricity, and water for irrigating an extra million acres of land. After initial delays at the time of the Suez Crisis, work on the dam eventually got under way and the project was completed in 1971. With all going well at home and the prospect of effective help from Iraq and Syria, Nasser seems to have decided that the time was ripe for another attack on Israel. He began to move troops up to the frontier in Sinai, asked the UN to remove its troops policing the narrow strip of land along the coast connecting Gaza with the rest of Egypt, and close the Gulf of Aqaba (May).

(iv) *Syria, Jordan and Lebanon also massed troops along their frontiers with Israel* while contingents from Iraq, Saudi Arabia and Algeria joined them. Israel's situation seemed impossible.

(v) *Moshe Dayan*, the new Israeli Minister of Defence, decided that the best policy was to *attack first* rather than sit about waiting to be destroyed. It has been suggested that Israel wanted a war to unite the country, solve the unemployment problem and attract American dollars. Seizing the opportunity provided by the ponderous Arab troop build-up, the Israelis launched a series of *devastating air strikes which destroyed most of the Egyptian air force on the ground (5 June)*.

Israeli troops moved with remarkable speed, *capturing the Gaza strip* and the *whole of Sinai* from Egypt, the *rest of Jerusalem and the West Bank from Jordan* and the *Golan Heights from Syria*. The Arabs had no choice but to accept a UN cease-fire order (10 June). Reasons for the brilliant Israeli success were their superiority in the air and inadequate Arab preparation and communications.

(b) Results of the war

This time the Israelis *ignored a UN order to return captured territory*. This meant that defence would be easier but it left them with the problem of how to deal with an extra million Arabs who now found themselves under Israeli rule; many of these were living in the refugee camps on the West bank and in the Gaza Strip set up in 1948. The Arab states, though humiliated, were no less determined on the ultimate destruction of Israel.

26.5 THE YOM KIPPUR WAR 1973

Two elements combined to produce a *joint Egyptian–Syrian attack on Israel in October 1973*.

(i) Pressure was brought on the Arab states by the Palestine Liberation Organisation (PLO) under its leader Yasser Arafat for some action. The PLO tried by committing acts of terrorism, to draw world attention to what it considered to be the grave injustice done to the dispossessed Arabs: hijacking aircraft, shooting down passengers waiting in airport lounges, and killing members of the Israeli team at the 1972 Munich Olympics. However, such outrages only *alienated world sympathy*.

illus 26.2 *The child soldiers of the Palestine refugee camps; trained from the age of seven, these boys and girls would be ready for front-line service by the age of 15*

(ii) Egypt (ruled since 1970 by President Sadat) and Syria re-equipped their armies with Russian help, and felt justified in attacking Israel to *regain territory lost in 1967*. They were probably incited by the Russians who informed them, incorrectly, that Israel was about to attack them.

Egyptian and Syrian forces attacked early on the feast of *Yom Kippur*, a Jewish religious festival, hoping to catch the Israelis off guard. After initial Arab successes the Israelis, using mainly American weapons, were able to turn the tables, managing to *hang on to all territory captured in 1967 and even crossing the Suez Canal* into Egypt. This time the fighting was more evenly balanced and both sides were glad to accept a cease-fire organised by the USA and the USSR with UN co-operation. At the end of the war came a glimmer of hope for some sort of permanent settlement when Egyptian and Israeli leaders came together (though not in the same room) at Geneva. The Israelis agreed to move back from the Suez Canal (closed since the 1967 war) which enabled the Egyptians to clear and open the canal in 1975 (but not to Israel).

An important development during the war was that the *Arab oil-producing states* tried to bring pressure to bear on the USA and western European states friendly to Israel by *reducing oil supplies*. This caused serious oil shortages especially in Europe. At the same time producers, well aware that oil supplies were not unlimited, saw their action as a way of preserving resources. With this in mind, the Organisation of Petroleum Exporting Countries (OPEC) began to raise oil prices substantially, *contributing to inflation and causing an energy crisis in the world's industrial nations*.

26.6 CAMP DAVID AND THE EGYPTIAN–ISRAELI PEACE 1978–9

Egypt and Israel showed a readiness to continue negotiations and President Sadat took the courageous step of becoming the first *Arab leader to talk peace to Israel*. Even to talk with Israeli leaders meant a recognition of the lawful existence of the state of Israel, and this would be resented by the PLO and the more aggressive Arab states, Iraq and Syria. However, Sadat was becoming increasingly convinced of the foolishness of squandering Egyptian resources on fruitless wars; at the same time Israel, in spite of her success in farming, industry and commerce, was facing *economic problems* partly caused by her enormous defence expenditure, and partly by the world recession. The USA, apparently growing impatient with the Middle East situation, pressed Israel to settle her differences with at least some of the Arabs. Sadat visited Jerusalem (November 1977) and Menahem Begin, the Israeli Prime Minister, visited Egypt the following month. President Carter of the USA played a vital role in bringing about the opening of negotiations between the two leaders at *Camp David* (near Washington) in September 1978. With Carter acting as intermediary, the task resulted in a *peace treaty being signed in Washington (March 1979)* which ended the state of war that had existed between Egypt and Israel since 1948. Israel promised to make a phased withdrawal from Sinai, while Egypt undertook not to attack Israel again and guaranteed to supply her with oil from the recently opened wells in southern Sinai.

The treaty was condemned by the PLO and most Arab states (except Sudan and Morocco), and there was clearly a long way to go before similar treaties could be signed by Israel with Syria and Jordan. World opinion began to move against Israel and to accept that the PLO had a case, but when the USA tried to bring Israel and the PLO together in an international conference, the Israelis declined to co-operate. In November 1980 Begin announced that Israel would never return the Golan Heights to Syria even in exchange for a peace treaty, and would not allow the West Bank to become part of a Palestinian state, which would be a mortal threat to Israel's existence. At the same time resentment among West Bank Arabs mounted at the Israeli policy of establishing Jewish settlements on land owned by Arabs. Many observers feared fresh violence unless Begin's government adopted a more moderate approach.

The peace also seemed threatened for a time when President Sadat was assassinated by some extremist Muslim soldiers while he was watching a military parade (October 1981). This showed how risky it was for a moderate Arab leader to try and restore peace to the Middle East; if it meant *acknowledging the lawful existence of Israel* it was seen by the fundamentalists as a *betrayal of the Muslim cause*. However, Sadat's successor, Hosni Mubarak, bravely announced that he would continue the Camp David agreement.

For most of the 1980s the Arab-Israeli feud was overshadowed by the Iran–Iraq War (see below), which occupied much of the Arab world's attention. But in December 1987 there were *massive demonstrations by Palestinians* living in the refugee camps of the Gaza Strip and the West Bank. They were *protesting against Israeli repressive policies* and the brutal behaviour of Israeli troops in the camps and in the occupied territories. An Israeli clampdown failed to quell the unrest, which gained momentum during the early part of 1988; the tough methods of the Israelis earned them UN and worldwide condemnation. Palestinian demands included: an end to Israel's 'iron fist' policy, withdrawal of troops from Arab towns and refugee camps, free elections and no more confiscations of land.

26.7 THE IRAQI–IRANIAN WAR 1980–

The Middle East and the Arab world were thrown into fresh confusion in September 1980 when *war erupted between Iraq and Iran* over the disputed Iranian province of Khuzestan, peopled largely by Arabs and over control of the Shatt-el-Arab waterway, which formed part of the frontier between the two states.

The war began when the President of Iraq, Saddam Hussein, ordered the seizure of the Shatt-el-Arab, which had once been completely under Iraqi control. Five years earlier the Shah's government had forced Iraq to share control of the waterway with Iran. In 1980 Iran seemed to be in chaos as Khomeini carried out his Muslim revolution; Saddam apparently thought Iran would be weak and demoralised and expected the war to be short. But it soon became clear that he had miscalculated: the Iranians quickly reorganised and began mass infantry attacks against heavily fortified Iraqi positions. On paper Iraq seemed much the stronger, being well supplied with Soviet tanks, helicopter gunships and missiles. However, the Iranian *revolutionary guards* fought with fanatical determination, and eventually they too began to get modern equipment (anti-aircraft and anti-tank missiles) from China and North Korea (and, secretly, from the USA). As the war dragged on, Iraq concentrated on *strangling Iranian oil exports* which paid for their arms supplies; Iran meanwhile captured Iraqi territory, and early in 1987, their troops were only ten miles from Basra, Iraq's second city, which had to be evacuated. By this time the territorial dispute had been lost in the *deeper racial and religious conflict*: Khomeini had sworn never to stop fighting until his Shia Muslim fundamentalists had destroyed the hated Saddam regime. The war had important international repercussions:

(i) The *stability of the entire Arab world was threatened*: the more conservative states – Saudi Arabia, Jordan and Kuwait gave cautious support to Iraq, but Syria, Libya, Algeria, South Yemen and the PLO were critical of Iraq for starting the war at a time when, they believed, all Arab states should have been concentrating on the *destruction of Israel*. The Saudis and the other Gulf states, suspicious of Khomeini's extreme brand of Islam, wanted to see Iran's ability to dominate the Persian Gulf controlled. As early as November 1980 an Arab summit conference in Amman (Jordan) to draw up new plans for dealing with Israel, failed to get off the ground, because the anti-Iraq states, led by Syria, refused to attend.

(ii) The attacks on Iran's oil exports threatened the *energy supplies of the West*, and at various times brought American, Soviet, British and French warships into the region, raising the international temperature. In 1987 the situation took a more dangerous turn as all oil-tankers, whatever their nationality, were threatened by mines, though which side was responsible for laying them was open to debate.

(iii) The *successes of Iran's Shia fundamentalist troops*, especially the threat to Basra, alarmed the non-religious Arab governments and many Arabs were afraid of what might happen if Iraq was defeated. Even President Assad of Syria, at first a strong supporter of Iran, was worried in case Iraq split up and became another Lebanon (see next section), which could well destabilise Syria itself. An Islamic conference held in Kuwait (January 1987) was attended by representatives of 44 nations, including Syria and Libya; but Iran's leaders refused to attend and the conference failed to agree on any action to bring the war to an end. After six and a half years, the conflict seemed certain to continue for the foreseeable future.

26.8 CHAOS IN THE LEBANON

(a) Successful beginnings

Once part of Syria, the Lebanon had enjoyed *independence since 1920*; after the Second World War it was a *prosperous state*, making money from banking and from serving as an important outlet for the exports of Syria, Iraq and Jordan. The country was a bewildering mosaic of different religious groups, some Christian, some Muslim, separated originally by mountain ranges. There were four main Christian groups – Maronites (the wealthiest and most conservative), Greek Orthodox, Roman Catholics and Armenians, and three Muslim groups – Sunni, Shia and Druze. The *Shia* were the largest and were mainly a poor, working class group, while the *Sunni* were wealthier and had more political influence. The *Druze* were a comparatively small group who lived in the centre; mostly poor peasants, they were a closely-knit group with an hereditary leader, Kamal Jumblatt, and an aggressive left-wing outlook. There was a long history of hatred between Maronites and Druze, but this seemed to be kept in check by the carefully framed constitution which tried to give fair representation to all groups. The *President* was always a *Maronite*, the *Prime Minister* a *Sunni*, the *Speaker* a *Shia*, and the *chief of Staff* a *Druze*. Of the 44 seats in Parliament, the Maronites were allowed 13, Sunni 9, Shia 8, Greek Orthodox 5, Druze 3, Roman Catholics 3, and Armenians 2. The situation was further complicated by the *influx since 1948 of Palestinian refugees from Israel*. By 1975, there were perhaps half a million of them living in squalid camps away from the main centres of population. The Palestinians were not popular in Lebanon because they were continually involved in frontier incidents with Israel, provoking the Israelis to hit back at the Palestinians in southern Lebanon. In particular the Palestinians, being left-wing and Muslim, alarmed the conservative and Christian Maronites who saw the Palestinian presence as a dangerous destabilising influence.

(b) Civil War 1975–6

The delicate balance was preserved until 1975 when a dispute between Christians and Muslims over fishing rights led to *civil war*. Beginning as an apparently minor incident, the dispute escalated when some Palestinians sided with the Muslims, whereupon a group of right-wing Christians known as the Phalange, began to attack Palestinians. Soon a full-scale civil war developed: the Maronites saw it as a chance to expel the Palestinians who had formed an alliance with the Druze (seizing the chance to strike at their old enemies). For a time, the Druze seemed poised for victory, but in 1976 President Assad of Syria sent troops into the Lebanon. Order was restored and the Lebanon was preserved; it was a defeat for the Druze and for the PLO and its leader, Yasser Arafat, who had to agree to withdraw his armed troops from the Beirut area.

(c) Chaos continued

Complete peace was never quite restored and strife of various kinds continued. Fighting soon broke out in the south between Palestinians and Christians; the Israelis seized this opportunity to send troops in to help the Christians. A small semi-independent Christian state of Free Lebanon was declared under Major Haddad, and supported by the Israelis as a buffer zone to protect them from further Palestinian attacks. The Palestinians and Muslims counter-attacked, and although by 1982 there were 7000 UNIFIL (United Nations Interim Force in the Lebanon) troops in the area, it was a constant struggle to keep the peace. Meanwhile the Druze leader, Jumblatt had been assassinated, allegedly by the Syrians, and then in 1980 the two main Maronite groups (the Gemayel and Chamoun families) fought each other and the Gemayels won.

In *1982*, in reprisal for a Palestinian attack on Israel, *Israeli troops invaded Lebanon and penetrated as far as Beirut*. For a time the Gemayels, supported by the Israelis, were supreme in Beirut. During this period the Palestinians were expelled from Beirut and from then on the PLO was divided. The hard-liners went to Iraq and the rest dispersed into different Arab countries where they were, on the whole, not welcome. The Israelis withdrew and a multi-national force (made up of troops from USA, France, Italy and Britain) took their place to maintain the peace. However a spate of suicide bombings forced them to withdraw.

In 1984 an alliance of Shia militia (known as Amal) led by Nabih Beri, and Druze militia led by Walid Jumblatt, and backed by Syria, drove President Gemayel out of Beirut. Then the Shia and Druze themselves came to blows in a struggle for control of West Beirut (November 1985). Yasser Arafat used the general confusion to rearm his Palestinians in the refugee camps.

Towards the end of 1986 the situation was extremely complex: Shiite Amal militia backed by Syria, alarmed at the renewed strength of the PLO which seemed likely to set up a state within a state, were besieging the camps, hoping to starve them into surrender. At the same time an alliance of Druze, Sunni and Communists was trying to oust Amal from West Beirut. Another more extreme Shia group known as Hezbollah ('Party of God') heavily backed by Iran, was also involved. Early in 1987 fierce fighting again erupted between Shia and Druze militia for control of West Beirut. Several European and American hostages were seized, including Terry Waite, the Archbishop of Canterbury's special envoy, who had gone to West Beirut to try and negotiate the release of earlier hostages. The situation seemed desperate when *President Assad of Syria*, responding to a request from the Lebanese government, *again sent his tanks and troops into West Beirut (February 1987)*. Within a week calm had been restored and the militiamen cleared out of the capital. Druze, Shia and Sunni leaders were brought together under Syrian supervision to find a workable plan for the Lebanon's future. But the difficulties were more complex than in earlier days: there was the problem of the ever-multiplying militia groups, now numbering about 40; in particular there was Hezbollah, thought to be responsible for some of the kidnappings. Above all there loomed the problem of what to do about the Palestinians, and their undying and embarrassing determination to destroy Israel. In June 1987 there was a new crisis: the Sunni Prime Minister, Rashid Karami, was assassinated in a helicopter explosion, and the Shia Speaker resigned, complaining that the Christian President Gemayel was not doing enough to find out who was responsible.

QUESTIONS

1. The formation of Israel
Study the Sources below, and then answer the questions that follow.

Source A
A cartoon in the *News Chronicle* (Fig. 26.2), 28 April 1948, commenting on the retreat of Bevin and Creech Jones (see Source B) from Palestine.

Fig. 26.2

Source B
An English journalist's comments on the end of the mandate.

It is painful for an Englishman to tell of the last phase of the Palestinian mandate. It is like recalling a case of mass lunacy. The main facts are these: in December 1947 the Colonial Secretary, Arthur Creech Jones, announced that Britain would withdraw totally from Palestine on 15th May 1948. The UN then asked for permission to send some officials to Palestine to arrange an orderly transfer of power. This was emphatically refused. A secret agreement between Bevin [Britain's Foreign Secretary] and King Abdullah of Jordan in late 1947 arranged that the well-disciplined Arab Legion would take over the military positions in the non-Jewish area. But the agreement was not honoured. In April 1948, the British, seeking to please King Farouk of Egypt, who saw Abdullah as his rival for the leadership of the Arab world, ordered the Legion to withdraw. At the same time the British knew that Arab guerrilla bands were entering the country from Syria, but did nothing to stop them. British policy seemed determined to end the mandate in the most disorderly way possible.

Source C
From a document setting out the Arab case against creating Israel, 1946.

1. The whole Arab people is opposed to the attempt to impose Jewish immigration and settlement upon it, and to establish a Jewish state in Palestine.
2. The entry of wave after wave of immigrants prevents normal economic and social development and disturbs the country's life.
3. Continued land-purchase and immigration by Jews is pushing the Arab population to the poorest land or turning them into a landless peasantry.
4. If Israel is established the Palestinians will be a minority in their own country; a minority which can hope for no more than a minor share in the government, for the state is to be a Jewish state.

Source D
A map of Israel and her Arab neighbours (Fig. 26.3).

Source E
Israel under attack, 1948.

Palestinian Arabs suffered a number of defeats at the hands of well-armed Zionists before the end of the British mandate, and then Egypt, Syria, Jordan and Iraq declared war on Israel, the newly-proclaimed Jewish state. Britain had managed to pull out successfully from the Palestinian problem, but, as had long been threatened, war flared up between Arabs and Jews in the Middle East.

The struggle lasted from May 1948 to February 1949. The Arabs were defeated partly because their leaders quarrelled among themselves about who should lead the Arab world. As a result Israel not only survived but actually increased her share of Palestinian territory. A million Arabs fled from Israel, homeless refugees. Neither side regarded the war as having settled anything.

Source: J. B. Watson, *Success in Twentieth Century World Affairs* (John Murray, 1977)

Fig. 26.3

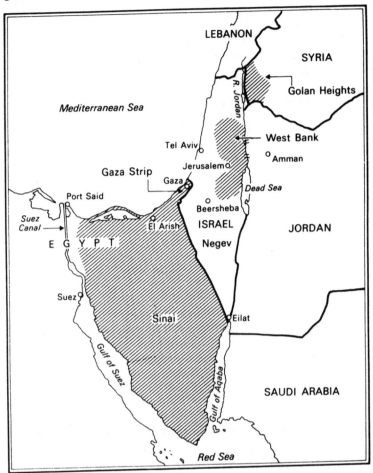

Territory conquered by the Israelis, June 1967

(a) How does the cartoon in Fig. 26.2 (Source A) make clear the opinion that British control of Palestine had not been successful?

4(a)

(b) (i) What backing does Source B offer for its accusation of 'mass lunacy'?

4(a)

(ii) How does the author of Source B show his disapproval of British policy with regard to the withdrawal from Palestine?

4(a,b)

(c) What evidence can be drawn from Sources C and D to show the difficulties that the partition of Palestine would create for the new Israel?

4(a,c)

(d) **(i)** How does Source E differ from Source B in its attitude to the British withdrawal from Palestine? **4(a,b,c)**

(ii) On what major point does Source E support a view expressed in Source B? **4(a,c)**

(iii) In what way is the gloomy fear of the cartoonist in Fig. 26.2 (Source A) confirmed in Source E? **4(a,c)**

(iv) How does Source D (the map) show that the end of the war in February 1949 was only a temporary lull in the struggle between Israel and the Arab states? **4(a)**

(e) **(i)** How justified, since Israel was set up, have been the Arab fears as expressed in Source C? Explain your answer. **1,2,4(a)**

(ii) How has the Soviet Union been able to take advantage of Arab hostility to Israel? **1,2**

[Southern Examining Group, Specimen Question.]

2. The Suez War, 1956

Study the Sources below, and then answer the questions that follow.

Source A

The rise of Nasser to power in Egypt was welcomed at first by Israel. Indeed the aims of the revolution and initial contacts with Nasser's regime inspired hope for the future. But Nasser's mixture of radicalism and extreme Arab nationalism, coupled with an ambition to achieve leadership in the Arab world, pre-eminence in the world of Islam and primacy in the so-called 'non-aligned' group of nations . . . gradually came to expression in a bitter, blind *antagonism* to Israel.

Antagonism – hostility, hatred.

Source: C. Herzog, *The Arab–Israeli Wars* (Arms and Armour Press, 1982).

Source B

In the excitement following his daring action [the nationalisation of the Suez Canal] Nasser became the hero of the Arab world. He had defied the imperialists. If attacked by Israel, France or Britain he could probably rely on support from the USA or Russia. What he did not foresee was an attack by all three of his enemies at once.

Source: L. E. Snellgrove, *The Modern World Since 1870* (Longman, 1968).

Source C

If Eden had come with the British Navy and tried to invade Egypt I think the Egyptians would have forgiven and forgotten once it was all finished. Even if he had come with the French we would have said that perhaps he needed an ally. But to bring the Israelis into an adventure against the Arabs was very foolish. We were used to hating British policy, but then we began to despise British policy. I hate to use the word 'despise' but it is the only one.

Source: R. Lawless, *The Middle East* (Batsford, 1980).

Source D
(Fig. 26.4)

Fig. 26.4

(a) Who was, or were:
    (i) the imperialists (Source B)?   1
    (ii) Eden (Source C)?   1

(b) Read Source A. What specific events in the two years before the Suez Crisis help to explain Israel's changing views on Nasser?

                                                        1,2,4(a)

(c) In many ways the Suez Crisis was a crushing military defeat for Egypt, but Nasser turned it into a propaganda victory. How do the Sources help to explain this?   4(a,c)

(d) In Source B Snellgrove claims that Nasser became 'the hero of the Arab world'.

    Using all the Sources, explain how the events of 1956
    (i) helped bring this about;
    (ii) tended to hide the weakness of Nasser's leadership.   4(a,c)

                                          4(a,c)

(e) What are the advantages and disadvantages for a historian of the Middle East in using the following sources as evidence:
    (i) the memoirs of a politician who was involved in events, as in Sources A and C?
                                        4(a,b)
    (ii) cartoons, as in Fig. 26.4 (Source D)?
                                        4(a,b)

    [Reproduced by permission of the Midland Examining Group.]

3. The Iran–Iraq War

Study the Source below, and then answer the questions that follow.

An article in the *Observer*, 24 May 1987.

For the first time, the leader of the only formal opposition party still allowed in Iran has called on Ayatollah Khomeini to end the Gulf War. In an open letter to Khomeini, the former Prime Minister Mehedi Bazargan, criticises the government for making no attempt to end the seven-year-old war with Iraq. The letter says:

The Iranian people are asking why their leadership has given top priority to prolonging the war, while those same people responsible for the war have told them, if the war is prolonged, the only benefit is for countries like Israel and the superpowers. While people have been told to fight the war to their last reserves to safeguard Islam, important issues such as health, education and housing have been ignored by the government. What is the purpose of all these killings?

Bazargan was appointed by Khomeini as Iran's first Prime Minister after the Islamic Revolution in 1979. He resigned in protest against the storming of the US embassy, which was welcomed by Iran's fundamentalist clerics . . . Bazargan, a liberal, has come under fire from the clerics for his views on the aims of the Islamic Revolution.

(Adapted extracts.)

(a) (i) Who is the Ayatollah Khomeini?   1,4(a)
    (ii) From the evidence of the article, who is Mehedi Bazargan?
                                        4(a)

(b) **(i)** According to the article, why does Bazargan think the war between Iraq and Iran should be brought to an end? **4(a)**

(ii) How had Bazargan earlier shown his disapproval of Khomeini's policies? **4(a)**

(c) **(i)** Describe what happened at the time of 'the Islamic Revolution in 1979', mentioned in the article. **1,2,4(a)**

(ii) Explain why the war between Iraq and Iran started in 1980. **1,2**

(iii) Do you agree that Israel and the superpowers had benefited from the war? Explain your answer. **1,2**

(d) **(i)** What other attempts had been made to end the war and why had they failed? **1,2**

(ii) From the evidence of the article, and your own knowledge, explain what effect you think Bazargan's letter was likely to have on the Ayatollah Khomeini. **1,2,4**

4. It is late in 1972 and there is to be an international conference to discuss events of recent years to do with the Middle East. These events are the hijacking of aircraft, the shootings at Tel-Aviv airport, and the attack on Israeli athletes at the Munich Olympic Games.

   (a) Write a draft of a speech to be made by a representative of the Palestinian Liberation Organisation. The speech will put the Palestinian case and try to justify these actions.

   (b) Write a draft of a speech to be made by a member of the Knesset (the Israeli parliament). The speech will put the Israeli case and try to persuade the conference to condemn these actions. **1,2,3**

   [Southern Examining Group, Specimen Question.]

5. **(a)** Why did President Nasser of Egypt decide to nationalise the Suez Canal in 1956?

   (b) Describe the main events of the Suez War of 1956.

   (c) How did the war of 1956 change the international situation in the Middle East? **1,2**

6. Describe and show the importance of *two* of the following in the history of the Middle East:

   (a) Arab–Israeli War of 1973;

   (b) the Camp David Agreement;

   (c) events in the Lebanon since 1975;

   (d) the Iran–Iraq War which began in 1980. **1,2**

FURTHER READING

This list contains books suitable both for the general reader and for GCSE students. Those marked with an asterisk * are particularly suitable for GCSE students. Those marked ** are suitable for GCSE students and contain source material. 'Purnell' refers to *Purnell's History of the Twentieth Century* (10 volumes), London: BPC Publishing, 1969. The place of publication is London unless otherwise stated.

CHAPTER 1

** Brooman, J., *The End of Old Europe* (Longman, 1985)
Tuchman, B. W., *The Proud Tower* (Macmillan, 1966)
Turner, L. C. F., *Origins of the First World War* (Arnold, 1970)

CHAPTER 2

* Clark, A., *Suicide of the Empires* (Macdonald, 1970)
* Crinnion, V., *The Great War* (Macmillan, 1980)
** Evans, D., *The Great War* 1914–18 (Arnold, 1987)
* Gibbons, S. R., and Morican, P., *World War One* (Longman, 1972)
* Horne, A., *Death of a Generation* (Macdonald, 1970)
Horne, A., *The Price of Glory* (Macmillan, 1962)
Liddell-Hart, B., *The First World War* (Cassell, 1970)
* Taylor, A. A., *The First World War* (London University Tutorial Press 1972)
Taylor, A. J. P., *The First World War* (Harmondsworth: Penguin, 1966)

CHAPTER 3

* Austin, M., *The Great Experiment: a Study of Russian Society* (English Universities Press, 1975)

** Aylett, J. F., *Russia in Revolution* (Arnold, 1987)
 * Catchpole, B., *A Map of History of Russia* (Heinemann, 1974)
   Freeborn, R., *A Short History of Modern Russia* (Hodder & Stoughton, 1966)
 * Fry, D., *Russia: Lenin and Stalin* (Hamish Hamilton, 1966)
   Hill, C., *Lenin and the Russian Revolution* (English Universities Press, 1970)
   Kochan, L., *The Making of Modern Russia* (Harmondsworth: Penguin, 1970)
 * Pickering, S., *20th Century Russia* (Oxford: University Press, 1970)
 * Pimlott, T., *The Russian Revolution* (Macmillan, 1984)
 * Quinn, J. G., *The Russian Revolution* (London University Tutorial Press, 1972)
** Stacey, F. W., *Lenin and the Russian Revolutions* (Arnold, 1970)
   Taylor, A. J. P., *Lenin: October and After* (Purnell, vol. 3, ch. 37)

CHAPTER 4

   Lloyd, T. O., *Empire to Welfare State* (Oxford: University Press, 1970)
** Lowe, N., *Mastering Modern British History*, 2nd edn (Macmillan, 1989)
   Marquand, D., *Ramsay MacDonald* (Jonathan Cape, 1976)
   Medlicott, W. N., *Contemporary England 1914–64* (Longman, 1976)
   Montgomery Hyde, H., *Stanley Baldwin* (Hart-Davis, 1973)
   Morris, M., *The General Strike* (Harmondsworth: Penguin, 1976)
   Mowat, C. L., *Britain Between the Wars* (Methuen, 1976)
 * Mowat, C. L., *The General Strike 1926* (Arnold, 1969)
   Rowland, P., *Lloyd George* (Barrie and Jenkins, 1975)
   Seaman, L. C. B., *Post-Victorian Britain, 1902–1951* (Methuen 1975)
   Taylor, A. J. P., *English History 1914–45* (Harmondsworth: Penguin, 1965)

CHAPTER 5

 * Bury, J. P. T., *France: The Insecure Peace* (Macdonald, 1972)
   Bury, J. P. T., *France 1814–1940* (Methuen University Paperback, 1976)
   Cobban, A., *A History of Modern France*, vol. 3 (Harmondsworth: Penguin, 1970)
 * Holland, P., *20th Century France* (Oxford: University Press, 1970)
 * Knapp, W., *France: Partial Eclipse* (Macdonald, 1972)
   Shirer, W. L., *The Collapse of the Third Republic* (Heinemann, Secker & Warburg, 1970)
 * Williams, B., *Modern France* (Longman, 1983)

CHAPTER 6

** Gregory, D., *Mussolini and the Fascist Era* (Arnold, 1968)
Hibbert, C., *Benito Mussolini* (Harmondsworth: Penguin, 1965)
* Rowlands, B. R., *Modern Italy* (London University Tutorial Press, 1970)
Tannenbaum, E., *Fascism in Italy* (Allen Lane, 1973)
Wiskemann, E., *Fascism in Italy: its Development and Influence* (Macmillan, 1970)
** Wolfson, R., *Benito Mussolini and Fascist Italy* (Arnold, 1986)

CHAPTER 7

* Bassett, M., *The American Deal* (Auckland: Heinemann, 1977)
* Catchpole, B., *A Map History of the United States* (Heinemann, 1972)
* Conkin, P. K., *The New Deal* (Routledge, 1968)
Galbraith, J. K., *The Great Crash* (Harmondsworth: Penguin, 1969)
* Hill, C. P., *A History of the United States* (Arnold, 1974)
* Hill, C. P., *The USA Since the First World War* (Allen & Unwin, 1967)
McCoy, D. R., *Coming of Age: The United States during the 1920s and 1930s* (Harmondsworth: Penguin, 1973)
Morgan, T., *FDR* (Grafton/Collins, 1985)
** Scott-Baumann, M., *The USA Since 1919* (Arnold, 1985)
* Traynor, J., *Roosevelt's America 1932–41* (Macmillan, 1983)
* Triggs, T. D., *Boom and Slump in Inter-War America* (Macmillan, 1984)
Zinn, H., *A People's History of the United States* (Longman, 1980)

CHAPTER 8

** Aylett, J. F., *Hitler's Germany* (Arnold, 1987)
Bullock, A., *Hitler – A Study in Tyranny* (Harmondsworth: Penguin 1969)
* Bumstead, P. J., *Hitler* (London University Tutorial Press, 1977)
* Catchpole, B., *20th Century Germany* (Oxford: University Press, 1970)
Craig, G. A., *Germany, 1866–1945* (Oxford: University Press, 1978)
* Delmer, S., *The Weimar Republic* (Macdonald, 1972)
Fest, J., *Hitler* (Weidenfeld and Nicolson, 1974)
Hiden, J. W., *The Weimar Republic* (Longman, 1974)
** McKay, M., *Germany between the Wars 1919–45* (Longman, 1988)
** Phillips, D. M., *Hitler and the Rise of the Nazis* (Arnold, 1968)

Ryder, A. J., *Twentieth Century Germany from Bismarck to Brandt* (Macmillan, 1973)
* Williams, *The Rise and Fall of Hitler's Germany* (Macmillan, 1985)

CHAPTER 9

* Austin, M., *The Great Experiment: a Study of Russian Society* (English Universities Press, 1975)
** Aylett, J. F., *Russia under Stalin* (Arnold, 1986)
** Bassett, J., *Socialism in One Country* (Auckland: Heinemann, 1978)
   Conquest, R., *The Great Terror* (Macmillan, 1968)
   Freeborn, F., *A Short History of Modern Russia* (Hodder and Stoughton, 1966)
   Grey, I., *Stalin* (Weidenfeld, 1979)
   Kochan, L., *The Making of Modern Russia* (Harmondsworth: Penguin 1973)
   Montgomery Hyde, H., *Stalin* (Hart-Davis, 1971)
* Pickering, S., *20th Century Russia* (Oxford: University Press, 1970)
   Stacey, F. W., *Stalin and the Making of Modern Russia* (Arnold, 1970)
** Warnes, D. J., *Russia – A Modern History* (Unwin Hyman, 1986)

CHAPTER 10

* Allen, L., *Japan: the Years of Triumph* (Macdonald, 1971)
** Fewster, S., *Japan 1850–1985* (Longman, 1988)
* Mitchell, D., *The Spanish Civil War* (Granada, 1972)
   Snellgrove, L. E., *Franco and the Spanish Civil War* (Harlow: Longman, 1965)
   Storry, R., *A History of Modern Japan* (Harmondsworth: Penguin, 1975)
   Thomas, H., *The Spanish Civil War* (Harmondsworth: Penguin, 1968)
* Williams, B., *Modern Japan* (Longman, 1987)

CHAPTER 11

* Power, E. G., *Modern Ireland* (Longman, 1988)
* Watson, J. B., *Empire to Commonwealth, 1919 to 1970* (Dent, 1971)
   Woodward, G. W. O., *Divided Island: Ireland, 1910–1949* (Auckland: Heinemann Educational, 1976)

CHAPTER 12

* Fitzsimmons, O., *Towards One World* (London University Tutorial Press, 1974)
* Gibbons, S. R., and Morican, P., *League of Nations and UNO* (Harlow: Longman, 1970)
  Henig, R., *The League of Nations* (Edinburgh, 1976)

CHAPTERS 13 AND 14

  Allen, L., *Japan: The Years of Triumph* (Macdonald, 1971)
  Bullock, A., *Hitler – A Study in Tyranny* (Penguin, 1969)
* Bumstead, P. J., *Hitler* (London University Tutorial Press, 1977)
  Fest, J., *Hitler* (Weidenfeld & Nicolson, 1974)
  Gilbert, M., *Appeasement in Action* (Purnell, vol. 4, ch. 57)
  Gilbert, M., and Gott, R., *The Appeasers* (Weidenfeld & Nicolson, 1963; paperback ed., 1967)
* Henig, R., *Versailles and After 1919–33* (Methuen, 1984)
* Henig, R., *The Origins of the Second World War* (Methuen, 1985)
  Mowat, C. L., *Britain Between the Wars 1918–1940* (Methuen, 1955; paperback ed., 1968)
* Rowlands, B. R., *Modern Italy* (London University Tutorial Press, 1973)
  Seaman, L. C. B., *Post Victorian Britain 1902–1951* (Methuen, 1966; paperback ed., 1970)
* Stone, R., *The Drift to War* (Auckland: Heinemann, 1975)
  Storry, R., *A History of Modern Japan* (Harmondsworth: Penguin, 1960)
  Tannenbaum, E., *Fascism in Italy* (Allen Lane, 1973)
  Taylor, A. J. P., *English History, 1914–1945* (Harmondsworth: Penguin, 1965)
  Taylor, A. J. P., *The Origins of the Second World War* (Harmondsworth: Penguin, 1964)
  Thorne, C., *The Approach of War, 1938–1939* (Macmillan, 1967)
** Wolfson, R., *From Peace to War: European Relations 1919–39* (Arnold, 1985)

CHAPTER 15

* Arnold-Forster, M., *The World at War* (Collins, 1973)
** Bayne-Jardine, C., *The Second World War and its Aftermath* (Longman, 1987)
  Calvocoressi, P., and Wint, G., *Total War* (Penguin, 1974)
** Evans, D., *The Second World War* (Arnold, 1985)
  Liddell-Hart, B. H., *History of the Second World War* (Cassell, 1970)

* Mortimore, M. J. A., *The Second World War* (London University Tutorial Press, 1974)

Taylor, A. J. P., *The Second World War* (Hamish Hamilton, 1975)

CHAPTER 16

Bown, C., and Mooney, P. J., *Cold War to Détente 1945–83* (Heinemann, 1984)

Feis, H., *From Trust to Terror: The Onset of the Cold War 1945–1950* (Blond, 1970)

Frankland, M., *Khrushchev* (Harmondsworth: Penguin, 1966)

** Hartley, L., *Superpower Relations Since 1945* (Unwin Hyman, 1987)

* Heater, D., *The Cold War* (Oxford: University Press, 1970)

Higgins, H., *The Cold War* (Heinemann, 1984 edition)

Knapp, W., *A History of War and Peace 1939–1965* (Oxford: University Press, 1967)

Laqueur, W. Z., *Europe Since Hitler* (Harmondsworth: Penguin, 1972)

** Sayer, J., *Superpower Rivalry* (Arnold, 1987)

CHAPTER 17

* Fitzgerald, C. P., *Communism Takes China* (Macdonald, 1969)

Higgins, H., *Vietnam* (Heinemann, 1978)

Matthews, H. L., *Castro* (Allen Lane, 1969)

* Mitchison, L., *China in the Twentieth Century* (Oxford: University Press, 1970)

** Morrison, D., *The Rise of Modern China* (Longman, 1988)

* Roper, M., *China in Revolution 1911–1949* (Arnold, 1969) (documentary)

* Tarling, N., *Mao and the Transformation of China* (Auckland: Heinemann, 1977)

Thomas, H., *Cuba or the Pursuit of Freedom* (Harper & Row, 1971)

CHAPTER 18

* Allan, P. D., *Russia and Eastern Europe* (Arnold, 1984)

Frankland, M., *Khrushchev* (Harmondsworth: Penguin, 1966)

Morgan, R., *Tension in Eastern Europe* (Purnell, vol. 5, ch. 80)

Morgan, R., *Eastern Europe: Hopes and Realities* (Purnell, vol. 6, ch. 83)

Morgan, R., *The Czechoslovak Spring* (Purnell, vol. 6, ch. 94)

Westwood, J. N., *Khrushchev and After* (Purnell, vol. 6, ch. 83)

CHAPTER 19

Bown, C., *China 1949–76* (Heinemann, 1978)
Gray, J., *China under Mao* (Purnell, vol. 6, ch. 89)
Harkness, D., *The Post-War World* (Basingstoke: Macmillan, 1974)
** Morrison, D., *The Rise of Modern China* (Longman, 1988)
Moseley, G., *China, Empire to People's Republic* (Batsford, 1968)
** Steele, P., *China Under Communism* (Arnold, 1987)
* Tarling, N., *Mao and the Transformation of China* (Auckland: Heinemann, 1977)
** Williams, S., *China Since 1949* (Macmillan, 1986)

CHAPTER 20

* Fitzsimmons, O., *Towards One World* (London University Tutorial Press, 1974)
* Gibbons, S. R., and Morican, P., *League of Nations and UNO* (Longman, 1970)

CHAPTER 21

Cobban, A., *A History of Modern France*, vol. 3 (Harmondsworth: Penguin, 1970)
Crozier, B., *De Gaulle: the Statesman* (Methuen, 1974)
Farr, W., *Daily Telegraph Guide to the Common Market* (Collins, 1972)
** Hall, D., *Unity in Europe* (Unwin Hyman, 1986)
Lacqueur, W., *Europe since Hitler* (Harmondsworth: Penguin, 1972)
** Lowe, N., *Mastering Modern British History* (2nd edn, Macmillan, 1989)
Ryder, A. J., *Twentieth Century Germany from Bismarck to Brandt* (Macmillan, 1973)
* Seaman, R. D. H., *Britain and Western Europe* (Arnold, 1984)
Wiskemann, E., *Italy since 1945* (Macmillan, 1971)

CHAPTER 22

* Bassett, M., *The American Deal, 1932–64* (Auckland: Heinemann, 1977)
Beals, C., *Latin America: World in Revolution* (New York: Abelard-Schuman, 1963)
** Fewster, S., *Japan 1850–1985* (Longman, 1988)
* Hill, C. P., *The USA Since the First World War* (Allen & Unwin, 1967)
* Lancaster, A. B., *The Americas* (Arnold, 1985)

** Scott-Bauman, M., *The USA Since 1919* (Arnold, 1985)
** Simkin, J., *USA Domestic Policies 1945–80* (Spartacus, 1986)
   Snowman, D., *America Since 1920* (Heinemann, 1978)
   Storry, R., *A History of Modern Japan* (Harmondsworth: Penguin, 1975)
   Zinn, H., *A People's History of the United States* (Longman, 1980)

CHAPTER 23

   Courriere, Y., *The Algerian War* (Purnell, vol. 6, ch. 81)
   Davidson, B., *Africa in Modern History* (Allen Lane, 1978)
 * Hatch, J., *Africa – the Rebirth of Self-Rule* (Oxford: University Press, 1970)
   Horne, A., *Dien Bien Phu* (Purnell, vol. 6, ch. 81)
   Horne, A., *A Savage War of Peace* (Algeria) (Macmillan, 1972)
   Moon, P., *India: Independence and Partition* (Purnell, vol. 5, ch. 75)
   Phillips, D., *Cyprus: The Failure of Force* (Purnell, vol. 6, ch. 91)
   Rose, S., *Indonesia Gains Independence* (Purnell, vol. 5, ch. 75)
** Simkin, J., *Africa Since 1945* (Spartacus, 1986)
 * Taylor, J. K. G., and Kohler, J. A., *Africa and the Middle East* (Arnold, 1984)
   Watson, J. B., *Empire to Commonwealth* (Dent, 1971)

CHAPTER 24

   Davidson, B., *Africa in Modern History* (Allen Lane, 1978)
   Hoskyns, C., *Two Tragedies: Congo and Biafra* (Purnell, vol. 6, ch. 85)
   Mackie, J., *The Indonesian Confrontation* (Purnell, vol. 6, ch. 91)
   Pandey, B. N., *The Rise of Modern India* (Hamish Hamilton, 1972)
** Simkin, J., *Africa Since 1945* (Spartacus, 1986)
   Stephens, I., *The Pakistanis* (Oxford: University Press, 1968)
** Walker, A., *The Modern Commonwealth* (Longman, 1975)
 * Watson, J. B., *Empire to Commonwealth* (Dent, 1971)

CHAPTER 25

   Davidson, B., *Africa in Modern History* (Allen Lane, 1978)
   Hoskyns, C., *Two Tragedies: Congo and Biafra* (Purnell, vol. 6, ch. 85)
 * Le May, G. L., *Black and White in South Africa* (Macdonald, 1969)
   Luthuli, A., *Let My People Go* (Fontana, 1963)
   Mason, P., *Rhodesia: Great Britain's Dilemma* (Purnell, vol. 6, ch. 81)
** Roberts, M., *South Africa* (Longman, 1987)

Simkin, J., *Africa Since 1945* (Spartacus, 1986)
* Watson, J. B., *Empire to Commonwealth* (Dent, 1971)

CHAPTER 26

Bullard, R., *The Persian Oil Crisis* (Purnell, vol. 5, ch. 80)
Dodd, C. H., and Sales, M., *Israel and the Arab World* (Routledge, 1973)
Hunter, R. E., *The Six Day War* (Purnell, vol. 6, ch. 94)
* Jones, D., *The Arab World* (Hamish Hamilton, 1969)
* Nussbaum, E., *Israel* (Oxford: University Press, 1968)
* Perkins, S. J., *The Arab-Israeli Conflict* (Macmillan, 1982)
* Scott-Bauman, M., *Israel and the Arabs* (Arnold, 1986)
Sykes, C., *The Birth of Israel* (Purnell, vol. 5, ch. 78)
Thomas, H., *The Suez Affair* (Weidenfeld & Nicolson, 1967)

INDEX

A

Abyssinia *see* Ethiopia
Adenauer, K. 381, 403–4
Afghanistan 297, 318–19, 321,
  334, 375, 421
Africa ch. 25, 30, 180–1, 268, 306,
  337, 371, 439, 443–6, 465–78
Agadir 5
Albania 5, 21, 95, 227, 229, 253,
  266, 282
  since 1945 277, 338, 342
Algeria 258, 381, 399–400, 439,
  503, 510, 514
Allende, S. 297, 314–16
Alsace-Lorraine 2, 28, 30
America *see* Latin America,
  South America, United States of
  America
Andropov 319, 321, 334
Anglo-German Naval Agreement
  (1935) 224, 228, 231, 236
Anglo-Irish Agreement (1985) 456
Angola 180, 297, 440, 446, 486,
  489, 494
Anti-Comintern Pact (1936) 224,
  226, 229, 232
apartheid 484, 488, 491–6
appeasement 232–6, 238–40
Arab League 504
Arabs ch. 26, 187–90, 371
Arusha Declaration 474–5
Attlee, C. R. 281, 387, 441
Australia 20, 180–1, 254, 305,
  306, 382, 454, 455, 464
Austria (since 1918) 133, 227–8
  and the Peace Settlement 33–4
  and union with Germany
    (1938) 225, 231–2
  after Second World War 267,
    279, 282, 287, 384
Austria-Hungary (before
  1918) 1–3
  and responsibility for First World
    War 6–9

during First World War 22, 27,
  51
autocracy, meaning 2

B

Baghdad Pact 505, 507
balance of payments 388–9,
  390–4, 420, 423, 467
  meaning 380
Baldwin, S. 65, 66, 69–73, 187,
  234
Balfour Declaration (1917) 189
Balkan Wars 5–6
Bangladesh 454, 459, 461–2
battles
  Adowa (1896) 228
  Arnhem (1944) 264
  Atlantic (1942–3) 260–1
  Britain (1940) 252–3, 261
  Cambrai (1917) 25
  Caporetto (1917) 25
  Dien Bien Phu (1954) 310, 399
  El Alamein (1942) 249, 258–9
  Falklands Islands (1914) 22
  Jutland (1916) 23
  Marne (1914) 18
  Masurian Lakes (1914) 19
  Midway Island (1942) 249,
    257–8, 261
  Monte Cassino (1944) 263
  Passchendaele (1917) 24
  Somme (1916) 21
  Stalingrad (1942) 250, 259–60
  Tannenberg (1914) 19
  Verdun (1916) 21
  Vittorio Veneto (1918) 27
  Ypres (1914) 19; (1915) 19;
    (1917) 24
Belgium 1, 10, 28, 29, 88–9, 180,
  209, 212, 218, 249–52, 282,
  285, 305, 369, 374, 383, 440,
  485
Bengal 442, 456

Berlin 252, 262, 265, 338, 405, 416
  divided after Second World War 284, 288
  Blockade and airlift 284–5
  wall 286, 288
Beveridge Report 267, 387
Bhutto, Z. A. 459, 461–2
Biafra 469–71
Bolsheviks 44, 49–54
  beliefs 46
  coming to power 48–50
Bosnia 4, 6
Botha, P. W. 494–6
Brandt, W. 381, 405
Brezhnev, L. 317, 319, 333–4, 336, 346
Briand, A. 86, 208, 210, 213–14
Britain 157, 167, 175, 282
  and Germany before 1914 1–2, 4–8
  during First World War 17, 19–27
  and the Peace Settlement 27–8, 33, 34–6
  internal affairs between the wars ch. 4
  foreign policy between the wars 175, 209–11, 212, 218, 228, 232–40
  and Russia 4, 52, 63, 214–16, 235
  and League of Nations 197–8, 202
  and Germany 211, 212, 232–8
  and India 183–7, 440–2
  and Ireland 182–4, 392, 393
  during Second World War 249–66
  and the Middle East 505–9
  since 1945 285, 305, 319, 368, 376, 386–98
  and the empire 180–1, 185–9, 374–5, 395, 397, 439–46, 484
  and the commonwealth 181, 384–5, 454–5
  and South Africa 493–5
  and Europe 380–6, 391, 393, 395
  and Suez 372, 389, 505, 507–9
Bukhari, Major General 471
Bulgaria 5, 20, 27, 200
  and the Peace Settlement 34

  since 1945 277, 282, 344
Burma 180, 249, 255, 261, 439, 454
Butler, R. A. 387, 389–90
Butskellism 389

C
Cambodia (now Kampuchea) 297, 310, 313, 321–2, 465
Camp David 421, 512–13
Canada 180–1, 217, 285, 305, 382, 454
Carter, J. 317–18, 420–1, 429, 512
caste system 457
Castro, F. 297, 307–9
Ceausescu 343
Central African Federation 445, 487
Chamberlain, N. 69, 184, 225, 234, 236–40
Chanak 35, 63, 168, 181
Chernenko 319, 334
Chernobyl 336, 338, 339, 406
Chiang Kai-Shek 225–6, 296, 299–302, 304–6, 317
Chile 297, 314–16, 412, 425–6
China 170, 208–9, 219, 268, 277, 296–302, 315, 342, 346, ch. 19, 368, 397, 476
  under Sun Yat-sen 299
  under Chiang Kai-shek 299–302
  becomes communist 277, 300–2
  under Mao Tse-tung 352–6
  and Korea 302–6
  and USA 208–9, 301, 317–18, 321
  and USSR 318, 321–2, 352
  and Japan 170–1, 202, 208–9, 219, 225–6, 301–2, 431
  and India 454, 458–9
  and Vietnam 310, 313
Chirac, J. 402–3
Chou En-Lai 299, 301–2, 305, 356
Churchill, Sir W. 69, 70, 185, 187, 279–82, 381, 384, 386, 389, 445
  during Second World War 251–2, 279–82
Civil Rights Acts (USA) 415, 417–19
Clemenceau, G. 25, 27, 33, 86, 211
Cold War ch. 16, ch. 17, 268, 303–6, 308

meaning 277
collective farms 53, 153, 158–9, 332–3, 353–4
collective security 198, 228, 239
Comecon 283, 336, 343
Cominform 283, 287, 336
Comintern (Communist International) 224
Common Market *see* European Economic Community
Commonwealth, British ch. 24, 70, 484, 488, 493, 495
definition 454–5
communes, in China 354–5, 357
communism ch. 16, ch. 17, ch. 19
in Russia 44, 50–4, ch. 9
in Eastern Europe 281, ch. 18
in China 296, 300–2, ch. 19
in Chile 297, 314–16
Congo, the (Zaire since 1971) 180, 371, 374, 440, 465, 484–6
Council of Europe 380, 382
credit squeeze, meaning 390
Cruise missiles 318–21, 396, 421
Cuba 297, 306–9, 315, 424–5, 489
missile crisis (1962) 287–8, 297, 308, 333, 416
Cultural Revolution, Chinese 352, 355–6
Cyprus 374, 439, 443, 454
Czechoslovak Legion 51–2
Czechoslovakia 133, 213, 234, 267, 281, 330, 342, 344–6
creation of 33
and Germany 143, 197, 210, 225, 234, 236–7
becomes communist 277, 283–4, 344
1968 rising 330, 334–5, 374

D
Daladier, E. 83, 86, 87, 237
Danzig 29, 31, 237–9, 339
Dardanelles 20
Dawes Plan (1924) 68, 85, 126, 131, 209
democracy 2, 168, 170, 456
meaning 2
Deng Xiaoping 352, 356–9
Denmark 249, 250, 282, 384, 385

Depression, the Great *see* World Economic Crisis
D'Estaing, G. 381, 401
détente 317–22, 420
meaning 317
disarmament 199, 202, 208, 210–11, 334
German 29, 32
Dominican Republic 424, 426
Dubček, A. 283, 334, 344
Dumbarton Oaks Conference (1944) 367
Dunkirk 89, 252
Dutch East Indies (*see also* Indonesia) 255, 268, 371, 439, 440

E
East Germany *see* Germany
Eden, Sir A. 389, 443, 507
Education Act (1944) 387
Egypt 180, 253, 261, 372, 503–4, 507–9, 511–13
Eire 183–4, 285, 385, 396
Eisenhower, D. D. 264–5, 287–8, 308, 312, 414–15, 428, 505
Enabling Law (German) (1933) 137
enosis 443
Eoka 443
Estonia 29, 51, 250, 267
Ethiopia 181, 197, 202, 224, 228, 266
Europe, Council of 380, 382
European Coal and Steel Community (ECSC) 383, 404
European Economic Community (EEC) 380, 383–6, 393, 395, 404, 431, 455
European Free Trade Association (EFTA) 384
European Movement 380–6

F
Falklands War (1982) 375, 395
fascism 94–103, 119, 135, 143–4, 171
principles 98–9
Finland 51, 199, 250, 267, 287
First World War
events leading up to 2–7
causes 7–10

First World War (*cont'd*)
events during (*see also*
battles) 17–26
reasons for German defeat 27
Peace Settlement 27–36
Ford, G. 317, 420
Formosa *see* Taiwan
Fourteen Points *see* Wilson, W.
France 4–5, 52, 129, 131, 156,
157, 198, 202, 209
during First World War 17–19,
21–2, 24–5, 26–7
and the Peace
Settlement 28–30, 36
internal affairs between the
wars ch. 5
foreign policies 209–10, 211–14,
216, 224, 228, 235–8
and the empire 180, 188, 310,
381, 398–401, 439–40
during Second World War 83,
87–9, 249–52
reasons for defeat 87–9
since 1945 285, 297, 305, 310,
368, 381, 398–403, 431
and Europe 282, 380–6, 400–1
and Suez 372, 399
Franco, F. 167, 173–5, 229, 381
Fulton Speech (Churchill) 281

G
Gallipoli Campaign 20, 167
Gandhi, Mrs I. 455, 456–7, 459
Gandhi, M. K. 185–7, 440, 442
Gandhi, R. 455, 458, 495
GATT (General Agreement on
Tariffs and Trade) 382
Gaulle, General C. de 88, 381,
382, 385, 398–401
General Strike (1926) 69, 70–3
Germany 77, 114, 157, 175, 180,
200, 208
and Britain before 1914 1–2,
4–8
and responsibility for First World
War 8–10
during First World War 17–27
reasons for defeat 26–7
and the Peace Settlement 27–33
Weimar Republic 126–7, 140
and Russia 2, 8–9, 19–20, 25–6,
153, 209, 215–16, 229, 238

under Hitler 136–45, 175, 227,
229–32, 236–9
and Poland 197, 200, 209–10,
213, 225, 229–31, 237–8
and France 209, 212–14
and Britain 211–14, 232–8
and Austria 225, 227, 232
and Czechoslovakia 197, 209,
225, 229, 236–7
during Second World
War 249–66
reasons for defeat 265–6
divided after Second World
War 279, 284, 317
Germany, East 277, 285, 288,
315, 344, 404–5
Germany, West 285, 287–80, 319,
346, 381–3, 397, 403–7
glasnost 336
Ghana 439, 444, 466–9, 488
Gold Coast 439, 444
Gorbachev, M. 319–22, 335–6,
346, 422
Government of India Act
(1919) 185
Gowon, General Y. 469, 471
Great Leap Forward 352, 354–5
Greece 34–6, 200–1, 227, 253–4,
282, 305, 386, 443, 454
Guatemala 308, 425–6, 428–9
Guevara, 'Che' 307–9

H
Hammarskjöld, D. 369, 372, 374,
485–6
Heath, E. 385, 392–3
Helsinki Agreement (1975) 317,
318, 334, 405
Herriot, E. 86, 208–9, 213
Hindenburg, P. von 19, 127, 135
Hinduism 440–2, 457–8
Hitler, A. 87–8, 98, 102, 126–7,
153, 175, 189, 202, 207, 211,
224
Munich putsch 129
rise to power 133–5
internal policies 135–6
foreign policies 143, 215–16,
227–8, 229–32, 236–40
during Second World 249–55,
261, 265–6
Ho Chi Minh 310–13, 317

Holland 249–52, 282, 285, 305, 369, 383
and her empire 180, 371, 439–40
Hoover, H. 108, 114–15
Hoxha, E. 342
Hundred Flowers Campaign 353–4
Hungary 227
and the Peace Settlement 33–4
since 1945 277, 281, 340–2, 344
1956 rising 287, 330, 340–2, 373
Husak 344, 346
Hu Yaobang 357, 359

I
imperialism, meaning 2
India 180, 185–7, 374
becomes independent 440–2
since independence 454–60
Indo-China 180–1, 255, 257, 306, 381, 399, 439–40
Indonesia 371, 454, 464
Industrial Relations Act (1971) 393
Indus Waters Dispute 459
inflation 61, 129–31, 212, 315, 338, 358, 390–5, 398, 402, 404–5, 468
International Court of Justice 198, 213, 369
International Labour Organisation (ILO) 199, 370
International Monetary Fund (IMF) 337, 339, 357, 370, 392, 464, 466, 475
IRA (Irish Republican Army) 182–3, 392, 393, 396
Iran (Persia) 503, 505, 514–15
American hostages 421
Irangate 423, 430
Iran-Iraq War 375, 513–15
Iraq 34, 180, 188, 200, 503, 510, 513–15
Ireland 180, 181–4, 392, 393
Easter rebellion (1916) 182–3
Irish Free State 181, 183–4
Iron Curtain 281
Israel 371, 503, 506–7, 515
wars with Arabs 371, 372, 506–13
Italy 144, 175, 180, 197–8, 200, 217, 224, 234

during First World War 21, 25, 27–8
and the Peace Settlement 34, 207
problems after First World War 94–9
becomes fascist 94–101
under Mussolini 99–103, 200–1, 226–9, 231
foreign policy between the wars, 175, 200–1, 202, 219, 226–9, 231, 236
during Second World War 249–63, 267
since 1945 285, 287, 381, 383

J
Japan 4, 52, 210, 218, 224, 412
during First World War 170
between the wars 167, 170–1
and China 171, 181, 208–9, 219, 225–6, 431
and the USA 171, 208–9, 218, 431
invasion of Manchuria 171, 197, 202, 219, 225–6
and League of Nations 197–8, 202, 219, 226
during Second World War 171, 249, 255–68, 281
since 1945 277, 382, 397, 412, 430–2
Jaruzelski, General 339–40
Jews (see also Israel) 133, 136, 138, 140, 143, 188–9, 256–7, 371, 503, 506–7
Jinnah, M. A. 187, 440, 460
Johnson, L. B. 312, 418–19
Jordan 188, 503–4, 507, 510, 514

K
Kadar, J. 340–2
Kashmir 374, 454, 459–60
Katanga 485–6
Kaunda, K. 445, 476–8
Kellogg, F. 208, 218
Kemal, Mustapha 34, 167–9
Kennedy, J. F. 288, 308, 312, 412, 416–17, 426
Kenya 439, 444–5, 466, 472–4
Kenyatta, J. 445, 472–3

Kerensky, A. 48–9
Keynes, J. M. 33, 70, 77
Khan, M. Ayub 459, 461
Khrushchev, N. 285, 287, 308,
    318, 331, 336, 338, 340, 342
    internal policies 331–3
    foreign policies 285–8, 308, 333,
        337, 415
King, M. L. 413, 419
Kohl, H. 381, 406–7
Korea 277, 296–7, 322
    war in 285, 297, 302–6, 372,
        389, 431
Kosygin, A. 333, 346, 459
Ku Klux Klan 110
Kulaks 45, 155, 158
Kuomintang 226, 296, 299–302,
    352

L
Lancaster House Conference
    (1979) 490
Laos 297, 310, 313
Latin America 297, 306–9,
    314–16, 333, 412, 424–30
Laval, P. 88–9, 228, 235
Lawrence, T. E. (of Arabia) 36,
    187
League of Nations 29, 68, ch. 12,
    208, 210, 213, 224, 226, 228,
    230, 235, 239, 367, 370–1
Lebanon 188, 375, 503, 510,
    515–17
Lebensraum 229, 254
Lee Kuan Yew 464
Lend-Lease Act (U.S.A.)
    (1941) 255
Lenin, V. 153–4, 161, 318
    and the Russian revolutions 44,
        46–9
    domestic policies 49–54
    foreign policies 214
Libya 253, 259, 397, 422, 503–4,
    514
Lithuania 29, 51, 200, 218, 237,
    250
Lloyd George, D. 60–3, 198, 207,
    209, 214–15
    during First World War 22, 24,
        27–8
    statement of war aims 27
    and Ireland 63, 182–3

Local Government Act (1929) 69
Long March 296, 300
Ludendorff, E. 26, 127, 129
Luthuli, A. 492

M
MacArthur, D. 258, 304–5, 372,
    430
MacDonald, J. R. 65, 67–8, 73–5,
    187, 189, 201, 208–9, 214–15,
    218, 234
Macmillan, H. 77, 380, 384, 389,
    396, 443–5, 493
Maginot Line 88, 250
Malawi (see also Nyasaland) 439,
    445, 455, 487
Malaya 180, 249, 255, 268, 439,
    442–3, 462–3
Malaysia 439, 454, 462–5
Manchuria 171, 197, 202, 219,
    225–6, 305, 321
mandates 29, 30, 34, 187–90, 200,
    208, 369, 506
Mandela, N. 494–5
Mao Tse-tung 277, 296, 300–2,
    342, 352–6
Marshall Plan 282–3, 380, 382,
    388, 414
Marx, K. 46, 98, 155, 161, 318
McCarthyism 413, 415
Mein Kampf 134, 239
Memel 237
Middle East ch. 26, 187–90, 268,
    443
Mitterrand, F. 381, 400–3
Moi, D. arap 473
Monckton Commission (1960) 445
monetarism, meaning 394
Montagu–Chelmsford
    Reforms 185
Morley–Minto Reforms 185
Morocco 4–5, 171, 173, 174, 180,
    258, 399, 440, 503
Moscow Olympics (1980) 319
Mozambique 180, 297, 440, 446,
    477, 489, 494
Mugabe, R. 489–90
Munich Conference (1938) 225,
    232, 234, 236–7
Muslims 440–2, 444, 460–1, ch. 26
Mussolini, B. 135, 143–4, 175, 224,
    237

rise to power   94–8
domestic policies   99–103
foreign policies   175, 201, 202,
   207, 219, 226–9, 235–6
during Second World
   War   102–3, 249, 253, 266
downfall   103, 262

O
Oder-Neisse Line   281, 405
OPEC (Organisation of Petroleum
   Exporting Countries)   512
Organisation of African Unity
   (OAU)   467, 476, 489, 493
Ostpolitik   405

N
Namibia   see South-West Africa
Nasser, G. A.   333, 372, 504,
   507–9
National Economic Development
   Council (Neddy)   391
National Health Service Act
   (1946)   387, 397
NATO (North Atlantic Treaty
   Organisation)   285, 318, 375,
   380, 382–3, 400, 404
naval warfare   22–4, 251, 260–1
nazism   127, 129, 136–45
programme and
   principles   133–4, 135–6
and facism   143–4
Nehru, J.   185, 187, 440, 455–7,
   459
Netherlands   see Holland
New Deal (Roosevelt)   109,
   115–19
New Economic Policy (NEP)
   (Lenin)   53, 155, 158
New Zealand   20, 180–1, 254, 258,
   305, 306, 384, 464
Nicaragua   319, 421, 423, 429–30
Nicholas II, Tsar   44–7
Nigeria   439, 444, 454–5, 465,
   469–72, 488
Nixon, R. M.   313–14, 317, 343,
   412, 419–20
Nkomo, J.   445, 487, 489–90
Nkrumah, K.   444, 466–7, 469
Normandy Landings (1944)   250,
   262, 263–4
Norway   249, 251, 282, 285, 369,
   384
nuclear weapons   267, 288, 308,
   318–22, 400, 406, 421
Nyasaland (see also Malawi)   439,
   445
Nyerere, Dr J.   444, 466, 474–5

P
Pakistan   187, 306, 374, 439, 454,
   459–61, 505
creation of   440–2
Palestine   34, 188–90, 371
Palestine Liberation Organisation
   (PLO)   510, 512–13, 514, 516
Papen, F. von   134–5, 142
Paris Peace Settlement
   (1919–20)   27–36
Pearl Harbor   249, 255–6
perestroika   335
Persia   see Iran
Petain, H. P.   24, 88–9, 252
Philippines, the   249, 255, 261,
   305, 306
Poincaré, R.   83, 85, 212, 213
Poland   28, 29, 30, 34, 51, 77, 133,
   200,
foreign policy   213, 216, 218–19,
   225
and Germany   143, 197, 200,
   229–31, 237–8, 278
during Second World
   War   249–50, 267, 279–81
since 1945   277, 330, 334,
   338–40, 341, 344, 405
Polish Corridor   31, 229, 230, 234,
   237–8
Pompidou, G   381, 385, 401
population problems   425, 457
Portugal   8, 180, 282, 285, 381,
   384, 386, 446, 488
Portuguese colonies   8, 180, 297,
   440, 446, 458
Posen (Poznan)   29, 338
Potsdam Conference (1945)   279,
   281
Prohibition   110–11, 118
protection   see tariffs
Punjab, the   185, 442, 458

R

racial problems 476, 486–90,
    491–6
  in USA 110, 413, 415–16,
    417–19
  in Germany 143–4, 506
Rahman, Tunku Abdul 462–3,
    465
Rawlings, J. J. 468–9
Reagan, R. 319–21, 376, 421–3
reparations 29–30, 33, 85, 127,
    129, 207, 210–12, 217–18
Representation of the People Act
    (1918) 60
revisionism 318, 333, 352, 356
Rhineland 29, 33, 211, 224, 229,
    231–2
Rhodesia 439, 445–6, 455, 476–7,
    484, 486–90
  Northern (see also
      Zambia) 439, 445, 476
  Southern (see also Zimbabwe)
      445–6
Rome-Berlin Axis 224, 229, 232
Roosevelt, F. D. 108
  and the New Deal 115–19
  during Second World War 279
Ruhr, the 157, 262
  French occupation 85, 129, 131,
    207, 209, 212
Rumania 28, 34, 36, 213, 267
  since 1945 277, 330, 334, 341,
    342–4
Russia (USSR after 1917) 4, 8,
    143, 175, 200, 209, 218–19,
    235, 330–6, 369
  during First World War 17,
    19–22, 25–6
  and the Peace Settlements 36
  under Nicholas II 44–7
  revolutions in 44, 47–9, 61
  civil war in 50–3, 214
  under Lenin 50–4
  under Stalin ch. 9, 278–87,
    330–1
  foreign policies 175, 209,
    214–16, 238, 240
  during Second World
      War 249–68
  under Khruschchev 330–3,
  foreign policies since 1945 ch.
    16, 296–7, 304–6, 313, 317–22,
    335, 372, 405

  and China 318, 321, 352
  and Eastern Europe ch. 18, 373
  and Africa 486
  and Middle East 372, 505, 507,
    511–12

S

Saar, the 29, 199, 211, 231
Sadat, President 504, 511–13
SALT (Strategic Arms Limitation
    Talks) 317, 318–19, 421
Samuel Commission 70–1
Sankey Commission 61–2
Sarajevo 6–7
Saudi Arabia 503–4, 510, 514
Schleicher, K. von 134–5
Schlieffen Plan 10, 17–18, 27
Schmidt, H. 381, 405
SEATO (South East Asia Treaty
    Organisation) 306
Second World War 197, 224, 310
  events leading up to 224–39
  causes of 239–40
  events during (see also
      battles) 249–65
  results 266–8, 310, 439, 506
self-determination 28, 181
  meaning 28
Serbia 2–7, 20, 27
  becomes Yugoslavia 33–4
Sharpeville 492, 494
Shastri, L. B. 455, 456, 459
Siegfried Line 250, 264
Simon, Sir J. 72, 186–7, 225, 234
Singapore 249, 255, 268, 442, 463,
    464
Sinn Fein 61, 63, 182–4
Six Day War 509–10
Smith, I. 476, 487–90
'Socialism in One Country' 155,
    278
South Africa 180–1, 369, 422, 446,
    455, 476, 484, 491–6
  and Rhodesia 488, 489
South America 217, 297, 309,
    314–16, 395, 424–8
South-West Africa (Namibia) 30,
    369, 493
space exploration 332, 415, 420,
    422
Spain 167, 180, 381, 386, 440
  civil war 167, 173–5, 225, 229,
    234, 236

under Franco 174–5, 381
Spartacist Rising 126, 128
Special Areas Act (1934) 78
Specialised Agencies (United
    Nations) 370
Stalin, J. 278, 330–1, 336–7, 338,
    340, 342
  rise to power 153–5
  internal policies 155–61
  the purges 159–61
  foreign policies 215–16, 278–85,
    330
Stalingrad 250, 259–60
START (Strategic Arms Reduction
    Talks) 319, 321
Star Wars 320–1
Stolypin, P. 45–7
Stop-go policies 390–3
Stresa Front 224, 228, 231, 236
Stresemann, G. 126, 130, 131,
    208–9, 213, 234
Sudetenland, the 225, 236–7
Suez Canal 189, 258, 508, 512
Suez Crisis (1956) 372, 504, 507–9
Sun Yat-sen 296, 297–8
Sykes-Picot agreement 188
Syria 34, 181, 188, 397, 503–4,
    509–10, 514, 516

T
Taiwan (Formosa) 296, 302,
    305–6, 317
Tanganyika 30, 439, 444, 474
Tanzania 337, 439, 466, 474–6,
    488
tariffs 65, 75, 84, 112, 118, 132,
    218, 383–4
Thailand 305, 306, 464–5
Thatcher, M. 385–6, 394–8, 421,
    455, 495
Third World 268, 306, 371, 375,
    426–7, 455, 458, 466
Tito, J. 281–2, 287, 330, 336–8
Trade Disputes Act (1927) 73, 388
Transjordan see Jordan
treaties
  Austrian State (1955) 287
  Berlin (1926) 216
  Brest-Litovsk (1918) 28, 30, 51
  Brussels (1948) 383
  INF (1987) 320–1
  Lausanne (1923) 35, 168, 181
  Locarno (1925) 70, 181, 201,
      208, 210, 231
  London (1915) 21
  Neuilly (1919) 35
  Rapallo (1920) 219
  Rapallo (1922) 209, 215–16
  Riga (1921) 52, 218
  Rome (1957) 383
  San Francisco (1951) 267, 430
  St Germain (1919) 33–4
  Sèvres (1920) 35, 167
  Trianon (1920) 34
  Versailles (1919) 28–33, 94,
      108, 127, 133, 142, 197, 200,
      231, 239, 369
  Washington (1922) 217, 218
tribalism 444–5, 465, 468–72, 476,
    486, 490
Trotsky, L. 44, 49, 51, 52, 53,
    153–5, 160
Truman, H. S. 265, 278–82,
    304–5, 414
  Doctrine 282, 414
Tunisia 259, 399, 440, 503
Turkey 17, 19–20, 27, 63, 167–9,
    180, 188, 199–200, 227, 277,
    282, 305, 374, 382, 443, 454,
    505
  and the Peace Settlement 34–6,
      207
  under Kemal 167–9
Tutu, Archbishop 494, 496

U
U-2 Affair 288, 415
Uganda 439, 444–5, 472, 475
Ulster 182–3
underdevelopment 424–6, 466
unemployment
  in Spain 173
  in Japan 171
  in Britain 62, 64, 73–4, 75–8,
      391–3, 397
  in USA 113–15, 118–19, 413,
      417, 419
  in Germany 131–3, 140, 404–6
  in Italy 95, 102
  in Cuba 307
Union of Soviet Socialist Republics
    (USSR) see Russia
UNESCO 370, 375–6
UNICEF 370
United Arab Republic 504

United Nations Organisation (UNO) ch. 20, 268, 283, 287, 298, 302–6, 317, 382, 426, 454, 463–4, 476, 484–7, 493, 506, 509, 510, 516
United States of America 157, 171, 182, 207, 226, 368, 488, 489
  constitution and parties 108
  during First World War 17, 24–7
  and the Peace Settlement 28, 36, 108, 211–12
  and Russia 52, 419, 421–3
  and Japan 171, 208–9, 430–1
  and China 301–2, 317–18, 419, 421
  and Germany 24, 26, 126, 131
  internal affairs between the wars ch. 7
  and world economic crisis 111–19
  foreign policies 208, 210, 211, 217–18
  and League of Nations 198, 200–1, 217
  during Second World War 249–66
  internal affairs since 1945 412–23
  foreign policies since 1945 ch. 16, 301–2, 304–6, 317–22, 372, 376, 382, 395, 416–17, 419, 423, 430–1, 489, 506, 512–13
  and Vietnam 310–14, 413, 418, 419–20
  and Latin America 306–8, 315–16, 417, 421, 423, 426–30
  'Uniting for Peace' resolution 369, 371, 372
USSR (Union of Soviet Socialist Republics) see Russia
U Thant 369, 371, 486

V
Venezuela 427–8
Verwoerd, H. 491–3
Victor Emmanuel III, King 94, 97, 103, 144
Vietcong 312–14

Vietminh 310, 311
Vietnam 297, 310–14, 318, 321–2, 413, 419–20, 465
Vilna 218
Vorster, J. 491, 493

W
Wagner Act (USA)(1935) 118
Walesa, L. 339
Wall Street Crash (1929) 73, 108, 111, 126, 131, 171, 210
Warsaw Pact 287, 334, 340, 343, 344, 374, 382
Washington Conferences (1921–2) 208–9
Watergate 314, 412, 420
Weimar Republic see Germany
West Irian 371, 464
Westminster, Statute of (1931) 70, 181, 454
Wilson, H. 389, 391–2, 394, 446, 487–8
Wilson, W. 26, 108, 181, 197–8, 200, 217
  his 14 Points 28, 30
World Bank 339, 357, 370, 459, 472
World Disarmament Conference 202, 208, 210–11, 230
world economic crisis (1929–33) 108, 126, 131, 170–1, 239
  causes 111–13
  effects 85, 102, 113–15, 131–3, 170–1, 202, 239
World Health Organisation (WHO) 370

Y
Yalta Conference (1945) 279, 282
Yom Kippur War 510–12
Young Plan (1929) 33, 73, 131, 210
Yugoslavia 34, 36, 95, 207, 213, 219, 227, 235, 254, 267, 330
  since 1945 277, 281–2, 287, 336–7

Z
Zaire (Congo) 446, 465, 484, 486
Zambia (see also Rhodesia, Northern) 439, 445, 476–8, 487, 488

Zhao Ziyang   321, 357–9
Zia ul Haq, General   460, 462
Zimbabwe (*see also* Rhodesia,
    Southern)   421, 484, 490–1,
    494

Zinoviev Letter   68, 215
Zionism   189–90